THE FIRST DAY ON THE EASTERN FRONT

THE FIRST DAY ON THE EASTERN FRONT

Germany Invades the Soviet Union, June 22, 1941

CRAIG W. H. LUTHER

STACKPOLE
BOOKS

GUILFORD, CONNECTICUT

Published by Stackpole Books
An imprint of The Rowman & Littlefield Publishing Group, Inc.
4501 Forbes Blvd., Ste. 200
Lanham, MD 20706
www.rowman.com

Distributed by NATIONAL BOOK NETWORK
800-462-6420

British Library Cataloguing in Publication Information available

Library of Congress Cataloging-in-Publication Data

Names: Luther, Craig W. H., author.
Title: The First Day on the Eastern Front : Germany invades the Soviet Union,
    June 22, 1941 / Craig W.H. Luther.
Description: Guilford, Connecticut : Stackpole Books, 2018. | Includes
    bibliographical references and index.
Identifiers: LCCN 2018017491 (print) | LCCN 2018017951 (ebook) | ISBN
    9780811767651 (e-book) | ISBN 9780811737807 (hardback : alk. paper)
Subjects: LCSH: World War, 1939-1945—Campaigns—Eastern Front. | World War,
    1939-1945—Soviet Union.
Classification: LCC D764 (ebook) | LCC D764 .L8765 2018 (print) | DDC
    940.54/217—dc23
LC record available at https://lccn.loc.gov/2018017491

Printed in the United States of America

To my dear wife, Maria Therese, who has supported my many years of book-writing activity with grace, dignity, and most of all, with a patience I did not deserve.

I am convinced that our attack will sweep over [Russia] like a hailstorm.
   —Adolf Hitler to Field Marshal Fedor von Bock, February 1, 1941[1]

If it were necessary to organize a provocation, then the German generals would bomb their own cities. Hitler surely does not know about it.
   —Joseph Stalin reacting to initial reports of Germany's surprise attack, June 22, 1941[2]

22 June 1941: Das Oberkommando der Wehrmacht gibt bekannt: "An der sowjetrussischen Grenze ist es seit den frühen Morgenstunden des heutigen Tages zu Kampfhandlungen gekommen."
   —German Armed Forces High Command announcing the outbreak of hostilities with Soviet Russia[3]

Contents

APPENDICES

NOTES ON STYLE

MAPS USED IN THE PREPARATION OF THIS BOOK WERE EXCLUSIVELY GERMAN OR ENGLISH in origin; no Russian-language maps were used. For consistent spellings of towns, cities, and other geographical features, I have relied in part on recent publications on the Russo-German War 1941–1945 by experts such as Colonel David M. Glantz (U.S. Army, ret.) or Evan Mawdsley; I have also used a selection of maps from Colonel Glantz's fine atlas of the battles along the Russo-German frontier in late June 1941. For more obscure towns and villages recorded in the war diaries of German units—or in the field post letters or diary entries of German soldiers used in this narrative—I have in some cases simply retained the original German spellings. Due to centuries of Germanic influence, proper spellings of towns and cities in Lithuania can pose a challenge to historians of the Second World War—e.g., Daugavpils (Dünaburg/Dvinsk), Siauliai (Schaulen), Tauroggen (Taurage), and so forth; in each instance, I have selected a spelling that appears consistent with that used by most English-language historians. For the proper names of Soviet personages (marshals, generals, etc.), I have also relied on the most common current spellings used by Glantz, Mawdsley, and other experts, as well as on *The Oxford Guide to World War II* (I. C. B. Dear, ed.).

I have sought to employ reasonably consistent protocols for German and Russian military units. German armies are spelled out, as in German "Fourth" Army, while Russian armies are always numbered, as in Soviet "11 Army." Military units, regardless of their size (or whether German or Russian), are generally referred to with the unit number followed by the type of unit, for example: 3 Panzer Group, 9 Army Corps, 24 Panzer Corps, 6 Infantry Division, 77 Infantry Regiment, etc. Sometimes shortcuts are taken; for example, 9 AK for 9 Army Corps, 6 ID for 6 Infantry Division, or 98 Geb.Jg.Rgt. for 98 Mountain Regiment. In the translated German texts (letters, personal diaries, official unit war diaries, etc.), and in my own narrative, I have, on occasion, for units below division and regiment level, elected to use abbreviated German unit designations, such as III./PzRgt 18 (in lieu of 3rd Battalion, 18 Panzer Regiment), or 3./IR 18 (in lieu of 3rd Company, 18 Infantry Regiment). While this may seem inconsistent, it made sense for reasons of economy, while also enabling me to retain a bit of the original German "flavor" in the narrative. In Chapter 6, addressing the operations of the German air force (*Luftwaffe*) on June 22, 1941, I have typically used the German abbreviations for units such as bomber or fighter wings; this, however, should be easy to follow, for I have also compiled detailed orders of battle for each German air fleet juxtaposing the English and German terminology. In any case, readers unfamiliar with German military terminology are urged to consult the List of Abbreviations in this book.

When introducing German officers I have elected in most cases to give their ranks in German—e.g., "*Oberst* Hans von Greiffenberg," "*Generalmajor* Walther K. Nehring," "*Generalleutnant* Friedrich Paulus," "*General der Panzertruppen* Joachim Lemelsen," "*Generaloberst* Heinz Guderian," and so forth.[1] This was purely an aesthetic choice, with the goal of adding a touch of authenticity to the book. For economy's sake, I have used the German abbreviations for "General of Panzer Troops" (*Gen.d.Pz.Tr.*), "General of Infantry" (*Gen.d.Inf.*), etc. I have also attempted in each case to introduce Russian generals with their full name and rank. For a table of U.S. and German equivalent military ranks, please consult Appendix 1.

Throughout the narrative I have used the American-style dating standard, i.e., June 22, 1941, not 22 June 1941. For denoting distances kilometers are generally used; in quotations where distances are given in miles, I have left them as is and not converted them to kilometers. For denoting time, three variants are used; for example, 0315 hours, 3:15 in the morning, or 3:15 A.M.

In the summer of 1941, the Germans put their clocks forward an hour as an important wartime daylight-saving measure; hence, German timings for June 1941 (in German summer time) were just one hour behind Soviet time (instead of the two-hour difference normally separating Berlin and Moscow). To eliminate any confusion over the timing of key events, I have sought to change the times in Soviet military documents to German summer time. In other words, if a Soviet *front* commander states that the German attack began at 4:15 on the morning of June 22, 1941, I have moved it back an hour to 3:15 A.M. German summer time is the standard used by most western military historians to denote the time of events along the Eastern Front.

Finally, because I make such extensive use of official operational war diaries of German units ranging from army groups to divisions, and regularly mention these war diaries in the text, I have, for sake of variation, sometimes referred to them simply as "diaries" or "journals," instead of war diaries (e.g., "journal" of 18 Panzer Division, instead of "war diary" of 18 Panzer Division). Again, this is nothing more than an aesthetic choice on the part of the author.

LIST OF MAPS[1]

LIST OF ABBREVIATIONS

(German, English, and Russian)

AA	*Aufklärungsabteilung*: reconnaissance battalion
AA	antiaircraft
Abt.	*Abteilung*: branch (administrative), battalion, or unit, depending on the context employed
a.D.	*ausser Dienst*: retired
AFV	armored fighting vehicle
AK	*Armeekorps*: German army corps
Anl.	*Anlage:* enclosure
AOK	*Armeeoberkommando*: German army headquarters staff
APC	armored personnel carrier
AR	*Artillerie-Regiment*
Arko	*Artilleriekommandeur*: artillery commander
BA-MA	*Bundesarchiv-Militärarchiv* (the German Federal Military Archives in Freiburg, Germany)
Battr.	*Batterie* (artillery)
Bd.	*Band*: volume (of book or journal)
Bf	*Bayerische Flugzeugwerke*
Brig.	brigade
Brig.-Gen.	brigadier general
Btl.	battalion
CAD	composite aviation division (Soviet)
CAS	close air support
C-in-C	commander-in-chief
CP	command post
d.G.	*des Generalstabes*: of the General Staff
DR	*Das Reich*
DRZW	*Das Deutsche Reich und der Zweite Weltkrieg* (German quasi-official history of World War II, see Select Bibliography)

FHO	*Fremde Heere Ost*: Foreign Armies East
FHq	*Führerhauptquartier*: Hitler's military headquarters
Fla	*Fliegerabwehr*: air defense (antiaircraft)
Flak	*Fliegerabwehrkanone*: antiaircraft artillery
Fw.	*Feldwebel*: technical sergeant
GAF	German Air Force
Geb.Jg.Rgt.	*Gebirgsjäger-Regiment* (mountain regiment)
Geb.K.	*Gebirgs-Korps* (mountain corps)
geh.	*geheim*: secret
Gen.d.Art.	General of Artillery
Gen.d.Inf.	General of Infantry
Gen.d.Kav.	General of Cavalry Troops
Gen.d.Pi.	General of Engineer Troops
Gen.d.Pz.Tr.	General of Panzer Troops
GenLt	*Generalleutnant*
GenMaj	*Generalmajor*
GenQu	*Generalquartiermeister*: chief supply officer of German Army General Staff
GenSt	*Generalstab*: German Army General Staff
GenStdH	*Generalstab des Heeres*: German Army General Staff
GFM	*Generalfeldmarschall*
GHQ	General Headquarters
gK.Chefs	*geheime Kommandosachen-Chefsachen*: the highest routine security classification
GKO	State Defense Committee (Stalin's war cabinet)
GRU	Main Intelligence Directorate of the Soviet General Staff
HE	high explosive
HF	high frequency
HGr	*Heeresgruppe*: army group
HKL	*Hauptkampflinie*: main battle line
Hptm	*Hauptmann*: captain
HQu	*Hauptquartier*: headquarters
HVP	*Hauptverbandsplatz*: main dressing station
Ia	*Erster Generalstabsoffizier*: An operations officer responsible for operational issues at the division, army corps, army, and army group levels.
Ib	*Zweiter Generalstabsoffizier*: Supply officer responsible for supply at the division level

Ic	*Dritter Generalstabsoffizier*: An intelligence officer responsible for enemy intelligence and counterintelligence (*Abwehr*); position was clearly subordinate to that of the Ia
ID	*Infanterie-Division*
ID (mot.)	*Infanterie-Division* (motorized)
IfZ	*Institut für Zeitgeschichte*: Institute of Contemporary History (Munich and Berlin)
IG	*Infanterie-Geschütz*: infantry gun
i.G.	*im Generalstab*: a member of the German General Staff
IR	*Infanterie-Regiment*
JG	*Jagdgeschwader*: fighter wing
K	*Kradschützen*: motorcycle riflemen
KDC	Karlsruhe Document Collection
Kdr	*Kommandeur*
Kfz	*Kraftfahrzeug*: motor vehicle
KG	*Kampfgeschwader*: bomber wing
KGr	*Kampfgruppe*: battle group
KIA	killed in action
Kom.Gen.	*Kommandierender General*: commanding general (army corps level)
Korück	*Kommandant des rückwärtigen Armeegebietes*: commandant of rear army area
Kp	*Kompanie*
KTB	*Kriegstagebuch*: war diary
KV	*Klementi Voroshilov*: for KV-1 and KV-2 tanks (Soviet)
le.FH	*leichte Feldhaubitze*: light field howitzer
le.Gr.W.	*leichter Granatwerfer*: light mortar
le.IG	*leichtes Infanterie-Geschütz*: light infantry gun
le.MG	*leichtes Maschinengewehr*: light machine gun
Lkw	*Lastkraftwagen*: truck or transport vehicle
Lt.	*Leutnant*
Lt.-Col.	lieutenant colonel
Lt.-Gen.	lieutenant general
Maj.-Gen.	major general
MC	Mechanized Corps (Soviet)
MD	Mountain Division
MG	*Maschinengewehr*: machine gun

MGFA   *Militärgeschichtliches Forschungsamt*: Research Institute for Military History (Potsdam, Germany)

MIA   missing in action

Mot.   motorized

N   *Nachlass*: personal papers

NCO   noncommissioned officer

NKGB   People's Commissariat of State Security (Soviet Union)

NKO   People's Commissariat of Defense (Soviet Union)

NKVD   People's Commissariat of Internal Affairs (Soviet Secret Police)

OB   *Oberbefehlshaber*: commander-in-chief

ObdH   *Oberbefehlshaber des Heeres*: Commander-in-Chief of the German Army

Oblt.   *Oberleutnant*: first lieutenant

Obst.i.G.   Colonel in the General Staff

Obstlt.   *Oberstleutnant*: lieutenant-colonel

Offz.   *Offizier*

OKH   *Oberkommando des Heeres*: High Command of the German Army

OKL   *Oberkommando der Luftwaffe*: High Command of the German Air Force

OKW   *Oberkommando der Wehrmacht*: High Command of the German Armed Forces

OpAbt   *Operationsabteilung*: Operations Branch of the German Army High Command

OQu   *Oberquartiermeister*: Deputy Chief of the Army General Staff

OQu I   *Oberquartiermeister I*: Deputy Chief of Staff for Operations in the Army High Command

OT   Organisation Todt

Pak   *Panzerabwehrkanone*: antitank gun

PD   Panzer Division

Pi.   *Pionier*: engineer soldier

PR   Panzer Regiment

Pz   panzer

Pz I   Panzer I (tank)

Pz II   Panzer II (tank)

Pz III   Panzer III (tank)

Pz IV   Panzer IV (tank)

Pz 35(t)   Panzer 35(t) (tank of Czech origin)

Pz 38(t)   Panzer 38(t) (tank of Czech origin)

PzJg   *Panzerjäger*: antitank troops

PzK	*Panzerkorps*
PzRgt	Panzer Regiment
RAD	*Reichsarbeitsdienst*: Reich Labor Service
RC	Rifle Corps (Soviet)
RD	Rifle Division (Soviet)
Rgt	Regiment
RH	*Reichsheer* (Denotes German army records at BA-MA)
RL	*Reichsluftwaffe* (Denotes *Luftwaffe* records at BA-MA)
SD	*Sicherheitsdienst*: Security Service (Branch of the SS)
s.FH	*schwere Feldhaubitze*: medium field howitzer
s.Gr.W.	*schwerer Granatwerfer*: medium mortar
s.IG	*schweres Infanterie-Geschütz*: medium infantry gun
s.MG	*schweres Machinengewehr*: heavy machine gun
SP	self-propelled
SPW	*Schützenpanzerwagen*: armored personnel carrier
SR	*Schützen-Regiment*: rifle regiment (in motorized infantry and panzer divisions)
SS	*Schutzstaffel*: elite guard of the Nazi Party
Stavka	Soviet High Command
StG	*Sturzkampfgeschwader*: divebomber wing
StuG	*Sturmgeschütz*: assault gun
(t)	*tschechisch*: Czech (origin)
TD	Tank Division (Soviet)
Uffz	*Unteroffizier*: noncommissioned officer
USAF	United States Air Force
USSR	Union of Soviet Socialist Republics (Soviet Union)
VA	*Vorausabteilung*: forward detachment
VB	*Vorgeschobener Beobachter*: forward observer (artillery)
VVS	*Voenno-vozdushnikh sil*: Soviet Air Force
WFSt	*Wehrmachtführungsstab*: Armed Forces Operations Staff (OKW)
z.V.	*zur Verfügung*: at the disposal of (e.g., *z.V. AOK 16*)

FOREWORD

ON JUNE 22, 2016, THE GERMAN PARLIAMENT IN BERLIN OBSERVED THE SEVENTY-FIFTH anniversary of Germany's surprise attack on the Soviet Union. The *Bundestag* deputies solemnly remembered the twenty-seven million soldiers and civilians of that multinational state who fell victim to National Socialist Germany's war of annihilation and conquest between 1941 and Germany's capitulation in 1945. Even today Operation *Barbarossa*, Hitler's surprise attack on Soviet Russia, remains in both East and West a highly charged topic laden with emotion. In this volume Dr. Craig Luther has sought to describe and analyze the circumstances of the attack on the Soviet Union in an objective fashion. In doing so, he has focused his efforts on the very first day of the war.

In Hitler's "Third Reich," the war against Soviet Russia was characterized by National Socialists as the Russian or eastern campaign (*Russland- oder Ostfeldzug*), while to the Russians it became known as the Great Fatherland (or Patriotic) War. The war began on June 22, 1941, with the surprise attack of the German *Wehrmacht* (armed forces) on the Soviet Union and ended after the battle of Berlin on May 8, 1945, with Germany's unconditional capitulation. Along with the twenty-seven million dead of the USSR, more than four million German soldiers perished on the Eastern Front. Indeed, virtually every family in Germany lost family members in this terrible conflict. Thanks to the efforts of the former West German chancellor Dr. Konrad Adenauer, the final German prisoners of war in the Soviet Union returned home between October 1955 and January 1956—that is, more than ten years after the war's end and almost fifteen years after the attack on the Soviet Union in June 1941.

The generations of the former USSR and Germany who lived through, or who were otherwise touched by, the Russo-German war, with its boundless suffering and death, have never forgotten it. To this day, the war has helped to shape who they are. Those who took part directly in the war have now largely passed on, yet subsequent generations vividly recall the many stories told by their fathers and grandfathers. For both sides, Russian and German, the war remains to this day—to reemphasize a vital point—a theme burdened by emotions still raw and deep.

On November 17, 2017, Nikolai Desyatnishchenko, a sixteen-year-old Russian student from the Siberian town of Nowy Urengoi, who along with two other Russian and three German students was taking part in an exchange program sponsored by the German War Graves Commission, spoke before the German *Bundestag*. In his speech, on the occasion of the Day of National Mourning (*Volkstrauertag*) in Germany, he expressed sympathy for those individual soldiers of the *Wehrmacht* who had not supported Hitler's eastern campaign but had been pressed into service there and later perished in Soviet captivity. Sadly, the young man's conciliatory sentiments were met by a wave of hatred and outrage in Russia. Such Russian-German exchange programs have taken place for many years now, and they have made their contribution to ongoing efforts at Russian-German reconciliation. Yet the young man's speech to the *Bundestag* on this November day, and its explosive impact, reveal just how difficult the process of reconciliation remains—seventy-seven years after the war began. To promote the necessary healing, Germans must continue to emphasize that they make no attempt to equate victims and evildoers and that Hitler's attack on the Soviet Union was a criminal war of aggression (*verbrecherischer Angriffskrieg*).

In this emotionally riveted environment the American military historian Dr. Craig Luther, a former Fulbright Scholar (Bonn, West Germany) and retired U.S. Air Force historian, has addressed the first twenty-one hours of Nazi Germany's surprise attack on the Soviet Union, harnessing a wide range of both German and Soviet documentary evidence; he thereby makes an important contribution to documenting this difficult chapter in German-Russian history. His account, which builds on his several decades of research and study of German military operations during the Second World War and, most notably, on his recent work, *Barbarossa Unleashed*, offers significant new insights into the start of the Russian campaign.

In the first two chapters Dr. Luther examines in some detail the military and political background to the start of the campaign from the vantage point of both Germans and Russians, bringing his expert grasp of the material to the subject at hand. Based on his intensive evaluation of both German and Russian primary materials, as well as his inspections of former battlefields along the old Russo-German frontier—such as the bunkers at Akmenynai, Lithuania, which were captured at such great cost to the Germans—he then explores in unusual depth the first day of Operation *Barbarossa* along the entire length of the Eastern Front. In several chapters he describes the operations of the German infantry and panzer divisions based on official German war diaries and the personal accounts of both German and Russian soldiers who took part in the fighting. His account of operations on the ground, which sometimes follows the action on a minute-by-minute basis, is followed by a chapter addressing the virtual destruction of the Russian air force by the *Luftwaffe* on June 22, 1941.

On that day, the strongest and best-equipped army in the world, the German army, struck the totally unprepared Red Army. The Germans possessed the experience, were far superior to their adversary in leadership, and were utterly relentless in their operational approach. The German army began its surprise attack with over three million soldiers, 3,600 tanks and assault guns, and supported by nearly 3,000 aircraft; it was the largest attacking force the world had ever seen. The front line stretched for nearly 2,000 kilometers from the Baltic to the Black Sea. The Germans advanced in three great spearheads (*Stosskeile*) toward Leningrad, Moscow, and into the Ukraine. Although they failed to take Leningrad, they cut it off and surrounded it, resulting in the starvation of hundreds of thousands of civilians. In the south, the German army reached Crimea and, in 1942, pushed all the way to the Caucasus. Yet in 1941, the primary push was made by the German central army group, which, by December 1941, had been stopped before the gates of Moscow by mud and snow, but mostly by the tenacity of the Red Army. All of that, however, transpired well after June 22, 1941, which was really *the* decisive day; indeed, because *Barbarossa* ended in dismal failure, that terrible Sunday marked the beginning of the end for Hitler's Third Reich.

In his study of that first day of war on the Eastern Front, Dr. Luther, as noted, does not limit his account to the German perspective, but is careful to examine the course of those twenty-one bloody hours through the lens of Soviet experience as well. Working together with Dr. Richard Harrison, a superb Russian translator, Dr. Luther gained access to a large tranche of official Red Army documents, enabling him to balance his narrative with meaningful insights into the Soviet side of the fighting on June 22, 1941.

As far as I am aware, no American historian prior to Dr. Luther has ever addressed the planning and course of operations on the first day of *Barbarossa* from the standpoints of both German and Russian combatants in such detail. As such he has made a major contribution to our understanding of this decisive chapter of the Second World War. Surely he has succeeded in reaching his goal of furnishing the reader with unprecedented insight into the opening hours of Nazi Germany's war of aggression against the Soviet Union; moreover, the book is eminently accessible to both the professional historian and casual reader.

On June 22, 2016, *Bundestag* president Dr. Norbert Lammert, in his introductory remarks to the German parliament on the seventy-fifth anniversary of the German attack on the USSR, spoke of a "war of annihilation without precedent in eastern Europe, which had its origins in the disdain for human life and racist ideology of National Socialism." And if today Germany remembers this surprise attack, "we confirm our will to do justice to the lessons of a history for which our country bears more responsibility than all others," he continued. In *The First Day on the Eastern Front*, Dr. Luther makes a valuable contribution to our understanding of that history.

Dirk C. Frotscher
Oberst d.R.
(Colonel in the Reserves, German Army)

Acknowledgments

Voltaire, the great writer and philosopher of the eighteenth-century French Enlightenment, once observed: "To hold a pen is to be at war" (*Qui plume a, guerre a*). While I'm no philosopher, and not privy to the precise context of Voltaire's remark, every author knows through his or her own travails that there is more than a touch of verisimilitude to those few simple words. Writing is hard. At times, every sentence can be a struggle. And self-doubt is always looming just beneath conscious thought. That is one reason that for myself, and most authors, preparing the acknowledgments is such a joy—it is a time to simply unwind and thank all the good souls without whose patience, advice, and moral support—mostly patience—no author's book, surely not mine, would ever see the light of day.

Let me begin by thanking Stackpole's senior history editor, David Reisch, without whose support this book would surely never have happened. And that I mean quite literally, for it was David who asked me one day if I had any books left in me and, if so, might I like to write one for Stackpole? I had, for some time, been intrigued by the concept of a book examining in detail the first day of war on the Eastern Front—Sunday, June 22, 1941. So, I mulled over David's question and, within forty-five minutes, I emailed him a proposal for just such a book. During the many months of research and writing, David was always there when I needed help; it was a pleasure to work with him. Among David's colleagues who also deserve a "shout out" are production editor Meredith L. Dias, assistant editor Stephanie Otto, and copy editor Joshua Rosenberg, the latter for his remarkable edit of my manuscript, which clearly was not ready for "prime time" before he got hold of it. Thanks also to proofreader Shana Jones and layout artist Sue Murray.

Another man who deserves to be at, or near, the top of my acknowledgments is the CEO of Schiffer Books, Peter Schiffer. Peter published two of my books in recent years and did a fine job with both of them; the only reason I was even able to move forward with Stackpole on this book project was because Peter graciously let me do so by releasing me from my Schiffer obligations. Peter Schiffer is a good man and I will always remember his kindness.

Before getting too far along I must certainly acknowledge Herrn Dirk C. Frotscher, a colonel in the reserves of the German military (*Bundeswehr*), for his thoughtful foreword to the book. His words capture the essence of *The First Day on the Eastern Front,* and for that I am most grateful.

A number of professional colleagues, historians who have written many fine works of their own (often on the Eastern Front, 1941/45), also merit high praise. So my most profound thanks and gratitude go to Dr. Jürgen Förster (Freiburg, Germany), Dr. David Stahel (University of New South Wales, Australia), and Dr. Jonathan Roth (San Jose State University, California) for always being available to respond to a difficult question, provide constructive criticism, or for simply letting me "think out loud" at their expense. Dr. Stahel took time from his own very busy—and most productive!—writing schedule to carefully read the entire manuscript, offering many useful suggestions and, simply put, making this book a better book; in addition, he provided me with several key primary documents I had missed in my research.

Without the gracious assistance of Colonel David M. Glantz, my "vision" for *The First Day on the Eastern Front* would certainly have fallen short. David is—as all historians of World War II would acknowledge—the Western world's foremost expert on Eastern Front operations 1941/45. He provided me with essential documentary materials, responded patiently (and often in meticulous detail) to my many queries, read the manuscript, and offered his invaluable professional critique. Due to David's support, I gained access for the first time to official Russian primary documents—records of Soviet *fronts*, armies, etc.—that enabled me to cover the "Other Side of the Hill" in more detail than I had in my recent book, *Barbarossa Unleashed*. David also got me in touch with Dr. Richard Harrison, one of the finest Russian translators in the country, who patiently translated dozens of pages of documents that provided me with many new insights into June 22, 1941, from the Soviet perspective. So forgive me for a repetitive thought, but without the kindness and professional acumen of Colonel Glantz and Dr. Harrison, this book would not have come about.

A woman dear to my heart is Dr. Madeleine Brook (now teaching at the University of Stuttgart in Germany). Dr. Brook, who prepared most of the translations for *Barbarossa Unleashed*, helped ensure that my translations for this book at least approached her (unapproachable) standard of excellence. Over the years, I've learned so much from this exceptionally gifted young woman about translating text from German to English, and I trust this book benefited from that. Madeleine also researched and provided me with a large tranche of German field post letters and diaries from the Library of Contemporary History (Stuttgart, Germany) that helped to enrich my narrative. I'd also like to extend my thanks to Frau Irina Renz, the head of special collections at the library, for graciously assisting Madeleine and helping to ensure that she gained access to what I was looking for.

Librarians and students who assist us authors often get short shrift in the acknowledgment pages, but not here, not ever. For I am fully aware of the great lift given to my work by Mr. Nyle C. Monday, the history librarian and faculty member at San Jose State University, and Mr. Spencer Brophy, an SJSU graduate student and ROTC cadet. Nyle acquired, when necessary via interlibrary loan, a number of books I needed to fill the lacunae in my research, and patiently scanned many pages from them. Spencer located dozens of books in the SJSU library system vital to my research and photocopied many hundreds of pages—liberating me from the onerous prospect of a round-trip of 750 miles to do the work myself. I should add that SJSU boasts such a fine collection of books and documents addressing German operations in World War II due to the efforts of the late (great) Dr. Charles Burdick, who taught history for decades at the university and, over the decades, assembled one of the finest collections of such materials in the United States.

While sincerely hoping I neglect no one, I must also acknowledge my dear friend and U.S. Air Force command historian, Dr. Deborah C. Kidwell, for patiently reading the manuscript and offering many useful suggestions; Oleg Beyda (doctoral candidate, University of New South Wales), who located and transcribed a large number of official Soviet military documents; Herr Arne Schrader and Christian Reith (German War Graves Commission), for permission to use their agency's photographs; Mr. Rupert Harding (Pen & Sword Books, U.K.), for permission to use several photographs; Herr Kurt Arlt, who located and transcribed (from Russian to German) several graphic accounts by Russian soldiers; Mr. Dirk Burgdorf (AAA Research), who provided me with hundreds of pages of German war diaries, maps, and other records from the National Archives in Washington, DC; Henley's Photo Shop (Bakersfield, CA), for producing the most exquisite (and reasonably priced!) photographs and maps that are in this book; the German-Russian Museum Berlin-Karlshorst, for kindly allowing me to use a particularly important photograph from their fine collection; and, finally, I once again owe a special debt of gratitude to my first publisher and friend of forty years, Mr. Roger Bender of Bender Publishing, for graciously furnishing several of the photographs of German generals and German military equipment used in this book.

Most of all, however, I must salute my dear wife, Marie Therese, who spent far too many nights alone while I jabbed at my keyboard until the wee hours of the morning, struggling to reach my writing goal for the day. Without her patience, her support, and most of all, her love, I cannot conceive of this book ever being finished. So I thank you from the heart, my dear wife; perhaps another jaunt to Europe (to research the next book, naturally) will help to make amends?

PREFACE

The first day in the campaign against Russia. We have a hard day behind us! The Russians fought like devils and never surrendered, so we engaged in close combat on several occasions; just now, half an hour ago, another four Russians were struck dead with the butts of our rifles.

—Dr. Heinrich Haape, 18 Infantry Regiment[1]

During the night the messenger Anisimov of the border guards of the 98 Border Detachment dropped by. He reported to us that the Germans were placing small boats in the Bug river and preparing to cross. We received no orders from the divisional staff. The wire communications had been cut by saboteurs.

—Anatolij Kazakov, 178 Artillery Regiment[2]

Barely thirty-one years of age, American journalist Henry C. Cassidy was the Associated Press bureau chief in Moscow[3] when, at dawn on June 22, 1941, Adolf Hitler unleashed his still undefeated legions against Soviet Russia. Two years later, in 1943, after Hitler's legions were broken and annihilated in the epic battle of Stalingrad, Cassidy published an account of his observations of the Russo-German war from the Soviet capital. Issued by Houghton Mifflin, *Moscow Dateline 1941–1943* began (literally) with atmospherics before noting the cynical policy of government-induced ignorance prevailing in Moscow on the eve of the German invasion:

Spring came late to Moscow in 1941. Well into April, the heavy winter clouds that fell lower and lower, until every breath of the damp, compressed air rasped like a file in the lungs, hung over the Byzantine turrets of the Kremlin. Not until June 6 did the last snow fall. Those who had to stay with it cursed the dirty coat of ice, the soggy piles of snow that clung to the cobblestoned streets, and longed for the warmth of spring, not knowing that with it would come war.[4]

"Everyone," Cassidy went on, "except those who should know," was aware that war between Germany and Russia, the two great totalitarian powers on the European continent, was simply a matter of time; it was coming, inexorably and unavoidably, bearing down on the Russian people—metaphorically, at least—like that proverbial runaway train. Reports of impending war abounded—"for two cents, you could read in all the newspapers of America reports from Ankara, Berne, and London that Germany was to attack the Soviet Union." And yet, Cassidy recalled:

> *In the censor-tight cylinder of Moscow, no one knew, not the foreigners, not the Russian people, not the Soviet leaders.*
>
> *The reason we did not know there would be war was that we did know the Soviet Union wanted peace at almost any price, would make almost any concession, even unasked, to escape war. What we could not know was that Germany was determined, in any case, to attack.*
>
> *So we went on, cursing the tardiness of spring, and leading the strange life of that last winter of peace in Moscow.*[5]

Yet even a totalitarian state like Soviet Russia in 1941, dominated though it was by the brutal and murderous stewardship of Joseph Stalin, cannot stop people from thinking nor rumors from spreading—and by June 1941, the rumors of approaching war had become rampant and unnerving in the Soviet capital and throughout the infinite reaches of the Soviet multinational state. On June 14, with the German invasion barely a week away, Stalin, perhaps in an act of sheer desperation, felt compelled to publish "that famous TASS communiqué," which was to "figure prominently in all Soviet histories of the war written under Khrushchev as the most damning piece of evidence of Stalin's wishful thinking, short-sightedness and total lack of understanding of what was going on in Germany even at that late hour."[6] The text of the rather garrulous communiqué included the following passages:

> *Even before Cripps'*[7] *arrival in London and especially after he had arrived there, there have been more and more rumors of an "early war" between the Soviet Union and Germany. It is also rumored that Germany has presented both territorial and economic claims to the Soviet Union . . . All this is nothing but clumsy propaganda by forces hostile to the USSR and Germany and interested in an extension of the war . . .*
>
> *2) According to Soviet information, Germany is also unswervingly observing the conditions of the Soviet-German Non-Aggression Pact, just as the USSR is doing. Therefore, in the opinion of Soviet circles, the rumors of Germany's intention to tear up the Pact and to undertake an attack on the USSR are without any foundation. As for the transfer to the northern and eastern areas of Germany of troops during the past weeks, since the completion of their tasks in the Balkans, such troop movements are, one must suppose, prompted by motives which have no bearing on Soviet-German relations.*

3) As is clear from her whole peace policy, the USSR intends to observe the conditions of the Soviet-German Pact, and any talk of the Soviet Union preparing for war is manifestly absurd . . .[8]

While the TASS communiqué no doubt mollified the fears and anxieties of many, it bore no relationship to reality and signified nothing more than the culmination of Stalin's frantic attempts to appease his nemesis, Adolf Hitler, and to preserve peace—in the words of Henry C. Cassidy—"at almost any price."[9] Moreover, it had a pernicious effect on Red Army readiness:

Such an announcement from an authoritative government body dulled the troops' vigilance. Among the command element it gave birth to the confidence that there were some kind of unknown circumstances that enabled our government to remain calm and confident in the security of the Soviet frontier. The commanders stopped spending the night in the barracks. The troops began to undress at night.[10]

Ivan Kovaljov, in 1941 a first lieutenant in a Soviet rifle division posted in the far south, at the Prut River, recalled the impact of the TASS communiqué on the Russian people and his comrades:

Saturday evening [June 21, 1941]. Throughout the country, except on the western border, which has grown more restless over the course of the year, the typical hustle and bustle before a day of rest holds sway. For most people the thought was barely discernable that, in 10 hours, the word "war" would ring out. Only the highest military-political leadership of the country were aware of Germany's preparations for war and the surprise attack on the Soviet Union long before that tragic day.

Our army and our people had a boundless trust in Stalin's "genius" and allowed themselves, just a week before the outbreak of war, to be taken in by the TASS communiqué, according to which Germany, under no circumstances, would violate the non-aggression pact and attack our country. Even experienced professional soldiers did not doubt the credibility of the official propaganda. It was hardly a coincidence that also in our division, which was stationed close to the western frontier on the Prut, many officers, among them the regimental commander of 256 Rifle Regiment, Safonov, were granted leave and left their garrisons in Moldavia. Yes, the trust in our leadership was boundless, although [millions] of German soldiers and their allies had already deployed on our border.[11]

But it was much too late for hollow gestures of appeasement, for there was nothing the almighty Joseph Stalin could do to turn back the malevolent and deadly runaway train bearing down on him and his unsuspecting countrymen at such frightening speed.

In fact, literally thousands of trains were now rumbling east into German-occupied Poland and East Prussia, shepherding the troops, tanks, trucks, artillery, and armored personnel carriers of Hitler's eastern army (*Ostheer*) toward the frontier with Russia in the final phase of the German buildup for Operation *Barbarossa*—Hitler's surprise attack on the Soviet Union.

If the reader will indulge me a repetitive thought—that attack commenced at dawn, on Sunday, June 22, 1941—in other words, more than seventy-seven years ago. And yet, despite the historical remoteness of that day, the "post-modern" world of the twenty-first century has yet to shake off its terrible, and enduring, impact. The destruction of European Jewry in the Holocaust, the creation of the state of Israel, the decades-long division of Europe into two armed and antagonistic camps and, ironically, even the eventual collapse of the Soviet Union and its empire, all have their origins in that fateful day. Moreover, the current efforts of President Vladimir Putin to promote the rise of Russia to Great Power status—in some cases via the application of military power—can be interpreted as an attempt by the Russian strongman to recapture at least a portion of the former Soviet Union's superpower status that had its origins in the USSR's territorial acquisitions at the end of World War II and its acquisition of nuclear weapons (accomplished with the support of captured German scientists).

As noted English historian Paul Johnson posited in his epic account of recent world history, 1941 was the "watershed year" of the twentieth century, "from which mankind has descended into its present predicament."[12] The year, of course, culminated in the surprise Japanese attack on the U.S. Pacific Fleet at Pearl Harbor and against American, British, and European possessions in the Pacific region and Southeast Asia. Yet the *pivotal* event of this "watershed year" had occurred months earlier, on June 22, with the launch of Germany's "*Blitzkrieg*"-style campaign against Soviet Russia—a campaign, Hitler and his General Staff calculated, that would crush the hated and feared Bolshevik enemy in a mere matter of weeks.

The late Alan Clark, English politician, diarist, and accomplished historian, penned the first full-length narrative of Operation *Barbarossa* in the English-speaking world; his still classic study, first published more than a half-century ago (1965), amplifies the preceding observations:

> *What an appalling moment in time this is! The head-on crash of the two greatest armies, the two most absolute systems, in the world. No battle in history compares with it. Not even that first ponderous heave of August 1914, when all the railway engines in Europe sped the mobilization, or the final exhausted lunge against the Hindenburg Line four years later. In terms of numbers of men, weight of ammunition, length of front, the desperate crescendo of the fighting, there will never be another day like 22 June 1941.*[13]

Using any benchmarks, the war that began that day—when, "as they had in all other cities of Europe, the lights of Russia were blacked out so, all unwilling, Russia became Armageddon"[14]—was the most gigantic, monstrous, and costly war the world has ever witnessed:

- The main Russo-German front reached a maximum length of 2,050 kilometers in 1942, while the maximum depth of the German advance (also 1942) was 1,730 kilometers from the *Barbarossa* start line.[15]

- From 1941 to 1944, some ten million German soldiers saw active military service in the cities and towns, the forests and swamps, and endless steppe lands of the Eastern Front,[16] and more still in the final battles for Hitler's 1,000-Year Reich in the winter/spring of 1945. More than 4.5 million of these men lost their lives, including over one million who died in Soviet captivity.[17] The average life expectancy of a German lieutenant in the East was eighteen days; of a company commander about twenty-one days; and of a battalion commander roughly thirty-two days.[18]

- During the war 34.5 million men (and women) served in the Soviet armed forces. According to highly credible new research into recently declassified Soviet military archives, the Red Army's "demographic" losses (i.e., those who were killed in battle; died from wounds, illness, or accidents; perished in captivity,[19] went missing and never returned, or were executed by their own people) amounted to nearly 14.6 million men (and women),[20] while the total number of Soviet citizens (soldiers and civilians) who died in the war is estimated at about 27 million.[21]

- The economic impact of the war was also staggering. The areas ultimately occupied by the German invaders embraced two-fifths of the grain and four-fifths of the sugar beets produced in the Soviet Union, as well as about one-quarter of the country's farm animals, tractors, and combine harvesters. Between them, the Germans and Russians destroyed 1,710 towns, 70,000 villages, 32,000 industrial plants, and 65,000 kilometers of railway track. "In the Russian republic alone 23,000 schools were razed to the ground. Damage to basic industry was particularly severe. Between half and two-thirds of Soviet basic industrial capacity was put out of action."[22]

In the spring of 2014, I published *Barbarossa Unleashed*,[23] which recorded in fulsome detail the blood-stained drive of German Army Group Center through central Russia in the summer of 1941. The research for the book claimed more than a decade of my life and, originally, was intended to produce a book focused on Operation Typhoon (*Taifun*), the final German advance toward Moscow, which began on October 2, 1941. However, after completing the obligatory chapters on the background to Hitler's attack on Soviet

Russia, I did something I had not expected to do—I composed an entire chapter (nearly 25,000 words) addressing just the first day of the war along the front of Field Marshal Fedor von Bock's Army Group Center. It was at that point I realized I would be writing a very different book from the one originally envisaged; yet the abrupt *volte-face* was inescapable, for the material I had collected on June 22, 1941, was so dramatic, so ineluctable, I simply couldn't avoid it.

The war between Germany and Soviet Russia lasted for 1,418 dreadful days, and yet the war's very first day echoes so many of the themes that characterized the conflict until Hitler committed suicide in his bunker and the victorious Red Army raised its battle flag above the *Reichstag* in Berlin in May 1945. The vast expanse of the battle space, the many millions of combatants, the large and unremitting slaughter, the primordial cruelty and barbarism (on both sides), the heroism of men in often desperate situations—all of this is strikingly evident in the first twenty-one hours of Operation *Barbarossa* (the German assault began just after 3:00 A.M.).

What also became evident—and surprisingly so—as I drilled down deeper into my research was that, despite obvious similarities, the events of those initial twenty-one hours often played out quite differently along each of the three main axes of the German attack. Oddly enough, it was, in some respects, almost as if the Germans fought three separate wars that day.

From the very first moments of that very first day, the German *Ostheer* encountered an adversary who, while far from fully prepared for war, often resisted tenaciously—even savagely—as a generation of Communist rule and propaganda had prepared the Red Army soldier *psychologically* for war in a way the czars could have but envied. And if the invading Germans registered truly impressive successes on June 22, 1941, they also encountered disturbing auguries of what the future held in store: the 6 Infantry Division's bitter and costly battle for the bunkers at Akmenynai, just across the frontier inside Soviet-occupied Lithuania; the savage struggle for the old Polish fortress of Brest-Litovsk along the Western Bug River,[24] which took such a heavy toll on the Austrians of 45 Infantry Division; the fanatical Red Army defense of the fortified border town of Oleszyce in the Ukraine against the stalwart veterans of General Hubert Lanz's elite 1 Mountain (*Gebirgs*) Division—all of these actions, and many more, are described in graphic detail in the narrative that follows.

To construct an account that offers an intimate glimpse inside the first day of war on the Eastern Front—and does so from the perspective of the common soldier (the view "from below") as well as of the military-political leadership of both antagonists (the view "from above")—I was able to assemble a voluminous array of both primary and secondary materials. To tell the German side of the story I have made extensive use of the military records at the German Federal Military Archives in Freiburg, Germany (*Bundesarchiv-Militärarchiv*, or BA-MA), and at the National Archives and Records Administration (NARA) at College Park, Maryland; these include official war diaries

(*Kriegstagebücher*) of the army groups, armies, panzer (tank) groups, and divisions that took part in the start of Operation *Barbarossa*, as well as maps, photographs, and other key documents. The Library of Contemporary History (*Bibliothek für Zeitgeschichte*, or *BfZ*) in Stuttgart, Germany, boasts one of the finest collections of German field post letters from the Second World War, and I have put them to good use. I also fully exploited my own personal archive—collected over many years—which encompasses hundreds of books, dozens of published and unpublished unit histories, military maps, and hundreds of photographs.

Working together with Russian-speaking scholars, I made significant use of primary Russian materials in an effort to provide some balance to the narrative by offering English-speaking readers new insights into June 22, 1941, from the vantage point of the Red Army and the Soviet leadership. In doing so, however, due to the often prohibitive costs involved—not to mention the sheer volume of Russian archival documents now becoming available—I was, at best, only able to scratch the surface of these vital Russian materials. And yet I did manage to glean meaningful insights from dozens of translated Russian documents, which, I believe, palpably enriched the narrative. Russian primary sources consulted for this book include: (a) several volumes of the series *Sbornik Boevykh Dokumentov* (Collection of Combat Documents), which, *inter alia*, embrace documents covering combat activities of Soviet *fronts* (army groups) and their constituent armies on a daily basis for the initial period of the war; and, (b) a small selection of documents (among the many thousands) recently placed on the World Wide Web by the Central Archive of the Ministry of Defense of the Russian Federation.[25] There is also a wonderful website (available in both the Russian and English languages)[26] that offers hundreds of firsthand accounts of the experiences of Russian soldiers and civilians alike in what the Russians still refer to with pride as the "Great Patriotic War" against Nazi Germany. And, of course, I have once again relied on the works of Russian scholars Colonel David M. Glantz, John Erickson, Chris Bellamy, Evan Mawdsley, Gabriel Gorodetsky, Constantine Pleshakov, and others.

Because for the first time in my modest career as a writer I found myself under the "tyranny" of a word count—albeit a flexible word count, due to the graciousness of my Stackpole editor—I have, perforce, limited my discussion of topics that precede the events of June 22, 1941. What this essentially means is that Chapter 1 (*Planning for Armageddon—Adolf Hitler and His General Staff Prepare to Unleash War on Soviet Russia*) is limited in scope, and that many issues fundamental to Operation *Barbarossa* (e.g., was Hitler's surprise attack on Russia preventive, or even preemptive, in nature?) were only addressed in passing, while others (e.g., Hitler's reasons for turning against the USSR, German General Staff planning, the actions of the Soviet leadership and Red Army in the months preceding the German invasion) could only be examined in largely general terms. For more detailed discussions of background issues germane to Operation *Barbarossa*, the reader is directed to my book *Barbarossa Unleashed*, to several excellent books recently published by historian David Stahel, and to the dozens of works produced over several decades by Colonel Glantz.

If I have succeeded in my efforts, this book will fully immerse the reader in the terror, confusion, and horror of a distant time and place, when Adolf Hitler decided to "play chess with humanity"[27] by unleashing Armageddon—his criminal war of annihilation (*Vernichtungskrieg*)—against the Soviet people. "Subject to those inevitable 'modifications in practice,'" observed historian Chris Bellamy in his excellent study of Russia at war, "the war on the eastern front was probably the most 'absolute' war ever fought, on both sides."[28] These words have the ring of verisimilitude, for if any war in recorded history inclined toward Clausewitz's theory of war in the *abstract*—that is, toward *absolute violence*, as opposed to how soldiers actually practiced it—it was surely the war that began when Hitler's *Soldaten* poured across the Russo-German frontier on the morning of June 22, 1941.[29]

CHAPTER 1

Planning for Armageddon—
Adolf Hitler and His General Staff Prepare to
Unleash War on Soviet Russia

When Barbarossa begins the world will hold its breath.

—ADOLF HITLER[1]

Don't ever underestimate your enemy, but put yourself in his situation—what would I do if I were him?

—FREDERICK THE GREAT[2]

How could it be expected, assuming a German victory, that the situation in the east would be other than that so mordantly described by Tacitus, ubi solitudinem faciunt, pacem appellant, *"where they make a wilderness, they call it peace"?*

—HISTORIAN RONALD LEWIN[3]

❧

IN HIS NEW YEAR'S ADDRESS TO THE *WEHRMACHT* (GERMAN ARMED FORCES) ON JANUary 1, 1941, Adolf Hitler began by fulsomely praising his soldiers for the "glorious" and "unique" victories they had achieved during the previous year of war. "With unprecedented boldness," they had "smashed the enemy on land, at sea and in the air," he said. All of the tasks that he, the "*Führer*," had been "forced" to set for them, his *Soldaten* had solved through their "heroic spirit" (*Heldenmut*) and soldierly virtues. Hitler ended his address by predicting that "the year 1941 will bring the completion of the greatest of all victories in our history."[4]

What could the Nazi leader have meant by such a bold statement? How should his armed forces and the German people have understood it? Only twelve months before, Hitler, in his New Year's message had said, "may the Year 1940 bring the decision!" And

I

he had not been disappointed. In April 1940, German land, sea, and air forces, in a daring display of initiative and flexibility, had seized Norway. On the heels of this great victory came an even greater victory—"the most glorious victory of all time," Hitler proclaimed on June 24, 1940[5]—over France, which Germany's armies and air force (*Luftwaffe*) had vanquished with dazzling speed and Teutonic precision. Yet Great Britain was still resisting, and mightily so, having beaten back the *Luftwaffe's* furious assaults in the battle of Britain in the summer/fall of 1940, forcing the *Führer* to first postpone, and then cancel, Operation *Sealion*, the planned invasion of Britain. So perhaps Hitler's curious New Year's statement was aimed at Winston Churchill's brave and defiant little island?

That would have made for an obvious, and logical, inference, but it would have been wrong. For by January 1941, Hitler was looking east, and only east. In fact, just weeks before, with most of the war planning already completed by his General Staff, he had put his signature to the "*Führer* directive" for "Case *Barbarossa*," the attack on the Soviet Union, to be launched in the spring of 1941.

In 1941, Germany and Russia were at peace. In August 1939, Europe's two totalitarian giants, in one of the slickest diplomatic démarches in world history, had shocked contemporaries by signing on to a non-aggression pact. The pact, which had partitioned Poland between them and, in secret protocols, carved up Eastern Europe into zones of influence, had freed the *Führer* to attack and destroy Poland in September 1939,[6] and then to move against the western powers, England and France, without fear of danger on his eastern flank. The pact had also led to significant economic cooperation between Germany and Russia; in 1940, in fact, 65 percent of Germany's chrome ore supplies, 55 percent of its manganese, 40 percent of its nickel imports, and 34 percent of its imported oil were supplied by Russia. It is hardly an overstatement to posit that such economic support from the USSR helped to maintain Hitler's armies in the field. To quote the quartermaster-general of the German army, Colonel Eduard Wagner, "the conclusion of this treaty [i.e., the 'gigantic' trade deal of February 1940] has saved us."[7]

Yet for both Hitler and Stalin—albeit for quite different reasons—the non-aggression pact, and the broader political settlement that ensued, had never signified anything more than a marriage of convenience, for however long it was convenient to maintain it. Indeed, for Hitler, the pact "was nothing more than what the 1918 Brest-Litovsk Treaty with Germany had been for Lenin: a distasteful necessity, which, with luck, would not endure very long."[8] And by New Year's Day, 1941, it had outlived any long-term usefulness for Germany's dictator, who had concluded months before that realization of his fantastical plans of global conquest and empire required, as *the* fundamental prerequisite, the destruction of Bolshevik Russia and the systematic pilfering of its resources. Yet there had never really been the slightest doubt that Hitler would, at first opportunity, turn against Russia, and the critical decision to do so was taken by him almost at once in the wake of the French Campaign of 1940.

1.1: Prologue—France 1940 and the Nimbus of Invincibility

The German offensive against France and the Low Countries (Holland, Belgium, and Luxembourg) began shortly after dawn on May 10, 1940. On the fourth day of the campaign (May 13), German ground forces (all told, 136 divisions, including ten panzer and seven motorized divisions, supported by some 2,500 combat aircraft)[9] crossed the Meuse River at Sedan, achieving a decisive breakthrough. The *Wehrmacht*'s armored spearheads then raced rapidly to the west, toward the English Channel; soon the panzer divisions were sweeping across the bloody battlefields of 1914/18 and, on May 19, advance elements of a panzer corps reached the English Channel near Abbeville, having thrust 320 kilometers in a mere ten days. Elite units of the French army and the British Expeditionary Force (BEF) were now trapped in a huge pocket with their backs to the sea and, in the desperate days that followed, the French and British evacuated more than 350,000 Allied soldiers (including the entire BEF) from Dunkirk, the last remaining Channel port in Allied hands. By June 4, "the battle was over"—the Allies having lost 50 percent of their forces and over 75 percent of their best weapons and equipment. "The flower of the French Army was behind wire, the majority of the British humiliated and back in Britain."[10]

The final phase of the campaign began on June 5, the Germans wheeling southward against French forces dug in along the Somme and the Aisne—the so-called Weygand Line. But it was a "line" in name only, and although the French, now hopelessly outnumbered, often fought with more tenacity than they had on the Meuse, the Germans rapidly broke through. On June 14, Paris fell, and elements of the German 87 Infantry Division marched triumphantly through the undefended city, weeping Parisians looking on in disbelief. Three days later, the aged Marshal Pétain, hero of World War I, having already formed a new government, informed the French people that negotiations for an armistice were underway.

American journalist and war correspondent, William L. Shirer, had "followed the German Army into Paris that June." On the 19th, he "got wind" of the location, in northern France, where Hitler planned to "lay down his terms" for the armistice requested by Pétain. So late that afternoon Shirer drove out there. It was a small clearing in the forest at Compiègne, the same spot where Imperial Germany had capitulated to France and its allies on November 11, 1918. When he arrived, Shirer found German army engineers "demolishing the wall of the museum where the old *wagon-lit* of Marshal Foch, in which the 1918 armistice was signed, had been preserved." By the time he drove away, the engineers, "working with pneumatic drills, had torn the wall down and were pulling the [railway] car out to the tracks in the center of the clearing on the exact spot, they said, where it had stood at 5:00 a.m. on November 11, 1918, when at the dictation of Foch the German emissaries put their signatures to the armistice."[11]

Two days later (June 21), Shirer returned to the clearing in the forest at Compiègne "to observe the latest and greatest of Hitler's triumphs":

It was one of the loveliest summer days I ever remember in France. A warm June sun beat down on the stately trees—elms, oaks, cypresses and pines—casting pleasant shadows on the wooded avenues leading to the little circular clearing. At 3:15 P.M. precisely, Hitler arrived in his big Mercedes, accompanied by Göring, Brauchitsch, Keitel, Raeder, Ribbentrop and Hess, all in their various uniforms, and Göring, the lone Field Marshal of the Reich, fiddling with his field marshal's baton. They alighted from their automobiles some 200 yards away, in front of the Alsace-Lorraine statue, which was draped with German war flags so that the Führer could not see (though I remembered from previous visits in happier days) the large sword, the sword of the victorious Allies of 1918, sticking through a limp eagle representing the German Empire of the Hohenzollerns. Hitler glanced at the monument and strode on.[12]

Hitler and his entourage soon climbed into the armistice railway car, the *Führer* no doubt relishing the brutal irony of it all, seating himself in the same chair Marshal Foch had sat in almost twenty-two years before. Minutes later, the French delegation arrived, led by General Charles Huntziger, commander of the Second Army at Sedan. To Shirer they "looked shattered," yet retained, he thought, "a tragic dignity."[13] As *Gen.d.Art.* Franz Halder, chief of the German Army General Staff, later jotted in his diary, the French delegation had "no warning that they would be handed the terms at the very site of the negotiations of 1918. They were apparently shaken by this arrangement and at first inclined to be sullen."[14]

Hitler and his party departed the railway car after *Generaloberst* Wilhelm Keitel, chief of staff of the Armed Forces High Command (OKW),[15] had read out the preamble of the armistice terms to the French, leaving Keitel to preside over the negotiations, albeit with strict instructions not to depart from the terms Hitler himself had laid down. The French, finding the terms "hard and merciless," much more severe in fact than those France had imposed on Germany in 1918, struck a defiant pose, with the result that the negotiations dragged on into the next day. Yet with no realistic alternative—and facing an ultimatum from Keitel—the French delegation relented and signed the armistice at precisely 6:50 P.M., June 22, 1940.[16]

The defeat of France marked an extraordinary victory for German arms; moreover, it had been achieved at a relatively modest cost, with losses (army and air force) amounting to 163,213 men, including 29,640 fatal losses.[17] In fact, since September 1939, the German armed forces had only sustained about 200,000 casualties, including some 60,000 fatalities, in the Polish, Scandinavian, and French campaigns combined. If by today's standards these figures seem exorbitant, they are equal to about half the losses suffered by the Kaiser's Army in a single engagement—the battle of the Somme in 1916.[18] To offer another comparative statistic: By the end of 1914—that is, after just five months of fighting in World War I—total German losses had amounted to 840,000, of which roughly 150,000 were fatal losses.[19]

Having subdued France, Germany's historic arch-enemy (*Erzfeind*), Adolf Hitler stood at the pinnacle of power. In barely six weeks he had done what Imperial Germany had been unable to do in four long bloody years of war. His Third Reich, his *Wehrmacht*, dominated Europe from above the Arctic Circle to Bordeaux, from the English Channel to the Bug River in eastern Poland. The former corporal and regimental dispatch runner on the Western Front in World War I had become "the greatest of German conquerors."[20] He had reached a peak in popularity among the German people he would never again enjoy; his political authority was beyond challenge. When the victorious dictator returned to Berlin in early July, he was "driven to the Reich Chancellery on a carpet of flowers. According to press reports 'the mile-long route from the Anhalter Station to the Chancellery was a perfumed avenue of greens, reds, blues and yellows flanked by cheering thousands who shouted and wept themselves into a frantic hysteria as the Führer passed.'"[21]

Hitler's spectacular victory in the West, of course, was a vital prerequisite for turning to the East, for the (eventual) launch of a war of conquest against the Soviet Union. Had Germany become bogged down in a war of attrition in France, as had been Stalin's sincere desire when he signed the non-aggression pact in August 1939, history would have charted a much different course—one that most likely would have ended with Soviet Russia emerging as the dominant power on the European continent and, perforce, arbiter of its affairs. In any case, Stalin was demonstrably frightened by the rapidity and thoroughness of the German victory—even in the spring of 1940, France was perceived by most contemporaries to be Europe's premier military power—and his immediate response was to annex the Baltic States (June 15–17) and to seize Bessarabia and Northern Bukovina from Romania (June 28) as a *cordon sanitaire* against Germany,[22] in the process moving Soviet Russia's borders closer to Romania's oil fields, which were essential to Germany's war effort.

To contemporary observers, the *Wehrmacht*'s victory over France signified the apotheosis of Germany's new style of "*Blitzkrieg*," or "lightning," warfare, based on an innovative combination—and coordination—of mechanized forces (tanks and motorized infantry), combat aircraft, and radio communications. The Germans, with the enthusiastic support of the *Führer*, had pioneered the new techniques in the 1930s, before unleashing them on Poland in September 1939. Yet if the German armed forces—exquisitely trained, equipped, and disciplined as they were—had begun to assume something approaching a nimbus of invincibility, the reality was that the German Reich had built a war machine that harbored many well-concealed shortcomings, including serious shortages of critical raw materials as well as aircraft and other major weapon systems already on the cusp of obsolescence, not to mention an economy still lumbering along on a peacetime footing. Moreover, the German armed forces had entered hostilities in September 1939 with no serious plans to fight a major war. As historian Ian Kershaw put it, "Nothing at all had been clearly thought through. The *Luftwaffe* was the best equipped of the three branches of the armed forces. But even here, the armaments program had been targeted at 1942, not 1939. The navy's operational planning was based upon a fleet that could not be ready before 1943."[23]

Even the victory over France was not quite what it had seemed to be, for the decisive breakthrough early in the campaign owed as much to *fortuna* as it did to German tanks and *Luftwaffe* divebombers: French forces, responding to a report—false as it turned out—that enemy tanks had already crossed the Meuse, collectively panicked, with the result that the French line folded up like a "house of cards," enabling the Germans to break through at Sedan. The rapid *Blitzkrieg* that followed, far from being planned, was largely due to the arbitrary and, at times, even insubordinate, actions of "panzer leader" Heinz Guderian who, galvanized by the dramatic and unanticipated success of his tank corps at Sedan, drove for the Channel at breakneck speed, ignoring orders of his superiors in the process; as a result, Guderian created—as one author described it[24]—an avalanche-like effect that pulled other panzer units along with him. The operations thus developed a dynamic all their own, with even the General Staff at times losing control over them. In this manner, despite General Staff planning that had been fundamentally cautious in its approach—albeit bold and innovative—the campaign unfolded in a *Blitzkrieg*-like fashion that was less the outcome of intent than of a series of fortuitous and unpredictable events.

Yet Hitler and his generals, largely oblivious to the pivotal roles accident and chance had played in France, were indubitably intoxicated by their historic victory over their long-standing nemesis.

> *Seduced by the "miracle of Sedan," and the putative "lessons learned" from 1940, they fell victim to the illusion that had animated Count Alfred von Schlieffen prior to World War I—that a materially superior enemy could be quickly and decisively overcome in a rapid war of movement culminating in a decisive battle of annihilation, what the Germans were fond of calling a* Vernichtungsschlacht. *In other words, to General Halder and his colleagues, the Battle of France had proven, beyond doubt, that victory in battle was simply a matter of working out the proper operational formula, even against an industrial power significantly larger than Germany, like Soviet Russia. Such thinking, an outcome of the badly misconstrued lessons of 1940, exercised a pernicious influence on German doctrine and, perforce, on planning for the Russian campaign.[25]*

In Greek tragedy, hubris denotes "excessive pride toward or defiance of the gods, leading to nemesis." The fall of France fundamentally changed the mindset of Hitler and his General Staff. As for the generals, they now largely entertained the conviction that there was simply nothing the German soldier could not do; no mission he could not perform. As for the German dictator, "his victory in France had given him a feeling of immortality."[26] In its immediate aftermath, Hitler, "drunk on victory" (*siegestrunken*) informed General Keitel, "Now we've shown just what we're capable of. Believe me, Keitel, in comparison [to France] a campaign against Russia would be little more than child's play!"[27]

1.2: HITLER AND RUSSIA I—THE *FÜHRER*'S STRATEGIC (POLITICAL-MILITARY) CASE FOR WAR

The *Sieg über Frankreich* (victory over France) was perceived by most contemporaries as a "colossal personal triumph" for Hitler.[28] The future course of the war—indeed, the fate of all Europe—seemed in the months that followed to hinge largely on whatever decisions he would make. As Hitler's propaganda minister, Joseph Goebbels, noted in his diary on July 12, 1940: "Everyone waits on the decisions of the Führer."[29] And yet, in a paradox of sorts, Germany's strategic position in the summer of 1940 was actually surprisingly fragile.

> *Many scholars of this period refer to Germany's strategic dilemma in the interregnum following the French campaign—a dilemma which, in Hitler's mind, was only resolved in December 1940, when he finally issued his* Barbarossa *directive for the attack on Soviet Russia. The crux of the matter was simple, if not the solution: How was Germany to bring the war to a successful conclusion? How was she to vanquish Great Britain and, ultimately, America and Soviet Russia, before they could bring to bear the collective weight of their material might and trap the Reich in a protracted war of attrition—a repeat, in effect, of 1914–18? A dilemma to be sure; however, one might also posit that what Germany faced that summer was a simple paradox: She was the uncontested master of most of continental Europe, yet faced certain defeat in the years ahead if her statesmen and generals failed to quickly and decisively overcome her strategic conundrum.[30]*

For Germany, the primary long-term threats were the two great continental powers on its flanks—America and Russia. The United States, of course, was still neutral, but was growing increasingly hostile as President Roosevelt moved his country inexorably closer to Great Britain; Hitler calculated that the United States would be ready to enter the war against Germany in 1942. As far as Russia was concerned the problem seemed more pressing. While few details were known—German intelligence was largely unable to penetrate the Soviet Union's solid wall of secrecy—it was generally clear that the Soviet Union was rearming at a rapid pace. Moreover, its occupation of the Baltic States, Bessarabia, and Northern Bukovina meant that its behavior was becoming more aggressive, more threatening.

Yet in the summer of 1940, after the *Sieg über Frankreich*, Hitler had a more immediate problem on his plate—Great Britain. For Hitler, the primary option vis-à-vis Britain was not war but peace; in fact, he genuinely sought an arrangement with the brave island nation. He hoped that his victory in the West might suffice to bring about a general settlement: Britain would accept its exclusion from the European continent and, in return, be allowed to keep its global empire, whose breakup, Hitler feared, would only benefit Japan, the United States, and Soviet Russia. On July 19, 1940, in his victory speech to the *Reichstag*, the *Führer* made a final passionate appeal to the British to "see reason" and seek an arrangement with the Reich. But Churchill, who had become prime minister on May 10, 1940—the very day the Germans launched "Case Yellow," the invasion in the West—"was determined to continue to war." To underscore the point, the RAF conducted bombing raids on cities in western Germany, while the Royal Navy blasted the French fleet in the Algerian port of Mers-el-Kébir to keep it from falling into German hands. On July 23, following a broadcast by Britain's foreign secretary, Lord Halifax, Hitler was forced to accept that the rejection of his offer was final.[31]

Great Britain's refusal to make peace robbed Hitler of the biggest potential political payoff of his triumph in the West. He now "cast around" for alternatives to force Britain to come to terms. Already, on July 16, 1940, he had issued a directive for preparations to begin for an invasion by the middle of August. However, he was skeptical that his navy would be able to pull it off, thus the invasion was soon pushed back to mid-September, at the earliest. He pondered other options as well, such as the capture of the British stronghold of Gibraltar, which, if successful, would close off the western entrance to the Mediterranean to the Royal Navy. In the end, however, he kept coming back to Russia. Flummoxed by the fact that Great Britain was still in the fight, despite its desperate situation—to Hitler Britain's position was "militarily hopeless"—he told Halder (the army chief of staff) on July 13 that the key for Britain was Russia. "The *Führer*," Halder informed his diary that day, "is greatly puzzled by Britain's persisting unwillingness to make peace. He sees the answer (as we do) in Britain's hope on Russia."[32]

By mid-July 1940, the impetuous German dictator was urging General Walther von Brauchitsch (C-in-C of the army) to explore the prospects of an invasion of Russia that very fall. In Berlin (July 21), Hitler met with Brauchitsch, Grand Admiral Erich Raeder (C-in-C of the navy), and Air General Hans Jeschonnek (*Luftwaffe* chief of staff) at the Reich Chancellery. As recorded by Halder (who was briefed by Brauchitsch the next day), the *Führer* insisted that he "will not let the military-political initiative go out of his hand." He repeated his remark to Halder of a week before that Britain was putting her "hope in Russia," while "Stalin is flirting with Britain to keep her in the war and tie us down, with a view to gain time and take what he wants."[33] Hitler went on to indicate that he was prepared, if necessary, to postpone a decision on *Sealion*, the planned invasion of Britain, until next spring, and to move against Russia that very autumn. He had been advised that his armies could be regrouped for the attack in as little as four to six weeks; the objective would be: "To crush [the] Russian army or at least take as much Russian territory as is necessary to bar enemy air raids on Berlin and Silesian industries. It is desirable to penetrate far enough [into Russia] to enable our air force to smash Russia's strategic areas." Eighty to one hundred divisions, Hitler estimated, would be required for the attack.[34]

On July 26, Hitler arrived at the *Berghof*, his idyllic mountain sanctuary on the Obersalzberg, above Berchtesgaden, in the Bavarian Alps. Over the next few days, he conducted a series of conferences with Balkan potentates. The Russians, it was now evident, had placed strong forces in the former Romanian provinces of Bessarabia and Northern Bukovina, among them cavalry and mechanized forces; Hitler was troubled by the proximity of Russian air forces to Romania's oil fields, so vital to Germany's ongoing war effort. One morning, after the scheduled war conference in the *Berghof*'s Great Hall, he queried the chief of his OKW Operations Staff, *Gen.d.Art.* Alfred Jodl, about the prospect of striking at Russia in a "lightning" campaign before winter set in. Jodl, sober military analyst that he was, demurred; he doubted that the army could redeploy from the west and prepare for such an immense task in just a few short months. Ever dutiful, however, he promised to explore the matter. Several days later, Jodl returned to the *Berghof*, bringing along his operations staff's analysis of the potential for an autumn attack: "Spreading out railway maps on the large red marble table at the *Berghof*, he had to advise Hitler that for transport reasons alone it would be impossible to attack Russia that autumn." The *Führer* responded by ordering OKW to assign top priority to expanding the capacity of the railroads in the East.[35]

Finally abandoning his unrealistic notions of an autumn offensive, Hitler privately informed Jodl on July 29 that he had decided to attack the Soviet Union in the coming spring, and that preparations should now begin.[36] Two days later (July 31), in the "great conference on the overall war situation"[37] at the *Berghof*, Hitler informed his top military advisors of his decision. The conference began with Grand Admiral Raeder reporting on the state of preparations for a landing in England, the details of which need not concern us here. After Raeder departed the conference, Hitler quickly got to the heart of the matter, his train of thought captured in the shorthand notes of the chief of the Army General Staff:

> Britain's hope lies in Russia and the United States. *If Russia drops out of the picture, America, too, is lost for Britain, because elimination of Russia would tremendously increase* Japan's power *in the Far East* . . . Russia is the factor on which Britain is relying the most . . . *All that Russia has to do is to hint that she does not care to have a strong Germany, and the British will take hope* . . . With Russia smashed, Britain's last hope would be shattered. *Germany then will be master of Europe and the Balkans.* Decision: Russia's destruction must therefore be made a part of this struggle. Spring 1941.[38]

The sooner Russia was "crushed," the better, he went on. But the attack, he admonished, would only achieve its purpose if Soviet Russia were "shattered to its roots with one blow"—a conviction which, as it turned out, would guide German planning for the Russian campaign like a lode star. Hitler proceeded to outline the operation as he saw it unfolding; he figured that Germany needed 180 divisions to complete its future tasks, 120 of which would be earmarked for the East.[39] Because preparations would not be complete until the following spring, Hitler laid down May 1941 as the "provisional date" for the attack.[40] Historian Ian Kershaw observed:

It was a momentous decision, perhaps the most momentous of the entire war. And it was freely taken. That is, it was not taken under other than self-imposed constraints. It was not taken in order to head off an immediate threat of attack by the Soviet Union. There was no suggestion at this time—the justificatory claims would come later—of the need for a pre-emptive strike. Hitler himself had acknowledged 10 days earlier that the Russians did not want war with Germany. Nor was the decision taken in response to pressure from the military, or from any other lobby within the power-echelons of the regime . . .

The pressure upon Hitler was subjective: his sense that no time could be lost before striking at the Soviet Union if the overall initiative in the war, based on the balance of power and armed might, were not to drain away from Germany toward Britain and, ultimately the United States.[41]

It is, perhaps, one of history's great ironies that Hitler's stated reasons for attacking Russia—which at once unleashed a flurry of planning activity by concerned military staff agencies—were based on a serious misreading of the intentions of his English adversary. As argued by the late German historian Andreas Hillgruber in his analysis of Anglo-American strategic planning over the period 1940/41:

It is striking that the Soviet Union was to play no part in the long-term strategic planning [of the U.S. and Great Britain] . . . the USA and Great Britain were planning to conduct a global war alone against Germany and Japan. Contrary to what Hitler always presumed in his situation analyses, in the course of their strategic planning the USA and Great Britain, whose strengths lay in the area of sea and air power, had not in any way assumed the necessity of a "continental sword," of including the Soviet Union in the "Anti-Hitler Coalition."[42]

In other words, Hitler's basic assumption—"Britain's hope lies in Russia and the United States"—which exercised such a powerful influence on his determination to turn to the east in 1941—was half wrong. While in the coming months the ties between Britain and America would grow closer, and the strategic planning more active, Britain never looked to Russia to function as its "continental sword." This was due, certainly, to Britain's deep mistrust of the communist nation, as well as to its low opinion of Russia's prowess as a military power, perspectives shared, it seems, by civilian and military policy makers in the United States.

In the weeks that followed, the skies above England were filled with Messerschmitt Bf-109s, Heinkel bombers, Spitfires, and Hurricanes—the epic battle of Britain ending in a bitter defeat for Göring's *Luftwaffe*. In October, the German dictator turned diplomat, as he sought—unsuccessfully, to be sure—to harness Franco's Spain and Vichy France to the ongoing war effort. On November 12, 1940, "a dark drizzling day," the Soviet commissar for foreign affairs, Vyacheslav Molotov, arrived in Berlin. "Driving up the Linden to the Soviet embassy, he looked to me," American journalist William L. Shirer wrote in his diary, "like a plugging provincial schoolmaster. But to have survived in the cutthroat competition of the Kremlin he must have something."[43]

The talks that followed "went badly." Molotov's counterpart, German foreign minister Joachim von Ribbentrop, sought in vain to gain Russia's adherence to the recently signed Tripartite Pact between Germany, Italy, and Japan. Direct discussions between Molotov and Hitler himself yielded no better results. Other matters of mutual concern were taken up, but no progress was made. Perhaps underscoring the futility of it all, a "celebratory" dinner at the Soviet Embassy the next day was abruptly broken off due to the arrival of British bombers over Berlin, the talks continuing in Ribbentrop's own air raid shelter. When his German interlocutor insisted that Britain was defeated—her empire ripe for partition among the Axis powers—Molotov acidly replied: "If that is so, why are we sitting in this air-raid shelter?"[44]

Besides its obvious failure, the larger meaning of the Molotov mission was that Hitler felt "wholly vindicated in his view that the conflicting interests of Germany and the Soviet Union could never be peacefully reconciled. A clash was inevitable. Hitler saw Molotov's visit as confirmation that the attack envisaged since July could not be delayed."[45] Two days later, he ordered construction of a field headquarters for the impending Russian campaign—deep in the gloomy forests of East Prussia, near Rastenburg.[46]

Shortly before year's end (December 17, 1940), he informed General Jodl, one of his closest military advisors, that Germany must be prepared to solve all of its "continental European problems" in 1941, because the United States would be able to intervene in the war from 1942 onward.[47] The next day, December 18, Hitler signed "*Führer* Directive" No. 21 ("Case *Barbarossa*"), the Russian campaign directive.[48]

Hitler was well aware that, due to the radically altered situation in Europe resulting from the fall of France, a narrow window of opportunity had opened to settle the score with Russia. As he put it: "In the spring [of 1941], we will be at a discernable high in leadership, material, and troops, and the Russians will be at an unmistakable low."[49] To wait to strike until 1942, he realized, was out of the question, for by then Russia would be ready and America would most likely be in the war—the window slammed shut. He was "convinced, therefore, that time was not on Germany's side. Continental dominance, the end of the European war and the impregnability this would bring had to be attained in 1941 before any conflict with the United States ensued."[50]

1.3: Hitler and Russia II—The *Führer*'s Programmatic (Ideological) Case for War

Biographers of Adolf Hitler and historians of the Third Reich have for decades sought to determine why the German dictator took the fatal step of attacking the Soviet Union in June 1941. Some have focused on the political-military situation in Europe that emerged from the first ten months of war; others have emphasized the ideological convictions held by Hitler since the 1920s, or argued for a synthesis of the two. Recent scholarship has made the compelling case that Hitler made war on Soviet Russia because that was the war he had wanted all along. It was—to invoke the words of Manfred Messerschmidt in his introduction to volume four of the quasi-official German history of the Second World War—"Hitler's real war" (*eigentlicher Krieg*).[51]

In other words, the war he unleashed in June 1941, which would "decide the future of the Continent of Europe,"[52] signified much more than simply an attempt to escape from a strategic dilemma. A dilemma there surely was, and I have touched on it in the preceding paragraphs. To recapitulate: With Great Britain's determination to continue the war after the debacle in France, Hitler needed a way to hold on to the initiative and bring about a decision favorable to Germany before America entered the fray (most assuredly, he thought, in 1942). Yet to effectively challenge Anglo-American air and naval power, he needed to bring the entire European continent under Germany's control, and that could only be done through the conquest of Soviet Russia. The absorption of Russia's vast space would give Germany control over its (Russia's) prodigious bounty of raw materials—its oil, ores, rubber, grain, etc. This, in turn, the *Führer* reasoned, would give the Reich a redoubtable European base of operations and a position of economic self-sufficiency (autarky). In fact, "autarky, in Hitler's thinking, was the basis of security. And the conquest of the east, as he had repeatedly stated in the mid-1920s, would now offer Germany that security."[53]

Here we can begin to discern the conflation of Hitler's long-standing *programmatic* objectives (as adumbrated in *Mein Kampf*), with the political and military imperatives of the moment. Looking back to the 1920s, one discovers strong elements of continuity in Hitler's thinking—his "*Weltanschauung*," or world view—from that period right up to the summer of 1941. In *Mein Kampf*, Hitler had posited that it was Germany's "mission" to conquer Russia.[54] Germany, he insisted, required "living space" (*Lebensraum*) for its expanding population, and this could only be got in the East. By the 1930s, his ideas had grown even more radical.

> On several occasions following his seizure of power, between 1933 and 1939, Hitler was surprisingly open with his generals about the ultimate aims of his policies, letting slip that they embraced violent expansion in the east with pronounced racial and ideological overtones. On one occasion shortly before the outbreak of war, in February 1939, he intimated to a gathering of officers that Germany's present Lebensraum was insufficient; she would have to take more. He also left no doubt about the character of the coming war: "a purely ideological war, i.e., consciously a national and racial war."[55]

Just what this signified in human terms would become all too apparent on June 22, 1941, and throughout the years of subjugation and genocide that followed. Indeed, Hitler's war on Russia—and its people—would more closely resemble a European colonial war of the nineteenth century than a modern military conflict. And yet in his mind, he was simply fighting "fire with fire."

> *Hitler was a realist . . . He expected the war in the Soviet Union to be merciless and to obey no conventional rules. For twenty years he had been fighting Bolshevism, and its face had changed but little in those two decades. Bolshevik methods were familiar to him . . . The horrors of the Cheka were part of history, but the brutality of the Bolsheviks in the Spanish Civil War, in Stalin's half of Poland, and most recently in the hapless Baltic States . . . indicated that this was a permanent trait. In the French campaign, German troops had found ten of their infantry comrades bound hand and foot with their eyes torn out, and an antiaircraft gunner with his feet sawn off; the culprits turned out to be Spanish Red Guards (all were executed). In the Baltic countries, Stalin had appointed commissars who had supervised the deportation and liquidation of the entire intelligentsia within a matter of weeks (as had been done in Poland already); these commissars—said to have been Jewish—had then been replaced by Russians who had disposed of their predecessors.[56]*

German occupational policies, as they took shape before the outbreak of war with Russia—and then grew increasingly extreme as the war went on—envisaged the ruthless "Germanization" of the captured eastern territories. They were to be repopulated by Germans, or European peoples of German descent (*Volksdeutsch*) at the expense of the indigenous Slavic populations, millions of whom would be displaced or simply left to starve to death. Millions more were to be enslaved, while the Jews—in Hitler's mind the ultimate purveyors of "Bolshevism"—along with the intelligentsia, Red Army political officers (commissars),[57] and other "undesirables," were to be liquidated. In the final analysis, "Hitler conceived the war between Germany and Russia as an ineluctable confrontation—an apocalyptic struggle between two mutually exclusive *Weltanschauungen* culminating in a racial war of extermination."[58] More than three decades ago, a celebrated German historian, the late Andreas Hillgruber, laid out the four fundamental programmatic objectives of Hitler's *Ostkriegkonzeption*; his insights remain valid to this day:

> *a. The extermination of the Soviet Union's "Jewish–Bolshevik" ruling elite, including its purported biological mainspring, the millions of Jews in eastern central Europe;*

> *b. The acquisition of colonizing space for German settlers in those areas of Russia reputed to be the best;*

> *c. The decimation of the Slavic masses and their subjugation to German authority in four "Reich Commissariats," Eastland (Belorussia, Lithuania, Latvia, Estonia), Ukraine, Muscovy, and Caucasus[59] . . . under the leadership of German "viceroys," as*

Hitler termed it, borrowing from his "ideal" model of colonial power, the role of Great Britain in India . . . And finally,

d. The autarky of a "large territory" in continental Europe under German authority was to be achieved that would be secure against blockades and for which the conquered eastern territories were to provide an allegedly inexhaustible reservoir of raw materials and food stuffs. This appeared to be the decisive condition for Hitler's Reich to prevail against Anglo-American sea power in war and for it to be equal to any imaginable new "world war" in the future. It was already presupposed in the guidelines for the "Wirtschaftsstab Ost" [Economic Staff East] of 2 May 1941 that the aim alone of provisioning the German Army exclusively from Russia would mean that "x-million people" would starve.[60]

In the months prior to the start of the Russian campaign, Hitler was careful to keep his plans to wage a war of annihilation (*Vernichtungskrieg*) in the East mostly to himself. Not even his generals—to whom, we have seen, he articulated his aims in traditional military-strategic jargon—were made privy to the true nature of the impending struggle until the end of March 1941, with *Barbarossa* but weeks away. The generals, steeped for the most part in their own fears and racial prejudices about Soviet Russia, put up no resistance to their *Führer's* murderous and genocidal plans; rather, at the highest echelons of command they took part in preparing them. In any case, by March 1941, operational planning was complete, and a vast migration of men, horses, and weapons of war underway toward the eastern frontier, poised to unleash "the cruelest military campaign ever fought."[61]

1.4: GERMAN GENERAL STAFF PLANNING—JULY TO DECEMBER 1940 (A CONCISE OVERVIEW)

Even before the "great conference" at the *Berghof* on July 31, 1940, when Hitler had announced his intention of moving on Russia the following spring, the *Wehrmacht's* planning organs had done some preliminary work of their own. The C-in-C of the army, *Generaloberst* Walther von Brauchitsch—about to become a field marshal along with a number of other top generals, their reward for the victory over France[62]—had ordered his staff at OKH to "do some operational thinking" about such a possibility; moreover, Foreign Armies East (*Fremde Heere Ost*, or FHO), the army agency responsible for evaluating military intelligence about the Soviet Union, was ordered to investigate the distribution of Red Army forces facing Germany. Following Hitler's decision, staff work on a possible war with Russia went forward with a heightened sense of purpose. While the Army High Command (OKH) was primarily responsible for the effort, departments within OKW also participated, among them *Generalmajor* Walter Warlimont's National Defense Branch (Warlimont was Jodl's deputy) and *Gen.d.Inf.* Georg

Thomas's War Economy and Armaments Branch. For the most part, Hitler, who was surprisingly literate in military affairs,[63] left the military planning to his General Staff professionals; not until early December 1940 would he be briefed on the operational plans of the Army High Command.[64]

The man who would exercise a decisive influence over those plans was Army Chief of Staff Halder; in fact, the plan of operations that ultimately emerged from the months of map exercises, number crunching, and war games largely incorporated his ideas on how best to defeat the Red Army. As his adjutant, *Hauptmann* Conrad Kühlein, recalled shortly after the war, the fifty-six-year-old Halder was "a tireless worker who [during the Russian campaign] put his health at stake, in that he was active until the early hours of the morning for months at a time. I repeatedly saw him leave his desk at 7:00 in the morning when I arrived in the barracks for the early situation briefing. Then at 9:00 [A.M.] he would reappear for duty."[65] On a more typical day, Halder arrived at work at about 8:00 A.M., worked well past midnight, then read for a while before turning in. "In this sense he tried to personify Moltke the Elder's dictum 'Genius is diligence,' and he expected no less from those who worked under him."[66]

In July 1940, the Army High Command established its headquarters at Fontainebleau, about 50 kilometers southeast of Paris. The Château de Fontainebleau had once belonged to the kings of France, and the history of the region dated to the twelfth century; in all, some three dozen French sovereigns had spent time there over the centuries. One of Halder's first discussions about how to address the problem posed by the Soviet Union took place at Fontainebleau on July 3, 1940, with the chief of his operations branch, *Oberst* Hans von Greiffenberg. Both men started from the assumption that a "blow against the Soviet Union" would shatter the hopes of Great Britain of remaining in the war.[67]

As first measures, the army *Stabschef* asked for an intelligence survey of Soviet strength and dispositions and assigned a specially selected General Staff officer—*Generalmajor* Erich Marcks, chief of staff, Eighteenth Army—with the task of preparing a strategic campaign study. Prophylactic measures to thwart any unwanted surprises on the part of the Russians had already been set in motion, including the transfer from the West to the eastern occupied areas of fifteen infantry divisions, six panzer divisions, and three motorized divisions, along with the headquarters of the Eighteenth Army.[68]

On July 22, Halder began to explore the question of Russia in more detail. Over the next few days, he held discussions with Greiffenberg and the chiefs of Foreign Armies East, Cartography, and Signal Communications. Based on such conversations, Halder reached some (highly tentative) conclusions about potential requirements. He assumed that one hundred divisions would be needed for the invasion force, and that it would take four to six weeks to concentrate them (a highly inaccurate estimate as matters turned out). He readily concluded that the only operational solution to the strategic problem of subduing Russia was to aim the army's primary thrust at Moscow.[69] In addition to its political and psychological value, Moscow (and its region) was a leading industrial center—by 1941 "at least as important to the Soviet war economy as Leningrad or the Ukraine"—and the hub of Russia's railway network.[70] Throughout the planning process—and during the campaign of 1941—the Army General Staff would cling to the concept of a direct advance on Moscow as the *sine qua non* of victory.[71]

In response to Hitler's orders of late July, efforts got underway to upgrade transportation and supply infrastructure in East Prussia and occupied Poland, a directive to this effect—entitled *"Aufbau Ost"* ("Buildup East")—signed by Field Marshal Keitel[72] at OKW on August 7, 1940.[73] The decision was also taken to increase the size of the army to 180 divisions, with the new divisions to be formed by the spring of 1941; among them were ten new panzer divisions (doubling the number that had existed in May 1940) and eight new motorized infantry divisions.[74] The existing ten panzer divisions were to be reorganized and partially reequipped with more medium tanks; however, due to the low production figures for tanks in 1940/41, the only way to double the size of the panzer force was to dramatically reduce the number of tanks in each division. In fact, the average number of tanks assigned to the panzer divisions would be reduced from 258 in 1940 to just 196 following the reorganization and expansion, while the actual number of tanks in the divisions would range from 147 to 299.[75]

General Marcks arrived at OKH headquarters in Fontainebleau on July 29 and, after an exchange of views with Halder, began work on his study. Completed in just five days (on August 5), it was called "Operational Draft East" (*Operationsentwurf Ost*). The Marcks plan was a "comprehensive survey"; it also "reflected fully Halder's ideas about the Russian campaign and formed the basis for more detailed staff work."[76] The army's primary mission was to destroy Red Army forces by means of a powerful thrust north of the Pripiat' Marshes[77] and then drive on Moscow, the "economic, political and spiritual center of the USSR," whose capture would "shatter the cohesion of the Russian Reich."[78] Following the capture of Moscow, this main force (*Schwerpunkt*) was to wheel to the south and, in cooperation with a southern force grouping, seize the Ukraine. The final stage would be an advance on a broad front at least as far as the line Rostov–Gorki–Archangel, which would place Germany well beyond the range of Soviet airstrikes. To execute these tasks, Marcks proposed an invasion force of 147 divisions, among them twenty-four panzer and twelve motorized. The northern (main) group was to consist of sixty-eight divisions and the bulk of the armored forces (fifteen panzer and two motorized divisions), while armies in the southern group were to have thirty-five divisions (including five panzer and six motorized divisions). The OKH was to hold forty-four divisions in reserve (including four panzer and four motorized). The time needed to conduct the campaign was estimated at nine to seventeen weeks.[79]

The Marcks plan envisaged the decisive battles being fought along the Russo-German frontier in the opening weeks, with the armored forces doing the heavy lifting. The study posited only a slight numerical advantage for the *Ostheer*, which would enjoy a decisive advantage in training, experience, and quality of weaponry. Once German troops had broken through the enemy's frontier defenses and begun to exploit into the interior, Marcks believed the Soviet system of command and control would simply collapse, enabling surviving enemy forces to be defeated in detail.[80]

Further German staff studies[81] followed the direction taken by Marcks, and although "certain problems" emerged in wargaming the operation—among them the great distances involved in a Russian campaign—"most officers concurred with the proposed strategy with its emphasis on gaining a swift military victory by advancing on Moscow."[82] Hitler, however, did not, at least not fully.

> *In his view, after successful execution of the frontier battles, the drive on Moscow should not take place until Leningrad in the north had been captured and the Baltic region secured. The "Führer" also placed greater importance on gaining key economic targets, while the Army stressed military factors. Here then, was the genesis of a serious conflict between Hitler and his Army High Command on how the war in the east should be waged; and while the conflict would be contained—or simply ignored—during the planning phase, it would burst out into the open in the summer of 1941, at a critical juncture in the Russian campaign.[83]*

On September 3, 1940, Halder appointed *Generalleutnant* Friedrich Paulus, chief of staff of Sixth Army, as the new *Oberquartiermeister I* (OQu I, or deputy chief of staff for operations) in the Army High Command. In this position, Paulus, a respected panzer specialist, would serve as Halder's immediate deputy and have responsibility for coordinating all OKH planning pertaining to a potential campaign in the East. Working closely with the OKH Operations Branch, he was to further develop the operational details as well as plans for the German force buildup and concentration against Russia. Paulus threw himself into his work, often engaging Halder in animated discussion well into the night. Between the two men a bond of trust and friendship developed, which soon grew into social contacts between the two families.[84]

By mid-September, Paulus had completed initial planning for the deployment of German forces in the East (*Aufmarsch Ost*). Using this as a foundation, he worked out an overall concept for conduct of the Russian campaign. He supported Hitler's belief that no more than 128 divisions would be needed to crush a Russian army estimated at 188 divisions, a perspective encouraged by intelligence reports of Foreign Armies East (FHO), which posited that the Red Army had no more than fifty to seventy-five "good" divisions. (In the ensuing months, FHO would continuously revise its estimation of Soviet forces upward.) In their essence, however, Paulus's basic campaign concepts differed little from those of General Marcks.[85]

In October 1940, the OKH left Fontainebleau and moved to Zossen, some 30 kilometers south of Berlin. Here, at the former Imperial German Army training complex, it would remain for the remainder of the war, amidst the massive underground bunkers and flak towers that had been finished just prior to the outbreak of war in September 1939. Toiling late into the night, Paulus would often bring working papers home—not classified documents, but maps, materials about geographical and climatic conditions in the Soviet Union, and the like. Naturally, he was unable to keep his work completely hidden from his two lieutenant sons and, more importantly, from his wife, "Coca" (Constance). For Paulus, this soon resulted in rather disquieting discussions about the nature of his work. While Paulus—buried as he was in the minutiae of planning a war—wasted little time pondering potential moral questions inherent in his activities, his wife had other thoughts. Simply put, she raised robust moral and religious objections to an attack on the Soviet Union—a prospect that she found "unjust," even "disastrous." Paulus understood her protests, yet he was a soldier who carried out his orders and, in any case, was not responsible for policy. One of Paulus's sons recalled a particularly stormy encounter between the two:[86]

> *At any rate, one day, in the presence of we two sons, then lieutenants, she strongly rebuked my father on this count. My father argued to the contrary that these were questions of policy, the individual was not asked for his opinion. And there were in fact important military viewpoints in support of such an undertaking. When my mother asked what would happen to our soldiers, indeed, to us, who would even survive that, my father responded that there was the possibility, the hope, that a decisive victory could be achieved as early as 1941 . . . It could even be the case that the campaign would be over after only 4–6 weeks. Perhaps the whole lot would tumble down like a house of cards after only the first push.[87]*

By late November 1940, the OKH plan of campaign—based largely on the operational insights of Halder, as expressed initially in the Marcks study and then refined in weeks of meticulous staff work by General Paulus—was essentially complete. Under his direction, the many assumptions developed over the weeks and months of planning were put to the test in two major war games (*Planspiele*)—the first on November 29 at Zossen, in the bunker complex "Maybach 1," the second taking place several days later (December 3). The principal insight to emerge from both games was that a major task of the army groups on the wings was to provide flank protection for the central group, which was to carry out the "decisive" push along the Minsk-Smolensk axis, toward Moscow. After conducting the initial stage of the operation—an advance to the Dnepr River—a three-week pause was planned to replenish and restock the forces. The attack on Moscow was to commence on the fortieth day of the campaign.[88]

On December 5, 1940, a wide-ranging conference on the future conduct of the war took place at the *Reichskanzlei* in Berlin. For the first time, OKH—Brauchitsch and Halder—briefed the Russian campaign plan to Hitler. Also present were the heads of OKW, Keitel and Jodl. Brauchitsch spoke first, among other things discussing time requirements for the Russian campaign. Hitler then held forth: "The Russian armed forces," he insisted, "were inferior to those of the *Wehrmacht* in terms of matériel and personnel, especially in leadership. The present moment, therefore, is especially auspicious [*besonders günstig*] for an eastern campaign." It could be anticipated, he averred, that "once the Russian army has incurred a serious blow, it would suffer an even greater collapse than had France in 1940."[89]

Halder then outlined the operation in detail. He began by surveying the geographical features of the Russian theater of war, as well as the Soviet centers of war production (*Rüstungszentren*), the most important of which lay in the regions of Leningrad, Moscow, and the Ukraine. The theater of operations, he continued, was divided by the Pripiat' Marshes into a northern and southern sector; yet the northern sector, with its superior road and rail network, offered more favorable conditions for large-scale maneuvers. It was apparent, he stated—erroneously, as it turned out—that the Soviet High Command had concentrated most of their forces close to the Soviet-German frontier. The decisive objective, which was to be secured by German armored wedges (*Panzerkeile*) driving deep behind the Soviet front, was to encircle and destroy Red Army forces at or near the frontier, thus preventing them from withdrawing intact to the line of the Dnepr and Western Dvina Rivers. Three army groups were earmarked for the offensive: Army Group North, advancing on Leningrad; Army Group Center, the strongest of the three, moving from the area of Warsaw toward Moscow; and Army Group South, advancing on Kiev in the Ukraine. All told, 105 infantry and thirty-two panzer and motorized divisions would make up the German invasion force. The final territorial objective would be the line of the Volga and the area of Archangel.[90]

Hitler approved the plan in principle, adding that the "most important objective is to prevent the Russians from withdrawing in an unbroken front." The German advance, he said, would have to "carry far enough east so that the Russian air force is no longer able to attack the Reich, and conversely [far enough east] so the *Luftwaffe* is able to raid and destroy Russian armament centers." Hitler expounded at length on the operational principles he hoped to see applied. In doing so, he indicated that, despite his expressed agreement with the OKH plan, his operational concepts diverged fundamentally from those of his army chief of staff. Simply put, he sought the decision on the flanks, with eccentric drives by the northern and southern army groups—not in the center with one concentric thrust on Moscow. In fact, after successful completion of the frontier battles, the central army group, instead of moving on Moscow, was to be ready to wheel north with strong elements to assist in encircling Red Army forces in the Baltic area. In the south, a secondary thrust was to aim for the Dnepr near Kiev, then swing southeast to trap Soviet forces in the western Ukraine. Earlier in the conference, as Halder jotted in his diary that day, Hitler had gone so far as to state that Moscow was of "no great importance."[91]

Apparently, neither Brauchitsch nor Halder raised any objections at the time to Hitler's contrary views. In any case, Hitler, OKH, and OKW were of one mind about the opening phase of the campaign: The mass of the Red Army was to be encircled and destroyed west of the Dnepr–Western Dvina River barriers, and its withdrawal into the interior was to be prevented. Halder may well have thought that the emerging differences between himself and his *Führer* were, ultimately, of no great issue, for once the powerful drive in the center had gathered momentum toward Moscow—sweeping away everything before it—no one would dare to stop it before it reached its objective. The next day (December 6), General Jodl instructed his staff to codify the results of the conference in new directives, including one for the invasion of Russia based on the army's plan and Hitler's intentions.[92]

Less than two weeks later, at the *Berghof* on December 17, 1940, General Jodl, OKW operations chief, presented a first draft of the Russian campaign directive to Hitler, who summarily rejected it. The document, it seems, had (furtively, no doubt) incorporated the primary intent of the Army High Command—that is, an advance by the main force via Minsk-Smolensk to Moscow—and ignored Hitler's design that the main thrust be directed through the Baltic toward Leningrad.[93] The directive, redrafted in accordance with the dictator's desires and retyped on the large "Führer typewriter," was resubmitted to Hitler the next day, December 18,[94] and signed by him as "Führer Directive" No. 21, "Case *Barbarossa*." Only nine copies of the eleven-page document—"in its top-secret cover, scarlet with a diagonal yellow line"—were made; they were to be carried "by hand of officer, only."[95]

The decision to name the operation after Frederick I, "Barbarossa" (ca. 1123–1190), appears to have been Hitler's alone. Frederick I had become Holy Roman Emperor in 1152, the sobriquet a reference to his red beard. He was a "bold and skillful" commander and an "astute ruler." After participating in the Second Crusade in 1188, he had, the following year, led the greatest ever medieval crusading army back toward Palestine, only to drown crossing the Calycadnus River (in modern Turkey) in June 1190. In Germanic folklore he was to become the equivalent of the British (Celtic) King Arthur. As legend has it, he is not dead, but sleeps with his knights in a cave beneath the Kyffhäuser mountains in central Germany; one day—the story goes—Barbarossa will rise up from his resting place and, once again, take up the call to arms. It was a "brilliantly evocative and apposite code-name for the 1941 offensive, 'arrogant in its recall of medieval splendors and menacing in its hints of medieval cruelties.'"[96]

The directive began by stipulating that the "German Armed Forces must be prepared, even before the conclusion of the war against Britain, to *crush Soviet Russia in a rapid campaign*" (*Sowjetrussland in einem schnellen Feldzug niederzuwerfen*). All preparations for the attack were to be in place by May 15, 1941. The bulk of the Red Army in western Russia was to be annihilated (*vernichtet*) by means of "daring operations led by deeply penetrating armored spearheads" and the enemy's withdrawal into the interior prevented. The final objective of the campaign was to "erect a barrier against Asiatic Russia on the general line Volga-Archangel." If necessary, surviving industrial areas in the Urals could be taken out by the *Luftwaffe*.[97]

Having "turned the switch" on war with Russia, Hitler departed his mountain retreat and set off to celebrate Christmas with his soldiers along the English Channel. Something "distantly resembling the spirit of Christmas overcame him":

> *He instructed the* Luftwaffe *to suspend bombing missions against Britain until Christmas was over. A fortnight of aimless meandering ensued . . . Keitel, Halder, and much of Jodl's staff had gone on leave. Protected by extra antiaircraft trains, Hitler set out with his personal staff on a Christmas tour of the western front. He wanted to inspect the big gun batteries which Todt's organization had installed to command the Channel coast— the sites had names like "Great Elector," "Siegfried," and "Gneisenau"—and he wanted to celebrate the holiday with the aircrews of Göring's fighter and bomber squadrons . . . One of Hitler's secretaries wrote to a friend: "We have not stopped moving since December 21. Christmas on the French coast—Calais and Dunkirk. As we were eating dinner in the dining car of our special train on the 23rd at Boulogne, the British came and started bombing, and our antiaircraft guns roared back at them. Even though we were shunted into a safe tunnel"—guarded by antiaircraft trains at each end—"I couldn't help feeling 'a bit queer' . . . On New Year's Eve the mood was more than painful . . ."* [98]

With the promulgation of Directive No. 21, planning for the Russian offensive was essentially complete, with the exception of the army's detailed deployment directive (discussed in Section 1.5). What then can said about the feasibility (or want thereof) of the war plans developed by Hitler and his High Command for their impending *Blitzkrieg* campaign against the Soviet Union?

In theory at least, the operational plan was "elegant in its clarity and simplicity of purpose: The main Red Army forces were to be enveloped, encircled and annihilated by the German armored spearheads west of two great river lines, the Dnepr and Western Dvina, in a spectacular *Vernichtungsschlacht*—a super 'Cannae,' whose doctrinal antecedents were to be found in the theories of Clausewitz, the elder Moltke and Schlieffen."[99] Yet when one drills down into the details of the planning process, the set of assumptions made by planning staffs and the decisions that emerged from them, a disturbing picture emerges.

Most significantly, in preparing the *Barbarossa* campaign, Hitler and his General Staff grotesquely overestimated the capabilities of their own forces while largely dismissing the unique challenges posed by an operation against the Soviet Union. The Germans had carefully observed the poor performance of the Red Army in Poland in 1939 and Finland in 1939/40, and concluded that their impending adversary was far from ready to fight a major war. In addition, Stalin's purges of the late 1930s, which had decapitated much of the Red Army leadership, meant that Russians would be no match for the well-trained and highly experienced *Wehrmacht*.

For Halder and the Army High Command, success in battle, even against an industrial power like the Soviet Union, was simply a matter of devising and executing the proper operational formula. The campaign in France, as noted above, had reinforced this perilous conviction and, in any case, the German (and Prussian) Army had a long tradition of over-emphasizing the operational and tactical imperatives of war at the expense of other critical factors, such as intelligence and logistics.[100] "And so 22 June came. At the operational level the Germans expected to destroy the Red Army in the frontier zones. But beyond that the German High Command had not decided the campaign's next objectives—largely because Halder and Brauchitsch feared that a decision by Hitler would force them to focus on Leningrad and the Ukraine, which they did not want to do."[101]

In his book *Hitler's War*, David Irving stated that "probably no major military campaign has ever been launched upon less intelligence. The services had furnished Hitler—to say nothing of their lower commands—with only the most inadequate information on the Russians. They were certain of only one thing: the German fighting man's inborn superiority. All else was the product of rumor, speculation, and fragile calculations."[102] To be fair, my research informs me that the Germans, via aerial reconnaissance and wireless intercepts, had managed to put together a tolerably accurate picture of Red Army forces at or near the frontier; and yet, in perusing the war diaries of German divisions attacking on June 22, I was struck by the repeated admissions of how little they often knew about the enemy forces facing them. Perhaps even more significant, the Germans "were totally ignorant of Soviet mobilization capabilities, specifically, the quantity of reserve armies the Soviet Union could raise and deploy forward into new defensive positions east of the Western Dvina and Dnepr Rivers."[103]

Logistical planning for the campaign was equally hapless. Which is hardly surprising, for logistics had always been a "stepchild" of sorts in the German (Prussian) military: "Even the famous Moltke and Schlieffen treated it with disdain since it was not directly operational."[104] Yet the logistical challenges were staggering, the daily requirements of a single infantry division in the East amounting to about 170 tons of supplies per day (food, fuel, munitions, spare parts, etc.), while the needs of panzer or motorized divisions were correspondingly greater.[105] And yet the assumptions made by German logistical planners on vital issues ranging from rates of fuel consumption to ammunition expenditures were characterized by a careless optimism; moreover, it was calculated that the system of supply could sustain an advance of about 500 kilometers beyond the frontier—that is, to the line of the Dnepr-Dvina Rivers—beyond that point planning could not be adequately projected.[106]

Yet the obsession with operational planning, the shortfalls in intelligence and logistics, don't get to the core problem, which was this: the German attack on Russia was "seriously underpowered in terms of the magnitude of its objectives."[107] The Germans would begin the campaign with a force of about 150 divisions (less than three dozen of which were armored or motorized). They were so confident of victory that the army's force structure for *Barbarossa* was only slightly larger than that deployed during the

French campaign, although the theater of operations was roughly twenty times the size of France![108] And while these forces were marginally better equipped than in 1940 (more medium tanks, a smattering of upgraded antitank guns, assault guns for the infantry, and so forth), they would, in the end, be overwhelmed by a Soviet mobilization system that would put more than fifty new armies in the field between June and December 1941.[109] It was, opined historian Walter S. Dunn, Jr., "Soviet divisions, not cold weather, [that] stopped the Germans."[110]

In the final analysis, in assessing German planning for Operation *Barbarossa* one is struck by the almost preternatural arrogance of Hitler and his military planners. These were not stupid men, and they were acutely aware of the difficult challenges posed by a campaign in the endless expanses of European Russia. In the end, however, blinded by hubris and a *Russland-Bild* (Russia picture) predicated upon unalloyed feelings of racial and cultural superiority, they simply ignored or dismissed those challenges. The "hyperoptimism" of army C-in-C Field Marshal von Brauchitsch was characteristic: Buoyed by the rapid conclusion of the Balkan campaign (against Greece and Yugoslavia), on April 30, 1940, he predicted that the war in the East—after a series of tough border battles—would essentially be over in four weeks; after that, it would simply be a matter of mopping up.[111]

Before moving on, one further issue merits our attention (if only briefly): Was Adolf Hitler's attack on the Soviet Union in any way justified as a preventive or even preemptive attack? The second part of the question is easily disposed of: Operation *Barbarossa* was in no way a preemptive assault—that is, an action to "forestall or deflect a threat which is 'imminent and overwhelming.'"[112] Indeed, "if Hitler and his generals in the weeks before 22 June were occasionally discomfited by the accelerating pace of Soviet war preparations, there are absolutely no indications—neither in contemporary documents nor memoirs— that anyone was unduly concerned about the prospect of *Barbarossa* being pre-empted."[113] German military intelligence offered no indications of an impending Soviet attack,[114] while Army Chief of Staff Halder (June 1941) characterized Soviet dispositions along the Russo-German frontier as "purely defensive" (*rein defensiv*) and rejected the prospect of an attack on Germany as "nonsense" (*Unsinn*). German thinking at the time is succinctly summed up by German historian Jürgen Förster:

> *Since Stalin was not presumed to harbor aggressive, but rather defensive, intentions, Hitler and his military command were not alarmed by the capacity of the Red Army for war. Its concentration in the advance areas around Lemberg and Belostok was actually quite convenient for them. The greater concern for Hitler was rather that Stalin might spoil his bellicose idea with a political gesture of good will.*[115]

The issue of preventive war—an action "to prevent a threat from materializing which does not yet exist"[116]—is rather more intriguing. While an in-depth discussion is beyond the scope of this narrative, suffice it to say that recent scholarship, particularly the pioneering research of Polish-born scholar Bogdan Musial into Soviet archives hitherto inaccessible to western scholars, has confirmed that Stalin, too, was preparing to unleash a big attack of his own. Observed Musial:

> *What is undeniable is that in spring 1941, Stalin was in the process of building up the largest invasion force of all time along the German-Soviet border in order to attack his German ally at the right moment. This intention was not the result of the fear that Germany would soon attack the Soviet Union, but rather of the Communist ideology of world revolution. The aim was to implement the next and decisive stage of the world revolution, to sovietize Central and West Europe, indeed the whole of Europe. For a victory over Germany would then have meant mastery of all Europe. The German attack on 22 June 1941 caught this invasion force off guard in the midst of its preparations.[117]*

Since the early 1930s, Stalin, Communist revolutionary that he was, had been pinning his hopes on the Red Army as the sole means of spreading revolution to Germany and the West. Like Hitler, he considered war inevitable; and if Germany had not struck in 1941, Stalin conceivably would have done so himself the following year (1942), when his army and air force had completed their reorganization and were reequipped with modern weapons. And if the Russian archives have yet to produce a "smoking gun," the basic objectives of Stalin's Russia, its foreign and defense policies prior to 1941, lead to the reasonable conclusion that Hitler's attack on the Soviet Union, while hardly planned as such, served a preventive function.[118]

Musial, however, rightly rejected the notion that Germany's attack on Soviet Russia was in any way preemptive. As his book clearly revealed, Russia was in no way prepared for war in June 1941, while the Germans were largely unaware of the actual strength of the Red Army and of ongoing Soviet preparations for their own war of aggression, which were "in full swing" (*auf Hochtouren*). The adrenal shock these preparations would administer to the invaders was evident from the first day of the war in the observations and experiences of more than a few German soldiers and airmen.

1.5: *AUFMARSCH OST:* THE GERMAN STRATEGIC FORCE BUILDUP IN THE EAST (JANUARY–JUNE 1941)

The initial movements of German forces to the east had begun in the summer of 1940. First to deploy was Eighteenth Army, followed in September by the Fourth and Twelfth Armies and, in the second half of October, by the headquarters of Army Group B. Furthermore, three panzer and two motorized infantry divisions were routed back to eastern Germany "to retrain for combat in the east and prepare deployment areas and communications networks required for the coming flood of German forces. Masking the buildup was essential to German plans. The initial movements could be explained as a covering force. Thereafter the problem [was to become] more complex as the tempo of deployment picked up."[119]

After the basic concepts and guidelines for the Russian campaign had been outlined in "*Führer* Directive" No. 21 (December 18, 1940), the Army General Staff began to bring its operational plans and timetables into bolder relief. In a "flurry of purposeful activity," General Staff planners crafted the army's deployment directive (*Aufmarschanweisung Barbarossa*), issuing a first draft of the document on January 22, 1941, and submitting a "final" version[120] to Halder nine days later (January 31). It began by again emphasizing the requirement to smash the bulk of the Red Army in the western border regions through daring operations of armored forces driving deep behind the front and preventing the organized withdrawal of enemy forces into the depths of the Soviet Union. The second section of the directive—"Enemy Situation" (*Feindlage*)—began with the pivotal assumption that the Russians would accept battle west of the Dnepr and Dvina Rivers "with at least strong elements of their forces," thus fulfilling a key German requirement for the destruction of the main Soviet forces.[121]

The deployment directive went on to outline in some detail the individual tasks of the three army groups—Army Group South, under Field Marshal Gerd von Rundstedt; Army Group Center, under Field Marshal Fedor von Bock; and Army Group North, under Field Marshal Ritter von Leeb—as well as their assigned armies and panzer groups.[122] The mission of the *Luftwaffe* was briefly addressed—"eliminate as much as possible the influence of the Russian air force while supporting the Army's conduct of operations at its points of main effort [*Schwerpunkten*], in particular by Army Group Center and on the main wing of Army Group South."[123]

Signed by Field Marshal von Brauchitsch, the directive also warned the troops to be ready for the Russians to use chemical weapons, even dropping them from the air.[124] The warning was no "one off," for the Germans were, in fact, acutely concerned about the potential use of gas, as well as the contamination of land and water wells, by Red Army forces. In general, they were prepared for the Russians to respond to the German attack with "harshness and brutality" (*Härte und Brutalität*) far in excess of earlier campaigns—a foreboding not without basis in fact.[125] On the eve of the eastern campaign, Brauchitsch visited his army field commanders in the East, informing them that the Russians could be expected to use flamethrowers and gas and to contaminate wells and stocks of supplies. On June 12, 1941, he told the staff of Fourth Army to be prepared for the enemy to wage "war by all possible means" (*Krieg mit allen Mitteln*).[126] As Brauchitsch predicted, the Red Army would fight with virtually every means at its disposal from the very first day of the war, often in violation of the laws and usages of war; yet despite more than a few scares among German troops at the start of the campaign, there is no evidence the Russians ever resorted to poison gas (though water wells were indeed poisoned by withdrawing Red Army troops).

Meanwhile, taking into account the suddenly changed situation in the Balkans—on April 6, 1941, the Germans had launched Operation *Marita*, an attack on both Greece and Yugoslavia—the army's Operations Branch amended the deployment directive for *Barbarossa* on April 8. In this revised version of the document, the German Twelfth Army was replaced in Romania by the smaller Eleventh Army in the order of battle of Army Group South—a change that would have a significant impact on the army group's operational plan.[127] A "definitive" version of the deployment directive was issued just days before the start of *Barbarossa*, on June 8, 1941.[128]

The strategic concentration of forces in the East—based on the intricate timetable for assembly and concentration of forces laid out in the OKH deployment directive—was carried out primarily by rail movements (*Eisenbahnaufmarsch*)—an effort so enormous that it required thousands of trains to transport millions of men, thousands of tanks and artillery pieces, and hundreds of thousands of vehicles to the new theater of operations. In October 1940, the High Command had issued a new set of guidelines to German rail authorities calling for expansion of stations, rail lines, and other infrastructure of the *Ostbahn*, with the objective of more than doubling rail capacity by May 10, 1941. The entire effort came under the purview of the "Otto" Program (prior to promulgation of the *Barbarossa* directive, the Army High Command had generally referred to planning for Russia under the code name "Otto"), which in the intervening months made dramatic improvements to rail lines and facilities, including new west-east lines, new stations, platforms, signal installations, an expanded telephone net, and other improvements. As a result, the flow of trains transiting the borders of the Reich to the East increased over time from approximately eighty per day to more than 200 per day, enabling the transfer of troops, tanks, vehicles, equipment, and supplies to proceed according to plan (*planmässig*). In fact, from February to mid-July 1941, well over 10,000 trains were unloaded in the East; yet despite this colossal effort, German and Polish rail lines were not stretched to their limits during this time.[129]

The army's deployment plan envisaged this vast movement of men and matériel taking place in five distinct phases—the fifth, and final phase, not beginning until after the start of hostilities and embracing mainly the OKH reserves. Six primary rail truck lines were to be used for these movements. Most of the marching infantry divisions were to be transported in the initial phases, while rail transport of the panzer and motorized units was not to begin until the final few weeks before the invasion. Road movements, mostly from detraining points to more forward assembly areas, were carefully integrated into the progression of rail movements to ensure a smooth flow of men, equipment, and supplies. Until three weeks before the campaign was to begin, new formations arriving in the East were not to go beyond a line marked by Tarnow-Warsaw-Königsberg. Beyond that "invisible barrier," authority for dispositions became the responsibility of the army groups and armies. The execution of those final movements was to be scrupulously concealed, meaning that most movements, particularly those of the armor, were to occur only at night.[130]

As briefly discussed above, even before the buildup began in earnest, the Germans had deployed significant forces in the East. In September 1940, they had come under the command of Field Marshal von Bock and his Army Group B headquarters (soon to become Army Group Center for the Russian campaign). One of Bock's primary tasks was to (quietly) continue the incipient buildup and, by the end of the year, total German divisions in the East had risen from twenty-three (July 1940) to thirty-four, including six panzer divisions.[131] Four of these formations, however, were quartered in Austria due to the increasing uncertainty in the Balkans; in addition, in early February 1941, the OKH dispatched another four divisions from German-occupied Poland to the southeast, leaving Bock with twenty-six divisions (there were also two German divisions stationed in Romania). Thus, when the strategic concentration (148 divisions) for the Russian campaign began on February 7, 120 divisions still had to be moved by a combination of rail and road, twenty-two of them (along with two reinforced regimental combat teams) twice due to the intervening requirements of the Balkan campaign.[132]

With the completion of the first three phases (1.-3. *Aufmarschstaffeln*) of the rail assembly in the East—Phase I: February 7–March 17; Phase II: March 16–April 10; Phase III: April 13–May 20—the majority of the marching infantry divisions had been deployed.[133] While the sources differ, it seems that some sixty German marching infantry divisions had been transferred to the Eastern Front by May 20, 1941.[134] At first most formations were stationed well back from the Russo-German demarcation line; however, in the final ten days of May, entire divisions began to close up to the frontier in a series of night marches. All movements were conducted with great security and with disinformation measures calculated to conceal their actual intent from the Russians.[135]

By late May 1941, with the start of the fourth (and final) phase of the prewar rail movements, the buildup for the attack on Russia reached a fever pitch, German military authorities flooding the frontier zones of the *Generalgouvernement* (in occupied Poland) and East Prussia with two or more divisions per day.[136] The fourth phase was divided into two parts: May 23–June 2 (nine infantry divisions from the West), and June 3–June 23 (twelve panzer and twelve motorized divisions from the Reich, the West, and the Balkans).[137] For reasons of security, the deployment of these twenty-four mobile divisions—the backbone of the *Barbarossa* invasion force—took place at the last possible moment. The frantic pace of these final deployments is reflected in the example of the 8 Panzer Division. The division departed from the area around Prague on the afternoon of June 16, its transport requiring 101 trains; within fifty-one hours it had reached its temporary billeting area north of Insterburg in northern East Prussia.[138] Only on the final four nights before *Barbarossa* was to begin (June 18–June 21) would the mobile divisions move up to their assigned positions at or near the frontier.[139]

The final prewar deployment phase also witnessed the assignment of the heavy rail-borne artillery, which had been brought up from the Channel coast and distributed among the three army groups: Four "K5" (each with ninety rounds of ammunition) and two type "*Karl*" pieces were assigned to Army Group South; eight "K5" guns and two of type "*Karl*" to Army Group Center; and four guns, type "*Bruno*" (short), with 300 rounds to Army Group North.[140] The transport of these super-heavy guns and the construction of their positions required a major effort.

> *Stretches of track had to be kept clear and improved. Work on the track alone, it was*
> *calculated, would take two engineer battalions two weeks per unit. In view of the pro-*
> *longed blockage of the railway routes during deployment as well as the impossibility of*
> *camouflaging such extensive installations, Seventeenth Army HQ [Army Group South]*
> *and Army Group North wanted to forgo the use of those batteries altogether. In the end*
> *they were employed at the points of main effort of the breakthrough.*[141]

The short nights in June complicated efforts to complete the final concentration of forces, while the troops were discomfited by a plague of mosquitoes "of biblical pro-portions," the result of an unusually wet spring. Transportation and assembly schedules encountered a number of unexpected challenges, among them the last-minute decision to move the *Luftwaffe*'s 8 Air Corps across the east-west lines of communication to East Prussia. After supporting the attack in Greece, the air corps (personnel and vehicles) had been shipped by rail to Silesia, detraining on May 31; it then marched some 500 kilo-meters with 8,000 motor vehicles—"the lateral move [threatening] to tie up every main artery from the Reich to the eastern front." Facing the prospect of a "major traffic snarl," Army Group Center solved the problem by appointing a special road communications staff commanded by a general, who enforced strictest control and march discipline. Ger-man field commands were also concerned about potential forest fires, which the Russians could have easily started by dropping incendiary bombs, wreaking havoc among the many fuel and ammunitions dumps scattered among the forests. "The fact that the Russian air force did not interfere with the concentration was probably the biggest break the Ger-mans got. All other problems that arose during the tense weeks of the final buildup could, in the end, be solved."[142]

Improvements to roads and reinforcement of bridges and culverts went forward to the final minute, the Organization Todt (OT), Reich Labor Service (*Reichsarbeitsdienst*), and army engineers cooperating in these efforts. Some of the biggest "headaches" occurred in the primitive Suwalki triangle—the salient where 3 Panzer Group (Army Group Cen-ter) was to concentrate—due to the absence of paved roads. Due to a deficit of heavy construction equipment, the Germans were unable to adequately reinforce the roads in this backwater region opposite the Russo-German frontier; the result was that the roads were not strong enough to handle some of the heavy weapons—such as the 300mm mortars—that Ninth Army intended to commit to "crack the big bunkers of the Soviet border defense line."[143] Despite such challenges, by June 22, 1941, 122 divisions had been deployed to the Eastern Front (the three army groups' full complement of 120 divisions and two divisions of the OKH reserve), along with General Headquarters (GHQ) troops, supply services, and the bomber, fighter, and ground attack squadrons of the *Luftwaffe*.[144] Twelve divisions of the OKH reserve were in transport (scheduled to arrive in the East by the first week of July), while most of the fourteen remaining reserve divisions were scheduled to reach the front by mid-July—all in the final phase of the German strategic rail deployment.[145]

In the final weeks before the start of war with Russia, as the troop trains clattered day and night across the trunk lines running east, the German General Staff put the finishing touches on a series of orders designed to ensure that "Hitler's war" would indeed be the "war of annihilation" he intended it to be. That his top generals, most of them, supported such a war is an undeniable historical fact. Field Marshal von Brauchitsch, speaking to the top commanders of the *Ostheer* at Zossen on March 27, 1941, lectured them on the "special character" of the impending campaign. About the treatment of the enemy, he declared: "The troops have to realize that this struggle is being waged by one race against another, and proceed with the necessary harshness."[146]

> *What, exactly, did [Field Marshal] von Brauchitsch mean by "harshness?" It encompassed many things: a plan to starve large portions of the population; rear area "security measures" that amounted to widespread mass murder; orders to shoot political commissars and other "undesirables;" the use of forced labor on a massive scale; and criminal negligence toward prisoners of war. Absolute ruthlessness was the rule by which the Germans intended to conquer and "pacify" their new realm.[147]*

The criminal orders approved and promulgated by the German High Command (OKW and OKH), when necessary in cooperation with the SS, are well known, and need not be recapitulated here.[148] Suffice it to say that they helped to ensure that June 22, 1941, would be the beginning of the most radical, destructive, and barbarous military campaign the world has ever seen. And they beg the question: Just how prepared was Soviet Russia to fight a war for its very existence?

1.6: THE STATUS OF THE RED ARMY (SPRING 1941)

Under the brutal stewardship of Joseph Stalin, the Soviet Union had undergone a remarkable transformation from an economic backwater into an advanced industrial and military power by the late 1930s. As is well documented, however, this achievement was only accomplished at the cost of millions of ordinary Soviet citizens, many of whom perished during the forced collectivization, while others were worked to death in the factories and labor camps. Yet without its blood-stained emergence into the modern world, the Soviet Union would most surely have been unable to survive the German onslaught in 1941.

Due to the iron will of the Soviet dictator, the *vozhd* (leader) who had led the Soviet state since the mid-1920s, and the efforts of Russian military theorists like Marshal M. N. Tukhachevsky, the Red Army grew from what was essentially a "foot-and-hoof" army— that is, an infantry and cavalry force—of marginal capabilities[149] into a modern military force informed by an innovative doctrine of offensive warfare that envisaged armored and motorized forces (supported by infantry, artillery, and airborne units) striking deep behind the enemy front to disrupt lines of communication and supply. While Tukhachevsky perished in the purges in 1937, the doctrine he helped to develop survived, only to be adopted by German armored theorists in the 1930s and used against the Russians in Operation *Barbarossa*.[150]

By the spring of 1941, the Red Army had become the "largest and most complex fighting force in the world,"[151] boasting larger mechanized, cavalry, and airborne forces than any other nation; all told, the Russian military was composed of more than five million men arranged in twenty-seven armies and 303 divisions outfitted with 17,000 to 24,000 tanks[152] and nearly 20,000 aircraft. In the midst of a massive force restructuring when the Germans struck, the Soviet armed forces were developing modern new weapons systems, among them KV (*Klementi Voroshilov*) heavy and T-34 medium tanks (about which the Germans had little intelligence), BM-13 "Katyusha" ("*Little Kate*") multiple rocket-launchers, and a new generation of fighter, bomber, and ground attack aircraft. In his memoirs, Soviet marshal G. K. Zhukov, whom Stalin appointed chief of the Army General Staff in January 1941, cited an impressive array of statistics illustrating the frenetic pace of the Soviet military buildup as the Soviet state responded to the challenges posed by Germany's burgeoning military might and the increasingly threatening international situation; from them I have culled the following:

- From 1939 through June 1941, the rifle divisions received 105,000 light, mounted, and large-caliber machine guns, and 100,000 submachine guns. In the spring of 1941, 500,000 men and NCOs were called up and dispatched to the border military districts to "augment infantry divisions there, bringing up the strength of each to at least 8000." An additional 300,000 reservists were called up only days later to man the fortified regions with specialists and to support other arms and services. In sum, the Red Army got an addition of nearly 800,000 men on the eve of the war in what amounted to a "partial secret mobilization."[153]

- By 1938 the production of tanks had "more than trebled" in comparison to the early 1930s. From January 1939 to June 22, 1941, the Red Army received more than 7,000 tanks, including 1,861 of the new KVs and T-34s. "The new tanks began appearing in the tanks schools and in the border military districts only in the latter half of 1940." In 1940, the activation of new mechanized corps got underway, but they were far from fully outfitted when war broke out.

- Archival records reveal that, between January 1, 1939, and June 22, 1941, the Red Army took receipt of 29,637 field guns and 52,407 mortars—the total number of new artillery pieces and mortars (including tank guns) amounting to 92,578. This equipment was "mostly organic to the units in the field," while the High Command Reserve consisted of just sixty howitzer and fourteen artillery regiments on the eve of war—a number which, "considering the specifics of war with Germany, was totally insufficient." In the spring of 1941 the Red Army began to form ten antitank artillery brigades, "but failed to man them to prescribed strength by June."

- Archival records also reveal that, from January 1, 1939, to June 22, 1941, the Red Army received 17,745 combat planes, among them 3,719 of the "latest models." A "new stage" began in aircraft construction, with new designs including the Yak-1, MiG-3, and LaGG-3 fighters, the Il-2 ground attack plane, the Pe-2 bomber, and others, "some 20 types in all." In late 1940 "batch production was stepped up of the best types of aircraft. But industry could not keep pace with the needs of the time. Old types of aircraft were still plentiful on the eve of war. Some 75–80% of the planes were technically inferior to their German counterparts. New aircraft were still in the testing stage; only 21% of the air units had been rearmed."

- The buildup of naval forces was accelerated. The first eleven months of 1940 witnessed the launch of one hundred destroyers, submarines, minesweepers, and torpedo boats—"all of them highly effective in combat." Some 270 ships of all types were constructed in 1940, while new naval bases were established. "On the whole, the Soviet Navy was impressive on the eve of the war, and gave the enemy a fitting reception."

- The construction of new fortified regions on the western frontier had begun in early 1940, yet had not been completed by June 1941. By the outbreak of war, some 2,500 reinforced concrete structures had been built, 1,000 being equipped with "appropriate" fortified-area artillery, and the other 1,500 outfitted only with machine guns. "As for the Ukraine, the Rava Ruska and Peremysl' [fortified regions] were best prepared for combat in June 1941."[154]

As Zhukov's account illustrates, despite the tremendous strides made in preparing the Red Army for war, much remained to be done. In general, Soviet rifle divisions were short of personnel, weapons, and equipment;[155] moreover, much of the artillery of the divisions in the border districts had yet to undergo range firing and, accordingly, was "practicing at the ranges when the *Wehrmacht* struck."[156] The mechanized corps were largely made up of outmoded tank models and, as of June 15, 1941, 29 percent of these older tanks were in need of major repairs, 44 percent in need of lesser maintenance. Of the 1,861 new KVs and T-34s, only 1,475 were "distributed unevenly" among the mechanized corps in the western military districts.[157] As noted by Zhukov, the great majority of the Red Army's combat aircraft[158] were also obsolete designs, *Luftwaffe* pilots having encountered most of them during the Spanish Civil War in the late 1930s. Not to be overlooked were the serious shortfalls in training and experience; indeed, it was not uncommon on the eve of war for the crews of the new tanks and pilots of the new aircraft models to have logged no more than a few hours of training time.[159]

At the strategic level, Soviet war planning was seriously hamstrung by several unfounded assumptions that, in the end, nearly proved fatal. In an "extraordinary example of strategic blindness," the Soviet political and military leadership "prepared for war on a false assumption":

> *that there would be time to mobilize and concentrate the Red Army before the main fighting began.* Vnezapnost' ("suddenness," the element of surprise) was for Soviet commanders a key element in warfare. The USSR would choose when war would break out—as had been the case with Finland in 1939. The Soviet generals could not grasp that it was the Red Army that could be caught by surprise. The Soviet military leaders also expected—at least until late spring of 1941—that it would take several weeks for the Germans to concentrate their forces for an attack against Russia. They believed that this German concentration could not be carried out secretly. They also supposed that their covering forces on the border could hold any German attack for three or four weeks while the Red Army was mobilized and concentrated. These assumptions were not consistent with the intelligence that was coming in, nor with the knowledge of the sudden attacks that the Germans had mounted against Poland, Scandinavia, and France. By May 1941 the Red Army had finally concluded that the German armed forces were already mobilized and that a large German force had been concentrated in East Prussia and Poland, but Stalin still did not order a change to existing plans.[160]

Another serious misjudgment of Stalin and his generals was their decision to concentrate their main forces in the Ukraine instead of in Belorussia (along the Belostok-Minsk-Smolensk axis), where the main German attack would come. A total of about sixty divisions (including sixteen tank and eight motorized), far more than in any of the other military districts, was stationed in the Kiev Special Military District, covering the Ukraine. Red Army air regiments were also heavily deployed in the district.[161] Some revisionist historians have interpreted the conspicuous Soviet concentrations in the Ukraine as proof that Stalin and his generals were planning a preemptive strike against Germany. Certainly, had Stalin decided to launch a preemptive strike—and Zhukov had prepared such a plan in mid-May 1941[162]—an advance from the Ukraine into Poland, across relatively open country, through Lublin and Cracow (Kraków) and Upper Silesia, would have outflanked the German forces in Poland and threatened their communications to the Balkans; moreover, it signified a better option than attacking out of Belorussia, which would have meant an advance through the lakes and forests of East Prussia with its prepared German fortifications.[163] Yet there are simpler, less sinister explanations for the Soviet decision to deploy their largest force grouping away from the main axis of the German advance (serious error though it was). First, by placing such large forces in the south, they shielded the grain of the Ukraine, the coal and minerals of the Donbas, and beyond that, the oil of the Caucasus region; second, Stalin and his generals were simply acting in accordance with traditional Soviet military doctrine, which envisaged immediate offensive action—even when attacked—to take the war to the enemy's territory. In any case, regardless of whatever aggressive designs the Russians may have entertained in the 1930s, by 1940/41—and certainly after the *Wehrmacht*'s stunning victory over France in May/June 1940—Soviet military preparations were driven largely by the fear of an impending German attack. Indeed, as Stalin is said to have remarked after Germany's defeat of France, "The Germans will now turn on us, they will eat us alive."[164]

Soviet military planning in the months prior to the German assault was also disrupted by the movement of the frontier more than 300 kilometers to the west, following annexation of the Baltic States, eastern Poland, and Bessarabia in 1939/40. Before 1939, the Red Army had built robust defensive positions along and behind the USSR's old border, fortifications the Germans christened the "Stalin Line." The Stalin Line, however, was not really a line at all, rather a system of fortified regions (*ukreplennyi raion*, or UR), each outfitted with bunkers, light artillery, machine guns, and tank traps.[165] A German training film offered a fascinating glimpse of these Soviet border defenses following their capture in July 1941: On display are tank traps, water obstacles, wire entanglements, crisscrossed steel beams (tank obstacles), bunkers (concrete, wooden, earthen), earthworks of timber and soil, houses and barns used to conceal weapon positions, even flamethrowers with remote ignition.[166] One of the oldest fortified regions along the Stalin Line was Polotsk, which sat astride the Dvina River where the Soviet, Polish, and Lithuanian frontiers came together. (In 2016, I visited Polotsk on a research trip; several of the concrete bunkers, slashed and cut by German shelling, are still there—looming over the landscape like forgotten sentries of a bygone era.)

In an effort to transform the newly occupied territories in the West into a kind of strategic *glacis*, the defenses along the old 1939 frontier—that is, along the Stalin Line—were stripped to furnish weapons and matériel for new fortified regions at the Russo-German border. The outcome was predictable: When the Germans struck the Stalin Line had been seriously compromised, but not nearly enough had been done to create the fortified regions along the new border. Moreover, on *Barbarossatag*, most of the Red Army divisions manning the frontier were without their engineer battalions (which had been detailed to construct new bunkers and obstacles), seriously degrading their combat effectiveness.[167]

From the preceding analysis, which barely scratches the surface of the Red Army's many strengths and weaknesses, one can draw the logical conclusion that Soviet armed forces were far from prepared for war as war loomed that spring of 1941. They were, at best, months away from being ready, but perhaps even more time was needed to effectively integrate the myriad changes in personnel, training, weapons systems, and organization resulting from the Red Army's remarkably rapid growth. That duly noted, one issue inseparable from this discussion has yet to be addressed—that being the nature of the Russian fighting man.

Prior to the start of Operation *Barbarossa*, the propaganda branch of the German Armed Forces High Command (OKW), working closely with the Army High Command (OKH), developed the "Guidelines for the Conduct of Troops in Russia" (*Richtlinien für das Verhalten der Truppe in Russland*). On May 19, 1941, they were distributed to the individual *Wehrmacht* commands, but were only to be released to the troops on the eve of the invasion.[168] The guidelines embraced several key notions that were to guide the behavior of German troops:

I. 1. Bolshevism is the mortal enemy *[Todfeind]* of the National Socialist German people. Germany's struggle is aimed against that disruptive ideology and its exponents.

2. That struggle demands ruthless and energetic action against Bolshevik agitators, guerrillas, saboteurs, Jews *and the complete liquidation of any active or passive resistance.*

II. 3. Extreme reserve and most alert vigilance are called for toward all members of the Red Army—*even prisoners—as treacherous methods of fighting are to be expected. The* Asiatic soldiers *of the Red Army in particular are inscrutable, unpredictable, insidious, and unfeeling.*

4. After the capture of units the leaders *are to be* instantly separated *from the other ranks.*[169]

As the guidelines clearly reveal, the average German soldier—the *Landser*—was being admonished to wage ruthless war upon the hated, feared, and barely understood Bolshevik enemy. But older German officers, at least those who had fought against the Russians in the Great War of 1914/18, had a more nuanced view of things and, in general, had learned to respect the Russian fighting man and admire his impressive fighting abilities (if often unable to shake ancestral prejudices about Russian Asiatic troops). One of those German officers was Günther Blumentritt, in June 1941 a colonel and chief of staff of Field Marshal Günther von Kluge's Fourth Army. In a wide-ranging interview with British historian B. H. Liddell Hart shortly after the war, he made the following observations about the Russian soldier:

In 1914–18, as a lieutenant, I fought for the first two years against the Russians, after a brief contact with the French and Belgians at Namur in August 1914. In our very first

34

attack on the Russian front, we quickly realized that here we were meeting essentially different soldiers from the French and Belgian—hardly visible, entrenched with consummate skill, and resolute! We suffered considerable losses.

In those days it was the Russian Imperial Army. Hard, but good-natured on the whole, they had the habit of setting fire on military principle to towns and villages, in East Prussia when they were forced to withdraw, just as they always did thereafter in their own country. When the red glow from the burning villages lit up the horizon at evening, we knew that the Russians were leaving . . . That was the Russian way, and had been so for centuries.

When I referred to the bulk of the Russian Army as good-natured, I am speaking of their European troops. The much harder Asiatic troops, the Siberian corps, were cruel in their behavior. So, also, were the Cossacks. Eastern Germany had plenty to suffer on this score in 1914.

Even in 1914–18 the greater hardness of war conditions in the East had its effect on our own troops. Men preferred to be sent to the Western rather than the Eastern front. In the West it was a war of material and mass-artillery—Verdun, the Somme, and so on. These factors were paramount, and very grueling to endure, but at least we were dealing with Western adversaries. In the East there was not so much shellfire, but the fighting was more dogged, as the human type was much harder. Night fighting, hand-to-hand fighting, fighting in the forests, were particularly fostered by the Russians. In that war there was a saying current among German soldiers: "In the East the gallant Army is fighting; in the West the Fire Brigade is standing by."

It was in this war, however, that we first learnt to realize what "Russia" really means. The opening battle in June 1941, revealed to us for the first time the new Soviet Army. Our casualties were up to 50 percent . . . A women's battalion defended the old citadel at Brest-Litovsk for a week, fighting to the last, in spite of bombardment with our heaviest guns and from the air. Our troops soon learnt to know what fighting the Russians meant . . .

The Red Army of 1941–45 was far harder than the Czar's Army, for they were fighting fanatically for an idea. That increased their doggedness, and in turn made our own troops hard, for in the east the maxim held good—"You or I." Discipline in the Red Army was far more rigorous than in the Czar's Army . . . Wherever Russians have appeared in the history of war, the fight was hard, ruthless, and involved heavy losses. Where the Russian makes a stand or defends himself, he is hard to defeat, and it costs a lot of bloodshed . . . The East and the West are two worlds, and they cannot understand each other.[170]

Blumentritt's characterization of the Russian fighting man was, of course, right on the mark. And from the very first day of the campaign the German soldier on the Eastern Front would experience a remarkably brutal and unforgiving style of warfare unlike that encountered in any previous campaign.

CHAPTER 2

On the Cusp of War—Berlin, Moscow, and the Eastern Front

It all starts in a few hours!—Our regiment is positioned at the very front line. The resistance must be broke, despite bunkers, hordes of men, and any amount of devilry. It is a war for Germany's greatness and future.
— Dr. Heinrich Haape, German 6 Infantry Division, June 21, 1941[1]

The evening before the war with Russia began, we were all quite aware of its imminence. I was called by the official chaplain of the division and asked if I would hear the confessions of soldiers in one of the nearby churches of Eastern Catholics. A great many soldiers made their confessions that evening.
— Bernard Häring, German medic and Catholic priest, June 21, 1941[2]

There was the feeling everywhere that war was approaching. Night after night tanks, artillery and infantry would pass by us along the road only to disperse and become camouflaged during daytime hours. Troops were being assembled up along the border, meaning that war was imminent. We, though, were convinced that we would smash them (the Germans). The saying at the time went like this: "Leave us alone and we'll leave you alone, but put one finger on us and you'll get no quarter."
—Ivan Konovalov, Red Army bomber pilot trainee[3]

⌒

As dawn broke on Saturday, June 21, 1941, two colossal armies sat on the Russo-German frontier along a front stretching for 1,800 kilometers from the Baltic to the Black Sea.[4] One of these armies, the largest invasion force the world had ever seen, having finally lurched into place, was the newly minted *Ostheer*—made up of three-quarters of the German army's field strength, splendidly trained and equipped, and poised to unleash the 1941 equivalent of a nuclear first strike. To cite specific numbers, Hitler's eastern army consisted of 148 divisions earmarked for the main battle front,[5] including nineteen panzer[6] and fourteen motorized infantry divisions; 120 of these divisions, distributed among three army groups, made up the first assault wave, while twenty-eight were assigned to the OKH reserve. All told, the invasion force embraced some 3.3 million men, 3,350 tanks, 250 assault guns, 7,146 artillery pieces, 600,000 vehicles, and 625,000 horses. This enormous array was supported by a *Luftwaffe* force structure in the East of nearly 3,000 aircraft (of which 2,250 were combat ready). Allied forces included about 500,000 Finnish troops (sixteen divisions with adequate modern equipment) and some 150,000 Romanian troops with largely outmoded equipment.[7]

The other army, the Red Army, was inexperienced, ill prepared, and ignorant of the fate about to befall it. Of the Red Army's total force structure (more than five million men and 303 divisions),[8] field forces (*Deistvuiushshaia armiia*) deployed in the western frontier region were distributed among five military districts—the Leningrad Military District; the Baltic, Western, and Kiev Special Military Districts; and the Odessa Military District. The forces assigned to these military districts boasted a total strength of about 2.9 million men organized into sixteen armies with 163 divisions (ninety-seven rifle, forty tank, twenty mechanized, and six cavalry divisions), forty-one fortified regions, and eighty-seven artillery regiments. (Immediately after the German invasion these districts would become the Northern, Northwestern, Western, Southwest, and Southern Fronts, respectively.)[9] In addition to the forces of the western military districts, there were five reserve armies (fifty-seven divisions) under the centralized control of the Soviet High Command.[10]

The Red Army forces in the western Soviet Union were arrayed in great depth in two strategic echelons. The first strategic echelon, comprising the field forces (163 divisions) of the western military districts (along with eight divisions of the High Command reserve) was deployed in three operational belts extending from the border to positions several hundred kilometers beyond the frontier.[11] The twenty mechanized corps in this first echelon were outfitted with more than 10,000 tanks.[12] The second strategic echelon consisted of the five reserve armies of the Soviet High Command. When war came, these reserve armies—"virtually invisible" to German intelligence—were in the process of assembling along the line of the Dvina–Dnepr Rivers; their mission was to conduct a counteroffensive in conjunction with counterattacks by the armies of the forward fronts. On June 22, however, "neither the forward military districts nor the five reserve armies had completed deploying in accordance with the official mobilization and deployment plans. As in so many other respects, the German attack . . . caught the Soviets in transition."[13]

2.1: BERLIN—A CITY AND ITS *FÜHRER* ON EDGE

By the spring of 1941, the four million inhabitants of Berlin were growing accustomed to the hardships of the war. Since the war began they had been living with rationing and blackouts. Rationing, in fact, was introduced on August 27, 1939, just days before the invasion of Poland; after that, the distribution of most foods, clothing, footwear, and coal was strictly controlled. There was, moreover, the increasingly discomfiting reality of air raids over the city:

> *The first British air raid over the Reich's capital, a rather trifling affair, had taken place on 26 August 1940. By the autumn of that year, however, the raids had become a regular occurrence; and, following a brief hiatus in the first months of 1941, had resumed again in March with desultory attacks over the central areas of the city. While the damage from the RAF bomber "offensive" was normally slight at this time, a heavy raid on 10 April caused serious damage to the State Opera House and other key buildings, eliciting outrage from Hitler and a furious argument with Air Marshal Göring.* [14]

As the days and weeks went by, Berliners began to speak openly about the prospects of war with Russia. On May 24, Marie Vassiltchikov, a perceptive twenty-four-year-old White Russian émigré, wrote in her secret Berlin diary that people were talking about troop concentrations along the border with Russia, and that "nearly all the men we know are being transferred from the west to the east. This can only mean one thing." Less than three weeks later (June 10) she observed: "Most of the German army seems to be massing on the Russian border."[15]

By mid-June 1941, such talk had escalated into a flood of rumors about what lay ahead for German-Russian relations. Some Berliners sought psychological refuge in wishful thinking, for example, convincing themselves that Stalin had agreed to cede the Ukraine to Germany for ninety-nine years, or that Russia was on the verge of adhering to the Tripartite Pact, or even that the Soviet dictator would come to Berlin to work out a deal with the *Führer*. Still others—if "only a minority" according to a June 12 report of the SS Security Service (*Sicherheitsdienst*), which carefully monitored the mood of the German people—suspected the scenario that would soon come to pass; that is, that German-Russian relations had essentially collapsed and that "an invasion of Russia would begin around the end of the month."[16]

At the Reich Chancellery in Berlin, Hitler passed the final days prior to start of the Russian campaign in a state of growing agitation. As Nicolaus von Below, Hitler's *Luftwaffe* adjutant, recalled in his memoirs, the German dictator seemed "increasingly nervous and troubled. He was garrulous, walked up and down continuously and seemed to be waiting anxiously for news of something."[17] Moreover, "the old familiar bouts of insomnia began to attack him as the last days before *Barbarossa* dragged by." At night, he would lie awake and ask himself, "what loopholes in his grand design the British might yet exploit. He believed he had plugged them all . . . Yet Hitler could still only go to sleep with sedatives, even after staying up until three or four each morning discussing Turkey, Russia, war, and warfare with dutiful but weary henchmen like Himmler, Ley, Hewel, Ribbentrop, and Seyss-Inquart."[18]

Surely, at some level, Hitler, a man of superior intellect and keen instincts, must have been aware of the brittle foundation upon which his Russian campaign was built. Such an awareness would help to explain his anxious and agitated behavior in the days preceding the outbreak of war. On June 20, less than forty-eight hours before the launch of *Barbarossa*, the *Führer* joined his female secretaries for the coffee break he shared with them daily at the Reich Chancellery in Berlin. He told them that there was something sinister (*unheimlich*) about Russia—something that reminded him of the ghost ship (*Gespensterschiff*) in *The Flying Dutchman*. When *Fräulein* Schroeder, "a clever, critical, and often dangerously outspoken" thirty-three-year-old stenographer, asked him why he always seemed to stress that the decision to attack Russia was his most difficult yet, he replied: "Because we know virtually nothing about Russia. It could turn out to be a big soap-bubble, or it might be something quite different."[19]

Five days before, on the afternoon of June 15, Hitler had summoned Goebbels to the Reich Chancellery. After greeting his propaganda minister with "great warmth," he went on to discuss the coming campaign. On this occasion, Hitler radiated confidence. The attack, he said, should begin in about a week, as soon as the troop deployments were completed. "It will be an enormous attack [*Massenangriff*] on the grandest of scale, very likely the most powerful history has ever seen," the *Führer* assured him. This was necessary, he said, because Stalin simply wanted to wait until Europe had bled itself out (*bis Europa ausgeblutet sei*) in order to "Bolshevize" it. His own apprehensions about war with Russia allayed by Hitler's optimism, Goebbels confided in his diary the next day: "Bolshevism will collapse like a house of cards. We stand on the cusp of a victorious advance [*Siegeszug*] without equal. We must act . . . Our operation is as well prepared as is humanly possible."[20]

Hitler's activities over the next few days are briefly adumbrated in German historian Max Domarus's unique chronicle of the *Führer*'s daily activities, speeches, and proclamations: On June 17, he dispatched a telegram to Admiral Horthy, the Regent and head of Hungary, congratulating him on his birthday; on June 18, in an attempt to secure Germany's southern flank, a treaty of friendship (*Freundschaftspakt*) was signed in Ankara between Germany and Turkey, eliciting an exchange of telegrams between the German dictator and the Turkish head of state on the 18th and 19th. On June 19, Hitler greeted Field Marshal List, fresh off his victories in the Balkan campaign, at the Reich Chancellery; the *Führer* thanked him "with heartfelt words and boundless recognition for the splendid performance of both the leadership and the troops."[21] On Friday evening, June 20, in accordance with Hitler's orders, General Jodl, chief of the OKW Operations Staff, released the prearranged code word, "Dortmund," notifying all service branches that Operation *Barbarossa* was to go forward as planned.[22]

Hitler had already dictated his proclamation "To the Soldiers of the Eastern Front" (*Tagesbefehl an die Soldaten der Ostfront*). In his diary, Army Chief of Staff Halder characterized it as a "long-winded manifesto," and that it surely was—an effusive and self-serving document ("its language must have been far above the average soldier's head")[23] that sought to justify the surprise attack on Soviet Russia as a preemptive measure, while offering a *tour d'horizon* of German foreign policy since the start of the war in September 1939. The proclamation was printed in the hundreds of thousands and issued in absolute secrecy to the service branches; it would not be read out to the troops until the evening of June 21.[24]

Saturday, June 21, 1941, broke warm and sunny in Berlin. In his diary, *Generaloberst* Halder recorded the latest developments:

Situation Conference:
a. Codeword "Dortmund" has come through . . .
d. Hungary has effected certain improvements to its border defenses (anti-tank guns) . . .

General Brand; General Buhle:
a. Artillery developments. General Staff comments on development program of Chief of Armaments.
b. Brand reports on his inspection tour: Artillery assembly in the east.
c. Ratio of combined German and Romanian artillery to Russian is 2.2 : 2.9 . . .

Wagner-Baentsch:
a. Possible transport difficulties at the Lublin tip. If necessary, coordination with troop transports.
b. Embargo on field post letters [Feldpostsperre] from Germany to the Army: B+1 to B+5 . . .

Heusinger: . . .
d. Luftwaffe (Waldau) reports that it is ready . . .

Enemy Intelligence:
At several locations increased watchfulness on the part of the Russians reported. (Enemy has occupied its positions in front of 8 Army Corps.) Mobilization proclamations reported to have been posted in Finland.[25]

In one of his official acts on the 21st, Hitler honored *Luftwaffe* fighter ace, Adolf Galland, who had recently been shot down and wounded in aerial combat with British Spitfires, with the first ever award to a *Wehrmacht* officer of the Oak Leaves with Swords to the Knight's Cross in recognition of his seventieth aerial victory.[26] At the Russian embassy in Berlin, however, there were more pressing matters at hand. Soviet ambassador Vladimir Dekanozov had received another report warning of a German attack the next day; while this "fell upon the ambassador's disbelieving ears," the information was dutifully transmitted to Moscow, which, that morning, instructed the embassy to arrange an interview with Ribbentrop. The Russians wanted to demand "an explanation from the

German government of the concentration of German troops on the Soviet frontier." The Soviet embassy was informed that the German foreign minister was "out of town," and everybody else, it seems, was "out" as well.[27]

Ribbentrop, of course, was simply making himself scarce. That night, "over the air waves between Berlin and Moscow," he dispatched a long coded radio message to the German ambassador in Moscow, Count Friedrich Werner von der Schulenburg. The message was marked "Very Urgent, State Secret, For the Ambassador Personally." It began: "Upon receipt of this telegram, all of the cipher material still there is to be destroyed. The radio set is to be put out of commission. Please inform Herr Molotov at once that you have an urgent communication to make to him . . . Then please make the following declaration to him." The declaration, which "topped all the previous ones for sheer effrontery and deceit," laid out Germany's "justifications" for attacking the Soviet Union and would be read out by Schulenburg to a stunned Molotov at dawn, June 22.[28]

At some point on June 21—according to William L. Shirer it was in the afternoon—Hitler finally sat down and composed a letter to the Italian dictator Benito Mussolini, explaining his reasons for attacking the Soviet Union. ("As in the preparation of all his other aggressions he had not trusted his good friend and chief ally enough to let him in on his secret until the last moment."[29]) The letter was delivered to Mussolini's foreign minister, Count Ciano, in Rome at 3:00 the next morning, just minutes before German troops were to cross the Russian border. Mussolini, who was relaxing at his summer place at Riccione, had to be roused from his sleep to receive the news.[30] Hitler's long missive began: "Duce! I am writing this letter to you at a moment when months of anxious deliberation and continuous nerve-racking waiting are ending in the hardest decision of my life." Once again, Hitler fell back on the same old arguments, all based on the need for a preemptive strike. Time, he insisted, was not on Germany's side. In a year's time, Soviet Russia would be stronger, and Great Britain, its hopes resting on Russia, even less prepared to make peace; and by then the mass deliveries of war material from the United States would be having an effect. In ending his letter, the *Führer* could not resist lying even to Mussolini, while also expressing his great relief at having finally made his decision:

> *Whatever may come, Duce, our situation cannot become worse as a result of this step; it can only improve . . . Let me say one more thing, Duce. Since I struggled through to this decision, I again feel spiritually free. The partnership with the Soviet Union, in spite of the complete sincerity of our efforts to bring about a final conciliation [!], was nevertheless often very irksome to me, for in some way or other it seemed to me to be a break with my whole origin, my concepts and my former obligations. I am happy now to be relieved of these mental agonies.[31] [Ich bin glücklich von dieser Qual befreit zu sein.][32]*

By now, spring 1941, Mussolini was "completely a prisoner" of the Germans, something he knew only too well and resented. He was sure that Germany would defeat Russia and yet, as he confided to Ciano: "I hope for only one thing, that in this war in the east the Germans lose a lot of feathers." Still, he also knew that his own future hinged wholly on the success or failure of German arms. He at once issued orders for a declaration of war on Soviet Russia.[33]

That evening, as the Chancellery burst with energy and excitement on the eve of the new campaign,[34] Hitler again summoned Goebbels to him. Hitler himself was, by now, utterly exhausted, but he soon became carried away by his remarks about the war about to break. For three hours the two men paced up and down inside the cavernous building. For an hour or so they tried out the new fanfares to be broadcast over the radio to announce *Wehrmacht* victories in the East. Slowly, Hitler began to unwind. "The *Führer* is freed from a nightmare the closer the decision comes. It's always so with him," Goebbels wrote in his diary. At 2:30 in the morning, with the start of the campaign less than forty minutes away, Hitler retired to bed.[35]

It was not until 3:30 A.M. that Goebbels, having returned to his ministry through the blacked-out streets of Berlin and put his staff in the picture, retired to his room. By then, "the most destructive and barbaric war in the history of mankind" had already begun.[36] In his diary Goebbels wrote:

> *Now the artillery is thundering. God bless our weapons! . . . I pace restlessly up and down in my room. I can hear history breathing. Great, wondrous time in which a new Reich is being born. In pain, it is true, but it rises upwards to the light.*[37]

2.2: "*SOLDATEN DER OSTFRONT!*"—THREE MILLION MEN ARE POISED TO STRIKE!

By late morning, June 21, 1941, the "Dortmund" code word released by General Jodl at OKW had arrived at the headquarters of all three army groups in the East; it was then transmitted via secure communications to the staffs of the armies, panzer groups, corps, and divisions at the front. Thus had the long and increasingly stressful months of meticulous staff work and planning finally culminated—"according to plan" (*planmässig*) as recorded in the war diary of Army Group South's elite 1 Mountain Division[38]—in the *Wehrmacht* High Command's order for the surprise attack on the Soviet Union, to begin at dawn the next morning.[39]

In the final days before the attack the commanders of the army groups worked tirelessly to bring their preparations to a successful conclusion and to make sure that not even the slightest detail was neglected or overlooked, for that, of course, could mean lives lost. Field Marshal Fedor von Bock, Commander, Army Group Center, drove out frequently to the Russo-German frontier,[40] deliberating with front-line commanders, poring over maps and battle plans, examining the terrain, receiving updates on enemy intelligence, and coordinating last-minute details or changes of plan. Since October 1940, Bock's headquarters had been located in the city of Posen, in occupied Poland; on June 21, however, he relocated his headquarters much farther to the east, to the village of Rembertov on the eastern outskirts of Warsaw.[41]

Shortly before *Barbarossa* began, Bock found himself in a dispute with Field Marshal Ritter von Leeb, Commander, Army Group North. While Bock wanted the attack to begin at a uniform time (0315 hours), Leeb was adamant about starting his artillery preparation ten minutes earlier, at 0305 hours; apparently, his rationale for the staggered start times was that sunrise occurred minutes earlier farther north—not only in the sector of Army Group North but on the left wing of Army Group Center as well.[42] While Bock vigorously disagreed with Leeb about staggering the timing of the attack, he was overruled by OKH. "So I'm the one who has to suffer and have to attack with my right wing at Rundstedt's time [0315] and with my left wing at Leeb's time," Bock recorded in his diary two days before the attack.[43]

Meanwhile, final preparations for the impending campaign included the calibration of communications links between Hitler's new headquarters outside Rastenburg, East Prussia, and the army groups, while signal troops completed installation of telephone trunk lines from higher headquarters to ground and air units along the forwardmost line.[44] The pressures on commanders and their staffs, the weight of their responsibilities, were immense in these last days prior to the onset of war. At least one superior and trusted officer, Dr. Seidel, chief intelligence officer (*Luftflotten-Nachrichtenführer*) in Field Marshal Albert Kesselring's 2 Air Fleet, collapsed under the strain and took his life. Kesselring himself, whose air fleet (*Luftflotte 2*) was responsible for providing Bock's army group with air support, made numerous flights in his twin-engine Fw-189 tactical reconnaissance aircraft, from south of Brest-Litovsk (Brest) to the border of East Prussia, to better acquaint himself with the deployment areas of his wings, groups, and squadrons. One of his last acts before the war began was to visit Field Marshal von Bock on the evening of June 21. He found the army group commander, in distinct contrast to their final encounters before previous campaigns, downcast [*niedergeschlagen*] and pensive—no doubt weighed down by the solemn responsibility he alone shouldered for the more than one million men in his army group.[45]

As noted in Chapter 1 (Section 1.5) the deployment by rail of twelve panzer and twelve motorized divisions to the East was—for security reasons—not to begin until early June; these formations signified the tip of the *Wehrmacht's* spear, and OKH sought to conceal their movements (and their presence) from the Russians as long as possible. The movements of the mobile units to the eastern frontier, which took place from June 3 to June 23, will now be examined in some detail below.

One of the mobile units arriving in Poland in early June 1941 was General of Panzer Troops (*Gen.d.Pz.Tr.*) Joachim Lemelsen's 47 Panzer Corps (Army Group Center). Its 17 Panzer Division, moving by road and rail, had transited the German border, detrained, and motored on to Warsaw, arriving there about June 11. The division then laagered temporarily near the Polish capital, while Lemelsen's two other mobile divisions (18 Panzer and 29 Motorized Infantry Divisions) were assembling southeast and south of Warsaw. In an early postwar study of the initial attack of 17 Panzer Division at the start of the Russian campaign, the author, a former commander of the division's 39 Panzer Regiment, outlined the elaborate efforts of his regiment in the days before June 22 to conceal its preparations for war with Russia. For example, regimental insignia on uniforms, standards, and unit symbols on motor vehicles had been removed before entraining for the journey eastward. In addition, a news embargo was imposed and all outgoing mail restricted. To avoid detection by Russian listening posts, radio traffic was prohibited, while movements during daylight hours were mostly forbidden to guard against potential aerial reconnaissance. All motor vehicles, in particular armored fighting vehicles, were carefully camouflaged. To provide additional security, the movements of local inhabitants were restricted to limited areas around German occupied villages and to certain hours of the day. Headquarters, along with military and regular police units, had special authority to enforce the strictest secrecy as well as the requisite camouflage measures.[46]

A history of 40 Rifle Regiment (17 Panzer Division), compiled after the war by former members of the regiment (*Kameradschaft* Regiment 40), offers further insight into this last phase of the German *Ostaufmarsch*, while also typifying the confidence of the German invaders. In early June, the regiment, in motorized march and by means of rail transport, crossed the Elbe and Oder Rivers, advancing into Poland. ("Traces of the German-Polish war of 1939 are still visible everywhere.") After unloading at Kalisz and Lódz, the motorized march continued through Warsaw on "poor, dusty roads." By June 16, the regiment had arrived at Siedlce–Konstantinov, not far from the Russo-German frontier.

> *The regimental staff has already driven ahead toward Wiśniew in trucks . . . Positioning and assembly for attack are completed without a hitch. The Russians notice barely anything of our intentions to attack. On 16.6.41, the divisional order arrives for the regiment to move into the assembly area at Derlo—15 kilometers north of Brest-Litovsk . . . Parts of 3 Company take over surveillance and security along the Bug River, after men from our regiment, disguised in customs uniforms, have carried out reconnaissance and soundings on the Bug beforehand. Firing positions and observation posts for the heavy weapons are determined. Frequent discussions have taken place concerning the method of carrying out the attack. The remaining elements of the regiment arrive in the staging area by the evening of 21.6 . . .*
>
> *Since there is sufficient time available, the attack is thoroughly prepared. The surveillance of the enemy river bank provides a clear picture of the enemy. The favorable terrain permits a move under cover into the staging area. Officers Bapst and Steiner swim across the Bug repeatedly and tap the Russian telephone lines. The sand on the Russian riverbank is regularly smoothed over in order [not] to detect any footprints.*

> *In view of our superiority of personnel and matériel (240 guns have been posi-*
> *tioned in a sector of approximately 8 km), we are certain that our mission will lead*
> *to success.*[47]

Only from June 18 to June 21 were the panzer and motorized divisions to move into their assigned concentration areas (*Aufmarschräume*) near the border or attack assembly areas (*Bereitstellungsräume*) directly adjacent to the border with Russia;[48] as much as possible, these movements were to take place under cover of darkness. Among the panzer and motorized units rolling toward the eastern frontier were those of General Hermann Hoth's 3 Panzer Group (Army Group Center). A report in the panzer group's official records describes the movements of its divisions into the Suwalki triangle, a depressed region dotted with forests and lakes opposite Soviet-occupied Lithuania and the panzer group's assigned assembly area for the attack. The problems encountered with poor roads—not to mention the paucity of roads in general—were only too typical; in this case, however, good traffic discipline proved its worth:

> *The deployment of 3 Panzer Group in the Suwalki triangle proceeded according to plan from 19.–22.6.[41]. The three short nights that were available, as well as the avail-ability of only two roads for moving up the troops, made it necessary to move elements into the assembly areas during the day . . . Despite this, secrecy was maintained, as the later attack demonstrated.*
>
> *All deployment movements proceeded smoothly amid good traffic discipline . . . The strict separation of combat vehicles and vehicles that were to follow had proved its worth. All vehicles required for combat, as well as those extensively equipped with bridging columns, reached the designated areas on time along poor roads. The strict sepa-ration of the sectors assigned to the panzer corps and infantry corps for their movement, repeatedly requested by the* Panzergruppe, *had already borne fruit for the deployment.*
>
> *The divisions, well camouflaged, prepared for the attack under the protection of the artillery, heavy weapons and Flak. At 0200 hours on 22.6.[41], the assembly was com-pleted without disruption, which in itself was an achievement, since a Russian attack into our troop movements and assembly areas could have caused a difficult situation.*[49]

By the night of June 21/22, 1941, the panzer divisions of Army Group Center's two panzer groups earmarked for the initial assault had reached their jump-off positions in the forests, hills, meadows, and fields along the demarcation line with Russia. The situa-tion map of the German Army General Staff's Operations Branch reveals that the two forwardmost panzer corps of Heinz Guderian's 2 Panzer Group—easily identifiable on the ground from the white "G" (for Guderian) emblazoned on all tanks and vehicles as a tactical identification sign—were in position on either side of the Soviet fortress of Brest-Litovsk (Guderian's other panzer corps was in reserve). Several hundred kilometers to the north, at the other end of Field Marshal von Bock's long and meandering front, the tanks and motorized infantry of Hoth's 3 Panzer Group, as briefly described above, were assembled for the attack.[50]

Meanwhile, on the southern wing of the front, in the sector of Field Marshal Gerd von Rundstedt's Army Group South, the tanks, armored personnel carriers, and motorized artillery of General Ewald von Kleist's 1 Panzer Group were lurching into position in German-occupied Poland. Due to the strong Soviet fixed fortifications along the front of his army group, Rundstedt's plan of attack was for the initial breakthrough to be made exclusively with infantry divisions and, as a result, six infantry divisions were allotted to Kleist's panzer group, while the panzer and motorized infantry divisions were kept back from the frontier.[51] As registered in the war diary of 1 Panzer Group, by late evening of June 20, 1941, the mobile formations had reached their assigned concentration areas, which stretched from about 15 kilometers from the border (11 Panzer Division) back to behind the Vistula River some 150 kilometers from the front (16 Panzer Division).[52] "The morale of the troops is excellent," noted the war diary of the panzer group's 14 Panzer Division on the last day of peace. "But everywhere the great questions: What effect will the initial artillery barrage have on the Russians? Will they be surprised by our attack, or has the enemy already got wind of the enormous movements of our strategic deployment?"[53]

The same process was repeated along the front of Field Marshal Ritter von Leeb's Army Group North. Here, however, as with Army Group Center, the panzer divisions (three in all, assigned to General Erich Hoepner's 4 Panzer Group) were pushed right up to the frontier to participate in the initial attack. Leeb's attack sector was the narrowest of the three army groups, which led to difficult challenges as men, tanks, and other vehicles closed up to the frontier. To facilitate movement across the Nemen River, German engineers constructed pontoon bridges, while laborers with the Reich Labor Service cut lanes and reinforced roadways through the forests of East Prussia. Recalled Erhard Raus, in June 1941 a colonel in 4 Panzer Group's 6 Panzer Division:

Just prior to the beginning of Operation Barbarossa, 6 Panzer Division, which had originally occupied the area around Deutsch Eylau and Torun, assembled in the area around Osterode, Riesenburg, and Deutsch Eylau. From this point the buildup for the attack proceeded in a succession of four night marches. The assembly movements proved very difficult because of the sheer mass of troops in Army Group North that were approaching the border and their often conflicting routes of march. Crossing the [Nemen] River turned out to be particularly difficult. Our lighter vehicles crossed at Schreitlauken on an auxiliary bridge over which a test run had only been driven at the last moment. Tanks and heavier vehicles moved across the Memel' bridge at Tilsit, which also had to be used by 1 Panzer Division, so that two parallel columns converged at a single point. Nevertheless, the entire assembly succeeded without any major stoppages, with all movements restricted to hours of darkness and never allowed to extend into daytime.[54]

A former officer with 1 Panzer Division remembered the final days before the onset of war:

The forward detachments of 1 Panzer Division marched from 16 June into the Eighteenth Army assembly area west and northwest of Tilsit along the [Nemen] River . . . 1 Panzer Regiment with approximately 160 tanks left its garrison at Zinthen, 50 kilometers west of Königsberg, on 17 June. All armored units were ordered to march only during the night. Officer reconnaissance teams, clad like civilian hunters or farmers, were dispatched into the countryside to take a short look at the area east and southeast of Tilsit and west of Tauroggen. However, the area [five kilometers] west of the former German/Lithuanian border remained strictly "off limits!" A few selected advance assault teams moved into the frontier section during the night of 21 June through 22 June. No armored movements were permitted after the initial assembly of the division. There we waited calmly for the final orders to arrive. Hq., 1 Panzer Division, covered by a deep forest, was located near the small village of Kullmen. Now everything was thoroughly prepared and organized.[55]

The fear that the Russians had already caught on, that the invasion would not catch them napping, must have kept many a German field commander and staff officer up late at night. "Tensions rose steadily on the German side," wrote then colonel and chief of staff of Fourth Army, Günther Blumentritt, after the war:

By the evening of the 21st we assumed that the Russians must have realized what was happening, yet across the River Bug on the front of Fourth Army and 2 Panzer Group . . . all was quiet. The Russian outposts were behaving quite normally. At a little after midnight, when the entire artillery of the assault divisions and of the second wave too was already zeroed in on its targets, the international Berlin-Moscow train passed without incident through Brest-Litovsk. It was a weird moment.[56]

General Lemelsen (47 Panzer Corps) was convinced that the Russians had long ago put "two and two" together:

Saturday, 21.6.41 (B-1 Day)

It really is a strange state of affairs: the Panje-horses are still running around everywhere here right up to the Bug and they haven't been evacuated, but no doubt it is to preserve the element of surprise as much as possible. Even so, we are certain that the

*Russians have known for some time about what is going on here. They are working
further forward, but it seems as if they have left only the weaker forces up front in order
to fight with the bulk of the army further back. That would not be very pleasant for us.
At this time tomorrow we shall know more.*[57]

That morning, the war diarist of Seventeenth Army (Army Group South) noted
that the "enemy picture" was essentially unchanged—that while the Red Army field
positions at the border were still only partially manned, significant entrenching activity (*Schanztätigkeit*) had also been observed.[58] Hundreds of kilometers to the north,
in a dreary East Prussian forest, 1 Panzer Division bore witness to more disturbing
developments, while rejecting the prospect of the Russians launching an attack of their
own: "The opinion of the division this morning [June 21] is that the enemy must have
detected our movements, or that he at least expects an immediate attack. Artillery
observation posts are now recognized as being occupied; the Russians are equipped for
battle (*feldmarschmässig ausgerüstet*) and have put on steel helmets. But it's now too late
for the Russians to attack."[59] Even Field Marshal von Bock found that keeping secrets
in wartime was no easy matter: "Today [June 20] my Polish cleaning lady proved how
hard it is to keep something secret in wartime; she asked me to see to it that she kept
her position as I was after all going away!"[60]

As dawn broke on June 21, 1941, and the final hours of peace ticked irretrievably
away, millions of ordinary German soldiers across the vast reaches of the eastern frontier
made their final preparations for battle, just like soldiers everywhere on the eve of a great
new campaign. What was different in this case, however, was that the overwhelming
majority of the *Landser* had no firm grasp on just what that campaign might be. It was,
in fact—perhaps largely on an emotional or psychological plane—inconceivable to most
of them that they were about to wage war on the Soviet Union. Such a bold statement
may seem extravagant, but it is true. After all, since August 1939, Germany had had a
non-aggression pact with Russia that had brought many tangible benefits to the Reich.
Would the *Führer* truly contemplate breaking such a pact? Besides, Germany was still
at war with Great Britain, and hadn't Hitler promised that he would never commit the
Reich to a two-front war?

As the troop trains trundled east, across Germany, the Elbe, and into Poland and East
Prussia, the men had wondered where they were going and why they were going there.
They knew nothing of course, yet it soon began to dawn on them that something big,
extraordinarily big, was in the air. To explain what they could not know, the men—as all
men do in times of war—resorted to rumors, often the wildest of rumors, and all pointing away from war with Mother Russia. "The craziest rumors about Russia are making
the rounds here," wrote *Leutnant* H.H. (258 Infantry Division) in a field post letter to
an unknown recipient on May 20, 1941. "Some are saying that we've leased the Ukraine
for the next 90 years and received permission to march through Turkey to Iraq . . . Every

latrine rumor is closely followed by another."[61] *Gefreiter* Hubert Hegele (1 Mountain Division), in a long diary entry on June 21, wrote:

> *Many rumors have been floating about recently, from the one about Molotov's revolution—which, if need be, we would support—to the right of transit through Russia in order to assist hard-pressed Iraq against its English attackers. An attack on the Soviet Union? Well, we don't believe that at all. First of all, Germany has a friendship pact and a non-aggression pact with the Soviet Union; and secondly—a battle against this vast empire? No, that won't happen. What is truth—what is rumor? What do we little wheels in this vast machinery of war know? Nothing, absolutely nothing. Only the unrest in our hearts about whatever's looming ahead of us. That something is coming, we surely know that.*[62]

Waffen-SS officer Otto Skorzeny (SS Motorized Infantry Division "Viking"), who in September 1943 would lead the successful mission to rescue Benito Mussolini, who had been overthrown and taken prisoner, recalled in his memoirs:

> *In mid-June 1941 our division was transferred by rail to Lódz in Poland. After all vehicles and supplies had been loaded onto the flat cars, we boarded our passenger cars and enjoyed the journey without worry.*
>
> *For hours we speculated about our next military objective, but none of us envisioned that we would soon embark on a war against Russia. To the contrary, the most persistent rumor was that our objective would be the oil fields of the Persian Gulf. Russia would grant the German Army free passage and we would march across the Caucasus into Iran . . .*
>
> *Another rumor was that we would march via Turkey into Egypt and surround the English Near-East Army in a pincer action. As a result of this conjecture I took along the book* The Seven Pillars of Wisdom, *by T.E. Lawrence. The tempting Orient provided us with many hours of conversation while we were transported in a wide arc around Bohemia and Moravia to reach Poland via Upper Silesia.*[63]

Still others at the front sought to manage the stress and uncertainty of what the days ahead held in store by making friendly wagers:

> *We all have a lot to do but time is running very short, for we're supposed to move to a new forest billet in a couple of hours. Otherwise I'm doing well. And the weather is beautiful—warm and sunny. Today I made a wager—"Will there be war the day after tomorrow or not?" But it's only for two liters of beer. I'm in for "ja," and my partner says "nein." Would sure be good if I lost this bet, but most likely I'll win it.*[64]

In addition to inspecting weapons and equipment and doing requisite maintenance, some of the *Landser* marked their final days before "B-Tag" with soccer games and equestrian competitions.[65] Others simply sought to survive difficult conditions in the field that could border on the intolerable. Recalled a soldier who served in a field replacement battalion (*Feldersatzbataillon*) with 8 Panzer Division:

> On 17 June we packed up our things again and, leaving behind the motor vehicles we had just received, marched on foot at night until we were right at the Lithuanian frontier, not far from the small border town of Eydtkau, in a humid forested area. Between the thickets of pine and fir trees we built tents for four persons out of triangular shelter halfs and camouflaged them. The region was dominated by an unimaginable plague of mosquitoes. Myriads of these blood-sucking pests [Plagegeister] could bring one to the point of desperation. These June days were hot and oppressive and, at least for me, filled with great worry and inner tension.
>
> On one occasion, I was sent to Eydtkau to receive orders and found the town to be oddly unfamiliar and practically deserted by civilians.[66]

Conditions were no better in the primitive backwater of the Suwalki triangle, where the 20 Motorized Infantry Division was completing its assembly in the final days before war with Russia. Recollected an artillerist in the unit:

> I think that it was on the 19th of June, 1941 . . . we left our quarters in the morning and traveled over primitive and dusty roads. In the late afternoon, we passed the little town of Suwalki at the border of Lithuania and soon thereafter dismounted in a dense forest covered with thick underbrush. We were advised that we would stay there over night and would receive new orders the next morning. The night turned out to be horrible.
>
> We were surrounded by swamplands. It was very hot and humid. But the worst were the thousands of big mosquitoes infesting the area. There was not a single minute without several stings from these tiny beasts. After about an hour my hands and face started to swell from all the bites, and so was it with my comrades. We saw no other way out but to build some fires and assemble around it in small groups. Fortunately, there was no wind going at all, so the smoke stayed concentrated around the fire, which kept the mosquitoes more or less away. But instead, we had now to contend with the heat from the fire and the dense smoke, which burned our eyes. It was a miserable night, and no one could find any sleep.[67]

The panzer divisions, before slipping into their attack assembly areas, carefully reconnoitered their approach routes, as well as the assembly areas themselves, which, if possible, were concealed in forests. Once in their assembly areas, the panzer units rapidly made ready for combat, which included clearing all barriers and obstacles—such as barbed wire entanglements—along their attack frontage.[68] Radio silence was strictly enforced, ammunition quietly brought forward, and extra containers of fuel hung on tanks and vehicles. Artillery and other heavy weapons were shepherded into their firing positions. Telephone wire was laid between the gun batteries and the forward observation posts. Dr. Alfred Opitz, then a thirty-year-old *Obergefreiter* in 18 Panzer Division, recalled after the war:

> On 21 June the noise of motors and vehicles began to roar and drone in the broad extent of forest to our rear. Tanks and heavy artillery seemed to be moving up from there. Now and then a reconnaissance aircraft circled over the river terrain. The air was thick enough to stifle, it smelled of something horrendous [es roch nach Ungeheuerlichem].[69]

Last-minute reconnaissance of terrain and enemy forces beyond the frontier was carried out, with some of the reconnaissance teams going out to inspect border regions disguised as local hunters and farmers, and even carrying farm implements to complete the ruse. Liaison was established with supporting combat and combat-support units, while front-line commanders were briefed on their missions. In some cases, chocolate and cigarettes were distributed to troops, some of whom were fortunate enough to receive an allotment of *Schnapps*, one bottle for every four men.[70]

Hans Jochen Schmidt, a young *Leutnant* who would be killed in Russia in 1942, noted in his diary on June 21:

> We then also moved off at dusk and occupied an assembly area in a depression at the Suwalki tip. Each of us received 60 rounds of live ammunition. From that point forward our rifles stayed loaded. There could be no thought of sleep. But we had a radio, which unfortunately quit on us much too early. No one suspected anything yet in the Reich and they were enthusiastically playing dance music, which we let trickle comfortingly over our souls. The route of advance [Vormarschstrasse] was alive with traffic. Vehicle after vehicle. At 2400 hours the proclamation of the Führer was read out to us, and the tension became almost unbearable.[71]

During the afternoon and evening of June 21, 1941, German commanders throughout the East, their men huddled around them in small groups, read out Hitler's proclamation to the "Soldiers of the Eastern Front," thus putting an abrupt end to the weeks and months of anxious speculation about what the future was to bring. The proclamation included the following passages:

Soldaten der Ostfront!

Troubled by deep concerns, condemned to months of silence, the hour has finally arrived in which I may speak to you, my soldiers, openly . . .

At this very moment, Soldiers of the Eastern Front, a concentration of forces is underway which, in its extent and scope, is the largest the world has ever seen . . . When this greatest front of world history now advances, then it will not only be to secure the conditions for the final conclusion of this great war in general, or to protect those countries affected at this moment, but rather to save the entire European civilization and culture.

German soldiers! You are thus entering into a struggle that is both difficult and laden with responsibility. For:

The fate of Europe, the future of the German Reich, the existence of our Volk *now lie in your hands alone.*

May the Lord God aid us all in this struggle!

Adolf Hitler
Führer *and Supreme Commander of the* Wehrmacht [72]

Because the march into Russia was to begin in a matter of hours, the soldiers had no time to process the enormous and unfathomable implications of it all. They had, in effect, been confronted with a *fait accompli*; in fact, in what can only be characterized as a surreal irony, not only the Russians, but a significant majority of the German soldiers themselves were taken completely by surprise by Hitler's decision to attack the Soviet Union.[73] Some officers took it upon themselves at—literally—the last minute, to attempt to steel their soldiers psychologically (and ideologically) for the immense struggle ahead. In 26 Army Corps (Army Group North), all unit commanders, guided by the *Führer*'s proclamation, spoke at length with their men in an effort to drive home the requisite "*Furor Teutonicus*" (Teutonic fury) that would be necessary to bring the war with Russia to a victorious decision.[74]

And yet from my examination of hundreds of German field post letters and diaries it is evident that most *Landser*—even those who were not convinced National Socialists, and even those who had dismissed the possibility of such a war (many others, of course, had surmised correctly)—welcomed Hitler's decision to finally settle the score with Soviet Russia. For some, war with Germany's arch ideological foe was simply inevitable, while others were convinced of the need to eliminate once and for all the existential threat posed by the sinister and secretive Bolshevik state. A diary entry of a regimental adjutant (45 Infantry Division) is, in this context, illustrative:

Today [June 16, 1941] the order came. So it is getting serious. The Führer *has decided, after the collapse of the peace efforts with England, to first overthrow Russia. Only the How and When still present us with a conundrum. With no declaration of war? But:*

it will be war against the archenemy [Erzfeind] of our idea, Bolshevism. And we will know how to conduct it, grimly and resolutely...[75]

On June 21, a battalion commander in 1 Mountain Division assured his men that the struggle on which they were about to embark was a "struggle [*Kampf*] for the life or death [*Sein oder Nichtsein*] of our people and it must end with the complete destruction of the Bolshevik Army."[76] For *Leutnant* Helmut D. (4 Mountain Division), the war was justified because Germany required space (*Lebensraum*) to feed her people: "Since early this morning at 0300 hours, we have a state of war with Russia . . . Even for us it came as quite a surprise, but after the explanation of the Führer much has become clear. Naturally, the question of food [*Ernährungsfrage*] is also important. With Russia we will be able to feed ourselves."[77] The same day (June 22), *Unteroffizier* Wilhelm Prüller (9 Panzer Division) responded in his diary to the onset of the Russian campaign and the reaction of his comrades:

Some of us simply gaped with astonishment, some took it with equanimity, some are horrified . . . Personally I think it's a good thing that we face the fight squarely and save our children from having to do it. For this reason: in the long run it would have proved impossible for two such giant nations, living right next to each other and with completely different ways of life, to exist side by side in peace and understanding. The fight between Communism, which is rotting so many peoples, and National Socialism was bound to come. And if we can win now, it's better than doing it later. And the Führer will know what he's doing. Above all, I'm sure it'll end well.[78]

In a similar vein, *Soldat* Erich N. (SS Motorized Infantry Division "*Das Reich*") wrote in a letter: "This morning you have also surely heard the proclamation of the *Führer*'s that was read by Dr. Goebbels. That comes as a big surprise. *Na ja*, sooner or later this conflict between the two world views had to come. May our trusty fortune in war [*Kriegsglück*] also lead us to a swift victory in this struggle!"[79] *Hauptmann* Dr. H.U., having just heard the first radio reports of a state of war existing between Germany and Soviet Russia, jotted in his diary:

We are thunderstruck [by the news]. The truce that had existed with the Soviets, the most bitter enemy of National Socialism, had always seemed so curious to us. We put up with it as a political necessity to avoid a two-front war . . . We had gotten a free hand in France, Poland, Belgium, Holland, Yugoslavia and Greece . . . Yet in spite of all the unique successes of the German armed forces in every theater of war, which often bordered on the fantastic, both of us always had a rather strange and uncomfortable feeling, most likely knowing that this [war] would become, must become, a most bitter and difficult struggle—where two completely opposite world views [Weltanschauungen] strike each other with the force of arms. It was clear to me at once where I would do my fighting: in the East![80]

For many other soldiers, any misgivings they may have had about war with Russia were submerged in their sublime sense of duty to country and boundless faith in their *Führer*. "I do my duty as a decent soldier," wrote *Gefr.* Gerhard S. (98 Infantry Division)[81] on June 22. "I would like to make my modest contribution to Germany coming out of this war victoriously. Look, what is most important now is to be hard against oneself. Our personal desires mean nothing. We must begin to adopt the very essence [*Wesen*] of the front soldier of 1918. I will gladly give all for our nation because, in this fateful time, that is our highest and purest experience."[82] For *O'Gefr.* Werner E. (73 Infantry Division),[83] the attack on the Soviet Union was an opportunity to reaffirm his faith in Adolf Hitler: "So now the dance of war has also embraced Russia . . . We soldiers are not exactly enthusiastic about the new theater of war, but we will follow the *Führer* with unyielding resolve."[84]

The typical German soldier was also imbued with an exalted sense of moral and martial superiority vis-à-vis his Russian opponent, despite knowing very little about him, which also served to inform his views about a war with the Soviet Union. In a diary entry on June 21, Private First Class Hänseler (123 Infantry Division) wrote: "Our commander read to us what many could not at first believe: the order to attack Russia. At 11:00 p.m. our company was to be ready to start. I'm in high spirits. At last my most cherished wish is coming true. I hope I'll live to see what I have always been dreaming about."[85] Noted an officer in 4 Panzer Division: "Most of us are awfully pleased that it's finally come to blows again."[86] In 296 Infantry Division the sense was that Russia would collapse after just a few weeks of fighting. "It'll go quite fast with the Russians, even if many of us will bite the dust" (*wenn auch mancher ins Gras beissen muss*), predicted a soldier in the division. "But it won't be in vain, it will be for Germany's future."[87] At midnight (June 21), a soldier in an artillery regiment (in sublime confidence or simply to reassure loved ones, or both) wrote home:

In three hours we will relay by radio the commands to open fire, which, when received by the batteries, will unleash a barrage on the Russian positions that will destroy everything. You will sleep peacefully, while we, who are in the first wave, begin the Vormarsch *into enemy territory. However, in the morning you will also know what hour has struck, and you will think of me . . . [but] you need have no worries, because everything has been so well prepared that almost nothing can go wrong.*[88]

And *Unteroffizier* Eberhard Krehl, who served on the staff of an artillery commander, would later remember:

Two days before the attack against Russia, we were transferred to Suwalki . . . Shortly before daybreak on 22 June 1941, Oberleutnant Wieland turned up in our quarters with the words: "It's all kicking off against Russia. I've just come from a meeting with the generals of the panzer units. One declared, 'In five weeks I'll be in Moscow,' then the next: 'I'll be there in four at the latest,' then the last retorted: 'I'll make it in three.' So it's going to go very quickly."[89]

For twenty-two-year-old Hermann Stracke, a soldier somewhere along the Eastern Front and, no doubt, for other *Landser*, the impending war with Russia was willingly embraced as an opportunity to prove one's manhood in the hard and merciless crucible of combat—a point of view expressed by Stracke in a letter to loved ones composed on the morning of June 22, 1941:

Last night the Oberleutnant *read out to us the proclamation of the* Führer, *so now this time we will finally be playing our part . . . If at this moment the designs of fate stand uncertain before me, and one ultimately must be prepared for anything, ready for anything, then believe me that I will go into battle confidently, joyously and undaunted* [unverzagt]. *And that I will proudly take on this trial of life* [Lebensprobe].[90]

There were others, however, who took a much dimmer view of the matter. For at least some of the men in 121 Infantry Division, the order to invade Russia evoked "not a trace of enthusiasm" (*von Begeisterung war keine Spur*); to be sure, they were confident men, but the prospect of war in the endless spaces beyond the frontier, against an enemy about whom they knew little, filled them with a certain foreboding for the future of their Fatherland, their families, and themselves.[91] Dr. Alfred Opitz (18 Panzer Division) recalled that the soldiers of his company responded to the order with "icy silence"; not even a joke by his company commander—that their division commander was so sure of a rapid victory, he'd already put in for leave in mid-August—managed to break the ice among the men.[92]

For most German soldiers, however, it is a fair judgment that the profound and implicit faith they had in their *Führer*, and his military leadership, outweighed any scruples they may have had about the coming campaign. And it would take many defeats, many unexpected and shocking setbacks in the months and years ahead to even begin to shake their confidence in him.

The night of June 21/22 was "clear and warm,"[93] with only a "faint crescent of the waning moon."[94] Concealed in forests, farmsteads, fields, and meadows along the frontier, the "Soldiers of the Eastern Front" hunkered down in their attack assembly areas. Formidably armed and equipped, their weapons ready to fire, their hand grenades armed, taking their last, deliberate draws on their cigarettes, they waited in burgeoning and increasingly unbearable tension, staring at the luminous dials of their watches as the final hours and minutes of peace ticked forever away. "The summer night lay over the banks of the River Bug," recalled a soldier with 18 Panzer Division. "Silence, only now and then a brief clanking somewhere. Over by the water, the frogs croaked. Anyone who was there in an assault detachment, or who was among the attack spearhead in the Bug meadows up front that night of 21–22 June 1941, will never forget the creaking courting calls of the Bug frogs."[95] A postwar account published by veterans of 77 Infantry Regiment (26 Infantry Division) also offered vivid recollections of those final hours before war began:

> *Without making a sound the units of 77 Infantry Regiment emerge from their quarters after dark and move silently into their assembly areas . . . Only the clouds of dust kicked up along the dry dirt roads offer hints as to where the field gray columns are moving toward the border. An eerie silence lies over the land. The hours of waiting that follow tear at our nerves . . . What will the "X-Hour" bring? Are the enemy positions really just weakly occupied over there, on the other side? Or will we be met by a hurricane of fire? What will the coming weeks and months bring?*
>
> *Cigarettes, whose glow we conceal in our cupped hands, provide some comfort. Only now and then can a whispered word be detected, as the men re-check their combat readiness. Finally, the high summer night begins to yield to the first faint rays of morning light. To the north, the large surface of Lake Wystiter throws off a silver glow. Otherwise it's calm. The calm before the storm?[96]*

Disciplined soldiers that they were, they methodically went through their last-minute checks: Were rifles loaded and safety catches on? Were helmet straps adjusted properly and uniforms buttoned up? Were hand-grenade arming mechanism screws easy to adjust? Few but the most seasoned veterans were able to snatch a few hours of sleep before the guns began to thunder. What, they wondered, would they encounter beyond the border? Were the Russians waiting for them, or were they still largely in the dark about the firestorm about to break?

In the final hours before the start of war, German special forces belonging to Regiment 800, the so-called *"Brandenburgers,"* many of them Russian speaking and clad in Red Army uniforms—or, more likely, uniforms of the Russian security forces—infiltrated or were dropped by parachute behind Soviet lines. Once in place, they began to blow up or otherwise incapacitate power and signal stations, activate German "sleeper" agents, seize bridges vital for German operations (and secure them from demolition), cut communications, spread false messages and fake orders and, in general, foment alarm and confusion.[97] The mission of the *Brandenburgers* was unwittingly assisted by the Russians themselves: "Soviet communications security was appalling, particularly for a country which was so paranoiac about such matters. The fact that German special forces managed to crack the Soviet communications across the 1800 kilometer front from the Baltic to the Black Sea

. . . was a stupendous achievement for them. It was also a disgrace for the Red Army, the NKVD and the Soviet government."[98]

2.3: MOSCOW—STALIN STILL IN DENIAL ABOUT THE IMPENDING GERMAN ATTACK

In 1811, the year before Napoleon's ill-fated invasion of Russia, a comet swept across the skies of Europe. On March 25, 1811, Honoré Flaugergues, observing the night sky from his makeshift observatory in Viviers, discovered the comet "in the now defunct constellation of Argo Navis." The next day, he observed it again and began to track its flight:

The comet was low in the south and was moving northward and brightening. On 11 April it was spotted by Jean Louis Pons in Marseille, and on 12 May by William J. Burchell in Cape Town. The comet soon became visible to the naked eye, and by the late autumn it lit up the night sky from Lisbon to Moscow. People gazed up at it, some with interest, many more with a sense of foreboding.

This seemed to increase the further east one went in Europe. "As they contemplated the brilliant comet of 1811," recalled a parish priest there, "the people of Lithuania prepared themselves for some extraordinary event." Another inhabitant of the province never forgot how everyone got up from dinner and went out to gaze on the comet and then talk of "famine, fire, war and bloodshed." In Russia, many linked the comet to a plague of fires that swept the land that summer and autumn, and a blind terror gripped them as they looked on it. . . .

In St. Petersburg, Czar Alexander himself became fascinated by the phenomenon, and discussed it with John Quincy Adams, the American ambassador at his court. He claimed to be interested only in the scientific aspects of the comet, and made fun of all those superstitious souls who saw in it a harbinger of catastrophe and war.

But he was either being disingenuous or he was deluding himself, for the machinery of war had already clanged into gear.[99]

Joseph Stalin, of course, was not so fortunate as to have a terrifying comet to alert him to the impending arrival of Armageddon. What he did have was "perhaps the most effective intelligence apparatus of any"; and parts of it operated "right at the heart of German decision-making."[100] On the other hand, German counterintelligence agencies "had little sense of the true depth and breadth of Soviet intelligence penetration."[101] Soviet agents were practically ubiquitous across Germany and Europe and included the German Communist sympathizers Harro Schulze-Boysen (code name "Starshina," or "the Elder") and Arvid Harnack (known as "Korsicanets," or the "Corsican"). Exploiting his family connections (his father was a nephew of Adm. Alfred von Tirpitz, the former head of the German navy; his mother a relative of Hermann Göring) Schulze-Boysen joined *Luftwaffe* headquarters in 1941 as an officer, gaining access to top-secret material. Harnack, a lawyer who had studied in the United States and a nephew of the eminent theologian, Adolf von Harnack, had worked since 1935 at the Economics Ministry in Berlin; he, too, had access to classified information. Both men, who had been recruited in the summer of 1940 to work for Soviet intelligence, "were able to tap sources close to the heart of Nazi military and economic planning." They were found out and executed in 1942.[102]

Soviet espionage groups also operated throughout German-occupied Europe and neutral Switzerland, among them the "Lucy" spy ring—based in Lucerne, Switzerland, and run by an émigré German anti-Fascist publisher named Rudolf Rössler.[103] Because of the very high-value information provided by "Lucy," historians had long speculated that the ring may have been used by the British as a covert way to pass ULTRA-derived intelligence to the Soviets. (ULTRA was the code name for British signal intelligence derived from radio traffic encrypted by the Germans on their high-grade electrical cipher machines, known as ENIGMA.)[104] Such speculation is now known to be false. Another extremely well-informed source of information on German intentions was Richard Sorge ("Ramzai"), a Soviet spy embedded in the German embassy in Tokyo. British, American, and other foreign governments also provided Stalin and his cohorts with a plethora of intelligence (and, at Churchill's behest, with some of the British intelligence gleaned directly from ULTRA), much of it highly accurate. Moreover, by the spring of 1941, a disturbing amount of tactical intelligence was reaching Moscow from the Soviet western border military districts.

From late July 1940 to June 22, 1941, no less than ninety separate warnings of an impending German attack were passed on to Stalin by his intelligence apparatus,[105] each report first having been carefully evaluated and interpreted before being briefed to the *vozhd*, as the Soviet leader was called. Outlined below are several of the warnings received by Stalin in June 1941; they offer fascinating insights into the nature of the information Stalin was getting—and just days before the German attack—as well as his response to that information:

- *June 1941: The German ambassador in Moscow, von Schulenburg, warns the head of the Soviet International Affairs Department: "I am going to tell you something that has never been done in diplomacy before," he says. "Germany's state secret number one is that Hitler has taken the decision to begin war against you on 22 June." Stalin's response is indignant. He tells the Politburo that "Disinformation has now reached ambassadorial level!"*
- *12 June 1941: Stalin receives information from "Starshina," that the decision has been taken to attack Russia. The same day, a report reaches the Foreign Ministry and Central Committee, indicating that, between 1 January and 10 June 1941, German planes had violated Soviet airspace more than 2,000 times; including ninety-one violations in the first ten days of June.*

- *Mid-June 1941: A report arrives from "Lucy," stipulating the date of the attack (22 June) and furnishing details of the German operational plan. Stalin remains in complete denial.*
- *17 June 1941: Another warning arrives from "Starshina," indicating that all German military measures for an attack are complete and that the blow may come at any moment. Reliable reports have also been received from the German Economics Ministry, indicating an imminent attack. In the margins of the report, Stalin hisses: "You can send your source from the staff of the Luftwaffe to the devil. He's not a source, he is providing disinformation."*
- *18 June 1941: When Army Chief of Staff Zhukov suggests that the Red Army be placed in alarm readiness, Stalin replies: "So you want a war? Don't you have enough decorations and isn't your rank high enough?"[106]*

With each such warning—and there were many more like them—it became increasingly difficult for Stalin to justify his headstrong and dangerous policy of avoiding any military move in the western border districts that might be construed by the Germans as a "provocation." "In the last days and weeks [before war]," noted Rodric Braithwaite, British ambassador to Moscow from 1988 to 1992, "Stalin's mind was increasingly closed to reason as the rationale for his policy ebbed away."[107] The *vozhd*, it seems, had become obsessed with the idea that nothing—nothing at all—could be done that might be interpreted by the Germans as a provocation, which, in Stalin's mind, could very well elicit a full-up German attack.

When the Soviet defense commissar, Marshal S. K. Timoshenko, and chief of the Army General Staff, General G. K. Zhukov, informed Stalin of their evidence of German intentions, the Soviet dictator "threw it back in their faces."[108] "Hitler and his generals," Stalin insisted, "are not so foolish as to start a two-front war. The Germans broke their neck on this in World War I. Hitler would never risk such a thing."[109] Yet as the first weeks of June 1941 slipped away, and with evidence of an imminent German assault having reached staggering proportions, Stalin's top military leaders were becoming increasingly desperate to force the dictator's hand and take action before the Germans struck.

On June 15, 1941, Timoshenko and Zhukov requested permission from Stalin to move the covering forces along the frontier to stronger defensive positions. The *vozhd* bluntly rejected their request. "We have a non-aggression pact with Germany," Stalin reminded them. "Germany is up to her ears with the war in the West and I am certain that Hitler will not risk creating a second front by attacking the Soviet Union. Hitler is not such an idiot and understands that the Soviet Union is not Poland, not France, and not even England."[110] Stalin told his generals to take their cues from the communiqué issued by the Soviet news agency TASS on June 14—to wit, that the rumors of an "early war" between Germany and Soviet Russia were "nothing but clumsy propaganda by forces hostile to the USSR and Germany and interested in the extension of the war." The combative communiqué clearly implied that the "hostile forces" were the British government and its ambassador in Moscow, Sir Stafford Cripps.[111]

In the final days of peace, it appears that Stalin's "dogged confidence" finally "began to crack." On June 17, he ordered his advisors to summarize all of the intelligence they had collected: "They produced a list of 41 reports received from Berlin over the previous nine months. Some were the usual gossip that agents are prone to pass on. Some were red herrings. Some were contradictory. But taken as a whole the weight of the intelligence was clear. Alas, by the time it was ready, the document was already only of historical interest. It reached its readers after the Germans had already attacked."[112]

The next day Timoshenko and Zhukov, as they had been doing for days, sought once again to prevail upon Stalin and the Politburo to place the army on full alert. The meeting went on for three long hours.

> *The more Zhukov spoke, the more irritable Stalin became. He accused Zhukov of war-mongering and became so abusive that Zhukov fell silent. But Timoshenko persisted. There would be havoc, he said, if the* Wehrmacht *struck the troops in their present positions. Stalin was furious. "It's all Timoshenko's work," he told the others. "He's preparing everyone for war. He ought to have been shot, but I've known him as a good soldier since the Civil War." Timoshenko reminded Stalin that he had told the cadets on 5 May[113] that war was inevitable. Stalin replied furiously, "I said that so that people would raise their alertness. But you have to understand that Germany on her own will never fight Russia. You must understand this." He stormed out, then suddenly put his head round the door and shouted, "If you're going to provoke the Germans on the frontier by moving troops there without our permission, then heads will roll, mark my words." In Stalin's mouth, that was not a figure of speech.[114]*

On the same day, June 18, the Soviet embassy in London cabled that Sir Stafford Cripps (who had been recalled to London for consultations) was "deeply convinced" that war between Germany and Russia was inevitable, and that war should start "not later than the middle of June." And yet the Red Army went on with its normal training routine, while the political instruction in its ranks did not change. Neither the NKVD border guards nor the forces of the special military districts received any special orders.[115] And when the orders finally did arrive, it was too late.

Stalin's "wishful thinking" had become a tragic obsession. As Winston Churchill would later "acidly" recall: "Nothing . . . pierced the purblind prejudice and fixed ideas which [he] had raised between himself and the terrible truth . . . The wicked are not always clever, nor are dictators always right."[116]

If today, several generations removed from the tragic events of June 1941, it seems inconceivable that Stalin would respond so dismissively to the flood of warnings pointing to an imminent German attack, one must also consider that much of the intelligence that made its way to the Soviet dictator's desk was much less clear cut than the examples cited above; indeed, some of it was plainly unreliable or contradictory in nature. Top lieutenants, such as Lavrenti Beria, sinister head of the NKVD (Soviet Secret Police), or F. I. Golikov, head of the GRU (Main Intelligence Directorate of the General Staff), often simply told Stalin what he wanted to hear, reinforcing his own prejudices and misconceptions. Moreover, in assessing Stalin's failure to accurately discern German intentions one cannot overlook the role played by Germany's exquisitely effective disinformation campaign, which brilliantly exploited and manipulated his catastrophic illusions.[117]

In Moscow it had rained heavily for several days, but on Saturday, June 21, Midsummer's Day, the sun broke through and throngs of people set out for the city's parks. Others left to relax in their dachas, toil in their vegetable gardens, or to picnic and fish in the Moscow River, while those who lacked the means for such luxuries, or who were tied down by work or still had exams to take, remained behind in the city of some four million people. "In the memories of survivors, that last day of peace has the golden quality of an idyll."[118]

Despite the disquieting rumors of impending war with Germany, the official mood in Stalin's capital was one of confidence. The citizens of Moscow, too, having been subjected to a steady diet of Soviet propaganda, mostly believed that, if the Germans struck, they would rapidly be pushed back and the Red Army would carry the fight to the invader's homeland within days, whereupon the German workers would rise as one to greet them and victory would be had at a minimal cost in blood. This had been the comforting message of the popular film *If War Should Come Tomorrow*—and, tomorrow, it *would* come.[119]

Stalin did not arrive at the Kremlin until late that Saturday, in the early hours of the afternoon. The massive fortress, one of the largest structures in Europe, was now more than four-and-a-half centuries old, its imposing red brick walls and tall towers looming menacingly over the city.[120] By now, the Soviet dictator must have been aware that events were rapidly slipping from his grasp; yet one can only wonder what was passing through his mind at this time. Surely, he did not want to take any rash or premature action; and he was, of course, determined to steer clear of any move that might be interpreted as a "provocation." Late in the afternoon, however, he began to act "as if he sensed greater danger" and, about 5:00 P.M., "set about some precautionary moves of his own."[121] He ordered the Moscow Party bosses, A. S. Shcherbakov and V. P. Pronin, to come to him in the Kremlin; once there, the *vozhd* instructed them to direct all Party *raikom* (district) secretaries to stay at their posts, and under no circumstances were they to leave their particular towns. "'*Vozmozhno napadenie Nemtsev,*' 'The Germans might attack' was the cryptic formula he used to cover all these instructions." But there were still no orders for the military, and time was running out.[122]

At some point, Stalin spoke with I. V. Tyulenev, commander of the Moscow Military District, and queried him about the readiness of Moscow's antiaircraft defenses. After hearing Tyulenev's report, Stalin replied: "Listen, the situation is uncertain and therefore you must bring the anti-aircraft defenses of Moscow up to 75 percent of their readiness state." Tyulenev passed the order posthaste to Maj.-Gen. Gromadin, the antiaircraft defense commander in Moscow.[123] That the state of the city's AA defenses would surface to the top of Stalin's mind at this point is perhaps not surprising. The "Winter War" with Finland (1939/40) had revealed the inadequacies of the Soviet air defense system, and the military leadership had issued repeated orders for their improvement, and yet little was done. Perhaps Stalin had suddenly recalled the excruciatingly embarrassing incident of May 15, 1941, when a German Ju-52 military transport plane had flown (without permission) from German-occupied Poland all the way to Moscow. The Soviet air defenses had failed to react. Timoshenko and Zhukov had investigated the incident and, on June 10, 1941, had issued a "furious" order.

> *Ground observers, they said, had mistaken the (three-engined) Ju 52 for a scheduled (two-engined) Soviet DC3. The Belostok airfield had failed to inform the local air defense units of the intrusion because their communications had broken down. The people in Moscow had not only failed to stop the aircraft; they had given it permission to land there! Timoshenko and Zhukov called for remedial measures, reprimanded those responsible, and—surprisingly belatedly—ordered that silhouettes of German aircraft should be distributed to all ground observers. The arrests and beatings started almost immediately.[124]*

Meanwhile, furious diplomatic maneuvers were in full swing. As we have seen (Section 2.1), all attempts by the Soviet embassy in Berlin to arrange a dialogue with Ribbentrop on June 21 had proved futile, as Hitler's foreign minister had deliberately departed Berlin early that morning, leaving instructions with his staff to hold the Russian ambassador at bay.[125] Rebuffed in Berlin, the Soviets turned frantically to the German ambassador in Moscow, Schulenburg, rushing him to the Kremlin at 6:00 P.M., where he encountered an agitated Molotov. The Soviet foreign minister complained about the ongoing violations of Russian airspace by German military aircraft; then he proceeded to barrage Schulenburg with questions. He, Molotov, wanted to know why members of the German embassy staff, and their wives, had suddenly left the country, resulting in rumors of imminent war. Why had the German government failed to respond to the "peace loving" TASS communiqué? What was behind the German discontent—"if it actually exists"—with the Soviet Union? Schulenburg's replies failed to restore Molotov's rattled composure. The German ambassador did, however, drop "his final hint about the German intentions, which obviously he did not report home. He admitted that 'posing those issues was justified,' but unfortunately he was in no position to answer, as Berlin 'kept him entirely in the dark.' Rather pathetically, Molotov whined that 'there was no reason for the German government to be dissatisfied with Russia.'"[126]

If diplomacy was proving to be frustratingly ineffectual, the situation at the western frontier was causing growing alarm. Early in the evening, Lt.-Gen. M. A. Purkayev, chief of staff of the Kiev Special Military District, reported that a German NCO had crossed the border and told Soviet frontier guards that a German attack was due in a matter of hours—on the morning of June 22. General Zhukov reported the news to Defense Commissar Timoshenko and to Stalin; the latter then ordered Timoshenko, Zhukov, and his deputy, N. F. Vatutin,[127] to the Kremlin posthaste.

The conference at the Kremlin began about 8:50 P.M.[128] Along with the top Soviet generals, Molotov and Beria were also among those present. Stalin asked his defense commissar what should be done; Timoshenko proposed that forces at the frontier should move up to their battle stations. But Stalin still resisted. "It's too soon," he said. "Perhaps we can still solve the problem by peaceful means." Although he was now worried, he was still unable to face head-on the disaster about to strike; he flirted with the idea that the German generals had deliberately sent the defector to "provoke a conflict." "No," his generals replied, "we think the deserter is telling the truth." The troops on the western frontier had to be put on combat alert at once, they insisted.[129]

After lengthy discussions, Stalin finally directed Zhukov to draft a "short general warning to the frontier armies." The result, Directive No. 1, was a "deeply confusing document." On the one hand, the troops were warned that a German attack could begin at any time; they were to secretly man their "firing points," while also dispersing and camouflaging their planes. On the other hand, they were "to avoid provocative actions of any kind, which might produce major complications." They were to take no further action without specific instructions. And yet it hardly mattered, for the directive was far too late. It would, for example, not reach the headquarters of the Western Special Military District until just before 1:00 A.M. on June 22; it would not be passed on to subordinate units until 2:30 in the morning, while Soviet frontier detachments, their communications cut by German saboteurs, would never receive the message.[130] And just as Timoshenko and Zhukov predicted, the directive would only cause more confusion: What should the commanders expect—border clashes or a major war? If they were not to yield to provocations, should they react at all? Stalin's notorious influence was all over the document.

The night of June 21 had been "sultry, hot and windless" in Moscow. Then, at 10:00 P.M., the thunder rolled[131]—an unusual summer storm punishing the city with torrential rain and driving gusts of wind, like a freakish harbinger of the storm of iron and steel about to break across the Russo-German frontier. And like claps of thunder, reports from the western border were now rolling in to the Kremlin, each one more worrisome than the one before it. The chief of staff of the Baltic Special Military District reported that "the Germans have finished the construction of the bridges across the [Neman River] . . . The civilians have been advised to evacuate to a depth of 20 kilometers from the frontier." The chief of staff of the Western Special Military District, Maj.-Gen. V. E. Klimovskikh, reported that the Germans had removed wire obstacles from the border near the Augustov-Seiny road, and that from the woods the distinct sound of engines could be heard; moreover, "violations of the state border by German aircraft along the Augustov direction" had taken place and, "according to data from a border detachment, the aircraft were carrying bombs under their wings." Col.-Gen. M. P. Kirponos, C-in-C of the Kiev Special Military District, reported that the war would start in a matter of hours. These reports, and others like them, were dutifully passed along to Stalin that evening at the Kremlin.[132]

Having done what he could—or, at least, what he was willing to do—Stalin left the Kremlin shortly after 11:00 P.M. and returned to his nearby Kuntsevo dacha, where he "carried on carousing" until perhaps 2:00 in the morning.[133] According to one account, Molotov and other Politburo members joined him there to watch a short film.[134] While the *vozhd* relaxed, a thousand kilometers to the west, on the far side of the frontier, the separate German army commands in the East were transmitting their call-signs signifying "full and final" readiness to attack—"*Kyffhäuser*" from Kluge's Fourth Army, "*Wotan*" from Rundstedt's Army Group South. "Panzer leader" Heinz Guderian, Commander, 2 Panzer Group, struck out for his forward command post, while the first wave of German assault troops was slipping quietly into position along the thick, green banks of the Bug River.[135]

After departing the Kremlin, Timoshenko and Zhukov, hardly satisfied by the general warning to the troops, had returned to the Ministry of Defense, where they remained on alert. About midnight, once again in the Kiev Special Military District, a second defector, a soldier from a German infantry division, swam across the river to the Soviet side of the frontier west of Vladimir-Volynski (Wlodzimierz) and informed the NKGB border police that the invasion was to begin at 4:00 that morning. General Kirponos reported the information over the high-frequency telephone to Zhukov at the defense ministry. At 12:30 A.M. the Red Army chief of staff telephoned Stalin. "Did you send the directive to the military districts?" Stalin asked. Zhukov replied that he had. And that was the "end of the exchange."[136]

Aware that his Red Army was still not ready for war, but also convinced that Hitler would not be so reckless as to open a second front before he had finished with Britain, Stalin continued to cling tightly to his illusions until the moment arrived when he could cling to them no more. That moment was now but a few hours away, and it would signify the complete collapse of Stalin's efforts to appease Germany's dictator and avoid a war at any cost.

2.4: The Red Army Courts Disaster at the Western Frontier

By June 18, 1941, Soviet border guards and troops along the Russo-German frontier were registering increasingly ominous observations. The noise of tank engines and motor vehicles from the woods across the border was becoming increasingly prevalent, almost omnipresent, one might believe, from the number of reports arriving at various Red Army headquarters. In some places, the Russians looked on from their observation posts as German soldiers dismantled barbed wire barriers and brought forward pontoon equipment, sectional bridges, and ammunition, while the railroads leading up to the front were bursting with activity. And then there were the overflights—dozens of them—of Soviet frontier positions, towns, and cities; yet even when the German reconnaissance aircraft were low enough in the sky to be taken under fire, the Russian antiaircraft batteries had explicit orders not to do so. When the either very brave, or foolishly reckless, commander of 97 Detachment had defied these orders and opened fire on German aircraft he was "very nearly shot for it."[137]

Despite the escalating signals that a German assault was imminent, Soviet troops at the frontier, "apart from stray instances of individual foresight"[138] or acts of individual courage on the part of their commanders—who were acutely aware of Stalin's orders that no action be taken that might be construed as a provocation—had as yet received no formal guidance or instructions; and, of course, Stalin stubbornly refused to place them on alert. So the Red Army soldiers soldiered on with their normal peacetime routines—conducting routine drills and field exercises; practicing at artillery ranges; constructing or improving lines of communication; building fortifications, billets, supply dumps, rifle ranges, armor training grounds; and working feverishly on the dozens of new airfields under construction in the western frontier zone (the vast majority of which were incomplete when the *Luftwaffe* smashed them on the first day of the war). To cite but one example: On June 10, 1941, several additional rifle battalions were detailed for construction work in the Brest Fortified Region.[139] All of this activity—purposeful though it was—weighed heavily on combat readiness, for the German attack would find many Russian units at the frontier scattered widely about, instead of at their assigned combat posts ready to fight.

On June 19, just two days after Stalin had been handed reports of the NKVD and the frontier guards command that the German invasion was expected for the night of June 21/22, Defense Commissar Timoshenko finally ordered that forward airfields, military units, and military installations be properly camouflaged. The special order noted the "bad state of airfield camouflage and the congestion of the parked aircraft; in the armored units, and in the artillery, tanks and guns were painted in a way which made them far too visible from ground and air level. Like the planes on the ground, tanks and armored vehicles were bunched up, presenting splendid targets. Dumps and installations were also far too plainly visible."[140] Unfortunately, little progress was made toward satisfying Timoshenko's order before the Germans attacked.

Another problem that bedeviled the Red Army on the eve of war was, in essence, a problem of Soviet military culture. The Soviet officer corps was distrustful of wireless communications, which seemed to them much too vulnerable to interception in a society obsessed with secrecy and control. As a result, the military districts in the western frontier zones were procuring radios slowly, while those they did receive they were hesitant to put to use, in part because of certain technical challenges. For example, each radio network required its own operational and reserve frequencies, and each radio its own call sign. The wartime frequencies and call signs were, of course, different from the ones used in peace-time, and military staffs assumed it would take too long to introduce them to each army unit down to battalion level. The upshot of this was that, on June 22:

The Red Army radios were not used.

Cable communications were mistakenly believed to be more reliable. In fact, only the last few miles of cable, in the immediate vicinity of front *headquarters, ran under-ground. Most of the hundreds of miles of telegraph wires hung on poles lining the coun-try's highways and railroads—an obvious and easy target for Hitler's commandos. All a saboteur had to do to disable a division was to cut out 100 feet of cable at the highway nearest its headquarters. In something approaching criminal negligence, the telegraph lines had been left unprotected on the night of 21 June. Neither the army nor the police, Zhukov nor Beria, the local field commanders nor the police chiefs had bothered to take the most obvious precaution . . .*

The worst news by far [at the start of the German invasion] was that Hitler's com-mandos had managed to break the Red Army communication lines. An army deprived of communications in the first minutes of a foreign invasion is virtually disabled. As with many of that morning's mishaps, this one could have been prevented.[141]

On June 15, 1941, Soviet district commanders had been granted permission from the NKO (People's Commissariat of Defense) and the Red Army General Staff to shift forces positioned deep inside their districts to positions further forward in accordance with prevailing defense plans. In response, some deployments were conducted by rail, but most went on foot and at night to avoid detection. During these movements, however, the NKO "categorically prohibited military district commanders from redeploying first echelon forces or improving their forward defenses"—moves that (once again) could be interpreted by the Germans as provocative.[142]

There was, however, one "brave" military district commander willing to flout these instructions from his superiors. On the same day (June 15), Col.-Gen. F. I. Kuznetsov, Commander, Baltic Special Military District,[143] alarmed by intelligence reports detailing the threatening German buildup along the East Prussian border with Soviet-occupied Lithuania, issued a "lengthy order" with the objective of increasing force readiness along the border. Without referring directly to the German offensive preparations, Kuznetsov criticized some of his division commanders for "laxness and sloppiness" in maintaining combat readiness. "Today, as never before," he insisted, "we must be fully combat ready. Many commanders do not understand this. But all must firmly and clearly understand that at any moment we must be ready to fulfill any combat mission." He ordered his subordinate commanders to implement certain "passive measures" to enhance combat readiness and defenses.[144]

That same day, the district Military Council "reiterated combat alert procedures" in a directive that began: "In the event of enemy violation of the border, a surprise attack by large [enemy] forces, or an overflight of the border by [German] aviation formations, I am establishing the following notification procedures." On June 18, following receipt the day before of a detailed and threatening intelligence summary, Kuznetsov ordered his three armies and ancillary units to full military readiness. The order mandated full combat readiness for district air defense, signal, and ground transport systems; it also instructed his 8 and 11 Army commanders to "prepare engineer bridging and minelaying, [while providing] instructions to all other force commanders to make appropriate defensive preparations."[145]

In adherence to the district commander's orders, both 8 and 11 Armies were to form "mobile anti-tank mining squads" and to establish dumps of AT mines and explosives. Demolition squads were to be in place by June 21 on bridges from the frontier to the line Shauliya-Kaunas (Kovno)-Nemen River; in the sector of 11 Army, on the Neman bridges, a bridging regiment was assigned to blow up the bridges on direct orders from the army commander.[146]

The activation and laying of minefields came to an abrupt halt on June 21: Maj.-Gen. V. F. Zotov, chief of the Baltic military engineers, had begun to enlist local civilians to dig trenches and positions along the frontier; when cows from a collective farm detonated some of the mines, he was forced to "call off" his engineers—an order issued to prevent "the spread of panic." The combat readiness of air defense systems was hampered by a shortage of crews and trained officers for the antiaircraft gun sites. Kuznetsov did manage to get some artillery units on their way to their combat positions, but a paucity of gun-towing equipment disrupted movement, and even when some of the guns reached their positions they were still short of ammunition.[147] In other words, despite Kuznetsov's "courageous" attempts to ready his forces for battle, "there is no evidence that the additional preparations made any difference in district combat performance when war began."[148]

Finally, on the night of June 21/22, 1941, just hours before the *Ostheer* struck, Soviet 8 Army ordered one of its rifle divisions—48 Rifle Division, which had been posted north of Siauliai—to move southward and into position behind 125 Rifle Division, whose forwardmost positions were directly at the frontier. This movement was underway when the Germans attacked, with 48 Rifle Division spread out along the road from Raseinai (lead elements) to north of Siauliai (Schaulen) (rear elements).[149] Activities on the Soviet side of the frontier were carefully monitored by the Germans, as indicated by this report in the journal of 1 Panzer Division (June 21): "New enemy reports seem to indicate that Tauroggen [Taurage] is held by two Russian rifle regiments. A strong artillery group is reported in the woods east of Tauroggen astride the road. It appears that the edges of woods have been built up into a second line of resistance. The organization of terrain, tank traps and gun positions has also been reported there."[150]

Stationed in the center of the western frontier zone was the Western Special Military District, commanded by Army-General D. G. Pavlov. On March 26, 1941, the district command had issued Order 008130, calling for all formations to achieve full strength by June 15; the order would fall far short of expectations.[151] Just like Kuznetsov's command, the rifle and mechanized corps under Pavlov's control found themselves dangerously scattered "both by deployment and by training plans" on the eve of Operation *Barbarossa*. Many units in the Western Special Military District[152] were out on field exercises or away from their posts for other reasons. For example, 28 Rifle Corps (responsible for the defense of the fortress of Brest-Litovsk and contiguous areas) had nine rifle, three artillery, and all of its engineer battalions working on defenses; its antiaircraft guns and crews off at Minsk at practice ranges; and its signal battalions in camp. The corps commander reported that it would require "not less than 1–1 ½ days" to reassemble his corps. Meanwhile, behind the thick walls of the imposing Brest fortress, Red Army soldiers carried on with their routine drills, "complete with band," while German troops across the Bug River looked on, no doubt with some amusement. At night the Germans could see Russian troops, by the bright illumination of searchlights, working on the fortifications and earthworks of the Brest Fortified Region, which, like everywhere else, were far from complete. Elsewhere on the Soviet side of the river the frontier seemed quiet.[153]

As the days and weeks of June 1941 slipped by, many inside the Brest fortress "sensed the menacing atmosphere" as the signs and rumors of impending war metastasized. Commissar Pimenov, head of political propaganda for 6 Rifle Division (a component of 28 Rifle Corps), wrote to General Pavlov, requesting permission to take up defensive positions and evacuate the wives and children who were living inside the fortress. For his efforts he was branded a "panic-monger."[154] N. G. Mishchenko, a soldier in a rifle regiment, wrote:

> I'm living well thus far, but within a hair's breadth of something. Meanwhile we have a lot of news, but I won't be writing. The entire country should learn about our news, but to this point nobody knows it. I ask you to write letters more often, while you still have someone to write. If you're interested . . . I ask that you keep your mouth shut.[155]

The chief of the operations section of 28 Rifle Corps, Major E. M. Sinkovsky, recalled the uneasy mood of his men:

> Soon after the TASS announcement [of June 14, 1941], I was in the fortress with the 333 Rifle Regiment. Together with the regiment commander D. I. Matveev, I spent time among the units. One of the soldiers asked, "Tell me, Comrade . . . , when will they pull us out of this mousetrap?" Matveev vaguely answered, referring to the

69

TASS announcement, but it was perceptible that the soldiers weren't satisfied with the response.[156]

The staff of the NKVD frontier troops in Belostok—a town right in the middle of a salient that projected deep into the German lines—placed the border posts on alert on June 18, 1941. About the same time, Soviet antiaircraft batteries had begun to move into firing positions behind the fronts of both the Western Special and Kiev Special Military Districts, in the Grodno–L'vov (Lemberg) zone to the Minsk–Novograd–Volynski line; yet a large number of the batteries of Pavlov's district were away at gunnery exercises at Camp Krupki.[157]

Throughout Friday, June 20, Maj.-Gen. V. E. Klimovskikh, chief of staff of the Western Special Military District, received a stream of reports addressing German activities at the frontier; they were quickly passed on to Pavlov and then—like all the previous reports—sent along to the General Staff in Moscow. Yet as General Klich, the district's artillery commander, noted, the response was always the same: "Don't panic. Take it easy. 'The boss' knows about it." As for General Klich himself, he had his own worries, namely too many untrained gunners and immobilized guns.[158] But the artillery was only one headache among many. In April and May, Pavlov's mechanized corps had received hundreds of new KV and T-34 tanks, but their drivers had not been assigned until late May or early June and many were still untrained. Moreover, many of the new heavy KV models, along with not being bore-sighted, were unable to fire their guns because they had no ammunition. The armored formations of the Western Special Military District were also badly scattered; indeed, none of the district's mechanized corps had all their forces in a single location.[159]

Saturday evening, June 21, 1941—for most Red Army soldiers "there was nothing as yet, apart from private premonitions," to distinguish this weekend evening from any other of recent memory. In fact, it promised to be, as Colonel Sandalov (chief of staff of the Western District's 4 Army) characterized it, "quite ordinary." Soviet officers, of both senior and junior rank, ready to relax and enjoy an evening of entertainment, struck out for the numerous garrison shows and theaters; many others were at home with their wives and children.[160] Ivan Konovalov, who was training to be a bomber pilot at a flying school behind the western frontier, recalled that "on Saturday the officers had gone off on leave to their families at the garrison. At the airfield all that were left were the students and a few duty officers."[161]

As for General Pavlov, he was 250 kilometers beyond the frontier, in the Minsk Officers Club, where the popular comedy, *The Wedding at Malinovka*, was playing to a packed house; also in attendance were his chief of staff, Maj.-Gen. Klimovskikh, and district deputy commander, Lt.-Gen. V. I. Boldin. Despite the burgeoning signs of an imminent German attack, Stalin had ordered his commanders not to worry; thus Pavlov considered it his patriotic duty to showcase his *sangfroid* in spite of what was happening. The evening's entertainment was briefly interrupted when Colonel Blokhin, chief of intelligence for the Western Special Military District, visited his commander's box and whispered that "the frontier was in a state of alarm"—German troops at the border were now at full combat readiness and the firing of weapons had been reported in some sectors.[162] Pavlov brushed the warnings aside: "Nonsense," he said, "this simply cannot be."[163] And yet: While General Pavlov enjoyed the play, German commanders along the Eastern Front were reading Hitler's proclamation to their men "by the dim illumination of shielded flashlights."[164]

Earlier that evening, when Lt.-Gen. V. I. Kuznetsov, Commander, Soviet 3 Army, reported that the Germans had dismantled barbed wire barriers along their side of the frontier and that the sound of engines could be heard from the woods,[165] Pavlov had dismissed the news: "Believe me, Moscow knows the military and political situation and the state of our relations with Germany better than we do." When his chief of staff proposed that combat readiness be increased, an infuriated Pavlov swept a map from the table and hissed: "War is possible, but not in the near future. Now we must prepare for the fall maneuvers and make sure that no alarmist answers German provocations with fire."[166] And yet: Klimovskikh would sign off on a highly disturbing intelligence report on the "Disposition of German Forces on 21 June 1941" at the Russo-German frontier, which noted, *inter alia*:

> *The main part of these forces are located in a 30-kilometer zone from the border. In the Suwalki-Arys area troops and rear establishments continue to be moved up to the border. The artillery is in its firing positions ... Troop observation has systematically noted the large-scale movement of troops in groups in the Terespol-Janov Podlaski-Sokolov Podlaski area, primarily to the east, as well as entrenching work along the western bank of the Western Bug River. 40 trainloads of crossing materials (wooden girders and iron pontoons) and munitions arrived at Biala Podlaska [just west of Brest-Litovsk] on 20.6.41 ...*

> *Conclusion:*

> *According to available information, which is being checked, the main part of the German Army in the zone opposite the Western Special Military District has occupied jump-off positions. The bringing up of units and reinforcements to the border has been noted along all axes.[167]*

Immediately after the play, General Pavlov took part in an "awkward briefing" with several of his staff officers; then, at 1:00 in the morning, he was summoned to district headquarters to take a telephone call from Timoshenko, who was on the line from Moscow. The Soviet defense commissar asked about the situation at the border: "Well, how is it where you are? Quiet?" Pavlov replied that there had been significant German activity at the border; he specifically mentioned a buildup of German motorcycle regiments and special forces. "Just try to worry less and don't panic," Timoshenko responded. "Get the staff together anyway this morning, because something unpleasant may happen perhaps, but don't rise to any provocation. If there is a specific provocation, call me," he said.[168]

Pavlov later recollected that he spent the next two hours with his senior officers. One by one they reported on their troops, on the dismal problems of supply, and on their lack of readiness for battle. Some units had been dispersed on exercises, others needed stocks of fuel or ammunition, and all were more or less paralyzed by inadequate or poorly organized transport. The railways were still running on peacetime schedules, and almost every front-line regiment was short of motor vehicles. The army could not even requisition trucks, for there were almost no civilian cars in Stalin's Soviet Union. Pavlov and his men were still busy with these questions at 3:30 a.m., the moment scheduled for the German land assault.[169] Coincidentally, it was also the time when Timoshenko called again. "He asked me what was new," Pavlov recalled. "I told him that the situation had not changed." By then, a dozen cities in the borderlands had been engulfed in flames.[170]

Meanwhile, at 2:00 in the morning, Lt.-Gen. A. A. Korobkov, Commander, Soviet 4 Army, had fielded a call from the border city of Brest. The power, he was told, was out, and there was no running water. Minutes later, the town of Kobrin, the site of 4 Army headquarters, also went "dark." Thirty minutes after that the general became aware that all communications with Pavlov's headquarters and with his troops along the border had been cut.[171] For the catastrophic failures of his command on June 22 and throughout the initial days of the war, Pavlov would be shot for treason.

Finally, what was the situation in the south, in the sector of the Kiev Special Military District? As discussed above (Section 1.6) this military district—commanded by Col.-Gen. M. P. Kirponos and covering the Ukraine, where the main German attack was expected—possessed the largest force grouping of the military districts in the western border region.[172] Kirponos's forces, however, "suffered from common Red Army weaknesses," including: (a) inexperienced and poorly trained officers and NCOs (particularly at the headquarters level); (b) a shortage of radios and of qualified radio operators (communications for echelons above corps level was by telegraph, which was immobile and vulnerable to destruction by German special forces, Ukrainian saboteurs, or through *Luftwaffe* interdiction); and, (c) logistical units that were incomplete and poorly trained for their vital support mission.[173]

The forces of the Kiev Special Military District, in particular Kirponos's heavy contingent of armor—the largest and most powerful in the western frontier zone—were "echeloned in strength and in depth," which helps to explain why, in a relative sense, they had more success at the start of the war than the forces of the Baltic and Western Special Military Districts. The district's mechanized corps, however, evinced the typical shortcomings of Soviet mechanized units everywhere, among them the sorely incomplete training of the crews of the new KV and T-34 tanks, shortages of ammunition, and inadequate logistical support. For example, the 41 Tank Division, which was on field exercises north of Vladimir-Volynski when the Germans struck, would go into combat with no ammunition for its KV tank or antiaircraft battalions.[174]

In June 1941, Kirponos's 9 Mechanized Corps was commanded by Maj.-Gen. K. K. Rokossovsky, who, although briefly imprisoned during Stalin's purges, would go on to become a Marshal of the Soviet Union and "one of the most important and capable Soviet commanders of WWII."[175] Rokossovsky's memoir first appeared in the 1960s; in the 1990s, a post–Soviet era version became available, containing critical passages not included in earlier editions:

> *Even when the Germans set about concentrating their forces close to our border, moving them from the west, about which the General Staff and the KOVO [Kiev Special Military District] could not but have known, there were no changes on our side. An atmosphere of incomprehensible tranquility continued to predominate among the district's forces . . .*
>
> *It became known that the headquarters of the KOVO had begun to move from Kiev to Tarnopol. What brought this about, no one informed us. In general, I must once again repeat that some kind of lull reigned and no kind of information came from above. Our press and our radio also transmitted only calming messages.*
>
> *By the start of the war our corps was almost fully staffed with personnel, but was not supplied with basic equipment: tanks and motor transport. The matériel provisioning of this equipment did not exceed 30% of authorized strength. The equipment was worn out and not good for prolonged activity. To put it simply, in this condition the corps, as a mechanized formation, was not capable of combat activities. Both the headquarters of the KOVO and the General Staff could not but have known this.[176]*

In the final days before the outbreak of war, Russian officers of the Kiev Special Military District discussed with border guards the steadily escalating reports of German movements on the far side of the frontier and the sinister sounds of tank and motor vehicle engines. On June 18, Colonel I. I. Fedyuninsky, Commander, Soviet 15 Rifle Corps, received an urgent telephone call from the local NKVD border troops—a German deserter had crossed over with "very important information." The German corporal, who was fleeing German military justice, told his captors that the German army would launch its attack on Sunday, June 22. Fedyuninsky promptly passed the news on to his superior, Lt.-Gen. M. I. Potapov, at 5 Army. The army commander, however, like so many other high-ranking Soviet military officers, simply dismissed the information as another "provocation."[177] After all, "because everyone was terrified of [Stalin], and also believed that he 'always knew best,' no one openly opposed him over . . . his prognosis of German timing and targets. Nor, therefore, did anyone have the energy or initiative to think for themselves."[178]

One key area where the Kiev Special Military District made significant progress was in the construction of fixed and field fortifications. The fixed fortifications encompassed a series of fortified regions, and in this district included the Rava Ruska and Peremysl' fortified regions, which, as the Germans were soon to discover, were well outfitted for combat when the war began. In the interior there existed a second, older grouping of fortified regions, which anchored the Stalin Line along the former (1939) Polish-Russian border. In theory—if not always in fact—each was manned by a regiment of troops and embraced a veritable maze of artillery, machine-gun, and antitank bunkers. After March 1941, Kirponos had "put maximum effort" into building up the new fortified regions, employing more than 40,000 construction workers per day.[179] The work on the frontier fortifications would go on right up to the outbreak of war. The German 298 Infantry Division, which sat on the border opposite the Vladimir-Volynski (Wlodzimierz) Fortified Region, noted in its daily report on June 20: "Expansion of the [Red Army] fortifications is continuing in the entire sector; [the enemy] has been observed bringing artillery into position." The 298 ID would find these positions tenaciously defended on June 22, 1941.[180]

On the evening of June 21 near Sokal' (north of L'vov), another German defector, confessing to be a Communist, stole across Soviet lines.[181] He was taken posthaste to the area officer, a Major M. S. Bychkovskii, who heard him say that a German attack was scheduled for dawn the next day; German guns were in their firing positions and armor and infantry at their jump-off points. Bychkovskii at once notified his immediate superior and passed the information on to General Potapov (5 Army). He followed up these moves by ordering the guard in his area to be doubled and a close watch to be kept on things. A short while later, "on his own initiative—dangerous enough—he ordered preparations for blowing up the bridge into Sokal'; he sent one of his officers into the Strumilov [Fortified Region] to get more explosives, but this was far from easy, since most of the Red Army officers had gone to L'vov for their free day on Sunday."[182]

At midnight, the commander of the German 48 Panzer Corps reported that "Sokal' is not blacked out. The Russians are manning their posts that are fully illuminated. Apparently they expect nothing." The report—and others like it—merely confirmed what "German officers had themselves seen and could still see, crouched and waiting as they were on the Soviet frontiers, with their armor, artillery, assault and bridging units at the ready"[183]—that is, that the Russians were not prepared to do battle. One exception to such reports[184] was General Kirponos. The clearly alarmed commander of the Kiev Special Military District was already at his battle headquarters at Tarnopol by midnight, June 21, 1941.[185] And yet, to belabor a point—too many of Kirponos's units, both at the frontier and in the interior, were not properly assembled for war and/or tragically ignorant of the terrible fate that awaited them (as elsewhere, the alert order—Directive No. 1—finally issued by the Soviet High Command arrived much too late). To cite the example of one Otroschenkov Sergei Andreyevich:

I was on active military duty in the town of Guive near Zhitomir. I did my military service in the 40 Tank Division, 79 Tank Regiment. By the time the war started I had the rank of junior sergeant and was a driver-mechanic of the light T-26 tank . . .

On Saturday evening 21 June, the contingent of the regiment was brought to a stadium. The unit was being prepared for a sports festival. We practiced in performing exercises and were flourishing arms. And the next morning the Germans "bugled" us a wakeup. A bomb landed right into a courtyard of a brick-built, three-story U-shaped building of our barracks. It shivered all the window panes right away. The Germans finished their bombing and many soldiers got wounded or killed before even waking up, let alone fighting. Can you imagine how that hurt the morale of the 18–19 year old boys?[186]

PHOTO ESSAY: COMMANDERS AND WEAPONS

Adolf Hitler at the Wolf's Lair (*Wolfsschanze*) in East Prussia on June 24, 1941 (R. BENDER)

Field Marshal Walther von Brauchitsch, C-in-C of the German army (R. BENDER)

General Franz Halder, chief of the German Army General Staff (R. BENDER)

Field Marshal Ritter von Leeb,
C-in-C Army Group North
(R. BENDER)

Field Marshal Fedor von Bock,
C-in-C Army Group Center
(R. BENDER)

Field Marshal Gerd von Rundstedt,
C-in-C Army Group South
(R. BENDER)

Panzer III tank in Russia (R. BENDER)

Panzer IV tank (R. BENDER)

Close-up view of German 75mm assault gun. The German infantry loved this weapon.

German 105mm light field howitzer in open firing position on Eastern Front

German 150mm medium field howitzer in action in Russia (NATIONAL ARCHIVES, HEREAFTER CITED AS "NA")

88mm flak gun in action against Red Army tanks

Weapons of a German infantry company
in 1941. Shown here clockwise from
upper right-hand corner: the Mauser
98K bolt-action rifle, twelve MGs, three
AT rifles, three mortars. (NA)

A Bf-109 fighter taking on fuel (R. BENDER)

He-111 medium bombers in flight (BUNDESARCHIV, BILD 101I-408-0487-10, FOTO: MARTIN, 1940/41)

Flight of Ju-87 *Stuka* divebombers over the Eastern Front

Joseph Stalin, in June 1941 the unchallenged leader (*vozhd*) of the Soviet state

Soviet marshal S. K. Timoshenko, People's Commissar of Defense
(D. M. GLANTZ)

Army-General G. K. Zhukov, chief of the Red Army General Staff
(D. M. GLANTZ)

Col.-Gen. F. I. Kuznetsov, C-in-C
Soviet Northwestern Front
(D. M. GLANTZ)

Army-General D. G. Pavlov, C-in-C
Soviet Western Front
(D. M. GLANTZ)

Col.-Gen. M. P. Kirponos, C-in-C
Soviet Southwestern Front
(D. M. GLANTZ)

BT-7 light tank, one of several BT models in service in 1941 (D. M. GLANTZ)

T-34 medium tank, one of the best tanks produced by any combatant during World War II (D. M. GLANTZ)

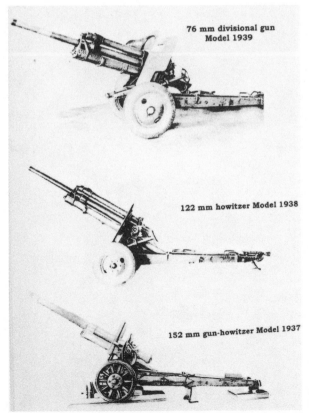

76 mm divisional gun
Model 1939

122 mm howitzer Model 1938

152 mm gun-howitzer Model 1937

Selection of Soviet artillery pieces
(D. M. Glantz)

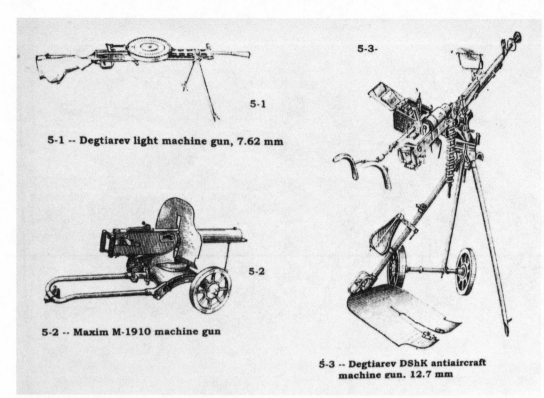

5-1 -- Degtiarev light machine gun, 7.62 mm

5-2 -- Maxim M-1910 machine gun

5-3 -- Degtiarev DShK antiaircraft machine gun. 12.7 mm

Soviet machine guns (D. M. GLANTZ)

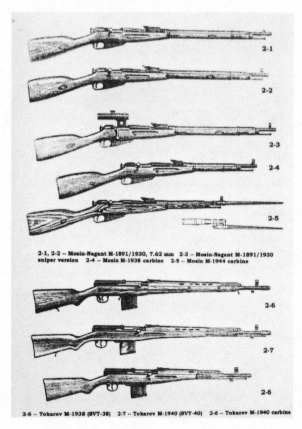

2-1, 2-2 -- Mosin-Nagant M-1891/1930, 7.62 mm 2-3 -- Mosin-Nagant M-1891/1930 sniper version 2-4 -- Mosin M-1938 carbine 2-5 -- Mosin M-1944 carbine

2-6 -- Tokarev M-1938 (SVT-38) 2-7 -- Tokarev M-1940 (SVT-40) 2-6 -- Tokarev M-1940 carbine

Selection of Soviet infantry weapons
(D. M. GLANTZ)

3-1 -- Degtiarev M-1934/38 (PPD-34/38)   3-2 -- Degtiarev M-1940 (PPD-40)
3-3 -- Shpagin M-1941 (PPSh-41)   3-4 -- PPSh-41 modified

Selection of Soviet infantry weapons (cont.) (D. M. GLANTZ)

COMBAT AIRCRAFT

I-16 fighters

MiG-3 fighter

Iak-3 fighter

La-5 fighter

Selection of Soviet aircraft (cont.) (D. M. GLANTZ)

COMBAT AIRCRAFT

SB bomber, 1935

TB-3 (ANT-6) heavy bomber, 1930

Reconnaissance flying boat MBR-2

Selection of Soviet aircraft (D. M. GLANTZ)

INTERMEZZO: OPERATION *BARBAROSSA* BEGINS— FROM THE BALTIC TO THE BLACK SEA

SUNDAY MORNING, JUNE 22, 1941, FOLLOWED THE FIRST DAY OF SUMMER AND THE shortest night of the year, known as "white nights" in northern Russia because the sun never really sets there.[1] Shortly after 0300 hours, thousands of German guns, ranging from super-heavy rail-borne artillery to light and medium howitzers and infantry mortars, unleashed a storm of shellfire shattering the morning calm along the 1,800-kilometer front, while senior German officers, high atop their observation towers, trained their binoculars on the initial targets along the frontier. As the first slivers of light peeked tentatively over the horizon far to the east, the first wave of more than three million German soldiers swarmed across the Russo-German demarcation line from Memel' on the Baltic coast south to the Hungarian border. Overhead, squadrons of *Luftwaffe* bombers struck towns and cities as far afield as Sevastopol, Kiev, Minsk, Kronstadt, and the Baltic ports of Tallin and Riga, while divebomber, ground attack, and fighter aircraft obliterated dozens of forward Soviet airfields and destroyed hundreds of Red Army planes on the ground. The *Luftwaffe* also targeted ammunition and fuel depots, fortifications, barracks, bunkers, artillery positions, and Red Army headquarters.[2] The "border battles" of 1941—the "*Grenzschlachten*" to the Germans and the "*pogranichnaia srazheniia*" to the Russians—had begun.

As contemporary accounts confirm, all three German army groups achieved total tactical surprise on their respective attack frontages. Within a few hours, German assault detachments had captured intact every bridge along all the border rivers. Dazed and disoriented, many Red Army troops were caught unprepared in their camps and barracks.[3] The results of the initial hours of the attack were documented in the war diary of OKW:

> Between 0305 and 0330 hours Army Groups South (without Eleventh Army) Center and North begin the surprise attack on Russia according to plan (planmässig). Throughout the morning the impression grows that surprise has been achieved in every sector. The enemy is only able to resist the attack with weak forces. Already in the morning hours, along the entire front, German forces are able to advance to a depth of four to five kilometers and breach the enemy border defenses.[4]

The diary notes of *Generaloberst* Franz Halder, chief of the Army General Staff, were equally ebullient:

> *The morning reports indicate that all armies (except Eleventh) have started the offensive according to plan. Tactical* surprise *of the enemy has apparently been achieved along the entire line. All bridges across the Bug River, as on the entire river frontier, were undefended and are in our hands intact. That the enemy was taken by surprise is evident from the facts that troops were caught in their quarters, that planes on the airfields were covered up, and that enemy groups faced with the unexpected development at the front inquired at their [headquarters] in the rear what they should do. More effects of the surprise may be anticipated from the assaults of our armor, which have been ordered in all sectors. The navy reports that the enemy seems to have been taken by surprise also in their zone of action. His reactions to the measures of the last few days were of a purely passive nature, and he now is holding back his naval forces in ports, apparently for fear of mines.*[5]

Yet if Soviet resistance was at first surprisingly light (Soviet artillery fire was scarcely detected), NKVD border guards, recognizable by green collar tabs and green bands around their caps, and in most cases the first troops encountered by the Germans, often resisted fiercely. Within a few short hours, however, German tanks, assault guns, artillery, and motorcycle troops were rolling across the captured bridges—or over pontoon bridges hastily erected by German engineers—their movements secured by a protective umbrella of *Luftwaffe* fighters. By midday, the Red Army's frontier defenses were mostly shattered, as the assault teams of the *Ostheer* drove relentlessly toward their assigned objectives. Disoriented by the suddenness and *force majeure* of the German attack, their communications disrupted, the Soviet High Command issued no counterattack order to the three Soviet *fronts* defending the frontier (the Baltic, Western, and Kiev Special Military Districts were renamed Northwestern, Western, and Southwestern Fronts, respectively, upon the oubreak of hostilities) until the war was several hours old; and even then the *front* commanders were instructed not to let ground troops cross the German frontier without "special authorization."[6]

At about 0300 hours, in the sector of GFM von Leeb's Army Group North, seventy-six bomber and ninety fighter aircraft of Keller's 1 Air Fleet crossed the border at altitude and headed for seven specially selected Soviet airfields, while other German aircraft deposited minefields (*Minensperren*) in the waters about Leningrad and the Soviet naval base at Kronstadt.[7] On the army group's 300-kilometer front the artillery bombardment began precisely at 0305 hours and was of short duration.[8] As the mist still shimmered in the forests, meadows, and valleys along the East Prussian frontier, German infantry emerged from their assembly areas and plunged across the border, while the tanks of Hoepner's 4 Panzer Group poured out of the woods. As recorded in the army group's war diary, the attack began—as it did across the entire Eastern Front—"according to plan"; by 0432 hours, Leeb's headquarters was informing the Army High Command (OKH) that initial reports from the front, although still incomplete, were noting little to no enemy resistance.[9]

CHAPTER 3

Armageddon Unleashed (I)— Army Group North Goes to War

0305 hours: The attack begins with the enormous concentrated blow of our artillery firing from all barrels. The roar of the shells as they leave the guns virtually shakes the heavens. Taking full advantage of the massed artillery fire the battalions move out to the attack. At first there are no reports of Russian artillery fire. The surprise attack seems to have succeeded completely. All three battle groups cross the border according to plan.
—WAR DIARY, 1 PANZER DIVISION[1]

After telephone discussions with our neighbors to the right and left, it is apparent that they have the same impression of things as we do at 4 Panzer Group—that the enemy is weak along the entire front, well camouflaged, in some cases in bunkers, and defending himself skillfully and with toughness.
—WAR DIARY, 4 PANZER GROUP[2]

[Soviet air forces] to launch a powerful attack, with bombers and fighter-bombers, on the enemy airfields and the main groupings of ground forces and destroy them. The air attack is to be directed into the depth of the German territory, up to 100–150 kilometers. Königsberg and Memel' are to be destroyed with bombs.
—ORDER OF SOVIET 8 ARMY TO ITS AIR ELEMENTS AT 0715 HOURS[3]

⌐⌐

THE SIXTY-FOUR-YEAR-OLD COMMANDER OF ARMY GROUP NORTH AND DEFENSIVE warfare specialist, Field Marshal Wilhelm Josef Franz Ritter von Leeb, was a descendant of an old Bavarian military family. During the Great War (1914–1918) he saw action as a General Staff officer in France (including the battle of Verdun), Galicia, Serbia, Russia, and Romania. After the war he was accepted into the 100,000-man *Reichswehr* and promoted rapidly, rising to the rank of General of Artillery (*Gen.d.Art.*) in 1934. "Astute and morally solid," and a devout Catholic, Leeb was no friend of Hitler (to whom Leeb was an "incorrigible anti-Nazi") and his National Socialist movement; he found himself under Gestapo surveillance as early as 1934. Under pressure from Hitler, he retired from the *Wehrmacht* in March 1938, only to be recalled later that year to command an army during the Sudetenland crisis. After returning to his retirement in Bavaria, he was again recalled to active duty in 1939. At the time of the German invasion of Poland (September 1939) he was in command of Army Group C, which successfully guarded Germany's western border with an assortment of second and third class formations. Raised in rank to full general (*Generaloberst*) in November 1939, Leeb also led Army Group C during the invasion of France in 1940; for his role in defeating the French in Alsace-Lorraine he was honored with the Knight's Cross to the Iron Cross on June 24, 1940, and, on July 19, 1940, promoted to field marshal. Leeb's Army Group C was re-designated as Army Group North for the Russian campaign.[4]

Facing Field Marshal von Leeb across the frontier was the much younger (forty-two years of age) Col.-Gen. F. I. Kuznetsov, the commander of the Baltic Special Military District (renamed Northwestern Front upon the outbreak of war). Born to a peasant family, Kuznetsov joined the Czarist army in 1916 and fought in World War I as a platoon and infantry scout commander. He commanded a detachment of Red Guards in October 1917 and joined the Red Army in 1918. After the civil war, he commanded a rifle regiment and a brigade and, in the 1930s, served in various academic positions, including that of department head of the prestigious Frunze Military Academy. In July 1938 Kuznetsov was appointed deputy commander of the Belorussian Special Military District. He successfully led a corps during the Winter War with Finland (1939/40) and, following short assignments as chief of the General Staff Academy (July 1940) and as commander of the North Caucasus Military District (August 1940), he was appointed commander of the Baltic Special Military District in December 1940. He was promoted to colonel-general in 1941. Despite his experience and recognition as a serious military theoretician, the Soviet official history of the war noted that Kuznetsov evinced the same liabilities characteristic of most other *front* commanders; that is, he was "unprepared to cope with the exceptionally complicated task" and "lacked the necessary operational and strategic preparation and practice." He would hold on to his post as commander of the Northwestern Front for less than two weeks.[5]

3.1: OPPOSING FORCES AND BATTLE PLANS (NORTHERN AXIS)

The smallest of the three army groups, Army Group North (headquarters in Waldfrieden) comprised twenty-nine divisions (twenty infantry, three panzer, three motorized infantry, and three security divisions) organized primarily into the Sixteenth and Eighteenth Armies and 4 Panzer Group; total personnel was roughly 640,000 men.[6] Commanded by Panzer General Erich Hoepner, 4 Panzer Group possessed about 600 tanks, distributed among its three panzer divisions.[7] Three of Leeb's infantry divisions were held in his army group reserve, while two divisions of the Army High Command reserve were in transport and earmarked to arrive by July 4, 1941. General Headquarters (GHQ) troops (*Heerestruppen*) allotted to Army Group North (and distributed among its two armies and panzer group) included the following:

- 11 150mm medium field howitzer (*s.F.H. 18*) battalions
- 6 105mm cannon battalions
- 4 210mm heavy howitzer (*Mörser*) battalions (mot.)
- 2 mixed artillery battalions
- 2 150mm cannon battalions
- 1 240mm heavy artillery battalion (mot.) for flat trajectory fire (*Flachfeuer*)
- 3 antitank battalions
- 1 assault gun (*Sturmgeschütz*) battalion
- 5 assault gun batteries
- 1 *Nebelwerfer* rocket projector regiment (*Nb.Werf.Rgt.*)[8]
- 2 *Nebelwerfer* battalions
- 1 decontamination battalion (*Entg.Abt.*)
- 1 machine-gun battalion (mot.)
- 2 flak (*Fla*) battalions
- 7 flak (*Fla*) companies
- 2 army flak battalions
- 4 type "*Bruno*" (short) heavy rail-borne artillery pieces[9]

Additional GHQ resources in the army group's order of battle included thirteen engineer (*Pionier*) battalions, five bridge-building battalions, thirty-nine bridge columns "B" (*Br.Kol.B*),[10] twenty-one construction battalions (*Bau-Btle.*), and eight battalions for road construction and repair. The army group was also supported by the Organization Todt and the Reich Labor Service (*Reichsarbeitsdienst*).[11] *Luftwaffe* units assigned for tactical support included short- and long-range (strategic) reconnaissance and courier squadrons,[12] as well as light and mixed flak battalions. Security behind the front was the mission of the three weak security divisions under Commander, Rear Army Area 101 (*Befehlshaber rückwärtiges Heeresgebiet 101*).[13]

Providing air support for Field Marshal von Leeb's ground forces was the relatively tiny 1 Air Fleet (*Luftflotte 1*), commanded by *Generaloberst* Alfred Keller; it began the Russian campaign with 453 combat-ready aircraft, but only 211 of these were bombers and 167 were fighter aircraft.[14]

Leeb's assigned sector of the Eastern Front was relatively narrow, extending nearly 300 kilometers from the northern edge of the Suwalki triangle north and northwest along the East Prussian border to the Baltic Sea just above the town of Memel'. His attack frontage fell on the entire Soviet 8 Army, but only covered part of Soviet 11 Army, whose southern wing was included within the boundaries of neighboring Army Group Center. (Both of these Soviet armies belonged to Kuznetsov's Baltic Special Military District.) The army group's forces were arranged with General Ernst Busch's Sixteenth Army on the right and General Georg von Küchler's Eighteenth Army on the left; between them were the two panzer corps of Hoepner's 4 Panzer Group. Although the tactical grouping of Leeb's forces was not ideal—his two armies and two panzer corps were committed side-by-side with no depth and little in reserve—the Germans did manage to secure a "devastating superiority of numbers and firepower at the [point] selected for their armored penetration." In fact, the army group's 600 tanks, along with two supporting infantry divisions, were assembled on a narrow attack frontage of approximately 40 kilometers; facing them was a single weak Russian rifle division.[15]

Simply stated, the mission of GFM von Leeb's Army Group North was to destroy Soviet forces in the Baltic region, capture Leningrad, and establish a junction with Finnish forces astride Lake Ladoga. The instructions to Leeb's army group were laid out in some detail in the army's deployment directive:

> *The mission of Army Group North is to destroy enemy forces in the Baltic area and, by taking possession of the Baltic ports, and eventually of Leningrad and Kronstadt, to deprive the Russian fleet of its bases. Cooperation with strong mobile forces of Army Group Center, which are to drive on Smolensk, will be arranged by OKH in timely fashion.*
>
> *Within the scope of this mission, Army Group North is to break through the enemy front, with the main effort [Schwerpunkt] in the direction of Daugavpils [Dünaburg], and drive its strong right wing—its mobile forces in advance beyond the Dvina—as rapidly as possible into the area northwest of Opochka, in order to prevent the withdrawal of combat capable Russian forces from the Baltic region to the east and thus to establish the prerequisite for a further rapid drive in the direction of Leningrad.[16]*

The axis of advance of Army Group North would take it through territory that had been Germanized by Teutonic knights and Hanseatic traders for 500 years; moreover, the Baltic region had produced many of the families that had "officered the Prussian and German armies throughout their history. Manstein and Guderian, who were to win Hitler his greatest eastern victories, descended from landowners of those parts."[17] It was assumed that the population of this region, which was to be "liberated" from Soviet rule, would be friendly. It was also uncertain if Soviet forces would even defend the Baltic

States. German intelligence suggested that the enemy's strong frontier defense forces had been pulled back, thus it was all the more critical to rapidly engage and destroy the mass of Red Army forces before they could withdraw behind the formidable barrier of the Western Dvina River.[18]

Defending the northwestern strategic axis and the approaches to Leningrad, Kuznetsov's Baltic Special Military District, composed of three armies and two mechanized corps, was the weakest of the three military districts in the western frontier zone. Lt.-Gen. P. P. Sobennikov's 8 Army and Lt.-Gen. V. I. Morozov's 11 Army, supported by the 3 and 12 Mechanized Corps,[19] made up Kuznetsov's first echelon, with Maj.-Gen. M. E. Berzarin's 27 Army forming the second echelon. Kuznetsov's primary forces consisted of nineteen rifle, four tank, and two motorized divisions; his total force (including several fortified regions, independent artillery regiments, antitank, and antiaircraft units) was made up of 370,000 men (44,000 in schools), with 7,019 guns and mortars, 1,549 tanks (1,274 combat ready), and 1,344 aircraft (1,150 combat ready) on June 22, 1941.[20] While "powerful on paper," the military district's forces "suffered from the same debilitating deficiencies that plagued the entire Red Army on the eve of war and were only partially reorganized, trained and equipped." The district's rifle divisions were only at about 60 percent strength, averaging roughly 8,700 men each, while its mechanized corps boasted only 109 KV and T-34 tanks (12 Mechanized Corps, which was earmarked to be the primary counterattack force, having no KV or T-34 tanks at all).[21] In addition, Kuznetsov's forces embraced a number of divisions of the former Lithuanian, Latvian, and Estonian armies, which had been integrated into the Red Army in 1940; these formations, the Germans believed, "would be unlikely to give a good account of themselves."[22]

In the Baltic Special Military District's first echelon, 8 Army made up the right wing, extending to the Baltic coast, while 11 Army anchored the left wing extending south and southwest and covering the approaches to Kaunas and Vilnius. Sobennikov's 8 Army held a front 160–170 kilometers in length,[23] with its 10 and 11 Rifle Corps possessing between them five rifle divisions; three of these rifle divisions—10 and 90 RD of 10 Rifle Corps and 125 RD of 11 Rifle Corps—were defending the frontier zone from the Baltic Sea southeastward to the Nemen River.

The general deployment of rifle forces [of 8 Army] was in single echelon configuration. The two rifle corps . . . were positioned side by side. The 10 Rifle Corps had its two divisions deployed forward, although the bulk of the troops of those divisions were in lagers, or camps, on the morning of 22 June. The 10 Rifle Division had all its regiments in camps on line across the front at a depth of about 10 to 15 kilometers, with scattered elements from company to battalion strength actually deployed along the border. This amounted to roughly an 80 kilometer front for the division.

The main Soviet defenses along the border were manned by 10 border guards detachments, whose positions ran the entire length of the border . . . The 90 and 125 Rifle Divisions deployed with elements of two regiments forward and one regiment well to the rear.[24]

In several German primary accounts—among them a detailed chronology of the start of the Russian campaign prepared by the operations branch (Ia) of Army Group North and the personal diary of GFM von Leeb[25]—the assumption is that, beginning about June 18, 1941, the bulk of Red Army forces in the Baltic Special Military District posted at the border were quietly withdrawn to unknown (to the Germans) locations in the interior. As a result, the Germans were convinced that most of the Russian forces encountered on the first day of the war along the northern axis were Soviet border guards and/or rearguards, but not the main enemy forces. Be that as it may, Soviet defense plans for the Baltic region indicate that they intended to mount a vigorous defense along the Russo-German frontier. The Baltic Special Military District's top secret "Covering Plan" of June 2, 1941, approved by Marshal Timoshenko, included the following points under Section 2, "Covering Missions:"

1. Do not permit violation of Baltic Special Military District territory by either enemy land or naval forces.

2. Repel the enemy offensive by stubborn defense along the line of the frontier [author's emphasis] in the positions of existing fortified regions, and protect mobilization, concentration, and deployment of district forces . . .

5. Gain air superiority and destroy and retard concentration and deployment of enemy forces by strikes against railroad junctions, bridges, staging yards, and force groupings.

Under the section entitled "Covering Region 2—8 Army" the plan called for "defense of the state border along the front from Palanga to the Nemen River."

Missions:

a. Firmly cover the Memel', Tel'shiai and Tilsit, Tauroggen and Siauliai axes by defensive field fortifications along the line of the state border and the existing Tel'shiai and Siauliai Fortified Regions.

b. Prepare for a counterattack by 12 Mechanized Corps, 9 Anti-Tank Artillery Brigade, and four rifle divisions along [several axes]. Conduct the counterattack in cooperation with front aviation.[26]

Without question, General Kuznetsov was a serious commander who did what he reasonably could—despite the frustrating restraints Moscow placed on his ability to prepare his troops for battle—to augment the combat readiness of the forces under his command. Indeed, as we have seen, he even took courageous risks in an effort to do so. And yet, when war came, and "amid the chaos, thousands of stunned Red Army officers and soldiers muttered grimly, '*Eto nachalo*' (It has begun),"[27] Kuznetsov's armies would be shattered by the initial German assault.

3.2: SIXTEENTH ARMY OPERATIONS

German Sixteenth Army (headquarters in Trakehnen) was commanded by the fifty-five-year-old *Generaloberst* Ernst Busch; his chief of staff was *Obst. i.G.* Wuthmann. The army consisted of about 140,000 men[28] (eight infantry divisions) distributed in the main over three army corps (from right to left): *Gen.d.Inf.* Walter Graf von Brockdorff-Ahlefeldt's 2 Army Corps (12, 32, 121 ID); *Gen.d.Inf.* Mauritz Wiktorin's 28 Army Corps (122, 123 ID); and *Gen.d.Art.* Christian Hansen's 10 Army Corps (30, 126 ID). In army reserve was 253 Infantry Division.[29] General Headquarters (GHQ) troops assigned to Sixteenth Army included:

- 2 battalions of *Nebelwerfer* rocket projectors (2 AK)
- 5 batteries of assault guns (*Sturmgeschütze*) (3 to 2 AK; 2 to 28 AK)
- 6 battalions of 150mm medium field howitzers (2 each to 2, 10, and 28 AK)
- 3 105mm cannon battalions (1 each to 2, 10, and 28 AK)
- 2 battalions 210mm heavy howitzers (*Mörser*) (2 AK)
- 1 mixed artillery battalion (2 AK)
- 1 240mm heavy artillery battalion (mot.) for flat trajectory fire (*Flachfeuer*) (253 ID)
- 1 150mm cannon battalion (253 ID)
- 1 mixed army flak battalion (*z.V. AOK 16*)[30]
- 3 flak (*Fla*) companies (1 to 253 ID; 2 *z.V. AOK 16*)

Among other GHQ troops allocated to Sixteenth Army were: seven engineer battalions, two bridge-building battalions, fifteen bridge columns "B," nine construction battalions, and three road construction and repair battalions. *Luftwaffe* units assigned to the army for tactical support embraced three short-range reconnaissance squadrons (*Aufklärungs-Staffel*)—one each to 2 and 28 Army Corps; one *z.V. AOK 16*—and three mixed flak battalions (*z.V. AOK 16*).[31]

Forming the right wing of Army Group North, Sixteenth Army was assigned an attack frontage of more than 100 kilometers, stretching from a point opposite the Lithuanian border village of Vištytis (just above Lake Wysztyter) northward to where the

Neman River crosses the East Prussian frontier (Maps 2 and 10).[32] The army's basic mission was to break through the enemy's border positions in the general direction of Kaunas, cross Neman River, and, following in the wake of 4 Panzer Group, secure the far bank of the Dvina River around Daugavpils.[33] As outlined in the Army High Command's deployment directive:

> *Sixteenth Army, in cooperation with 4 Panzer Group, is to break through the enemy front with its main effort [Schwerpunkt] astride the road from Ebenrode to Kaunas. Driving forward with its strong right wing behind the [panzer troops] it is to reach the northern bank of the Dvina at and below Daugavpils as soon as possible. Following behind 4 Panzer Group, the army will then rapidly reach the area of Opochka.[34]*

The Lithuanian border region—like the Baltic States in general—was largely flat, with occasional uplands; thickly wooded areas were common, while rivers and streams posed potentially significant obstacles. On the frontier in the sector of Sixteenth Army were several river barriers, among them the Šešupė River (*Ostfluss*, or East River, in German accounts),[35] which ran north along the border from the East Prussian village of Schirwindt for some distance before veering west into East Prussia and emptying into the Neman. Roads were generally poor, often no more than sandy tracks.[36]

Sunday morning, June 22, 1941, dawned clear and bright. At 0305 hours, Sixteenth Army put in its attack. In its sector—and across the front of Army Group North— concentrated artillery fire only preceded the attack in specific areas (for example, in the sector of 4 Panzer Group); for the most part, the initial wave of infantry and assault sappers "rose silently from their dugouts among the crops along the frontier" and sought out the enemy.[37] Facing Busch's infantry were border guard detachments, construction battalions, and the forward elements of Soviet 11 Army's 16 Rifle Corps. The German assault took the Russian defenders—whose prepared positions were only partially occupied, if occupied at all—by complete surprise. Within forty-five minutes, the first corps reports were filtering back to Sixteenth Army headquarters, leaving the impression that enemy resistance was weak. By 0445 hours, the bridges at Schirwindt, Naumiestis, and Eydtkau (Eydtkuhnen) had been captured intact.[38]

Led by *Generalmajor* Walther von Seydlitz-Kurzbach, the assault troops of 12 Infantry Division (2 Army Corps) debouched from their attack assembly areas in the woods and stormed across the border not far from the East Prussian town of Stallupönen (east of Gumbinnen), where in August 1914 German and Russian forces had fought the opening battle of World War 1 on the Eastern Front. They crossed the frontier without meeting any enemy resistance.[39] "In the morning, at 0305, we began the attack without preparatory time-on-target artillery fire," recalled Heinz-Georg Lemm, then a company commander in the division's 27 Infantry Regiment:

In the beginning of the attack the resistance of the Russians was weak and consisted of individual fire with guns, light machine guns and the irregular fire of a light artillery battery. My company advanced well, but the very great physical efforts required for passage through the roadless, sometimes sandy, sometimes swampy terrain, the wading through several swampy brooks with all our weapons and ammunition boxes in a sun now standing high, exhausted many soldiers. All were very thirsty. The village of Debiliniai, in Lithuania, was conquered at 0450. The first Russian prisoners appeared happy that for them the war, although hardly begun, was over. From the population nobody was to be seen and the cattle were gone as well. At the village well I had my men fill their canteens. Soon enemy resistance with gun and machine gun fire became stronger.[40]

Yet the soldiers of the 12 ID were hardly prepared for the combat methods of their adversary: When the Russians fell back, they left behind small pockets of resistance, which, after letting the German assault parties pass by, opened fire on them from behind—a method of warfare that the Germans found to be malicious (*heimtückisch*) yet cunning (*verschlagen*).[41]

Operating on the left (northern) flank of 2 Army Corps, the 121 Infantry Division crossed the border at Eydtkau, east of Stallupönen and opposite the Lithuanian frontier town of Kybartai. At 0305 hours, the division's *Panzerjägerabteilung* 121 (Antitank Battalion 121) fired the first shot as a signal that the war had begun. Then the AT guns opened up on known enemy defensive positions and on Kybartai. For reasons unclear—perhaps due to local tactical imperatives—the divisional artillery did not open fire until 0344 hours. The division's three regiments (405, 407, 408 IR) made good progress. By 0345, lead elements of 407 and 405 Infantry Regiments had linked up on the highway (*Rollbahn*) east of Kybartai; minutes later, the rail and road bridge at Kybartai was in German hands. In the town itself, the Russian defenders fought doggedly in their bunkers and cellars; the situation was precarious enough that the division commander, *Generalmajor* Otto Lancelle, intervened personally to direct the attack on the town.[42] (On July 3, 1941, General Lancelle would be killed in the fighting at the Krāslava bridgehead at the Dvina River.)[43]

Not until 0455 hours did the Russian artillery make its presence felt, shelling the railway station at Wirballen (Virbalis). While German engineers labored furiously to erect military bridges over water obstacles, the 121 ID continued to press forward. At 0550, 407 IR seized Hill 114 and the northeast corner of the woods just south of Wirballen. By 0600, Wirballen was in German hands, taken without enemy resistance by III./IR 405, while I./IR 405 had reached the line Wirballen-Karalinavas; yet the intense battle at Kybartai continued (II./IR 405).[44] Only minutes before (0545), Col.-Gen. Kuznetsov, Commander, Soviet Northwestern Front, attempted to strike back with airpower. Russian bombers sought out targets in East Prussia, dropping bombs on the bridge at Wischwill

(Viešvilė) to no discernable effect and unloading about twenty bombs on the railway station at Eydtkau, causing minor damage to rail lines and destroying the engine of an armored train (*Pz. Zug*).[45]

Farther north, on the left wing of Sixteenth Army, in the sector of Hansen's 10 Army Corps, the first infantry assault teams of 126 Infantry Division crossed the Šešupė River in pneumatic boats (*Flossäcke*) shortly after 0300 hours.[46] The Russian border guards were caught by surprise and quickly put out of action; by 0315, the attacking troops were across the river at several points.[47] The division's engineers hastily assembled some makeshift ferries (*Behelfsfähren*), and by 0445 hours, all three of the division's regiments were over the river; meanwhile, the construction of bridges had already begun, and soon the artillery and other heavy weapons would be crossing into enemy territory.[48] The early going had been easy—too easy, perhaps; but some serious fighting would come later in the day.

The soldiers of 126 Infantry Division, storming into Lithuania on the morning of June 22, found themselves suddenly in a land that appeared to be a cultural backwater, a place fundamentally alien when compared to their German and East Prussian homeland. As recalled in a divisional history published in 1957: "The first glimpse of the land beyond the border was unforgettable. The difference between East Prussia, with its well-kept streets, villages and cities, and Lithuania, with its bottomless sandy paths and miserable peasant huts, revealed that another world began here."[49] And yet the Lithuanians, whose country had been brutally occupied by the Russians in 1940 along with the rest of the Baltic States, welcomed the Germans as liberators from Russian oppression; they greeted the invaders "enthusiastically, with flowers and, probably more welcome to hard-fighting combat troops, coffee, milk, eggs, bread and butter laid out on tables in front of their houses." Within hours of the German invasion, Lithuanian resistance groups sprang into action, firing on withdrawing Soviet troops and seizing government buildings in Kaunas. The Germans, however, did not seem prepared to exploit the unexpected support they were receiving.[50]

On the far left (northern) flank of Sixteenth Army, at the Neman River west of Jurbarkas, was 30 Infantry Division, also a component of 10 Army Corps. The division's assault parties crossed the Reich border (*Reichsgrenze*) "according to plan," meeting only negligible opposition; within minutes they had already secured the first farmsteads beyond the frontier.[51] And yet, at 0403—in other words, barely an hour after the start of the German assault—the division's war diary recorded: "Impression of the enemy: Enemy consists of young men [*junger Leute*], outfitted with semiautomatic rifles [*Selbstladegewehren*]. They have defended courageously."[52] The 30 ID's experiences on the first day of the Russian campaign are graphically portrayed in Paul Carell's classic account, *Hitler Moves East 1941–1943*:

*The men of 30 Infantry Division . . . had no water obstacles to overcome on their first day. The sapper platoon of their advance detachment [*Vorausabteilung*], under* Oberleutnant *Weiss, crept up to the barbed wire. For days they had been observing every detail. The Russians patrolled the wire only intermittently. Their defenses were farther back, along some high ground.*

Softly. Softly . . .

The wire-cutters clicked. A post rattled. Quiet—listen. But there was no movement on the other side. Keep going. Faster. Now the passages were clear. And already the men of 6th Company were coming up on the double, ducking as they ran. Not a shot was fired. The two Soviet sentries stared terrified down the carbine-barrels and raised their hands.

Keep going.

The observation towers on Hills 71 and 67 stood out black against the sky. There the Russians were established in strong positions. The Landser *were aware of it. And so were the gunners of the medium battalion of 30 Artillery Regiment waiting in the frontier wood behind them. The Russian machine guns opened up from the tower on Hill 71 . . . Immediately the reply came from the well-camouflaged medium field howitzers of 2nd Battalion, 47 Artillery Regiment, in position behind the regiments of 30 Infantry Division on the road from Trappen to Waldheide. Where their shells burst there would be no grass growing for a long time.*

*Assault guns forward! Ducking behind the steel monsters, Weiss's advance detachment was storming the high ground. Already they were inside the Soviet positions. The Russians were bewildered and taken by surprise. Most of them were not even manning their newly built, though only partly finished, defenses. They were still in their bivouacs. These were Mongolian construction battalions, employed here on building frontier defenses. Wherever they were encountered, in groups or platoon strength, manning those defenses, they fought stubbornly and fanatically [*verbissen und fanatisch*].*[53]

Despite pockets of stubborn Soviet resistance, the first few hours of the German assault had been strikingly successful. The enemy border posts had been overwhelmed, and Sixteenth Army's seven attacking infantry divisions were steadily moving east. The initial impression at Hansen's 10 Army Corps headquarters, to cite but one example, was that enemy resistance was everywhere weak—if slightly more vigorous before 126 ID—an impression confirmed (for the most part) throughout the day.[54] As of 0600 hours, as recorded in a detailed account later prepared by the operations branch (Ia) of Army Group North, Busch's infantry had reached the following points:

12 ID roughly 7.5 kilometers east of Schlossbach;

32 ID penetrated into the woods 5 kilometers east of Vištytis;

121 ID attacking directly west of Wirballen; house-to-house combat still ongoing in Kybartai;

123 and 122 ID in line 3 kilometers east of Naumiestis—8 kilometers west/northwest of Sintautai;

126 ID with forwardmost elements 12 kilometers west/southwest of Sakiai;[55]

30 ID elements 3 kilometers southwest of Jurbarkas.

All bridges at the border (including the railroad bridge at Kybartai) in sector of the Army have been captured intact.[56]

On the right flank of Sixteenth Army, 2 Army Corps had gained more ground by 0800 hours: 121 Infantry Division was now 3 kilometers east of Wirballen;[57] 32 Infantry Division had pushed beyond the woods at Skardupiai, and 12 Infantry Division had captured the town of Kunigiskiai. Again, the recollections of company commander Heinz-Georg Lemm (12 ID):

At 0730 the regiment was able to report the capture of Kunigiskiai. Here, in the sandy hilly terrain, the Russians had built bunker positions reinforced with wooden timbers and had dug fox-holes and ditches on both sides of the village. They defended those fortifications tenaciously and bravely. Despite its frontal attack, our 3rd Battalion remained immobile for almost one hour and encountered its first noticeable losses, whereas the 1st Battalion, to which also my 2nd Company belonged, was able to advance past the village, turn in and enter the village from the rear, thus blocking the way for Russians who attempted to make a fairly orderly retreat.

The Russian losses were very high and about 60 prisoners were taken. Many Russians—primarily Uzbeks and Tartars—surrendered voluntarily, and Ukrainians also threw away their weapons and left their well-camouflaged combat positions. The losses on our side were numerous as well. As far as I can remember they amounted to ten or eleven killed and more than 20 wounded. During the last minutes of the assault, while we were already seizing one house after the other in the village of Kunigiskiai, a Russian battery moved into an open firing position about 800–1,000 meters away and opened rapid fire from all six guns which, however, hit the Russian defenders more than us and decisively contributed to the accomplishment of our mission. Yet we were happy when the artillery observers who advanced with our infantry companies concentrated the fire of three of our own batteries on the Russian guns which were completely visible targets and destroyed that enemy battery within a few minutes.[58]

At 0850, 2 Army Corps notified army headquarters that aerial reconnaissance was reporting that enemy forces were continuing to withdraw to the east. Less than an hour later, the corps reported again to army headquarters, this time to inform them that 121 Infantry Division had captured Alvitas and was advancing on Vilkaviskis (ca. 20 kilometers northwest of Mariampole). At 0935, 10 Army Corps reported in, noting that the enemy appeared to be conducting a systematic withdrawal eastward (*Gegner setzt sich anscheinend planmässig ab*). Thirty-five minutes later (1010), the chief operations officer (Ia) of Sixteenth Army summed up the results of the first seven hours of the Russian campaign, informing Army Group North that "the enemy has not defended his prepared positions at the border," and that the army had begun a general pursuit (*Verfolgung*) of the enemy with the objective of reaching the Neman River as soon as possible.[59] Five minutes later, the army chief of staff, *Obst. i.G.* Wuthmann, amplified the observations of his "Ia" with a more detailed report to the army group:

> *The chief of staff of Sixteenth Army reports: The enemy is withdrawing without putting up resistance. Hitherto, all bridges have been taken intact. The enemy's field fortifications were not defended. There's been little to no enemy artillery activity. It is not yet clear whether the enemy is falling back on a prepared rear line of defense, or if the deployment (Aufmarsch) of the enemy had not yet been completed.[60]*

Meanwhile, Lt.-Gen. V. I. Morozov's Soviet 11 Army was preparing its own reports at its headquarters in Kaunas. In "Intelligence Report No. 5" (0900 hours) it noted that,

> *1. Following an artillery preparation, the enemy, supported by aviation, began an offensive at 3:00 A.M. on 22.6.41.*

> *2. By 8:00 A.M. the enemy, along the 16 Rifle Corps' front, captured Jurburg, Wladyslawow, Kybartai, and Lubovo, attacking in separate groups of up to a battalion in the area of Jurburg, up to a regiment in the Wladyslawow—Virbalis [Wirballen] area.[61]*

In "Combat Report No. 6," the chief of staff of 11 Army, Maj.-Gen. Shlyomin, assessed the situation in more detail as it existed at 0800 hours along the tottering front of 16 Rifle Corps (5, 33, 188 Rifle Divisions):

> *FIRST: The enemy, having violated the state boundary at 3:00 A.M. on 22.6.41, went over to the offensive along the army's entire front, launching his main attack and pushing our units to the east.*

> *SECOND: Along the 16 Rifle Corps' front, by 8:00 A.M. the enemy had captured Jurburg, Silininkai, Wladyslawow, Virbalis, and Kalvaria.*

A. Along the 5 Rifle Division front, its right flank fell back to the line Jurburg-Angladegiai woods. There is no information on the rest of the front.

B. The 33 Rifle Division is securely holding its main defensive line: Pranskabudis-Tumpai-Rumokai-Vailiskiai-Rudkiskiai.

There are communications with the division and corps.

Communications have been lost with the 188 Rifle Division and there is no information . . .

SIXTH: During 3:30–4:30 A.M. the enemy air force carried out bombing against the following airfields: Kedainia, Karmelava, Kaunas, Alytus.

The enemy lost five planes to anti-aircraft fire and in air battles, with three pilots captured.[62]

In general, the two reports of Soviet 11 Army accurately reflected the situation along the front of its severely stressed 16 Rifle Corps, even if the army, its communications badly disrupted, only had an incomplete picture of events (for example, bitter house-to-house combat in Kybartai was still going on at 0900 hours; in fact, the tenacious Russian garrison there would not be completely cleared from their bunkers and cellars until the next morning).[63]

During the afternoon the relentless advance of Sixteenth Army continued, with the most progress being made on its right wing. At 1300 hours, GFM von Leeb, at his headquarters in Waldfrieden, noted that 2 Army Corps had pushed some 12 kilometers beyond the frontier and that aerial reconnaissance was reporting "retrograde movements" (*rückgängige Bewegungen*) of enemy forces at Mariampole and Pilviskiai. Yet Soviet forces were slowly recovering from the initial shock of invasion and, as German reports indicated, enemy resistance was beginning to stiffen. By mid-afternoon, elements of 121 Infantry Division (2 Army Corps) were approaching the town of Pilviskiai (northeast of Vilkaviskis), astride the Šešupė River; the division's reconnaissance battalion, however, was soon brought to a halt before a group of field fortifications bitterly defended by Russian troops (to get the battalion moving again it was reinforced by infantry, a battalion of artillery, and two assault guns).[64] By late afternoon, Russian opposition in the sector of 121 ID had increased substantially. As recorded in the journal of 2 Army Corps: "Every bunker, every field fortification and every farm house had to be taken out individually in hard fighting supported by artillery."[65]

At 1600 hours, Wiktorin's 28 Army Corps, in the center of the Sixteenth Army front, reported to army headquarters that "the impression exists that enemy resistance before the corps' front is increasing." In fact, Wiktorin's corps would suffer the loss of ten officers killed in combat on this day.[66] Meanwhile, in the sector of Hansen's 10 Army Corps, 126 Infantry Division was learning some bitter lessons of its own about the nature of combat on the Eastern Front:

> *The 2nd Battalion, 422 Infantry Regiment, suffered heavy losses. Parts of a Soviet machine gun picket had hidden themselves in a cornfield and allowed the first wave of the attack to pass by. In the afternoon, when Captain Lohmar unsuspectingly led his battalion from reserve positions to the front, the Russians in the crops suddenly opened up. Among those killed was the battalion commander, among those seriously wounded was his adjutant. It took an entire company three hours to flush the four Russians out of the field. They were still firing when the Germans had got within 10 feet of them, and had to be silenced with hand grenades.[67]*

As noted in the 126 ID war diary, due to such combat methods on the part of the enemy—methods that the Germans found highly unpleasant (*unerfreulich*) and that were attributed largely to Russian Asiatic troops—422 Infantry Regiment lost three officers and a large number of NCOs and men on this first day of the war.[68]

While small pockets of Soviet border troops resisted furiously, by late afternoon signs of disintegration among the Red Army defenders were becoming readily apparent. At 1620 hours, the reconnaissance battalion of 121 Infantry Division reported that discarded uniforms of Russian officers and soldiers had been discovered lying about in the battalion area, arousing the suspicion that some of the enemy were exchanging their uniforms for civilian clothing.[69]

The Army Group North situation map for the evening of June 22, 1941, reveals that the greatest progress on this day was made by Graf von Brockdorff-Ahlefeldt's 2 Army Corps. Having pushed more than 40 kilometers beyond the frontier, the advance detachment of the corps' 32 Infantry Division had reached the outskirts of Mariampole,[70] while both 12 and 121 ID had covered some 30 kilometers and ended the day in positions east of Vilkaviskis; moreover, 121 ID reported the capture of some 500 prisoners along with significant booty (artillery pieces, tanks, and weapons of all types). In the center Wiktorin's 28 Army Corps had made less progress, the corps reporting to Sixteenth Army at 2008 hours that the advance of its right wing had been slowed by superior enemy forces in heavily wooded terrain; its two divisions had still managed to advance 10–15 kilometers beyond the border. On the left (northern) wing of Sixteenth Army, the two infantry divisions of Hansen's 10 Army Corps had advanced 20–25 kilometers—30 ID along the southern bank of the Neman River (east of Jurbarkas) and 126 ID in action farther south (Maps 3 and 11).[71] The forward progress of 30 ID was helped along by the brilliant operations of its neighbor to the north, 8 Panzer Division of 4 Panzer Group;[72] before the day was over, an advance detachment of 30 ID had secured a bridgehead over the Neman at Panemune and then held on to it against a Red Army counterattack with tanks.[73]

All things considered—despite the inevitable setbacks resulting from friction and enemy countermeasures—the first day of Operation *Barbarossa* had been a good one for General Busch's Sixteenth Army. While the enemy border guards had fought bravely, they had simply been overwhelmed by the superior firepower of the attacking German forces; enemy air activity had been negligible.[74] As the first day drew to a close, many *Landser* no doubt shared the convictions of *Gefr.* Otto S., who served in the ration supply office of a large construction staff unit in Gumbinnen:

> *Today is the memorable day of the advance into Russia! My first thoughts were of you— how you're most likely overcome with worry about me. How I wish this letter would reach you on the fastest way possible! But you'll probably have ten anxious days, before this letter arrives. I can well imagine how things look to you now.*
>
> *I had slept peacefully and awakened about 5.45 in the morning, when a comrade insisted there was an air raid warning. I really had no desire to climb out of my "nest," but then someone burst in our room and said, "The* Führer *is speaking!" and that he'd heard it. So quickly out of bed and turn on the radio—and we heard the news, which astounded us all, of the invasion of Russia. We also heard that a mail embargo was now in effect, so you can't write to me!*
>
> *Last Sunday I said that on Saturday—that is, yesterday—it would all kick off. I was only off by a few hours! And still, again and again I had my doubts, if it would really begin in the East. But everything that was going on here could not, in the end, lead to any other conclusion. What a remarkable deployment took place here! . . . It is . . . something that the world has never seen before! And just how fast is it all going. The word is that our troops have already advanced quite far.*
>
> *Everything is quiet here. In the morning the local population was understandably somewhat agitated, but already by midday it was a typical Sunday. People are taking walks and have complete trust in our* Wehrmacht. *I believe that it will also end very quickly with the Reds. I believe that now the final decision is coming. And as Russia goes, so goes England. So it's at least possible that this accursed killing will come to an end this year.*[75]

Despite such optimistic assessments, to officers and men alike it had become increasingly clear as the day wore on that their Russian adversary was unlike any other they had hitherto encountered:

> *The German troops were beginning to realize that this was not an opponent to be trifled with. These men were not only brave but also full of guile. They were masters of camouflage and ambush. They were first-rate riflemen. Fighting from an ambush had*

always been the great strength of the Russian infantry. Forward pickets, overrun and wounded, would wait for the first German wave to pass over them. Then they would resume fighting. Snipers would remain in their foxholes with their excellent automatic rifles with telescopic sights, waiting for their quarry. They would pick off the drivers of supply vehicles, officers, and orderlies on motorcycles.[76]

The next morning, 28 Army Corps reported to Sixteenth Army that individual enemy groups in its combat sector were resisting chaotically and without any real cohesion (*zusammenhanglos*). "Our losses due to this unfamiliar method of fighting," the report conceded, "are heavy."[77]

3.3: 4 PANZER GROUP OPERATIONS

The 4 Panzer Group (headquarters in Pogegen) was commanded by the fifty-four-year-old *Generaloberst* Erich Hoepner; his chief of staff was *Obst. i. G.* Chales de Beaulieu. Among the thousands of general officers who served in Germany's armed forces during the Second World War, Hoepner was one of the more complex, even tragic figures. From early on he feared that Hitler's expansionist policies would lead to disaster and did not feel bound by his oath of allegiance to the German dictator. As noted by a sympathetic biographer, Hoepner was a member of the military resistance to Hitler from its "first to the last hour";[78] there is also some evidence that he was opposed to an attack on the Soviet Union. As a former officer, who for three years had been among the panzer general's closest confidants, recalled long after the war: "Hoepner believed a war against the Soviet Union to be out of the question and the whole deployment to be a bluff . . . It is utterly impossible that Hoepner could ever have considered war against the USSR to be unavoidable, or to be a fight for survival that had been imposed on us. Three or four days before the attack [began] he said to me: 'This cannot be true, this is our hara-kiri!'"[79] That duly noted, the preponderance of historical evidence supports the view that the *Generaloberst* strongly supported the attack on Soviet Russia. He was, after all, despite his pronounced anti-Hitler leanings, a member of the conservative German officer caste, and he shared its bedrock convictions about the existential danger posed by Soviet Bolshevism to the Reich's survival and the superiority of German culture to that of the Slavic east. Which explains a secret order of the day of May 2, 1941, that bears his signature:

The war against Russia is an essential stage in the struggle for existence [Das-einskampf] of the German people. It is the age-old struggle of the German against the Slav, defense of European culture against the Muscovite-Asiatic inundation, resistance against Jewish Bolshevism. The objective of this struggle must be the utter destruction [Zertrümmerung] of today's Russia and, as a result, it must be conducted with unalloyed hardness. In design and execution every engagement must be guided by the unbending will to completely and mercilessly destroy the enemy. For the purveyors of the present Russian-Bolshevik system in particular there will be no mercy.[80]

In the late autumn of 1941, the surviving remnants of Hoepner's 4 Panzer Group would come closest to Moscow of all German forces. In January 1942, in violation of a Hitler order to stand fast, Hoepner withdrew troops that otherwise would have been surrounded and destroyed. In a rage, the *Führer* relieved Hoepner of his command for "cowardice and disobedience" (*Feigheit und Ungehorsam*) and ordered that he be "expelled from the Army with loss of pay, pension, and the rights to wear the uniform and decorations." According to Samuel W. Mitcham Jr., "Hoepner demanded a court-martial. In early 1942, the military courts still worked, or at least to a degree, so Hitler was faced with a choice: allow a court-martial or restore Hoepner's rights and pension. With typical bad grace, the *Führer* chose the latter. He had, however, earned Hoepner's undying hatred."[81] On August 8, 1944, Hoepner was hanged in Plötzensee prison in Berlin for his role in the anti-Hitler resistance.

The 4 Panzer Group's order of battle for Operation *Barbarossa* comprised about 125,000[82] men (eight divisions) and 602 tanks arranged in two panzer corps—*Gen.d.Inf.* Erich von Manstein's 56 Panzer Corps (3 ID [mot.], 8 PD, 290 ID) and *Gen.d.Pz.Tr.* Georg-Hans Reinhardt's 41 Panzer Corps (1 PD, 6 PD, 36 ID [mot.], 269 ID)—with one motorized division (SS "*Totenkopf*") in group reserve. Manstein's sole panzer division possessed a total of 212 tanks; however, 118 of these were tanks of Czech manufacture, the Pz 38(t), adapted by the Germans to fit a four-man crew. Although reliable mechanically, the Pz 38(t) was a light tank, its main armament being a 37mm gun, supported by two 7.92 machine guns. Reinhardt's two panzer divisions boasted a total of 390 tanks, yet 155 of these (all in 6 PD) were the Pz 35(t), which was also of Czech design and manufacture. While slightly heavier than its sister tank, the Pz 35(t) was also outfitted with a 37mm main armament and two 7.92 machine guns; moreover, it was already out of production, making spare parts difficult to come by. In all, more than 40 percent of the panzer group's tanks were of Czech manufacture; only 150 were medium Pz III and Pz IV models—the former equipped with 50mm, the latter with 75mm main armament. The remainder of the panzer group's tanks were light—and obsolete—Pz IIs, with a main armament of one 20mm gun and a 7.92 machine gun.[83]

Among the principal General Headquarters units allocated to Hoepner's 4 Panzer Group were:

- 1 105mm cannon battalion (41 PzK)
- 1 mixed artillery battalion (56 PzK)
- 2 medium field howitzer battalions (41 PzK)
- 1 210mm heavy howitzer battalion (mot.) (41 PzK)

- 2 antitank battalions (SP) (1 to 56 PzK; 1 *z.V.Pz.Gr.*)
- 1 army flak battalion (41 PzK)
- 1 *Nebelwerfer* rocket projector regiment (41 PzK)

Additional GHQ troops allotted to the panzer group included three engineer battalions, one bridge-building battalion, a minimum of twelve bridging columns "B," and five construction battalions. *Luftwaffe* formations assigned for tactical support included six reconnaissance squadrons (five short-range squadrons allotted to the two panzer corps and one long-range [strategic] reconnaissance squadron [4.(F)/33] controlled by panzer group headquarters); three light flak battalions (one to each panzer division) and two mixed flak battalions (one to each panzer corps).[84]

In violation of Army High Command orders, Hoepner, with Field Marshal von Leeb's approval, had made Reinhardt's 41 Panzer Corps (deployed on the panzer group's left) stronger than Manstein's 56 Panzer Corps (on the right), by assigning it two of the three panzer divisions. Recalled Adolf Heusinger, then Chief, OKH Operations Branch, long after the war:

> *After I examined 4 Panzer Group's order of battle for the attack, and without Halder being present, I went to [C-in-C of the Army] Brauchitsch and said: "Something doesn't look right! We ordered that the main effort be made on the right [Schwerpunkt rechts], but the panzer group has given most of its panzer divisions . . . to Reinhardt on the left!" Whereupon Brauchitsch replied: "Ja, I'm aware of that. But Halder and Leeb are compatriots [Landsleute] and get along well together. We'd best leave it alone!"*[85]

As noted above (Section 3.1), 4 Panzer Group's attack frontage north of the Neman River was only about 40 kilometers in length and roughly in the center of Army Group North's front, with Sixteenth Army on the panzer group's right, and Eighteenth Army on its left. Because the assembly area in the sector of Manstein's 56 Panzer Corps was so cramped, only its 290 Infantry Division and 8 Panzer Division were able to deploy forward in the first echelon, while its 3 Motorized Infantry Division was held south of the Neman; in fact, 8 Panzer Division was to be put in its attack along a front of barely 5 kilometers. Reinhardt's 41 Panzer Corps had slightly more space at its disposal, thus it was able to concentrate three of its four divisions along the frontier, with 1 Panzer Division forming the corps' (and the panzer group's) left flank astride the main road leading from Tilsit via Siauliai (Schaulen) to Riga (Map 4).[86] The terrain at the border was heavily wooded and partly swampy; east of the border were numerous rivers and streams, in particular the Dubyssa River valley, which posed a potentially serious obstacle to the movement of mobile forces. In general, the movement of troops and supplies would be rendered more difficult by the paucity of roads and highways.[87]

In response to the OKH deployment directive of January 31, 1941, Army Group North had issued its own deployment order (*Aufmarsch- und Kampfanweisung Barbarossa*) on May 5, 1941; in it, the initial tasks of Hoepner's 4 Panzer Group were laid out in some detail:

> *4 Panzer Group, in cooperation with the Sixteenth and Eighteenth Armies, and with its forces tightly concentrated and supported by its two subordinated infantry divisions, is to break through the enemy border zone between the Neman River and the highway from Tilsit to Riga (inclusive). [It is then to secure] the Dubyssa sector between the mouth of the river and the area about Siauliai. After that, the panzer group is to advance as rapidly as possible toward the Dvina sector Daugavpils–Jekabpils [Jakobstadt] and establish bridgeheads, with the weight of the main effort [Schwergewicht], so far as possible in the situation, in the area of Daugavpils.[88]*

The first intermediate objective of the panzer group was the line Kedainiai (56 Panzer Corps)–Siauliai (41 Panzer Corps). Hoepner's armored spearheads were then to advance furiously toward Daugavpils (56 Panzer Corps) and Jekabpils (41 Panzer Corps); after forging bridgeheads over the Dvina River, the two panzer corps were to push on to the area about Opochka, and from there wheel north or northeast,[89] with the ultimate objectives of trapping and destroying Soviet forces in the Baltic, capturing Leningrad and Kronstadt, and linking up with Finnish forces. For Manstein, the initial objective was the big highway bridge (viaduct) across the gorge of the Dubyssa River at Ariogala; it lay some 75–80 kilometers to the northeast, but it had to be taken intact the very first day.[90] In his postwar memoirs, Manstein described what success, or failure, at the Dubyssa would signify:

> *I knew the Dubyssa sector from World War I. What we should find there was a deep, ravined valley whose slopes no tank could negotiate. In the First War our railway engineers had labored there for months on end to span the gap with a masterly construction of timber. If the enemy now succeeded in blowing up the big road viaduct at Ariogala, the [panzer] corps would be hopelessly stuck and the enemy would have time on the steep far bank of the river to organize a defense that would in any case be extremely difficult to penetrate. That we could thereafter no longer expect to make a surprise descent on the Daugavpils bridges was perfectly obvious. The Ariogala crossing was indispensible to us as a springboard.[91]*

And success or failure would depend on Manstein's 8 Panzer Division, which, supported by 290 Infantry Division, would have to pierce the line of enemy pillboxes at the border and then push on, without regard to its flanks, without stopping, until it had reached its objective.[92]

The initial task of Reinhardt's 41 Panzer Corps, which was to conduct its attack on a broader front, was to smash the Soviet border fortifications around and east of Tauroggen (Taurage), the town itself located less than 10 kilometers inside the frontier. Enemy forces appeared to be stronger in this sector of the panzer group's front—the Germans had observed work on field fortifications along the main road heading northeast from Tilsit and south and southeast of Tauroggen—which explains why Hoepner had allotted a second panzer division to Reinhardt, and why most of the *Heeresartillerie* and the *Nebelwerfer* rocket projector regiment had been assigned to his corps. After piercing the enemy's border defenses, Reinhardt's corps was to gain some depth beyond the frontier before wheeling northeast toward the Dvina River.[93]

Because speed and freedom of movement were essential, the army group commander did not subordinate Hoepner's panzer group to an infantry army (in contrast to the other three panzer groups); both Sixteenth and Eighteenth Armies would have to "adjust their respective wings to the movements of the rapidly advancing armored group, cover its flanks, and 'round up' remnants of overrun enemy forces."[94]

In assessing the operational plans of 4 Panzer Group, two critical factors deserve our attention. Firstly, there are the ambitious distances involved—nearly 300 kilometers (in a straight line) from the frontier to the first major objective, the Dvina River crossings, and 800 kilometers to the ultimate objective of Leningrad. Secondly, due to the depth of the theater of operations, the problems posed by terrain and by poor road and rail conditions—and, of course, by the Red Army itself, which would grow stronger as German forces, dangling at the end of supply lines stretching back hundreds of kilometers, grew weaker—it was apparent to both Army Group North and 4 Panzer Group that the forces assigned for the mission were not sufficient.[95] Indeed, Hoepner's group would begin the Russian campaign with only one division in reserve, and that wasn't even a panzer division.

Not until the night of June 21/22, 1941, did 4 Panzer Group's three panzer divisions enter their attack assembly areas north of the Neman River, crossing by way of the Tilsit roadbridge and two pontoon bridges hastily erected after dusk. Second echelon units closed up tighter to the frontier. The movements were carried out without incident. On the Russian side of the border all seemed quiet. According to an entry in the panzer group's war diary, at 2:50 in the morning, just fifteen minutes before the attack was to begin, both panzer corps reported that all units had finally reached their jumping-off points and were ready to go.[96]

Shortly before daybreak, General Hoepner drove out to the forward command post (CP) of 41 Panzer Corps to observe the start of the attack at Tauroggen, where the Germans expected to meet the toughest resistance. At 0305 hours, across the front of the panzer group, hundreds of artillery tubes, *Nebelwerfer*, and heavy railway guns shattered the pastoral morning calm with an intense barrage, which, in most sectors, was of relatively short duration. Overhead, waves of *Luftwaffe* medium bombers, and their fighter escorts, slowly vanished in the mists beyond the border as they droned on toward their targets. From panzer group headquarters in Pogegen, north of Tilsit, one could make out the dull, distant thud of thirty batteries of all calibers (120 guns) as they struck identified enemy targets in and around Tauroggen. To the southeast, the three artillery battalions of 80 Artillery Regiment (8 PD) dropped shell after shell on Soviet bunkers in the woods just beyond the frontier. All told, as many as 600 guns participated in the panzer group's artillery bombardment.[97]

Capitalizing on the devastating—and disorienting—effect of the barrage, the assault groups of 56 and 41 Panzer Corps stormed across the frontier and surged down the forest tracks. In line with long-standing German doctrine, the attacking forces of all three panzer divisions were organized into battle groups (*Kampfgruppen*)—combined arms teams made up of motorized infantry, tanks, mobile artillery, antitank guns, and engineers. The weather was fine and dry—"a beautiful, clear summer day," that stood out incongruously against the murderous task at hand, recalled then chief of staff of 4 Panzer Group, Chales de Beaulieu[98]—and initial enemy resistance ranged from light to nonexistent. As noted in the journal of 1 Panzer Division: "The surprise [of the enemy] appears to have succeeded completely; all three battle groups are crossing the border according to plan."[99] Initial reports from both corps were that enemy resistance was everywhere weak.[100]

The 4 Panzer Group attack struck at the junction of Soviet 8 and 11 Armies; more specifically, it fell directly on the forward elements of Maj.-Gen. P. P. Bogabgun's 125 Rifle Division (11 Rifle Corps, 8 Army), which covered the Tauroggen-Siauliai axis (Map 2). In the words of military historian and Russian expert John Erickson, the German assault hit 125 RD "with a massive armored fist" (three panzer and two infantry divisions), while the sorely overmatched General Bogabgun sought in vain to "stem this armored tide with three guns to the kilometer."[101]

The 56 Panzer Corps' 8 Panzer Division was commanded by *Generalmajor* Erich Brandenberger, a "cool and controlled commander who radiated calm everywhere he went." He was, in fact, "tactically brilliant. He almost never made a mistake and took advantage of every opportunity. The senior German officers came to recognize this, even at *Führer* headquarters."[102] To conduct his attack across the frontier, Brandenberger had organized his division into several battle groups, the most important of these being *Kampfgruppe* Crisolli and *Kampfgruppe* Scheller. *Oberstleutnant* Crisolli's[103] battle group was made up of the bulk of 8 Rifle Regiment,[104] Motorcycle Battalion 8 (K8), a battalion of tanks of the division's 10 Panzer Regiment (II./Pz.Rgt. 10), a company of engineers, and flak troops to defend bridge-crossing sites. Operating on 8 PD's right (southern) flank, along the northern bank of the Neman River, Crisolli's group had as its first objective the bridges over the Mituva River, which were to be seized in a *coup de main* (*handstreichartig*). On the division's left (northern) flank, *Oberst* Scheller's battle group (28 Rifle Regiment, I./Pz.Rgt. 10, an advance detachment [*Vorausabteilung*] under *Hauptmann* v. Wolff, engineers, flak troops, and other units) was to cross the frontier at Antschwenten, traverse the Mituva, and, as the stronger of the two groups, make the decisive breakthrough toward the day's objective—the Dubyssa River viaduct at Ariogala. The attacks of both battle groups were to be supported by the infantry of 290 ID, which was to open a path for the armored spearheads by breaching the enemy's frontier defenses.[105]

To gain surprise, the 501 and 502 Infantry Regiments of *Generalleutnant* Theodor *Freiherr* (Baron) von Wrede's 290 Infantry Division attacked without a preparatory artillery barrage. Advancing across the frontier stream and through thickly wooded terrain, the going was initially slow,[106] the assault troops sustaining heavy casualties. The division's other infantry regiment (503 IR), directly subordinated to Brandenberger's 8 Panzer Division, registered at least seven dead and three wounded in the first minutes of combat.[107] The Russian border guards, well camouflaged and, in some cases, defending bunker positions, acquitted themselves well, fighting with skill and tenacity; yet they were far too few in number to halt the German assault detachments, which were soon making good progress. In the sector of *Kampfgruppe* Crisolli, combat engineers led by *Hauptmann* Hallauer cleared mines and other obstacles from the road, often under fire; at 0310 hours, Crisolli's lead platoons of motorcycle riflemen and tanks crossed the frontier stream at Pasvenciv—the bridge there taken by surprise by Hallauer's *Pioniere*—and rolled on toward the Mituva. For his role in opening the way for Crisolli's battle group, *Hauptmann* Hallauer would become the first German soldier to be awarded the Knight's Cross (*Ritterkreuz*) in the Russian campaign; badly wounded during the fighting he died two days later.[108]

Less than an hour after the start of the attack (0400), the diarist of 8 Panzer Division noted that "the panzers are advancing [*im Vorrollen*]; on the Mituva enemy resistance weak; no artillery fire."[109] Advance elements of Battle Group Crisolli were soon beyond the Mituva and facing little to no opposition. At 0445 hours, the lead tanks of II./Pz.Rgt. 10, at the edge of a wood near Susmuk, suddenly encountered a Russian light T-26 tank, which was rapidly disposed of with a few well-placed shells. An hour later (0540), the panzers were rumbling into Jurbarkas, at the confluence of the Mituva and Neman Rivers; at 0620 hours, 8 Panzer Division reported to Manstein's headquarters that its tanks were at the eastern edge of the town and that the bridges there had been captured intact. At the same time, infantry of 290 Infantry Division was across the Mituva 12 kilometers northwest of Jurbarkas. With his attack developing smoothly, Crisolli received orders at 0650 to push posthaste toward the Dubyssa; in response, his motorcycle riflemen and tanks rumbled northeast, while the companies of 8 Rifle Regiment were ordered to protect the two bridges at Jurbarkas.[110]

As noted, General Brandenberger had placed the *Schwerpunkt* of his advance on the northern wing, with *Kampfgruppe* Scheller; this force, however, quickly ran into serious trouble, including delays caused by the marshy, heavily wooded terrain, a less well-developed road system, and robust enemy resistance. Supported by 503 Infantry Regiment (290 ID), Scheller's group had to battle its way through a line of bunkers, reinforced with antitank and machine-gun positions, which held up its advance for many hours.[111]

Responding vigorously to the new reality, General Brandenberger had, by 0740, decided to shift the main weight of his attack from Scheller's to Crisolli's group, which was moving much more fluidly while encountering fewer natural obstacles or Russian resistance; moreover, he personally joined up with Crisolli to help accelerate his group forward. The situation as it existed at mid-morning is outlined succinctly by the late military historian R. H. S. Stolfi:

> *Battle Group Crisolli was little delayed by the Soviets, cross country terrain, river, road, or other similar factors on 22 June. In contrast, the other half of 8 PD in terms of the deployment for the advance over the border—the Advanced Detachment and Battle Group Scheller—was slowed and then blocked by Soviet resistance in a system of obstacles, field fortifications, and concrete bunkers. Battle Group Scheller did not subdue the Soviets in these defenses until after a difficult battle lasting 13 hours. At that moment, it lay approximately half a day behind Battle Group Crisolli, which was now reinforced by most of the tanks of the division and had become the strongest battle force . . . By approximately 0740, 22 June, Battle Group Crisolli had become, in effect, 8 PD, being simultaneously the leading and the* Schwerpunkt *force for the advance on Daugavpils.*[112]

With Scheller's group now reduced to a temporary non-factor, Crisolli's reinforced battle group continued to drive east along the northern bank of the Neman. At 1100 hours, near Elecnorova, the *Kampfgruppe* encountered "active resistance" for the first time—Red Army soldiers in construction battalions—which was quickly overcome. At 1130, *Generaloberst* Hoepner arrived at the CP of 8 Panzer Division, now just east of Jurbarkas, where he was briefed on the situation. He ordered that the Dubyssa be crossed at Ariogala that evening, and the closing up of the entire division, which was now badly strung out back to the border. The current intentions of the panzer division, as registered in its war diary less than an hour before, were to advance northeast on Ariogala and the Dubyssa with all available forces. Motorcycle Battalion 8 (K8), however, on special orders of the division commander, was to drive due east, capture the town of Seredzius (at the confluence of the Neman and the Dubyssa), and establish the first bridgehead over the Dubyssa there.[113]

The *Kradschützen* (motorcycle riflemen) of K8 had motored into Seredzius by early afternoon; roadblocks, which were not defended, were quickly brushed aside and the bridge over the Dubyssa seized intact; moving on, by 1430 hours, the bulk of the motorcycle battalion was just 7 kilometers southwest of Ariogala. Yet despite being overmatched by the speed and force of the German Blitz, the Russian frontier troops often resisted fiercely; in some cases, they continued to fight even after being badly wounded, while others sought to even the odds by ambushing German soldiers or fought effectively as snipers.[114] Facing tenacious resistance, Scheller's former *Schwerpunkt* battle group did not break through the Soviet bunker positions at Girdziai, only 13 kilometers beyond the Russo-German demarcation line, until 1600 hours.[115]

At 1620, General Manstein appeared at the 8 Panzer Division command post, where he conferred with the division's chief operations officer (Ia); amplifying the points made earlier by Hoepner, he ordered that, before day's end, all combat units were to reach the east bank of the Dubyssa at Ariogala. Manstein also ordered the division to throw forces beyond the river toward Kedainiai, while holding open the Seredzius crossings at the mouth of the Dubyssa.[116]

The final push by Battle Group Crisolli to seize the highway bridge (viaduct) across the Dubyssa River now got underway. At 1515 hours, his group had crossed the big ford over the Dubyssa just southwest of Ariogala, but the real prize, the viaduct over the river gorge, still had to be seized. At about 1530, General Brandenberger, riding with Crisolli's battle group, ordered the attack to begin:

> *The tank battalion with Crisolli and one motorized infantry company in armored, three-quarter-tracked vehicles [were to cross] the ford immediately to seize the eastern heights above the river and the city. With this attack accomplished, the division commander ordered an immediate push to take the highway bridge over the Dubyssa gorge lying 2.5 kilometers northwest of Ariogala. Elements of Battle Group Crisolli seized intact the big bridge on the unpaved but well constructed* Autobahn *(main highway) running through the city.*[117]

As noted by the war diarist of 8 Panzer Division, the highway bridge was captured at 1725 hours: "The *Autobahnbrücke* was strongly defended and was attacked from behind by 8 Rifle Brigade with tanks and artillery."[118] In his memoirs, *Gen.d.Inf.* Manstein observed:

> *Excessive though Corps H.Q.'s requirements may appear to have been, 8 Panzer Division (General Brandenberger), with which I spent most of the day, still fulfilled its task. After breaking through the frontier positions and over-running all enemy resistance further back, it seized the Ariogala crossing with a reconnaissance in force by the evening of 22 June. 290 [Infantry] Division followed, marching at record speed;[119] and 3 Motorized Infantry Division, which had started moving over the Nemen at noon, was directed toward a crossing south of Ariogala.*[120]

The lead elements of 56 Panzer Corps were now approximately 80 kilometers beyond the East Prussian border. At 1800 hours, Manstein directed Brandenberger to move on Kedainiai, the next major city on the road to Daugavpils and the Dvina River crossings. The division commander, in turn, ordered *Obstlt.* Crisolli to continue the advance with the available elements of his group. The tanks of II./Pz.Rgt. 10, at least those that still had adequate fuel, roared off; 12 kilometers east of Ariogala, in the area of two bridges over large streams that crossed the highway, the tanks of the panzer regiment encountered strong enemy resistance from motorized infantry, artillery, antitank guns, and light tanks belonging to the Soviet 5 Rifle Division (16 Rifle Corps, 11 Army) and were ordered to halt for the night. It was now 2300 hours, and the forward units of 8 Panzer Division stood 92 kilometers by road from where they had begun their assault at 0305 hours that day (Map 3).[121]

Years later, Manstein recalled the day's successful outcome: "As it turned out—and as we had hoped—the corps had the good fortune to strike a weak patch in the enemy's defenses. Despite repeated enemy counterattacks, some of which entailed hard fighting, the divisions were able to break this resistance relatively quickly."[122] It was, without question, a brilliant day's work for Manstein and his 56 Panzer Corps—a fact also reflected in the surprisingly light casualties—twenty killed in action, sixty-five wounded—sustained by 8 Panzer Division.[123]

Yet for Manstein—and, no doubt, for many *Landser* at the forward edge of battle—the first day's combat had brought the sobering realization that the Russian adversary posed unprecedented challenges:

> On this very first day the Soviet Command showed its true face. Our troops came across a German patrol that had been cut off by the enemy earlier on. All its members were dead and gruesomely mutilated [grauenhaft verstümmelt]. My A.D.C. and I, who often had to pass through sectors of the front that had not been cleared of the enemy, agreed that we would never let an adversary like this capture us alive. Later on there were more than enough cases where Soviet soldiers, after throwing up their hands as if to surrender, reached for their arms as soon as our infantry came near enough, or where Soviet wounded feigned death and then fired on our troops when their backs were turned.[124]

While Manstein's tanks were racing for the Dubyssa gorge, the armored forces of *Gen.d.Pz.Tr.* Reinhardt's 41 Panzer Corps put in their attack on the left wing of 4 Panzer Group. Reinhardt's corps began its assault along a front of about 30 kilometers directly south and southwest of Tauroggen. On the corps' right was *Generalmajor* Ernst von Leyser's 269 Infantry Division; in the center, *Generalmajor* Franz Landgraf's 6 Panzer Division (245 tanks); and on the left, *Generalleutnant* Friedrich Kirchner's 1 Panzer Division (145 tanks) (Map 4).[125] In reserve, below the Neman, was *Generalleutnant* Otto-Ernst Ottenbacher's 36 Motorized Infantry Division.[126]

The initial objectives of Reinhardt's two panzer divisions were extremely ambitious, which was only fitting for the victorious panzer generals of Hitler's *Wehrmacht*. Landgraf's 6 Panzer Division was to break through the enemy border positions in the heavily wooded country south of Tauroggen, advance via Kongayly (Kangailai)—Stegvilai to Raseinai (Rossinie) and, as the day's objective (*Tagesziel*), gain bridgeheads over the Dubyssa River northeast of Raseinai. As expressed in the division's attack order, securing this "*Tagesziel*" was of decisive importance (*von entscheidender Bedeutung*).[127] Kirchner's 1 Panzer Division was to drive northeast across the Jura River, crossing the water obstacle on both sides of Tauroggen; it was then to gain the "big highway" northeast of Tauroggen, before pushing rapidly via Skaudvile (Skaudvila) and Kelme toward the city of Ponjevits, which was "the first objective of the assault."[128] Each of the panzer divisions had gathered its assault units into two main battle groups for the thrust across the frontier. On the panzer corps' right wing, von Leyser's 269 ID was reinforced with a company of tanks from 6 PD.[129]

At 0305 hours, the German artillery, including *Nebelwerfer* Regiment 52 and a battalion of 210mm heavy howitzers, loosed a devastating barrage on Russian positions in and about Tauroggen. Recalled Helmut Ritgen, then a young adjutant in a tank battalion in 11 Panzer Regiment (6 PD), "an artillery preparation of five minutes on known targets [preceded] the infantry attack" (in his division's sector).[130] This is supported by an entry in the journal of 4 Panzer Group, indicating that the attack began with a "short [but] effective" barrage on Tauroggen.[131] Yet as recorded in an official Soviet document (a coded message from 8 Army headquarters), "the enemy's artillery preparation was continuing at 0420 along the 11 Rifle Corps' front, with the shells landing between the forward edge and the defensive zone, with some shells falling on Tauroggen, with the latter burning."[132] The "shock effect" (*Schockwirkung*) of the German barrage was readily apparent when, at 0400, the *Luftwaffe* reported that thirty to forty trucks, loaded with Russian infantry, had been observed fleeing the battlefield along the Tauroggen-Siauliai highway to the northeast.[133]

Following the artillery bombardment, a Fieseler "Storch" liaison plane saw to it that a wooden machine-gun tower outside of Siline was put out of action, after which the assault troops of 6 Panzer Division crossed the frontier south of Tauroggen.[134] Enemy resistance was at first negligible. Within minutes of the start of the attack, 6 Panzer Division was reporting enemy columns—on foot and horse-drawn—in full flight from Tauroggen.[135] Throughout the day, *Luftwaffe* bomber and fighter aircraft would mercilessly assail withdrawing Soviet forces, inflicting serious casualties. Another easy target for General Alfred Keller's 1 Air Fleet (*Luftflotte 1*) were the tens of thousands of Soviet citizens of non-Baltic origin: "soldiers' families, airfield and port construction workers, police and administrators who had been engaged in sovietizing and russifying the new territories, [and who now] flooded the few roads back to the Soviet Union, impeding the movement of Red Army reserves. These would-be colonizers suffered many casualties from German air attack and were sped on their way by the incursions of armed Lithuanians and Latvians."[136]

Along the attack frontage of 41 Panzer Corps, progress was slowed by the bad routes and narrow sandy tracks that intersected the many wooded ravines and gullies; furthermore, from 0400 hours, the German spearheads were reporting serious Russian resistance at Tauroggen, while in the center and on the right flank of Reinhardt's panzer corps, both 6 Panzer Division and 269 Infantry Division were experiencing "spirited" combat as they struggled through the wooded terrain.[137]

Leading the assault of 6 Panzer Division was the battle group of *Obstlt.* Erich *Freiherr* von Seckendorff, based on the division's 114 Rifle Regiment; it attacked through the village of Siline and succeeded in rapidly clearing the road to Kongayly. In the woods east of that town, however, two Russian companies—according to then *Oberst* Erhard Raus, the commander of 6 PD's other battle group—"put up a defense more tenacious than any so far seen in the war." The German infantry would not succeed in annihilating the last of this resistance until mid-afternoon.[138] "As soon as a state of war existed," noted the journal of 6 PD's 6 Rifle Brigade, "Motorcycle Battalion 6 and *Kampfgruppe* Seckendorff began their attack."

> *If the Russians—as was later confirmed by the statements of prisoners—had already evacuated most of their troops from a wide belt [along the frontier], the few who remained there put up considerable resistance. Skillfully concealed in the terrain, they held their position to the last man and literally had to be struck dead [erschlagen] in their fox holes. Because of this resistance, a swift advance was already made more difficult. The advance was also frustrated by the difficult terrain and poor roads. Marshy areas that could not be navigated and unpassable sandy tracks alternated in swift succession.*[139]

Despite the often vigorous—even fanatical—resistance of Soviet border troops, the first impression of Reinhardt's headquarters was that his panzer corps had not encountered well-prepared defenses.[140] In most cases, enemy resistance was quickly broken and, despite the challenges posed by poor roads and unfavorable terrain, the German assault was making good progress. Once again, however, the Russian defenders, although weak in numbers, fought with a doggedness to which the Germans were not accustomed. "Enemy resistance in our sector was much stronger than excepted," remembered Helmut Ritgen (6 PD):

> *Up to six anti-tank ditches in a series had been dug and these were stubbornly held by riflemen supported by snipers in trees. Fortunately no enemy anti-tank guns or mines were in position. Since nobody surrendered, almost no prisoners were taken. Our tanks, however, were soon out of ammunition, a case which had never happened before in either Poland or France. Resupply depended on the arrival of supply trucks that were unable to overtake us as they tried to cope with the traffic jams on the narrow track.*
>
> *On a motorbike I tried to assemble the ammunition trucks. Driving was exciting because of the presence of snipers, which could not be located. Their victims were hit primarily by gun-shots in the head. A few hours later I witnessed an incident, which characterizes the fanaticism of the Soviet soldier. Beyond the forest we were waiting for resupply for at least two hours near a cornfield. Suddenly two Russians jumped out of the field with their hands raised. A sergeant waved to them to come to us. At that*

moment they dodged, while one threw a hand grenade and the other fired a pistol at the sergeant, who was wounded. The Russians must have hidden motionless in this field for three or more hours.[141]

On *Gen.d.Pz.Tr.* Reinhardt's left wing, *Generalleutnant* Kirchner's 1 Panzer Division was beginning its advance on Tauroggen. Kirchner's assault forces were organized into two main battle groups—one led by *Oberst* Franz Westhoven (bulk of reinforced 1 Rifle Regiment; one mixed tank company under *Leutnant* Fromme); the other by *Generalmajor* Walter Kruger (bulk of 113 Rifle Regiment, 1 Panzer Regiment, and one artillery battalion).[142] Both *Kampfgruppen* had crossed the frontier according to plan (*planmässig*) in the wake of the German artillery barrage and registered impressive initial gains, capturing border villages and putting enemy bunkers out of action.[143] Westhoven's group attacked with the reinforced 2nd Battalion, 1 Rifle Regiment (II./S.R. 1) in the vanguard and "advanced against heavy enemy mortar and artillery fire." After routing a force of stubbornly defending Soviet infantry, the battle group reached the Jura River sector near Tauroggen.[144]

On Westhoven's left, *Kampfgruppe* Kruger advanced toward the Jura River with his forces organized into two assault groups. Spearheading the attack, the reinforced 3rd Company of 113 Rifle Regiment (sixteen armored personnel carriers [APCs], two AA-Flak guns [20mm SP], ten Pz III and two Pz IV tanks, and one light 105mm field howitzer battery) crossed the border shortly after 0300 hours, reached the Jura River after a short march, and forced the steep riverbank by way of a newly discovered ford. The initial advance of Kruger's battle group was supported by regimental sappers in the first assault wave who removed masses of Soviet mines; the attackers then smashed their way through wire obstacles covering a row of concrete pillboxes along the first line of fortifications about Tauroggen. The net effect of such actions was to open the way for Kruger's main body.[145] As recorded in the journal of 1 Panzer Division, by 0510 hours, 1st Battalion, 113 Rifle Regiment had encountered heavy enemy resistance along the Jura; about the same time, the tanks of 1 Panzer Regiment were able to ford the river and, in the face of stubborn enemy resistance, slowly gain ground while pressing forward their attack.[146]

By 0600 hours, significant progress had been made across the front of 41 Panzer Corps. On the right wing, 269 Infantry Division was now 12 kilometers north of Wischwill and attacking at Sakalyne (Sakaline),[147] where it fought its way through wooded terrain against Red Army forces in prepared positions; in the center, *Kampfgruppe* Seckendorff (6 PD) had seized intact the bridge over the Sesuvis River at Kongayly, just 4 kilometers south of Tauroggen; on the left wing, *Kampfgruppe* Westhoven (1 PD) was on the outskirts of Tauroggen.[148]

By 0610 hours, 489 Infantry Regiment (269 ID)[149] had seized intact the rail bridge over the Jura south of Tauroggen and, soon thereafter, Westhoven's battle group, in hard and costly fighting, had captured the road bridge over the river (though the Russians had already destroyed it) and built a small bridgehead in the southern environs of Tauroggen. The city was staunchly defended by the Russians, the Germans subjected to increasingly intense enemy artillery fire; soon, the attackers had identified thirteen Soviet artillery batteries in action against them. German forces attacking Tauroggen were also struck repeatedly by Soviet air forces.[150]

Although elements of 1 Panzer Division had pushed through the city by 0815, the bitter fighting there would drag on for hours. The intensity of the combat is captured in this short entry in the 1 PD war diary: "In Tauroggen the fighting is dogged [*hartnäckig*] and house-to-house. The combat style of the enemy is tenacious and cunning [*zäh und hinterlistig*]. Enemy snipers make their appearance. The civilian population is also taking part in the battle."[151] In an effort to crush Soviet resistance inside the city as rapidly as possible, 1 Panzer Division brought forward some of its heavy artillery. At 1130 hours, German units inside the city included 2nd Battalion, 1 Rifle Regiment (Battle Group Westhoven) and 489 Infantry Regiment, which had come to the former's aid. Westhoven, however, soon poured fresh forces into the melee:

> *Fourteen APCs of 1st Battalion, 1 Rifle Regiment, supported by mixed Tank Company Fromme of 1 Panzer Regiment crossed the steep river banks in this sector at about 1300 and forced their way into [Tauroggen] . . . Later in the afternoon strong, stubborn and cunning Russian infantry, fighting with anti-tank guns and light tanks, were thrown back. They defended from house to house and road block to road block, until German assault troops using flamethrowers and demolition charges, cleared the passage.* [152]

At 1445 hours, *Kampfgruppe* Westhoven was on the move again—this time heading for the town of Batakiai (northeast of Tauroggen). At 1600, after 489 Infantry Regiment had cleared out the last enemy pockets in Tauroggen, the city was reported free of the enemy (*feindfrei*). With enemy resistance now tapering off, the division had already transmitted the code word "*Ziethen*" to *Kampfgruppe* Kruger—the signal for it to begin advancing toward the town of Skaudvile (Skaudvila), astride the big highway northeast of Tauroggen.[153]

If Hoepner's 4 Panzer Group had experienced daunting challenges on this first day of the war, they paled in comparison to those faced by Col.-Gen. F. I. Kuznetsov, Commander, Soviet Northwestern Front. From his operational CP at Suboch, he had sought in vain to rally his forces throughout the day, but German air superiority had thwarted any effective countermeasures at the border. With links to forward commands often disrupted (even his command post came under ferocious *Luftwaffe* attack), he had dutifully attempted to implement prepared defense plans, "but given the precipitous and violent German attack, did so in wooden and haphazard fashion."[154] Of particular concern to Kuznetsov were the dangerous penetrations made by the German armored spearheads; in response, he struggled to assemble his 3 and 12 Mechanized Corps for a major counterstroke that would strike the advancing German armor in the flanks and smash it. And yet the reality was that a situation that had begun badly had only continued to deteriorate as the day wore on.[155]

There was very rapid German forward progress, in particular by the armored elements. Lead elements of 8 Panzer Division were already [advancing far to the east] . . . [and] 1 and 6 Panzer Divisions [were] beginning their dash northward to Raseinai. There was a considerable amount of confusion in the Northwestern Front (formerly Baltic Military District) headquarters after the attack began. This confusion reigned throughout the Soviet Union and in all border military districts. Generally the confusion could be characterized first, by disbelief; and second, by conflicting reports from the border areas; and finally, by conflicting orders from higher headquarters. Along the border, units suffered heavy initial losses and issued desperate cries for help, while confusion reigned at army and front *level as commanders sought in vain to obtain guidance from Moscow. Generally the guidance from Moscow at this stage [i.e., in the initial hours of the German attack] was to "do nothing, and do not provoke the Germans." By late evening, the "do not provoke" orders changed into orders "to launch counterattacks and expel the Germans." Of course, at this point, the orders to launch counterattacks were virtually futile.*[156]

The reader will recall that the full weight of the 4 Panzer Group attack had struck the hapless Soviet 125 Rifle Division (11 Rifle Corps, 8 Army) defending along the Tauroggen-Siauliai axis. Throughout the day, the Russians issued situation reports that chronicled the division's uneven struggle against the overwhelmingly superior German forces. In a morning report (0900) prepared for the commander of 8 Army, Lt.-Gen. P. P. Sobennikov, it was noted that the "enemy had occupied Tauroggen," and that the regiments of 125 RD were "falling back under pressure." German intentions were seen as "trying to envelop the 125 Rifle Division along two flanks."[157] An hour later, another report (a telegram to 8 Army headquarters) indicated that "[German] motorized infantry has penetrated to Tauroggen and has been met by our heavy artillery fire." Although a number of key words are missing, the report also noted that *Luftwaffe* attacks had been "unceasing."[158] In a detailed combat report later that day (1800 hours), the 8 Army chief of staff observed (to be sure, too optimistically, but with a partially accurate picture of the German order of battle):

1. The 8 Army forces . . . during the course of 22.6.[41] held off through a stubborn defense an offensive by up to six infantry divisions, three motorized and more than one tank division. The enemy, launching his main attack [along the Tilsit–Siauliai axis], is attempting to encircle the 8 Army's [illegible] . . .

3. On the 11 Rifle Corps' front the enemy captured Tauroggen and is striving to turn the 125 Rifle Division's units from both flanks from Pagramantis and Gavri. There are up to three infantry divisions and two tank regiments opposite the 125 Rifle Division's front.

The 125 Rifle Division is suffering heavy losses and gradually falling back, while putting up stubborn resistance to the enemy. The 48 Rifle Division's left flank is falling back, while holding its position in the center . . .

5. The army's air force bombed Tilsit throughout the day and operated against the enemy's attacking troops opposite the army's front. The enemy air force bombed Siauliai and units of the 48 Rifle Division in consecutive raids throughout the day.[159]

A combat report filed by 11 Rifle Corps—regrettably, there is no time recorded on the document—indicated that the losses of 125 Rifle Division[160] were mounting dangerously: the division's 657 Rifle Regiment had already lost most of its 3rd Battalion, while its 466 Rifle Regiment had forfeited some 40 percent of its combat strength.[161] An entry in the war diary of 1 Panzer Division noted the destruction of fourteen batteries of 125 RD's artillery, with five of the batteries eliminated by the panzer division's tanks.[162] Although some elements of Bogabgun's 125 ID would somehow contrive to avoid annihilation by escaping to the northeast, by the end of the day the division "had already been smashed by the initial [German] attack."[163]

Of course, the example of 125 Rifle Division—perhaps an extreme example because the division had to absorb single-handedly 4 Panzer Group's initial assault—only mirrored what was occurring to Kuznetsov's 8 and 11 Armies at the frontier along the entire length of Northwestern Front. Simply put, their first echelon forces were being surgically taken apart by the unprecedented violence of the German attack both on the ground and through the air.

While the breakup of Northwestern Front's border defenses signified a severe blow to Kuznetsov and his command, it was not nearly so ominous as the much larger threat that loomed over his *front* late on June 22, 1941:

While Kuznetsov planned to block or to chop off the German spearheads, he either did not know or failed to grasp that the bottom of his front was in some danger of falling out. Army Group Center's success against Kuznetsov's 11 Army, which had brought it across the Neman bridges, simultaneously threatened Pavlov's right flank 3 Army (of what was now the Western Front) with a deep outflanking movement. The junction of the Northwestern with the Western Front had already begun to sway ominously.[164]

The above paragraph was written by John Erickson in the 1970s, when Western historians lacked access to key Soviet military documents. While Erickson's analysis is accurate as to the course of events—Army Group Center's 3 Panzer Group had indeed pried open a dangerous gap between Soviet Northwestern and Western Fronts and had begun to envelop the latter's 3 Army—it is wrong about Kuznetsov. As we now know,[165] the commander of Northwestern Front was well aware of the serious danger developing at the junction of the two *fronts*; that evening, in fact, he reported to People's Commissar of Defense Timoshenko that "a gap has opened with the Western Front." The problem was that he "lacked the strength" to do anything about it. In his report to the defense commissar, Kuznetsov also noted the "enemy's absolute air superiority," and that because wire communications had been "cut by the enemy," he was now "maintaining communications with the armies by radio."[166]

By early afternoon, with most enemy resistance broken, the armored columns of Reinhardt's 41 Panzer Corps had begun to wheel northeast toward Raseinai and the Dubyssa River, with surviving Red Army forces withdrawing in the same direction. At this point, 4 Panzer Group headquarters thought it likely that the Russians would attempt a renewed stand west of the Dubyssa.[167] The positions reached by Reinhardt's three attacking divisions by late evening are outlined (from right to left) in the paragraphs below (Map 3).

The lead elements of *Generalmajor* von Leyser's 269 Infantry Division had reached the woods south of Palsaltuonis—east of Tauroggen and about 20 kilometers beyond the border.[168] The division had spent much of the day in difficult combat in wooded areas, and had suffered losses as a result. It should be noted that forest fighting was one area in which most German soldiers had received little, if any, specialized training prior to the start of Operation *Barbarossa*. The Russians, of course, were masters of combat in wooded regions, which functioned as force multipliers for their defending forces. In the opening weeks of the campaign, the Germans would pay a heavy price for this training deficit.[169]

Generalmajor Landgraf's 6 Panzer Division, although by nightfall widely scattered back toward the frontier, had, by late evening, reached the town of Erzvilkas (on the Saltuona River), which was captured by *Kampfgruppe* Seckendorff at 2230 hours.[170] After the forest belt had been cleared (by about noon), the division's progress was "hindered more by the deep sandy track and the lack of supplies than by enemy action. No bridges had been blown up but their low load capacity forced tanks and heavy trucks to ford the streams."[171] As a result, 6 Panzer Division failed to reach its objective for the day, the Dubyssa River crossings northeast of Raseinai. Moreover, the division's other battle group, *Kampfgruppe* Raus, delayed for hours by the difficult terrain and the lack of good roads, never got into action on this day. Raus's battle group did not begin to move forward until late in the morning, its engineers having to locate and slash new routes—including the construction of corduroy roads—through the swampy, heavily wooded belt along the border; by 1900 hours, the head of Raus's column, thick on the heels of Motorcycle Battalion 6 (K6), had only reached Kongayly, some 6 kilometers beyond the frontier.[172] In the fighting on June 22, 6 Panzer Division sustained twenty dead, ninety-two wounded, and two missing.[173]

The battle groups of *Generalleutnant* Kirchner's 1 Panzer Division had advanced about 20 kilometers by the end of the day, with *Kampfgruppe* Westhoven gaining the area about Lapurvis (10 kilometers northeast of Tauroggen, along the highway to Skaudvile). "Here the soldiers took a well-deserved rest . . . ordered by Lt.-Gen. Kirchner, who followed the assault in his command APC, along with Colonel West-hoven's Forward HQ (six APC and four Flak-20mm [SP]). Shortly after, four logistical teams, which were transported by a few APCs, appeared for resupply of gasoline and ammunition. By 0100, our master-sergeants showed up with food, cigarettes and repair teams."[174]

Oberst Westhoven's battle group was soon on the march again, securing the town of Batakiai (south of Skaudvile) and a bridgehead over the Ancia River in the early morning hours of June 23.[175] Because *Luftwaffe* aerial reconnaissance had observed numerous Russian tanks, artillery, and the movement of motorized forces about 40 kilometers southwest of Siauliai, 1 Panzer Division was reinforced late on June 22 with Antitank Battalion 616 (*Pz.Jg.Abt. 616*), hitherto in panzer group reserve. As noted by the war diarist of 4 Panzer Group late on June 22: "It is likely that, in the morning, the first clash with [an enemy] motorized (mechanized) brigade will occur."[176]

While the panzer group had failed to secure all its territorial objectives, its war diary put a positive "spin" on the day's results:

> *In the face of a weak, well camouflaged adversary, who fought with particular tenacity and doggedness [zäh und verbissen] against 41 Panzer Corps, the panzer group has succeeded in breaking through the border defense zone along its entire front . . . In conclusion it can be said of the first day's combat that 4 Panzer Group, despite regrettably high losses, fought quite successfully . . . A breach has been been smashed in the enemy's border defenses. [Das Loch in die feindliche Grenzverteidigung ist geschlagen.][177]*

The panzer group, however, was still unsure of its adversary's ultimate intentions along its front:

> *Aerial reconnaissance this morning [early on June 23] has picked up the movement of tanks heading northeast along the road Jonava-Kedainiai, and motorized forces—which yesterday were detected in the area southwest of Siauliai—advancing to the north, northeast and southeast.*
>
> *Is the enemy pulling back? When will he try to intercept the advance of the panzer group with his strong motorized forces? Will he wait to do so until he has clearly recognized our line of advance?[178]*

In a letter home on June 23, *Generaloberst* Hoepner, the clear-eyed commander of 4 Panzer Group, offered a more sober assessment of the first day of war on the Eastern Front than had his war diarist.

> *Today is already the second day of operations. Yesterday didn't go exactly as I had hoped. The fighting at Tauroggen was quite difficult. Despite the fact that we mounted an enormous fireworks [i.e., the opening barrage], which I myself witnessed from close up, the Russians fought back tenaciously. They were from the Caucasus, and as prisoners they made for an uncivilized[179] impression—yellowish-brown, narrow-eyed; wide, coarse heads, closely shaved; powerful, wiry physiques. Many of them were asleep when our artillery fire began, and were so startled that they only had on a single piece of clothing—a shirt, underwear, or a coat. With the exception of a few houses, the entire city of Tauroggen is burned to the ground. On the other wing of my attack [i.e., by 56 Panzer Corps], it turned out better. There the Dubyssa 70 kilometers beyond the border was reached at two points.[180]*

3.4: EIGHTEENTH ARMY OPERATIONS

German Eighteenth Army (headquarters in Matzicken) was commanded by the sixty-year-old *Generaloberst* Georg von Küchler (in January 1942 he would become commander of Army Group North and, in June 1942, he was promoted to field marshal); his chief of staff was *Oberst i.G.* Hasse.[181] The army consisted of some 120,000 men in seven infantry divisions (three army corps). Forming the army's right wing was 1 Army Corps (1, 11, 21 ID), under the command of *Gen.d.Inf.* Kuno-Hans von Both; on the army's left was 26 Army Corps (61, 217 ID), commanded by *Gen.d.Art.* Albert Wodrig. Anchoring the army's far left flank (and directly controlled by Eighteenth Army) was the strongly reinforced 291 Infantry Division, whose left flank rested on the Baltic shore north of Memel'. The 38 Army Corps (58 ID), commanded by *Gen.d.Inf.* Friedrich-Wilhelm von Chappuis, was in army reserve. Deployed in the sector of Eighteenth Army astride the Neman River was 254 Infantry Division, one of Army Group North's three reserve divisions.[182]

An examination of the General Headquarters troops assigned to Küchler's Eighteenth Army reveals that Both's 1 Army Corps had been earmarked as the *Schwerpunkt* corps of the army:

- Assault Gun Battalion 185 (1 AK)
- 2 105mm cannon battalions (1 each to 1 and 26 AK)
- 3 medium field howitzer battalions (1 AK)
- 1 210mm heavy howitzer battalion (all batteries with 1 AK, except one battery assigned to 291 ID)
- 1 150mm cannon battalion (1 AK)

- 2 rail batteries (1 each to 1 AK and 291 ID)

- 3 army coastal artillery battalions (2 to 291 ID; 1 under direct control of Eighteenth Army headquarters [*z. V. AOK 18*])

- 1 antitank battalion (26 AK; except one platoon *z. V. AOK 18*)

- 1 machine-gun battalion (mot.) (291 ID)

- 1 flak battalion (1 AK, except one company *z. V. AOK 18*)

- 3 flak companies (1 each to 26 AK and 291 ID; 1 *z. V. AOK 18*)

- 1 army flak battalion (mixed) (*z. V. AOK 18*)[183]

Other GHQ units allotted to Eighteenth Army included: two engineer battalions, one bridge-building battalion, six bridge columns "B," six construction battalions, three road-building battalions, and several Organization Todt and Reich Labor Service (RAD) units. *Luftwaffe* units assigned for tactical support included four reconnaissance squadrons: one short-range squadron each to 1 and 26 AK; one *Kette* (flight of three aircraft) of a short-range squadron to 291 ID; one short-range squadron (less one flight) and one long-range (strategic) squadron (3.(F)/22) under direct army control. In addition, three mixed *Luftwaffe* flak battalions were controlled by Eighteenth Army headquarters (*z. V. AOK 18*).[184]

Forming the left (northern) wing of Army Group North, Eighteenth Army was deployed along a front stretching more than 100 kilometers from west of Tauroggen to the coast of the Baltic Sea (Map 2). The basic mission of Küchler's army was to clear the Baltic States of Red Army forces while supporting the left wing of 4 Panzer Group as it pushed along the more direct route to Leningrad. With its main effort on the right (on and east of the main road from Tilsit to Riga, as noted in the deployment directive of the Army High Command), Eighteenth Army was to break through the enemy's border defenses and, in close cooperation with Hoepner's armor,[185] advance to the Dvina River, capture the crossings at Jekabpils (Jakobstadt) and Jaunjelgava (Friedrichstadt), and isolate and destroy Soviet forces remaining west of the Dvina. The ports of Liepaja (Libau) and Ventspils (Windau) were to be secured with minimal expenditure of force, while Riga, the Latvian capital, was to be captured by a flanking maneuver from the east side of the Dvina. Air support was the responsibility of General Keller's 1 Air Fleet, which, for naval targets and sea search and rescue, included an "Air Leader Baltic" (*Fliegerführer Ostsee*).[186]

In the final hours before Operation *Barbarossa* began, commanders across the Eastern Front issued special orders of the day to motivate their troops for the decisive struggle ahead. Preserved in the records of 21 Infantry Division (1 AK) are two of these special orders—the first issued by the commander of 21 ID, *Generalmajor* Otto Sponheimer; the second by 1 Army Corps commander Both. While Sponheimer struck an ideological tone, Both made the (propaganda) point about the putative preemptive nature of the German attack.

21 Infantry Division

Commander

<u>*Soldiers!*</u>

As in years past, the division will attack today at a decisive point. Remembering the great achievements of the division in both East and West I look upon you with great trust. I know that you will fight relentlessly in the days ahead, with bold determination [mit kühner Entschlossenheit] and the most joyous commitment to duty until this enemy is also crushed.

    The war against Russia is similar to the struggle against Poland and France. It must be conducted to achieve final victory in this war that has been forced upon us by England. It is, however, also necessary in order to finally destroy the Jewish and Bolshevik warmongers and firebrands [Kriegshetzer und Brandstifter].

    With this in mind [we fight] for the future of our homeland and for the existence of the German people.

    Forward!

Heil Hitler!
[signed by Sponheimer]
Generalmajor *and Division Commander*[187]

━◆━

The Commanding General of 1 Army Corps　　　　　*21.6.1941*

<u>*Soldiers of the 1 Army Corps!*</u>

The Führer and Commander-in-Chief of the Wehrmacht *had ordered that war be made on Bolshevik Russia.*

    Russia, having already seized parts of Finland and Romania and subjugated the Baltic States against the will of the Führer, *has deployed its entire armed forces along our border. Russia has become a present and continuous danger to the German living space.*

    The German Wehrmacht, *which has everywhere been victorious on land, at sea and in the air, will also smash this enemy and give its very last for* Führer *and Fatherland.*

    We enter this battle, which has been thoroughly prepared by our leadership with all means available, with complete confidence in our abilities and the capabilities of our weapons . . .

I know that the troops subordinated to me will fight with the same courage, and emerge victorious, just as they have done in Poland in 1939 and in France in 1940.

[Signed] von Both
General der Infanterie[188]

The initial waves of the six attacking infantry divisions of *Generaloberst* Georg von Küchler Eighteenth Army crossed the Russo-German frontier shortly after 0300 hours on June 22, 1941.[189] The attack struck the forward battalions of the Soviet 10 and 90 Rifle Divisions (10 Rifle Corps), the right flank of 125 Rifle Division (11 Rifle Corps), and the ubiquitous Soviet border guard detachments. As noted above (Section 3.1), the 10 Rifle Division held a front some 80 kilometers in length, from the Baltic coast north of Palanga running southeast to Svekana; the front of the adjoining 90 Rifle Division was much shorter, extending southeast past Naumiestis and meeting the right flank of 125 Rifle Division west of Tauroggen (Map 2).[190]

Beginning at 0330, the two attacking infantry corps (1, 26 AK) and 291 Infantry Division were reporting to Küchler's headquarters that they had met weak opposition along the border from Russian infantry. Desultory enemy artillery fire had been experienced in some sectors (none in others).[191] The 26 Army Corps reported fighting in the frontier town of Gargzdai (east of Memel') while 291 ID indicated that its advance was being assisted by heavy fog. At 0450, 26 Army Corps reported by telephone that the Minge River bridge at Gargzdai had been captured intact, while a scouting party (*Spähtrupp*) had met more robust enemy resistance at Jarniai. Also at 0450, on the far left flank of Eighteenth Army, 291 ID reported it had pushed through Krottingen (the capture of the town would not be reported until several hours later).[192] Based on these early reports, and the good progress being made, Eighteenth Army headquarters soon formed the opinion that "the enemy, against our expectations, is, in general, only resisting with weak forces directly at the border." Army headquarters also concluded that the enemy had been taken completely by surprise by the German attack.[193]

Attacking on the army's right wing, and supporting the attack of 1 Panzer Division, Sponheimer's 21 Infantry Division was to put in the main effort along the front of Both's 1 Army Corps. The mission of 21 ID was to rapidly break through the Soviet border defenses along the Jeziorupa, a water obstacle—characterized as a "*Bach*," or stream, in German accounts—about 8 kilometers beyond the border and running parallel to it. After crossing the Jeziorupa, the division would have to make its way through the difficult (swampy) terrain of the Bagno Plenoje, before pushing on to the more imposing water obstacle of the Jura River, with its steep banks, roughly 12–15 kilometers beyond the frontier. In the days prior to the start of *Barbarossa*, the Germans had observed the construction of numerous fortifications along the Jura, which cut across the line of advance of 26 Army Corps. After gaining the northern bank of the Jura, 21 ID, pushing on through wooded country northeast of the river, was to take possession of the high ground north and northwest of Upynas.[194]

To carry out its ambitious assignment, Sponheimer's division was reinforced with an artillery staff unit, an additional battalion of artillery (II./AR 37 [mot.]), an army flak battalion (*Heeres-Fla-Btl. 605*), and a battery of assault guns (*3./Stug-Abt. 185*). The division planned to attack with two regiments in front (45 IR right, and 24 IR left) with the main effort (*Schwerpunkt*) on the left; more specifically, 45 Infantry Regiment was to advance on Prismantai and 24 Infantry Regiment on Zygaiciai. In addition to these actions, an advance detachment of the division (reconnaissance troops, antitank guns, and an artillery battery) led by *Obstlt*. Matussik and operating inside the left boundary of 4 Panzer Group, was to advance directly behind the spearheads of 1 Panzer Division; after crossing the Jura, it was to wheel westward and hold open the Jura bridges at and south of Pagramantis for the advancing 21 Infantry Division. The division's 3 Infantry Regiment, initially in reserve, was to follow behind 24 IR.[195]

By 0200 hours, the assault parties of 21 Infantry Division, huddled in their attack assembly areas, were ready for combat. At precisely 0305 hours, the rumble of artillery fire out of the east—4 Panzer Group bombarding Tauroggen—announced the start of Operation *Barbarossa*. With but a sorely incomplete picture of the enemy forces at the border,[196] Sponheimer's infantry moved out to attack without a systematic (*planmässig*) artillery preparation. The battalions of 21 ID crossed the *Reichsgrenze* along an 8-kilometer front without encountering serious enemy resistance. After several hours, the initial objective was reached and elements of the division were now north of the Aukstupiai-Zygaiciai road. Then the movement of the division slowed dramatically as the regiments struggled to navigate the almost primordial thickets of the swampy woodlands of the Bagno Plenoje.[197] Somewhat earlier, at 0520, 1 Army Corps reported that its divisions had advanced an average of 3 to 4 kilometers beyond the border, and that the town of Naumiestis—where the Russian defenders had fought to the last man (*bis zum letzten*) in the cellars of the houses[198]—had been captured by 11 Infantry Division. Meanwhile, Both's 1 Infantry Division (21 ID's neighbor on the left) had struck the seam between the Soviet 90 and 125 Rifle Divisions and swiftly gained ground.[199]

On the left flank of Eighteenth Army, *Generalleutnant* Siegfried Haenicke's 61 Infantry Division (26 AK) was to breach the enemy border defenses between Picktassen and Liewern and then drive northeast, past Varniai and Lake Plinsker, in the direction of Telsche. Earmarked to lead the division's attack was its 151 Infantry Regiment, which was to pave the way for the rest of the division; after gaining the hills around Girininkai, an advance detachment (*Vorausabteilung* Clausen) was to be sent forward to conduct reconnaissance. On 151 IR's left, 176 Infantry Regiment was to seize the bridge over the Minge River at Gargzdai in a sudden attack (*handstreichartig*), while also taking possession of the border village.[200]

The troops of 61 Infantry Division launched their assault from an assembly area astride the East Prussian town of Schnaugsten (southeast of Memel'). While 151 Infantry Regiment made rapid progress,[201] the fighting for Gargzdai was intense and resulted in serious German casualties.

The powerful barrage soon fell silent. The enemy could not be made out in the thick ground fog. Resistance was negligible. When the fog lifted about 0500 hours, the forwardmost elements of the division were already three kilometers beyond the border. Scattered enemy forces and snipers [Baumschützen] with automatic weapons harried the German troops, but could in no way slow down the rapid advance. At 0730, the hills east of Girininkai were reached. The advance continued through forested and marshy meadows in the face of negligible enemy resistance. Humble straw cottages, rutted marshy pathways, and large boulders on the sandy fields reminded one of a primeval landscape. Recently prepared roadways and concrete bunkers still under construction offered a picture of the military preparations that were underway here. Following the capture of the Minge bridge by Kampfgruppe Bülow,[202] the bulk of 176 Infantry Regiment pressed into the tenaciously defended town of Gargzdai, where it sustained serious losses. Lt. Dreyer (I./IR 176), Lt. Friebe (9./IR 176), Lt. Wandelt (10./IR 176), Oblt. Eisenblätter (11./IR 176), Lt. Hannemann and Lt. Penner (6./IR 176) were killed in action.[203]

(Note: According to reports of German troops who fought in Gargzdai, a number of the civilians there also took up arms against the invaders; as a result, a police action took place that resulted in the execution of some of the town's people. The incident became the subject of a criminal trial in Ulm, Germany, in 1958. During the trial it was determined that no members of the combat troops [*Angehörige der kämpfenden Truppe*] had taken part in the executions.)[204]

Attacking on the far left (northern) flank of Eighteenth Army, directly on the Baltic coast, was *Generalleutnant* Kurt Herzog's reinforced 291 Infantry Division, whose tactical sign was the elk's head in honor of its Masurian homeland.[205] For centuries the Masurian region, with its beautiful lakes and rivers, had served as a base for the Teutonic Knights and their impregnable fortresses, while the Great War had seen major battles in the region (1914/15). Now, once again, Teutonic invaders from Masuria were conducting a *Drang nach Osten* (drive to the east)—this time in an effort to destroy Soviet Russia and the hated Bolshevik enemy.

On the morning of June 22, the infantry and combat engineers of 291 ID's three attacking regiments (504, 505, 506 IR) traversed the border and cautiously felt their way through a miasma of thick ground fog causing conditions of zero visibility.[206] A combat report (*Gefechtsbericht*) prepared in July 1941 by 504 Infantry Regiment vividly re-created the opening minutes of the attack:

The morning of 22 June 1941 has dawned bright and early and brings the unpleasant surprise of a completely impenetrable ground fog. The minutes move by faster than we would like toward the "X" time, and our hopes for better visibility—right up to the time of attack—are all for naught. Support of the attacking infantry by artillery observers is thus ruled out.

0305: "X"-Time

A profound silence holds the fog-covered landscape in its grip. [Suddenly] the strident crack of two antitank shells ruptures the morning peace and is the signal to unleash the rolling fire of our artillery. Right on target, the antitank shells strike the housing of the Russian observation tower south of Krottingen. At the same time, the attacking infantry are set in motion. The armored train, hissing and steaming, discharges great clouds of smoke and rumbles right on past the regimental command post; it then stops, according to plan, in front of the railway station Bajohren, from where it is to first take out the water tower in Krottingen—which is most likely an enemy observation post—with the fire of its two 75mm cannon.

The tension that holds sway at the regimental CP is unbearable. Tak, tak, tak—the sound of sporadic machine-gun fire. Will everything go as planned and as it's been ordered? The fog prevents one from seeing anything. All of the observation posts [B-Stellen] for the artillery, which were built among the trees with so much effort, were built for naught.

About 0310 a telephone call from Assault Detachment von Bistram brings the relief we've all been waiting for: "The first objective of the attack on the southern edge of Krottingen, beyond the customs house . . . along the road has been reached. Weak enemy resistance broken."[207]

Their movements concealed by the dense fog, the assault troops of 291 ID advanced according to plan and, at 0342 hours, the division reported to Eighteenth Army that opposition was so far negligible. At 0344, Artillery Commander 104 (*Arko 104*) reported that 505 Infantry Regiment had reached the ravine at the western bank of the Tenza, 500 meters beyond the frontier, and that the western fringe of Krottingen was on fire. Minutes later 504 IR observed that there was still no visibility, but that ground signals (*Leuchtzeichen*) indicated that the troops were advancing *"planmässig."* Meanwhile, a flight of short-range reconnaissance aircraft (2.(H)/21) aborted its mission due to the thick ground fog.[208]

While the border towns of Krottingen and Palanga gradually went up in flames—victims of the German artillery fire plan—an advance detachment of 505 Infantry Regiment, led by the regimental commander, *Oberst* Karl Lohmeyer, was soon racing ahead. It promptly broke through the forward line of pillboxes of a startled Soviet border position whose defenders, under cover of the ground fog, sought to pull back quickly. The relentless Lohmeyer gave them no respite, beginning an extraordinary advance that, by nightfall, would take him and his men all the way to the Latvian-Lithuanian frontier.[209] Yet that was still hours away and, in the meantime, the division had some difficult fighting to do. Indeed, at both Krottingen and Palanga the 291 ID met strong opposition; at 0825, however, the division reported the capture of Krottingen (after street battles in the town), and that 505 IR was closing on Darbenai about 15 kilometers from the frontier, while Palanga was still occupied by the enemy.[210]

As the morning went on, reports from the front continued to flow in to the headquarters of Küchler's Eighteenth Army. At 0830 hours, 26 Army Corps reported on the latest developments in the sectors of its 217 and 61 Infantry Divisions, citing progress along the front of each division. Fifteen minutes later, *Oberst i.G.* von Kries, Chief of Staff, 1 Army Corps, reported that, at 0820, advance elements of Sponheimer's 21 Infantry Division had reached the Jura River near Didkiemis; the overall impression of 1 Army Corps was that the enemy's main forces had yet to commit to battle. At 1000 hours, the war diary of Army Group North recorded the capture of Darbenai and Palanga by 291 ID, and that in Palanga ten enemy planes had been captured intact. Conversely, as the hours passed, it became apparent that Russian resistance was becoming particularly robust in the combat sector of 1 Panzer Division (4 Panzer Group), and that this was adversely affecting the operations of the Eighteenth Army's right wing (21 ID).[211]

By late morning, the overwhelming weight of Küchler's attack against the relatively weak Russian border defenses was taking its toll. At 0930, in a "personal note for the commander of 8 Army," Maj.-Gen. I. F. Nikolaev, Commander, 10 Rifle Corps, lodged a plea for assistance:

To the commander of the 8 Army.

The enemy, in strength up to a regiment, broke through the front in the direction of the village of Jakuliai, 6 kilometers east of Varnaiciai and is developing the attack on height 147.4 (south of the village of Kuliai).

The 204 Rifle Regiment's 2nd Battalion and the 140 Howitzer Regiment's 1st Battalion are fighting in encirclement and the 62 Rifle Regiment's 1st Battalion is in danger of being encircled. On the right flank, the enemy, in strength of up to 2 [illegible] is developing the attack west of Kretinga to the north.

The 10 Rifle Division's situation is difficult . . . I don't have any real strength. I need serious aid.[212]

A summary of operations of Eighteenth Army through December 1941, prepared by the army's operations branch (Ia), began with the following observations about the first day of war on the Eastern Front:

During the day, the enemy picture was clarified to the extent that the army command came around to the view that the fighting so far has only been against the enemy's rearguards [Nachhuten]. Where the bulk of the enemy forces were located (according to statements of prisoners and local civilians they were pulled back [from the border] beginning on 18 June) could not even be satisfactorily clarified by aerial reconnaissance, which had been carried out as far as the Dubyssa–Venta line.[213]

This situation assessment must have taken shape by midday. At 1135 hours, the chiefs of staff of Army Group North and Eighteenth Army engaged in candid discussion about the events of the first eight-and-a-half hours. The army chief of staff, *Oberst i.G.* Hasse, told his counterpart that he believed the main enemy forces (*aktive Truppen*) had indeed been at the frontier (*dass sie da waren*), only to be withdrawn in the days immediately preceding the German attack. *Oberst* Hasse's assessment was shared by GFM von Leeb and others; in fact, despite the heavy fighting that took place at many points along the border, a consensus of sorts seems to have emerged among the Germans that the enemy was only fighting a rearguard action on June 22, while his main forces had been withdrawn at the last moment. The weak Russian troops at the border; the fact that many fortified positions were not well defended (or defended at all); and, of course, the statements of POWs and civilians alike—all contributed to this viewpoint shared by many top German field commanders. And while it was clear that Russian forces at the border were caught napping by the German attack,[214] it was not clear that the same could be said of the Soviet military leadership.[215]

By midday, Eighteenth Army was reporting that its divisions had everywhere advanced 8 to 10 kilometers beyond the border against light enemy resistance.[216] At 1220, the operations officer for 1 Army Corps, *Major i.G.* Weber, reported to army headquarters that a regiment of 11 Infantry Division had already (1030) crossed the Jura River at Zwingiai, although the bridges there were destroyed.[217] As noted above, the forwardmost elements of 21 Infantry Division had reached the river earlier that morning, but, as expected, enemy resistance stiffened along the river line and the division was brought to a temporary standstill. Russian defenses along the Jura included concrete emplacements; many of them, however, were still under construction, and the Russian defenders did not possess a large number of heavy weapons. That said, the geography of the river itself provided the Russians with an eminently defensible position, while posing a serious obstacle to the attackers. The Germans, moreover, consigned to the sandy tracks through the heavily wooded terrain south of the Jura, struggled to bring their artillery forward; the situation by 21 Infantry Division was so bad that some of its artillery was temporarily immobilized.[218] Further complicating matters was the fact that enemy resistance about Tauroggen had delayed the mission of the advance detachment commanded by *Obstlt.* Matussik.[219]

Despite such challenges, during the afternoon and evening elements of both 1 and 11 Infantry Divisions were able to cross the Jura. Facing fewer terrain obstacles than 21 ID, and exploiting a weak spot in the Russian river defenses, a regiment (22 IR) of 1 ID traversed the river at 1210 hours.[220] The last to cross was 21 Infantry Division, which, building on the success of its neighbor on the left (1 ID), managed to get over the Jura by about 2000 hours, but not before assembling and attacking with all three of its regiments; by dusk, the division's 3 Infantry Regiment had established a 2-kilometer-deep bridgehead across the river at Didkiemis.[221]

In the sector of Wodrig's 26 Army Corps, 61 Infantry Division, pushing aside light enemy resistance, continued to make good progress;[222] however, a battalion of its 176 Infantry Regiment (III./IR 176) was still locked in bitter house-to-house fighting in the border town of Gargzdai. As noted in the journal of 61 ID, "every house had been made into a bunker," and each one had to be taken in deadly close combat. The situation at Gargzdai must have caused Wodrig some anxiety, for at 1300 both he and his chief of staff drove out to the battlefield there for a firsthand look.[223] Yet by 1330, the town had been secured, and the division could report that it had "broken through the enemy border positions along its entire front. The attack to gain our day's objective [*Tagesziel*] can now continue."[224]

The advance of 61 Infantry Division continued throughout the afternoon without further incident, and by 1710, 151 Infantry Regiment, without making contact with the enemy, had reached its day's objective—the high ground beyond Girininkai (Hill 147).[225] At 2100, 162 Infantry Regiment reported that it too had reached its *Tagesziel*—the high ground northwest of Zadeikiai. In fact, all of the division's regiments and independent detachments had gained their objectives. Despite the division's success, the final entry in its diary for June 22 (2300) struck a cautionary note: "While the division has reached all its assigned objectives, the difficult battles of this first day still offered a foretaste [*Vorgeschmack*] of what's to come."[226]

Meanwhile, with *Oberst* Lohmeyer at the helm, the advance detachment of 505 Infantry Regiment (291 ID) was continuing its lightning strike across Lithuania toward Latvia. Before noon, it had pushed aside the Soviet 67 Rifle Division and stormed northward, paying no attention to its flanks or rear. Field Marshal von Leeb, no doubt tracking Lohmeyer's progress with great interest, noted in his diary at 1830 that the advance detachment of 505 IR was approaching Skuodas.[227] Two hours later, 291 Infantry Division reported the capture of the town,[228] its advance detachment having reached the Lithuanian-Latvian frontier. Lohmeyer's startling achievement was briefly summarized in a report prepared by Army Group North:

At the head of his regiment, Oberst *Lohmeyer (Commander, 505 Infantry Regiment), after breaking through a defended, fortified field position, conducted a relentless pursuit [of the enemy] and within 16 hours had advanced 65 kilometers, taken Darbenai in combat, and subsequently gained a bridgehead north of Skuodas.*[229]

To follow up this stunning success, the impetuous commander of 291 Infantry Division, *Generalleutnant* Herzog, hoped to continue the advance by striking quickly toward the port of Liepaja (Libau). At this point, however, the chief of staff of Eighteenth Army gently intervened and counseled caution—the division should first clarify the situation on its flank, which only meant that it should moderate (*mässigen*) the tempo of its advance, not stop it.[230]

Before concluding this account of the operations of Eighteenth Army on *Barbarossa-tag*, we should again examine the situation as it appeared on the "Other Side of the Hill," that is, to the Russians. At 1800 hours, the chief of staff of Lt.-Gen. P. P. Sobennikov's 8 Army signed the following combat report (excerpts only):

2. The 10 Rifle Corps is fighting along its main defensive line.

A. Units of the 10 Rifle Corps abandoned Palanga, Kretinga, Kartena, and Vezaiciai. Up to two enemy infantry divisions are attacking opposite the front. The enemy's main efforts are being aimed along the following axes: Kartena and Kuliai. By 1000 the enemy had managed to penetrate along the boundary of the 1st and 2nd battalions of the 204 Rifle Regiment and capture Iekule. The 204 Rifle Regiment's 2nd Battalion and the 140 Howitzer Regiment's 1st Battalion are fighting in encirclement. Elements of the 204 Rifle Regiment were fighting stolidly and have suffered significant losses, which are being determined. [Handwritten note in red:] As a result of stubborn fighting, the 204 Rifle Regiment broke out of the encirclement.[231]

B. Along the 90 Rifle Division's[232] *sector the enemy reached the Jura River at 0730. The division's units were holding the forward edge of the main defensive zone. Up to two infantry divisions and one tank regiment are operating along the division's front, as well as motorized units. A large concentration of tanks and motorcyclists has been established in the following areas: the woods south of Didkiemis; in the Trinapolis area (3 km southwest of Pagramantis). At 1500 in the Kamsciai-Didkiemis area the enemy, in strength up to an infantry regiment, managed to break through the forward edge in the direction of Silale.*[233]

By the time most combat operations had come to an end on this first day of the war, the attacking divisions of *Generaloberst* von Küchler's Eighteenth Army had all made respectable, if not dramatic gains—the exception of course being the 65-kilometer odyssey of the advance detachment of 291 Infantry Division on the army's far left wing. All three divisions (1, 11, 21 ID) of General von Both's 1 Army Corps had established bridgeheads across the Jura River, while registering gains of about 20 (21 ID), 20 (1 ID), and 25 kilometers (11 ID), respectively.[234] As noted by the war diarist of 11 Infantry Division: "The day was hot and sunny. For many soldiers of the division it was their baptism of fire [*Feuertaufe*]. Troop morale is excellent, and their attitude radiates confidence and a spirit of attack."[235]

In the sector of Wodrig's 26 Army Corps, both 61 and 217 Infantry Divisions had advanced roughly 20 kilometers beyond the frontier—217 ID to Endriejavas and 61 ID past Gargzdai on the east and approaching the town of Kuliai (Map 3). To close the gap that had opened up between Both's 1 and Wodrig's 26 Army Corps, Küchler ordered 58 Infantry Division (38 Army Corps) forward,[236] while 254 Infantry Division (Army Group North reserve) was crossing the Russo-German border (by 2300 hours) and moving up behind the right wing of 1 Army Corps.[237]

3.5: *ABENDLAGE:* PRÉCIS OF THE COMBAT ACTIONS OF ARMY GROUP NORTH

At dawn on June 22, 1941, GFM Ritter von Leeb's Army Group North launched its attack along a front of almost 300 kilometers with—from right to left—Sixteenth Army, 4 Panzer Group, and Eighteenth Army. The first attack wave was made up of eighteen divisions—fifteen infantry and three panzer divisions. Enemy resistance was at first desultory to nonexistent, only to increase as the day wore on and the shock of invasion wore off. Exploiting the advantage of surprise, the army group managed to seize virtually every bridge intact, while the attacking divisions registered gains of at least 15–20 kilometers by the end of the day—the most noteworthy advances having been made by 4 Panzer Group's 8 Panzer Division (90 kilometers) and Eighteenth Army's 291 Infantry Division (65 kilometers). Despite the overall success of Leeb's army group, casualties had sometimes been heavy, with serious fighting taking place at Kybartai (Sixteenth Army), Tauroggen (4 Panzer Group), Gargzdai (Eighteenth Army), and other locations along the frontier. Entries in German war diaries reveal that the invaders quickly became aware that the Russians often fought tenaciously—even fanatically—and that the war on the Eastern Front would pose a more formidable challenge than the campaigns in Poland, France, and the Balkans.

As the initial hours of Operation *Barbarossa* passed by, GFM von Leeb and his top field commanders soon concluded that they were mainly fighting Soviet border guard units and Red Army rearguards, while the main Soviet forces seemed to have withdrawn from the frontier even before the start of the attack. This was a disappointment to the field marshal and his lieutenants,[238] and made it imperative that the German advance go forward at breakneck speed in the days ahead to cut off and destroy Soviet forces before they could reach the protective barrier of the Dvina River. The achievement of this objective would depend largely on the operations of Hoepner's panzer group.

At 1915 hours on June 22, Leeb offered this assessment of the first day's action along the front of Army Group North:

Along the entire front of the army group, the enemy did not have strong forces at the border, but apparently only rearguards. There is no clarity concerning the whereabouts of his main forces. As a result, our armies, despite enemy resistance and terrain difficulties (road conditions) are far out in front. In general the enemy does not appear to have been surprised [by our attack], because he has evidently pulled back the bulk of his forces. On the other hand, it seems that here and there he was taken by surprise locally [örtlich] due to the early hour of the attack. It is particularly significant [besonders bedeutungsvoll] that 4 Panzer Group, despite tenacious Russian resistance at Tauroggen, has already succeeded today in advancing to the Jura and capturing intact the bridges across the Dubyssa at Seredzius and Ariogala, so that tomorrow we can count on a further rapid advance toward the east.[239]

Field Marshal von Leeb's Soviet counterpart, Col.-Gen. F. I. Kuznetsov, Commander, Northwestern Front, did his best to respond to the imposing power and violence of the German attack but found himself thwarted at every turn. With his communications in tatters and his forces under relentless attack from the air, confusion reigned as he sought without success to rally the troops and to implement his prepared defense plans. The greatest threat, he fully understood, was posed by the rapidly advancing German armored spearheads, and he needed to find a way to stop and defeat them. Yet the counterattack plans he drew up for his two mechanized corps bore no relationship to the reality of the rapidly changing situation at the front. Making matters worse, and significantly so, was the success of German Army Group Center, whose deep penetrations on its left wing threatened to tear apart the junction of Northwestern and Western Front.

On June 24, 1941, Kuznetsov would finally launch his tanks—including the super heavy KV models, which administered an adrenal shock to the German invaders—against the advancing armor of Reinhardt's 41 Panzer Corps at Raseinai. In the ensuing two-day engagement, the Russian mechanized forces would be cut to pieces, forcing the two shattered armies of Northwestern Front to withdraw in disorder toward the Dvina River. Kuznetsov "had clearly lost control." On July 4, 1941, he was dismissed by the Soviet High Command and replaced by Lt.-Gen. Sobennikov, the former 8 Army commander.[240] Yet unlike the tragic General D. G. Pavlov of Western Front, Kuznetsov went on to hold other major commands throughout the war. Indeed, within a few weeks of being dismissed from Northwestern Front, he assumed command of the newly formed Central Front (July–August 1941); before the end of 1941, he was also assigned to several army commands and served as deputy commander of Western Front. During the course of his military career, Kuznetsov would be decorated with two Orders of Lenin, three Orders of the Red Banner, the Order of Suvorov 2nd Class, the Order of the Red Star, and other honors.[241]

CHAPTER 4

Armageddon Unleashed (II)—
Army Group Center Goes to War

At exactly 0310 on 22 June 1941 we were ready to fire. Somewhat restively I followed the minute and second hands of my watch until the firing order came. At 0315 a lightning bolt of gigantic dimensions tore through the night. Thousands of artillery pieces shattered the silence. I will never forget those seconds. But just what they signified for the world, for Germany—that was beyond comprehension.

—*Leutnant* Heinz Döll, 18 Panzer Division[1]

[Early that morning] the artillery preparation began. It roared and thundered as if the world was going under and then, at 0400, the firing ceased and the attack got underway. The enemy was certainly knocked on his heels by the force of the attack, but with what doggedness did these Russian soldiers fight! Of course we had the bad luck on this first day to encounter Stalin cadets. They were aspiring officers and political officers [Politruks] who refused to surrender. Rather they fought to the last man and had to be formally beaten or shot to death in their rifle pits. The nature of the war had fundamentally changed, and it was alien to us.

—NCO Fritz Hübner, opposite the town of Belostok[2]

To the commander of the Western Special Military District. I report: At 0315 on 22.6. the enemy began to shell the fortress of Brest and the area of the city of Brest. The enemy simultaneously began to bomb the Brest, Kobrin and Pruzhany airfields. By 0500 the artillery shelling had increased in the Brest area. The city is on fire. The 42, 6 and 75 Rifle Divisions and the 22 and 30 Tank Divisions are moving to their areas; there is no information on the 49 Rifle Division. I have no information as of 0530 of the enemy forcing the Western Bug River . . . The 22 Tank Division is moving to its area in disorder under artillery fire.

—Lt.-Gen. A. A. Korobkov, Commander, Soviet 4 Army[3]

⌐⌐

Field Marshal Fedor von Bock, the sixty-year-old commander of Army Group Center, was born in Küstrin (now Kostrzyn, Poland), a fortress city astride the Oder River in the province of Brandenburg. His father, General Karl Moritz von Bock, had commanded a division during the Franco-Prussian War; his mother, Baroness Olga Helene von Falkenhayn von Bock, was related to General Erich von Falkenhayn, a former chief of the Imperial German General Staff (*Oberste Heeresleitung*). As a child, Bock "yearned for a career in the army." Educated at the Potsdam Cadet School and the Gross Lichtefelde Military Academy, he "grew into a strong-willed, efficient, and arrogant young man. Although not brilliant, he became an excellent tactician and a good linguist, being fluent in French and fair in Russian and English. He was a fanatical soldier who, in later years, often lectured his men on how it was an honor to die for the Fatherland." Due to his steadfast patriotism and unbending will, he received the sobriquet "the Holy Fire of Küstrin."[4] Simply put, Fedor von Bock became a man for whom the military was his entire world—a man who was so consumed by his military life that he looked upon the civilian world with contempt.

In March 1898, at the age of seventeen, he passed the selection board and was commissioned as a second-lieutenant with the 5 Foot Guards Regiment in Berlin-Spandau. Effective September 10, 1908, he was promoted to first lieutenant (*Oberleutnant*). From 1910 to 1912 he took part in General Staff training and was promoted to captain (*Hauptmann*) in March 1912. During this period, he joined the Army League, where he first had contact with several of the future Third Reich's top military leaders—Brauchitsch, Halder, and Rundstedt. During World War I, the future field marshal saw action on both the Western and Eastern Fronts, doing duty in General Staff positions and as a battalion commander in the field. He proved to be a fearless leader of men, and was awarded the Iron Cross, First and Second Class, the Order of the House of Hohenzollern and, in April 1918, the coveted *Pour le Mérite*. He ended the war as a major.[5]

After the war, as one of Imperial Germany's finest soldiers, Bock was absorbed into the 100,000-man *Reichswehr*. Throughout the next decade and beyond he held important staff positions and field commands, attaining the rank of *Generalleutnant* in 1931. In 1933, when Hitler seized power, he commanded Military District 2 (*Wehrkreis 2*), headquartered in Stettin.[6] While much has been written about Bock's attitude toward Hitler and National Socialism, suffice it to say that Bock was never a Nazi; in fact, during the war in Russia, he even tolerated the presence of a large anti-Hitler cabal among his top staff officers. On the other hand, he was much too cautious, vain, and ambitious to ever make common cause with the military resistance. Moreover, it appears that he—like many politically conservative German generals—was captivated by the *Führer*'s dramatic successes during the 1930s and early years of the war.

Bock's rise in stature continued throughout the mid- and late 1930s. In 1935, he was promoted to *General der Infanterie* (Lt.-Gen.). During the *Anschluss* in March 1938, he marched into Austria at the head of Eighth Army and was promoted to *Generaloberst* (full general). By now, Hitler was beginning to notice Bock, who made a favorable impression on Germany's dictator; conversely, he was not an easy man to work with and could be hard on subordinates. As a man, history has judged him harshly: "Arrogant and cold-blooded, Bock's humorless, vain, inflexible, and irritating personality earned him many enemies, both in the Army and in the Party."[7]

Having played an integral part in operational planning for the attack on Poland, Bock was given command of Army Group North for the campaign, which began on September 1, 1939, and unleashed the Second World War. In this initial demonstration of *Blitzkrieg*, he evinced a mastery of fast-moving operations and the control of large formations. For his part in the campaign, Bock was one of the first to be awarded the Knight's Cross. In October 1939, he was transferred to the Western Front, his army group now renamed Army Group B. With this army group he participated in the French campaign of 1940, albeit in a secondary role. He was, however, given the honor of reviewing the military parade through Paris on June 14, 1940, at the Arc de Triomphe, and was among the twelve German generals promoted by Hitler to *Feldmarschall* on July 19, 1940. In October 1940, Bock's headquarters was transferred to Poland, where it orchestrated the buildup of German forces in the East. Perhaps a reflection of the *Führer's* favor, Bock was selected to command Army Group Center—the largest and most important of the three army groups—for Operation *Barbarossa*.[8]

Facing Field Marshal von Bock across the Bug River in Poland was the forty-four-year-old Army-General D. G. Pavlov, the commander of the Western Special Military District (renamed Western Front upon the outbreak of war). Pavlov had served in the Czarist army since 1914 and fought in World War I as a senior NCO. He joined the Red Army in 1919, commanded a platoon and cavalry squadron, and was an assistant commander of a cavalry regiment on various fronts. He completed the Omsk Higher Cavalry School in 1922 and the Frunze Military Academy in 1928. From 1928 he commanded cavalry and mechanized regiments. Pavlov took part in the fighting along the Chinese Eastern Railway in 1929 and completed academic courses with the Military-Technical Academy. From 1934 to 1936 he was commander-commissar of a mechanized brigade; and, in 1936 and 1937, he led a tank brigade in Spain during that country's civil war, for which he was made one of the first "Heroes of the Soviet Union." In November 1937 Pavlov was appointed chief of the RKKA[9] Armor and Tank Directorate. During the Winter War with Finland (1939/40), Pavlov "led one of Timoshenko's corps in a daring march across the frozen Vyborg Bay to outflank the defenses of the Mannerheim Line, an action that forced the Finns to make peace. By prewar (and post-purge) standards Pavlov was well trained." In June 1940 he was named head of the Belorussian (Western) Special Military District and promoted to General of the Army in 1941.[10]

Beginning on June 22, 1941, Army-General Pavlov would struggle desperately with his poorly prepared forces to halt the advance of Bock's powerful Army Group Center, only to see his frontier armies surrounded and annihilated. With an enraged Stalin demanding a scapegoat, Pavlov was accused of cowardice, a lack of initiative, indecisiveness, and of actively trying to disrupt troop control. He was removed from his post and arrested (June 30) and executed on July 28, 1941. Pavlov was posthumously rehabilitated in 1957. For his military service, Pavlov was awarded three Orders of Lenin and two Orders of the Red Banner.[11]

"We can only speculate," opined historian Evan Mawdsley, "what kind of 'war' Pavlov would have had, had he been stationed somewhere else. Like Zhukov, he had been an example of the kind of brave, energetic, youthful—and ruthless—middle-level leader that Stalin liked to pick out and promote. Pavlov was probably no better and no worse than the other generals commanding army groups and armies on the western frontier in June 1941."[12]

4.1: OPPOSING FORCES AND BATTLE PLANS (CENTRAL AXIS)

The largest of the *Ostheer*'s three army groups, Army Group Center (headquarters at Rembertov)[13] was composed of 50.5 divisions (thirty-one infantry, nine panzer, six-and-a-half motorized infantry, three security divisions, and one cavalry division), organized largely into two infantry armies (Fourth and Ninth Armies) and two panzer groups (2 and 3 Panzer Groups);[14] total personnel (including GHQ troops) amounted to 1,308,730 men. Led by Heinz Guderian (2 Panzer Group) and Hermann Hoth (3 Panzer Group), the two panzer groups possessed collectively more than 1,900 tanks, considerably more than the other two army groups combined. While Bock had only one division in army group reserve (293 ID), six infantry divisions of the OKH reserve were in transport and earmarked to arrive by July 4, 1941.[15] The army group's impressive lineup of GHQ troops included:

- 22 artillery commanders (*Arko*)
- 17 artillery regimental staffs
- 6 assault guns battalions (of the 11 on the Eastern Front)
- 15 105mm cannon battalions
- 16 150mm medium howitzer battalions
- 5 mixed artillery battalions
- 17 210mm heavy howitzer battalions (10 motorized; 7 with "limited mobility")
- 3 150mm cannon battalions
- 3 305mm heavy howitzer battalions for high angle fire (*Steilfeuer*)
- 2 heavy artillery battalions (210mm and 240mm) for flat trajectory fire (*Flachfeuer*)
- 4 *Nebelwerfer* rocket projector battalions

- 2 *Nebelwerfer* regiments
- 2 decontamination battalions (*Entg.Abt.*)
- 1 machine-gun battalion (mot.)
- 6 antitank battalions
- 9 flak battalions (5 *Fla* and 4 *Heeres Flak Abt.*)[16]
- 9 flak (*Fla*) companies
- 2 flamethrower (*Flammenwerfer*) tank battalions (*Pz.Abt.Flamm.*)
- 4 batteries 280mm "K5" heavy rail-borne artillery[17]
- 1 battery 600mm "*Karl*" heavy rail-borne artillery[18]

All told, Army Group Center would begin the Russian campaign with 750 batteries of artillery,[19] including the super-heavy, rail-borne artillery (eight "K5" and two type "*Karl*" guns). Additional GHQ resources in the army group's order of battle included twenty-three engineer battalions; twelve bridge-building battalions, seventy-four bridge columns "B," thirty-five construction battalions, and eleven battalions for road construction and repair. The army group was also supported by the Organization Todt and the Reich Labor Service (*Reichsarbeitsdienst*).[20] *Luftwaffe* units assigned for tactical support included short- and long-range (strategic) reconnaissance squadrons,[21] as well as a generous allocation of light and mixed flak battalions.

The vast armada of men and machines that made up GFM von Bock's powerful army group was supported by GFM Albert Kesselring's 2 Air Fleet (*Luftflotte 2*), the largest of the three air fleets on the Eastern Front. The air fleet possessed a total of 1,367 front-line and transport machines, of which 994 were combat ready on June 22, 1941; the combat-ready aircraft comprised 222 bombers, 323 *Stuka* divebombers, sixty destroyer (*Zerstörer*) ground attack aircraft, 284 fighters, sixty-nine transports, and thirty-six "other." Kesselring also had control over the powerful 1 Flak Corps, whose complement of 88mm guns would prove highly effective in both an air and ground support role;[22] moreover, in 1941, these excellent high-velocity, multi-purpose weapons were often the only answer to the Soviet T-34 and KV tanks, against which the standard German 37mm and 50mm AT guns were practically useless.[23]

The infantry, panzer, and motorized divisions of Army Group Center were deployed along a stretch of the frontier 500 kilometers in length—from the northern tip of the Suwalki triangle south past the Soviet fortress of Brest-Litovsk. Most of the southern half of the army group's front—from the point northeast of Warsaw where the Bug River crossed the frontier into German-occupied Poland, southeast to the junction with Army Group South—ran along the Bug River for more than 200 kilometers.[24] Bock's attack frontage fell squarely on the forces of Army-General D. G. Pavlov's Western Front and also faced the left wing of Soviet 11 Army of Kuznetsov's Northwestern Front. The army group's forces were deployed in the following order (right to left): 2 Panzer Group (Guderian), Fourth Army (Kluge), Ninth Army (Strauss), 3 Panzer Group (Hoth).[25] The tactical dispositions of Bock's army group, with a panzer group poised to attack on each wing, prefigured the intention to rapidly encircle and destroy Pavlov's forces as close to the Russo-German frontier as possible.

The plan of attack was indeed for Army Group Center to destroy Soviet Western Front forces in Belorussia by means of an ambitious double envelopment aimed at the Belorussian capital of Minsk, some 250 to 300 kilometers from the border.[26] This was to be the task of the two panzer groups, with Hoth advancing from north of the Belostok salient, out of the Suwalki triangle; and Guderian debouching from south of the salient—out of German-occupied Poland—on either side of Brest-Litovsk, via Slutsk toward Minsk. A shorter double envelopment—well inside the pincers of the panzer groups—was to be carried out by Ninth Army on the northern wing and Fourth Army in the south, with the goal of encircling Western Front forces directly within the Belostok salient. After securing these objectives, 2 and 3 Panzer Groups were to prevent surviving Western Front forces from reestablishing lines of resistance along the Dvina-Dnepr Rivers, traverse both of the river barriers, and link up again near the ancient city of Smolensk, some 600 kilometers from the start line and for Bock's army group the first operational objective of the campaign.[27]

As stipulated in the original *Barbarossa* directive of December 18, 1940 (and also in the OKH deployment directive), after the Red Army had been routed in Belorussia, Army Group Center was to send "strong mobile forces" north to support the drive of Leeb's army group through the Baltic region toward Leningrad. Only after securing the essential objectives in the north—most significantly, Kronstadt and Leningrad—was the attack to be resumed toward Moscow, fully 1,000 kilometers from the Army Group Center start line.[28]

To challenge Bock's formidable array and defend along the Belostok-Minsk-Smolensk axis, Pavlov's Western Front could muster four armies (3, 4, 10, and 13),[29] including six mechanized corps; the armies were deployed in single echelon, with three armies well forward and the field headquarters of 13 Army far behind the frontier. In terms of personnel and weaponry, Pavlov's command consisted of 671,165 men (including 71,715 in schools), 2,900 tanks (2,192 operational), 14,171 guns and mortars, and 1,812 combat aircraft (1,577 combat ready). On June 22, only thirteen of Western Front's rifle divisions were manning border defenses, and most of these divisions were deployed with one regiment forward and two in garrison.[30] In addition, much of Pavlov's armor was still quartered in its peacetime garrisons and, thus, not prepared to make a rapid transition to mobile wartime operations.[31]

Despite its impressive size (and numerical superiority in tanks, artillery, and aircraft to Bock's army group and 2 Air Fleet), Pavlov's *front* was not the center of gravity of the Soviet deployment. As discussed in Chapter 1 (Section 1.6), the Soviet High Command had positioned significantly larger forces farther south, in the Ukraine, from where they could mount offensive operations into southern Poland. Pavlov's forces were also "in a particularly dangerous geographical position. The Soviet army groups to the north and south at least had their flanks covered, one by the Baltic and the other by the Carpathian Mountains and the Black Sea. In contrast, both of the [Western Front's] flanks were open to attack."[32] But the situation was far worse than that, for the mass of Pavlov's troops, including three of his prized mechanized corps, were crammed into a large salient (150 kilometers deep and 200 kilometers wide) around the town of Belostok,[33] which jutted deep into German-occupied Poland. As a result, these forces were already deeply enveloped by Bock's panzer and infantry units on both wings of his army group—a situation, the field marshal realized, that would render his operational task that much easier (Map 6).[34]

Adding to the arguably insurmountable challenges facing Pavlov's Western Front was the fact that the border fortifications in his sector were far from complete (as, of course, was the case across the frontier for the Red Army). In this context, the example of Lt.-Gen. A. A. Korobkov's 4 Army is illustrative:

> By June 1941 . . . Korobkov's 4 Army . . . was covering 150 kilometers of the USSR national border on the Brest–Minsk axis . . . By 22 June, Korobkov had been commanding the army for two and a half months. As [army chief-of-staff Colonel L. M.] Sandalov recalled, the army commander himself acknowledged that he was better suited to command a rifle corps . . .
>
> The construction of defensive works in the 4 Army's first (and main) line of defense—pillboxes and additional field-type positions in the Brest Fortified [Region]—began back in 1940 at the beginning of the summer. Its forward line (and by June 1941 only it had been completed; work in depth had not even begun), ran along the eastern bank of the Bug River . . .
>
> The pillboxes of the Brest Fortified [Region] were two-tiered concrete blocks; the embrasures of the upper casemate, divided by a wall into two caponiers, were almost at ground level . . . The upper level had casemate guns with shortened barrels or machine guns in the caponiers. The pillboxes as constructed were primarily of a single- or twin-embrasure machine-gun, artillery machine-gun or artillery style. Key positions were guarded by pillboxes with three to five firing ports. The walls were 1.5 to 1.8 meters thick, while the roofs were up to 2.5 meters thick (calculated to withstand a direct hit by a 250 kg bomb). Certain pillboxes contained one 76mm gun and two heavy machine guns each, while others had a 45mm gun with a tandem DS-39 machine gun. The pillbox garrisons consisted of 8 to 9 men or 16 to 18 men.[35]

By June 21, 128 concrete pillboxes had been built in the Brest Fortified Region; however, only twenty-three of them were combat ready (eight of which were in the Brest area, mainly within the fortress of Brest-Litovsk). Moreover, the pillboxes in the battalion sectors were poorly positioned, plainly visible to the Germans from their observation posts, and vulnerable to destruction from artillery fire.[36]

The Brest Fortified Region also encompassed fieldworks located between the pillboxes; in response to an alarm, they were to be occupied by troops of 4 Army. The fieldworks, laid out in the form of strongpoints and battalion boxes, were mostly earth and timber structures as well as entrenchments (mostly rectangular rifle pits, lacking communication trenches and camouflage) and a few obstacles that offered minor protection against tanks (i.e., ditches and log post obstacles). There was a paucity of command posts, observation posts, and shelters.[37]

Work on the fortifications "progressed slowly and could not be completed by [June] 1941. The positioning of the units assigned to man them, which were frequently based 15–50 kilometers away from their designated sectors, discounted the possibility of a surprise attack."[38]

4.2: OPENING ACTS ALONG THE ARMY GROUP FRONT

As addressed in Chapter 2 (Section 2.2), German special forces, the *Brandenburgers* of Regiment 800, had infiltrated behind Soviet lines in the final days and hours before the start of the Russian campaign. Along the front of Bock's Army Group Center, primary objectives of the *Brandenburgers* were the fortress of Brest-Litovsk and the bridges over the Bug River, which were to be secured from demolition by Soviet border troops. Some of the special forces, secreted across the frontier on Saturday, June 21, on goods trains, or hidden beneath loads of gravel in rail cars, hid out in the city of Brest for many hours before the attack began. From Kobrin, east of Brest and in the middle of Bock's attack frontage, Soviet 4 Army command, at 0220 Moscow time, having interrogated yet another German deserter, attempted to alert subordinate units to this latest confirmation of the impending attack. But the news never got out: German special forces had already severed the telephone lines to a depth of 50 kilometers beyond the border. Operation *Barbarossa* was less than two hours away.[39]

At exactly 0300 hours, thirty Heinkel He-111 and Dornier Do-17 medium bombers, flying in groups of three, droned across the Russo-German demarcation line at maximum altitude. The vanguard of the *Luftwaffe's* eastern air fleet, the clutch of bombers—their hand-picked crews with many hours of night-flying experience—set out to strike Soviet fighter bases between Belostok and Minsk and other key locations along the central axis of the German attack. The bombers flew over sparsely populated areas of marsh and forest, their aircrew scanning the terrain for navigational clues; ahead of them, the first yellow and red hues of a new day crept above the horizon. As the aircraft closed on their targets—still undetected—they started their descent. By 0315 hours they were roaring in at low level, preparing to disgorge hundreds of small SD-2 fragmentation bombs from their open bomb bays.[40]

On the ground, in the sector of Geyr von Schweppenburg's 24 Panzer Corps (2 Panzer Group), the capture of the highway bridge across the Bug River at Koden, 40 kilometers south of Brest-Litovsk, was a vital prerequisite to the deployment and advance of his corps' armor. As a result, an engineer assault group of 3 Panzer Division had orders to seize the bridge by surprise just minutes before the start of the main attack, to neutralize the Russian bridge guards on the far side, and to remove all explosive charges. The bold action succeeded and the bridge was in German hands at 0310, barely five minutes before the start of the artillery barrage. To the immense relief of *Generaloberst* Heinz Guderian, Commander, 2 Panzer Group, 24 Panzer Corps had gained a bridgehead that would ensure its tanks access to Panzer Route 1—the *Panzerstrasse* leading by way of Kobrin and Slutsk to Bobruisk.[41]

As the final minutes before the launch of *Barbarossa* faded away, senior German commanders and staff officers assembled at observation posts across the front of the army group. Guderian, having shortly after midnight received the code word "*Kyffhäuser*" from all his corps, signifying they were ready for action, set out at 0210 hours on that "fateful" (*schicksalschwer*) morning[42] for his forward command post at Hill 158, south of the town of Bohukaly. It was still dark when he arrived there at 0310. Atop the hill, overlooking a bend in the Bug River, was a wooden observation tower—from here, the panzer general could make out the lights of the city of Brest-Litovsk, 15 kilometers to the southeast. The formidable citadel just outside the city, "with its forts and casemates pointing at the German line like an anchored battleship, lay in darkness."[43] In *Hitler Moves East*, Paul Carell offered a gripping portrait of Guderian's CP on the cusp of war:

> At the foot of Hill 158, in a patch of wood, was the advanced command post of 2 Panzer Group, the brain of Guderian's tank force. "The white G's," the men called the group, because of the large white letter "G" that all vehicles bore as their tactical identification sign. "G" stood for Guderian. At a glance a vehicle was recognized as "one of ours." Guderian had introduced the idea during the campaign in France. It had proved so successful that Kleist [1 Panzer Group] had adopted it and had ordered all the vehicles of his panzer group to be painted with a white "K."
>
> During the preceding night, the night of 20/21 June, the staff officers had arrived in greatest secrecy. They were now sitting in their tents or office buses, bending over maps and written orders. No signals came from the aerials: strict radio silence had been ordered, lest the monitoring posts of the Russians became suspicious. Use of the telephone was permitted only if strictly necessary. Guderian's personal command transport [Befehlsstaffel]—two radio vans, some jeeps, and several motorcycles—stood parked behind the tents and buses, well camouflaged. The command tank [Befehlspanzer] approached. Guderian jumped out. "Morning gentlemen."

The time was exactly 0310. A few words, then Guderian drove up the hill with his command transport to the observation tower. The luminous minute-hands of their wrist-watches crept round the dials.

0311 hours. In the tent of the operations staff the telephone jangled. Oberstleutnant Bayerlein, the Ia, or chief of operations, picked up the receiver. Oberstleutnant Brücker, the chief of operations of 24 Panzer Corps . . . was on the line. Without greetings or formality he said, "Bayerlein, the Koden bridge was all right."

Bayerlein glanced across to Freiherr von Liebenstein, the chief of staff, and nodded. Then he said, "That's fine, Brücker. So long. Good luck." He replaced the receiver.[44]

Panzer General Joachim Lemelsen, the commander of 47 Panzer Corps (also 2 Panzer Group), drove down to the Bug River with his escort officer to observe his riflemen and combat engineers in their assembly areas, directly northwest of Brest. The night before, in a brief moment of reflection, he had jotted in his diary: "It is profoundly peaceful everywhere, the cows and horses are in the field and the *Panje*-horses are raking the potatoes, and what will it look like tomorrow morning? The bombs and shells will explode everywhere and the houses will burn, the residents flee. The contrast is too unreal."[45]

Generalfeldmarschall Günther von Kluge, Fourth Army commander, and his staff were in the sector of 31 Infantry Division, almost directly opposite Brest and only a few kilometers from the Bug. As Kluge's chief of staff, *Oberst* Günther Blumentritt later recalled: "We watched the German fighter planes take off and soon only their tail lights were visible in the east . . . As [zero hour approached], the sky began to lighten, turning to a curious yellow color. And still all was quiet."[46]

Suddenly, at 0305 hours, thousands of German guns and mortars—e.g., light and medium field howitzers; 105mm and 150mm cannons; 210mm, 240mm, 305mm heavy howitzers; super-heavy rail-borne artillery—supported by army and *Luftwaffe* flak batteries and *Nebelwerfer* rocket projectors, opened fire along the left wing of Army Group Center (Ninth Army and 3 Panzer Group).[47] Ten minutes later (0315), thousands more guns and mortars began to bellow along the right wing of the army group (2 Panzer Group, Fourth Army). For the preparatory fusillade, Bock had assembled more than sixty battalions of GHQ artillery, supplemented by the massive organic firepower of his own infantry and panzer divisions, along his 500-kilometer front. As noted, the army group bristled with 750 batteries of artillery of all types.[48]

While the opening barrage was of relatively short duration (in some sectors lasting no more than a few minutes), no one who took part in it—or witnessed it—was ever to forget it. In his war memoir, published in 1957, Dr. Heinrich Haape (6 Infantry Division), graphically recounted the moment:

One minute to zero hour! There is nothing of which we can think, except what will happen when the next second and the next have ticked by. The tense moment holds us breathless. We wait, our faces rigid, pulses racing. The whole world seems to be waiting . . .

A mighty clap of thunder as thousands of guns roar forth at one stroke. Their flashes turn dawn into daylight. In a split second, [the front] is electrified into action. Hell is let loose and history is made. Guns of every caliber fire point-blank at the Russian lines. With a heavy, droning hum, mortar shells arc over our heads toward the enemy. Machine guns and automatics rattle out their urgent salvos. The Russians return the fire. We hear the whine as heavy shells rend the night above us. But the German fire intensifies into an overwhelming crescendo as our forward storm troops and infantry battalions pour into the enemy's frontier defenses. And the panzers, we know, are crushing their way forward, spitting fire. The East is aflame.[49]

To *Oberst* Blumentritt, it was as if "a miracle happened" when the Russian artillery (for the most part) failed to return fire: "Only very rarely did a gun open fire from the far bank."[50] *Soldat* Franz Frisch, an artillerist in a motorized *Heeresartillerie* battalion (105mm cannon) who took part in the cannonade, recalled that the sustained "drumfire," which soon rose to an infernal roar, produced a level of noise that was "incredibly uncomfortable."[51] *Soldat* Paul B. was awed by the mighty rumble (*schwere Grollen*) of the heavy guns and proud that his flak unit was at the forward edge of battle.[52] *Unteroffizier* Helmut Pabst, attached to an artillery unit on the central front, looked on as the "Russian watch-towers vanished in a flash."[53] "The thunder of guns awakened us at 0315 in the morning," wrote a soldier who hailed from Berlin:

34 batteries are firing. We can see the barrage from the edge of the forest, since we are merely 7 kilometers away from the frontier (Bug). Soon towns are burning, white flares shoot up, the front rages like a storm. When there is flak fire, gray streaks rise into the sky, slowly drifting away. A plane goes down burning. The sky, at first clear and red, gradually turns purple mixed with green. There is a gigantic smoke cloud behind the low silhouette of the horizon and it drifts leadenly to the right.[54]

Oberleutnant Siegfried Knappe commanded an artillery battery in 87 Infantry Division. His guns were in position in a woods and, as he circulated among his 180 men to conduct final checks, he was struck by the pungent odor of the pine needles. The men, he knew, were supremely confident—in fact, "their confidence was total, like that of a diamond cutter taking a chisel to a priceless gem. Now they sat about in groups, joking bravely about everything except what lay immediately ahead of them. I was confident the world had never seen anything like them," he later recalled. Knappe checked out the forward observation post. Then, at the designated moment, his battery opened up on the small village of Sasnia, a few kilometers beyond the border:

I was not in the front line with the infantry but at a little hill about a half kilometer away, which I thought would be a good place from which to watch the effectiveness of our fire. I could see our shell bursts clearly from my observation post, as well as the oily black-and-yellow smoke that rose from them. The unpleasant, peppery smell of burnt gunpowder soon filled the air as our guns continued to fire round after round. After 15 minutes we lifted our fire, and the soft pop-pop-pop of flares being fired replaced it as red lit up the sky and the infantry went on the attack.[55]

During the barrage, an artillery soldier in 19 Panzer Division was struck by the peculiar juxtaposition of the shellfire with the dance music that drifted from the radios of some of the nearby panzers:

The tension became unbearably high. Nerves seemed to vibrate. A great offensive, the likes of which no member of the regiment had ever experienced, was imminent . . . A few minutes before 0300 . . . the hum of motors in the West made the presence of the first German bombers felt. At exactly 0300 hours, they crossed the frontier. [At 0305 hours] the artillery fire began abruptly from all gun barrels positioned along the front line. The all-encompassing tension like that before a storm was discharged in a thundering artillery barrage at the start of the attack. Everyone felt this deafening declaration of intent by a great Army to be a powerful event that would never be forgotten by any participant, regardless of its damaging impact on the peace of nations. We were proud to take part in such an event as a small cog in the vast army machinery—an event that would later be regaled by the history books . . . If, in this strange atmosphere, this electrically charged mood, you could even hear dance music from some of the tanks, this produced a rather incongruous atmosphere. The German radio station broadcast dance music all night with rolling news bulletins, for which everyone waited eagerly.[56]

In the sector of 17 Panzer Division, northwest of Brest-Litovsk, 240 guns were in place along an 8-kilometer front. At precisely 0315 hours, they unleashed a storm of steel across the Bug—80–90 meters wide in this sector—against known Russian field positions and bunkers. A postwar history of the division's 40 Rifle Regiment recorded the regiment's role in the bombardment:

The air roars. Commands can barely be understood. Our infantry guns fire 60 rounds per gun in 10 minutes. Flak guns finish off the bunkers along the enemy bank. Soon, fires on the other side of the Bug can be seen. At 0340 hours, the bombs from the Stukas *strike the enemy positions. From 0415 hours, the transport [of troops and weapons] across the river begins.*[57]

Along the front of 18 Panzer Division, fifty batteries of all calibers loosed a furious barrage and a protective smoke screen.[58] *Leutnant* Georg Kreuter supported the bombardment with his two 150mm medium infantry guns (s.IG 33). Because the guns' shellfire merged with the general cannonade, he was unable to discern its effects on the far side of the Bug. What he did observe, however, was an unfortunate Ju-87 *Stuka* divebomber, which plunged to the ground after being struck by a shell from a German gun. Such "friendly fire" incidents were far from uncommon on this first day of the war, or any other day throughout the eastern campaign.[59]

At no point on the Eastern Front was the opening barrage more intense, more devastating, than against the fortress of Brest-Litovsk, where the Germans unleashed a veritable whirlwind of fire—the progressive stages of the concentrated fire plan given the names of flowers—"Anemone," "Crocus," "Narcissus," etc.[60] Rudolf Gschöpf, a chaplain in 45 Infantry Division, later likened the bombardment of the fortress to a "hurricane," which "broke loose and roared over our heads, the likes of which we had never experienced before and never would again."[61] To *Leutnant* Erich Bunke, watching in awe in the sector of the adjoining 31 Infantry Division, it was as if the "jaws of hell" (*Schlund der Hölle*) had opened, while the thousands of shells arcing across the dawn sky made the "air vibrate."[62] *Gefreiter* Herbert R., an infantry squad leader (*Gruppenführer*) in the reserve regiment of 45 ID, found the fire raining down on the fortress to be quite "unimaginable" (*unvorstellbar*):

> It was early morning and suddenly thousands of guns opened up all at once . . . it was truly an inferno. It was already becoming light, but after a while a wall of black smoke rose into the sky, and it again became black as night—and that only because of the explosions. I was lying on my back in my foxhole, and was so startled by the sudden artillery fire that the burning cigarette, which was up near my service coat, fell on me and burned a hole in my chest. That was my first wound in Russia.[63]

The 10 Panzer Division (2 Panzer Group) was held in reserve on June 22 and did not take part in the opening assault; its artillery batteries, however, were posted to 18 Panzer Division (also 2 Panzer Group) for the opening barrage. A history of the division, published by its veterans' organization (*Traditionsgemeinschaft*) in 1993, provides a graphic account of the meticulous preparations for the artillery barrage, as well as of the barrage itself:

> In the late afternoon of 21.6.[41], the observation posts are manned, the computing units [Rechentrupps] move into the firing positions. When evening falls, the Führer's proclamation is read out, which begins with the words: "Soldaten der Ostfront!" And suddenly all the guessing games that had been going on are at an end, everybody knows that the weapons will be doing the talking once again . . .

Weather reports, known as "Barbara Reports" by the artillerymen, have been coming in every two hours since evening at the batteries' computing section posts. The trajectory of the shells is, of course, influenced by various factors, such as temperature, air pressure, humidity, wind direction, and wind force. When firing blind, these variables have to be taken into account, and so every two hours the computing units calculate all the firing commands for the planned barrage [Feuerschlag] anew. And then the X-hour is announced: 22.6., 0315 hours!

At 0300 hours, the firing commands are adjusted for the last time, there is nothing more for the computing units to do. The guns are aimed and loaded, the battery officers have the handset of a field telephone to their ear; they look at their watches. The artillery commander has reserved for himself the order to open fire. Over on the horizon, a pale light, just a narrow sliver, is very weakly discernable. A quiet shiver, more like a thrill, takes hold of the soldiers standing in the night. The battery officer repeats the words that are coming out of the telephone: "10 minutes more."—"5 minutes more."—"1 more minute."—"30 seconds more."—"15 seconds more,—and 10 seconds,—8, 7, 6, 5, 4— battery. . ." He raises his arm and thrusts it down, the command "Fire!" erupts from his mouth like thunder and lightning—a single bolt of lightning flashes across the whole sky, a deafening crash tears through the silence. And then shell after shell speeds across the Bug, rising to a drumfire [Trommelfeuer] due to the sheer numbers of batteries standing to the left and right.

Over there, a wall of dense smoke and dust rises sluggishly, blotting out the pale slivers on the horizon. Then suddenly German rocket projector batteries join the fray: howling and whining, whole series of rockets with long trails of fire and smoke sweep across into the inferno. The first rays of sun light up the edges of the clouds and the wall of smoke in a bloody red. And with the first light come the Stukas, seeking out their targets, positioning themselves in a row, circling and plunging earthward, dropping their bombs and pulling up again. And behind them, black smoke pours up into the sky again . . .

When day has come and the rolling barrage has ended at the limit of the artillery's range, as the gunners from 90 Artillery Regiment collect the empty cartridges and the ammunition boxes and the sounds of combat across the advancing front rumble like a receding storm, suddenly Russian bombers appear above the German positions, approaching in strict formation, as if on maneuvers.[64]

German fighters, Messerschmitt Bf-109s, from the airfield at Biala Podlaska, rose to intercept the enemy bombers. Pouncing on their prey from behind, the nimble Bf-109s fired short bursts from their 20mm cannon. One of the intruders was soon hit and plunged earthward, trailing thick plumes of smoke in its wake; then a second bomber went into a spin and broke apart in midair. None of the Russian bombers made it through to their objective that day.[65]

4.3: 2 Panzer Group Operations

The commander of 2 Panzer Group was the fifty-three-year-old *Generaloberst* Heinz Guderian; his chief of staff was *Obstlt.i.G. Freiherr* von Liebenstein. A bold, daring, and charismatic leader of men, who drove himself (and his men) hard, Guderian had led 19 Panzer Corps with great distinction in Poland, Belgium, and France; during the final phase of the French campaign, his command was enlarged to embrace three corps and re-designated as Panzer Group Guderian. In recognition of his singular achievements, he was promoted to full general rank (*Generaloberst*) on July 19, 1940, and, in November 1940 his command was upgraded to 2 Panzer Group.[66] His prewar role as a military innovator and theorist, who played an integral part in crafting the concept of *Blitzkrieg* warfare—based on the combined operations of tanks, motorized infantry, and aircraft, linked by modern (radio) communications—is well known, even if he most certainly exaggerated his contributions in this arena.

Heinz Guderian has been lionized by many as the legendary father of the German armored force and brilliant practitioner of "blitzkrieg" maneuver warfare. Guderian created this legend with his own highly-influential, yet self-serving and distorted memoir, which remains one of the most widely read accounts of the Second Word War. Unfortunately, too many of Guderian's biographers have accepted Guderian's view of his accomplishments without sufficient critical scrutiny. The result has been an undeserved hagiography of Guderian. While undoubtedly a great military figure, Guderian was a man of appreciable ego and ambition—a volatile, impetuous, and difficult personality determined to achieve his vision of a war-winning armored force, irrespective of the consequences . . . In the end, he proved to be a man prepared to distort the truth in order to establish his place in history. In doing so, he denigrated the myriad important contributions of other Germans as he took personal credit for what were, in reality, collective accomplishments.[67]

As noted in Chapter 1 (Section 1.1), Guderian also evinced the disturbing proclivity to ignore orders of his superiors; early on in the Russian campaign this would get him into serious trouble and, ultimately, be his undoing: During the retreat from Moscow in December 1941, Guderian's repeated acts of insubordination would finally result in his dismissal from command of 2 Panzer Army (as his panzer group was re-designated in October 1941). Although he would go on to hold other key commands (in March 1943, Hitler appointed him inspector general of panzer troops and, in 1944/45, he would serve as acting chief of the Army General Staff), Guderian never again led forces directly into battle.[68]

Guderian's 2 Panzer Group was the largest of the four panzer groups committed to the Russian campaign. It consisted of approximately 240,000 men in 15.5 divisions (five panzer divisions, three motorized infantry divisions, six infantry divisions, one cavalry division, and one motorized infantry regiment) organized into three panzer corps and one infantry corps—the latter assigned temporarily to Guderian's group to assist with the breakthrough at the border. One infantry division (255 ID) made up the panzer group reserve. The three panzer corps were: 24 Panzer Corps (1 KD, 10 ID [mot.], 3 PD, 4 PD, 267 ID),[69] commanded by *Gen.d.Pz.Tr. Freiherr* Geyr von Schweppenburg; 46 Panzer Corps (SS "Reich" [mot.], 10 PD, IR *"Grossdeutschland"* [mot.]), commanded by *Gen.d.Pz.Tr.* Heinrich von Vietinghoff; and 47 Panzer Corps (17 PD, 18 PD, 29 ID [mot.], 167 ID),[70] commanded by *Gen.d.Pz.Tr.* Joachim Lemelsen. The three panzer corps boasted an aggregate of 994 tanks (including fifty-seven command tanks)[71] distributed over thirteen tank battalions. The group's 12 Army Corps (31, 34, 45 ID) was led by *Gen.d.Inf.* Walter Schroth.[72] GFM von Bock was generous in assigning General Headquarters troops to Guderian's panzer group; they included the following:

- Assault Gun Battalions 192 and 201 (12 AK)
- 4 105mm cannon battalions (2 to 12 AK; 1 each to 24 and 47 PzK)
- 1 mixed artillery battalion (47 PzK)
- 4 150mm medium howitzer battalions (2 to 12 AK; 1 each to 24 and 47 PzK)
- 4 210mm heavy howitzer battalions (mot.) (1 each to 12 AK, 24 and 47 PzK; one directly controlled by 2 Panzer Group headquarters [*z.V.Pz.Gr.*])
- 1 210mm heavy howitzer battalion (limited mobility) (12 AK)
- 1 150mm cannon battalion (*z.V.Pz.Gr.*)
- 2 *Nebelwerfer* rocket projector battalions (12 AK)
- 1 *Nebelwerfer* rocket projector regiment (47 PzK [less one battalion]; 1 battalion to 24 PzK)
- Machine Gun Battalion 5 (*z.V.Pz.Gr.*)
- 3 antitank battalions (2 mot., 1 SP) (1 each to 12 AK, 24 and 47 PzK)
- 2 flak (*Fla*) battalions (1 12 AK; 1 *z.V.Pz.Gr.*)
- Flamethrower Tank Battalion 100 (*Pz.Abt.(F)100*) (47 PzK)[73]

Luftwaffe formations allotted to 2 Panzer Group included ten reconnaissance squadrons, eight of which were distributed among the three panzer corps,[74] one to 12 Army Corps, and a long-range (strategic) squadron (3.(F)31) controlled by Guderian's headquarters (*z.V.Pz.Gr.*). In addition, the *Luftwaffe's* 1 Flak Corps (two light and four mixed flak battalions) was assigned to the panzer group for both air and ground support. Rounding out the GHQ troops was a large contingent of engineer (*Pionier*) troops (including bridge-building battalions and bridge columns "B"), as well as construction and road repair battalions.[75] As one of Guderian's biographers observed: "It must have taken considerable effort, as well as all his power of persuasion (*Überredungsgabe*) to acquire [so many GHQ units for his panzer group]. He was also able to secure the support of large elements of the air fleet assigned [to Army Group Center]."[76]

Guderian deployed his forces for attack with three corps forward and one (46 PzK) in reserve. His attack frontage on the right wing of Army Group Center was 100 kilometers in length and followed the Bug River in a shallow arc that began about 40 kilometers northwest of Brest-Litovsk and ended some 50 kilometers southwest of the town and the fortress. On Guderian's right wing, Geyr (24 PzK) had concentrated his first echelon forces (3 and 4 PD) on a front of less than 20 kilometers southwest of Brest-Litovsk; in the center, Schroth (12 AK), whose corps straddled the citadel itself, had all three of his infantry divisions in the forward line; on the panzer group's left wing, Lemselen (47 PzK) had massed his first echelon divisions (17 and 18 PD) on a narrow front that began about 15 kilometers northwest of Brest[77] (Map 6).[78] Operating immediately to the left of 2 Panzer Group was GFM von Kluge's Fourth Army (to whom Guderian's group was subordinated for the attack on June 22), while to its right were the divisions of GFM von Rundstedt's Army Group South.

For Guderian's panzer group, and all of Army Group Center, the road east lay through Belorussia—a relatively primitive region in 1941[79] with its profusion of dilapidated farmsteads and hamlets. The terrain was dissected by numerous rivers and streams, permeated by lakes, bogs, and marshes, and covered with immense tracks of dense, primeval forest of spruce, oak, pine, and birch. Beginning on June 22, Guderian's panzer corps would have to cross through the deep belts of forest at the frontier, which, in some cases, stretched for nearly 100 kilometers before yielding to open country. Metaled roads were virtually nonexistent and, on many occasions, the barely navigable sandy tracks that passed for roadways would cause more problems for the panzers than enemy resistance. To the south of Belorussia, on the southern fringe of the panzer group's (and Army Group Center's) area of operations, lay the Pripiat' Marshes—an immense area of swamp land and primeval forest that began just beyond the Russo-German frontier, directly to the southeast of Brest-Litovsk. Simply put, the marshes formed an effective barrier to the movement of tanks and motor vehicles and divided the entire Eastern Front into a northern and southern theater.[80]

Because both of Guderian's attacking panzer corps were massed on very narrow fronts, they were able to concentrate overwhelming force at decisive points against defending Red Army formations. Providing close air support was the *Luftwaffe*'s 2 Air Corps (*Fliegerkorps II*), which included 115 Ju-87 *Stuka* divebombers and a complement of Bf-110 fighter-bombers.[81] The basic mission of 2 Panzer Group was elucidated in the deployment directive of the Army High Command:

> *2 Panzer Group, in cooperation with Fourth Army, is to break through the enemy forces along the border at and north of Kobrin and, through a rapid advance on Slusk and*

*Minsk in cooperation with 3 Panzer Group, which is advancing into the area north of Minsk, create the conditions for the destruction of all enemy forces in the area between Belostok and Minsk. Operating closely with 3 Panzer Group, it will then rapidly gain the area at and south of Smolensk, preventing the concentration of enemy forces in the region of the upper Dnepr and thereby securing freedom of action [*Handlungsfreiheit*] for the army group for its further tasks.*[82]

In an order to his subordinate divisions, the brilliant panzer general let it be known just how much he expected of his men:

Our panzer group, on the right wing of [Fourth Army] and advancing ahead of it, is to break through the frontier positions on both sides of Brest–Litovsk and strike out along Panzerrollbahn[83] *1 and 2 toward Slutsk and Minsk, and then into the area of Smolensk, in order to destroy the cohesion of the enemy army. After breaking through, it is of decisive importance to advance as far as the gasoline will take us, at full throttle, without pause or rest, marching day and night, without consideration for any threat to the flanks . . . The main thing is to advance far, and to shoot little. [*Es kommt darauf an, viel zu fahren, wenig zu schiessen.]*[84]

On June 20/21, Guderian had visited the forward units of his panzer corps to ensure that everything was in place for the attack. Careful study of the Russians just across the Bug had convinced him they knew nothing about the storm about to break over them. "We had observation of the courtyard of Brest-Litovsk citadel and could see them drilling by platoons to the music of a military band. The strong points along their bank of the Bug were unoccupied. They had made scarcely any noticeable progress in strengthening their fortified positions during the past few weeks. So the prospects of our attack achieving surprise were good."[85]

As dawn broke on June 22, 1941, first echelon forces of GFM von Bock's Army Group Center struck the left flank of Lt.-Gen. V. I. Morozov's 11 Army (Northwestern Front) and the entire span of General D. G. Pavlov's Western Front, achieving tactical surprise along the entire 500-kilometer front; as the field marshal recorded in his diary, "Everything began according to plan. Strangely, the Russians didn't blow a single one of the existing Bug bridges."[86] Under cover of protective barrages and artificial smoke, the German assault parties darted across the frontier, neutralizing stunned Soviet border guards with grenades or short bursts from automatic weapons and striking out for their initial objectives. On both wings of the army group the panzers and motorized infantry began to advance, supported by the fighters, fighter-bombers and *Stukas* of Kesselring's 2 Air Fleet. Naively believing that they had been freed from the yoke of Soviet oppression, many Polish and Lithuanian peasants greeted the invaders with gifts of salt and bread, their traditional gifts for travelers.[87]

For Guderian's 2 Panzer Group, the war began at 0315 hours, supported by an artillery barrage of at least thirty minutes' duration.[88] In the sector of the panzer group, where the frontier meandered along the Bug River, assault formations of infantry and combat engineers crossed in rubber dinghies or assault boats (*Sturmbooten*). Guderian's attack plunged headlong into the center of Lt.-Gen. A. A. Korobkov's 4 Army. Echeloned in depth, the spearheads of 24 and 47 Panzer Corps crossed the Bug on both sides of Brest-Litovsk, while in the center 12 Army Corps launched a furious assault on the fortress. Stunned by the suddenness and fury of the panzer group's assault, some of the Soviet border troops were caught in their barracks and could offer no resistance at all. Under relentless attack from both the ground and the air, many Soviet units collapsed in the first few hours; others, however, recovered from the initial shock of invasion and resisted tenaciously—for example, at the Brest fortress where, in many instances, the heroic defenders would literally fight until the last round of ammunition,[89] inflicting dreadful losses on the Germans.

Both 24 and 47 Panzer Corps attacked in the first assault wave because Guderian had prevailed over his superior, Field Marshal von Kluge (C-in-C Fourth Army), in a tactical dispute prior to the start of the campaign. Kluge, a more conservative and risk-averse commander, had argued that infantry—not armor—should make the initial penetration of the Russian frontier defenses; in his view, such an approach would preserve the tank forces from unnecessary losses and enable them to exploit the breakthroughs of the infantry. Guderian, however, demurred, insisting instead that his panzer units be committed immediately to effect and exploit their own breaches of the enemy lines, without the loss of time inherent in Kluge's approach. As Guderian recalled in his postwar memoir:

> *The panzer generals knew from experience in France what happens when the other system [i.e., Kluge's concept] is employed: at the critical moment of success the roads are covered with endless, slow-moving, horse-drawn columns of the infantry divisions, and the panzers as a result are blocked and slowed up. So they wished the panzer divisions to be put in front on those sectors where a breakthrough was desired; on other sectors, where the tasks were different, as for example the storming of fortresses [e.g., Brest-Litovsk], the infantry should lead the assault.*[90]

The panzer leader appealed to Bock, and the field marshal came down on Guderian's side, giving him "much freedom to execute operations as he saw fit and to commit his armor immediately as he desired."[91]

Southwest of Brest-Litovsk, Geyr's 24 Panzer Corps put in its main assault with 3 and 4 Panzer Divisions, holding its 10 Motorized Division in reserve. Led by *Generalleutnant* Walter Model, 3 PD possessed a total of 215 tanks (110 Pz IIIs and thirty-two Pz IVs), while *Generalmajor* Willibald *Freiherr* von Langermann und Erlenkamp's 4 PD boasted a complement of 177 tanks (105 Pz IIIs and twenty Pz IVs). Both divisions were to rapidly slip past the enemy border defenses from the area about Koden and begin to drive on the Belorussian capital of Minsk, more than 300 kilometers to the east—4 Panzer Division on the route designated as Panzer Route 1 (*Panzerstrasse 1*), which, as noted, led via Kobrin and Slutsk to Bobruisk, and 3 Panzer Division along a parallel track to the north.[92] For June 22—*Barbarossatag*—Geyr urged his panzer troops on with the slogan "Through and forward" (*Durch und vorwärts*).[93]

The attack of Erlenkamp's 4 Panzer Division commenced at 0315 hours with a thirty-minute artillery bombardment, which landed on the few barely observable Russian field positions at the frontier (most of which appeared to be unoccupied), while also striking areas where enemy resistance was anticipated. There was no response from the enemy. As one former 4 PD member recollected: "The massed fire [of the artillery] made a strong impression on the soldiers of the division, and most likely did so as well on the weak enemy border guard detachments. And so it fulfilled a purpose, even if it largely fell into a void (*ins Leere geht*)."[94]

At 0330 hours, the first wave of the division's 4 Rifle Brigade (*Schützenbrigade*) crossed the Bug on pneumatic boats (*Schlauchbooten*), encountering no enemy resistance; they were quickly followed by the forward observers of the division's 103 Artillery Regiment, while pneumatic ferries shepherded the first heavy weapons (including a light artillery battery) and a handful of motor vehicles across the river. The weather was clear and fine and the terrain (on the northern edge of the Pripiat' Marshes) mostly flat, though covered with wooded areas and heavy undergrowth and crossed by watercourses and swamplands, the few villages in the region poor and dilapidated. The single "road" heading east was simply a cross-country path mired in deep sand.[95] Recalled Hans Schäufler, a signal officer in 4 PD:

> *The first assault detachments crossed in assault boats and rafts. At 0400 hours, we moved to a staging area in a patch of woods right on the river [Bug]. The resistance across the way was slight. At 1200 hours, we crossed the river on pontoon ferries with our radio vehicles . . . Our vehicles wormed their way through the knee-deep sand of the Bug lowlands. The civilians, former Poles, were very friendly. They cooked eggs and milk for us.*[96]

While engineers of the division's Armored Engineer Battalion 79 (*Pz.Pi.Btl.79*) labored furiously to build a bridge over the Bug at Sostaki, 3 to 4 kilometers beyond the frontier Erlenkamp's infantry encountered stiff enemy opposition in a woods at Hill 149. Here the attacking German troops (12 Rifle Regiment) came up against well-defended bunker positions, while also taking fire from mortars and antitank guns. In response, the Germans brought up artillery, which fired on the bunkers from exposed positions (*aus offenen Stellungen*). As this first serious combat dragged on, the first Russian prisoners were taken. Meanwhile, at 1000 hours, 4 PD's 33 Rifle Regiment reached the town of Miedna, less than 10 kilometers from the border, without enemy opposition.[97]

Although the tanks and heavy weapons of 4 Panzer Division were soon rolling across the bridge at Sostaki, the going was slow—due to the difficult, marshy terrain around the bridge and the poor state of the route of advance (*Vormarschweg*) to the east—and would remain so throughout the day. Farther east, by mid-afternoon, the spearheads of 12 and 33 Rifle Regiments reached the towns of Brodziatyn and Orlanka, respectively, approximately 20 kilometers beyond the border. However, it was not until much later (2000 hours) that the division's 35 Panzer Regiment (with Motorcycle Battalion 34) began to advance northeast from Brodziatyn. Pressing on through the night, the tanks and motorcycle riflemen eventually gained the main road leading from Maloryta to Kobrin; by 0100 the next morning, the battle group, advancing without opposition, was only 25 kilometers shy of Kobrin and Panzer Route 1, although the panzers were now beginning to run out of fuel (as a result of the poor roads, fuel consumption had been much higher than anticipated).[98]

> *By evening of the first day of the attack, the lead elements of the division have advanced 45 kilometers as the crow flies [in Luftlinie].[99] Along exceptionally difficult roads, they reached the main road that leads northeast to Kobrin and thus to the* Panzerstrasse 1, *called the "Rollbahn." Resistance from the weak enemy border detachments was at times vigorous and led to delays. Without question, the attack succeeded in surprising the enemy, from which we gained an advantage. A more systematic defense, [by] stronger forces, would have made the success actually attained impossible. Already this first day has placed severe stress on the motor vehicles. The local Polish population treated the German soldiers in a most friendly manner.[100]*

General Model's 3 Panzer Division, the "Berlin Bear" division and left-hand division of Geyr's 24 Panzer Corps, also started its advance successfully (Map 7). Before addressing the division's combat action, a few words about its commander: Model had assumed command of 3 PD in November 1940; an exemplary leader of men, and a man of remarkable personal bravery, he could always be found at the forward edge of battle. Model would attain the rank of field marshal in 1944, by which time he had become one of the *Wehrmacht*'s most elite general officers and an acknowledged defensive expert due to his achievements on the Russian front. While much has been made by historians of his pro-Hitler, pro-Nazi views, other historians have offered persuasive evidence to the contrary.[101]

Punctually, at 0315 hours, the roar of hundreds of artillery pieces, including 210mm heavy howitzers, shattered the early morning calm; singled out for particular punishment was the border village of Stradecz, its church tower visible above the thick morning fog.[102] Protected by the hurricane of fire, infantry assault parties of 3 PD crossed the river in rubber boats, while motorcycle riflemen and reconnaissance troops drove unopposed across the bridge at Koden. At 0325, *Kampfgruppe* Kleemann[103] reported that enemy resistance was so far nonexistent (*gleich Null*), and that only a single round of artillery had been fired near the bridge. Five minutes later, *Kampfgruppe* Audörsch[104] reported no enemy reaction in its sector. By 0350, a complete battalion of the division's 3 Rifle Regiment (II./S.R. 3) was across the Bug, while the first tanks of its 6 Panzer Regiment were rolling over the bridge. Plunging directly through the waters of the Bug and crawling up the far bank was a small detachment of Panzer III tanks that had been specially modified for amphibious operations.[105]

Although the vital Koden bridge was in German hands, teams of engineers threw up additional spans several kilometers up and down the river to expedite the crossing of the division's armored fighting vehicles, trucks, passenger cars, and motorcycles, which together numbered in the thousands. At the same time, security teams fanned out along the eastern bank while motorcycle riflemen and reconnaissance troops rode east to seek out the main body of the enemy. As rapidly as they could get across the river, the larger battle groups into which Model had organized his division "formed up to follow in the wake of the scouting parties. There was an air of calm professionalism about these movements: Troops rode casually atop any moving vehicle, but the trained eye could not fail to observe that all eyes were scanning the road, the tree line, and the horizon, while every weapon was carried at the ready."[106]

Meeting only desultory defensive fire, after just a few hours the division's assault teams had cleared the east bank of the Bug and, after neutralizing a series of enemy bunkers, infantry of the 3 and 394 Rifle Regiments secured their first objective—the border village of Stradecz, defended to the last man by troops of the Soviet 75 Rifle Division.[107] At 1000 hours, the situation was well enough in hand that the main body of the division's tanks could begin to rumble across the Koden bridge, while the panzers of *Hauptmann* Schneider-Kostalski's 3rd Battalion (III./PzRgt 6)—in the van of Model's attack—took enemy strong points under fire.[108]

As of 0935 hours, as recorded in the war diary of 3 Panzer Division, enemy resistance remained "very weak." Within an hour, however, the division was running into serious difficulties—not due to enemy action but the result of massive vehicle congestion caused by "catastrophic road conditions" along the division's route of advance (*Vormarschweg*). Simply put, vehicles were becoming stuck in a swamp, making it impossible to continue on the planned road route. Model hastened to the site of the stoppage, only to have his vehicle get stuck as well.[109] After consulting with the commander of 24 Panzer Corps (Geyr), he ordered his troops (1500 hours) "to turn to the right" and use Panzer Route 1 for its further advance; in doing so, 3 PD would actually reach the *Panzerstrasse* before the lead elements of 4 PD (to whom, it will be recalled, the road was originally assigned). In any case, both panzer divisions were, by mid-afternoon, prepared to follow each other on the same route.[110]

The battle groups of 3 Panzer Division had by now already begun to engage the Red Army forces in their path. These included "disorganized bits and pieces" of 6 and 42 Rifle

Divisions of Maj.-Gen. V. S. Popov's 28 Rifle Corps. "Popov's men attempted to organize a defense under the worst possible conditions," posited military historian Steven H. Newton:

> Poorly trained to begin with, both divisions had been maintained at reduced manning levels and had recently been deprived of much of their field artillery. These men had not been at a high level of alert when the German bombardment started, and the efforts of their commanders to turn them out of their barracks into prepared defensive positions were hindered not only by enemy artillery but also by swarms of Luftwaffe fighter-bombers appearing with the dawn. When the main bodies of the divisions of the 24 and 47 Panzer Corps hit them, "the Russian defenses might have been a row of glass houses," observed one German lieutenant.[111]

By mid-afternoon, Model's 3 Panzer Division—now in the van *Kampfgruppe* Lewinski, consisting of the division's reconnaissance battalion, a motorized infantry battalion, a tank battalion, and two batteries of AT guns—had cleared the Soviet border defenses and was pressing for Kobrin; in doing so, Model's division, along with 4 Panzer Division on its right, and Lemelsen's 47 Panzer Corps on its left, had ripped a 50-kilometer gap in the front of Korobkov's 4 Army. In a desperate attempt to stop the advancing panzers, the two tank divisions of Soviet 14 Mechanized Corps (22 and 30 TD) had, by midday, begun to strike at the spearheads of Guderian's armor.[112] Commanded by Maj.-Gen. S. I. Oborin, the recently formed 14 Mechanized Corps was well understrength, having begun the day with only 518 tanks, all of which were older T-28 or BT models; in addition, some of the tanks were armed with no more than a machine gun and, in general, suffered from a paucity of armor-piercing ammunition and spare parts.[113] To make matters worse, Oborin's command post had been bombed by the *Luftwaffe* at 0500, knocking out his communication links,[114] while the opening German artillery barrage and aerial assault had produced 20 percent casualties in 22 TD[115] and demolished much of the division's ammunition and fuel stockpiles and artillery.

> During the enemy's artillery preparation, the [22 Tank Division], which was located in the southern military settlement of Brest, 2.5–3.5 kilometers from the state frontier, suffered huge losses. This settlement was situated on a plain and could be easily observed by the enemy. The artillery fire on the settlement and the subsequent air raids proved unexpected for the division. A large number of the rank and file and family members of the division's commanders perished and were wounded. This was made worse by the crowded situation of the division's units. A significant portion of the tanks, artillery and vehicles were destroyed, as well as more than half of the fuel trucks, workshops and kitchens. The division's artillery depot and a depot of fuels and lubricants caught fire (the first in the Brest fortress's Volhynia fortifications and the second in the village of Pugachevo). Attempts by the subunit commanders to remove the combat equipment

from their hangars and parks under enemy fire cost a lot of people their lives. That's
when the chief of the division's propaganda section, Regimental Commissar Illarionov,
perished. The chief of the division's medical service, Major Smirnov, led the evacuation
of the wounded from the southern military settlement to the rear under unceasing bom-
bardment. The doctor was unable to get out himself and he was captured.[116]

When the Soviet 22 Tank Division finally collided with Model's 3 Panzer Division, the results were preordained. Indeed, in the ensuing encounters—in some cases, Soviet tanks simply tried to slip past their tormentors and escape to the east[117]—the tanks of Maj.-Gen. V. P. Puganov's 22 Tank Division were smashed to pieces by Model's armor and wave after wave of screaming *Stuka* divebombers, turning the division's unwieldy march columns (which had no antiaircraft protection) into "long strings of blazing wrecks" along the few roads to the east of Brest. By day's end, the division had lost almost half its tanks and was low on ammunition and fuel;[118] the next day, its commander would be killed trying to launch a counterattack. As for Model's experienced and deadly efficient panzer crews, through June 23 they destroyed 197 enemy light tanks and several hundred guns of different calibers.[119]

Because forward progress was still slowed by traffic congestion and road condi-tions—which, it seems, were not much better on Panzer Route 1—it was after dark when the lead elements of 3 Panzer Division reached the Muchaviec (Mukhavets) River east of Brest-Litovsk. Since the wooden bridge there had already been burned down, movement came to a temporary halt. As a former platoon commander in the division's 6 Panzer Regiment summed up the day's events: "We had traveled a distance of only 18 kilometers when it should have been 80 kilometers!"[120] In its evening report to 24 Panzer Corps headquarters, 3 Panzer Division observed that the challenges of navigat-ing the swampy, sandy terrain had posed a greater hardship than had opposition from the enemy (Map 8).[121]

Forming the left wing of 2 Panzer Group, Lemelsen's 47 Panzer Corps launched its attack from astride the town of Pratulin (northwest of Brest-Litovsk) with its 18 Panzer Division on the right and 17 Panzer Division on the left (29 Motorized Division in reserve). The 18 PD began the Russian campaign with 218 tanks (114 Pz IIIs, thirty-six Pz IVs), including a special battalion of eighty amphibious tanks and a battalion of flamethrower tanks; its commander, *Generalmajor* Walther K. Nehring, was an inter-national expert on armored warfare who had worked closely with Guderian and others in the 1930s to develop tactical *Blitzkrieg* theory and create the German panzer arm.[122] *Generalleutnant* Hans-Jürgen von Arnim's 17 PD began operations with a complement of 202 tanks (106 Pz IIIs, thirty Pz IVs).[123] Along the front of 47 Panzer Corps there were no Bug bridges to capture; its engineers had to build them. What that meant was that Lemelsen's two panzer divisions had to rapidly establish a deep bridgehead—one strong enough to repel any Soviet attempt to crush it before the bulk of the corps' armor had been committed to the drive east. The main axis of advance was to be along Panzer Route 2 (*Panzerstrasse 2*), "an arbitrary link between the towns of Pruzhany, Slonim, and Minsk. Guderian's main effort was here."[124]

The terrain in the attack sector of 17 Panzer Division was described in detail in a study prepared for the U.S. Army in Europe in 1947 by Kurt Cuno, in June 1941 an *Oberst* in command of 17 PD's 39 Panzer Regiment; his observations on the state of Russian preparedness are also of interest:

> *The terrain over which the division was to advance consisted of rolling country with elevations ranging from 132–200 yards. It was intersected by numerous small creeks and streams that ran into the Bug River. The countryside consisted mainly of woods and meadows, and of cultivated land in the vicinity of scattered rural settlements most of which were hidden among clusters of tall trees. In mid-June and during good weather, the ground was dry and could support motor vehicles of all types. Depressions in the ground and gullies were partially muddy or swampy and impassable for wheeled motor vehicles. The low plain near the Bug River was partially covered with large marshes.*
>
> *The Bug River was from 55–110 yards wide, had a normal spring water level of 9–12 feet and a moderately strong current. The Bug was a winding river with numerous sharp bends. Its banks were covered with alder bushes and clumps of trees. Occasionally its banks descended gradually and sometimes fell off steeply, sometimes as much as 11 feet.*
>
> *No bridges existed and the river was not fordable. No improved approach routes led to the bank of the river. The terrain, generally, was favorable for the approach, assembly and attack. However, approach roads were required before motor vehicles could approach the banks of the Bug River.*
>
> *The enemy bank was protected by a weak, continuous wire entanglement along the river. Observation posts were located along the river at various points. Temporary and permanent field fortifications and various strong points were located behind the barbed wire along the banks and covered the river and its approaches with fire. Enemy defense installations were manned by squads or companies. Artillery positions, some poorly camouflaged and some still in the process of construction, were located in the rear area. Troops, apparently construction troops and reserves, were stationed in [several towns].[125]*

June 22, 0315 hours: In the "last shadows of the night," the first wave of assault troops, covered by a curtain of artillery fire and protective smoke screens, began to cross the Bug River in rubber rafts and assault boats. At 0340 hours, the first Ju-87B *Stukas* appeared above the battlefield, sirens howling as they dived at steep angles on their targets below. Fifteen minutes later (0355), the lead combat troops of both 17 and 18 PD were firmly on the eastern bank, their weapons including light antitank guns and heavy machine guns. Some Russian pickets opened up with automatic rifles and light machine guns but were soon silenced. So far at least, the German assault parties had encountered no enemy artillery fire. While the Germans dug in, "everything that could be pumped into the bridgehead was ferried across. The sappers at once got down to building a pontoon bridge."[126] In his personal diary, Erich Hager, a tank radio operator in 17 PD, scribbled down his first thoughts as the attack got underway:

> [0315] our artillery fire begins. A mighty display of firepower. We are standing ready for attack. However, the Russians skedaddle. At midday we come to the Bug [River], stand for an hour at the bridge, which has been built. See my first air battle. 8 bombers were shot down by our aircraft. Awful to watch. Crossed the Bug. We come to the first of our dead. Snipers were the culprits? Wounded Russians are still lying here. Password is drive and keep driving. All through the day and night.[127]

At 0443 hours, the first of eighty amphibious tanks (Pz IIIs and IVs) of Nehring's panzer division began to ford the Bug by diving straight into the river.[128] Originally destined for Operation *Sealion*, these special tanks were equipped with air intakes and exhaust snorkel pipes, while all openings had been carefully sealed to prevent water intrusion. The specter of "swimming tanks" created a sensation of sorts and, in one instance at least, more than a modicum of skepticism: "The artillerymen told me about an unbelievable experience," wrote an officer in 18 Panzer Division. "At our crossing point, they said, tanks dived into the Bug like U-boats and then reappeared on the east bank. Must be pretty strong tobacco that they're smoking, I thought to myself, but it was true."[129] And true it most certainly was:

> At [0443] hours Sergeant Wierschin advanced into the Bug with diving tank No. 1. The infantrymen watched him in amazement. The water closed over the tank. "Playing at U-boats!" Only the slim steel tube which supplied fresh air to the crews and the engine showed above the surface, indicating Wierschin's progress under water. There were also exhaust bubbles, but these were quickly obliterated by the current.
>
> Tank after tank—the whole of 1st Battalion, 18 Panzer Regiment, under the battalion commander, Manfred Graf Strachwitz—dived into the river. And now the first ones were crawling up the far bank like mysterious amphibians. A soft plop and the rubber caps were blown off the gun muzzles. The gun-loaders let the air out of the bicycle inner tubes round the turrets. Turret hatches were flung open and the skippers wriggled out. An arm thrust into the air three times: the signal "Tanks forward."
>
> Eighty tanks had crossed the frontier river under water. Eighty tanks were moving into action.[130]

Strachwitz's panzers landed on the far bank just in time to chase off a clutch of Soviet armored cars, knocking out several in the process. Wasting no time, General Nehring climbed into one of the assault boats of his combat engineers and crossed the river. After the vehicles of his tactical headquarters—the general's APC command vehicle, two Pz III command tanks, two SP flak guns, some thirty motorcycles, etc.[131]—had been shepherded across on pontoon ferries, Nehring, accompanied by several of his staff and *Graf* Strachwitz, joined his tanks as they began their advance. Commencing their "panzer raid" into Russia, they headed northeast toward Pruzhany, far outpacing the wheeled components of the division. At 0650 hours, Guderian crossed the Bug in an assault boat in the vicinity of Kolodno; as soon as his command car and two armored wireless trucks had been ferried into the bridgehead, he made out for Nehring's panzers: "I began by following the tank tracks of 18 Panzer Division and soon reached the bridge over the Lesna, whose capture was important for the advance of 47 Panzer Corps."[132] As noted in the war diary of Guderian's panzer group at 0800, both 17 and 18 Panzer Division were making good progress. At 1025, the leading tank company of 18 PD reached the Lesna River 10 kilometers north of Brest-Litovsk and crossed on the still intact bridge. With Guderian in tow, Nehring's tanks rolled on down Panzer Route 2, in pursuit of the still shaken enemy without regard to their flanks, while ignoring the fact that the mass of the division's armor was still well to the rear.[133] It was a textbook example of *Blitzkrieg* in action.

Across the front of 2 Panzer Group, nine bridges were in use by midday, three of them newly constructed by engineers.[134] In his diary, General Lemelsen (47 PzK) registered his satisfaction with the opening acts of the campaign:

> It was certainly a pretty grand experience, that start to the attack . . . At 0315 hours precisely . . . the hellish concert of the artillery let rip and, at the same time, the riflemen plunged into the water with pneumatic boats and made the crossing with those and assault boats. Contrary to expectations, the reaction of the enemy was extremely limited, which meant that construction of the bridge could start very quickly; astonishingly, neither did enemy artillery open up nor did their planes drop bombs. All the bunkers that had been located through weeks of observation were incomplete and unmanned. The greatest difficulties were caused by the very wet terrain on the other side of the Bug before you could get to a solid pathway. I soon crossed over the river in my command tank and accompanied the forward elements of 18 Panzer Division. Then we went inexorably onward along the Bug, at first straight to the east—the enemy had not thought of that—and then to the northeast across the Lesna. All the bridges were intact—our greatest concern—a sign that the Russians had been taken completely by surprise.[135]

If General Lemelsen was thrilled by the results of the first few hours of the campaign, the same cannot be said of Colonel L. M. Sandalov, chief of staff to Soviet 4 Army. Like his commanding officer, Lt.-Gen. A. A. Korobkov, and so many others, he had spent the days and weeks before June 22 refusing to believe that his country was on the cusp of war with Germany. Even after the bombs began to fall he clung to the conceit that war could somehow still be avoided.

> *Yes, until the last moment you [Korobkov] and I didn't believe it. Until we saw with our own eyes the ruins of the building that housed the army's headquarters, until we heard about the death of people close to us, everyone continued to hope that this still isn't war. We readily believed that some kind of hostile forces had cooked up an unheard of provocation and that if we didn't give in to it, then we could avoid war.*[136]

At some point that day, Colonel Sandalov drove out to the front to gain an appreciation of the disaster unfolding at the frontier. What he saw and experienced is recorded in his 1966 memoir.

> *The railroad tracks at Zhabinka station were clogged with rail cars smashed and burned by the enemy's aviation and the station was destroyed. An artillery cannonade could be heard from the direction of Brest. Enemy planes unceasingly strafing the troops who were hurriedly outfitting a new defensive line around Zhabinka [on the Muchaviec River]. Lines of civilian population moving to the rear stretched along all the roads and paths. From time to time uncoordinated groups of military personnel and even small subunits would appear on the roads. Blocking detachments would stop them and send them to the nearest units of the 28 Rifle Corps . . .*
>
> *Having set out on the Warsaw highway, I was constantly forced to pass individual cars and columns of trucks with belongings being evacuated from Brest. The people accompanying the freight intensely observed the sky and with the appearance of enemy planes would desperately knock against the driver's cabin, demanding that the vehicle get off the highway and into the woods. Carts with safes and archives from Party and Soviet institutions moved along the forest roads and the highway shoulder. From time to time we came across groups of freshly mobilized citizens, accompanied by representatives of the military commissariats. But there were a lot more refugees—men, women and children. They all had bundles, knapsacks and bags. Deathly tired, with sorrowfully sunken faces, they silently moved toward Kobrin, hiding under the trees and in the bushes from the enemy air force.*[137]

Meanwhile, the tanks and motorcycle riflemen leading the attack of Nehring's 18 Panzer Division had captured the village of Vidoml' as they pushed up Panzer Route 2 toward Pruzhany. At the same time, the tank regiments of Soviet 30 Tank Division (14 Mechanized Corps) had debouched from the woods southwest of Pruzhany and moved out to attack. "Fighting was going on along the approaches to Pilishchi,"[138] recalled Sandalov. "The forward edge of our defenses was clearly defined by the German aviation: It circled over the battlefield and through vertical strafing fire showed where our tanks were located."[139] Bypassing Vidoml' from the north, Sandalov headed for the town of Pilishchi. He arrived there at 1230 hours: "Just at that moment, right before our eyes, the troops deployed for battle and the main forces of both of 30 Tank Division's tank regiments attacked."[140]

In Sandalov's account, the weight of the Soviet tank attack sent the German panzers staggering back to Vidoml' ("the enemy did not withstand this impulsive attack and again rolled back to Vidoml'").[141] The war diary of 18 Panzer Division recalls the engagement quite differently, recording the destruction of thirty-six Soviet tanks by late afternoon (1730 hours) and that *Luftwaffe* bomber units had repeatedly and successfully intervened in the battle[142]—the latter point confirmed by a major Russian source, which notes that, beginning early that afternoon, Colonel S. I. Bogdanov's 30 Tank Division was "subjected to massed air strikes, suffering heavy losses."[143] As a result, after several hours of fighting—30 TD having incurred severe losses in both personnel and tanks[144]—the commander of Soviet 14 Mechanized Corps, Maj.-Gen. S. I. Oborin, decided to call off the uneven contest, issuing orders for the attack to be resumed early the next morning with all three divisions of his corps.[145] Yet the outcome would be no better; in fact, within forty-eight hours, Oborin would lose almost half of his 500 tanks.[146] The elation of 18 Panzer Division tank crews following their initial encounters with the Soviet armor was noted by the division's war diarist:

> *Despite the fierce battles, 18 Panzer Regiment [of 18 PD] has suffered hardly any losses from enemy fire. Renewed evidence for the absolute superiority of the German panzers . . . The morale in the panzer brigade is particularly strong thanks to the kill rate that it has achieved, since nobody reckoned with such great success and such clear superiority right from the first days of the campaign. The Bolshevist as an individual fighter [Einzelkämpfer] is extraordinarily tenacious and dogged. Since he has been incited against the Germans, he expects the worst if he is taken prisoner. On many occasions he tenaciously defends himself to the last round to avoid capture at all costs.[147]*

As darkness enveloped the battlefield, the vanguard of Nehring's 18 PD, chasing down *Panzerstrasse 2*, was only 20 kilometers southwest of Pruzhany. On its left, Arnim's 17 PD had reached the Lesna bridge at Rudaviec, 22 kilometers north of Brest-Litovsk (Map 8); the division's casualties on June 22 included twenty dead and twenty-four wounded in its 40 Rifle Regiment.[148] In an early evening conference at Guderian's headquarters, Field Marshal von Kluge argued that Russian forces were conducting a planned withdrawal (*planmässig ausweicht*) and intended to put up "strong organized resistance" in positions further to the rear. Guderian disagreed, pointing out that the enemy had been badly shaken by the initial German assault and was only capable of offering weak local resistance.[149] What was certain, however, was that German forces, in particular the panzers and motorized infantry, needed to rapidly and relentlessly exploit the confusion in the enemy's ranks by building on the day's successes and thwarting Soviet attempts to rebuild a stable front line in the interior.

While the armor advanced on the flanks, in the center of Guderian's 2 Panzer Group, *Gen.d.Inf.* Walter Schroth's 12 Army Corps (31, 34, 45 ID) had been engaged in a bitter and bloody struggle for the fortress of Brest-Litovsk. The Germans had sought to seize the citadel in a *coup de main*—as one author put it, Field Marshal von Kluge "hoped to capture the fortress before dinner"[150]—but would be bitterly disappointed by the outcome of the day's fighting. In fact, heroic Soviet resistance within the fortress would carry on for several weeks and become "a ghastly but epic illustration of how Russian infantrymen could fight in traditionally ferocious style."[151]

Founded in 1833, and expanded and strengthened in subsequent generations—the territory of medieval Brest was demolished to build it—the Brest fortress sat at the confluence of the Bug and Muchaviec Rivers, whose waters had been used to form four partly natural and partly artificial islands. The center island (Citadel Island), the smallest of the four, was the heart of the fortress, and was ringed by the three other islands to the south, west, and north; together, they formed the four fortified blocks of the massive citadel. The islands were studded with strong points of all kinds—hundreds of casemate and cellar positions, armored cupolas, dug in tanks, bastions or old casement forts complete with towers, etc.—with many of the fortifications concealed by thick undergrowth and clumps of tall trees. Even the barracks, which could accommodate 12,000 troops, were reinforced with walls 1½ meters thick that could withstand fire from all but the heaviest-caliber artillery. The south, west, and north islands, which provided an outer defensive belt, were ringed by earthworks nearly 10 meters high; deep moats filled with water posed another daunting obstacle. All told, the four fortified islands covered an area of about four square kilometers. Just outside the fortress was a gently undulating plain cut by river branches and streams, as well as several belts of forest, which, in swampy areas, gave way to patches of alder.[152]

The fortress was garrisoned by the 6 and 42 Rifle Divisions (28 Rifle Corps), the 17 Brest Border Guards Detachment, and the 132 Separate NKVD Military Escort Battalion. On June 22, however, these formations were not at full strength. Major elements of both rifle divisions were outside the fortress, participating in summer training exercises or, more likely, building fortifications in the Brest Fortified Region; in addition, a portion of 6 Rifle Division's artillery regiment had been moved out to the 4 Army's artillery firing range. Some of the troops inside the fortress did not have weapons, and many officers, spending the weekend at home, were absent. According to Russian journalist Rostislav Aliev, whose meticulously researched book (*The Siege of Brest 1941*) is the finest to date on the savage struggle for the fortress, there were about 9,000 Red Army soldiers inside the citadel on June 22; of these, about 1,100 "were part of alert units and thus presumably prepared to meet the German attack."[153]

As we have seen, Guderian's armor began its attacks on either side of the Brest fortress, whose two rivers and water-filled ditches rendered it, from the panzer commander's perspective, "immune to tank attack."[154] Thus an infantry corps, the 12th, commanded by one of the *Wehrmacht*'s most experienced corps commanders, was placed under Guderian and assigned the task of assaulting the fortress and protecting the inner flanks of the panzer corps as they traversed the frontier. The mission of seizing the fortress fell to 12 Army Corps' 45 Infantry Division (*Generalmajor* Fritz Schlieper), which, during the French campaign of 1940, had successfully forced the Aisne River while breaching a belt of concrete fortifications. In addition to seizing the citadel, the mostly Austrian division was to capture the four-span railway bridge over the Bug (at a point directly northwest of the fortress) and the five bridges spanning the Muchaviec south of the city of Brest, while securing the high ground just beyond the city. If successful, this would clear the way for the advance of Guderian's tanks along Panzer Route 1, the route toward Kobrin assigned to 24 Panzer Corps.[155]

The officers and men of Schlieper's 45 ID had no doubt about the outcome of the impending operation. *Leutnant* Michael Wechtler, commander of an infantry company in the division (5./IR 133), figured it would be "easy," noting that the first day's objective lay 5 kilometers east of Brest. Moreover, those who had observed the fortifications from a distance commonly believed "they were more like ordinary barracks than a fortress." Reflecting this optimism was the fact that only two of the division's nine infantry battalions were earmarked for the initial assault, while three battalions would still be deploying and four held in reserve. And yet "the assignment of such significant strength to the reserve more likely suggests the German command's lack of confidence and its wish to hold reserves ready to overcome any surprises. The first wave would thus be more like a reconnaissance in force."[156]

On hand to record the assault on the fortress were correspondents from the *Wehrmacht*'s main journals—*Die Wehrmacht* and *Signal*—as well as cameramen from the Reich's newsreel journal *Deutsche Wochenschau* (an indication of the propaganda value assigned to the operation). For the opening barrage the Germans had amassed an awesome display of firepower, including the nine light and three medium batteries of 45 ID; three batteries of 210mm heavy howitzers (nine guns); two 600mm "*Karl*" siege mortars (aptly christened "*Thor*" and "*Odin*," and in the *Wehrmacht* second in their power to only the 800mm "*Dora*" heavy guns);[157] and the 4 Rocket Projector Regiment (*Nebel-Rgt. z.b.V. Nr. 4*), whose nine *Nebelwerfer* batteries would drop 2,880 missiles on the fortress in rapid succession.[158] Artillery of the neighboring 34 and 31 Infantry Divisions was also part of the concentrated fire plan, which, in addition to smashing the fortress with thousands of shells, targeted Soviet positions along the Bug River, Soviet troop concentrations, and the exits from the fortress. In charge of coordinating the deadly hurricane of fire was *Generalmajor* Friedrich Krischer, under the headquarters of Artillery Commander 27 (*Arko 27*).[159]

At precisely 0315 hours, the guns opened fire and the earth began to shake. German soldiers and war correspondents who observed the spectacle were stunned by what they saw. "The sky was filled with bursting shells of every caliber," confessed one German veteran after the war. "It was an awful roaring, exploding, crackling and howling as if hell was actually about to come on earth." War correspondent Gerd Habedanck noted the "strong [drafts] of air [that] blew into our faces," and that "young willows were bent over as if in a storm."[160] Walther Loos, serving in the 45 ID's 130 Infantry Regiment, recalled the "thunder and howling of wailing shells," ranging from the smallest to the largest caliber, as they passed overhead and streaked toward their targets on the opposite bank of the river.

> *Involuntarily ducking our heads, we were almost forgetting to breathe. However, a second later the artillery fire of a different heavy gun gathered such a deafening and breath-taking strength like I never experienced later. Even those participants in the First World War among us later acknowledged that at that time, they had never experienced fire of such concentrated power. The sky turned red, and even though it was night, it became as light as day. Large trees fringing the Bug swayed wildly and were torn to pieces as if from an invisible force by the atmospheric pressure of the passing shells.*[161]

Within minutes the fortress was transformed into a sea of fire. From their command post in Terespol, officers of 45 ID could see tall columns of smoke and fire erupt across the river as fuel and ammunition dumps blew up. Among the first victims were Soviet border guardsmen, buried beneath the ruins of their building. The hospital on South Island, rocketed by the *Nebelwerfers*, erupted in flames, leaving terrified hospital staff and patients unable to escape to perish in inconceivable ways. Along with Red Army soldiers, women and children were blown apart by the heavy "*Karl*" mortar shells, or wounded by shell fragments. The "scale of destruction was stunning."[162] Decades later, A. A. Arschinowa, the wife of a commander inside the fortress on June 22, recounted the almost ineffable horror of that day:

> *I had three young children. The oldest was five, my daughter was three years old. We lived together with other families inside the citadel—in the East Fort [on North Island]. When the Fascists began their surprise attack, they bombarded the fortress to such an extent that we were totally dazed. Everyone ran about in all directions, the men, the women, the children. Everyone ran all around. We had no idea what we should do first . . . Those were large guns . . . With every shell burst I felt as if my head were about to explode. The children had blood running out of their ears and mouth. My daughter died. My son has been deaf ever since. He was five years old then. When I walk through the streets of Brest today, I can still see the destruction in my mind's eye, and it causes me pain.*[163]

The *Feuerschlag* lasted thirty minutes and, as noted (Section 4.2), unfolded in progressive stages; when it ceased (0345), swarms of *Stuka* divebombers appeared above the citadel, lunging earthward and loosing their bombs. Only minutes after the barrage began, the first German combat engineers and assault troops emerged from the thickets lining the Bug, crossed the river in rubber dinghies and assault boats, and began their attack on the fortress, meeting no enemy opposition. They did encounter their first Russians, however, "clustered in groups, stunned by the horror of the artillery barrage, or hiding one by one. They had faces pale with fear; many, it seemed, had lost the ability to speak and were surrendering in a daze."[164]

A group of nine assault boats, a mixed force of combat engineers and infantry led by *Leutnant* Kraemers, had been assigned the task of seizing several of the bridges over the Muchaviec. Four of the boats, however, were quickly put out of action: barely reaching the water, they were struck by "friendly" artillery fire falling short, leaving twenty men dead and wounded. Kraemers regrouped with the survivors and motored up the river, but soon two more boats were lost, this time to enemy fire. Pressing on with their three surviving boats, they captured the first two bridges by 0355 hours, supported by a *Stosstrupp* of 130 Infantry Regiment; at 0510, again with the support of 130 IR, as well as *Brandenburg* commandos, they took by storm bridge "*Wulka*," their final objective, along with eighty dazed prisoners. No doubt under enormous stress after losing most of his detachment, Kraemers, seeking to "crown the operation with [a] dramatic gesture," tried to raise a swastika flag over the bridge: He "probably didn't hear the single shot fired by some sniper. The others ran up to him, but it was already too late—Kraemers died, clutching the Reich flag, fatally wounded in the head."[165]

With 130 Infantry Regiment attacking south of the fortress and the city of Brest-Litovsk, all five of the still intact bridges over the Muchaviec River were soon in German hands. The Russians attempted to counterattack with tanks but were rapidly repulsed, losing twelve tanks for their efforts. Along the northern axis of the advance, 135 Infantry Regiment had captured the vital railway bridge in less than fifteen minutes (0327), and German armored cars began to roll across immediately; by 0415 hours, assault guns of 31 Infantry Division were also rumbling over the bridge. Initial progress against the fortress itself also appeared to be good, the attacking troops advancing swiftly across the outer island belt and, at some points, forcing their way inside the fortress's keep—the central island (Citadel Island). Both 12 Army Corps and 45 ID were encouraged by the early results, with the latter reporting at 0625 hours that "the division believes it will soon have the citadel firmly in hand."[166]

In a combat report filed later that morning, Colonel Sandalov, Chief of Staff, Soviet 4 Army, noted that the "Brest garrison has suffered heavy losses from the enemy's air and artillery, as a result of which the 6 Rifle Division was forced by 0600 to give up [the city of] Brest in fighting." Sandalov also reported that the 4 Army headquarters in Kobrin had been destroyed by air attack and that the army's air regiments had sustained "heavy losses."[167]

Yet within the fortress the situation soon began to take a turn for the worse for the attacking Germans. By 0730, 45 Infantry Division was reporting that strong elements of the garrison were now firing from behind on the forward assault units. In addition, the German assault detachments, scattered among the bushes, trees, buildings, and ruins of the fortress, had become so enmeshed among its defenders that artillery support was no longer an option. Sharpshooters concealed in the trees or firing from rooftop outlets began to take a heavy toll, particularly on German officers and NCOs. Others fired at the Germans from buildings, cellars, or sewers; even while hidden in garbage cans or behind piles of rags. Among the officers of 45 ID to perish this day were three battalion commanders—two belonging to 135 IR and the commander of 1st Battalion, 99 Artillery Regiment.[168]

While the fighting "swirled around numerous bridges, gates, buildings, mess halls and sections of barracks,"[169] confidence among the attackers soon began to yield to a growing pessimism. In an effort to regain the momentum, the division's 133 Infantry Regiment, hitherto 12 Army Corps reserve, was committed to battle by early afternoon. Infantry guns, antitank guns, and light field howitzers were brought forward to engage strong points with direct fire, while a battery of assault guns passing by was commandeered by the commander of 135 IR and thrown into the fray—all with little impact on the seemingly impervious fortifications. Some of the assault parties had also become cut off, with one group of seventy men trapped deep inside the fortress in the garrison church on Citadel Island.[170]

The war diary of 45 ID includes the following entry for 1300 hours: "In the citadel itself the division has yet to master the situation [*die Division ist noch nicht Herr der Lage*]. The enemy is putting up a defense that the division—after the strong barrage and the first confident reports from the combat units—had not anticipated."[171] Less than an hour later, General Schlieper, observing the faltering attack on Citadel Island, reached the only conclusion possible: the attempt to capture the fortress in a surprise infantry assault had failed. GFM von Bock, who had visited the CP of 12 Army Corps less than an hour before, came to the same conclusion. As a result, by mid-afternoon, Schlieper had decided to pull back his battered battalions under cover of darkness. The Russian garrison was to be tightly encircled and systematically reduced by artillery fire. Early that evening, GFM von Kluge, Commander, Fourth Army, arrived at the CP of 45 ID. He confirmed Schlieper's decision, pointing out that the fighting for the fortress was now of only local significance [*örtliche Bedeutung*], for the key bridges had all been captured and traffic across the railway and along Panzer Route 1 was now possible. Unnecessary losses were thus to be avoided; the enemy, Kluge averred, starved into submission.[172]

Shortly before Kluge had arrived at the 45 ID command post, the Germans had sent out Soviet prisoners and local residents bearing flags of truce in an effort to compel the Russians still holding out in the ruins of the fortress to surrender. The gesture was largely unsuccessful, and some of the flag-of-truce bearers were gunned down.[173] In a publication released by the *Wehrmacht* High Command (OKW) in 1943, a participant in the battle for the Brest fortress recorded his impressions of the savage fighting on June 22:

> *The battles on the islands extremely difficult. Complex terrain: groups of houses, clusters of trees, bushes, narrow strips of water, plus the ruins, and the enemy is everywhere. His snipers are excellently camouflaged in the trees. Camouflage suits made of gauze with leaves attached to them. Superb snipers! Shooting from hatches in the ground, basement windows, sewage pipes . . .*
>
> *First impression: the Bolshevist fights to his very last breath. Perhaps because of the threat of the commissars: those who fall into German captivity are shot. (According to statements by the first prisoners.) At any rate: no slackening of fighting power, even though resistance futile since citadel is surrounded.*
>
> *Silent night. We dig the first graves.*[174]

In response to Schlieper's order, the German assault troops were withdrawn and reorganized in the encirclement ring, with the exception of the exhausted and, in some cases, wounded men trapped inside the garrison church.[175] The abandoned positions were reoccupied posthaste by the surviving Russian defenders. The bitter and bloody fighting on this first day of the war had cost 45 Infantry Division 311 dead—twenty-one officers and 290 NCOs and enlisted men[176]—perhaps greater losses than those suffered by any other division of the *Ostheer* on June 22, 1941. Organized Russian resistance inside the fortress would not be broken until the end of the month. During the Soviet winter offensive in December 1941, the 45 ID would be overrun and sustain even more horrific casualties, only to be "laboriously rebuilt" in 1942.[177]

4.4: Fourth Army Operations

German Fourth Army (headquarters in Miedzyrzec Podlaski, more than 100 kilometers southeast of Warsaw) was commanded by the fifty-eight-year-old *Generalfeldmarschall* Günther von Kluge; his chief of staff was *Obst.i.G.* Günther Blumentritt. Kluge had assumed command of Fourth Army during the mobilization for war on August 26, 1939, and had led it with distinction during the campaigns in Poland and France. He was promoted to field marshal on July 19, 1940. In December 1941, he relieved GFM von Bock as C-in-C of Army Group Center, a post he would hold until October 1943, when he was seriously injured in an automobile accident. In July 1944, he replaced GFM von Rundstedt as C-in-C West, which included Army Group B, then fighting the Anglo-American armies in Normandy.[178]

Having served as Kluge's aide-de-camp in 1942/43, Philipp *Freiherr* von Boeselager[179] offered a balanced appraisal of the field marshal: He was "body and soul" (*Leib und Seele*) a soldier; "highly intelligent and brave" and an "outstanding military leader" who cared deeply for the well-being of his men. If he lacked the strategic vision of a Manstein, he still possessed a "clear strategic view and always grasped the interrelationship between the economy, geopolitics and military planning." Conversely, as a superior, he was "more than difficult," self-centered (*egoistisch*), insecure and extremely susceptible to criticism. Although he despised the Nazis—particularly men like Martin Bormann and Heinrich Himmler—he had an oddly ambivalent attitude toward Hitler, simultaneously admiring him while rejecting his unpredictability (*Unberechenbarkeit*) and contempt for mankind (*Menschenverachtung*).[180]

Kluge had no nose for politics—nor any interest in politics—and was fond of saying that he "understood nothing about it." Which is ironic when one considers that, during his tenure as C-in-C of Army Group Center, many of his closest staff officers were committed members of the anti-Hitler resistance. Kluge tolerated the anti-Hitler cabal in his midst and, for the most part, tried to "limit himself to an attitude of benevolent neutrality." This, however, was not enough to save him: On August 17, 1944, he was removed from his post as C-in-C West by Hitler on suspicion of involvement in the failed July 20, 1944, *Attentat* against the *Führer*. Two days later, on his way back to Germany, he stopped in Metz, the scene of some of his battles in the Great War of 1914/18. He "spread out a blanket, and ordered his driver to leave him. He then took a cyanide capsule. Hitler ordered that he be buried quietly, with military pallbearers but without military honors."[181] In the final analysis, Kluge was an extraordinary soldier, but a man with serious character flaws.[182]

Field Marshal von Kluge's Fourth Army consisted of some 205,000 men (twelve divisions) organized in four army corps (from right to left): *Gen.d.Inf.* Gotthard Heinrici's 43 Army Corps (131, 134, 252 ID); *Gen.d.Inf.* Hermann Geyer's 9 Army Corps (137, 263, 292 ID); *Gen.d.Art.* Wilhelm Fahrmbacher's 7 Army Corps (7, 23, 258, 268 ID); and (in reserve) *Gen.d.Inf.* Hans-Gustav Felber's 13 Army Corps (17, 87 ID). The 221 Security Division, under the Commander, Rear Army Area 102, was deployed on the army's far left flank on the boundary with Ninth Army.[183] General Headquarters troops assigned to Fourth Army included the following:

- Assault Gun Battalions 226 and 203 (9 and 7 AK, respectively)
- 4 105mm cannon battalions (2 to 43 AK; 1 each to 7 and 9 AK)
- 1 mixed artillery battalion (9 AK)
- 4 150mm medium howitzer battalions (2 to 7 AK; 1 each to 43 and 9 AK)
- 2 210mm heavy howitzer battalions (mot.) (1 each to 43 and 7 AK)
- 3 210mm heavy howitzer battalions (partially mobile) (1 each to 9 and 7 AK; 1 controlled by 4 Army [*z.V. AOK 4*])
- 1 heavy artillery battalion (210mm) for flat trajectory file (*Flachfeuer*) (*z.V. AOK 4*)
- 4 rail batteries (1 to 7 AK; 3 *z.V. AOK 4*)

- 1 battery "Karl" heavy artillery (assigned to attack on the Brest fortress)
- 1 flak (*fla*) battalion (43 AK)
- 3 flak (*fla*) companies (1 each to 43, 9, and 7 AK)
- 2 army flak battalions (*z. V. AOK 4*)[184]

Also distributed to Kluge's Fourth Army were five engineer battalions, bridge building troops and bridge columns "B" (*Br.Kol.B*); other units included nineteen construction and road repair battalions, four Organization Todt formations, and twenty Reich Labor Service (RAD) battalions. Among the *Luftwaffe* units assigned to Fourth Army for tactical support were five reconnaissance squadrons (one to each of the four army corps; one long-range squadron [1.(F)/33] directly under army control), and five mixed flak battalions (all *z. V. AOK 4*).[185]

The Fourth Army's attack frontage was more than 100 kilometers in length, stretching northwest from above Brest-Litovsk along (and beyond) the Bug River to the boundary with the neighboring Ninth Army; nine divisions made up the army's first assault wave, with three assembled just behind the front.[186] Operating in concert with Strauss's Ninth Army, Kluge's army corps were to carry out a relatively shallow envelopment of Soviet Western Front forces deployed within the Belostok salient, while Army Group Center's two panzer groups closed the outer encirclement ring at Minsk. The mission of Fourth Army was laid out in some detail in the Army High Command's deployment directive of January 31, 1941:

> *With its* Schwerpunkt *astride Brest-Litovsk,[187] Fourth Army is to force the crossing of the Bug River and, thereby, open the way to Minsk for 2 Panzer Group. Advancing with the bulk of its units across the Schara River at and south of Slonim, [the army], exploiting the rapid advance of the panzer groups, is to destroy the existing enemy forces between Belostok and Minsk in cooperation with Ninth Army. Advancing behind 2 Panzer Group, [the army's] further task will be, while securing its southern flank toward the Pripiat' Marshes, to force a crossing of the Berezina River between Bobruisk and Borysau and to gain the Dnepr River at and north of Mogilev.[188]*

Under cover of the preliminary barrage, and supported by fighters and fighter-bombers of Kesselring's 2 Air Fleet, Kluge's infantry began their assault at 0315 hours, striking the right wing of Lt.-Gen. A. A. Korobkov's 4 Army and the left wing of Lt.-Gen. K. D. Golubev's 10 Army—the latter, with its powerful 6 Mechanized Corps, defending in the apex of the Belostok salient (Map 6). The war diary of Fourth Army recorded the initial results of the attack:

0315: Following a powerful artillery barrage the army began to attack according to plan. After a short time the first reports were coming in, [stating] that the assault troops were making good progress and that the capture of the bridges had succeeded.

0420: It is being reported that all of the attacking divisions have crossed the Bug River and encountered little to no resistance.

0445: The divisional intelligence officer [Ic] reports his impression that the enemy has been completely surprised [völlig überrascht] by the attack. A [Soviet] air division has radioed for orders, asking what it should do; a command post in Minsk has done the same.

0530: Army chief of staff [Blumentritt] dictates an order to the corps, [stating] that the enemy has apparently been completely surprised and that the army commander has ordered the most rigorous assault [schärften Vorstoss] [on the enemy].[189]

In action on the right wing of Fourth Army were the three infantry divisions of Heinrici's 43 Army Corps. Max Kuhnert, a cavalry trooper in the corps' 131 Infantry Division, recalled the start of the assault:

At exactly 3:15 a.m., in the faint first light of day I was on my way to water the horses at the [Bug] river when the whole area exploded. All hell was let loose and I prayed for the strength to hold my two horses. The noise and sight were indescribable, the earth seemed to tremble, all the batteries came alive out of the darkness of the pine trees. Flames shot toward the border followed by the explosion of shells on the other side. All around us were what appeared to be great sheets of lightning, torn through by flames while thunder crashed and boomed. The barrage kept on and on, no one could hear anything else and orders had to be given by hand signal. We were ordered to march toward the river, where special units had already erected a pontoon bridge, over which, although we could not hear them, we could see our tanks rumbling.[190] *For an hour and a half the firing continued, and then we could hear the Russian planes attacking our invading troops; many of them got shot down by our fighters . . . Shells were now flying across from the opposite direction as well, and smoke was filling my nostrils. In fact, I prayed. This was really getting frightening.*[191]

The assault troops and combat engineers of 43 Army Corps crossed the Bug at Mielnik, east of the Polish town of Siedlce, beginning an advance that would take the corps' lead elements well beyond the frontier by dusk. An *Obergefreiter* (Corporal) H.S., on the staff of 1st Battalion, 431 Infantry Regiment (131 ID), penned a crisp note in his diary about the first hours of war on the Eastern Front: "The attack over the Bug began at 0315 hours. Everything came off without a hitch. We brought in the first prisoners."[192] Cavalry trooper Kuhnert elaborated at some length on the first Soviet prisoners captured by his regiment: "We already had some prisoners of war, most of them stragglers from the retreating Russian forces, looking very bedraggled indeed. What struck me about their appearance was their haircut—their heads were completely shaved. Now I understand why, when we had been called up and had our hair cut very short, we, as new recruits, had been called 'Russians.'"[193]

The commander of 9 Army Corps, *Gen.d.Inf.* Geyer, watched his attack go in from a farmstead behind the center of his front and just a few kilometers from the frontier. As he later recalled:

The barrage began suddenly at 0315 as ordered. I observed and heard our fire from an observation post [B-Stelle] of our artillery observation battalion. It was all most impressive! The enemy hardly responded, and it soon quieted down by us as well.

I quickly returned to my headquarters. Reports were coming in, indicating that our forwardmost detachments had all gained the opposite bank of the river, some in combat. The first prisoners were brought in. Our own losses appeared to be minor. All of the divisions were reporting that they had begun to build bridges. While not all of the reports were clear, the overall impression was satisfactory [befriedigend].[194]

The assault waves of Geyer's 9 Army Corps traversed the Bug east of the Polish town of Sokolov Podlaski. Because Geyer's three divisions had been assigned a sector of the border more than 60 kilometers in length, he had elected to consolidate his forces at decisive points for the leap across the frontier, thus ruthlessly denuding most of his front of troops. His attack across the Bug, however, was given a boost from the artillery, engineers, and heavy weapons of Felber's 13 Army Corps, which was in reserve behind Geyer's attacking divisions.[195] The 292 Infantry Division, on 9 Army Corps' right wing, recorded the start of its attack in its journal and noted that its three regiments were making good progress:

0300: About this time the sun rises up like a red sickle. The division commander [Generalmajor Martin Dehmel] is at the divisional observation post, east of Fw. Konczy-trudy.

0315: The extremely strong artillery fire begins . . . The Russian observation posts are blanketed by artificial fog. Within the first half hour all three regiments have crossed the Bug with 2–4 companies without meeting serious opposition. The surprise is complete.

0530: By [this time] the reinforced 508 Infantry Regiment has reached Hill 161.5 and the edge of the woods 1.5 kilometers southwest of Bujaki, while reconnoitering toward Zajeczniki, Bujaki and Rogavka. 509 Infantry Regiment has reached Volka Zamkova;

507 Infantry Regiment Milevo Minczevo. The first two prisoners, who had been work-
ing on field fortifications, confirm that they were totally surprised by our attack.[196]

Forming the center of 9 Army Corps, and putting in its main attack, was *Generalleut-*
nant Friedrich Bergmann's 137 Infantry Division. Supported by the concentrated fire of
fifty batteries[197] (including most all of the GHQ artillery assigned to the army corps) and
a battery of assault guns of Assault Gun Battalion 226, 137 ID crossed the frontier on a
narrow front of 6 to 7 kilometers with its three regiments launching their assaults on both
sides of Grodek.[198] Leopold Höglinger, a radio operator in the division, wrote in his diary
that "there was no resistance from the enemy [and] soon the first prisoners started coming in."[199] *Major i.G.* Meyer-Detring, chief operations officer (Ia) of the division, vividly
described the first hours of Operation *Barbarossa* along the 137 ID's front:

> *After careful preparations, in the night of 21.-22.6.[41] the regiments' assault com-*
> *panies had advanced to the west bank of the Bug. Pneumatic boats and assault boats*
> *for the crossing lay ready. Shortly after 0300 hours, General Bergmann arrived at the*
> *advance division command post on the river embankment of the Bug. The telephone*
> *operator at the switchboard in the cramped dugout recalled:*
> 　*"The matter was made more difficult because in the excitement we had forgotten*
> *the portable switchboard and now had to construct our own switchboard relay. We had*
> *connected both neighboring divisions, Artillery Commander 44 [Arko 44] and 9 Army*
> *Corps. For me, the humble soldier, the following hours were unforgettable. The general's*
> *calm, kind manner had impressed me deeply. That day was also a great experience for*
> *me from a military perspective, because the corps commander and the artillery com-*
> *mander came to the dugout later."*
> 　*The attack began in the early morning hours of the 22.6.[41]—0315 hours—*
> *with a barrage from all weapons and calibers lasting one minute. Under cover of*
> *this fire from around 200 barrels of between 100mm and 210mm, the first infantry*
> *formations embarked across the river and everywhere reached the opposite bank with-*
> *out a fight. Somewhere, a village was burning. Our own artillery then continued its*
> *incessant firing, now striking target areas located farther back, in line with the tacti-*
> *cal plan of fire, and after 25 minutes transitioned to observed fire. Large elements of*
> *the infantry were already on the opposite bank, and still nothing stirred on the enemy*
> *side. The surprise had succeeded flawlessly! Approximately one hour after the start of*
> *the attack, the first isolated pockets of resistance flared up in the bunkers, but were*
> *immediately quelled through rapid and ruthless action. Contrary to expectations, the*
> *enemy artillery also remained silent, so that the construction of the bridge could begin*
> *immediately. Eight hours later, the division's heavy weapons were already rolling*
> *across the completed bridge.*[200]

As recorded in the 137 ID war diary, the bridge was in operation by 1230 hours; assault guns, light field howitzers, and heavy infantry weapons were also ferried across the Bug. About noon, twelve Russian bombers, seeking out the newly constructed bridge, were pounced on by German fighters and targeted by German flak guns; all twelve of the bombers were shot down. It was, as Meyer-Detring recalled, "the first convincing proof of German superiority."[201]

The first difficulties for the division arose immediately upon crossing the Bug, when the decent roadways west of the river turned into barely traversable tracks of deep sand, slowing the advance and disrupting traffic on the bridge; as a consequence, vehicles were soon backed up for several kilometers. In an effort to break the logjam, vehicles had to be freed from the sand one at a time by "pushing details" (*Schiebekommandos*). "The first 100 meters of Russian territory," noted Meyer-Detring, "thus offered insight into the enormous terrain difficulties that would have to be overcome as the advance went on." Efforts to get an advance detachment underway—to take advantage of the weak enemy resistance—were also delayed by the bridge backup.[202]

On the left wing of Fourth Army, Fahrmbacher's 7 Army Corps attacked by the town of Malkinia, where the Bug River leaves the frontier and flows west into German-occupied Poland before joining the Narew River north of Warsaw.[203] The corps stormed into battle with three divisions in the first wave, one in reserve. Leading one of the assault parties of the corps' 23 Infantry Division was *Feldwebel* Becker. Under cover of the opening barrage, clutching his 9mm Walther P 38 pistol in his right hand, he rushed forward toward a railway embankment, motioning his men to follow; to their astonishment, they reached the embankment with no discernable reaction from the Russian border guards. Instinctively bent over for protection, the men scrambled up the embankment, crossed the tracks, and pressed on, the enemy now responding with isolated fire. On his right, out of the corner of his eye, Becker spied a German motorized column rumbling along a road; as far as he could see, German troops, widely dispersed and recognizable by their distinctive field gray uniforms, were advancing swiftly. The tension drained from Becker's body. The start of the attack had come off smoother than anticipated. He had not lost a single man.[204]

For many *Landser*, this Sunday, June 22, 1941, was their first day in combat—their baptism of fire (*Feuertaufe*). Such was the case for *Gefreiter* Kredel, another infantryman in 23 ID. At exactly 0315 hours, he leaped forward and began to run as fast as his legs could carry him, his light machine gun cradled in his arms. To allay his anxiety, a veteran had assured him that the first attack wave, due to the factor of surprise, usually made it through unscathed, while it was those coming after who would bear the brunt of the enemy's reaction. As he ran, he could hear bullets whistling past his helmet; they made an odd sound, he thought. Suddenly, a wooden observation tower, struck by a German anti-tank shell, disintegrated before his eyes, sending fragments of wood and Russian soldiers hurtling though the dawn sky. A German antitank unit (*Panzerjäger*) in open vehicles

(*Kübelwagen*) roared past him, their light 37mm guns in tow. In the next moment, German artillery fire began to drop short among the assault parties, evoking cries and curses from the wounded. Providently, the "friendly" artillery shifted its fire forward.[205]

Major Werner Heinemann, a decorated World War I veteran and battalion chief in 67 Infantry Regiment (23 ID), approached this first day of the war with palpable foreboding. An implacable anti-Nazi, the forty-two-year-old Heinemann had been put under house arrest in 1934 and, in response to his petition, released from active service in the *Reichswehr*. In 1940, he was put back on active duty and took part in the French campaign as a company and battalion commander. Now, on the eve of war with Russia, on the warm summer night of June 21/22, his men were quietly closing on the frontier and assembling for the attack. They had their work cut out for them: Dense thickets of barbed wire, some fifteen rows of them, lined the border. Heinemann's troops would have to cut through this wire before they could begin their assault; fortunately, an abundance of wire cutters were on hand.[206]

As the final minutes of peace slipped irretrievably away, Heinemann's thoughts turned to his experiences in Russia as a young soldier in World War I. His heart was troubled. He recalled the country's seemingly endless expanses and the difficulties encountered due to the terrain. More than most of his comrades, he recognized the formidable task now facing the German army in the East. And while he also knew that his men were in their highest state of readiness and strength, he could not shake loose from the thought that this imminent attack on Soviet Russia was an inconceivably irresponsible enterprise, not to mention a breach of the non-aggression pact that had been in place for the better part of two years.[207]

As the shortest night of the year slowly dissolved into sunlight, the artillery opened up along the front of 23 Infantry Division. Minutes later, Heinemann's two lead companies stirred into action, cutting through the thickets of wire and advancing in open order (*entfaltet*) toward their initial objective—a village just beyond the frontier. High above them, squadrons of German bombers, in tight formations, winged eastward toward their targets. On the ground, the artillery barrage was winding down, with the exception of several heavy howitzers. Yet here, too, the big guns fired short, their immensely powerful 210mm shells dropping among the forwardmost German infantry, sending impressive columns of dirt and smoke high into the air. Soon Very signal lights filled the dawn sky with their bright red bursts: "The artillery is firing short! Lift your fire!" (*Artillerie schiesst zu kurz! Feuer vorverlegen!*) Yet the damage was done, the battalion sustaining several wounded and its first dead soldier of the Russian campaign (a radioman in its signal section).[208]

After the assault groups had slipped through the lanes cut in the wire, *Major* Heinemann, at the head of his tactical operations staff, set out after them—a moment he recounted in his memoir (in third person):

Later, only many months later, his adjutant, Ekkehard Maurer, confided in him that he [Heinemann] had, back then, turned around at the entry point through the cut barbed wire entanglements and, to his adjutant and the special-missions staff officer, Zitelmann, who were following close behind him, said with an expression and tone more serious than any his long-trusted subordinates had ever seen in him: "Always remember this moment! It is the beginning of the end!" [Es ist der Anfang vom Ende!]

At that time, those words, which were even utterly forgotten by the commander, hardly penetrated the consciousness of his subordinates. In any case, they were young and more carefree than the "Old Man," and it seemed even to him that the deeply serious statement had arisen out of the unconscious of his heavy thoughts. But it happened just as it is described here and that is why it is reported, in order to show how the clash of arms back then was approached with the most insightful and grave misgivings.[209]

After visiting the front, Field Marshal von Kluge had returned to his headquarters by 0900 hours. Reports from the attacking formations revealed that, so far, few prisoners had been taken; however, among the Russians who had been captured, many had only been allotted fifteen rounds of ammunition—hardly enough rounds to mount even a pro forma defense of the frontier. Kluge and his staff were astonished by the virtual lack of enemy artillery fire in the opening hours of the attack, the army's war diary noting at 1000 hours that the Russians had responded with "only very weak artillery" (*nur ganz schwache Artillerie beim Feinde aufgetreten*). Although the army had already identified six Russian divisions opposite a narrow sector of its front, Kluge was convinced that the main Red Army forces had not been stationed at the frontier, but were somewhere farther back and would have to be found out. As a result, Fourth Army had, at about 0800, lodged a request with Kesselring's 2 Air Fleet to fly reconnaissance well behind the front to determine: (a) if the main enemy forces were falling back; or, (b) were already established in a prepared rearward position. By late afternoon, however, long-range aerial reconnaissance (*Fernaufklärung*) was reporting no signs of major Russian defensive preparations farther to the rear.[210]

Summing up the early results of the attack, the Fourth Army war diarist had, late that morning, noted that "the situation must indeed be quite difficult for the Kremlin."[211] While this was no doubt true, reports were now reaching Kluge's headquarters indicating that enemy resistance—if still largely desultory in nature—was beginning to stiffen up somewhat. At several points, the Russian border troops had fought with tenacity (*hartnäckig*); they had also mounted several minor counterattacks with tanks, which were easily repulsed.[212] Many of the Soviet frontier units, overwhelmed by the crushing German onslaught, had simply fled into the ubiquitous forests, marshes, and cornfields; after the main German assault columns had passed by, they often emerged from their hiding places to fall on German supply troops, medical personnel, motorcycle messengers, and other easy targets, or they simply shot at German soldiers from concealed positions. In innumerable contemporary German accounts—field post letters, personal diaries, war diaries—a word began to appear with disturbing frequency—*Heckenschütze*, or sniper. Indeed, from the first hours of the war, the German *Landser* faced a cunning and deadly adversary who was to torment him mercilessly throughout the campaign—the Red Army sniper.

Throughout the day, the divisions of Fourth Army continued to push beyond the frontier, often in the face of growing Soviet resistance. In its diary, 292 Infantry Division (9 AK) noted occasional firefights (*Schiessereien*) with Russian forces in the woods and cornfields.[213] That afternoon, ten to twelve hours after crossing the Bug, the attacking regiments of 137 Infantry Division (9 AK) encountered more serious enemy opposition, particularly in wooded areas. Recalled Meyer-Detring:

> *Very quickly we came to realize that forest fighting suited the Russians better than us. From the very first day the words "sniper," "tree sniper," "cunning [hinterhältig]*[214] *method of fighting," and so forth, showed up increasingly in the reports . . . The stiffening resistance was supported by disjointed counterattacks of the first enemy tanks. They were repulsed with ease. The [enemy's] light tanks and armored scout cars were greatly inferior to our anti-tank weapons. [So the thinking was]: If the Russians have nothing better to offer, nothing can go wrong!*[215]

Yet for those Germans on the receiving end of a Russian tank attack on this first day of the war, the experience could be a terrifying one, as this account by *Gefreiter* W. in 448 Infantry Regiment (137 ID) illustrates:

> *22.6.[41]. In the afternoon [there was] an enemy tank attack.* Obergefr. *Glaser got a direct hit and was dead immediately. We've now reached our objective for the day and are in a small patch of birch trees. I want to go to sleep, but I can't. So I'll keep writing. Finally our own tanks arrived [most likely he means the assault guns of Battalion 226], and the dreadful fear was finally over. My whole life over I will not forget this tank attack. I've never experienced anything in my life that was so dreadful [schrecklich]. As a simple rifleman one is entirely defenseless. But our defensive weapons are first class.*[216]

Even more dreadful was the experience of *Unteroffizier* Fritz Hübner, who made contact with the enemy somewhere west of Belostok. He described his shock and consternation—and that of his comrades—when confronted with gruesome atrocities perpetrated by Red Army soldiers.

> *We soon found the first reconnaissance patrols that had fallen into Russian hands. They had had their genitals cut off while still alive, their eyes gouged out, throats cut, or ears*

and noses cut off. We went around with grave faces, because we were frightened of this
type of fighting. Inevitably, we, too, developed an unnatural ruthlessness [unnatürliche
Härte] that had not been instilled in us during training.[217]

General Heinrici (C-in-C, 43 Army Corps) also found the first day of the war to be
a sobering one, despite the overall success of the attack. For as he, too, quickly discovered,
the "Russian way of war" was unlike anything hitherto experienced. His account, like
Hübner's, amplifies the insidious dialectic that would result in an ever expanding universe
of brutality and barbarism on the part of both antagonists across the Eastern Front.

Yesterday [June 22] we were facing a Russian division that, due to the surprise of the
attack, was utterly routed. Throughout the large forests and in the innumerable farm-
steads there are scattered [Russian] soldiers, who often enough shoot at us from behind.
On the whole, the Russian manner of fighting is insidious [hintertückisch]. As a result,
our troops have repeatedly mopped up without mercy.[218]

Yet the unprecedented challenges confronting Heinrici and his cohorts—serious
though they were—paled in comparison to the sheer ruination that threatened their
Russian counterparts. From the very first moments of the staggeringly powerful German
ground and air assault, Soviet Western Front began a slow, inexorable process of disintegration. The headquarters of Lt.-Gen. Korobkov's 4 Army, which, the reader will recall,
was destroyed by aerial assault at the start of Operation *Barbarossa*, was "never able to
establish reliable communications with headquarters above and below it." And although
Lt.-Gen. Golubev's 10 Army was in "tenuous communications with [Western Front]
headquarters," it was "hardly more functional as [a command element]."[219]

With his communications in shambles, Army-General D. G. Pavlov (C-in-C Western
Front) was largely unaware of the actual extent of the catastrophe taking shape along his
tottering front. By late morning, Pavlov, in an effort to gain some measure of control, had
ordered his deputy, Lt.-Gen. I. V. Boldin, to fly to 10 Army headquarters near Belostok to
organize a major counterstroke[220]—to be carried out by Golubev's 6 Mechanized Corps
and 11 Mechanized Corps of 3 Army (Lt.-Gen. V. I. Kuznetsov), "apparently in concert
with prewar operational plans."[221] Flying at low level through airspace swarming with German aircraft, and despite his plane absorbing twenty bullets from a Messerschmitt Bf-109,
Boldin somehow managed to reach Golubev's command post—two tents in a small copse
of wood by an airstrip. The 10 Army commander had been struggling to put up resistance
despite shattered telephones, constant radio jamming, and the chaos caused by multiple
teams of German *Abwehr* (counterintelligence) agents active at his rear. Over the next few
days, Lt.-Gen. Golubev would strike in vain at the spearheads of German Ninth and Fourth
Armies (north and south of Belostok, respectively), during which time his army practically
ceased to exist, except for stragglers desperate to break free of German encirclements.[222]

The chaos and confusion that prevailed among Red Army units bearing the full fury of the German assault is described in an operational review conducted by 1 Rifle Corps (10 Army) on the evening of June 22.

> *Approximately up to two infantry divisions of the enemy supported by artillery and aviation [on the morning] of June 22, 1941 violated the state border, overcame the resistance of the border guard units, and continued their advance to the east and southeast. The units of the 8 Rifle Division were not able to occupy the forward positions before the enemy got there and they are now on the defensive line Schuchyn-Grabovo-Vorkovo-Konty. During the day there was no communication with the HQ of the 10 Army either by radio or telegraph. Phone communications with the divisions is frequently disrupted. Heavy losses in the units are being reported.*[223]

By the time darkness had settled over the battlefield, the nine attacking infantry divisions of Kluge's Fourth Army, advancing from the southern shoulder of the Belostok salient, had pushed roughly 10–30 kilometers beyond the border, beginning the inner encirclement of Soviet Western Front in cooperation with Strauss's Ninth Army operating on the northern axis. The deepest penetration had been made by *Generalmajor* Ernst Haeckel's 263 Infantry Division (9 AK), which had covered 30+ kilometers to the town of Bransk, less than 50 kilometers southwest of Belostok (Map 8). The next day, the Russians would attack repeatedly with tanks in an effort to extrude German forces from Bransk; soon the road leading into the town was lined with burnt-out tanks, and inside them the carbonized bodies of their crews.[224] Visiting with Guderian in Pruzhany on the evening of June 23, Field Marshal von Kluge informed his chief of staff that, on the road leading up from the south were the charred remains of one hundred Russian tanks, which he contemptuously dismissed as "practically laughable little things" (*beinahe lächerliche Dinger*). The Fourth Army war diary, however, acknowledged that many of the Red Army men had fought bravely, even pouncing on the German tanks and shooting inside the hatches with their pistols.[225] In any case, the war had only begun, and the days when the handful of surviving *Landser* of Kluge's army would be fighting for their lives in the arctic wastes outside Moscow still lay many months ahead.

4.5: NINTH ARMY OPERATIONS

The Ninth Army was commanded by the sixty-one-year-old *Generaloberst* Adolf Strauss; his chief of staff was *Obst i.G.* Weckmann. In Poland Strauss had commanded an army corps and, in the spring of 1940, taken command of Ninth Army, which he led with distinction during the French campaign. Promoted to *Generaloberst* on July 19, 1940, Strauss and his Ninth Army had been assigned to the first wave of Operation *Sealion*, the abortive plan for the invasion of England, until transferred east for *Barbarossa* in the spring of 1941. Tall (6'1"), totally bald, and of impressive military bearing, he was "highly thought of by the Nazis and was certainly professionally competent, although pro-Nazi in attitude. He cooperated with the *Einsatzgruppen* (SS murder squads),[226] mistreated Russian prisoners and implemented the notorious Commissar Order."[227] As a commander, Strauss was not a risk taker, although he was certainly brave and almost always at the front with his troops; according to Günther Blumentritt, Strauss was a "quiet, prudent and experienced commander." Conversely, as a military thinker, he was not always one who grasped the larger picture of things. He would lead Ninth Army until relieved of command in January 1942 at his own request.[228]

Organized into three army corps with a total of eight infantry divisions, Strauss's Ninth Army consisted of approximately 140,000 men. On the army's right and center was 42 Army Corps (87, 102, 129 ID), commanded by *Gen.d.Pi.* Walter Kuntze; on the left wing, bunched together on the northern shoulder of the Suwalki triangle, where it protruded far into Soviet territory, were *Gen.d.Inf.* Friedrich Materna's 20 Army Corps (162, 256 ID) and *Gen.d.Art.* Walter Heitz's 8 Army Corps (8, 28, 161 ID). The allocation of GHQ artillery to Ninth Army makes clear that the army's *Schwerpunkt* was with Heitz's 8 Army Corps:

- Assault Gun Battalions 210 and 184 (20 AK and 8 AK, respectively)
- 4 105mm cannon battalions (2 each to 20 and 8 AK)
- 2 mixed artillery battalions (1 each to 20 and 8 AK)
- 5 medium howitzer battalions (2 to 20 AK; 3 to 8 AK)
- 2 210mm heavy howitzer battalions (mot.) (1 each to 20 and 8 AK)
- 3 210mm heavy howitzer battalions (limited mobility) (all to 8 AK)
- 3 305mm heavy howitzer battalions (mot.) (1 to 20 AK; 2 to 8 AK)
- 1 240mm heavy artillery battalion for flat trajectory fire (mot.) (8 AK)
- 1 150mm cannon battalion (8 AK)
- 2 *Nebelwerfer* battalions (8 AK)
- 1 SP antitank battalion (*z.V. AOK 9*)
- 1 flak (*Fla*) battalion (8 AK)
- 2 flak (*Fla*) companies (8 AK)
- 2 army flak battalions (1 88mm) (*z.V. AOK 9*)[229]

Also assigned to Ninth Army were five engineer battalions (3 to 8 AK; 1 to 20 AK; 1 z.V. AOK 9); two bridge construction battalions (1 to 20 AK; 1 to 8 AK); ample bridge columns "B"; ten construction battalions; two road repair battalions; four Organization Todt units, and sixteen RAD battalions. *Luftwaffe* formations assigned for tactical support included three reconnaissance squadrons: one short-range squadron each to 20 and 8 Army Corps, and one long-range (strategic) *Staffel* (4.(F)/14) under direct control of the army (*z.V. AOK 9*). The *Luftwaffe* also contributed five mixed flak battalions (all *z.V. AOK 9*).[230]

With a front approximately 200 kilometers in length, Strauss's Ninth Army took up most of the left wing of Bock's Army Group Center (with the army group's 3 Panzer Group on the far left wing). Elements of 42 Army Corps' three infantry divisions covered the wide expanse of the frontier along the Belostok salient from Augustov to Ostrolenka (and the boundary with Kluge's Fourth Army), while the five divisions of 20 and 8 Army Corps, assembled along a line of 50–60 kilometers within the Suwalki triangle northwest of the city of Grodno (on the Neman River about 30 kilometers beyond the border), were perfectly positioned to play their part in the encirclement and destruction of Soviet Western Front (Map 6).[231]

The mission of Strauss's Ninth Army was threefold: secure the left wing of Army Group Center at its junction with Army Group North; support the advance of the neighboring 3 Panzer Group while mopping up pockets of resistance left behind by the panzers; and, most importantly, execute the narrow envelopment of Soviet forces jammed into the Belostok salient in cooperation with Kluge's Fourth Army. Or as outlined in the Army General Staff's deployment directive:

> *The Ninth Army, in cooperation with 3 Panzer Group, and with the* Schwerpunkt *on its northern wing, is to break through the enemy forces west and north of Grodno, advance in the direction of Lida and Vilnius, and, taking advantage of the rapid advance of the panzer groups, destroy the existing enemy forces in the area between Belostok and Minsk in conjunction with Fourth Army. Following behind 3 Panzer Group, the army will then secure the Dvina River at and southeast of Polotsk.*[232]

Air support was the responsibility of Air General Wolfram *Freiherr* von Richthofen's 8 Air Corps, with its fleet of Ju-87 *Stuka* divebombers the only air corps in the *Luftwaffe* inventory specifically trained and equipped for the mission of close air support (CAS)—a capability for which the *Luftwaffe* as a whole was ill prepared.[233] A brilliant tactical innovator, Richthofen had, by June 1941, perfected a system of close air support—using *Luftwaffe* liaisons on the ground—that, *inter alia*, proved highly effective in reducing so-called "friendly fire" incidents and in directing *Stuka* attacks against fortified enemy positions.[234]

Across the frontier, opposite Strauss's Ninth Army, was the Soviet 3 Army, commanded by Lt.-Gen. V. I. Kuznetsov, and the 1 Rifle Corps (2 and 8 Rifle Divisions) on the right wing of Golubev's 10 Army. The primary components of Kuznetsov's 3 Army were 4 Rifle Corps, posted with two divisions forward (27 and 56 Rifle Divisions) and one in second echelon (85 RD); and 11 Mechanized Corps, outfitted with 414 tanks (including some new KV and T-34 tanks) and positioned just south of Grodno. Facing Strauss's 8 Army Corps was also the 68 Fortified Region (Grodno), which was "basically a rifle, machine-gun, and artillery outfit made up of separate battalions. In essence, it was a heavy border guards type defensive unit. It occupied positions along the border from the Neman River north of Grodno westward to Augustov [Map 6]."[235]

In distinction to the right wing of Army Group Center (i.e., 2 Panzer Group and Fourth Army), the attack on the army group's left wing started ten minutes earlier;[236] thus, Strauss's seven attacking divisions (102 ID of 42 AK did not see action on June 22) began their assault at exactly 0305 hours. Participating in the attack of Ninth Army was the thirty-year-old artillery *Unteroffizier* Helmut Pabst. From the start of the campaign, he "kept a diary in the form of letters to his parents and friends in Frankfurt-am-Main, and particularly to his father, who had served in the Russian campaign of 1914–17."[237] His diary, published posthumously in 1957, was one of the first accounts of the Russian campaign from a "simple" German soldier; it begins with the opening artillery barrage on *Barbarossatag*:

This time I was with the leading wave. The units moved up to their positions quietly, talking in whispers. There was a creaking of wheels—assault guns. Two nights before, we had looked over the ground; now we were waiting for the infantry. They came up in dark, ghostly columns and moved forward through the cabbage plots and cornfields. We went along with them to act as artillery liaison unit for the second battalion. In a potato field the order came "Dig in!" No. 10 Battery was to open fire at 0305 hours.

0305. The first salvo! At the same moment everything sprang to life. Firing along the whole front—infantry guns, mortars. The Russian watchtowers vanished in a flash. Shells crashed down on all the enemy batteries, which had been located long before. In file and in line, the infantry swarmed forward. Bog, ditches; boots full of water and mud. Ahead of us the barrage crept forward from line to line. Flamethrowers advanced against the strongpoints. The fire of machine guns, and the high-pitched whip of rifle bullets. My young wireless operator, with 40 pounds' load on his back, felt a bit queasy during the first half-hour. Then at [the] barracks came the first serious resistance. The company ahead was stuck. "Assault guns, forward!"

We were with the battalion commander on a small hill, 500 yards from the barracks. Our first man wounded—one of the runners. We set up the wireless. Suddenly we were fired on from close quarters. A sniper. We picked up our rifles for the first time. Although we were signalers, we must have been the better shots—the sniping stopped. Our first kill.

The advance went on. We moved fast, sometimes flat on the ground, but irresistibly. Ditches, water, sand, sun. Always changing position. Thirsty. No time to eat. By 10.00 o'clock we were already old soldiers and had seen a great deal: abandoned positions, knocked-out armored cars, the first prisoners, the first dead Russians.[238]

The assault detachments of *Generalmajor* Stephan Rittau's 129 Infantry Division (42 AK) crossed the Russo-German frontier southwest of Augustov and rapidly secured their initial objectives—the opening minutes of the division's attack recorded thusly in its *Kriegstagebuch*:

> *0305: The action begins . . . at the designated time . . . The infantry crosses the frontier and the artillery takes known enemy targets . . . under fire. Soon after the start of the barrage one can see the brightly burning [town of] Grajewo from the division's forward command post. The Russian observation tower, which can be seen from the division CP, is destroyed at 0315 hours by an antitank gun.*

> *0325: 2nd Battalion, 185 Infantry Regiment[239] has reached the burning [town of] Mierucie with its forwardmost elements.*

> *0330: [Elements of the division] have reached Grajewo.*

> *0340: 1st Battalion, 185 Infantry Regiment has reached Konopki, while the 2nd Battalion (II./IR 185) has seized the heights south of Mierucie.*

> *0355: The assault troops [Stosstrupps] in the sectors of 428 and 430 Infantry Regiments have all crossed the Reich's border according to plan. The observation towers along the border have been set ablaze and can no longer be used by the Russians. The assault troops in the sector of 430 IR have seized [several towns along the border]. The enemy, who has only put up minor resistance, appears to be withdrawing.*

> *0420: 428 Infantry Regiment captures the towns of Reszki, Rudki and Stare without enemy resistance.[240]*

By 0445 hours, Rittau's storm troops had seized their first prisoners, who were marched to the division CP for interrogation: "The prisoners give the impression that they had been taken completely by surprise by the attack. Some say that they had had neither weapons nor ammunition at hand; others claim they were surprised in their sleep (as a result, some of them appear without boots or socks)." While the prisoners were more than willing to talk, they knew nothing about the intentions of their superiors; they did "not even know the orders for the platoons or companies, or whether the frontier positions should be held or not."[241]

At 0935 hours, 185 Infantry Regiment reported that the enemy was pulling back along the regiment's entire front. As it advanced, however, 129 ID was at first unable to clear rear areas of all Soviet forces (an almost universal problem in the opening days of the campaign). Dispersed enemy troops often surfaced from their hiding places to attack the division's supply troops as they moved up behind the assault groups. From a farmstead captured by the advancing infantry early that morning, Soviet troops suddenly opened fire on German baggage train vehicles hours later. The Germans responded ruthlessly, pulverizing the farmstead with artillery fire, resulting in fourteen dead and seven wounded Russians. In a similar incident that afternoon, troops of 129 ID at the railroad station at Grajewo (captured that morning), came under fire from Soviet soldiers concealed in one of the local farmsteads. A platoon of the division's replacement battalion (*Feldersatz-Btl.*) summarily cleared out the enemy, losing two men in the process. From the papers of a dead Russian officer it was learned that Soviet battle groups had been ordered to let the German combat troops pass by, and then fall upon their supply traffic circulating on the roads behind the front. Such skirmishes, so typical of Red Army tactics, were to go on for days.[242]

Commanded by *Generalleutnant* Gerhard Kauffmann, the 256 Infantry Division (20 AK) launched its attack from due east of Augustov, its three infantry regiments debouching from the woods in the Suwalki triangle and crossing the frontier after a twenty-minute artillery preparation. While key terrain features and villages in the path of the advance were rapidly secured, the attacking battalions, on more than one occasion, were forced to clear tenaciously defending Red Army troops from their bunkers. In addition, a major route of advance taken by the division, as it pushed southward toward Novy Dvor and Dabrova (both west of Grodno), turned out to be little more than a "sea of sand," as explained in the division's war diary:

> *The division's route of advance [*Vormarschstrasse*] via G. Haczitowka to Kuryanka is in a very poor condition. On this side of the frontier it was alright, but immediately after crossing over the frontier, the road went through a sea of sand. Many vehicles got stuck and could only be put back to rights with the help of others. In addition to that, the bridge across the stream at the border collapsed after a short time as a result of the great strain and heavy use it was subjected to by the GHQ artillery and the assault guns, and it could only be used again after a lot of intense work.[243]*

Despite such difficulties—common of those experienced up and down the front by the attacking German formations—the combat infantry of 256 ID pushed on doggedly toward their objectives. By 1230 hours, lead elements of 481 Infantry Regiment reached an airfield several kilometers north of the town of Novy Dvor, just as a large group of Red Army aircraft were trying to get airborne. Supported by a battery of 75mm assault guns (Assault Gun Battalion 210),[244] the German infantry let loose a torrent of heavy machine-gun fire; together, they destroyed thirty-eight of the planes on the ground, along with several hangars in which other planes were housed. By 1315, Novy Dvor itself, with its thriving Jewish community dating back to the early sixteenth century, was in German hands.[245] At 1500, the Russians counterattacked Novy Dvor with tanks but were easily driven off. That evening, the division's 476 Infantry Regiment arrived at Dabrova and rapidly surrounded the town despite furious Russian opposition.[246]

As noted, the main effort of Strauss's Ninth Army was on its left wing, where the three divisions of Heitz's 8 Army Corps burst out of the Suwalki triangle from a start line east of Augustov and collided with Soviet 56 Rifle Division of Kuznetsov's 3 Army, which was covering the city of Grodno (prewar population 50,000).[247] Farther north, the lightning advance of Army Group Center's 3 Panzer Group was soon threatening Soviet 3 Army with envelopment. Lt.-Gen. Kuznetsov, his telephone lines down and his radio communications shattered, was at once in a perilous situation;[248] he tried to maintain "what contact he could by runners, but his troops were short of ammunition and he lacked any proper reserves."[249] Sometime before 0900 hours, Kuznetsov managed to get through to the headquarters of Western Front in Minsk, "personally" reporting that the "situation is worsening."[250] And indeed it was—for shortly thereafter Kuznetsov's 3 Army headquarters in Grodno was obliterated by the *Luftwaffe*. "We are through . . . everything destroyed," was the hysterical message intercepted by the Germans shortly after 0900 hours.[251]

The task of German 8 Army Corps (8, 28, 161 ID) was to protect the southern flank of 57 Panzer Corps (3 Panzer Group) by neutralizing the border defenses southeast of the Suwalki triangle and securing bridgeheads across the Neman River at and above Grodno.[252] To fulfill these objectives, 161 Infantry Division, advancing parallel to 3 Panzer Group, struck out for the Neman north of Grodno, while the 8 and 28 Infantry Divisions swept past the defenders of Sipotski (Sopotskii) and forced the Red Army troops back toward Grodno. In response, the Russians moved up their 85 Rifle Division to back up the remnants of 56 Rifle Division and establish a defensive line stretching southwest from Grodno (Map 9).[253]

Commanded by *Generalmajor* Gustav Höhne, 8 Infantry Division, on 8 Army Corps' right wing, had the ancient fortress city of Grodno directly within its line of attack. As the following account by the late Charles von Luttichau demonstrates, the fighting was ferocious from the moment the German assault troops crossed the frontier into the Soviet 68 Fortified Region (Grodno).

The bunker line on the border consisted of more than a dozen works clustered around Hill 150 that commanded the secondary road to Grodno. Under cover of an artillery barrage by 29 batteries, 38 Infantry Regiment, 8 Infantry Division, attacked the position. An engineer assault company, reinforced by an antitank platoon and an 88mm antiaircraft section, was attached to the regiment with the task of destroying the bunkers. The first resistance was encountered less than a mile from the border. A dug-in tank covered an antitank ditch, behind which stood groups of bunkers on both sides of the road. The preparatory fires had not silenced them. Antitank guns and machine guns concentrated their fires on the embrasures.

The engineer assault teams worked their way through wheat fields, fortunate to find cover in them and then behind earth mounds near the bunkers. Blinding the apertures with flamethrowers, individual engineers charged up to the bunker walls and with extension ladders scaled them. From the relative safety of their perches, they lowered explosive charges to the apertures, blasted holes into ventilation and periscope shafts, then poured gasoline into them followed by smoke grenades and chain charges. Meanwhile, other demolition teams blasted the often hidden entries to the bunkers.

In some of the storied bunkers, each level had to be destroyed in this manner, down to the basement. Rarely did the Russian crews, which numbered from 20–50 men, surrender, and most of the defenders fought to the death. In some instances survivors believed to be dead came to after hours and resumed the fight, requiring the same position to be neutralized all over again.[254]

At the start of the Russian campaign, then officer Alfred Durrwanger commanded the 13th Company (infantry gun company)[255] in an infantry regiment of *Generalleutnant* Johann Sinnhuber's 28 Infantry Division (8 Army Corps). Decades after the war, he discussed his experiences on June 22, 1941; because they are emblematic of the experiences of so many German soldiers on this first day of the war, they are quoted here at length.

After having crossed the Soviet border, the two other regiments of our division, believed to be confronted with the main forces of the enemy, advanced very quickly. Our regiment, considered to be a reserve, first remained on our side of the border. Only one battalion, accompanied by one of my platoons, had to cross the frontier, but only to protect the open flank of the other regiments. This battalion had to advance through a large forest and was then stopped unexpectedly by strong Soviet forces that fought vigorously. Here was the first indication that our knowledge of the enemy forces, even along the border, was inadequate.

At that moment my place as company commander of the 13th Company was near the command post of the regiment. The regimental commander, becoming a bit nervous because he had heard nothing about the progress of his battalion, ordered me to take a motor-bike, with a cyclist, to contact the battalion and find out what was going on. I remember very well the vast woods we both had to cross, with thinly scattered trees and a little brushwood on either side of a broad sandy road. You could not use this road with the motor-bike because there was so much sand. On both sides of the road, however, there was a small patch with solid, firm soil, so that the driver could proceed along it slowly. Both the driver and I had our loaded submachine-guns wrapped tightly around our shoulders.

While proceeding little by little forward, we saw now and then a German dispatch rider or runner of an ambulance. Finally we found the staff of the battalion and the commander explained the situation to me. Unexpectedly, there was very vigorous, strong opposition from an adversary who fought obstinately inside and outside of bunkers (pill-boxes), none of which had been marked on our maps . . .

After an hour we returned by the same broad road with the motor-cyclist ahead of me guiding the cycle slowly forward meter by meter along the small sandy path. We focused our attention only on the path but not on any enemy. Suddenly, a Red Army soldier stood five steps before us, aiming his Sten gun at us . . . In our confusion the cyclist and I remembered only one Russian word: Stoi (stop)! The Russian soldier stopped abruptly without doing anything . . . I tried eagerly to reach the trigger of my Sten gun, but it seemed to me an entire eternity before I got to it. My subsequent shots went into the blue sky and nothing happened! The Russian soldier, perhaps frightened by the shots, quickly disappeared . . . Carefully we proceeded several meters into the forest, but our Soviet acquaintance had disappeared completely. Whether he was hidden in a tree (that often happened in Russia), behind a tree or under the leaves or in a pit, we never discovered. This was perfect camouflage on his part, an evident sign of his great ability to adapt to the surroundings.

This was my first encounter with a Soviet soldier. I had to realize that we were confronted with another type of combat, that is, fights behind the front and behind the forward line. The German soldier was neither accustomed nor trained to accomplish such malicious procedures.

*My soldiers told me afterwards that they had observed a Soviet soldier who made signs of surrender. He was subsequently shot down by his own people. Another Russian soldier lying heavily wounded in a trench that had just been taken by us, put a hand grenade below his back and was blown apart at once. It even happened that some stragglers (*Versprengte*) occupied the recently destroyed bunkers anew and fought to their final extermination.*

All this proved that physically, as well as psychologically, the Soviet soldiers were extremely tough. Where did this come from? I think it was based in the first place on their ideological conditioning. We never expected nor were we trained for that kind of adversary.[256]

Despite such bitter Soviet resistance, Heitz's powerful 8 Army Corps continued its relentless drive toward the Neman River and Grodno. By the time Höhne's 8 Infantry Division reached the outskirts of Grodno, Kuznetsov had decided to counterattack with his 11 Mechanized Corps; however, only the corps' 29 Tank Division, posted south of Grodno, was able to respond on short notice. By midday, the tank commander, P. N. Studnev, had deployed his two understrength tank regiments, which together possessed no more than two KV tanks, twenty-six T-34s, and thirty-eight obsolete T-26 light tanks. Yet as noted by historian Robert A. Forczyk:

Interestingly, this was one of the rare occasions during the border battles when Red tank units were not exhausted by long marches and out of fuel, and they thus had real potential to inflict some damage on a German infantry formation. However, Studnev was not one of the rising stars of the Red Army; before the war he had twice been relieved of command and was only given a division command in 1941 because Stalin's purges had so thinned the ranks of senior tank officers.[257]

That afternoon, the Soviet 29 Tank Division's two tank regiments lurched into action, striking the right flank of 8 Infantry Division southwest of Grodno;[258] more specifically, Studnev's attack collided with a battle group of 8 ID's 84 Infantry Regiment, supported by assault guns from Assault Gun Battalion 184. After an advance of several kilometers, Studnev mistook the German assault guns for panzers; in response, he abruptly halted his tanks and elected to engage by fire, instead of maneuver, relinquishing the initiative to the Germans. Soviet tank crews had "not been trained in fire discipline" and they rapidly expended much of their ammunition, registering few hits. Because the short-barreled 75mm guns of the German assault guns, as well as the 37mm AT guns of the infantry, were "useless in a long-range gunnery duel against Studnev's T-34s, the Germans instead used their excellent radio communications to request close air support from [Richthofen's] *Fliegerkorps VIII* [8 Air Corps], which promptly dispatched Ju-87 *Stuka* dive bombers to the scene." For the ensuing four hours, Studnev's semi-stationary tanks were pummelled from the air and by German artillery, destroying most of his light tanks and some T-34s. "Finally, Studnev ordered his survivors to pull back after his division operations officer was killed and both his tank regiments became combat ineffective. For the loss of about half his sixty-six tanks, Studnev had inflicted only about fifty casualties on the [8 Infantry Division]."[259] After the failure of his counterattack, Kuznetsov decided to abandon Grodno and its fuel depot; the Germans, however, would not occupy the city until the next day.[260]

By the end of the day, the seven attacking divisions of Ninth Army had fought their way as far as 30 kilometers beyond the border—an advance detachment of 256 Infantry Division (20 Army Corps) pushing all the way to the outskirts of Kuz'nitsa (Kuznica), southwest of Grodno. All three divisions of Heitz's 8 Army Corps had seized bridgeheads across the Neman River,[261] protecting the right flank of Hoth's 3 Panzer Group. More significantly, Strauss's Ninth Army, as the northern arm of the pincer, had begun to carry out its mission of enveloping the forces of Soviet Western Front in conjunction with Kluge's Fourth Army to the south. (Maps 8 and 9.)

At 2100 hours, Pavlov's Western Front issued its "Operational Report No. 1,"[262] addressing the course of events on June 22. The document contains many interesting details, among them that the *front* had conducted "holding battles" while "putting up stubborn resistance to the enemy's superior forces" but, by late afternoon, had been forced to fall back. The report also noted that some of the strongest German attacks had occurred in the Grodno area, and that the city had been "subjected to particularly heavy bombing." And then there was this laconic entry: "The commander of 3 Army reported that [56 Rifle Division] has almost ceased to exist."[263]

Postscript: The reader will recall that, late on June 22, Army-General Pavlov had begun efforts to gin up a major counterstroke, to be orchestrated by his deputy, Lt.-Gen. I. V. Boldin. That attack finally got started on June 24, with two mechanized corps (6 and 11 MC) and a cavalry corps striking north from the area of Grodno in an effort to stop the steel juggernaut of 3 Panzer Group and thwart the impending encirclement of Western Front forces around and north of Belostok. Lacking effective communications, air cover, logistical support, or adequate numbers of modern tanks, the attack was "doomed from the start." Decimated by Richthofen's *Stukas*, the Soviet armor did not reach the Grodno region until long after Hoth's panzer group had pushed well beyond the frontier to Vilnius. The surviving Soviet tanks, infantry, and cavalry ended up engaging units of Strauss's Ninth Army, which dismantled Boldin's forces by means of devastating infantry ambush and screens of antitank guns.[264]

4.6: 3 PANZER GROUP OPERATIONS

The commander of 3 Panzer Group was the fifty-six-year-old *Generaloberst* Hermann Hoth; his chief of staff was *Obstlt. i.G.* von Hünersdorff. Hoth was the son of an army surgeon; after attending the Prussian War Academy (1910–1913) he became an intelligence officer. During and after World War I he held many staff positions, eventually becoming a specialist in armored warfare. In November 1938, he took command of 15 Panzer Corps, which played an integral part in both the Polish and French campaigns. On July 19, 1940, Hoth was promoted to *Generaloberst* (full general) and, four months later (November 1940), his corps staff was upgraded to 3 Panzer Group. A "calm, precise man," by 1941 Hoth had earned a reputation as one of the *Wehrmacht*'s finest commanders; he was highly respected by his men, to whom he was known affectionately as "Papa" Hoth.[265] In the assessment of the late R. H. S. Stolfi, Hoth "possessed boldness hard to parallel" in World War II.

> *In March 1941, for example, faced with putting together his scheme of maneuver within the advance of Army Group Center toward Moscow, Hoth would advise the ascetic but fiery commander of the army group, Field Marshal von Bock, that the initial encirclement of Soviet forces should close just east of Smolensk, an awe inspiring 700 km from the border. It is not clear just how Hoth envisioned the setting of lines of encirclement around the Soviet forces in so big a pocket. The pocket could be estimated as being 350 km long, 120 km wide and holding perhaps 1.1 million Soviet troops. Bock notes in his wartime diary, however, that he was in essential agreement with Hoth but that the High Command of the Army insisted on a more conservative encirclement closing approximately 350 km into the Soviet Union just east of Minsk. With such leadership above them in the chain of command, German division commanders could be expected to have advanced with a style exemplifying maneuver warfare.[266]*

Hoth's 3 Panzer Group comprised about 170,000 personnel in eleven divisions (four panzer, three motorized, and four infantry divisions) arranged in two panzer corps and two infantry corps—the latter assigned temporarily to Hoth's group to support the initial breakthrough at the border. The four corps and their commanders were: 57 Panzer Corps (12 PD, 19 PD, 18 ID [mot.]), *Gen.d.Pz.Tr.* Adolf-Friedrich Kuntzen; 39 Panzer Corps (7 PD, 20 PD, 14 ID [mot.], 20 ID [mot.]), *Gen.d.Pz.Tr.* Rudolf Schmidt; 5 Army Corps (5 ID, 35 ID), *Gen.d.Inf.* Richard Ruoff; and 6 Army Corps (6 ID, 26, ID), *Gen.d.Pi.* Otto-Wilhelm Förster. Between them the two panzer corps possessed 942 tanks (including thirty-six command tanks) distributed over twelve tank battalions. More than half of the tanks in the panzer group (507) were Pz 38(t)s, light tanks of Czech manufacture, whose main armament was only a 37mm gun; moreover, Hoth's group possessed not a single Pz III, the German army's main battle tank in 1941, while 278 of its tanks were the obsolete Pz I and Pz II models.[267] General Headquarters troops allocated to 3 Panzer Group included the following:

- 3 105mm cannon battalions (1 each to 57 PzK, 5 and 6 AK)
- 1 mixed artillery battalion (39 PzK)
- 3 150mm medium howitzer battalions (1 each to 57 PzK, 5 and 6 AK)
- 2 210mm heavy howitzer battalions (mot.) (1 each to 57 and 39 PzK)
- 1 150mm cannon battalion (39 PzK)
- 1 antitank battalion (SP) (39 PzK)
- 1 antitank company (SP / 88mm) (39 PzK)
- 1 flak (*fla*) battalion (39 PzK)
- 2 flak (*fla*) companies (6 AK)
- Flamethrower Tank Battalion 101 (*Pz.Abt.(F)101*) (39 PzK)[268]

Among other GHQ units assigned to Hoth's group were: six engineer battalions; four bridge-building battalions; a large complement of bridge columns "B," six construction battalions, and two road construction and repair battalions. Formations of the *Luftwaffe* assigned for tactical support included: eight short-range reconnaissance squadrons distributed among the panzer divisions, or assigned to the panzer and infantry corps; one long-range (strategic) reconnaissance squadron under direct control of the panzer group (2.(F)/33); four light flak battalions (2 each to 57 and 39 PzK); and two mixed flak battalions (1 to 57 PzK; 1 [minus one battery] to 39 PzK; one battery under panzer group control [*z.V. Pz.Gr.*]).[269]

The task of providing air support fell to Richthofen's 8 Air Corps, which included 158 Ju-87 *Stukas* and a complement of Bf-110 fighter-bombers;[270] as noted, Richthofen's air corps was the only air corps in the *Luftwaffe* specifically earmarked for the close air support (CAS) mission.

Forming the far left wing of Field Marshal von Bock's Army Group Center, 3 Panzer Group occupied a front of more than 75 kilometers in the Suwalki triangle on the border with Soviet-occupied Lithuania. Along the frontier from right to left were the first wave formations of 57 Panzer Corps, 5 Army Corps, 39 Panzer Corps, and 6 Army Corps. As the northern pincer of Bock's armored thrust, Hoth's two panzer corps were to press rapidly beyond the Soviet border defenses and—on June 22—drive 45–65 kilometers to seize bridgeheads over the Neman River at Alytus (Olita) (39 PzK) and Merkine (57 PzK). Both corps were then to advance east across Lithuania and Belorussia with the goal of enveloping Minsk from the north. Hoth's initial attack would exploit two distinct advantages: firstly, his deployments within the Suwalki triangle already projected deep into Soviet territory; and, secondly, his panzer group's axis of advance would strike at the boundary between the Soviet Northwestern and Western Fronts. The terrain, however, posed a challenge, as it was often heavily wooded and cut by innumerable rivers and streams. Simply put, Hoth's opening act "was to be literally a race" to the Neman River between his armored spearheads and Red Army forces attempting to erect defenses along the river line.[271] The Army General Staff's deployment directive laid out the panzer group's mission in the most general terms:

> *In cooperation with Ninth Army, 3 Panzer Group is to break through the enemy forces near the border in the area north of Grodno and, by advancing rapidly into the area north of Minsk in conjunction with 2 Panzer Group, which is advancing on Minsk from the southwest, create the conditions for the destruction of enemy forces in the region between Belostok and Minsk. Operating in close contact with 2 Panzer Group, [3 Panzer Group] will then rapidly reach the area at and north of Vitebsk [and] prevent the concentration of enemy forces in the region of the upper Dvina [River], thus preserving freedom of movement [Handlungsfreiheit] of the army group for further tasks.[272]*

Across the frontier, in the path of Hoth's impending juggernaut, were the forces that made up the left wing of Lt.-Gen. V. I. Morozov's 11 Army of Soviet Northwestern Front. As was so often the case across the Eastern Front, the border was only thinly covered in this sector, most notably by 128 Rifle Division, a regiment of 126 Rifle Division, and two battalions of 23 Rifle Division. The main forces of the latter two divisions were in camps behind the front (126 RD more than 70 kilometers to the rear in the region of Prienai, south of Kaunas), and would have to deploy forward in the case of a German attack. Morozov's 29 Rifle Corps, the so-called Lithuanian Rifle Corps (179 and 184 RD), was also posted well behind the frontier, south and southwest of Kaunas. Stationed just northeast of Alytus was Colonel F. F. Fedorov's 5 Tank Division of Maj.-Gen. A. V. Kurkin's 3 Mechanized Corps; it would acquit itself well in the fighting on June 22 (Map 10).[273]

During the starlit night of June 21/22, the divisions of Hoth's first attack wave (three panzer, four infantry, and elements of one motorized division),[274] protected by their artillery, heavy weapons, and flak batteries from any last-minute intervention by the Russians, moved up to the frontier; by 0200 hours, all of the divisions had reached their excellently camouflaged final assembly areas and were ready to go. After *Generaloberst* Hoth and his corps commanders had occupied their forward command posts, the 3 Panzer Group put in its attack at 0305 hours, the motorized infantry of the two panzer corps attacking dismounted along with the tanks in the forward line. While *Luftwaffe* bombers struck the border town of Kalvaria and, farther back, Alytus, encountering little in the way of Soviet air defenses, the assault units of the panzer group seized Red Army border positions and began their headlong dash for the Neman River crossings. Initial reports indicated that enemy resistance was weak, enemy artillery fire nonexistent; in fact, *Luftwaffe* reconnaissance counted just a single enemy artillery battery in its path. Overwhelmed by the merciless German onslaught, many of the Russian defenders simply melted away, fleeing into the woods or seeking other hiding places. As the war diarist of the panzer group observed: "The surprise appears to have succeeded . . . All along the border the enemy positions, especially artillery [positions], are proving to be more weakly held than expected."[275]

While the *Stukas* and fighter-bombers of 8 Air Corps flew rolling sorties to suppress Soviet defenses, Kuntzen's 57 Panzer Corps, on 3 Panzer Group's right wing, attacked with its 12 Panzer Division (220 tanks) and elements of 18 Motorized Infantry Division, holding its 19 Panzer Division (228 tanks) in reserve.[276] Rolf Hinze, a soldier in 19 PD, was awestruck by the elemental power of the "thundering artillery barrage" at the start of the attack, and by the waves of German bombers that passed overhead: "At first the explosions of their bombs were not so far off, so that the air pressure waves still reached the waiting troops and were felt distinctly in our ears. Very soon you heard the typical kinds of gun shots and short bursts of machine-gun fire—an indication that the infantry combat had gotten underway."[277]

The key objective of 57 Panzer Corps lay 45 kilometers to the east—the bridge over the Neman River at Merkine. In the diary of 3 Panzer Group, one can follow the advance of Kuntzen's tankers and motorized infantry as they secured one preliminary objective after another. The corps' progress, however, was soon disrupted by the numerous physical barriers (*Sperrungen*) placed in its path—and stoutly defended by the enemy—as well as by typical problems with the terrain.[278] Despite such difficulties, by 1715 hours a battalion of motorcycle troops had captured intact the bridge at Merkine and begun to cross the river. Ordered by Kuntzen to push on, by the end of the day, the 12 Panzer Division's 29 Panzer Regiment had pushed an additional 25+ kilometers to the northeast and reached the town of Varena. All told, the spearheads of 57 Panzer Corps had advanced some 70 kilometers from their start line—an impressive achievement![279] (See Map 11.)

Deployed between Hoth's panzer corps, the two infantry divisions of Ruoff's 5 Army Corps crossed the frontier about 30 kilometers northeast of Suwalki. *Generalleutnant*

Fischer von Weikersthal commanded the corps' 35 Infantry Division, affectionately labeled the "Fish Division" by its soldiers in his honor. Weikersthal issued an order of the day, insisting that the "victory must and will be ours," and rallying his troops with the motto "rapidly forward!" (*rasch vorwärts!*).[280] As *Luftwaffe* bombers and fighters roared overhead, *Gefreiter* Gerhard Bopp, a radio operator in the division's reconnaissance battalion, moved out with his unit at 0330 hours; at precisely 0403, they crossed the border—marked only by bundles of straw—and advanced into Lithuania, making their way through the largely open and undulating terrain. In his diary, Bopp recounted his experiences on the first day of the war.

> *All along the horizon columns of smoke from burning houses. The populace (Lithuanians) greets us joyfully, some with tears in their eyes. The girls and children throw flowers at us and all the vehicles are decked out with lilac blossoms, like in maneuvers . . . if there were no war.*
>
> *Around 0700, the first prisoners, shaved bald heads, Mongol faces, etc. Then the first fatalities . . . dead horses, etc.—through artillery fire before reaching the Kirsna River in the Didžioji region. Shells strike to the left and right of the road, but at great distances away. We get through unscathed. We capture the bridge over the Kirsna intact. After a brief stop, we continue to . . . where there has been intense enemy resistance since midday, which is only broken that evening. There, bivouac and provisions are in short supply, because the roads are sandy and in poor condition, and so the field kitchen can barely get through. There is only a little warm food and coffee.[281]*

Forming part of 35 ID's advance detachment (*Vorausabteilung*), Bopp's reconnaissance battalion had reached the Kirsna River crossing at Didžioji by 0925, while the division's 34 and 111 Infantry Regiments battled it out among enemy bunkers astride the town of Rudamina.[282]

On the right wing of 5 Army Corps was *Generalmajor* Karl Allmendinger's 5 Infantry Division, which attacked with two regiments forward, one in reserve. After clearing the enemy at the border, the division soon encountered much stiffer resistance near Lasdijai (ca. 10 kilometers inside the frontier), where Soviet bunker positions had to be systematically subdued—a process that tied down one of the attacking regiments for most of the day.[283] Defending the approaches to Lasdijai was the 128 Rifle Division—one of many divisions that largely disappeared from the Red Army order of battle over the course of the day. Despite its stubborn resistance at Lasdijai, the division was already in serious trouble by 0800 hours, as reported by the chief of staff of Soviet 11 Army: "The division is fighting halfway surrounded. The division commander issued orders to fall back. There are no communications with the division."[284]

Displaying the initiative and aggressiveness that so distinguished the German army during World War II, 5 Infantry Division's other forward regiment (56 IR) executed a spectacular foot march (*Fussmarsch*) of more than 40 kilometers and—despite difficult terrain and enemy resistance—reached the Neman River at Krikstoniai (northwest of Merkine) by 1815 hours. It was, recorded the war diary of 3 Panzer Group, a "brilliant feat" (*Glanzleistung*) by the infantry (although the bridge there had already been demolished), and one for which the name of the regimental commander, *Oberst* Thumm, was submitted for acknowledgment in a *Wehrmacht* High Command communiqué (Map 11).[285]

On its way to the Neman, however, Allmendinger's infantry had made an "unpleasant discovery: partisans!"

> *The two divisions of 5 Army Corps had to overcome a double defense position, the first one about five miles east of the border between the village of Lasdijai and the first of several finger lakes north of the Suwalki-Lasdijai secondary road. The second position was 10 miles farther east and just short of another village, Seirijai. Five miles beyond it was the Neman, the first day's objective. The 5 Infantry Division attacked with two regiments abreast. The bunker line north of Lasdijai stopped the left regiment for most of the day. But the right regiment [56 IR] cleared the village, broke through the second position, took Seirijai, and won a bridgehead over the Neman. By evening, the reserve regiment, moving forward to exploit the bridgehead, had reached Seirijai.*
>
> *As soon as it got dark, wild shooting broke out in the village. Division headquarters near the Neman could hear the noise, but attributed it to green German units shooting at each other in the night. Then a wounded motorcycle messenger brought the news that a bridge construction battalion, urgently needed at the bridgehead, had been ambushed from woods just northwest of Seirijai and that house-to-house fighting with "civilians" had erupted in the town. The first reaction to partisan warfare was disbelief and consternation.[286]*

By midnight, the Germans had once more cleared the village of Seirijai; yet the threat to their line of communications from the woods nearby remained, and Allmendinger ordered his reserve regiment to eliminate it. At first, just a single company, supported by heavy weapons, was sent to complete the task; but it made no headway, nor did the battalion sent after it. Eventually, the entire regiment, along with a battalion of artillery, had to be committed.

> *In the morning, the regiment attacked with two battalions, echeloned in depth, the third battalion was holding Seirijai and screening the open area beyond. Artillery fire proved to be of little value. Only after the Germans employed antitank guns and individual artillery pieces point blank, did the Russians break. Ferreting out positions one by one was a slow task and it took all day. Even then about a fourth of the 500-man partisan group escaped under the cover of darkness because the Germans had not drawn a tight ring around the woods. The partisans consisted of Red Army stragglers and Soviet Party functionaries who had joined them to organize a resistance.[287]*

The encounter described above offers a typical example of the first phase of partisan warfare in Russia. The Germans, hitherto without significant experience in partisan warfare in World War II, and, beyond that, lacking training for the forest fighting that would become such a dominant feature of the Russian campaign, made tactical blunders that cost precious lives. The action also revealed that Soviet soldiers and officials cut off behind German lines would continue to fight as partisans, while enlisting local civilians for the purpose. Simply put, the Germans were suddenly confronted by the "disturbing realization that it was no longer possible or safe to disregard, as in World War I, stragglers and isolated units behind the front. Eliminating partisan groups would be a problem [that required] both time and forces, commodities that were to become increasingly scarce as the campaign progressed."[288]

Before addressing the combat action of 39 Panzer Corps, a few thoughts about its commander, *Gen.d.Pz.Tr.* Rudolf Schmidt. He had assumed command of 1 Panzer Division in October 1937 and led it during the *Blitzkrieg* victory over Poland. In early 1940, he took over the 39 Panzer Corps, which he commanded successfully in the battle of France that spring. It is an interesting footnote to history that, during the campaign in the West, Schmidt had led the negotiations with Rotterdam in an unsuccessful attempt to bring about the Dutch city's capitulation and forestall the ruthless bombing of the city by the *Luftwaffe*'s 2 Air Fleet on May 14, 1940, "destroying the old city core and killing hundreds of civilians in a deliberate move designed to terrorize the Dutch into surrender."[289] Prior to the start of *Barbarossa*, he had evinced serious doubts about the forthcoming Russian campaign; having served on both the Eastern and Western Fronts in World War I, he was fully aware of the daunting challenges posed by war against the Soviet Union. A man of utmost decency, and no National Socialist, he led his men by his own example, gaining their respect and admiration; thus, it was not without justification that they referred to their commander affectionately as "Papa Schmidt," or simply as "Panzer-Schmidt."[290]

On the left wing of Hoth's panzer group, Schmidt's 39 Panzer Corps was deployed for combat on a front of approximately 20 kilometers—his two panzer divisions making up the first attack echelon, his two motorized infantry divisions in reserve.[291] On the corps' right was 7 Panzer Division (265 tanks), commanded by *Generalmajor* Hans *Freiherr* von Funk; on its left, the 20 Panzer Division (229 tanks), led by *Generalleutnant* Horst Stumpff. For the first day of the attack, 7 Panzer Division—the focus of the narrative below—was assigned four primary tasks: (a) break through the border fortifications (the division "knew no details about them"); (b) wheel to the east south of the town of Kalvaria; (c) advance on Alytus through the gap of Simnas (roughly halfway between Kalvaria and Alytus); and, (d) seize a bridgehead across the Neman River as the day's ultimate objective.[292]

With both panzer divisions attacking abreast at 0305 hours, the tanks and motorized infantry of 39 Panzer Corps crossed the frontier into Lithuania with Schmidt at the head of his combat engineers.[293] While their commander may still have had his doubts, the rank-and-file soldiers, more often than not, expressed unshakable confidence in what lay before them. *Oberleutnant* Richard D., a soldier in 7 Panzer Division, figured the worst of it would be over in two weeks:

> *And now at [0305] hours it all began, perhaps not as abruptly as it had in the west and not on the scale that it had in the World War, but a quarter of an hour later the first Luftwaffe air wings roared back, and now squadron after squadron travels eastward. And all the while the sun shone . . . You now know more than we do, because there is now no opportunity to listen to the radio, and everything will happen at once, and the spaces will be so vast that you can even find them on our wall map. We have maps that reach a long way to the east, and if you remember Napoleon's army did that on foot, but we're motorized and we'll get it done in 14 days.[294]*

No less confident was the NCO Helmuth Dittri, a soldier in 20 Panzer Division's 21 Panzer Regiment:

> *22/6. We have already been moving for three hours toward the Russian border. Our attack is to begin at 3:05 a.m. and should be a complete surprise to the enemy. The Russians haven't the faintest idea of what is going on! Their towns and villages along the border are brightly lit up.*
>
> *The Führer's proclamation is read to us. The time for a show-down has arrived. We'll show them which is the leading power of Europe. The front stretches from Finland to the Black Sea, a line as firm as a wall and exerting a pressure that no force in creation can withstand.[295]*

As was true most everywhere along the Eastern Front on this day, the lead combat units of both 7 and 20 Panzer Divisions easily traversed the frontier and advanced on their initial objectives: "At 0305 the first assault detachments [*Stosstrupps*] of 59 and 112 Rifle Regiments [20 PD] crossed the border and quickly seized the [enemy's] weakly held border posts. Only in Santaga was there tough house-to-house fighting with losses on both sides. The rifle regiments advanced so swiftly on foot that the artillery didn't need to intervene at first. Merely a battery of 105mm cannon contested a group of enemy motor vehicles at Hill 164.5."[296]

Bypassing the bulk of the Soviet 128 Rifle Division, by 0345 hours, both of 7 Panzer's motorized rifle regiments (SR 6 and SR 7) reported that they were only facing "weak enemy resistance";[297] moreover, there was only minor enemy artillery fire. Several hours later, the lead elements of 20 PD, having already dashed some 15 kilometers past the border, seized the burning town of Kalvaria, while south of the town the spearheads of 7 PD reached Rudeniskiai. By 0940, German aerial reconnaissance was reporting that the

Russians, in "small units," were streaming back toward the Neman, no doubt to build a new defensive line behind the imposing river barrier. The obvious objective for Schmidt's panzer corps was to beat the withdrawing Soviet formations to the river, thereby thwarting the enemy's design.[298]

The tanks of 7 Panzer Division's reinforced 25 Panzer Regiment, commanded by *Oberst* Karl Rothenburg, drove headlong for Alytus and the Neman; by 1245 hours, having thrust some 60 kilometers into enemy territory, they seized intact the massive structure spanning the river at Alytus[299] in a *coup de main* from a surprised NKVD guard detachment; a second bridge, directly to the south, was captured in a daring assault (*Sturmangriff*) by the division's 6 Rifle Regiment (SR 6). Stunned by this spectacular success, the journal of 3 Panzer Group plainly admitted: "No one had counted on that." (*Damit hatte niemand gerechnet.*) A captured Red Army engineer officer explained that he had orders to destroy both bridges at 1700 hours; unwilling (or unable) to exercise initiative on his own, he clung to his orders and made no attempt to demolish the bridges before the Germans arrived.[300] The highly decorated Rothenburg, holder of the *Pour le Mérite* (World War I) and the Knight's Cross, immediately began to push his tanks across the river in an effort to expand the bridgehead before the Russians could react. But react they would, and furiously so.

Col.-Gen. F. I. Kuznetsov, Commander, Soviet Northwestern Front, had already stripped his 3 Mechanized Corps of its 2 Tank Division (to support his impending counterstroke at Raseiniai, against 4 Panzer Group), leaving only Colonel F. F. Fedorov's 5 Tank Division available to check Rothenburg's rampaging battle group. Fedorov's tanks, which had begun the day laagered northeast of Alytus, had a 30-kilometer approach march to reach the city, and a number of them dropped out along the way due to mechanical problems; by the time 5 TD's lead elements had arrived, Rothenburg's tanks were already crossing the Neman. *Leytenant* Ivan G. Verzhbitsky, at the head of 2nd Battalion, 9 Tank Regiment, was the first to arrive, with forty-four T-34 tanks. One of the T-34s, commanded by a Sergeant Makogan, took the German tank column under fire and knocked out a Pz 38(t)[301] crossing the northern (Alytus) bridge.[302] At this point, Horst Ohrloff, on June 22 commander of the 11th Tank Company in 3rd Battalion, 25 Panzer Regiment, picks up the story:

> *After about 20 tanks of 3rd Battalion had crossed the northern bridge, the 21st tank was hit by a Russian tank that was in a well-concealed position near the bridge and could not be detected by the German tanks. The commander of the German tank, a second lieutenant, was killed and the Russian tank rushed back to its unit by passing approximately 30 German tanks that were dispersed throughout a large area. Several tanks including mine, tried to destroy the enemy tank using our 37mm gun. These attempts, however, had no effect on the T-34 that we were observing for the first time.*

The German forces did not succeed at first in expanding the northern bridgehead because it was impossible to destroy the Russian tanks standing in hull-down positions on the reserve slope . . . East of the southern bridge some German tanks were ambushed, and six were lost to antitank gun fire.[303]

The Soviet T-34, of course, was vastly superior to the German Pz 38(t); yet the Soviet tanks carried only a few rounds of armor-piercing (AP) ammunition, and the "drivers had no experience with their new tanks." *Leytenant* Verzhbitsky elected to deploy his tanks in defilade and wait for reinforcements, which soon arrived—twenty-four T-28 medium tanks of the 9 Tank Regiment's 1st Battalion. The German panzers, unable to close to the effective range of their 37mm cannons, were temporarily stymied by Fedorov's tanks. To break the logjam, Rothenburg summoned the *Luftwaffe*, which was soon pummeling the Soviet positions with high explosive.[304]

Determined to complete his mission, Fedorov would launch three counterattacks during the day, the ensuing tank-on-tank engagement dragging on for some six hours. While the aggressive Soviet tank commander did some damage to 7 Panzer Division, his own forces were at a distinct disadvantage and suffered accordingly. Unlike the Germans, Fedorov had negligible infantry and artillery support, and no air support at all; he also had far less fuel and shells for his tanks. Late in the day (1930 hours), Rothenburg was reinforced by the arrival of 21 Panzer Regiment (20 PD) at the northern bridgehead, whose defense it was ordered to assume, thus releasing the tanks of 25 Panzer Regiment to resume their attack.[305]

With its III./PzRgt 25 in the van, 7 Panzer Division burst from the bridgehead and "began to roll up Fedorov's tired tankers. By nightfall, Fedorov had to break off the action." According to German records,[306] the tank battle at Alytus cost the Soviet 5 Tank Division seventy to eighty tanks destroyed.[307] Yet Rothenburg's panzer regiment had also sustained significant losses: If only a handful of its tanks became permanent losses in the tank battle (the Germans retained possession of the battlefield and were able to salvage and repair many of the damaged panzers), many others had been destroyed along the approach routes to Alytus—victims of Soviet T-34s in good, hull-down fighting positions.[308] Some of the German tanks—mostly the light Pz 38(t)s—had their turrets blown clean off of their hulls.[309]

If the Russians had gotten the worst of the tank duel on the eastern bank of the Neman, they had also put on full display their "peculiar tenacity in defense, reckless courage in the attack, and unnerving capacity to take punishment."[310] Reflecting on the furious combat this day, Rothenburg called it the "toughest battle of his life." Even the war diarist of 3 Panzer Group conceded that "our own 7 Panzer Division has won its most difficult battle since the beginning of the war." According to Horst Ohrloff, "the tank battle near Alytus between German tanks and those of Soviet 5 Tank Division was probably the hardest combat ever conducted by 7 Panzer Division in the Second World War."[311] On

June 28, 1941, *Oberst* Rothenburg, the dashing commander of 25 Panzer Regiment, perished in the fighting near Minsk: After being wounded, and while being transported to a dressing station through territory still occupied by the Russians, his small convoy was ambushed, resulting in his death.[312]

Despite the intense, sometimes costly, fighting along the Alytus axis, it had been a day of spectacular results for "Papa" Schmidt's 39 Panzer Corps. By driving 60 kilometers or more into Soviet-occupied Lithuania and seizing intact the vital bridges over the Neman River at Alytus, Schmidt's panzer divisions (along with 57 Panzer Corps to the south) had set the stage for the rapid advance of 3 Panzer Group on Minsk and, perforce, the vast encirclement of the armies of D. G. Pavlov's Western Front in conjunction with Guderian's 2 Panzer Group.[313] Schmidt's operational breakthrough (again, supported by 57 PzK) had also begun to pry open a dangerous gap between the Soviet Northwestern and Western Fronts, which would expand to well over 100 kilometers within forty-eight hours.[314] As briefly discussed above (Section 3.3), the C-in-C of Northwestern Front, F. I. Kuznetsov, was acutely aware of the existential threat posed by the initial operations of 3 Panzer Group and, as Soviet documents reveal, he pleaded with Soviet Defense Commissar Timoshenko for support.[315] Yet for both Kuznetsov and Pavlov, things were only going to get much worse.

On the extreme left flank of 3 Panzer Group, on the boundary to Army Group North, were the 6 and 26 Infantry Divisions of Förster's 6 Army Corps. Commanded by *Generalleutnant* Helge Auleb, the 6 Infantry Division was one of the elite units of the German army; in 1943, after more than two years of bitter and costly fighting, it would be rated by the German General Staff as one of the three best divisions on the Eastern Front.[316] In June 1941, the division had a combat strength of more than 14,000 men and an array of weapons that included some 600 machine guns, 116 light and medium mortars, seventy-four antitank guns, forty-eight light and medium field howitzers, and twenty-seven flak guns (see, Appendix 3).[317] On Förster's right wing, 30 kilometers due north of Suwalki, the 6 ID was assigned a stretch of the border 10 kilometers in length, anchored on the right by the Šešupė River and extending to a wooded area on the left. The attack order (*Angriffsbefehl*) named Liudvinavas (7 kilometers south of Mariampole) as the day's objective (*Tagesziel*); the division was then to advance northeast, through heavily wooded terrain, and, by June 23, secure a bridgehead over the Neman River at Prienai, some 70 kilometers beyond the division's start line.[318] For a "foot-slogging" infantry division, it was an ambitious tasking order. Moreover, as their own observations and aerial reconnaissance had revealed, part of the Russian defensive line opposite the division consisted of well-prepared bunker positions that would have to be neutralized; as a result, *Generalleutnant* Auleb and his staff expected to encounter some serious enemy opposition directly at the frontier.[319]

Sometime between 0200 and 0300 hours, Auleb, in full battle kit (*feldmarschmässig*), climbed the hill to his advance command post. He was, as he observed in his unpublished recollections, fully aware of the "gravity and magnitude" (*Ernst und Tragweite*) of the mission at hand.[320] At 0305 hours, 6 Infantry Division attacked with all three regiments in the line—37 IR (right), 18 IR (center), 58 IR (left)[321]—the assault troops decamping from the Suwalki triangle in a thick fog that severely limited visibility. Silently, they cut lanes through the enemy's wire entanglements that snaked menacingly across the meadows and cornfields, and slipped across the frontier. Once again, enemy resistance was negligible in the opening minutes, and by 0330, the attacking regiments were already moving up their command posts.[322]

Putting in the division's main effort was its 18 Infantry Regiment, led by the forty-six-year-old *Oberstleutnant* Carl ("Corle") Becker, an "*Alte Hase*" (old-timer) who had fought with distinction in the Great War, being repeatedly wounded and garnering high military honors. The regiment's mission was twofold: (a) to capture the high ground astride the town of Galbanovka; and, (b) to break through the Russian defensive positions about Akmenynai, which consisted of a series of concrete bunkers stretching for several kilometers.[323] Fortunately, the war diary of 18 Infantry Regiment survived the war;[324] its account of the opening hours of Operation *Barbarossa* is detailed, graphic, and thus quoted here at length.

Sunday 22.6.1941. Regimental Command Post in Bojary (that evening moved to a farmstead 2 kilometers west of Bukta). The night passes without either side firing a shot, and there is no discernable change in the enemy situation. Shortly after 0200 hours every man along the entire front is in position, ready to spring, and carry out with machine-like precision all the assigned tasks for the leap across the border. The day promises to be a lovely one. It is still misty in the early morning hours, and the valley between Hill 224 and Hills 220 and 208 is nestled in a thick covering fog. Since 0200 hours, the regimental staff is also at the [CP] on Hill 224, where the [regimental] commander has spent the night in an isolated house.

At 0305 hours, the lead elements launch their attack according to plan. Silently, they cut their way through the enemy wire obstacles (Drahtverhau) along the border. The two assault companies—7th Company on the right and 3rd Company on the left— are far in front of both attacking battalions. At 0310 hours, a German Stuka wing is over Kalvaria and, in vigorous blows, smashes the rear-area troops of the enemy border garrison who are gathered there. Although in the sector of our neighboring regiment on the right one can already discern the sounds of heavy fighting, our own forward elements are closing on their initial objectives without a shot having been fired. The enemy is startled by our attack and is unable to fully occupy his defensive positions.

At 0340 hours, 1st Battalion reports that its 3rd Company, encountering only feeble enemy resistance, has seized Hill 220; a short time later, 2nd Battalion reports the capture of Hill 208, which was no longer occupied by the enemy. The division is continuously informed about the progress of the regiment. The regiment on our left is also making good progress against weak enemy resistance.

At 0430 hours, the lead elements of 1st Battalion, attacking rapidly beyond Hill 220, encounter considerable enemy resistance in front of the woods west of Pagrauziai, while 2nd Battalion, skirting the town of Liubavas, continues to advance steadily. The artillery concentrates its fire support on the battalion on the left [1st Battalion], loosing several barrages on the enemy strongpoint at Pagrauziai.

Starting at 0500 hours, the staff personnel, after struggling with their motor vehicles across cultivated fields and through marshy pastures, also make their way onto Hill 220. The 1st Battalion is still held up by the splendidly camouflaged enemy position west of Pagrauziai. Elements of the battalion have already by-passed a group of farmsteads and gradually reach the level of 2nd Battalion, which had already advanced beyond Epidemiai.

Locked in a bitter fight for Pagrauziai, the 2nd Company has, within an hour, already lost 24 men. However, [with 2nd Company] pinning down the enemy in the front, 3rd Company, led by the already wounded Oberleutnant *Sahrhage, succeeds in making a vigorous advance in the direction of Galbanovka. The company is soon followed by the battalion staff and most of the machine-gun company.[325] About 0700 hours, the report of 2nd Battalion comes in, indicating that its lead elements have already reached Galbanovka; as a result, the regimental commander decides to continue the attack at once, with the main effort on the right, especially since the neighboring regiment on the left has continued to advance against weak enemy resistance. 3rd Battalion, so far drawn up behind the 1st Battalion, is ordered to advance via Epidemiai to Galbanovka.*

At 0730 hours the regimental CP moves via Epidemiai to Galbanovka. There, at about 1030 hours, the following picture presents itself:

The 1st Battalion (without 2nd Company), on a good road that enabled heavy weapons and vehicles to be drawn forward rapidly, has by-passed the bunker line at Akmenynai *[underscore in original] to the north, while 2nd Battalion is tied down before the bunker line. The enemy there is fighting with bitter determination, which makes any advance across the bunker line impossible without artillery support. Since these enemy positions are capable of keeping all access roads to Akmenynai under fire, the regimental commander decides the bunkers must be taken.[326]*

For this purpose, 2nd Battalion is assigned an additional light antitank platoon and a 50mm antitank gun. After a change of position, III./AR 6 concentrates its fire on the bunker positions with several sudden barrages, yet to no discernable effect, while the repeated assaults of the 2nd Battalion against the splendidly ensconced enemy are simply too weak to dislodge him from his strong position. The thought of committing the regiment's 3rd Battalion to the attack was briefly considered, but quickly rejected, for under no circumstances can the mass of the regiment get bogged down by this pocket of resistance, which is well short of the day's assigned objective.

*During the fighting for Akmenynai, which broke down into a series of discon-
nected individual actions, Oberleutnant Grote, chief of 6th Company, and Leutnant
Mintrop, a platoon leader in 7th Company, distinguished themselves through their
special gallantry. In close combat, Grote knocked out two enemy armored scout cars
with hand grenades, while* Leutnant *Mintrop time and again led new assault detachments against the enemy bunkers. During these assaults* Leutnant *Stock, of [11th
Company],³²⁷ died a hero's death.* Leutnant *von Schrader, of 7th Company, was badly
wounded close to an enemy gun position; after the enemy sallied forth to attack, he was
murdered in the most beastly manner. His body was recovered by an assault detachment
led by* Leutnant *Mintrop . . .*

*Because the repeated assaults of the 2nd Battalion had still failed by 1400 hours
to achieve a breakthrough, the regimental commander decided to leave the task of
neutralizing the enemy bunker positions to 2nd Battalion alone (along with 7th Battery), while 3rd Battalion and the mass of the artillery were to follow the attack of 1st
Battalion (with elements of 2nd Battalion), which was making good progress toward
Mikalajavas . . .*

*At 1500 hours, 3rd Battalion struck out toward the north—while seeking to screen its
movements in the direction of Akmenynai—in order to reach the Liubavas-Mikalajavas
road by the shortest possible route. During the advance, the battalion was repeatedly fired
upon by enemy groupings from farm houses and cornfields; only by delaying the advance
[Vormarsch] could these enemy groupings be eliminated.*

*The reinforced 2nd Company, without bothering further with the costly attempt
to pin the enemy down before Pagrauziai, had joined the assault of the 1st Battalion.
Thus, this enemy force was also bypassed on both sides, in the reasonable hope that he
would give himself up to the following 37 Infantry Regiment. Later reports proved
otherwise. The cunningly concealed enemy succeeded on several occasions in taking by
surprise isolated supply columns of the regiment and the division.³²⁸*

Not until the next day was the determined Red Army resistance near Pagrauziai, and
of the bunker crews at Akmenynai, finally broken—the latter requiring the commitment
of both flak artillery and flamethrowers. As noted by *Generalleutnant* Auleb in his recollections, the bunkers were only secured after the German assault parties had incurred
"some grievous losses" (*einige schmerzliche Verluste*).³²⁹

One of the many splendid soldiers who made 6 Infantry Division such an extraordinary unit was *Assistenzarzt* (2nd Lt., Medical) Dr. Heinrich Haape. Son of a Lutheran
minister and a man of impressive intellect and strength of character, the thirty-one-
year-old Haape was working as a doctor at a hospital in Duisburg when drafted into the
military in July 1939. After basic training, he was transferred into the *Wehrmacht* medical
corps in October 1939. Several short assignments ensued and, in the fall of 1940, he
joined 6 Infantry Division, then stationed in Normandy, France. Dr. Haape would spend

more than two years on the Russian front, where he would become one of the most decorated doctors in the *Ostheer*, garnering the German Cross in Gold, the Iron Cross (First and Second Class), the Infantry Assault Badge, the Wounded Badge, and a decoration for personally destroying two Russian tanks in close combat.[330]

At 0345 hours, Dr. Haape's 3rd Battalion, 18 Infantry Regiment (III./IR 18), received the order to advance. For the good doctor, and many of the *Landser* in the 800-man battalion, the day would be their baptism of fire. And for many, Haape among them, the day would be filled with agony, death, and dreadful surprises—this first day in Hitler's war of annihilation against the Soviet Union.[331]

After hours of agonizing tension, the order to move out came as a relief: "We fall into position and move forward," Haape wrote in *Moscow Tram Stop*, his iconic account of his experiences during the first nine months of the Russian campaign. "It is a relief to be moving, but I sit astride my horse with a tense grip on the reins." Haape and his medical team quickly encountered their first wounded soldier—a superficial bullet wound in the arm. Haape removed the rubber tourniquet and emergency bandage applied by a stretcher-bearer at the front; in their place he fixed a pressure bandage and tied the arm in a sling. Haape then remounted his horse, "Lump," and galloped to the front of the column, where he met up with his battalion commander, *Major* Neuhoff, and the latter's adjutant, Hillemanns. Pointedly questioned by Neuhoff, Haape explained—to his superior's satisfaction—the measures he has put in place for evacuation and care of the wounded.[332]

Haape and his team were now beyond the burning customs house at the border and inside Soviet-occupied Lithuania. To Haape and his medical orderlies it looked like an alien world compared to their beloved Germany; they quietly took note of the "stony fields, with ill-kept houses and poorly-clad peasants." Civilians slowly crept out of their hiding places, looking "helpless and confused," but Haape had no time to stop and offer them advice: "Already the spearheads of our infantry were three miles inside enemy territory. And the panzers, we knew, were at this moment driving deep into the Lithuanian plains, beginning the first of many encirclement movements." As they advanced that morning, they observed "*Staffel* after *Staffel*" (squadron after squadron) of the *Luftwaffe*—Heinkel and Dornier medium bombers, *Stuka* divebombers, sleek Messerschmitt Bf-109 fighters—as they winged past in perfect order, on their way to distant objectives. They witnessed an attack by obsolete Russian divebombers—"they flew directly over our heads—we were not the target"—and gazed curiously at the first Russian prisoners: "They were about a platoon strong and wore shabby khaki-yellow uniforms, loosely-flapping, unmilitary-looking blouses and had clean-shaved heads. Their heavy faces were expressionless."[333]

From a farmhouse "came a shout for first-aid men." The doctor and his orderlies entered the house to find several civilians and wounded *Rotarmisten*. He administered first aid and moved on. Galloping through the cornfields alongside the road, he overtook the marching column of troops and again met up with Neuhoff, his battalion commander.

Then shots rang out barely 50 feet in front from a field of rye. Neuhoff and Haape dismounted as a burst of enemy fire arced directly over their heads. Hillemanns, the adjutant, and several other men darted into the cornfield, firing their rifles and automatics; a "melee" was on in the tall corn, "a confusion of revolver shots, upraised rifle butts and screams."

A tall infantryman from the H.Q. company brushed his way back through the rye. With his hands still gripping the barrel of his rifle, he shrugged and said: "Finished!" I noticed the butt of his rifle was splashed with blood. Neuhoff and I strode into the corn. A commissar and four Russian soldiers were lying on the trampled earth, their skulls battered into the soil, which had been freshly dug and thrown up into a mound for their suicidal ambush. The commissar's hands were still grasping uprooted corn stocks. Our casualties were negligible—one man with a bayonet wound in the arm, another man with a grazed calf. A little iodine, gauze and a couple of strips of adhesive plaster and they were ready to march on with the rest of us. Neuhoff, Hillemanns and I rode on together at the head of the column.

"I didn't expect that," said Neuhoff, rather shakily. "Sheer suicide, to attack a battalion at close quarters with five men." We were to learn that these small groups of Russians would constitute our greatest danger. The corn was high and made ideal cover for the small guerrilla bands, which stayed behind as the main body of the Russian forces rolled back. As a rule they were fanatically led by Soviet commissars and we never knew when we should come under their fire.[334]

The sun rose in the sky and the day grew hot; and "as the men marched the dust rose, until we were all covered in a light yellow coating—battledress, rifles, faces and hands. Men and vehicles assumed ghostly outlines in the dust-laden air. I wet my lips with a little water from my bottle and was glad when the order was given to halt." It was now noon, and they rested in a small wood. Suddenly, a flight of eight Russian bombers appeared overhead; Haape and the others looked on as the bombers were decimated with Teutonic precision by a clutch of Bf-109s:

[The Russian bombers] circled to make sure of their target. But this time they had to reckon with the Messerschmitts. The 109's swooped like hawks into a flight of pigeons. They attacked from the sun, firing as they dived. Breaking off the attack they zoomed to regain height for another attack and one by one the bombers were picked off. One Russian burst into flames, a second followed, and like two torches they sank toward the ground. It surprised me to see how slowly they fell. A wing broke off another bomber and the plane spun earthwards. I noticed two parachutes drifting gently above it. Our fighters continued the attacks until every bomber had been shot down.[335]

One of the downed bombers, however, had crashed into a divisional artillery column, causing serious casualties. Haape galloped to their aid, finding fifteen of the artillerymen already dead and nine others with serious burns: "Five of them were so badly burned that I held out no hope of their survival." He filled in casualty cards for the wounded and sent a dispatch rider for an ambulance. He stayed with the men for two hours, by which time he had temporarily lost touch with his battalion.[336]

Meanwhile, by early afternoon, matters were deemed well enough in hand by Förster's headquarters (6 AK) to order 6 Infantry Division to begin a general pursuit of the enemy. With Russian resistance largely shattered, the division's infantry marched eastward along two axes of advance (*Vormarschstrassen*) in the direction of the Neman River. By late afternoon, the 6 ID's improvised reconnaissance battalion,[337] commanded by Cavalry Captain (*Rittmeister*) Georg *Freiherr* von Boeselager, had already covered more than 50 kilometers. On orders from 6 Army Corps, Boeselager then made a spirited dash for the bridge over the Neman at Prienai, pushing hard through tracks of forest and marsh, only to be stopped in his tracks by a well-organized and superior enemy defense, which inflicted serious losses on his men. The capture of Prienai, the crossing of the Neman, would have to wait until the next day.[338]

By any measure, for *Generalleutnant* Auleb's 6 Infantry Division the first day of the campaign had been a successful one. By 2030, his spearheads had reached the day's objective—Liudvinavas astride the Šešupė River. Yet the Red Army nests of resistance outside Pagrauziai, and the stubbornly defended concrete bunkers at Akmenynai, had taken their toll—the division registering fifty-four dead (six officers), 106 wounded, and nineteen missing.[339]

As for Dr. Haape's 18 Infantry Regiment, its losses for the day amounted to thirty-one dead (two officers) and fifty-four wounded.[340] Moreover, by the end of the day, he had learned through hard experience that a Red Cross flag or armband, or a Red Cross symbol emblazoned on the side of an ambulance vehicle, offered no protection to German doctors or their medical staffs. As a result, he armed himself with an automatic weapon and grenades, and removed his Red Cross armband: "There's no Geneva Convention here," he said bitterly to one of his battalion's infantrymen. "I'm telling you . . . I'm a soldier like the rest of you now."[341]

As the harrowing and blood-soaked day neared its end, Haape managed to compose a letter to his fiancée in Duisburg.

The first day in the campaign against Russia. We have a hard day behind us! The Russians fought like devils and never surrendered, so we engaged in close combat on several occasions; just now, half an hour ago, another four Russians were struck dead with the butts of our rifles. Our regiment's losses on this single day are greater than during the entire French campaign . . . We were the focal point [Schwerpunkt] of the attack. Of the regiment's 6 doctors, one is KIA (shot to the head)[342] and another injured. In addition, 4 medical orderlies are also KIA. We have pushed the Russians back along the whole line, except for a few bunkers that have not yet fallen. There is still hard fighting. I had a lot of work to do and frequently had to bandage comrades under heavy machine-gun fire. I have not yet had anything to eat today and only a very little to drink; we are cut off from our supply line![343]

Posted on the left wing of Förster's 6 Army Corps, abutting the boundary with Army Group North, was *Generalmajor* Walter Weiss's 26 Infantry Division. Over the course of June 22, the division advanced more than 30 kilometers from its start line, reaching a point just south of Mariampole.[344] Like its neighbor on the right (6 ID), however, 26 ID also learned a bitter and costly lesson—the Russian soldier was not to be compared to earlier adversaries—as the following account of the initial attack of the division's 77 Infantry Regiment reveals.

"X-hour" has arrived. Whistles sound. Rifle squads leap up and storm forward across the frontier. Only quickly overcome the uncertainty! The nervousness subsides. Our soldiers are filled with resolve.

1st Battalion, on the right, has been tasked with pushing through to the hills directly in front of it and, after taking possession of them, to hold that position for the time being. 2nd Battalion, on the left, has the same mission, while the 3rd Battalion is to follow 2nd Battalion at staggered intervals and cover the Russian frontier posts identified to the north of the attack sector and to neutralize these in the course of the further attack.

While 1st Battalion reaches its objective in the shortest possible time without enemy contact, the 2nd Battalion first has to overpower a few Russian outposts, which had evidently been advanced there by the Russian border guards to the north.

The dogged fighting style of the Russians was evident, even in these early moments. Only by jumping quickly aside at the last minute did the commander of 2nd Battalion evade the detonation of a hand grenade, which a dying Russian, who had been shot down, had thrown between his legs. The 3rd Battalion had its first serious contact with the enemy. After reaching the NKVD frontier post, it did not, unfortunately, await the deployment and support of the heavy weapons, but instead swung into an attack against the outpost.

The officers and men were, no doubt, still overly influenced by the previous, relatively easy days of battle in France. This was to have dire consequences. The Russian NKVD garrison hadn't the slightest intention of surrender or flight. They opened fire with machine guns and rifles and fought tenaciously to the very last man. When the outpost was taken, 3rd Battalion had the lives of six officers, 12 NCOs and soldiers to mourn. Three officers and 46 NCOs and soldiers were wounded. A sad result.[345]

After securing its initial objectives, 77 IR sent out well-armed patrols to reconnoiter, but they reported no contact with the enemy, who had apparently withdrawn. By late morning, the regiment's battalions had reassembled and were ready to begin their pursuit march.[346] It was a march that they—along with dozens more of the foot infantry divisions—would continue for weeks, as they struggled to catch up with the panzer and motorized infantry divisions soon operating far beyond them to the east. For hundreds of kilometers they would march, in insufferable heat along sandy tracks—their boots kicking up clouds of fine dust that engulfed uniforms and equipment and filled every pore—across desolate terrain and through belts of primeval woodlands; all the while maintaining constant combat readiness because of the threat posed by dispersed Red Army units, which lingered in the forests, marshes, and cornfields, prepared to fight to the last man (and woman) rather than to surrender. The days and weeks ahead would often push the *Landser* to the limits of their physical and psychic endurance, and sometimes well beyond.

4.7: *ABENDLAGE:* PRÉCIS OF THE COMBAT ACTIONS OF ARMY GROUP CENTER

Typical of the German experience along the central axis on June 22, 1941, are these observations of Hoth's 3 Panzer Group:

General Impression:

Surprise of the enemy succeeded. The [enemy] resistance, while negligible at first, became stronger in spots. Very little enemy artillery was encountered, while the enemy fought in groups lacking cohesion . . . without centralized leadership. Individual field fortifications were not occupied at all or only weakly occupied, while some concrete bunkers were defended tenaciously. A number of small units had moved out without ammunition, apparently for an exercise.

On the whole, it appears that there were fewer enemy forces before the Neman River than the 3 to 4 divisions that were assumed there. Everywhere, the existing enemy forces withdrew to the east . . . apparently at this time they were not yet focused on the start of war.

Just as in Poland, the attacks of our Luftwaffe *drove the enemy off into the woods, from where he effectively waged guerrilla warfare [*Kleinkrieg*] against the rear elements and columns. This may also be a reason why, at first, surprisingly few enemy forces were encountered. Just how many of them have hidden in the woods . . . cannot yet be determined.*[347]

In assessing the results of the first day's combat operations along the 500-kilometer front of Field Marshal von Bock's Army Group Center, the most salient fact is that, on both wings of Bock's attack, the panzer groups had achieved dangerous operational breakthroughs of the Soviet border defenses. On the right wing, the operations of Guderian's

2 Panzer Group had yielded mixed results. Here, the advance of Geyr's 24 Panzer Corps had been slowed by heavily wooded, marshy terrain and poor roads; farther north, however, Lemelsen's 47 Panzer Corps had achieved a markedly better result, driving all the way to the outskirts of Pruzhany and, as noted by General Halder, chief of the Army General Staff, "gaining its operational freedom of movement" (*operativ Bewegungsfreiheit gewonnen*).[348] On the left wing of the army group the results were even better, with Hoth's 3 Panzer Group forging several bridgeheads across the Neman River well beyond the frontier and, in the words of Halder, "registering an especially robust success . . . In this sector, it appears that complete operational freedom has been attained."[349] The critical point here is that the impressive gains made by both panzer groups, coupled with the less spectacular, albeit clearly significant, progress made by the foot infantry divisions of Kluge's Fourth and Strauss's Ninth Army, meant that the battlefield had already been prepared—after barely twenty-one hours of war—for both the inner and outer encirclements of Pavlov's Western Front.

In achieving such remarkable success Bock's armies and panzer groups were able to fully exploit key advantages over their Russian opponent. As we have seen, the Germans managed to create overwhelmingly formidable force ratios at their key points of concentration across the central front—an effort facilitated by the largely weak Soviet forces posted at the frontier. This enabled the attacking panzers, motorized infantry, and foot infantry to rapidly overcome the enemy's frontier defenses and advance deep into Soviet territory, sowing chaos and confusion among the stunned, ill-prepared, and slow to react Soviet defenders. Also not to be overlooked was the tremendous advantage derived from the fact that the attacking German forces were able to seize intact every bridge across the Bug River; as noted (Section 4.3), on the front of Guderian's 2 Panzer Group alone, nine bridges were in use by midday.

And yet, from a broader perspective, what enabled the Germans to fight so much more effectively on this day—and in the weeks and months that followed—were their towering advantages in leadership, experience, and training over their Soviet counterparts. One can reasonably argue, as does celebrated military historian Dennis Showalter in his book, *Hitler's Panzers*, that the "relative tactical and operational superiority" of the German army's panzer forces over their opponents was never greater than at the start of Operation *Barbarossa*.[350] In fact, the *Wehrmacht* as a whole was at the very peak of its powers in June 1941, able to conduct combined operations of ground and air forces with a precision that the Russians could not begin to emulate (or even fully understand). The brilliantly executed operations of Guderian's and Hoth's panzer groups, along with those of Kesselring's 2 Air Fleet, amplify this point.

And yet, despite the successful start to Operation *Barbarossa*, there were unsettling omens: The savage opposition inside the fortress at Brest, the bunkers at Akmenynai, the NKVD border guards who fought to the last man, the deadly snipers in the trees and brush—these were all clear indications that the "Russian way of war" would confront the

Germans with daunting challenges in the days and months ahead. In a combat report covering the first days of the war, 3 Panzer Group was highly critical of Soviet command execution at all levels, observing that the influence of the enemy's higher level command (*höhere Führung*) was nowhere to be seen, while the tactical approach of lower-level command (*untere Führung*) organs was rigid, by the book (*schematisch*), and incapable of adapting quickly to the highly fluid tactical environment. Yet the report also acknowledged that the "individual [Russian] soldier was tougher [*härter*] than the soldier of [World War I], most likely a result of the Bolshevik idea, but also because he's been incited by his political commissars."[351] And one can only wonder what was going through GFM von Bock's mind when, on June 23, he jotted in his journal: "The Russians are defending themselves stubbornly. Women have often been seen in combat. According to statements made by prisoners, political commissars are spurring maximum resistance by reporting that we kill all prisoners! Here and there Russian officers have shot themselves to avoid being captured."[352]

In assessing the Soviet response to Army Group Center's attack, one must begin with the commanders of Soviet Western Front, and, to a lesser extent, Northwestern Front as well. As far as Army-General D. G. Pavlov was concerned, it can be frankly stated that he was not a man endowed with strategic foresight. He had no clear idea of what Bock's ultimate designs were and "spent the day of 22 June in anguish, shuttling between different units and vainly trying to figure out what was going on."[353] With his communications largely destroyed, he was unable to reach most of his generals and could do nothing to break his *front*'s descent into disintegration. Compounding Pavlov's problems was the fact that, on June 22, Soviet Western Front "was one big construction site. Fortifications, telephone and telegraph lines, roads, airfields, railroads, bridges, highways, fuel depots, and warehouses—everything was half finished. It was as hopeless to call such a *front* to order as it would be to transform a foundation into a fortress overnight."[354]

The disaster that ensnared Pavlov's Western Front from the very first moments of Operation *Barbarossa* was rendered infinitely worse by the loss of the *front*'s air forces—for the most part obliterated on their airfields in the opening German airstrikes. In the first few minutes alone, the squadrons of Kesselring's 2 Air Fleet destroyed more than 700 of the *front*'s aircraft, and the Germans had complete control of the skies; the despondent commander of Western Front's air forces, Maj.-Gen. I. I. Kopets, shot himself in disgrace.[355]

In 1965, Russian military historian V. A. Anfilov conducted a series of revealing interviews with Marshal G. K. Zhukov; due to Soviet-era censorship, Anfilov's article with the interviews did not appear until 1995. In one of the interviews, Anfilov asked: "What can you say about F. I. Kuznetsov [and] D. G. Pavlov?" Zhukov replied: "As commanders of operational major field units, they were poorly prepared. And in such a difficult situation they lost their head[s] entirely. Pavlov and Kuznetsov very poorly exercised control over combat activities." Zhukov, however, went on to say: "Of course [Pavlov] committed serious mistakes in troop control. But who didn't make them in that complex situation, when due to the lack of necessary information from the troops we did not know where and in what condition they were, and thus we were unable to make correct decisions."[356]

The unexpected velocity and power of the German ground and air assault evoked total chaos on the Soviet side, which, as historian David Stahel rightly observed, "was most strikingly evident" in Pavlov's Western Front, which had to bear the brunt of the main German assault. But whether or not Pavlov "lost his head," as Zhukov maintained, what is certainly true is Zhukov's second, and somewhat exculpatory, observation—that mistakes were inevitable due to the catastrophic lack of information required to make clear and meaningful decisions. Moreover, to a large extent, both Pavlov and Kuznetsov were victims of Stalin and the Soviet High Command, who rigidly adhered to prewar plans by demanding immediate and wide-ranging counterattacks when the conditions for such action did not yet exist. The inevitable result was a series of piecemeal attacks that ended disastrously for the attackers but barely delayed the advance of the German panzer units.[357]

Photo Essay: The Front—Operation *Barbarossa* Begins, June 22, 1941

Somewhere along the German-Soviet Demarcation Line prior to the start of Operation *Barbarossa* (NA)

Support vehicles crossing into Russia on the morning of June 22, 1941. The letter "G" emblazoned in white on the rear of vehicles indicates they belong to Guderian's 2 Panzer Group. (PEN & SWORD)

German troops cross the Bug River at the Russian fortress of Brest-Litovsk at 0315 hours on the morning of June 22, 1941. (MUSEUM BERLIN-KARLSHORST)

One of the Red Army's heavy concrete bunkers near Akmenynai just inside Soviet-occupied Lithuania, captured on June 22/23, 1941, by German 6 Infantry Division at a heavy cost in lives. Photograph taken in June 2016. (C. LUTHER)

German Pz IV tank and heavy machine gun at start of Russian campaign

Soviet aircraft destroyed at Kaunas, Lithuania, by the *Luftwaffe* on June 22, 1941

Aerial photograph of the fortress of Brest-Litovsk taken before the German invasion (NA)

German gunners prepare to bombard the fortress of Brest-Litovsk with the 600mm "Karl" siege mortar. This was the second-largest gun in the *Wehrmacht*'s inventory.

Fortress of Brest-Litovsk after its destruction by German artillery and the *Luftwaffe*

German motorcycle troops advance alongside a truck convoy shrouded in dust.

Troops of the elite 1 Mountain Division cross the frontier into Russia on the morning of June 22, 1941.
(BUNDESARCHIV, BILD 146-2007-0127, FOTO: KÖNIG)

On June 22, 1941, while the battle for the town of Oleszyce is still raging, General Hubert Lanz honors fallen soldiers of his 1 Mountain Division. Shortly after this picture was taken, the injured Lanz collapsed due to loss of blood. (BIBLIO VERLAG)

Battery of 150mm medium field howitzers in action

German 150mm *Nebelwerfer* rocket projector in firing position (NA)

The *Nebelwerfer* in action (NA)

A German machine-gun crew on the march

German forward observers directing fire of their artillery

German infantry on the march in the Baltic States; on their left an armored scout vehicle (Sd.Kfz 221).
(BUNDESARCHIV, BILD 101I-208-0027-04A, FOTO: NÄGELE, JUNE 1941)

At the start of the campaign, German soldiers were often greeted as liberators from Soviet Communist oppression. (BUNDESARCHIV, BILD 146-1974-109-25)

Four German Pz III tanks in position in a field (BUNDESARCHIV, BILD 101I-186-0199-08A, FOTO: SPRINGMANN, JUNE 1941)

A German soldier advances past a dead *Rotarmisten* and a burning BT-7 tank in southern Russia.
(BUNDESARCHIV, BILD, 101I-020-1268-36, FOTO: HÄHLE, JUNE 1941)

Soviet T-34 destroyed by German air attack, Dubno, Poland, in June 1941

Destroyed German Pz IV tank. Note the "G" on rear of tank, denoting that it belonged to Guderian's 2 Panzer Group. (D. GARDEN & K. ANDREW)

German infantry enjoy a brief pause before resuming the long march east. (PEN & SWORD)

Soviet T-26 tanks destroyed during the massive tank battles in the Ukraine in June 1941

The devastating German 210mm heavy howitzer in action (NA)

German machine-gun crew in firing position (NA)

German troops on the march through Russia (NA)

German tanks in the "fog of war" early in the Russian campaign (NA)

A German Military Cemetery somewhere in Russia. Over four million *Landser* would perish in the Russian campaign, along with more than fourteen million Russian soldiers. (NA)

CHAPTER 5

Armageddon Unleashed (III)—Army Group South Goes to War

Most of the bunkers on the Bug have been captured. Several are still firing, because the Russians are really tough. At the edge of the wood are a couple of houses, from which snipers are shooting at us. A few hand grenades and the straw roofs are burning like torches in the sun-filled morning . . . None of the civilians have fled. The war came as too much of a surprise to them.

—PAUL R., 44 INFANTRY DIVISION[1]

So, what say you about our new enemy? Perhaps father can still remember how I talked about the Russian army during my last leave. And even then I said that, over the long haul, we cannot maintain friendly relations with the Bolsheviks. Besides, there are still way too many Jews there. There's nothing new here. We sit continuously by the loud-speakers and listen to reports from the front.

—FELDWEBEL HANS M., 79 INFANTRY DIVISION[2]

The surprise attack launched by the enemy with enormous forces and his rapid advance into the depth of our territory stunned for a while our forces, which were not prepared for this. They were subjected to shock. A good deal of time was required in order to get them out of this condition . . . Instances were observed when even entire units, which came under a sudden flank attack from a small group of enemy tanks and aviation would panic . . . The fear of encirclement and fear of the enemy's imaginary parachute landings were a real sore point for a long time.

—MAJ.-GEN. K. K. ROKOSSOVSKY, COMMANDER,
SOVIET 9 MECHANIZED CORPS[3]

THE COMMANDER OF ARMY GROUP SOUTH WAS THE SIXTY-FIVE-YEAR-OLD FIELD MAR-
shal (Karl R.) Gerd von Rundstedt; his chief of staff was *Gen.d.Inf.* Georg von Sodenstern. The descendant of an old Prussian *Junker* family, Rundstedt entered the army in
1892 at age sixteen and was commissioned as a second lieutenant in the Prussian 83
Infantry Regiment (Kassel) the following year. A graduate of the prestigious *Kriegsakad-
emie* in Berlin, he saw duty as a staff officer on the Eastern and Western Fronts in World
War I, rising to chief of staff of an army corps and twice being recommended for Prussia's
highest military decoration, the *Pour le Mérite*. Following the Great War, his superior
abilities ensured his retention in Germany's 100,000-man *Reichswehr* and, rising rapidly
through the ranks, by the time Hitler came to power in January 1933, Rundstedt had been
promoted to General of the Infantry.[4]

While Rundstedt never hesitated to disparage Hitler in private, in public he evinced
unquestioning loyalty toward the *Führer*, in accordance with the Prussian military code
of honor, duty, and loyalty. Although he eschewed politics, the Nazis found him quite
useful, and Hitler seems to have taken a genuine liking to him. Erich von Manstein, his
chief of staff in 1939/40, later recalled that Rundstedt "had a charm about him to which
even Hitler succumbed."The German dictator, fully aware of Rundstedt's high reputation
among his brother officers, was quick to establish "a unique relationship with [him] in
order to ensure the loyalty of the officer corps." In March 1938, Rundstedt was promoted
to *Generaloberst* and, although he opposed the looming prospect of war with Czechoslo-
vakia (convinced as he was that Germany was not yet ready for war), he led the Second
Army during the Sudetenland crisis of 1938.[5]

Rundstedt retired from military service in November 1938 and was named honorary
colonel of 18 Infantry Regiment (he had led the regiment in 1925–1926)—a "distinction
he cherished above all others. From then on, he wore his regimental commander's uniform
exclusively and was often mistaken for a colonel by the lower ranks. Whenever that happened, Rundstedt laughed."[6] His retirement, however, was short-lived and, in May 1939,
he was appointed to lead a small working staff that played a major role in planning the
invasion of Poland. Working Staff Rundstedt soon became Headquarters, Army Group
South, which he commanded with notable success during the short Polish campaign of
September/October 1939. Following a brief stint as C-in-C East, he was transferred to
the Western Theater and took command of Army Group A, which had the leading role in
the six-week victory over France in May/June 1940. During the French campaign, it was
not Hitler but Rundstedt who, on May 20, decided to halt his panzers outside Dunkirk
and await the arrival of the trailing German foot infantry. While Hitler seconded the
decision, it was a fateful blunder—and one that Rundstedt later denied—that enabled
more than 300,000 British and French soldiers to escape certain death or capture.[7]

On July 19, 1940, Rundstedt was one of a dozen generals promoted by Hitler to the
exalted rank of field marshal. Although he had little faith in the project, he was given
command of the ground forces for the invasion of England. Following its cancellation, in

March 1941 Rundstedt was ordered to set up Headquarters Army Group South at Breslau for the impending invasion of Russia. While he viewed Operation *Barbarossa* with "foreboding," his army group would record some of the *Wehrmacht*'s greatest tactical and operational triumphs in the summer of 1941; yet the strain of the campaign in the East would also result in his first heart attack (a mild one) in November 1941. At the start of December 1941, Hitler peremptorily dismissed Rundstedt as C-in-C Army Group South—not for health reasons, but because he had withdrawn from Rostov-on-the-Don in the face of violent Russian counterattacks, violating the *Führer*'s order to stand fast at the city; however, "when Hitler was made aware of the facts, he quickly forgave him and sent him into retirement with a large financial reward, a gesture that embarrassed Rundstedt, who, while unable to refuse it, never personally touched the money." In March 1942, he would be recalled to active duty, this time as Commander-in-Chief West.[8]

It should also be noted that Rundstedt passed on Hitler's orders for the elimination of Red Army commissars "without question," although he did issue a "stream of orders" from his headquarters forbidding his soldiers from participating in the murderous actions of the *Einsatzgruppen*; however, and perhaps as an expression of his own gradual radicalization, Rundstedt did support Field Marshal Walter von Reichenau's notorious order of October 1941, which exhorted German troops "to revenge themselves on the Jews for atrocities committed against them"[9] (see, Section 5.4). Charles Messenger, in his balanced—and, at times, even sympathetic—biography of Rundstedt, offered an appraisal of the field marshal that included the following:

> On the surface, von Rundstedt represented the archetypal Prussian officer in character—stiff, unbending, emotionless. Underneath . . . lay a very different man. While he was shy and reserved toward those whom he did [not] know, he displayed warmth and humor when in the company of people who were familiar to him . . .
>
> [He] was not a man of great original thought nor an intellect, but never tried to conceal this. On the other hand, he had much commonsense, an ability to see both sides of an argument, and was possessed with clarity of thought, especially when it came to reducing a problem to its fundamental essentials quickly . . . His lengthy experience as a staff officer also made him recognize the ideal relationship between a command and his staff.[10]

Field Marshal von Rundstedt's opposite number across the frontier was forty-nine-year-old Col.-Gen. M. P. Kirponos, commander of the Kiev Special Military District (which became Southwestern Front upon the outbreak of war). During World War I, Kirponos served in the Czarist army from 1915 and did duty as a company medic. He joined the Red Army in 1918, serving as a regimental commander, an assistant division commander, and chairman of a revolutionary military tribunal. During the Civil War, he led a regiment and organized partisan detachments in the Ukraine. In 1919, he was an assistant chief of a school for red commanders in the Ukraine; and, in 1920, he was chief of a supply command and commissar of a school in Kiev. In the early 1920s, Kirponos held the post of deputy commander of a school for NCOs in the Ukraine. Following completion of the Frunze Military Academy in 1927, Kirponos commanded a rifle battalion, was an assistant chief of staff and chief of staff of a rifle division. From 1934 to 1939 he served as commandant of the Kazań Infantry School.[11]

Kirponos rose to prominence during the Russo-Finnish War of 1939/40, successfully leading one of Timoshenko's rifle divisions in the final attack on the Mannerheim Line in early 1940, an achievement for which he was made a Hero of the Soviet Union. Like D. G. Pavlov, Kirponos was an "example of the new blood promoted to senior commands after the Winter War with Finland." In April 1940, he was appointed commander of a rifle corps, and in June 1940, head of the Leningrad Military District. In February 1941, he replaced Zhukov as commander of the Kiev Special Military District. He was promoted to the rank of colonel-general in 1941. In about a year's time, Kirponos had gone from being a division commander to one of the top field commanders in the entire Red Army.[12]

While Kirponos appears to have done a better job than the commanders of the other western military districts in preparing for war—and in leading his *front* during the frontier battles of June and July—K. K. Rokossovsky, who, as commander of a mechanized corps served under him in the summer of 1941, was surprisingly harsh in his judgment of Kirponos:

> *The* front's *command post [July 1941] was in Brovary, on the eastern bank of the Dnepr. I spent the remainder of the night in* front *headquarters and in the morning presented myself to the* front *commander, Colonel General M.P. Kirponos. His obvious confusion very much amazed me. Evidently noting my amazement, he tried to put on an air of calm, but he was unsuccessful. He listened absentmindedly to my meager information about the situation on the 5 Army's and corps' sector and would often interrupt me, running up to the window and exclaiming: "What's air defense doing? . . . The planes fly and no one shoots them down . . . Disgraceful!" He would then order that instructions should be issued on increasing the activity of air defense and that the air defense chief be brought to him. Yes, this was confusion, insofar as in the situation that had come about at that time, another* front *commander, in my opinion, would not have worried about air defense.*
>
> *In these minutes I firmly came to the conclusion that such voluminous, complex and responsible duties were beyond this man and woe to the troops under his command. It was in this mood that I left the headquarters of the Southwestern Front, heading for Moscow.*[13]

On September 20, 1941, Kirponos, attempting to escape from the Kiev cauldron (where the Germans had surrounded most of Southwestern Front), was first wounded, then killed by a mortar shell in a wood near Lokhvitsa. Kirponos was awarded the Order of Lenin, the Order of the Patriotic War 1st Class (posthumously), and the medal "20 Years of the RKKA."[14]

5.1: OPPOSING FORCES AND BATTLE PLANS (SOUTHERN AXIS)

Forming the right wing of the Eastern Front, GFM von Rundstedt's Army Group South (headquarters at Rzeszów) was composed of forty-one divisions (twenty-five infantry, four light, five panzer, three motorized infantry, one mountain division, and three security divisions) arranged chiefly in three infantry armies and a single panzer group.[15] Total personnel (including GHQ troops) amounted to 972,000 men split into two distinct groups separated by a gap of 330 kilometers because Hungary was not participating in the initial German attack,[16] thus no German troops were stationed there. The first group, assembled north of the Carpathian Mountains in southern Poland and making up the main strike force, consisted of the Seventeenth and Sixth Armies and 1 Panzer Group. Commanding the panzer group was *Generaloberst* Ewald von Kleist, whose five panzer divisions had between them about 715 tanks, all of German manufacture. The second, and much weaker, grouping of forces was posted in Romania and included Eleventh Army along with the Romanian 3 and 4 Armies. While Rundstedt had just a single division in army group reserve (99 Light Division), two divisions of the OKH reserve (one infantry and one mountain division) were already in theater, with four more infantry divisions in transport and earmarked to arrive by July 4, 1941.[17] Among the General Headquarters troops allocated to Army Group South were the following:

- 16 artillery commanders (*Arko*)
- 9 artillery regimental staffs
- 4 assault gun battalions
- 7 105mm cannon battalions
- 10 150mm medium howitzer battalions
- 5 mixed artillery battalions
- 8 210mm heavy howitzer battalions (4 motorized; 4 with "limited mobility")
- 2 240mm howitzer (*Haubitze*) battalions (mot.)
- 2 150mm cannon battalions
- 1 210mm heavy artillery battalion for flat trajectory fire (*Flachfeuer*)
- 2 *Nebelwerfer* regiments
- 1 *Nebelwerfer* battalion
- 2 decontamination battalions (*Entg.Abt.*)
- 1 machine-gun battalion (mot.)

- 4 antitank battalions
- 6 flak battalions (2 *Fla* and 4 *Heeres Flak Abt.*)
- 12 flak (*Fla*) companies
- 1 Flamethrower tank battalion (*Pz.Abt.Flamm*)
- 4 280mm "K5" heavy rail-borne artillery pieces
- 2 600mm "Karl" heavy rail-borne artillery pieces[18]

Additional GHQ units in Rundstedt's order of battle included sixteen engineer battalions, eight bridge-building battalions, fifty-nine bridge columns "B," thirty-three construction battalions, and sixteen battalions for road construction and repair. Also supporting the army group were the Organization Todt and Reich Labor Service (RAD). As was the case with Army Groups North and Center, *Luftwaffe* units assigned for tactical support included short- and long-range (strategic) reconnaissance squadrons, along with seventeen light and mixed motorized flak battalions.[19]

Air support of Army Group South was the responsibility of *Generaloberst* Alexander Löhr's 4 Air Fleet (*Luftflotte 4*), which began the Russian campaign with a complement of 307 operational bombers and 272 combat-ready fighter aircraft. Yet because the Germans were not making their main effort along the southern axis, Löhr's air fleet was not fully resourced. For example, it possessed no *Stuka* divebombers and only minimal forces dedicated to the close air support (CAS) mission; moreover, significant air assets were committed to defending the vital Romanian oil fields from potential Russian air attack. Löhr's air fleet, however, did include the *Luftwaffe's* 2 Flak Corps, which controlled six of the seventeen flak battalions noted above, and which would play a significant role protecting the spearheads of Kleist's panzer group.[20]

The long front of Rundstedt's army group—by far the longest of the three army groups—stretched for many hundred kilometers from the Danube delta to the headwaters of the Pripiat' River, northeast of Lublin. Beginning at the Black Sea, the front twisted along the Romanian border for more than 600 kilometers and was lightly covered by the seven infantry divisions of German Eleventh Army (Schobert) and the two Romanian armies of limited utility. This was followed by the gap of more than 300 kilometers along the Hungarian frontier, which was only screened by a handful of Hungarian brigades. North of the Hungarian border began the army group's main front—more than 500 kilometers in length and mostly following the San and (Western) Bug Rivers to a point east of Lublin (in German-occupied Poland), where it met the southern boundary of Army Group Center. Here the mass of Rundstedt's forces were deployed in the following order (right to left): Seventeenth Army (Stülpnagel), opposite the Soviet fortified regions of Peremysl' and Rava Ruska; Sixth Army (Reichenau), one army corps east of Rava Ruska, a second army corps ca. 100 kilometers to the north, east of Chelm; and 1 Panzer Group (Kleist), on the inner flanks of Sixth Army's two army corps and opposite or south of the fortified region of Vladimir-Volynski.[21] Across the frontier, facing Rundstedt's *Schwer-punkt* grouping, were the 5, 6, and 26 Armies of Kirponos's Kiev Special Military District (Southwestern Front).

Army Group South's original plan of attack, as envisaged by both Rundstedt and Halder, had called for an ambitious double envelopment, conducted by Kleist's panzer group in the north with the support of a strong Twelfth Army coming out of Romania. Just weeks before the invasion, however, in March 1941, Hitler decided to reassign Twelfth Army to the impending Balkan campaign, replacing it in Romania with the headquarters of Eleventh Army and much weaker forces and ending plans for a major offensive across the Prut and Dnester Rivers. Hitler justified his decision by stating that "it would be fundamentally wrong to attack everywhere"; besides, he considered the Romanians to be utterly unreliable and without offensive strength. This meant that the success of Rund-stedt's operation would hinge entirely on 1 Panzer Group achieving a breakthrough of the Soviet border defenses and advancing deep into the rear of Soviet Southwestern Front. Yet because the Germans considered the Russian frontier defenses covering the Ukraine to be particularly robust, Rundstedt elected to make his initial assault with infantry forces, which would first pry open gaps in the Soviet defenses for the panzer units.[22] The terrain in the border region was partially wooded and gently undulating, not bad for tanks; but once clear of the frontier the land became increasingly suited for armored warfare in the treeless steppe of the Ukraine. Conversely, due to the dictates of geography, Army Group South would have more river lines to cross than the other two army groups.[23]

Rundstedt's final plan of attack was to use his strong left wing (Seventeenth and Sixth Armies, 1 Panzer Group) to break through the enemy lines between Rava Ruska and Kovel' and, advancing by way of Berdichev and Zhitomir, to gain bridgeheads over the Dnepr River at and south of Kiev. Kleist's tanks were then to drive southeast along the Dnepr, preventing the enemy from withdrawing past the river and defeating him in battle with an inverted front in cooperation with the advancing infantry. The success of this operation would enable subsequent operations to the east, in the direction of Rostov and Stalingrad, or to the northeast toward Khar'kov and Voronezh. On the right wing of the army group, Eleventh Army in Romania was to tie down enemy forces and prevent their orderly retreat into the interior (this army's forces, however, would not begin their attack across the Prut River until July 2).[24] The attack order for Rundstedt's Army Group South was laid out thusly in the OKH deployment directive:

> It is the mission of Army Group South to advance with a strong left wing—the mobile forces in the van—in the direction of Kiev, to destroy the Russian forces in Galicia and the western Ukraine west of the Dnepr River, and to secure the Dnepr crossings at and below Kiev as early as possible to ensure further conduct of operations beyond the Dnepr. The operation is to be conducted in such a manner that the mobile troops in the Lublin sector are concentrated for the breakthrough toward Kiev.[25]

Given the "great scope of his mission," Rundstedt was concerned about the relatively modest forces he'd been given to accomplish it. The closest objective, Kiev, was almost 500 kilometers ("as the crow flies") from the frontier. From his own experiences in World War I, he was aware of the great difficulties posed by the immense size of the theater of operations, the often extreme climate, the hazards of the terrain, and the inadequate road and rail infrastructure. Complicating matters was the fact that he would be attacking into the largest of the Soviet defensive groupings. To be successful in such a challenging environment, speed would be essential.[26]

On the "Other Side of the Hill," Col.-Gen. M. P. Kirponos would begin the campaign with an order of battle including 907,046 personnel (142,105 in schools), 16,997 guns and mortars, and 4,788 combat-ready tanks—organized in four armies and eight mechanized corps (sixty divisions in all, including sixteen tank and eight mechanized divisions). Nearly 2,000 operational aircraft (in ten air divisions) provided air support.[27] The mechanized corps between them possessed more than 500 T-34 and 270 KV I and II tanks; these, however, were unevenly distributed among the corps. The 4 Mechanized Corps (6 Army) boasted a total of 101 KVs and 359 T-34s; 8 Mechanized Corps (26 Army) had seventy-one KVs and one hundred T-34s; 15 Mechanized Corps (6 Army) was outfitted with sixty-four KVs and seventy-two T-34s; and 22 Mechanized Corps possessed thirty-one KV tanks and no T-34s. Three of the mechanized corps (9, 16, 24 MC) had no KVs or T-34s at all, while 19 Mechanized Corps had but six KVs and two T-34s. The great majority of the other tanks were the light, obsolete BTs and T-26s. In addition, Kirponos's mechanized units suffered from the typical shortages of equipment, training, and logistics.[28] That said, the sheer size of the Soviet mechanized forces, and their tenacity in battle, would pose a severe challenge to Rundstedt's army group at the start of the campaign.

A brief look at the deployment of Kirponos's Southwestern Front reveals that, while some of his units were stationed deep within the interior (including several mechanized corps), three of his armies and four mechanized corps (among them the powerful 4 and 8 Mechanized Corps), were posted in or about the L'vov salient, where they were positioned to clash directly with Rundstedt's main strike force.[29] The reader will recall that, in the months prior to June 22, Kirponos's military district had made good progress in the construction of fixed and field fortifications. The Rava Ruska and Peremysl' fortified regions in particular bristled with well-camouflaged pillboxes, heavy field artillery positions, and "cunning obstacles" that would turn the "first German leap across the frontier into a costly operation."[30] In any case, the mission for Kirponos and his Southwestern Front—the largest by far of the three *fronts* in the western frontier zone[31]—was clear-cut: Stop the German invaders dead in their tracks and, in accordance with prewar Soviet doctrine and operational planning, defeat the enemy by driving deep into his own territory.

5.2: Eleventh Army Operations

The Eleventh Army (headquarters in Piatra Neamt) was commanded by the fifty-eight-year-old *Generaloberst* Eugen *Ritter* von Schobert; his chief of staff was *Obst.i.G.* Wöhler. A pro-Nazi general who enjoyed Hitler's favor, Schobert had taken command of the army in Romania on May 24, 1941; he would be killed on September 12, 1941, while on a reconnaissance mission, when his Fieseler *Storch* landed in a Russian minefield near the front. In June 1941 his Eleventh Army comprised three army corps and seven infantry divisions—about 120,000 men: 11 Army Corps (76, 239 ID), commanded by *Gen.d.Inf.* Joachim von Kortzfleisch; 30 Army Corps (198 ID), under *Gen.d.Inf.* Hans von Salmuth; and 54 Army Corps (50, 170 ID), led by *Gen.d.Kav.* Erik Hansen. One division (22 ID) made up the army reserve, while most of another (72 ID) was assigned to protecting the vital Ploesti oil fields, which furnished Germany with about half of her oil needs. Indeed, Romania's huge petroleum reserves and long border with Soviet Russia made it indispensable to the Reich.[32] General Headquarters units assigned to Eleventh Army included:

- Assault Gun Battalion 190 (one battery to 11 AK; remainder *z.V. AOK 11*)
- 1 105mm cannon battalion (11 AK)
- 3 medium field howitzer battalions (1 each to 11, 30 and 54 AK)
- 1 mixed artillery battalion (30 AK)
- 1 antitank battalion (11 AK)
- 1 flak (*Fla*) battalion (*z.V. AOK 11*)
- 1 flak (*Fla*) company (*z.V. AOK 11*)

Other GHQ troops embraced the typical assortment of engineer and bridge-building battalions, bridge columns "B," and construction and road repair battalions. *Luftwaffe* units assigned for tactical support included three short-range reconnaissance squadrons (one to each army corps); one long-range (strategic) reconnaissance squadron (2.(F)/22) under direct army control; and three mixed flak battalions, all under direct army control (*z.V. AOK 18*).[33]

Serving alongside Schobert's Eleventh Army were the Romanian 3 and 4 Armies, led by Generals P. Dumitrescu and N. Ciupercă, respectively; together, they consisted of about 150,000 personnel in five army corps.[34] The question of command over the German and Romanian forces was resolved by placing them under the nominal command of the Romanian dictator, Marshal Ion Antonescu, while Eleventh Army headquarters staff was to "plan and supervise the actual execution of operations." On June 19, 1941, a new agreement was reached between Antonescu and Schobert, according to which the sector of Romanian 4 Army was left under Romanian army command, while Romanian 3 Army was excluded from controlling its units and placed directly under the control of Eleventh Army. Marshal Antonescu, it should be noted, was a stalwart supporter of Hitler's decision to attack the Soviet Union,[35] and the only Axis ally to put his entire armed forces at the disposal of the Reich.[36]

The bulk of Eleventh Army forces were concentrated in the center of the front, along the Romanian border (opposite the Prut River) on both sides of Iassy (Jassy). The Romanian 4 Army, on the right wing, was entrusted with the security of the Black Sea coast and the lower Prut, while 3 Army forces were distributed in the center and on the left wing.[37] The mission of Eleventh Army was as follows:

> *The Eleventh Army is to protect Romanian territory, which is vital [lebenswichtig] for the German conduct of the war, against any breach by Russian forces. Within the scope of the attack of Army Group South, it is to tie down enemy forces facing it by simulating the deployment of strong forces and, as the situation progresses, prevent an orderly withdrawal of the Russians across the Dnepr in cooperation with the* Luftwaffe.[38]

Simply put, Eleventh Army and Romanian forces were to be confined at first to the protection of the Romanian frontier and diversionary holding attacks, before going over to a limited offensive. That offensive would not begin until the start of July 1941, in part because most of Schobert's divisions (50, 72, 76, 198 ID) had only recently returned from the Balkan campaign and required a short period of refurbishment before they would be ready. Once underway, the objective of the attack would be to "clear Soviet forces from southern Ukraine and the Black Sea coast and, if possible, encircle Red Army forces in the Kamenets-Podol'skii and Vinnitsa regions in cooperation with the Seventeenth and Sixth Armies."[39]

To confront the modest Axis forces in Romania, the Soviet High Command would activate the Southern Front on June 25, 1941. Commanded by Col.-Gen. I. V. Tyulenev (a Red Cavalry veteran of the Civil War), it consisted of the 9 Army with two mechanized corps and 18 Army. The *front*'s task was to check Axis forces in Bessarabia, while giving Kirponos's Southwestern Front freedom to maneuver along the vital Kiev axis. Tyulenev left Moscow for his new command on June 22, arriving at his *front* headquarters in Vinnitsa on the 24th, where he found no telephones, telegraphs, or radios. But at least he had an extra ten days to prepare.[40]

While Operation *Barbarossa* began with a vengeance on the early morning of June 22 along the Eastern Front north of Hungary, in Romania there was no German artillery barrage and no attack across the frontier, only patrolling activity in pursuit of limited objectives. As Army Chief of Staff Halder jotted in his diary at 1330 hours: "Army Group South reports that own patrols have crossed the Prut River between Galatz and Huşi and Iassy without encountering any resistance. Bridges are in our hands."[41] Soviet patrols, which began about midday, were easily parried.[42]

At the front, *Gefreiter* Franz B., a soldier in a bakery company in 198 Infantry Division (30 AK), described his—rather more provincial—thoughts on the outbreak of the war in a letter to loved ones:

> *Since war with Russia has finally broken out, we will soon be receiving extra front pay. We can't really write anything in detail, and there is a very strict control of the mail. Up to the final minute everything was shrouded in secrecy . . . We were quite surprised [by the outbreak of war], for to the very last minute we had counted on a peaceful settlement with Russia. Last night our* Oberleutnant *visited our quarters and brought the news that tomorrow, at 0300 hours, it was going to start with Russia. So, early this morning, for our baking, we had to bring our steel helmets, gas masks, gas shelters, cartridges, guns and bayonets with us. But today has passed by peacefully. I'm quite eager to see what the night will bring us. We're all prepared for a major struggle [einen grossen Kampf]. We brought two light machine guns into position to protect our bakery area. It's the first time that we've had to take such extensive security precautions in our company.*
>
> *Rumor has it that the* Führer *was supposed to give a radio address today. But we didn't hear anything. It's also rather ridiculous—we don't have a newspaper and don't listen to the radio—so we know nothing in particular about the reasons for the conflict with Russia. For the moment, any thought of going on leave is out of the question.*[43]

At midday, the chief of staff of Eleventh Army, Colonel Wöhler, spoke by telephone with his counterpart at Army Group South, General von Sodenstern. Wöhler offered his assessment of the situation, noting that Eleventh Army (erroneously as it turned out) rated the enemy forces opposite its front as "very weak," and feared that they might soon begin to withdraw to the east. To prevent the enemy from doing so, and to ensure that Red Army forces stayed tied down by Eleventh Army, the two chiefs of staff discussed the option of launching a frontal attack toward the Dnester River, to begin as early as the evening of the 22nd. Such an action, thought Sodenstern, by placing the enemy's "Bessarabian front" under greater pressure, would also contribute to the confusion in the Soviet leadership. While Field Marshal von Rundstedt, the commander of Army Group South, and Colonel Adolf Heusinger, chief of the OKH Operations Branch, both supported the proposal, General Halder thought otherwise; in his diary, he noted: "The time is not ripe yet for a decision on how to employ Eleventh Army. Our assault troops have crossed the Prut River at various points and have seized the bridges. But there are no signs that the Russians are yielding the area between the Prut and the Dnester."[44]

At 2300 hours, Army Group South issued its orders to Eleventh Army for the following day: The army was to continue to defend the border, while aggressively conducting reconnaissance and expanding its small bridgeheads across the Prut. Romanian units, however, no doubt for political reasons, were not to be exposed to any possible setbacks.[45]

When the Axis offensive out of Romania got underway on July 2, 1941, Soviet Southern Front, well equipped with tanks, was ready for action. Eleventh Army infantry and the supporting Romanian forces, advancing without tanks and little to no air cover, averaged at first no more than 12/13 kilometers a day against Tyulenev's aggressive and mobile armored rearguards. Soviet fighters and bombers conducted harassing attacks, while the "frequent and sudden cloudbursts churned the rich black soil into liquid glue, bringing all wheeled movement to a halt for hours. Even field guns drawn by six pairs of horses came to a standstill."[46]

5.3: SEVENTEENTH ARMY OPERATIONS

The commander of Seventeenth Army was the fifty-six-year-old *General der Infanterie* (Lt.-Gen.) Carl-Heinrich von Stülpnagel; his chief of staff was *Obst.i.G.* Müller. Stülpnagel had led an army corps in the French campaign of 1940 and, on December 20, 1940, was named C-in-C of Seventeenth Army. He would continue to lead the army until October 1941 when, on his own wish, he was relieved of his duties and replaced by General Hermann Hoth.[47] In February 1942, he would be named C-in-C of German forces in France. As early as the fall of 1938, Stülpnagel had joined the military resistance to Hitler and, by the summer of 1944, had become one of its leading members. Fully compromised by the abortive attempt to assassinate the *Führer* on July 20, 1944, he was ordered to report to Berlin.[48]

> *Stülpnagel decided to go to Berlin by road. On the old Meuse battlefield north of Verdun he ordered his driver to stop and sent the car on. He walked down to the Meuse canal and shot himself through the head but without killing himself. Hearing the shot his escort turned back, found him floating in the canal and took him to a hospital in Verdun. He was operated on that night and, though his life was saved, he was blind.*[49]

General Stülpnagel was arrested by the Gestapo, condemned to death on August 30, 1944, and executed at Plötzensee prison the same day.[50]

Seventeenth Army (headquarters in Rudnik) began the Russian campaign with more than 200,000 men distributed over thirteen divisions and three army corps. On the army's right wing was *Gen.d.Inf.* Kurt von Briesen's[51] 52 Army Corps (101 Light [*Jäger*] Division, 444 and 454 Security Divisions); in the center, *Gen.d.Inf.* Ludwig Kübler's 49 Mountain Corps (Geb.K.) (68 ID, 257 ID, 1 Mountain Division); and, on the left wing, *Gen.d.Inf.* Viktor von Schwedler's 4 Army Corps (24, 71, 262, 295, 296 ID). In army reserve were the 97 and 100 Light Divisions.[52] Among the General Headquarters units distributed to Seventeenth Army were the following:

- Assault Gun Battalion 243 (4 AK)[53]

- 2 105mm cannon battalions (1 to 49 Geb.K.; 1 *z.V. AOK 17*)

- 4 150mm medium howitzer battalions (3 to 4 AK; 1 to 49 Geb.K.)

- 1 mixed artillery battalion (4 AK)

- 1 210mm heavy howitzer battalion (limited mobility) (4 AK)

- 1 280mm "K5" heavy rail-borne artillery battery (4 AK)

- 1 600mm "Karl" heavy rail-borne artillery battery (4 AK)

- 1 antitank battalion (49 Geb.K.)

- 3 flak (*Fla*) companies (1 each to 4 AK and 49 Geb.K.; 1 *z.V. AOK 17*)

- 2 army flak battalions (1 88mm) (*z.V. AOK 17*)

- Flamethrower Tank Battalion 102 (*Pz.Abt.(F)102*) (4 AK)

Also assigned to Seventeenth Army were: three engineer battalions, one bridge-building battalion, eight bridge columns "B," twelve construction battalions, and three road repair and construction battalions. *Luftwaffe* units subordinated to the army for tactical support encompassed three short-range reconnaissance squadrons (one to each army corps) and three mixed flak battalions (*z.V. AOK 17*).[54]

Forming the right (southern) wing of Rundstedt's main force grouping, Stülpnagel's thirteen divisions occupied a front of several hundred kilometers along the L'vov salient. While the two security divisions of Briesen's 52 Army Corps secured the army's right wing to a point near the Hungarian border, the main forces of Seventeenth Army were (as noted) deployed between Peremysl' and Rava Ruska, with several of the army's divisions behind the San River but the majority posted along a "dry" front on the northern shoulder of the L'vov salient.[55]

The assignment of Seventeenth Army was to break through the Soviet border defenses in the L'vov sector, destroy Soviet forces there, and, while protecting the southern flank of Reichenau's Sixth Army, advance rapidly to the southeast toward Tarnopol and, ultimately, Vinnitsa, where "the army was to stand in strength at the earliest possible moment. If in the advance contact with Sixth Army was lost, the army group would remedy the situation by bringing up reserves along the adjacent wings of the two armies."[56] As noted in the Army General Staff's deployment directive, the *Schwerpunkt* was on the army's left wing.

The Seventeenth Army is to break through the enemy border defenses northwest of L'vov. By advancing sharply with its strong left wing, [the army] must strive to throw the enemy back in a southeasterly direction and defeat him. Furthermore, the army, taking full advantage of the advance of the panzer group, is to quickly reach the area of Vinnitsa-Berdichev, in order to continue the attack to the southeast or east as the situation dictates.[57]

Defending along the frontier opposite Seventeenth Army were the first echelon forces of Lt.-Gen. N. I. Muzychenko's 6 Army and Lt.-Gen. F. Ia. Kostenko's 26 Army, supported by the typical array of border guard detachments. The Soviet 6 Army's order of battle included the powerful 4 Mechanized Corps, stationed at L'vov, and the 15 Mechanized Corps, posted around Brody (Map 13); attached to 26 Army was the 8 Mechanized Corps, behind the front astride the Dnester River. To break through at the border, Seventeenth Army would have to attack into the teeth of the Peremysl' and Rava Ruska fortified regions, whose fixed fortifications had been significantly upgraded over the previous months. For Stülpnagel's infantry and combat engineers, the first day of the Russian campaign was shaping up to be a very bloody day.[58]

At precisely 0315 hours, thousands of German guns of all calibers erupted in unison along the front of Rundstedt's Army Group South. The storm of steel crashed down on Soviet frontier posts, fixed and field fortifications, and other Red Army positions—targets that, for the most part, had already been accurately pinpointed. Overhead, *Luftwaffe* bombers and fighters crossed the frontier, their presence eliciting bursts of white recognition rockets from the German lines and responses from the aircraft. Under cover of the barrage, German assault boats slid into the San and the Bug—the latter on average some 70 meters wide in this southern sector—and made out for the opposite riverbanks. Once across, the German assault detachments struck out for their objectives, first among them the critically important bridges, while Soviet frontier troops fought back as best they could with their rifles, light machine guns and grenades. "Where possible, the unfortunate families of the frontier guards crowded into a blockhouse or took shelter in basements; at Sokal', Captain Bershadskii's detachment fought to defend the wooden bridge over the river, though his wife and 11-year-old son lay dead in the shattered buildings of the frontier post."[59]

Initial reports from the battlefront flowing back to higher German headquarters were encouraging. "Enemy resistance is negligible," recorded the war diary of Army Group South. "The bridges at the border rivers in the sector of the army group have not been destroyed. In general, the prevailing view is that the enemy has been surprised and overrun in his outposts." And the very next entry: "Over the course of the first morning hours the impression has grown stronger that, along the entire front, tactical surprise of the enemy is complete, while the enemy air force has also been thoroughly disrupted by our actions. So far, no enemy action in the air."[60] Affirming the observations of Army Group South was this report of Seventeenth Army: "0600 hours: Across the front the corps are reporting negligible enemy resistance. Contact initially only with border defense units [*Grenzschutz*]. The enemy seems to have been completely surprised. The bridge at

Peremysl' has not been destroyed; the bridge at Radymno has been seized intact. Everywhere progress is swift."[61]

Despite the inevitable initial setbacks, the Russians recovered rapidly along the front of Kirponos's Southwestern Front. Indeed, as soon as the German guns had opened fire, Red Army formations were decamping from their camps and barracks and racing for the frontier. Moving to their positions in the Rava Ruska Fortified Region were the divisions of Soviet 6 Army's 6 Rifle Corps; heading for their battle stations within the Peremysl' Fortified Region were the divisions of 26 Army's 8 Rifle Corps, which were in place by 0600 hours. The swift reaction to the German onslaught reflected the fact that the alert system functioned here, in the words of the chief of staff of 41 Rifle Division (6 RC), "without fuss." In addition, the lightly armed frontier detachments kept the Red Army informed of developments in their sectors, while also sending out pleas for reinforcements.[62]

This relative efficiency, which cost the Germans dear and which contrasted so sharply with the chaos of the Western and Northwestern Fronts, had been achieved in the face of considerable odds. The particular competence of the individual district commanders and their staffs clearly played a considerable part in determining the outcome on the frontiers: Pavlov at the center, disbelieving from the outset in the imminence of a massive German attack, clearly lost his nerve, while Kuznetsov in the Baltic command acted in a confused and half-hearted manner, disorganizing much of his own command. Colonel-General Kirponos at Kiev, in many respects a truly tragic figure, did not lose his nerve and he had behind him a tough chief of staff, [Lt.-Gen. M. A.] Purkayev, whose nerves were equally as good . . . On 21 June Kirponos had duly opened up his command post at Tarnopol. His stubbornness, persistence and foresight paid off in a few hours, for the German armies had to grind their way through his defenses.[63]

For the Russian defenders, however, "initial reversals and confusions" could "not be wholly avoided." The first German aerial bombings and artillery barrages had "wrought considerable havoc among military and civilians alike." When the officers of 41 Rifle Division occupied their CP at Hill 305 in the Rava Ruska Fortified Region, they could only watch as a long column of "disheveled women and weeping children, many the families of divisional personnel, [left] the exposed villages for Rava Ruska itself. As for the frontier guards, their families died with them or vanished as the battle swept over them."[64]

On the far right (southern) wing of Seventeenth Army, the 444 and 454 Security Divisions of Briesen's 52 Army Corps had a twofold mission—maintain contact with neighboring Hungarian forces while attacking at the San River to tie down opposing Red Army forces. It was an ambitious undertaking, for German security divisions, which only consisted of two infantry regiments with limited artillery (a light 105mm howitzer battalion) and no antitank battalion, were not intended for front-line taskings;[65] such divisions were also of limited mobility, while their personnel (some 10,000 in total) were older in comparison to line infantry divisions. Yet according to Carl Wagener, in his study of Army Group South, both divisions executed their mission effectively on this day, blasting Red Army forces across the San with "fire from all barrels." In the future course of the campaign, they would go on "to prove themselves time and again in open combat."[66]

An even more difficult task confronted Briesen's left wing division, the 101 Light (*Jäger*) Division, commanded by *Generalmajor* Eric Marcks, who, the reader will recall, had played a major part in the planning for Operation *Barbarossa* (Section 1.4). Simply put, Marcks's mission was to cross the San and push through the enemy fortifications at Peremysl' and, by securing the right flank of Kübler's 49 Mountain Corps, open the way for it to advance toward L'vov. Yet the San River, whose "bare banks provided the attackers with neither cover nor concealment,"[67] would pose difficulties for the German assault formations; moreover, as noted, Soviet rifle divisions had reached their positions in the Peremysl' Fortified Region by 0600 hours. Nevertheless, Marcks's 228 Infantry Regiment soon succeeded in capturing intact the important railway bridge in Peremysl' in a *coup de main*; and, by 1800, the German assault parties had captured most of the town. But the Russians responded an hour later—Colonel Dementyev's 99 Rifle Division launching a counterattack in a bid to retake the town. By the end of the day, 101 Light Division had achieved but modest success in its attempt to break through the enemy's strongly fortified positions—a tiny bridgehead across the San at Peremysl' held by a single (reinforced) company.[68]

In the center of Seventeenth Army's front were the three divisions of General Kübler's 49 Mountain Corps; together, they occupied an attack frontage of more than 60 kilometers, first running north along the San, then bending sharply east, away from the river in the direction of Rava Ruska. In the center of Kübler's line, 68 Infantry Division, commanded by *Generalmajor* Georg Braun, straddled the line of the San, with elements both west of the river and on a "dry" front to the east. Although the division's spearheads had, by 1015 hours, reached the town of Makoviska, enemy pressure increased as the day went on, the division undergoing difficult and costly fighting inside the enemy's frontier fortifications and in close combat within the fields of tall grain. As a result, 68 ID experienced local reverses and, in one case, its attack was halted by a Russian counterattack with tanks. By the end of the day, however, the division had posted "significant successes" (*beachtliche Erfolge*) in the face of tenacious enemy resistance. As for General Braun, he would not live to see the end of the year—blown up along with members of his staff in Khar'kov on November 14, 1941, by Soviet partisans.[69]

On the right wing of 49 Mountain Corps was the 257 Infantry Division, commanded by *Gen.d.Pi.* Karl Sachs. The division attacked across the San north of Peremysl', where the bank of the river was as "flat as a pancake—without woods, without ravines, without any cover for whole regiments." As a result, the assault formations of 257 ID had waited until the final hours of darkness before the attack to move to their assembly areas. To muffle any suspicious sounds, they had packed their weapons in blankets and wrapped bayonets and gas-mask cases in any soft material they could muster. The men were thankful for one thing—the frogs, whose "croaking drowned the creaking, rattling, and bumping of the companies making their way toward the river." At exactly 0315, the *Sturmbataillone* began to advance on both sides of Radymno, capturing the vital railway bridge there in a surprise strike.[70]

> *But in front of the customs shed the Russians were already offering stubborn resistance. Leutnant Alicke was killed. He was the division's first fatal casualty, the first of a long list. The men laid him beside the customs shed. The heavy weapons rolled on by him, over "his" bridge.*
>
> *In the south the Soviet alarm system functioned with surprising speed and precision. Only the most forward pickets were taken by surprise. The 457 Infantry Regiment had to battle all day long with the Soviet [NCO] Training School of Vysokoye, only a mile beyond the river. The 250 NCO cadets resisted stubbornly and skillfully. Not till the afternoon was their resistance broken by artillery fire. The 466 Infantry Regiment fared even worse. No sooner were its battalions across the river than they were attacked from the flank by advance detachments of the Soviet 199 Reserve Division.*
>
> *In the fields of Stubienka the tall grain waved in the summer wind like the sea. Into this sea the troops now plunged. Both sides were lurking, invisible. Stalking each other. Hand grenades, pistols, and machine carbines were the weapons of the day. Suddenly they would be facing one another amid the rye—the Russians and the Germans. Eye to eye. Whose finger was quicker on the trigger? Whose spade would go up first? Only with the fall of dusk did this bloody fighting in the rye-fields come to an end. The enemy withdrew.*[71]

In the journal of Seventeenth Army there is no mention of the dead and dying; nor of the anguished cries of the wounded, rising up out of the grain; nor of the desperate pleas for a life-saving stretcher. There is only this: "As a result of the tenacious resistance of small, local enemy groups, the ground gained by 257 Infantry Division was less than that of other divisions."[72]

One of the more dramatic stories to emerge from German operations along the Eastern Front on June 22, 1941, concerns Hubert Lanz's 1 Mountain Division (*1. Gebirgs-Division*), posted on the left wing of 49 Mountain Corps. Lanz had assumed command of the "*Edelweiss*" division on October 26, 1940, after relinquishing his position as chief of staff of 18 Mountain Corps; on November 1, 1940, he was promoted to *Generalmajor*.

Lanz's first assignment as division commander was to prepare for Operation *Felix*, Hitler's planned conquest of the British fortress of Gibraltar, for which the elite 1 Mountain Division was to provide the main strike force. After *Felix* was cancelled for political reasons, Lanz and his division fought in the Balkan campaign in the spring of 1941; in early June, the commander and his mostly Swabian and Bavarian mountain troops (combat strength of 14,684 personnel) began the transfer to Galicia in southern Poland as part of the buildup for Operation *Barbarossa*.[73]

A decent and brave man of deep Christian faith,[74] Lanz was not without his doubts about the entire Russian enterprise. On May 22, 1941, his forty-fourth birthday, he had met with his brother, Albrecht, an officer in the neighboring 71 Infantry Division of Schwedler's 4 Army Corps. Together, while enjoying a long walk, they openly discussed their fears for Germany's future—their worries over the impending war with Russia reducing both men at times to contemplative silence. From a professional standpoint, Lanz was concerned—among other things—by the relative paucity of forces assigned to the Russian campaign, given the enormity of its objectives.[75]

Yet there was no longer time for such thoughts, and Lanz, highly competent commander that he was, threw himself into the task of preparing his troops—and himself—for battle. He took part in major planning conferences (with Halder, Stülpnagel, Kübler, and others); disguised as a simple border patrol soldier, he carefully toured the frontier in his assigned sector, determining jump-off points, routes of advance, and locations from which to attack. The terrain was gently undulating—beyond the border a pair of water courses and ubiquitous patches of woods (Map 16). Several kilometers beyond the demarcation line, beyond the wire entanglements and numerous Russian observation towers, lay the village of Oleszyce, with its castle out of the middle ages; it sat in the middle of Lanz's attack zone and had been transformed into a veritable bastion by a Soviet border guard regiment. For days, Lanz had watched as the Russians labored industriously to improve their field fortifications, yet despite his best efforts, he was utterly in the dark about their strength and capabilities. And this despite the fact that his *Gebirgjäger* were to conduct the main push of 49 Mountain Corps toward L'vov.[76]

By June 20, the troops of 1 Mountain Division had reached the woods just north of the border. At 1130 hours on the 21st, Lanz's headquarters received a telephone call from 49 Mountain Corps with the simple message "Travel goal Dortmund!" (*Reiseziel Dortmund!*), signifying that the attack was to begin, according to plan, at 0315 hours the next morning. Lanz assembled his staff and, one last time, they carefully went over their assignments. The general notified key subordinates of Hitler's Commissar Order, but said he would not enforce it. Soviet commissars would be treated as normal prisoners of war; to do otherwise would be to violate the laws of war as well as his own religious faith.[77] At 1400 hours, Lanz released an order of the day, couched in the "jargon of the times," to all divisional units:

The 1 Mountain Division will drive the devil out of hell! [holt den Teufel aus der Hölle].

The devil stands before us!

We will destroy him!

Long live the Edelweiss!

Heil dem Führer![78]

In his history of 1 Mountain Division, published in 1954, Lanz described his feelings and those of his men on the eve of *Barbarossa*:

Now only a very few hours stand between us and the start of the greatest attack in all history. Each of us has the feeling that we are on the threshold of enormous events that will determine our fate. Despite our self-confidence, something we can't quite grasp, and almost oppressive, takes hold of us. We sense the vastness of the Russian space, the strength of her army, the passion of her people and their willingness to sacrifice. We sense it.[79]

On the night of June 21/22, the division's 98 and 99 *Gebirgsjäger* Regiments, led by *Oberstleutnants* Egbert Picker and Hermann Kress, respectively, occupied their well-camouflaged jump-off positions in the woods around the dilapidated Galician village of Dzikow—Kress on the right, Picker on the left—while the supporting artillery trundled into its firing positions. Attached to the division for the initial breakthrough was 188 Infantry Regiment (68 Infantry Division). At precisely 0300 hours, Lanz moved to his forward command post, which, aptly enough, was in a foxhole (*Erdloch*) in a cemetery almost flush with the Russo-Soviet demarcation line. For Lanz and his troops, the final minutes of peace were dominated by an eerie, oppressive calm. Now and then, the surroundings were bathed in the flickering light of a Soviet flare; but still no signs the enemy was aware of anything unusual. Enveloped in an early morning fog, the first assault teams and combat engineers debouched—ghostlike—from the woods and silently made their way toward the border.[80] In his diary, *Gefreiter* Hubert Hegele recorded the final minutes leading up to the assault:

0255 hours. Still 20 minutes to go until the start of the attack. Good Lord, the minutes pass by so begrudgingly today. Not a sound is to be heard. Only when you really perk up your ears can you detect some gentle whispering. We are just 20 meters from the border fence. The concentration of our assault troops has succeeded perfectly. The enemy has noticed nothing. The Russian sentries standing on their observation post haven't a clue. It's just two men, but they'll be the first to go down.

0306 hours. If I could only smoke a cigarette. The sky is now cloudless and the stars are shining down on us insignificant souls with their cheerful splendor, but the silver gray of the morning intrudes ever more strongly in their twinkling magnificence. You cannot grasp hold of sober thoughts in these final minutes—but you hardly need to. I make a little prayer and ask the Good Lord to stand by my side.

0310 hours. Still five minutes. The faces of my comrades look like gray masks. Their gaze is fixed straight ahead. The pounding in our chests grows stronger and stronger. The Pioniere *begin—very quietly, so you can hardly hear it—to cut a couple of pathways through the wire with their large shears. We still have two minutes to go. From some- where, far off in the distance, you can hear the call of a pack-animal.*

*0315 hours. Finally! A hand is raised up and gives the signal. As if drawn by a magnet, all eyes are on the hand of the assault troop leader [*Stosstruppführer*]. And with the raising of his hand, two shots from our sharpshooters resound through the night. The two Russian sentries collapse. The campaign against the Soviet Union has begun.*[81]

At 0315 hours, hell broke loose, only here without a preparatory artillery barrage. While German sharpshooters took out any Russian border guard unfortunate enough to show himself, and well placed artillery shells demolished the Russian watch towers, combat engineers blasted lanes through the wire for the surging assault teams. In its initial entry on the fighting, the division's war diary noted only isolated small arms fire, and that "the enemy appears to be completely surprised." At 0400, Picker reported that his group (98 Geb.Jg.Rgt.) had reached the village of Uskovca, just beyond the border. From his makeshift CP in the cemetery, Lanz first detected heavy firing erupting out on his right, in the sector of Kress's 99 Geb.Jg.Rgt. The assault troops of Picker's regiment soon joined in the deadly cacophony. Now the entire front was on fire. "*Der Angriff rollte.*" (The attack rolled.)[82]

The first objectives were Oleszyce and the patches of high ground that dominated the village—Hill 273 on the right and 242 on the left, the first to be taken by Kress's battle group, the second by Picker's. Exploiting the slow reactions of the Russian defenders, the Germans quickly captured a bridge north of Oleszyce. As the spearheads of Picker's regiment approached the village, which was nestled among groups of trees, the division's artillery opened up, while overhead, a squadron of Heinkel He-111 medium bombers drifted eastward. The Russians, however, recovering rapidly from the shock of invasion, responded with artillery fire of their own. Storming into Oleszyce, Picker's *Gebirgsjäger* (98 Geb.Jg.Rgt.) were suddenly locked in ferocious combat with the Soviet 97 Rifle

Division (6 Army)—a battle-tested unit—and a border protection unit made up of stout Mongolian troops.[83]

Lanz, in the meantime, had vacated his forward CP and accompanied the advance of Kress's 99 Geb.Jg.Rgt., which, within an hour after crossing the frontier, encountered bitter resistance at Hill 273 from so-called "Siberian" troops—or so they were characterized by the division's war diarist in what, no doubt, was a catch-all phrase for Russian "asiatic" troops in general. Kress's assault detachments soon secured the well-fortified hill, but not without sustaining casualties, giving Lanz his first indication that the Red Army soldier was an adversary who refused to sell his life cheaply. Kress's battle group then continued its advance toward Lipina, 6 kilometers from the regiment's start line.[84]

From the vantage point of Hill 273, Lanz could observe the bitter struggle being waged by Picker's troops in Oleszyce. To provide what support he could, the general rushed over to the village; when he got there, he found his men in hand-to-hand combat with spades, hand grenades, and pistols, the village in flames, and terrified women and children rushing aimlessly about—a consummate visage of hell. Russian sharpshooters, inside the burning castle and hidden in the trees, took aim at any German that moved, while the attackers employed assault guns and 20mm antiaircraft guns in an effort to crush Russian resistance. Yet the fighting in Oleszyce, at the castle and around the castle park, raged on, with both sides sustaining heavy casualties.[85]

That afternoon, the Germans finally captured the medieval castle and the tumult of battle was momentarily superseded by an eerie calm. Lanz, who had witnessed firsthand the splendid part played by his adjutant, *Hauptmann* Kopp, in breaking the enemy resistance, spontaneously affixed his own Iron Cross to Kopp's chest. Shortly thereafter, the Soviets counterattacked with strong forces. Lanz, who sought cover behind a wooden fence, was wounded when a shell grazed his shoulder and tore off his cross-straps, before striking the man next to him. While the wound bled profusely, it was not life-threatening, so the general refused to seek medical attention. Instead, he continued to race from one focal point of the battlefield to another, steadying his men, issuing orders, attempting to bring order out of chaos.[86]

Eventually, Picker's *Gebirgsjäger* secured Oleszyce and resumed their advance in the direction of L'vov along with Kress's 99 Geb.Jg.Rgt., now supported by 188 Infantry Regiment on the division's right flank. On the main road through Oleszyce, citizens of the village dug a long, cavernous trench to bury a group of dead German soldiers, all belonging to the 13th Company of 98 Geb.Jg.Rgt., among them the world champion Austrian skier, Willy Walch. The dead were laid to rest inside the trench and, as the Germans were honoring their fallen comrades, Lanz appeared by chance on the scene. At once grasping the situation, he climbed down into the trench, removed his cap, bent over his dead soldiers, and saluted them. It was a remarkable moment, but for Lanz it was a moment informed by the insight that the cost of war was great and, as he was beginning to fear, perhaps too great.[87]

Shortly thereafter, General Lanz, weakened by the gradual loss of blood from his wound, collapsed. His doctor demanded he return at once to his headquarters to recover. Lanz complied, but within an hour he was back at the front. By now, his regiments had pushed well beyond Oleszyce—across fields of grain, patches of forest, and through the many small settlements that dotted the region. By 1900 hours, his *Gebirgsjäger* had advanced 13–15 kilometers from their start line and crossed the Lubaczovka River, thereby reaching their day's objective (*Tagesziel*) (Map 16). And yet for such a modest gain—and although Russian losses had been enormous—the 1 Mountain Division had sustained its greatest losses to date for a single day's combat, among them eight officers killed and twelve wounded. The final entry in the divisional war diary for June 22 was a sobering one: "After the experiences and practices of the campaigns in France and Yugoslavia, the troops will have to get used to such a tough and skillful enemy [*zähen und gewandten Feind*] as the Russian has turned out to be." Or as Lanz's subordinate commanders put it at the evening situation conference that bloody day: "If it goes on like this, we're headed for difficult times."[88]

Finally, on the left wing of Stülpnagel's Seventeenth Army was Schwedler's 4 Army Corps of five infantry divisions, arrayed along a front of 50 kilometers on the northern shoulder of the L'vov salient. Schwedler, possessing the largest strike force of the army's three corps (his was the *Schwerpunkt* corps), attacked with four divisions forward—from right to left, 71, 295, 24, and 262 ID—and one in second echelon (296 ID). His task was a daunting one, for his infantry platoons would have to gnaw their way through the fixed fortifications of the Rava Ruska Fortified Region. The Russians, as described above, would react quickly and effectively in this sector, swiftly bringing up reinforcements and even counterattacking successfully. For the Germans, the gains would be modest, losses at times heavy; 4 Army Corps would also have to address a serious local crisis on its left (eastern) wing.[89] Characteristic of the combat along the front of Schwedler's infantry corps were the experiences of 24 Infantry Division, which are examined in some detail below.

The 24 Infantry Division—its tactical sign a "Polar Bear" (*Eisbär*)—was commanded by *Generalmajor* Hans von Tettau. In April 1941, the division was transported by rail from Belgium to Poland as part of the *Barbarossa* buildup; beginning in June, it marched into the region southwest of Tomaszov, laagering in the woods and villages not far from the Russo-German frontier. Soon its forwardmost battalions were ensconced directly along the border, facing Rava Ruska. From high atop their observation towers, the Germans looked on as the Soviets labored assiduously, with the help of searchlights at night, to complete their fortifications. In the final thirty-six hours before the attack, the bulk of 24 Infantry Division's troops slipped silently into their jump-off positions; thanks to meticulous staff work, and efforts of the troops themselves, these final movements went off largely without a hitch.[90]

As the *Schwerpunkt* division of Schwedler's 4 Army Corps, the mission of the "Polar Bear" division was to break through the Russian border fortifications and advance on Rava Ruska, some 15 kilometers inside enemy territory. To support its attack, 24 ID had assembled six light (105mm) and five medium (150mm) field howitzer battalions and three batteries of 210mm heavy howitzers—some 140 guns in all. The division was also supported by assault guns of Assault Gun Battalion 243. To preserve the element of surprise, no plans were made to conduct a preliminary barrage; however, the attack would begin with a portion of the artillery limbered up and ready to follow on the heels of the advancing infantry.[91]

At 0315 hours, *Generalmajor* von Tettau launched his attack, his two first echelon infantry regiments attacking abreast—31 Infantry Regiment on the right and 32 Infantry Regiment on the left. While combat engineers hastily assembled crossings for vehicles over the deep, wide antitank ditches, the weakly defended enemy border posts were overrun with barely a shot being fired. To the rear of the lead German battalions, however, Soviet border guard troops put up stubborn resistance, inflicting the first casualties on the attackers before being overwhelmed. Advancing over the gently rising ground, the German assault troops soon reached the first Soviet bunker line, which lay several kilometers beyond the border. The horse-drawn infantry guns and artillery batteries quickly arrived on scene, and several of the guns began to blast away at the bunkers from close range, while the infantry prepared to launch a systematic attack on the bunker positions (a task for which it was well trained).[92] In a postwar history of 24 ID co-authored by Tettau and based on veterans' accounts, the former division commander described the Soviet bunkers and the challenges they posed.

> *The Soviets, having learned from the German campaigns in both Poland and France, had outfitted their zone of fortifications primarily with robust, three-storied concrete structures. These enabled the bunker crews to withdraw into the lowest level when the bunker came under heavy fire, or if the enemy had forced their way into the higher levels. In the latter case, the bunker crews could offer serious resistance from within the structure with machine pistols and hand grenades. Toward the outside, these pillboxes [Kampfstände] were furnished with up to six firing ports [Scharten] for artillery and machine guns, and these were protected by highly-resistant steel covers. The bunkers were laid out in such a manner that they were mutually supporting, which meant that an attacker, when going after one bunker, would have to suppress or assault the neighboring bunker as well.[93]*

While 32 Infantry Regiment became bogged down in a protracted struggle for the bunker line, its neighboring regiment (31 IR), locating a weak spot in the enemy fortifications, was able to capture Hill 390 (northwest of Rava Ruska) and penetrate into the woods south and east of Monastyr. In doing so, the assault detachments of 31 Infantry Regiment had broken through the first line of resistance.[94]

Meanwhile, Army Group South, expecting Soviet resistance to stiffen after overcoming the initial shock of invasion, queried Seventeenth Army (0915 hours) if the commitment of 1 Panzer Group's 14 Panzer Corps would now be "advisable" (*zweckmässig*). Seventeenth Army put the question to Schwedler's 4 Army Corps, which responded that the "time was still somewhat premature" for such a move, since the Russians were building a new defensive line in front of Rava Ruska. As a result, Seventeenth Army, reporting back to Rundstedt's army group, advised that it was best to wait to employ the panzer corps until the sectors north and northwest of Rava Ruska were thoroughly cleared of the enemy—meaning that the tanks could begin to cross the border either that afternoon or early the next morning. Army Group South fully supported the army's assessment.[95]

During the afternoon, assault formations of 31 Infantry Regiment continued to advance, reaching the high ground west of Werchrata, signifying a push of 10 kilometers beyond the regiment's start line. Leaving its 3rd Battalion to contain the enemy bunker line, the bulk of 32 Infantry Regiment bypassed the bunkers to the west—its 2nd Battalion also reaching Werchrata and the high ground east of the village. By now, however, a serious situation was taking shape in the sector of 262 Infantry Division, the neighboring division on the left. On the front of 4 Army Corps, Soviet resistance had been increasing palpably since at least early afternoon. By 1335 hours, the Russians had put in counterstrokes with tanks, slowing the progress of Schwedler's infantry. By late afternoon, a major Soviet counterattack had torn through the right wing of 262 ID, opening a dangerous gap on the inner flanks of 262 and 24 ID. By 2000 hours, the war diary of Seventeenth Army was noting a "heightening [*Verschärfung*] of the crisis on the left wing of 4 Army Corps." To stabilize the situation and close the gap, which by evening had grown to 10 kilometers, 4 Army Corps had no choice but to insert its reserve division (296 ID) between 262 and 24 ID.[96]

If a full-blown crisis had temporarily disrupted the left (eastern) wing of 4 Army Corps, on the right wing, 71 and 295 Infantry Divisions had managed to break through the enemy's main bunker line after a day of hard fighting.[97] This success, coupled with the progress made by elements of 24 Infantry Division, meant that a good start had been made on breaking through the Rava Ruska Fortified Region. Indeed, the final entries in the journal of Army Group South for June 22 make clear that Rundstedt and his staff were confident the divisions of Seventeenth Army would complete the task of defeating enemy resistance along the border the next day, thus helping to create conditions for a successful continuation of operations along the army group's front. And yet the crisis on 4 Army Corps' left wing must have given pause for thought. In its diary, Army Group South recorded bluntly that 262 ID had fallen victim to a "*Russenschreck*," or Russian terror, and implied that elements of the division had abandoned their posts without orders. The war diarist, however, soon thought better of his choice of words, crossing out the sentence with "*Russenschreck*" and, one must assume, replacing it with something a little less inelegant.[98]

Be that as it may, the day ended with the infantry of Seventeenth Army, lacking armored support of any kind save for a single battalion of assault guns, still locked in bitter and costly combat among the bunkers of the Rava Ruska and Peremysl' fortified regions. Although several holes had been punched in the Russian defenses, Soviet forces had rapidly shaken off the effects of surprise and, in many cases, fought with skill and determination, keeping German gains in this sector to a minimum. On the other hand, efforts of Soviet 6 and 26 Armies in the L'vov salient to assemble their mechanized corps and shepherd them into position for the massive counterstroke being prepared by Col.-Gen. M. P. Kirponos, the commander of Soviet Southwestern Front, had been far less successful—as exemplified by the experiences of Lt.-Gen. D. I. Riabyshev and his 8 Mechanized Corps.

Riabyshev's 8 Mechanized Corps began the day assigned to Kostenko's 26 Army, but eventually was placed under command of Muzychenko's 6 Army, which was defending along the Rava Ruska-L'vov axis.[99] Riabyshev had spent the morning in the corps' compound at Drogobych, waiting for orders. While he waited, the *Luftwaffe* subjected his corps to merciless bombing attacks. At 1000 hours, a messenger finally arrived, informing Riabyshev that, by the end of the day, his corps was to relocate to the woods west of Sambor, which were just beyond the bend in the Dnester River and quite close to the frontier. Because no orders had been received to evacuate civilians, officers had to leave their families at the compound, which was now ablaze due to the aerial bombing.[100]

The march to Sambor was fraught with difficulties. The corps' 30,000 soldiers and nearly 800 tanks moved out slowly.[101] Only 171 of the corps' eight types of tanks were the new KVs and T-34s; the older tanks couldn't go more than 500 kilometers without repairs, and 197 of them already had serious mechanical problems. Most of the tanks ran on gasoline—three different types of gasoline—but others required diesel fuel. The tanks' main armaments were equally diverse—five types of guns requiring five types of shells. Such a situation was difficult enough to manage in peacetime, but it now became a logistical nightmare.[102]

To boost morale, the commissars painted bellicose slogans on the sides of the tanks, ranging from the uninspired ("Long Live Communism!") to the audacious ("To Berlin!"). Soldiers who had fallen for the propaganda now asked whether the German working class had already risen against Hitler. Many said that the war would be over in a few months. Riabyshev wasn't so sure.

The Eighth [8 Mechanized Corps] soon met the first refugees. Women and children sitting on bags and bundles in the open trucks looked frightened, but at least they didn't have to flee on foot—some kind army commander had provided them with transportation. Riabyshev's officers thought about their own families, abandoned at Drogobych, and their hearts ached. Almost every truck carried scores of wounded too. Many houses along the road had been blasted by German bombs, and several times the soldiers saw dead children lying in the rubble.

Someone in army headquarters had made a mistake, and Riabyshev soon discovered that while the Eighth was marching from Drogobych to Sambor, General N. K. Kirillov's 13 Rifle Corps was moving from Sambor to Drogobych along the same highway. The road was narrow, and the two corps had to sidle past each other. Riabychev's tank crews had a harder time than Kirillov's infantrymen, because bridges collapsed under the weight of their vehicles and the heat caused the tank wheels to tear up the road, making it almost impossible for those in the rear.[103]

When the tankers finally reached the woods near Sambor, they were stunned by what they saw. The *Luftwaffe* had clearly been there first, looking for Russian troops, for the trees were twisted, burned, and felled. It was a scene of total devastation and it frightened the men—"a hurricane of steel," someone mumbled. But Riabyshev had more important concerns, having just received a report stating that 200 of his precious tanks had already dropped out along the march route. Then a courier from *front* commander Kirponos showed up unexpectedly, bringing an order that made no sense at all: Riabyshev was to turn around, go back to Drogobych, then proceed north to L'vov, the capital of the western Ukraine. And he was to do so at once.[104]

No sooner had Riabyshev turned around his unwieldy mechanized columns than they were pounced on by German bombers. The men fled to the wheat fields, and it took precious time to coax them back to their vehicles, particularly after they'd seen their comrades lying dead on the ground. Though the men were by now exhausted, Riabyshev kept them moving throughout the night. When they arrived back at the compound in Drogobych, the town was on fire, but their families were still there. "The women asked why they could not leave, and their husbands didn't know what to say. Some of the women learned that they had already become widows; some officers found their families dead in the ruins."[105]

The next morning, the troops finally reached the headquarters of Muzychenko's 6 Army, northwest of L'vov. Muzychenko—apologetically, it seems—informed Riabyshev that his corps would once more have to change direction. And so, for the second time in forty-eight hours, it carried out a 180-degree turn, this time heading for Yavorov, close to the frontier. When they reached the town, Kirponos had another messenger waiting for them—they were to reverse course again and march a further 120 kilometers, northeast to Brody. This took Riabyshev's corps to L'vov a second time, only this time anti-Russian Ukrainian guerrillas were waiting for them, and they rained bullets down on Riabyshev's men. Unaware they had stumbled into a nationalist uprising, the men of 8 Mechanized Corps dealt with the snipers and continued on toward Brody, where a major tank battle was taking shape.[106]

At the end of June, Riabyshev filed a detailed combat report, addressing the actions of his 8 Mechanized Corps from June 22 to June 29. While it takes us well beyond the first day of the war, the focus of this book, Riabyshev's report adds further insight into the almost insurmountable obstacles faced by the Soviet mechanized corps during the initial days of Operation *Barbarossa*; thus, it is excerpted at length.

Conclusions

1. By the start of the war the corps was not fully outfitted with equipment. (For example, the corps had an authorized strength of 126 KVs and 420 T-34s; it actually had on 22.6.41 71 KVs, of which five were undergoing repair, and 100 T-34s. The latest tanks comprised 25–30%.)

The majority of the drivers of the KVs and T-34s had from three to five hours of practical experience. During the entire period of the corps' existence[107] the corps' combat equipment and rank and file were never fully taken out for tactical training and were not practically checked either on problems of march preparation or for activities in the main features of battle. Tactical cohesiveness was carried [to] no higher level than [that] of company and battalion, and partially that of a regiment . . .

2. During the period 22.–26.6.41 the corps carried out intensive "super forced" marches without observing the elementary regulation requirements for servicing the equipment . . . [and eventually] was put into the battlefield with its equipment having covered 500 kilometers.

Because of this, 40–50% of the combat vehicles were out of action due to technical reasons. (This was made more difficult because by the start of the war the old equipment had used 50% of its engine life.) The indicated 40–50% of the equipment was left behind along . . . the divisions' routes. The remaining equipment, as a result of such rapid marches, proved to be unprepared for battle in the technical sense . . .

3. The frequent and hurried changes of the corps' concentration areas by higher headquarters, as well as the headquarters' [lack of awareness] of the overall situation at the front and the enemy's actions led to a situation in which the corps, upon entering the fighting, lacked exact targets for its attack and was forced during the course of the fighting to change [direction] in search of the enemy's main group of forces. This led to the separation of individual units and subunits and to the dispersal of the attack.

4. The enemy's active air operations against the troops, both along the front and in the rear, and the careless attitude toward air defense measures . . . very often led to large and useless losses, to the disruption of combat orders and to the troops' demoralization.

5. The absence of the corps' cooperation with the air force, which was operating along the given axes, deprived the corps of air cover . . .

6. During the combat of 26.–29.6.41, despite the tasks assigned by the [Southwestern Front] to the corps for cooperating with the 15 and 4 Mechanized Corps, tank cooperation was not accomplished due to the lack of timely carrying out of the order by the cooperating formations, which led to the uncoordinated actions of the corps.[108]

The report, signed off by Riabyshev, cited other problems as well, including improper routing of the corps on the roads, the absence of traffic control, the absence of equipment to evacuate damaged vehicles (leading to unnecessary losses of equipment), the paucity of spare parts, and the assignment of "unrealistic missions" due to a "poor knowledge of tactics" and of the "technical capacity of equipment and weaponry on the part of a certain part of the command element."[109]

Finally, a postwar account by A. V. Egorov, chief of staff of a tank regiment in 32 Tank Division (4 Mechanized Corps), stationed near L'vov, epitomizes the confusion and chaos on the Soviet side that rendered clear, timely—and accurate—decision-making almost impossible on June 22, 1941. And as Egorov's account reminds us, Stalin and his High Command had instilled in all Red Army field commanders a visceral fear of provoking the Germans.

Out of the army staff [quarters], to where the C-in-C of the army had ordered the commanders of all troop elements stationed in L'vov, came Major Žeglov. He assembled the battalion and company commanders. With some difficulty, he began to speak: "This morning the Germans have dropped bombs on L'vov and opened up with artillery fire at the border—perhaps in an effort to cause a provocation. For this reason, we must be vigilant, but must not commit any provocations of our own. Our regiment is to march into the area of Sudova Višnja in the direction of Peremysl'."

We had hardly gotten under way, when we heard a new order: "Halt, everyone turn around!"

"What did that order mean—'Halt, everyone turn around!'?" I asked the regimental commander. "We've just got a new assignment, we're to go off in the direction of Rava Ruska. The Germans have broken through at the border there, at the village of Krakovec. We're supposed to drive the aggressors back and restore the situation."

As we approached the woods, shells suddenly began to strike to the right and left of us. The vehicle of the regimental commander increased its speed in an effort to evade the shell fire. I ordered my driver to follow behind Žeglov. To better understand what was going on, I opened the hatch. The first thing I noticed were groups of our infantry. Were they in fact falling back?

Žeglov halted his tank. The regimental commander dismounted and summoned one of the infantrymen to him. We also came to a stop. I only heard fragments of a sentence: ". . . German tanks have broken through." "Where are they?" "Right here, at the edge of the woods, and they're coming our way."[110]

5.4: SIXTH ARMY OPERATIONS[111]

The German Sixth Army (headquarters in Sulow, southeast of Lublin) was commanded by fifty-six-year-old Field Marshal Walter von Reichenau; his chief of staff was *Obst.i.G.* Heim. At the outbreak of war on September 1, 1939, Reichenau commanded Tenth Army, which formed the main German strike force for the attack on Poland; the general himself "was the first German soldier to cross the Vistula [River]. He swam it." Following the Polish campaign, his army was transferred to the west and re-designated as Sixth Army, which Reichenau led "with great success" in Belgium and France in 1940. He was promoted to *Generalfeldmarschall* on July 19, 1940.[112]

According to historian Samuel W. Mitcham Jr., Reichenau was probably the "most exceptional" of Hitler's field marshals. "Except for his pale blue eyes, he looked like a typical Prussian: he had a stern, cold and forbidding appearance, augmented by an ever-present monocle. He was also brutally ambitious. Walter Görlitz called him 'a man devoid of all sentiment, at times, indeed, a cold-blooded, brutal man.' On the other hand, he was very innovative, independently minded, and accessible to the troops, with whom he was quite popular."[113] Reichenau was also a stalwart pro-Nazi and supporter of Hitler's genocidal policies in the Soviet Union. On October 10, 1941, he promulgated a notorious directive—known to history as the "Reichenau Order"—justifying the annihilation of the "Jewish-Bolshevik" system and urging his soldiers to take the harshest measures against the "Jewish *Untermenschen.*"[114] In December 1941, Reichenau would replace Rundstedt as C-in-C of Army Group South. On January 15, 1942, he suffered a stroke and died two days later.[115]

For the initial breakthrough at the border, Reichenau had loaned six infantry divisions to Kleist's 1 Panzer Group; as a result, his army's order of battle on June 22 comprised only three army corps and six divisions (one security division and five infantry divisions), about 100,000 men.[116] The corps and their commanders were: 17 Army Corps (56 and 62 ID), under *Gen.d.Inf.* Werner Kienitz; 44 Army Corps (9 and 297 ID), led by *Gen.d.Inf.* Friedrich Koch; and, in reserve, 55 Army Corps (168 ID), under command of *Gen.d.Inf.* Erwin Vierow. The 213 Security Division was controlled by Sixth Army (*z.V. AOK* 6).[117] General Headquarters troops included:

- 1 150mm medium howitzer battalion (44 AK)
- 2 mixed artillery battalions (1 each to 17 and 44 AK)
- 1 210 heavy howitzer battalion (limited mobility) (44 AK)
- 1 150mm cannon battery (17 AK)

- 1 210mm heavy artillery battalion (mot.) for flat trajectory fire (*z. V. AOK 6*)
- 1 battery of a *Nebelwerfer* battalion (44 AK)
- 3 flak (*Fla*) companies (1 each to 17 and 44 AK; 1 *z. V. AOK 6*)
- 2 army flak battalions (1 88mm) (*z. V. AOK 6*)[118]

Among other GHQ troops allocated to Sixth Army were: two engineer battalions, two bridge-building battalions, eight bridge columns "B," ten construction battalions, and four road repair and construction battalions. *Luftwaffe* formations assigned for tactical support embraced two short-range reconnaissance squadrons (1 each to 17 and 44 Army Corps); one long-range (strategic) reconnaissance squadron under direct army control; and three mixed flak battalions (also *z. V. AOK 6*).[119]

Because half of Sixth Army's infantry divisions were in 1 Panzer Group's order of battle for June 22, it is, perhaps, not accurate to speak of an actual front held by the army; rather, the army's two attacking corps were posted like bookends on the southern (right) and northern (left) flanks of Kleist's panzer group. In the south were the two divisions of 44 Army Corps (9 ID and 297 ID) positioned along the northern shoulder of the L'vov salient (northeast of Rava Ruska) where it projected deepest into Soviet-held territory. Some 75 kilometers to the north began the positions of 17 Army Corps (62 ID and 56 ID), which extended 40–50 kilometers along the Bug River east of the city of Chelm. To the north of 17 Army Corps was the 213 Security Division, along the Bug just south of Włodawa, where it maintained contact with the right wing of Army Group Center. The 168 Infantry Division was in reserve.[120]

As outlined in the Army General Staff's deployment directive, during the initial phase of operations Reichenau's Sixth Army, in cooperation with Kleist's panzer group, was to break through the Russian defenses on both sides of Lutsk (Luck). The army's infantry was then to follow on the heels of the advancing armored wedge, destroying enemy forces left behind by Kleist's group, providing assistance with river crossings, and shielding the northern flank of Army Group South in the direction of the Pripiat' Marshes from enemy interference. Sixth Army was to rapidly gain the area Berdichev-Zhitomir (the latter city 300 kilometers from the frontier), thereby preventing the Red Army from making a stand in the fortifications of the Stalin Line. Reichenau's infantry was then to be prepared to pivot southeast to cut off the retreat of Soviet forces west of the Dnepr River in close cooperation with Kleist's panzer group on the left and Stülpnagel's Seventeenth Army on the right.[121]

Supported by GHQ troops, including a 210mm heavy howitzer battalion, a battery of *Nebelwerfers*, a 150mm howitzer battalion, and flak troops, Koch's 44 Army Corps attacked according to plan at 0315 hours. Forming the army corps' right wing was *Generalmajor* Siegmund *Freiherr* von Schleinitz's 9 Infantry Division, boasting a combat strength of just under 14,000 men (352 officers).[122] Schleinitz's assault formations attacked along a "dry" front west of the Bug River, pushing south into the Rava Ruska Fortified Region on the right wing of Soviet 6 Army. On the left wing of 44 Army Corps, *Generalleutnant* Max Pfeffer's 297 Infantry Division, advancing across the Bug at Krystynopol', struck the seam of Soviet 6 and 5 Armies, the division's *Stosstrupps* storming into the Strumilov Fortified Region, which covered the frontier between Krystynopol' and Sokal' (Map 13).

According to a credible German account, both of Koch's infantry divisions managed to breach the enemy's forwardmost fixed defenses on their first attempt, while infantry of the neighboring 48 Panzer Corps (1 Panzer Group) quickly seized a major Bug bridge south of Sokal', over which the tanks of its 11 Panzer Division were soon rumbling east.[123] By the end of the day, however, Schleinitz's 9 Infantry Division, trying to punch its way through the enemy bunker positions, had advanced less than 10 kilometers from its start line (Map 14).[124] For the infantry of 9 ID, the days that followed would get no easier—divisional records indicate that 9 ID sustained 431 casualties, including eighty-nine dead, through June 30, 1941.[125]

Although it registered greater territorial gains on *Barbarossatag*, 297 Infantry Division also encountered a determined and skillful enemy who inflicted serious losses on the invaders. Once again, it was a case where the German attack, which began easily enough, soon ran into serious opposition. The division crossed the Bug with elements of all three regiments (522, 523, 524 IR). The opening minutes of the assault are outlined in the division's war diary:

0325: So far, along the entire front, no [enemy] opposition.

0327: 524 IR reports: Bridge at Krystynopol' is in our hands. Everything is going according to plan.

0345: No enemy resistance in sector of 523 IR; regiment is crossing to the eastern bank [of the Bug].

0355: Most southerly company of 522 IR is one kilometer east of the Bug, at the edge of the woods. Peturzycka Wolka in regiment's hands.

0400: 523 IR has reached its first objective. Twin bunkers [Zwillingsbunker] in fog.[126] An attack on them is beginning.

0409: 524 IR has reached its first objective and is continuing to advance through the woods.

0415: 524 IR has captured the cemetery bunker [Friedhofsbunker].

0436: Order to the adjutant of the advance detachment: "Get ready to lead the advance."[127]

Yet the diary's very next entry (0453), less than two hours after the start of the attack, made it abundantly clear that the division's infantry, artillery, and combat engineers were now facing a difficult and costly task: "524 IR has encountered its second, strong bunker position. Despite the heaviest artillery and antitank fire, and small arms fire with armor piercing shells [*Pz. Gewehr-Feuer*], there was no effect on the bunkers. The enemy continues to fire from the bunkers. The 2nd and 3rd Battalions are advancing through a gap . . . in the direction of Pozdzimierz. The 1st Battalion is attempting to capture the bunker from the rear."[128]

Combat to neutralize the Russian bunker positions would continue throughout the morning, into the afternoon and evening. Short of explosives, without flamethrowers, their antitank guns and artillery often without effect, casualties quickly mounted. At 0615 hours, 522 Infantry Regiment reported seven dead and four missing (among the latter a company commander). At 0630, 523 Infantry Regiment reported that it had blasted one of the bunkers with twenty antitank shells to no effect. At 1210, Artillery Commander 15 (*Arko 15*), in charge of the GHQ artillery, reported that attempts to storm one bunker had resulted in serious casualties, and that the bunker was encased in such thick concrete that it was impervious to artillery fire. By early afternoon (1330), 524 Infantry Regiment had suffered twenty-one casualties (eight dead, twelve wounded, one missing) and, several hours later, Antitank Battalion 297 (*Pz.Jg.Abt.297*) reported that five of its guns were not fit for action (*nicht einsatzfähig*). Eventually, 210mm heavy howitzers were brought forward to engage the bunkers and, instead of costly frontal attacks, the German assault parties approached the bunkers from behind, a tactic that proved more successful; at 1405, 524 Infantry Regiment reported the destruction of four enemy bunkers in this manner. Yet in spite of the bitter and costly fighting, by day's end, the lead elements of Pfeffer's 297 Infantry Division had pressed 15 kilometers beyond the frontier to the southeast (Map 14).[129]

On the northern wing of Army Group South, Kienitz's 17 Army Corps was opposed by the two rifle divisions (45 and 62 RD) of Colonel I. I. Fedyuninsky's 15 Rifle Corps (5 Army) defending along the Chelm-Luboml-Kovel' axis. For unknown reasons, operations in the 17 Army Corps' area began at slightly different times—at 0315 in the sector of 62 Infantry Division, and at 0318 along the front of 56 Infantry Division.[130] One of the Russians on the receiving end of the opening German artillery barrage was Anatolij Kazakov, a soldier in 45 Rifle Division whose artillery regiment was stationed 13 kilometers east of the Bug.

During the night the messenger, Anisimov, from the border post of the 98 Border Detachment came by and reported that the Germans had set pontoons in the water and were preparing to cross the river.

No orders were received from the divisional staff. The wire communications had been cut by saboteurs.

About 0300 hours on 22 June the salvos of heavy German guns slammed into the regiment's quarters. We considered this sudden barrage to be a provocation in the sector of our division.

The initial salvo struck the barracks. Beams flew apart, ceilings collapsed, and walls crumbled. The crash of the explosions raised up dust into the air that held deadly shell fragments. The exploding shells spread to the horse stalls and the artillery park, where the guns and the ammunition boxes were located. In the opening minutes the staff tents were hit and the battalion commander wounded. His shattered hand hung down lifeless from his arm.

The battalion's chief of staff, Lieutenant Volčanskij, took command of the battalion. A general helplessness soon gave way to thoughtful action. Everyone sought to take up his assigned role in the unit.[131]

Good progress was made by both divisions of 17 AK, despite problems experienced by *Generalleutnant* Walter Keiner's 62 Infantry Division in building a bridge across the Bug. Possessing a combat strength of 13,537 men (4181 horses),[132] *Generalmajor* Karl von Oven's 56 Infantry Division began its attack with all three infantry regiments in the line—192 IR on the right, 171 IR in the center, and 234 IR on the left. Each of the attacking regiments was supported by a company of combat engineers and an antitank company, while the division's reconnaissance battalion secured the open northern flank. The first wave of Oven's infantry made it across the river in their rubber dinghies without a hitch, the Russian bunkers on the eastern bank barely offering a response. Indeed, the division's artillery fire "lay so squarely on the well-reconnoitered enemy positions" that the first assault detachments sustained practically no casualties. By mid-morning, a pontoon bridge was in place in the sector of 192 Infantry Regiment, and the artillery crossed at high speed.[133]

And yet again, the Russian defenders had soon collected themselves and, within hours, were putting up fierce resistance, even putting in counterattacks. For as the Germans discovered here, too, "the Russian of 1941 was no longer [the Russian] of 1914/18. To the older officers, who had taken part in World War I, this was soon clear. In contrast to the Russian soldier of nearly 30 years ago, the Soviet soldier fought with extraordinary bravery, toughness and fanaticism."[134]

The initial reactions of Soviet forces are described in graphic detail by I. I. Fedyuninsky in his memoirs. Shortly after the German attack began, he received a telephone call from Lt.-Gen. M. I. Potapov, the 5 Army commander, who ordered him to place the troops on alert; however, they were not yet to be furnished with live ammunition, no doubt due to Potapov's fear of causing a provocation. Fedyuninsky was left with the impression that no one at 5 Army headquarters was entirely sure if the Germans had actually started a war or not![135]

We had to occupy our defensive positions under the heaviest artillery fire and aerial bombardment. Our lines of communication were repeatedly interrupted. Operational orders only reached the units with significant delays. Yet the officers never lost control, and we reached the defensive positions, where the border troops had been waging an uneven battle for several hours. Even the wives of the border troops were on the firing line. They hauled up water and ammunition and cared for the wounded; some of the women actually shot at the attacking Nazis. But the lines of the border troops gradually disintegrated. Everywhere barracks and houses were engulfed in flames . . . Often our troops were not able to dig in, because they lacked even the most primitive equipment with which to do so. Because no spades were available, they dug out their rifle pits with their steel helmets.[136]

Along the Bug, at Wilczy-Przewoz, Red Army bunkers thought to have been neutralized sprung back to life, their crews refusing to surrender and fighting to the last man against the assault parties of 192 Infantry Regiment. After breaking this resistance, the regiment ran across serious opposition along the road and rail line leading from Chelm via Luboml to Kovel', a situation made worse because the neighboring 62 Infantry Division was grappling with major problems of its own on its left wing. With the onset of darkness, the division faced another crisis: Over the course of the day, 171 Infantry Regiment had fought its way through Soviet bunkers and field fortifications; in doing so, two of its battalions had advanced so impetuously they became cut off by Russian troops. Fortunately, the regimental commander, *Oberst* von Erdmannsdorff, responded with such decisiveness that disaster was averted and both battalions were soon freed from encirclement.[137]

On this first day of the Russian campaign, 56 Infantry Division dealt with yet another challenge, as recorded by veterans of the division:

During the course of the day, 56 ID faced a disturbing intervention by the headquarters of 17 Army Corps. Because the efforts of 62 ID to build a bridge had failed, but in the attack sector of 192 IR the military bridge was already operational in the morning, corps headquarters ordered all elements of [56 ID] off the bridge in favor of 62 ID, and this despite the fact that it was urgently necessary to bring forward the division's artillery. No doubt corps headquarters had plausible reasons for doing so . . . [Yet] for the division the result was a battle well east of the Bug without artillery support, in particular because the batteries of I./AR 156, which were already on the eastern bank of the Bug, had run out of ammunition. The battles of 192 IR were thus more costly than was necessary and, in places, quite serious.[138]

Despite the many challenges—most significant among them the tenacious enemy resistance—by day's end both divisions of Kienitz's 17 Army Corps had fought their way 14 kilometers beyond the border.[139] Casualty figures for 62 Infantry Division had amounted to fifty-two KIA, 126 wounded, and twenty-eight missing.[140] And the savage and costly fighting would go on in the days ahead. In the first seven days of the campaign, 56 Infantry Division would incur personnel losses of forty officers, 1,012 NCOs and men (KIA, wounded, and missing)—losses that included fully 20 percent of the infantry's combat strength (*Gefechtsstärke*). From June 22 to 29, 1941, 234 Infantry Regiment alone would lose 32 percent of its officers. The relentless attrition of the *Ostheer* had already begun.[141]

5.5: 1 PANZER GROUP OPERATIONS

In command of 1 Panzer Group (headquarters near the village of Wólka Łabuńska) was the fifty-nine-year-old *Generaloberst* Ewald von Kleist; his chief of staff was *Obst.i.G.* Zeitzler. Kleist was the descendant of a "long line of Prussian generals and aristocrats"; three members of his family had become field marshals, and thirty-one had garnered the highly prestigious *Pour le Mérite*. Throughout his long and brilliant military career, Kleist embodied the traditions of a Prussian officer and a Christian gentleman. Writes historian Samuel W. Mitcham Jr.: "There was never any hint of scandal in his life or background. Certainly the thought of cooperating with the *Einsatzgruppen* never entered his mind. He looked upon the Nazi Party with a distaste he did not bother to hide. Unfortunately, he was not the stuff conspiracies are made of. Along with the rest of the army, he swore an oath to Adolf Hitler in August 1934, and he would never go back on it."[142] Like other German generals who were—temporarily at least—in Hitler's favor, Kleist would accept a generous financial gift (*Dotation*) of 480,000 *Reichsmarks* from the *Führer* in September 1942.[143]

During the invasion of Poland in September 1939, Kleist commanded the 22 Army Corps and displayed an aptitude for leading large mobile forces in battle. As a result, in March 1940, the Army High Command put him in command of "Panzer Group Kleist" (*Gruppe von Kleist* [*mot.*]) and charged him with the task of leading Germany's main armored strike force in the Western campaign that began several weeks later—a task he fulfilled admirably despite some memorable clashes with the impetuous panzer leader Guderian.[144] On July 19, 1940, Kleist was promoted to *Generaloberst* and, in November, took control of 1 Panzer Group, which he led ably during the Balkan campaign in the spring of 1941. For his many notable achievements in the Russian campaign, including spearheading the German drive into the Caucasus in the summer of 1942, Hitler promoted Kleist to field marshal in February 1943.[145]

While his army was in the Caucasus region, Kleist sought to gain the acceptance of the local populace by granting them a large measure of autonomy. Simply put, he was convinced that the German army would only defeat the Soviet Union "if the Russian people know that we only want to liberate them from Bolshevism, but that we don't want to enslave them or carve up Russia." After the Stalingrad debacle, Kleist, now in command of Army Group A, withdrew from the Kuban bridgehead to the Crimea in September 1943. On November 29, 1943, he engaged Hitler in a dramatic, two-hour discussion, during which he expressed his concern about the conduct of the war in the East, recommending that Hitler relinquish his command of the *Ostheer* and focus on domestic and foreign policy. The *Führer*, of course, flatly rejected Kleist's démarche and, on March 30, 1944, the general was transferred to the reserve pool for high-ranking officers (*Führerreserve*). More than ten years later, on October 26, 1954, Kleist would perish in the Soviet POW camp Vladimir, 300 kilometers east of Moscow, after he had spent time in more than two dozen POW camps and prisons. Fellow prisoners fortunate enough to return home to Germany reported on Kleist's admirable bearing in captivity. Said one unnamed: "His energy, his sense of humor and his mental agility astounded us all."[146]

On June 22, 1941, Kleist's 1 Panzer Group boasted a personnel strength of about 225,000 men; all told, Kleist controlled fifteen divisions organized in three panzer corps, one army corps, and a panzer group reserve. The divisions broke down as six infantry, five panzer, and four motorized infantry divisions, including two *Waffen-SS* motorized infantry divisions. The five panzer divisions possessed between them about 715 tanks, including 355 Pz III (255 with a 50mm gun, 100 with a 37mm main armament), and 100 Pz IV tanks (75mm main armament). The panzer group's first echelon corps were organized as follows (from right to left): 48 Panzer Corps (57 ID, 75 ID, 11 PD), *Gen.d.Pz.Tr.* Werner Kempff; 29 Army Corps (111 ID, 299 ID), *Gen.d.Inf.* Hans von Obstfelder; and 3 Panzer Corps (44 ID, 298 ID, 14 PD), *Gen.d.Kav.* Eberhard von Mackensen. Forming the second echelon were *Gen.d.Inf.* Gustav von Wietersheim's 14 Panzer Corps (SS "Viking," 9 PD, 16 PD) and four divisions of the panzer group reserve: 13 PD, 16 ID (mot.), 25 ID (mot.) and SS "L.A.H."[147] To successfully complete its mission of breaking through the robust Soviet frontier defenses covering the Ukraine, Kleist's panzer group received a generous complement of GHQ troops:

- Assault Gun Battalions 197 and 191 (48 and 3 PzK, respectively)
- 4 105mm cannon battalions (2 to 48 PzK; 1 each to 29 AK and 3 PzK)
- 2 150mm medium field howitzer battalions (1 each to 48 and 3 PzK)
- 1 mixed artillery battalion (*z.V.Pz.Gr.*)
- 6 210mm heavy howitzer battalions (4 mot. and 2 limited mobility) (2 to 48 PzK; 1 to 29 AK; 3 to 3 PzK)
- 2 240mm heavy howitzer (*Haubitze*) battalions (1 each to 48 and 3 PzK)
- 2 150mm cannon battalions (less one battery) (3 PzK)
- *Nebelwerfer* Battalion 4 (less one battery) (48 PzK)
- *Lehr* (instructional) and 54 *Nebelwerfer* Regiments (48 and 3 PzK, respectively)
- 2 antitank battalions (1 to 3 PzK; 1 *z.V. Pz.Gr.*)
- 1 flak (*Fla*) battalion (3 PzK)
- 4 flak (*Fla*) companies (1 each to 48 PzK and 29 AK; 2 *z.V.Pz.Gr.*)[148]

Other GHQ units assigned to 1 Panzer Group included: five engineer battalions, two bridge-building battalions, twenty-six bridge columns "B," six construction battalions, six road repair and construction battalions, and five Reich Labor Service units (*Gruppen*). Among the *Luftwaffe* formations assigned for tactical support were nine short-range reconnaissance squadrons (allotted primarily to the panzer divisions), one long-range (strategic) squadron controlled by the panzer group (7.(F)/LG 2), and six flak battalions of 2 Flak Corps (*z.V.Pz.Gr.*).[149]

The six infantry divisions of Kleist's first echelon, earmarked for the initial assault, were arrayed along a relatively narrow front of 65 kilometers. On the panzer group's right wing, the infantry of 48 Panzer Corps (57 and 75 ID) were to attack into the Strumilov Fortified Region; in the center, 29 Army Corps (111 and 299 ID), and on the left wing, 3 Panzer Corps (44 and 298 ID), were to cut their way into the Vladimir-Volynski Fortified Region, which stretched from Ustilug in the north to Bilichi in the south. The main Red Army forces defending against Kleist's infantry were the 124 and 87 Rifle Divisions of 5 Army's 27 Rifle Corps, commanded by Maj.-Gen. P. D. Artemenko.[150] The 124 RD was deployed with one regiment forward and two regiments in camp behind the front; 87 RD was in laager directly east of Vladimir-Volynski with all three of its rifle regiments. The 27 Rifle Corps' other division (135 RD) was posted well behind the frontier, between Dubno and Ostrog. In support of the rifle corps, the Vladimir-Volynski Fortified Region had some units stationed along the border and interspersed with forces of the 90 Border Guards Detachment. Positioned well back from the frontier was the bulk of 5 Army's mechanized forces (22 and 9 Mechanized Corps); however, 41 Tank Division (22 MC)—with the exception of its motorized rifle regiment, which was garrisoned at Lutsk—was deployed well forward, conducting maneuvers close to the front north of Vladimir-Volynski (Map 13).[151]

Because it was standard German practice to subordinate a panzer group to an infantry army for the purpose of effecting the initial breakthrough, 1 Panzer Group was controlled by Reichenau's Sixth Army. The Ukrainian capital of Kiev, nearly 500 kilometers from the German start line ("as the crow flies") was Kleist's initial operational objective, as articulated in the OKH deployment directive:

> *The first task of 1 Panzer Group, in cooperation with the Seventeenth and Sixth Armies, will be to break through the enemy forces close to the border between Rava Ruska and Kovel' and, advancing via Berdichev–Zhitomir, rapidly gain the Dnepr at and below Kiev. From there it will, without delay, continue the attack along the Dnepr in a southeasterly direction according to the directive of the high command of the army group, with the objective of preventing enemy forces in the western Ukraine from withdrawing over the Dnepr and destroying them through an attack with an inverted front.*[152]

As soon as the infantry divisions had created the openings through the strong Soviet border defenses, the tanks and motorized infantry of Kleist's panzer divisions were to be ready to roll. The attack order (*Angriffsbefehl*) of 15 Panzer Regiment of 11 Panzer Division (48 PzK) underscored this point:

> *As soon as the infantry has smashed a hole [in the Soviet defenses], 11 Panzer Division, as the lead panzer division of the corps, is to advance along the central Panzerstrasse . . . and initially force a crossing of the Styr at Szczurowice. It will then advance relentlessly and without stopping [rücksichtslos und unaufhaltsam] via Dubno-Ostrog-Polonne-Berditchev to the Dnepr. It is of critical importance that any enemy resistance is broken by attacking immediately and, as much as possible, with the mutual support of the individual battle groups, and that all difficulties caused by roads and terrain are overcome quickly through the concerted action of all units. Enemy elements still holding out between the* Panzerstrassen *will be left to the armies moving up from behind. Enemy tank attacks are to be dispatched through immediate counterattacks with our superior armor-piercing weapons.*[153]

To inspire and motivate his troops, *Generaloberst* von Kleist issued an order of the day (*Tagesbefehl*) on the morning of June 22:

Soldaten der 1. Panzergruppe!

> *The* Führer *has decided to smash the Bolshevik-Soviet enemy before he tries to exploit our war with England by attacking us from behind due to his enduring hatred of National Socialism.*
>
> *In this campaign 1 Panzer Group has, once again, been deployed on an important sector [of the front]. With the subordinated infantry divisions, it will smash an opening through the Bolshevik border wall and then, with the mobile forces, drive far to the east. Then the Russian army in front of us will break apart [auseinanderfallen].*
>
> *Until that moment there will be no calm and no rest for us. We must advance without stopping, relentlessly and without restraint [unaufhaltsam, rücksichtslos und hemmungslos] until we've reached our objective.*
>
> *I am firmly convinced, that the* Gruppe von Kleist *will fulfill its new mission just as rapidly as in France and Serbia.*
>
> Es lebe der Führer![154]

The attack of Kleist's panzer group began with a thunderous artillery barrage up and down the front. On the right wing, the divisions of Kempff's 48 Panzer Corps unleashed a massive bombardment (*massierten Feuerschlag*) on Soviet targets across the Bug River with artillery of all calibers, *Nebelwerfer* rocket launchers, flak, infantry guns, and mortars.[155]

Witnessing the apocalyptic spectacle near Sokal', in the sector of 57 Infantry Division (48 PzK), was one Willibald G.:

> *At 0315 hours the spell-binding barrage got underway. We captured the bridge over the Bug at Sokal'. It was a fantastical firework display! Some 400 guns, including* Nebel-*werfer, fired in unison along a 5 kilometer front. The infantry made good progress, so we've already been able to make a change of position and cross over [the Bug]. Sokal' is in flames but we had to go through the city. The Russians put up no resistance. They didn't fire a shot across [the river], and there's not a single Russian plane to be seen. The Russians it seems were taken completely by surprise. Of course, the war has only just begun. Hopefully it will continue to go so splendidly! We are waiting in the first rays of sunlight for our horses.[156]*

Protected by the massive curtain of fire and smoke grenades, the assault detachments of *Generalleutnant* Oskar Blümm's 57 Infantry Division launched their attack—179 IR on the right, 199 IR on the left, and 217 IR in reserve—supported by combat engineers, assault guns, and flak units. Within fifteen minutes, the road bridge across the Bug at Sokal' was in German hands, captured in a *coup de main*. While the victorious *Stosstrupps* stormed across the bridge, other assault teams rapidly traversed the river in rubber dinghies and assault boats with only minor losses. Exploiting the factor of surprise, the attack on Sokal' and the tactically significant high ground in its vicinity was soon making good progress.[157]

The lead elements of *Generalleutnant* Ernst Hammer's 75 Infantry Division—forming the left wing of 48 Panzer Corps (north of Sokal')—were across the Bug by 0530 hours. The two attacking regiments then proceeded to storm the high ground on the far riverbank until they encountered a well-prepared defensive zone bristling with bunkers at the collective farm Kol. Rawszczyzna.[158] Here they were greeted by withering defensive fire that temporarily checked the division's advance. The attackers carefully probed the enemy bunker line, which was skillfully positioned and posed a formidable obstacle. Soon, however, 3rd Battalion, 202 Infantry Regiment, located a gap in the bunkers on the road leading from Sokal' to Tartakow; reacting swiftly, the battalion commander, *Hauptmann* Pintschovius, shepherded his companies through the opening and pressed on. The other two battalions of 202 IR also slipped through the gap, while elements of 222 IR managed to skirt the bunker line to the north. The elimination of the bunkers was left to II./IR 222, which was reinforced with special weapons (*Sonderwaffen*) for the purpose. Making good progress, 202 IR broke enemy resistance at Horbkow and advanced on Tartakow.[159]

In the center of 1 Panzer Group's attack, the two divisions of Obstfelder's 29 Army Corps—111 ID on the right, 299 ID on the left—crossed the Bug southwest of Vladimir-Volynski. Supported by the artillery regiment of 168 Infantry Division (the reserve division of Sixth Army), a battalion of 105mm cannon, and a battalion of 210mm heavy howitzers (GHQ artillery), Obstfelder's infantry clawed their way into the Soviet frontier defenses. Once again, the invaders took the Soviet garrison troops at the border by surprise; in some cases, elements of the Vladimir-Volynski Fortified Region were encircled, creating small pockets of resistance that would take the Germans as long as two to three days to subdue. In his remarkable wartime journal, Hans Roth, a *Panzer-jäger* (antitank trooper) in 299 ID, recorded a gripping account of the chaos, horror, and death that characterized the initial hours of the division's push across the frontier:

All of a sudden, at exactly 0315 hours, and apparently out of the blue, an opening salvo emerges from the barrels of hundreds of guns of all calibers. . . . It is impossible to comprehend one's world in such an inferno.

Our homeland is still innocently asleep while here death is already collecting a rich harvest. We crouch in our holes with pallid but resolved faces while counting the minutes until we storm the Bug fortifications . . . a reassuring touch of our ID tags, the arming of hand grenades, the securing of our [submachine guns].

It is now 0330 hours. A whistle sounds; we quickly jump out from undercover and at an insane speed cross the 20 meters to the inflatable boats. In a snatch we are on the other side of the river where rattling machine gun fire awaits us. We have our first casualties.

With the help of a few Sturmpionieren *[assault engineers] we slowly—much too slowly—eat through the barbed wire barriers. Meanwhile, shells fire into the bunkers at Molnikow . . .*

We finally get out of this mess. In a few short steps we are able to advance to the first bunker, arriving in its blind spot. The Reds fire like mad but are unable to reach us. The decisive moment is near. An explosive specialist approaches the bunker from behind and shoves in a short-fused bomb into the bunker's fire hole. The bunker shook, and black smoke emerged from its openings, signaling its final doom. We move on.

Molnikow is completely in our hands by 1000 hours. The Reds, hunted by our infantry, disperse quickly to Bisknjiczo-Ruski . . . We are ordered to cleanse the village of any remaining enemy combatants. The area is combed house by house. Our shelling has caused terrible damage. The Reds, however, have also done their fair share.

Slowly, our nerves grow accustomed to the all too familiar gruesome images. Close to the Reds' custom house lies a large mound of fallen Russians, most of them torn to shreds from the shelling. Slaughtered civilians lie in the neighboring house. The horridly disfigured bodies of a young woman and her two small children lie among their shattered personal belongings in another small, cleansed house . . .

We have taken our first prisoners—snipers and deserters receive their deserved reward.[160]

Over the course of the day, 29 Army Corps' 111 Infantry Division, led by *General-leutnant* Otto Stapf, succeeded in crossing the Luga at several locations, while the spirited attack of *Generalmajor* Willi Moser's 299 Infantry division split off the Soviet 124 Rifle Division from the 87 Rifle Division, beginning what was "essentially the first encirclement that would occur in the Southwestern Front sector."[161] To counter the dangerous German thrust, the Soviet 1st Antitank Brigade established a defensive shield in an effort to block the road running east to Lutsk (Maps 14 and 15).[162]

On the left wing of Kleist's panzer group, the two attacking divisions of Mackensen's 3 Panzer Corps—44 ID on the right, 298 ID on the left—supported by the "thunder" of 300 guns, "stormed across the Bug" from the area at and north of Hrubieszow.[163] According to the war diary of 14 Panzer Division (assembled directly behind the border south of Chelm), the barrage along the front of 3 Panzer Corps rumbled on for as long as two hours, the division's artillery supporting the advance of both of Mackensen's attacking infantry divisions.[164] In a letter to an unknown recipient, *Gefreiter* Franz S. (44 ID) recorded his thoughts on the start of the new campaign: "But just early this morning it's begun. The thunder of the guns rolls, and aircraft roar on by over our heads. So, of course, we won't be spared [a war] with the Russians. We've suspected that for quite some time."[165]

As always, when an attacking force has to overcome a major river barrier, the overriding imperative is to get safely, and swiftly, across to build momentum for the attack. Where bridges are available, seizing them intact is vital for the success of such an operation. Once again, on this first day of the war, the Germans succeeded in this task; indeed, by 0330 hours, the assault troops of 134 Infantry Regiment of *Generalleutnant* Friedrich Siebert's 44 Infantry Division had seized intact the bridge over the Bug at Grodek. Of course, bridges can also be built, which is why the attacking German forces were so generously equipped with bridging columns "B." Hence, at 0409 hours, 3 Panzer Corps ordered that the construction of military and emergency bridges (*Kriegs- und Befehlsbrücke*) was to begin at once. In the ensuing hours, reports flowed in about the capture of key objectives just beyond the frontier. At 0435, the division's chief operations officer (Ia) reported to the army corps that "Overture" (*Vorspiel*) had been reached. At 0845, the Ia again reported to the army corps, this time informing them that "Iron beard" (*Eisenbart*) had been reached by 134 Infantry Regiment, which was now engaging enemy bunkers south of Janow.[166]

In the sector of *Generalmajor* Walther Graessner's 298 Infantry Division, the first troops were crossing the Bug by 0319 hours, while the village on the far side was already in flames. At 0325 hours, Artillery Commander 3 (*Arko 3*) reported that the attack was going "according to plan" (*planmässig*), and that, so far at least, there had been no enemy resistance. Three minutes later (0328) *Leutnant* Müller, detailed to 526 Infantry Regiment as the division's forward observer (*vorgeschobener Beobachter*), reported that troops of one of the regiment's battalions were across the Bug and had already penetrated the enemy defenses; and, still, no sign of Russian infantry or artillery fire. Two minutes after that (0330), *Leutnant* Sperling, dispatched to 525 Infantry Regiment as the division's forward observer, also reported no signs of enemy small arms or artillery fire. As a result, at 0335, the division informed 3 Panzer Corps that the attack was going well with no discernable enemy response.[167]

Not until 0345 hours did the war diary of 298 Infantry Division note that the enemy still had a pulse (of sorts): "Lt. Müller reports: After reaching the edge of the woods, 526 IR [encounters] weak enemy resistance. The troops are advancing into the woods." Not until an hour after the initial assault (0410) did the Germans meet some serious resistance: "From 526 IR Lt. Müller reports by telephone: Northeast of Ustilug, along the road to Wydranka, considerable enemy resistance. *Obst.Lt.* Kempff killed in battle." Moreover, according to *Luftwaffe* reconnaissance, enemy motorized units (including infantry mounted on trucks), and a handful of enemy tanks (among them the "heavier types"), had left Vladimir-Volynski and were assembling in the wooded area 5 kilometers northwest of the city. Yet for the time being, the attack of Graessner's infantry rolled on; by 0425, forward elements had reached the outskirts of Ustilug, while prisoners were also being taken. Enemy resistance, however, was gradually increasing: By 0435, house-to-house combat was underway in Ustilug, and, at 0515, the diary of 298 ID mentions Russian bunkers for the first time, recording that 1st Battalion, 526 Infantry Regiment, had come to a halt before two enemy bunkers in the woods near Ustilug and was preparing to attack them.[168]

From their forward command post in the woods south of the village of Wólka Łabuńska, *Generaloberst* Kleist and his panzer group staff evaluated the reports pouring in from the front. As a result of the rapid progress of both 3 and 48 Panzer Corps, at 0700 hours the panzer group informed both corps that they could begin to bring their panzer divisions forward to the Bug River. After both panzer corps had secured further objectives—by 1100, the infantry of 48 Panzer Corps had taken Tartakow,[169] while 298 ID (3 PzK) had seized intact the bridge at Piatydnie—1 Panzer Group released 11 and 14 Panzer Divisions to begin their advance across the frontier, their initial objective the Styr River crossings. Shortly thereafter, a corresponding order arrived at the panzer group CP from Army Group South and Sixth Army.[170]

By 1200 hours, the reinforced Reconnaissance Battalion 231 of *Generalmajor* Ludwig Crüwell's 11 Panzer Division (143 tanks) had begun to roar across the Bug River at Sokal', heading east on the central *Panzerstrasse*. The battalion's advance, however, was held up initially by active enemy bunkers inadvertently left behind by the advancing German infantry. Despite deployment of a battery of 88mm flak guns, the indomitable Russian bunker crews would doggedly continue their resistance (and eventually require an infantry *Stosstrupp* to neutralize them). Yet they could not hold up a panzer division for long and, by 1500 hours, Crüwell's tanks were rolling over the Bug bridge and along the central *Panzerstrasse*. Other than minor skirmishes, 11 Panzer Division would see no action on this first day of the eastern campaign; by the end of the day, the division, advancing southeast, had reached the outskirts of Stoianov, more than 25 kilometers from its start line.[171] In doing so, 11 PD was the only one of Kleist's five panzer divisions to advance beyond the frontier on June 22 (Map 14).

If the day had been largely uneventful for the tankers and motorcycle riflemen of 11 Panzer Division, it had not been—uneventful—for *Unteroffizier* Alfred Höckendorf of the division's 15 Panzer Regiment. His astounding experience as a motorcycle messenger is outlined in the paragraphs below.

Following behind the tanks of his company [4./PzRgt 15], his motorcycle suddenly receives a direct hit in the rear wheel and is no longer operational. Fortunately, he is not injured as a result. Regrettably, however, this took place within a giant cornfield, which is still teeming with Russian soldiers. For a short time, Feldwebel *Bergander and his tank sticks close by [Höckendorf], but soon he has to drive off to catch up with the company. Now Höckendorf is alone and around him the Russians, who have let the German tanks roll by without revealing themselves.*

After a short while, the first enemy soldiers appear, and Höckendorf is soon engaged in a bitter man-against-man struggle. Yet he manages to take his first prisoners and to shoot down a Russian who had attempted to jump onto Feldw. *Bergander's tank. Although so far he's had luck on his side, what he needs to do now, and quickly, is to reach his own men. The positions of the German infantry are about 1 kilometer behind him yet, in his situation, that is a devilishly long way. But he has no choice. He must make it back, and so he stumbles off, driving his three prisoners before him as a shield.*

Again and again more enemy soldiers appear, some of whom he is able to disarm and take prisoner. So he's now up to six, and the farther back he goes, the more prisoners he takes. When he finally shows up at the rifle pits of the [German] infantry, the number of his prisoners has grown to 40, and the shock on the part of his comrades over his solitary feat is understandably great.

Left behind dead along Höckendorf's route were about 10 other Russians, who had preferred a struggle to becoming a POW.[172]

In the meantime, the border battles at the frontier had grown more intense and more costly for Kleist's infantry. As noted in the journal of 1 Panzer Group: "As the day progressed, resistance stiffened mainly in the sectors of 48 and 3 Panzer Corps. Individual bunker crews northeast of Sokal' fought bitterly and could only be neutralized one at a time by use of the heaviest weapons."[173] During the afternoon, the infantry of Blümm's 57 Infantry Division (48 PzK) ran across a group of well-camouflaged bunkers "of the most modern type"; unable to subdue them after protracted and bitter fighting, the infantry regiments simply bypassed the bunkers and continued to advance, leaving their destruction to follow-on assault teams.[174] In the sector of 75 Infantry Division (48 PzK), Red Army forces, with tanks, counterattacked at Tartakow, but each time were beaten back by the German defenders. The reader will recall that 2nd Battalion of 222 Infantry Regiment (75 ID) had, that morning, been assigned the task of taking out a particularly troublesome enemy bunker line at Kol. Rawszczyzna; by the end of the day, however, the battle for the bunkers was still going on. The battalion's infantry, having tightly encircled the bunkers, prepared to put in its final assault the next day, reinforced by combat engineers, a battery of 210mm heavy howitzers, two 150mm medium field howitzers, and two 88mm flak guns. By evening, June 23, despite fierce resistance, all eighteen of the bunkers were finally in German hands and, while "open resistance" had by then come to an end, the division found itself fighting in the villages against "guerrilla" forces (*Freischärler*) and "armed women" (*bewaffnete Frauen*).[175]

For the two infantry divisions of Mackensen's 3 Panzer Corps, struggling through the fixed fortifications of the Vladimir-Volynski Fortified Region, the going was no easier. At 1615 hours, 131 Infantry Regiment (44 ID), having happened upon Russian defenses consisting of four armored cupolas (*Panzerkuppeln*) and eleven additional gun positions, lodged a request with the artillery for artificial smoke. A short time later, Soviet bombers struck the sector of 131 IR and, at 1855, the impending assault of the regiment was called off. The division's other attacking regiment (134 IR) having, through armed reconnaissance, located "many new bunkers" along its line of advance, also postponed any further assault until the next day.[176]

The 44 IDs neighbor to the left, Graessner's 298 Infantry Division, experienced even more difficult fighting, as it sought to engage skillfully camouflaged and well-positioned Soviet bunkers in the heavily wooded terrain about Ustilug and Vladimir-Volynski. Although progress had at first been good—despite jittery (and, no doubt, spurious) rumors that the Russians were using gas, a common fear of German soldiers in the opening days of the campaign—by early afternoon the attacks of both the division's infantry regiments had come to a halt along a line running east of Piatnydnie and through Kol. Karczunek. While the Germans managed to subdue some of the enemy bunker positions, attempts to render them *hors de combat* as often as not led to serious casualties, as noted in the detailed German combat reports; even the assault guns of Assault Gun Battalion 191 proved useless against the Soviet bunkers at Kol. Karczunek. At 1945 hours, due to the staunch Russian resistance, which had "increased everywhere,"[177] Graessner decided to suspend the attacks and temporarily go on the defensive. A report filed by the division's 526 IR on June 24 noted that "the attack of the regiment [had] struck a strongly reinforced, cleverly laid out position in which the enemy fought to the end . . .[178] The strength of the enemy's battle positions was seriously underestimated."[179] During the night, fighting and skirmishing continued, with 298 ID forced to weather several "local crises" in its combat zone.[180]

In the final entries in its war diary for June 22, 1 Panzer Group offered at least a partial assessment of the first day's fighting: "On the entire front of the panzer group the enemy was surprised by the attack. The forward field fortifications [*Feldbefestigungen*] were only partially occupied and he was no longer capable of occupying the positions in a systematic fashion. Where the enemy succeeded in taking up his positions, he fought with tenacity. The [enemy's] bunker positions are only partially complete." The diarist went on to praise the support of the *Luftwaffe*—a topic that will be the focus of Chapter 6—which destroyed hundreds of Soviet aircraft, the bulk of them on the ground. The *Luftwaffe*'s 2 Flak Corps, while mostly in action along the German routes of advance to protect them from Soviet air attack, also committed some of its 88mm flak guns to contesting the enemy bunkers at the border.[181]

As we have seen, the thrusts of Kleist's panzer group developed along two primary axes. In the south, despite bitter Soviet resistance, 57 and 75 ID (48 PzK) succeeded in creating an opening for 11 Panzer Division, which, by mid-afternoon, was spearheading an advance southeast toward Dubno and Ostrog. In the north, the infantry of 44 and 298 ID (3 PzK)—again, in the face of often ferocious resistance—attacked toward Vladimir-Volynski and began to pry open a path for Kleist's armor along the Lutsk-Rovno axis. By June 24, four of Kleist's five panzer divisions (11, 13, 14, 16 PD) had poured through the breaches in the border defenses and were rumbling east.[182]

Soviet reactions to the attack of Kleist's forces on June 22 are concisely analyzed by Colonel David M. Glantz (U.S. Army, ret.):

> *During the first day of combat, the Soviet garrison troops along the border were surprised [and many were encircled]. The 87 Rifle Division reacted fairly quickly [all three of its regiments deploying forward] and the Soviets dispatched one of their 10 antitank brigades forward. In most of the major sectors the Soviets had one, two, or even three of these antitank brigades. The first units the Soviets dispatched forward on the expected axes of the German armored advance were these antitank brigades. . .*
>
> *On 22 June orders went out almost immediately from Kirponos' headquarters to the mechanized corps to close forward as rapidly as possible. The first corps to do so was 22 Mechanized Corps. Of course, that corps' 41 Tank Division was already located close to the attack sector and it was ordered to send elements southward to assist the 87 Rifle Division. Meanwhile, the 19 Tank and 215 Motorized Divisions hastened forward to join in the counterattack, which was anticipated somewhere in the area east of Vladimir Volynski. Similar orders also went out to Rokossovsky's 9 Mechanized Corps and [Maj.-Gen. N. V.] Feklenko's 19 Mechanized Corps.*
>
> *Essentially from Lutsk to Rovno, and from Korosten and Berdichev further to the rear, a solid stream of Soviet armor attempted to make its way forward. In most cases this movement was severely interdicted by German air strikes . . . In the south the 15 Mechanized Corps was ordered northward to strike at the German penetration forming near [Radekhov].*[183]

On June 23, 1941, the panzer regiment of *Generalmajor* Crüwell's 11 Panzer Division, reinforced with 88mm flak, would collide with the spearheads of Soviet 15 Mechanized Corps near Radekhov (Radziechov). In the ensuing battle, the German panzers—aided by fierce *Luftwaffe* interdiction—would destroy forty-six super-heavy KV-1 and KV-2 tanks, with minimal losses of their own.[184] At this brief moment in history, the German tank arm was the finest in the world, and the Russians—inexperienced, poorly trained, and outfitted with equipment they didn't yet know how to use—were not about to defeat them, as the days, weeks, and months ahead would demonstrate time and again.

5.6: *ABENDLAGE:* PRÉCIS OF THE COMBAT ACTIONS OF ARMY GROUP SOUTH

In its war diary, Army Group South offered this positive assessment of the first day's operations:

> *Due to the complete tactical surprise [along the front], the first day of combat exceeded the expectations of the high command of the army group. For the further course of operations in general favorable conditions have been created for both the army and the Luftwaffe . . . There is no cause to alter the basic objectives of the armies or to intervene in their conduct of operations. The issuance of the army group order merely serves the purpose of achieving exploitation of the day's initial successes by attacking boldly and of emphasizing once again the primacy of the attack.*[185]

In contrast to the operations of the other army groups, which saw the commitment of large panzer forces that advanced deep into the enemy's rear, in the sector of Rundstedt's army group the armor played virtually no part in the initial attack. Rather, it was a case of classic infantry combat—the German assault detachments, supported by artillery and other heavy weapons, seeking to break into, and through, the border defenses of Soviet Southwestern Front. Only after achieving these initial breakthroughs were the tanks to cross the frontier and drive east.

As a result of this tactical approach, made necessary due to the particular strength of the Soviet fortifications covering the Ukraine, the initial gains of Army Group South were not as impressive as those made in the central and northern sectors of the 1,800-kilometer Eastern Front. There were, however, gaps in the Soviet border defenses, which the Germans were able to exploit by committing Reichenau's Sixth Army and Kleist's 1 Panzer Group at the junction of the Rava Ruska and Strumilov fortified regions, against the left flank of Soviet 5 Army and the right flank of 6 Army. As a result, "by the morning of 23 June, German penetration at the junction [of the two Soviet armies] was an accomplished and menacing fact." Farther north, the left wing of Kleist's panzer group carved its way into the Vladimir-Volynski Fortified Region, creating another opening for the German armor. Due to these incipient German successes, "the threat of a deep penetration—and with it, the outflanking of the main Soviet forces from the north—was clearly developing."[186]

Recognizing this threat, M. P. Kirponos, the Soviet Southwestern Front commander, planned to strike at the flanks of Kleist's panzer forces "with every available armored formation."[187] Yet to do so, he would first have to concentrate these forces at the critical points in timely fashion. In the days ahead, however, factors ranging from insufficient intelligence and inexperience to the interdiction of his advancing armor by the *Luftwaffe*—attempting to avoid the relentless German aerial assault by staying off the roads, many Soviet tank units ended up stuck in swamps[188]—would force Kirponos to commit his mechanized corps in piecemeal fashion, resulting in their defeat in detail by the German panzer forces.

Finally, it hardly bears repeating that, once again, the Germans soon discovered that the war in the East would have a decidedly different character from the campaigns that had preceded it. Along the protracted front of Army Group South, from Peremysl' and the village of Oleszyce in the sector of Stülpnagel's Seventeenth Army, to the forests of Ustilug on the left wing of Kleist's panzer group, the Germans engaged a relentless and unyielding adversary who, as an individual fighting man, was every bit as tough as the Teutonic invaders.

As I bring my account of German ground operations to a close, I will leave the reader with the long and brutal diary entry of "Paul R.," who fought in a signals unit of 44 Infantry Division (3 PzK). His experiences encapsulate those of the hundreds of thousands of German soldiers who poured across the Russo-German frontier just before dawn on June 22, 1941.

During the evening we ride up over the hill, which is teeming with artillery pieces. The sun dissolved into the west and the dusk came—so peaceful, as if it weren't possible that, in just a few hours, a war would begin, more dreadful, more terrible than all those preceding it. Anxious hours. Stars fill the sky, bright and cold, and then the dawn comes. We check our watches. 0310—still five minutes to go.

Now comes the final judgment. I've never seen anything like it. Hundreds of incendiary shells and Nebelwerfer *rockets roar skyward, rolling over our heads and past us like fireworks. The heavens quake. A mighty hissing noise is in the air and it stuns us. Again and again flashes of light and piercing sounds. The horses rear up and those that are loose bolt across the gray fields. Then the furious fire from countless gun barrels merges into one terrible howl, which shakes even the strongest of men.*

Concealed by the fog, and under the influence of this holy hell, our assault detachments make their way over the Bug. We capture the bridge intact, so I'm able to make it across with the first troops. Then the struggle for the bunkers begins. I'm in the most forward line of infantry, on a slope where we're visible to the enemy, so we dig in and work our way forward in bounds. As if on a maneuver, I see everything spread out before me. But the more we advance up the slope, the stronger the enemy artillery fire becomes.

The command post moves up more and more quickly. I lay the [telephone] cable ahead through rustling cornfields and across the plowed brown fields, and I'm often only a few hundred meters behind the forwardmost troops. Most of the bunkers on the Bug have been captured. Several are still firing, because the Russians are really tough [wirklich zäh]. *At the edge of the wood are a couple of houses, from which snipers are shooting at us. A few hand grenades and the straw roofs are burning like torches in the sun-filled morning. The peasant woman lies in her blood on the road, her children cradled in her arms. The men are all being shot. None of the civilians have fled. The war came as too much of a surprise to them.*

It's finally becoming light. The enemy fire is growing stronger. The crisp clatter of the German machine guns alternates with the hollow crack of the Russian [machine guns]. But we are attacking. What then takes place cannot be put into words. It is the line between being and nothingness. In the blazing midday sun I move forward with three other men. All the necessary cable has to be carried along. And the enemy artillery crashes down, for hours, because they can see us. The shells strike in front of us, behind us, often so close to us that we're sprayed with clods of dirt. The shell splinters whiz past our heads so we press our heads into the earth. Stand up, then once again throw yourself to the ground, in the corn, in the blooming clover. They are hunting us. They are tormenting us. Time exists no longer.

A shell strikes my vehicle, which is behind us under cover. [One of my comrades] is so badly wounded that he dies that night. Four horses are dead, two are wounded. The enemy shell fire continues to grow stronger. Dear God, protect me! The exertions of this day are simply beyond words. This day has so drained us of strength, that the impact of the shells hardly registers any longer; we no longer care how close it is, whether it will bring death and silent oblivion. The hours are so filled with tension that this day seems like a year; like terror without end.

In the evening we dig in at the edge of the wood. The tree branches shatter, the trunks burst apart, and the crash of an explosion is twice as loud here. A telephone operator in my troop is wounded right next to me. I bind him up under fire, but he lies for hours beside me. The blood trickles out of the bandage. The puddle at my feet grows larger. For 30 hours nothing to drink, nothing to eat, and no sleep. The wounded man is groaning and the enemy shells hiss and burst. Is this why you've given birth to us, dear mothers? But don't ask, and don't think. Late in the evening German tanks go forward and silence the enemy batteries. The night is peaceful.[189]

CHAPTER 6

Death from the Sky—The *Luftwaffe* Wreaks Havoc and Smashes the Soviet Air Force

At last, a proper war!
—CHIEF OF THE *LUFTWAFFE* GENERAL STAFF, AIR GENERAL HANS JESCHONNEK.[1]

Our Luftwaffe *is apparently far superior [*turnhoch überlegen*] to the Russian's.*
—FIELD MARSHAL FEDOR VON BOCK, JUNE 22, 1941[2]

There is little doubt that the Luftwaffe . . . *prepared during the whole of its existence for a conflict such as the one that greeted it on the morning of 22 June 1941.*
—AIRPOWER HISTORIAN RICHARD MULLER[3]

In the initial stages of the attack, towns and villages were encountered lit up as if for peacetime, which made locating targets a great deal easier. Work on the [enemy] airfields was being done in part under floodlights. The element of surprise was total. Enemy defensive action barely had any appreciable effect and where it did, then only at a point when the main attacks had already been carried out.
—LOTHAR VON HEINEMANN, GERMAN 8 AIR CORPS[4]

During air raids, mothers put buckets on their children's heads to protect them from shrapnel . . . As soon as the Luftwaffe *came in sight, people covered up girls wearing bright colors with coats and jackets, fearing that a red dress would certainly catch the eye of a German pilot. Mothers stuffed birth certificates and home addresses in little bags and tied them around the necks of younger children so they would have some chance of being identified if the mothers were killed—and many were, particularly during the air raids . . . In a macabre twist, many highways were covered with scores of dolls that young girls had snatched up before fleeing and then lost to stampedes and death.*
—HISTORIAN CONSTANTINE PLESHAKOV[5]

━◦━

The author of the third epigraph above, airpower historian Richard Muller, would go on to write: "German bomber and fighter units exceeded the most optimistic hopes of their commanders when they virtually annihilated the Soviet air force during the first two days of the campaign . . . It is likely that this campaign against the VVS[6] at the [onset of Operation *Barbarossa*] was the *Luftwaffe's* major contribution to the course of the war."[7] Simply put, this was because the spectacular German victories of the summer and early fall of 1941 would most likely not have been possible without the general condition of air superiority (even air supremacy) established by the *Luftwaffe* at the very outset of the campaign.[8]

Although it had sustained much greater attrition than the German army in the first twenty-one months of the war, the *Luftwaffe* (like the army) was at the zenith of its powers in June 1941, its efficacy underscored by the easy and impressive victories in the Balkans and Crete. Like the army, it was well organized and experienced and, despite heavy losses in the air war against England, still possessed a strong and agile bomber force. There can thus be no doubt that the *Luftwaffe* entered the Russian campaign "in a spirit of the highest confidence as to the outcome of the result, emboldened further by the very poor showing of the Soviet air force in the Finnish Campaign of 1939/40, where 900 aircraft had been lost to a handful of obsolete fighters and guns."[9]

The operational objectives of the *Luftwaffe* at the start of the *Ostkrieg* were twofold: To achieve air superiority (and, in vital sectors, absolute air supremacy) by destroying Soviet air forces in the air and on the ground; and, after this objective had been fulfilled, to provide ground forces with direct and indirect support along the primary axes of advance. Direct support was the close air support (CAS) mission—that is, attacking enemy forces at or near the forward edge of battle. Indirect support embraced the interdiction of roads, bridges, rail lines, supply depots, troop concentrations and movements, and other assets of value to the enemy. *Luftwaffe* field commanders were accustomed to cooperating closely with the army and, thus, were largely comfortable with their supporting role. As with the ground forces, the basic tasks of the *Luftwaffe* were outlined in the army's deployment directive:

> *The mission of the* Luftwaffe *is to eliminate as much as possible the influence of the Russian air force while supporting the army's conduct of operations at its points of main effort* [Schwerpunkten], *in particular by Army Group Center and on the main wing of Army Group South. During major operations,* [the Luftwaffe] *will concentrate all its forces against the enemy air force and provide direct support to the army. Attacks on enemy industrial centers will only be carried out after the army has achieved its operational objectives.*[10]

Due to its enduring commitments in other theaters of war, the *Luftwaffe* was only able to commit 68 percent of its total actual front-line strength to the Russian campaign.[11] On

June 22, 1941, the *Luftwaffe* force structure in the East consisted of almost 3,000 aircraft, of which 2,255 were fully operational (*einsatzklar*); among the latter were 757 bombers, 360 Ju-87B *Stuka* divebombers, and 657 Bf-109 single-engine fighters. The aircraft were distributed over the four air fleets (1, 2, 4, 5) earmarked for the campaign.[12] Given its surprisingly modest number of aircraft—a problem that would become ever more acute as the months wore on—the *Luftwaffe's* accomplishments at the onset of the campaign were truly remarkable. At the beginning of German operations on *Barbarossatag*, *Generalmajor* Otto Hoffmann von Waldau, Chief, *Luftwaffe* Operations Staff, recorded in his diary that "complete tactical surprise" had been achieved, and that he expected "an outstanding success."[13] However, even he could not have dreamed that, by midnight on June 22, the German bombers, divebombers, and fighters would have destroyed 1,811 Soviet aircraft (according to official German figures), with the *Luftwaffe* losing only seventy-eight of its own planes.[14] It was the "greatest numerical success ever achieved in a 24-hour period in the battle between two air forces."[15]

Of course, the *Luftwaffe's* task was made that much easier by the Soviet air force's frightful lack of readiness for battle. In fact, the great majority of the VVS aircraft lost on the first day of the war never even made it into the air—often parked on the ground in neat, tidy rows on their airfields (many of which were close to the front yet still under construction), they were easy targets for the experienced German bomber crews and fighter pilots. Soviet aircrew that did get airborne were hopelessly handicapped by their lack of training, tactical doctrine, and obsolete bombers and fighters. In some cases, Soviet fighter pilots thought better of engaging their more experienced German adversaries in aerial combat, often turning away at considerable range if fired upon; others fought heroically, however, including fifteen Soviet fighter pilots who (suicidally) rammed German aircraft before the day was done as a final gesture of defiance.[16] Soviet bomber forces often displayed remarkable courage in what were little more than suicide missions. As we have seen, many German accounts report streams of VVS bombers heading west, in rigid tactical formations and without air cover, to attack German positions, only to be decimated by the packs of Bf-109s that rose to challenge them, or by well-placed antiaircraft fire.[17] Observing the slaughter firsthand from the second day of the war, Field Marshal Kesselring (C-in-C of 2 Air Fleet) called it "sheer 'infanticide'" (*der reinste "Kindermord"*),[18] while German soldiers watched in awe and fascination as the Soviet bombers tumbled slowly out of the sky. Indeed, the hopelessly one-sided aerial battles that filled the battlespace above them convinced many a *Landser* that victory would be easily come by.

6.1: A Brief Primer on *Luftwaffe* Organization and Combat Aircraft

For Operation *Barbarossa*, the basic *Luftwaffe* table of organization remained the one that had functioned so well in previous campaigns. "German air power was concentrated in a number of *Luftflotten*," or air fleets; in this chapter, we will examine the operations of *Luftflotten* 1, 2, and 4 which, as touched on in the preceding three chapters on ground operations, supported Army Groups North, Center, and South, respectively. (*Luftflotte 5* was a very small air fleet that operated in the far north in support of the German advance toward Murmansk; thus, its activities are beyond the scope of this narrative.) Each of the *Luftflotten* "was a self-contained air force command, analogous to an 'Air Force' within the United States Army Air Forces." In addition, the German air fleets were "operationally independent, and their relationship with the army groups was confined to cooperation and coordination."[19] A *Luftflotte* embraced all types of flying formations (fighter, bomber, divebomber, ground attack, reconnaissance, transport) along with the requisite signal and antiaircraft (flak) units. Each *Luftflotte* controlled one or more *Fliegerkorps* (air corps)— "smaller, multi-purpose air commands" that were also made up of a diverse mixture of flying formations. The composition of *Fliegerkorps V*, assigned to *Luftflotte 4* in the sector of Army Group South, was typical; it encompassed three bomber wings, one fighter wing, and the usual complement of communications, reconnaissance, and transport aircraft.[20]

Within each *Fliegerkorps*, combat power was organized according to mission and type of aircraft. The largest "homogeneous" flying unit was the *Geschwader* (wing), which comprised 90–120 aircraft (at full strength). Each *Geschwader* was, in turn, divided into *Gruppen* of thirty to forty machines. Finally, each *Gruppe* (Group) consisted of several *Staffeln* (squadrons) of twelve to fifteen aircraft each.[21] The main striking force of the *Luftwaffe* was concentrated in its bomber wings (*Kampfgeschwader*), outfitted with Heinkel He-111H/P, Dornier Do-17Z, and Junkers Ju-88A medium bombers—all combat-tested twin-engine designs. The Heinkel He-111 was a truly exquisite and beautifully handling aircraft, aerodynamically efficient, with elliptical wings and a completely glazed and streamlined fuselage nose. Unfortunately, as early as the outbreak of war in September 1939, the Heinkel bomber was on its way toward obsolescence; in particular, it was relatively slow, carried a light bomb-load (4,000+ lbs), and possessed an inadequate defensive suite.[22] In the West, against Britain's Royal Air Force, such shortcomings often proved fatal; yet under the radically different conditions in the East, the He-111 would often operate with devastating effectiveness—for example, on June 22, when waves of the bombers successfully struck cities, towns, airfields, and other key objectives. The Dornier Do-17 was the least modern of the three German medium bombers and had been the most disappointing in service. As a result, it was assigned a limited role in Operation *Barbarossa* as both a bomber and reconnaissance aircraft and would be withdrawn from front-line service by 1942. The sturdy, relatively well-armed Junkers Ju-88 would prove to be the *Luftwaffe*'s "most versatile bomber," and variants would fulfill a variety of different roles. By 1942, however, the speed and defensive armament of the Ju-88 would begin "to fall behind those of its opponents and it became increasingly vulnerable to enemy action."[23]

Complementing the German medium bomber force were the *Stukageschwader*, or divebomber wings, which operated the Ju-87B *Stuka* single-engine divebomber. Despite its slow speed and light armament—rendering it vulnerable to small arms fire—the Ju-87B was the nucleus of the *Luftwaffe*'s close air support (CAS) force for the Russian campaign. In Poland and France, the *Stuka* had become the frightening symbol of the invincible German *Blitzkrieg*, demonstrating its ability to accomplish not only the CAS but the interdiction mission as well. In an era before precision-guided munitions, the *Stuka* was a highly accurate bomber, able to strike its target in a diving attack at an angle of about 70 degrees with an accuracy of less than 30 yards. To enhance the psychological effect on enemy ground troops, the Ju-87B was outfitted with sirens operated by wooden propellers mounted on the craft's undercarriage spats; the pitch and intensity of the noise emitted by these "Jericho Trumpets" also managed to frighten many *Stuka* crews early in their training.[24]

The *Stuka*'s reputation took a beating in the battle of Britain, where its slow top speed of about 370 km/h (230 mph) and lack of defensive armament (several 7.92 MGs) had made it vulnerable to RAF Hurricanes and Spitfires. In Soviet Russia, however, under prevailing conditions of German air superiority, it often performed brilliantly. From June 22 onward, the *Stuka* pilots would maintain an almost inconceivably brutal pace of operations, going for weeks (even months) on end with virtually no rest while flying multiple sorties a day. The physical and psychological toll resulting from endless days of combat, under highly stressful conditions—the noise emitted by the sirens could shatter a crewmember's eardrum—could be catastrophic, culminating in a man's complete nervous collapse.[25] As for the Russians on the receiving end of the divebombers' attacks, they not only feared, they hated the German *Stuka* pilots. As one pilot recalled after the war: "Every time I was shot down behind Russian lines I was always prepared to shoot myself, because I never would have let them take me alive. I had seen the remains of *Stuka* fliers who had been massacred by Russian soldiers, their stomachs slit open, and so on. The Russians really hated *Stuka* crews."[26]

While the German bombers and divebombers were to play an integral part in the spectacular German victories of the summer and fall of 1941, protecting the bomber units and performing the air superiority mission was the responsibility of the Messerschmitt Bf-109 *Jagdgeschwader*. The sleek, single-seat, single-engine Bf-109 fighter was, at its inception, probably the best fighter in the world; by early 1941, it was only outclassed by the British "Spitfire." On June 22, German fighter wings in the East were outfitted with the Bf-109E (*Emil*) and Bf-109F (*Friedrich*) iterations of the aircraft. The "E" model, with a top speed of about 580 km/h (360 mph), featured two wing-mounted 20mm automatic cannon along with two 7.92 machine guns mounted over the engine nacelle. The newer "F" model, which had first appeared in late 1940, boasted a more powerful engine, attaining a top speed of about 625 km/h (390 mph) at 22,000 feet. Designed for precision shooting, the "*Friedrich*" was outfitted with one nose-mounted 15mm or 20mm automatic cannon and two 7.92 MGs. Both versions of the Messerschmitt Bf-109 "were vastly superior to almost all that the Soviets could launch into the air in 1941."[27] When the war began, the majority (thirteen) of the German fighter *Gruppen* in the East had received the newer, swifter Bf-109Fs, while the remainder were equipped with older Bf-109E models.[28]

For the Russian campaign, some Bf-109s were also equipped with bomb racks to perform as fighter-bombers (*Jagdbomber*). Moreover, the Bf-109 now had a new weapon in its arsenal that marked a major increase in the *Luftwaffe's* effectiveness. This was the SD-2 fragmentation bomb (*Splitterbomb*), the first true cluster bomb, which was far more lethal than conventional bombs when employed against ground troops or vehicles out in the open.

> Since each SD-2 was a container of ninety-six bombs that covered an area of a few hundred meters, one aircraft dropping two or three of the canisters could effectively wipe out an entire Soviet road column. The cluster bomb was so effective in the interdiction missions against the Red Army that it was accorded top priority for German munitions production. The U.S. Air Force found the SD-2 such an effective weapon that it copied and produced the bomb after the war; the SD-2 remained in the U.S. inventory as a standard munition into the 1960s.[29]

By June 22, only three fighter groups (and only Bf-109Es) had been equipped with the special mounts under the fuselage to carry the SD-2. Yet despite the weapon's devastating impact, serious problems with its employment became apparent from the onset. Pilots discovered that the suspension of the bomb racks under the fuselage adversely affected aerodynamic performance of the "*Emils*"; in addition, the "air pressure of flight" often caused the first row of bomblets to remain lodged in the bomb rack and fail to release. When the unsuspecting pilot returned to base, and throttled back to land, they "would tumble out one after the other—or wait till he was taxiing and explode just behind his machine." After some planes and pilots were lost, use of the cluster bombs (derisively labeled "Devil's eggs" by the Germans) by the Bf-109E was soon terminated. As it turned out, the SD-2 was employed more effectively by German bombers, which dropped the cluster bombs extensively during 1941. At the start of war with Soviet Russia, the Germans possessed an inventory of 2,298,500 of the SD-2 bomblets.[30]

In the *Luftwaffe's* order of battle in the East, the German fighter *Geschwader* were augmented by a small number of Messerschmitt Bf-110 *Zerstörer* (destroyer) aircraft.[31] While this twin-engine heavy fighter and light bomber was a personal favorite of Air Marshal Göring, that didn't keep it from getting badly mauled over the British Isles in the summer of 1940, when it proved to be "too heavy and too slow for modern fighter combat." Although it was heavily armed with two 20mm automatic cannon and five 7.92 machine guns (four in the nose, plus an aft machine gun), the heavy fighter had a poor turn radius and slow acceleration, making it easy prey for the RAF. The situation became so alarming that all Bf-110s were eventually withdrawn from the Channel coast. Once again, however, it would be a different story in the East, where the aircraft's range, top speed (ca. 550 km/h or 340 mph), varied weapon load, and ability to sustain serious battle damage gave it a new lease on life.[32]

In conclusion, the *"Luftwaffe* in 1941 was a formidable force"—well trained and equipped, highly experienced, doctrinally sound, and sublimely confident in its ability to accomplish the mission. Moreover, "the command organization of the German air force allowed for tremendous flexibility. Units could be transferred rapidly across vast sections of the front. An efficient signals network greatly eased the task of command and control of the scattered formations, thereby allowing the concentration of air power at any decisive point."[33] On June 22, 1941 (and in the days and weeks that followed), these and many other advantages would be fully exploited by the *Luftwaffe*, while the service's serious shortcomings—most significantly, a force structure simply too small to cover the burgeoning number of tasks it would be asked to perform in the endless spaces of the East—would only later become apparent.

6.2: *LUFTWAFFE* OPERATIONS IN SUPPORT OF ARMY GROUP NORTH

The two infantry armies (16, 18) and panzer group (4) of Field Marshal von Leeb's Army Group North were supported by the *Luftwaffe*'s 1 Air Fleet (*Luftflotte 1*), commanded by the fifty-eight-year-old *Generaloberst* Alfred Keller (headquarters in Norkitten, west of Gumbinnen). His chief of staff was *Generalmajor* von Wühlisch. In October 1939, Keller had assumed command of 4 Air Corps, which he led with "considerable success" in Poland and France, although he was "badly beaten" in the battle of Britain. While he was more adept at training and organization than as a tactical commander, he was appointed C-in-C of 1 Air Fleet on August 20, 1940; only weeks before, he had been promoted to the rank of *Generaloberst*.[34]

The reader will recall that Keller's air fleet was far and away the smallest of the three supporting the army groups on the main front from the Baltic to the Black Sea. The only flying formations assigned to the air fleet were: 1 Air Corps (*Fliegerkorps 1*) under *Generalleutnant* Helmuth Förster; and the Air Leader Baltic (*Fliegerführer Ostsee*), led by *Oberstleutnant* Wolfgang von Wild and responsible for naval targets. All told, Keller's 1 Air Fleet possessed just 592 front-line and transport aircraft, of which 453 were combat ready on June 22. Among the air fleet's operational aircraft were 211 bombers, 167 fighters, and 22 transports.[35] The fleet's order of battle is outlined below (aircraft types flown by the units—as far as I was able to ascertain them—are in bold type):

1 Air Fleet

Long-Range Recce Squadron 2 (C-in-C Luftwaffe) (**Do-215**)

Weather Observation Squadron 1 (**misc.**)

Air Transport Group 106 (**Ju-52**)

1 Air Corps

*Squadron 5, Long-Range Recce Group (*Gruppe*) 122 (5.(F)/122)*

*Staff 1 Bomber Wing (KG 1), with II and III Groups (***Ju-88A***)*

*Staff 76 Bomber Wing (KG 76), with I, II, and III Groups (***Ju-88A***)*

*Staff 77 Bomber Wing (KG 77), with I, II, and III Groups (***Ju-88A***)*

*Staff 54 Fighter Wing (JG 54), with I, II, and III Groups (***Bf-109***)*

*II Group, 53 Fighter Wing (II./JG 53) (without Squadron 6) (***Bf-109F***)*

Air Leader Baltic

Recce Group 125 (1., 2., 3. (F)/125) (**He-59, He-114,** *and* **Ar-95***)*

Coastal Air Group 806 (**Ju-88A***)*

Sea Rescue Squadron 9 (**He-59***)*

Air District 1 *(*Königsberg*)*

*Replacement Fighter Training Group 52 (JG 52) (***Bf-109E***)*

*Replacement Fighter Training Group 54 (JG 54) (***Bf-109E***)*[36]

The basic mission of *Generaloberst* Keller's 1 Air Fleet was to provide air support for Army Group North as it advanced from East Prussia across the Dvina River toward Leningrad. The objectives of the air fleet at the start of the campaign were: (a) rapidly gain air superiority by destroying Soviet airfields and aircraft; (b) provide fighter protection for the advancing ground forces; (c) interdict Soviet rail and road traffic between the Nemen and the Dvina Rivers; (d) directly and indirectly support the ground forces with bombers; and (e) attack the Soviet Baltic Fleet at sea and its bases with bombs and mines, while tying up merchant shipping in the Baltic. Within these basic parameters, the three bomber wings and lone fighter wing of Förster's 1 Air Corps were to focus their efforts in support of Hoepner's 4 Panzer Group as it began its drive toward Leningrad some 700 kilometers to the northeast ("as the crow flies"). The mission of the Bf-109s of 1 Air Corps' 54 Fighter Wing (*Jagdgeschwader 54*) was fourfold: (a) clear the airspace of enemy aircraft; (b) perform escort duty for bomber squadrons; (c) conduct general sweeps of the ground for targets, or the skies for enemy aircraft, an activity known in the idiom of the German fighter pilot as "*freie Jadg*" (free chases); and (d) conduct low-level attacks on enemy columns and, at a later time, contest enemy shipping in the Baltic Sea. Yet to discharge its many taskings, Keller's air fleet—with the exception of two Ju-88A bomber *Gruppen* outfitted to drop fragmentation bombs—had not been allocated any close-combat forces.[37]

The responsibilities of the Air Leader Baltic were equally ambitious. He had the "duty of guarding the coastal flank and keeping it safe from surprise attacks by Soviet surface or submarine naval units; he also had to mine the ports of Kronstadt and Leningrad, as well as the Neva as far as Shlisselburg, and later the White Sea Canal, and was required to operate against the locks on Lake Onega, protect convoy traffic in the Baltic [Sea] east of 13° [East longitude], and support the army in the seizure of the Baltic islands." The command authority in charge of the ground organization of 1 Air Fleet was Air District 1 in Königsberg (now Kaliningrad).[38]

At about 0300 hours, as the first shafts of sunlight lifted over the horizon in the east, hundreds of *Luftwaffe* fighters, bombers, and divebombers crossed the Russo-German frontier all along the 1,800-kilometer front[39]—"the bombers, to preserve the advantage of surprise, at operating ceiling even ahead of the army's attack."[40] The weather was ideal for flying—generally cloudless with just moderate ground haze throughout the morning hours. In waves, the attacking aircraft struck their targets in both high- and low-level attacks. Among the primary targets were more than sixty Soviet airfields, many of them just inside the border; in some cases, bomber squadrons carrying the SD-2 fragmentation bombs burst upon the Russian airfields at altitudes of 25 meters to drop their loads, leaving behind the burning, twisted wreckage of Soviet aircraft. Other bomber units moved in a wider arc deep into Soviet territory to strike cities and other targets as far afield as Sevastopol, Kiev, and Minsk, leaving "great flashes of fire and destruction" in their wake.[41]

Attacking *Luftwaffe* squadrons also strafed or dropped bombs on suspected quarters of Red Army staffs, soldiers' barracks, artillery positions, bunkers, ammunition depots, and oil storage facilities. Attacks on airfields were made much easier because the Soviets had done little to protect them. As a rule, the air bases were without antiaircraft protection. Astonished German pilots discovered some of the Russian planes uncamouflaged and parked wingtip to wingtip on their aprons, making them the easiest of targets. Few of the Russian planes made it into the air, not only because so many were smashed on the ground, but because ground crews—and the pilots themselves—were often asleep in their tents when the assault began. Those VVS fighters and bombers that did get airborne— without radios, without command and control (C2), and without modern tactics—were obliterated by squadrons of Bf-109 fighters that rose up to challenge them.[42] The nimble Bf-109s, emblazoned with their bold yellow (Russian) theater markings, were equally adept at obliterating Red Army forces on the ground. Aerial photographs snapped by *Luftwaffe* aircrew often depicted staggering scenes of death and destruction, with the twisted, charred remains of vehicles, artillery, men, horses, and equipment littering the roadways leading off from the frontier.[43]

As noted in the war diary of Army Group North, the first wave of Keller's 1 Air Fleet consisted of seventy-six Ju-88A bombers and ninety Bf-109 fighters, the latter operating from bases close to the frontier due to their limited range; together, they set out for seven Soviet airfields earmarked for destruction,[44] German air and ground reconnaissance having established a "clear picture of the condition of the Soviet flying forces, their strength, their composition, and the garrisoning of their bases.[45] On the ground, soldiers of 6 Panzer Division looked on as "wave after wave" of German fighters and bombers disappeared into the mists beyond the border. Far to the north, Air Leader Baltic began to deposit minefields in the waters about Leningrad and the Soviet naval base at Kronstadt, while also conducting attacks on enemy shipping in the Baltic Sea.[46] As a result of "teething problems" with new models of VVS aircraft just entering service, the front-line airfields in Lithuania were packed with aircraft of all types (both old and new), because the airfield construction program had not kept pace with the need to shelter such vast numbers of planes[47]—a state of affairs that rendered their destruction that much more inevitable.

It is thus hardly surprising that, to some of the airmen of 1 Air Fleet's 1 Bomber Wing (the "*Hindenburg*" wing), the first raid seemed like little more than a "gunnery training exercise." The first target of the Ju-88As of III./KG 1 was the airfield in Liepaja (Libau), on the Baltic coast nearly 200 kilometers from the bomber group's base in East Prussia. Recalled *Hauptmann* Gerhard Baeker, the group's technical officer: "At 0211 we took off on our first mission against the east. It was a clear night and the horizon was bright from the midnight sun in the far north. Our target was the airfield [Liepaja] in Lithuania. The base was occupied by a fighter unit, and its so-called [I-16] Ratas stood parked in nice, tight rows, offering us a good target in the bright night." The German medium bombers loosed their bombs onto "long rows of completely uncamouflaged aircraft standing in close formation as though on parade along the edges of [Liepaja] airfield," stated *Hauptmann* Manfred von Cossart, another participant in the raid that morning. The bomber group successfully fulfilled its mission and returned to base "undramatically" shortly before 0400 hours.[48]

Other Ju-88As of Keller's air fleet, escorted by *Major* Hannes Trautloft and Bf-109s of his JG 54, struck the Kaunas Airdrome in Lithuania early that morning, once again with telling effect:

> *Just as the bombers came in over the large grass-covered airfield, the sun rose above the horizon and cast its bright rays on the deadly birds. Trautloft watched as the fragmentation bombs exploded in devastating series among the double lines of neatly parked Soviet aircraft. Here dozens of I-153s of [13 Fighter Aviation Regiment] were turned into scrap within minutes. Only two airborne I-153s appeared in front of the attacking aircraft, but they left as quickly as they came. Returning from this raid, the* Luftwaffe *air crews reported seventy Soviet planes put out of commission.*[49]

As the Bf-109s and Ju-88s of the first wave returned to their bases, leaving in their wake blazing airfields and dozens of shattered Soviet planes, the aircraft of Keller's second wave were already over their targets. This went on all through the day, hour after hour. After landing, the aircraft were rapidly rearmed and refueled, then dispatched on new strikes against the Soviet airfields. At 0900 hours, the bombers of III./KG 1 lifted off for their second mission against Liepaja airfield. This time, they encountered antiaircraft fire and Soviet I-16 fighters, but only a few of the Soviet pilots dared to attack: "They came in individually, opened fire when still 550 yards distant, and attempted to escape in a dive as soon as their fire was returned." All of the German bombers returned safely to their base without battle damage.[50]

As briefly addressed in Chapter 3, Soviet bombers also attempted to strike targets inside East Prussia throughout June 22. At 0538 hours, the Bf-109Fs of II./JG 53, stationed near Tilsit, received the alarm that enemy bombers were approaching and responded with alacrity.[51]

All available fighters were scrambled and met a formation of the SB twin-engine bombers from [a Soviet high-speed bomber regiment]. At 0552, Hauptmann *Walter Spies shot down the first SB. In minutes, eight of the vulnerable Soviet bombers fell in flames. Following the escaping remainder of the Soviet formation, a desperate cry was suddenly heard over the German R/T: "My engine is hit, I'm wounded!" It was the voice of* Hauptmann *Heinz Bretnütz, one of the top aces of the* Luftwaffe *at that time. Bretnütz made a belly landing in enemy territory and was lucky to be hidden by friendly local people. But this could not save his life. Recovered by advancing German troops on June 26, this victor in thirty-seven aerial duels died of his wounds on the following day.*[52]

By midday, the sleek, fast Ju-88As[53] of *Luftflotte 1* had destroyed nearly a hundred Russian aircraft on the ground, while also targeting Siauliai, the Baltic ports of Tallinn and Riga, and Soviet command and control facilities; even the headquarters of Col.-Gen. F. I. Kuznetsov, Commander, Soviet Northwestern Front, was struck by the bombers, disrupting the *front*'s communications. The net effect of the *Luftwaffe* attacks on high-level Soviet communications was to throttle the flow of information to and from the front, seriously delaying the promulgation of key orders and directives to the troops. When Kuznetsov launched counterattacks with his two mechanized corps over the next few days, he would do so "without knowing where the advancing German forces were actually located or headed." The outcome was predictable.[54]

Throughout the day, Keller's fighters and bombers maintained a torrid pace of operations, flying multiple missions that also targeted Soviet ground forces in an effort to clear the way for the tanks of Hoepner's 4 Panzer Group. The Soviet 125 Rifle Division, which stood directly in the path of Hoepner's tanks, came under heavy air attack, as did the long, strung-out columns of 48 Rifle Division, which was attempting to move south and into position behind 125 RD.[55] (See, Section 3.3.) Moreover, tens of thousands of

Soviet citizens of non-Baltic origin, who had been engaged in sovietizing and russifying the recently acquired Baltic states, suffered serious losses from air attack as they sought to flee on the few available roads back to the Soviet Union, disrupting movements of Red Army reserves as they did so.[56] Air attacks such as this by German fighter planes on columns of civilians attempting to escape the battlefields are well documented in both German and Soviet accounts.

At 2340 hours, *Generalmajor* von Wühlisch, Chief of Staff, 1 Air Fleet, telephoned his counterpart at Army Group North, informing him that the operations of his air fleet had resulted in the destruction of 185 Soviet aircraft—forty-five shot down in aerial combat, 140 destroyed on the ground. Wühlisch also reported that, at 1530 hours, elements of the air fleet, alerted by aerial reconnaissance,[57] had conducted low-level attacks against a column of 150–200 Red Army tanks and vehicles west and southwest of Siauliai, destroying forty of them in the process.[58] Conversely, sporadic attempts of the Soviet air force to conduct attacks of their own were without success.

In a study completed in December 1953 by former *Luftwaffe* general Hermann Plocher for the U.S. Air Force, the author outlined the results of the start of the Russian campaign for Keller's 1 Air Fleet:

> In [Army Group] North, the opening attacks of 1 Air Fleet units took the Russians completely by surprise. A great part of the Soviet flying units were destroyed by these attacks and by those that took place during the following few days. Assessments made after the capture of the area yielded the same picture of tremendous destruction as had been found in [the sectors of Army Group Center and Army Group South]. Many hundreds of wrecked aircraft were found, mostly I-16 Rata fighters but also numerous so-called Martin bombers (SB-3s), burned out and torn to shreds on the airfields that had been plowed up thoroughly by German bombs of all sizes. The field installations, mostly of wood construction, were burned or otherwise destroyed. As a result, the Luftwaffe construction troops and the [Reich] Labor Service (Reichsarbeitsdienst) battalions later had to work long and hard to restore these airfields and to remove the gigantic quantities of debris.
>
> Through these annihilating blows, 1 Air Fleet achieved air superiority within the first few days in its zone of operations and induced the Russians to transfer their remaining air units behind the Dvina River. Then, the emphasis in air fleet operations shifted to the support of Army Group North's advance toward the Dvina, with the main effort over the sectors of the armored spearhead of 4 Panzer Group . . . The 1 Air Corps performed particularly valuable service to the ground forces by shattering a Soviet counterattack, heavily supported by tanks, in the area south and southwest of Siauliai. In close cooperation with the Army, the air arm destroyed more than 250 tanks.
>
> From the beginning of the Russian campaign, single planes and formations of planes of the enemy flew over East Prussian territory. These were so effectively met by

German antiaircraft artillery and fighters that after some three to four days no substantial penetration by Soviet aircraft occurred . . . The superiority of German fighters over Soviet bombers was especially impressive when an entire formation of 20 enemy bombers, returning from a largely ineffective attack on Gumbinnen, was intercepted and shot down between Gumbinnen and Goldap by a fighter group based at Trakehnen.[59]

6.3: *LUFTWAFFE* OPERATIONS IN SUPPORT OF ARMY GROUP CENTER

The two infantry armies (4, 9) and two panzer groups (2, 3) of Fedor von Bock's Army Group Center were supported by the *Luftwaffe's* 2 Air Fleet (*Luftflotte 2*), commanded by the fifty-five-year-old GFM Albert Kesselring (headquarters just outside Warsaw). Serving him as chief of staff was *Obst.i.G.* Hans Seidemann. Known as "smiling Albert," Kesselring was "an extremely able and popular commander."[60] At the helm of 1 Air Fleet during the Polish campaign, he "brilliantly" supported Bock's Army Group North. For the campaign in the West, he was given command of 2 Air Fleet, which he also led with great distinction, leading to his promotion to *Generalfeldmarschall* on July 19, 1940.[61] As the commander of 2 Air Fleet in Russia, Kesselring would cultivate a close relationship with Bock, working harmoniously with the Army Group Center commander and cheerfully accepting his supporting role.[62]

A military leader of genuine strategic aptitude, Kesselring soon came to the conclusion that the forces assigned to his 2 Air Fleet for Operation *Barbarossa* were altogether inadequate. Shortly before the start of the campaign, he took his concerns to Air Marshal Göring, as he described in his memoir:

At the beginning of 1941, I flew to Warsaw to confer with the commander-in-chief there, Field Marshal von Kluge, and to issue supplementary instructions about expanding the ground organization in that area. I went back again in May 1941 to patrol the deployment base for my air fleet in the East, and found that the work could not be completed before the beginning of June (primarily due to weather and ground conditions), but still with enough time for the rescheduled X-Tag (June 22) to be met. The operational and tactical inspections revealed that the attack by Army Group Center could not be supported to the best possible extent with the forces allotted me by the Commander-in-Chief of the Luftwaffe. *In a heated exchange in Göring's command train north of Paris, and with the support of my dear Jeschonnek ([Göring's] chief of staff), I succeeded in pressing my case and I was promised the minimum reinforcements of aircraft and flak troops that had been requested.*

I could sympathize with the irate Reichsmarschall *when he said that I was not the only one making demands, that England still had to be fought. But I had to insist that he appreciate my point of view that an attack should not be started if the forces necessary for it could not be assembled.*[63]

Field Marshal Kesselring did not depart the Channel coast—from where he was conducting the German air campaign against Great Britain—until June 12 or 13, heading first to Berlin for the final pre-*Barbarossa* conference. According to official German pronouncements, however, he was still with his bombers in the West, where bogus German wireless traffic sought to convey the impression that certain *Luftwaffe* units were still operating against England, instead of redeploying to the East. Several days later Kesselring flew on from Berlin, landing at an airfield outside Warsaw, where he joined his headquarters staff and threw himself into his final preparations for the impending air campaign.[64]

As briefly discussed in Chapter 4 (Section 4.1), Kesselring's 2 Air Fleet was the largest of the three *Luftflotten* assigned to the primary theater of operations (i.e., between the Baltic and the Black Sea). As noted, his air fleet began the war with Russia with 1,367 aircraft, of which 994 were combat ready, the latter including: 222 bombers, 323 divebombers,[65] 60 destroyers, and 284 fighter aircraft. In addition to the combat aircraft were some 200 operational reconnaissance and courier planes (tactically controlled by Bock's Army Group Center). The 2 Air Fleet consisted of two air corps—2 Air Corps, under Air General (*General der Flieger*) Bruno Loerzer, stationed on airfields in the Warsaw–Brest-Litovsk–Deblin area; and 8 Air Corps, led by Air General Wolfram *Freiherr* von Richthofen, with its airfields in the Suwalki triangle. Nearly all of the Ju-87B *Stuka* divebombers assembled in the East were massed under this air fleet, with the majority of them assigned to Richthofen's air corps. In addition, three bomber, one divebomber, one destroyer, and two fighter *Gruppen* of 8 Air Corps were outfitted with devices for dropping the 2-kg SD-2 fragmentation bombs. As Bock's Army Group Center began its advance across the frontier, Loerzer's air corps was to support Fourth Army and, more particularly, Guderian's 2 Panzer Group, while Richthofen's air corps cooperated with Ninth Army and the panzer spearheads of Hoth's 3 Panzer Group. Also controlled by Kesselring's air fleet was 1 Flak Corps (*Generalmajor* Walther von Axthelm), which was to support the armored forces during their penetration of the frontier fortifications and in subsequent operations.[66] The 2 Air Fleet's extensive order of battle is listed below:

2 Air Fleet

Staff Long-Range Recce Group 122, with Squadron 2 (2.(F)/122) **(Ju-88A, Bf-110, Bf-109E***)*

*Weather Operations Squadron 26 (***Bf-110, Do-17Z, He-111H***)*

*Staff 53 Fighter Wing (JG 53), with I and III Groups (***Bf-109F***)*

*Fighter Training Group 51(***Bf-109E?***)*

2 Air Corps

Squadron 1, Long-Range Recce Group 122 (1.(F)/122) **(Ju-88A, Bf-110***)*

Air Transport Group 102 **(Ju-52***?)*

Staff 210 Fast Bomber Wing (SKG 210), with I and II Groups **(Bf-110***)*

Staff 3 Bomber Wing (KG 3), with I, II, and III Groups **(Do-17Z, Ju-88A***)*

Staff 53 Bomber Wing (KG 53), with I, II, and III Groups **(He-111H, He-111P***)*

Staff 77 Divebomber Wing (StG 77), with I, II, and III Groups **(Ju-87B, Bf-110***)*

Staff 51 Fighter Wing (JG 51), with I, II, III, and IV Groups **(Bf-109F***)*

8 Air Corps

Squadron 2, Long-Range Recce Group 11 (2.(F)/11) **(Do-17P***)*

Air Transport Group 1 **(Ju-52***?)*

Staff 2 Bomber Wing (KG 2), with I, II, and III Groups **(Do-17Z***)*[67]

Staff 1 Divebomber Wing (StG 1), with II and III Groups **(Ju-87B***)*

Staff 2 Divebomber Wing (StG 2), with I and III Groups **(Ju-87B, Ju-87R, Bf-110***)*

II Group, 2 Training Wing (LG 2) **(Bf-109E***)*

Squadron 10, 2 Training Wing (LG 2) **(Hs-123A***)*

Staff 26 "Destroyer" Wing (ZG 26), with I and II Groups **(Bf-110***)*

Staff 27 Fighter Wing (JG 27), with II and III Groups **(Bf-109E***)*

II Group, 52 Fighter Wing (JG 52) **(Bf-109E, Bf-109F***)*

Air District 2 *(Posen)*

Replacement "Destroyer" Training Group 26 (ZG 26) **(Bf-110***)*

Replacement Fighter Training Group 51 (JG 51) **(Bf-109E***)*[68]

As the 2 Air Fleet's order of battle illustrates, Richthofen's 8 Air Corps was the larger of the fleet's two air corps. The 8 Air Corps had been heavily engaged in the recent capture of the island of Crete, with the result that it had little time to accomplish its transfer to the East and properly prepare for the impending Russian campaign (as Richthofen would complain to his diary). Not until June 19 did it deploy to its bases in the East from deep inside Germany, where it had replenished supplies and taken on new aircraft and aircrew. Still, 8 Air Corps would begin Operation *Barbarossa* short of some 600 motor vehicles, vital spare parts, and communications equipment, and with its air units at a 70 percent operational rate or even lower. Yet despite all transport and logistical problems, the air corps—the only dedicated close air support (CAS) formation in the *Luftwaffe*—was ready to perform its mission on *Barbarossatag*.[69]

The operations of Kesselring's *Luftflotte 2* got underway at 0300 hours, when thirty He-111 and Do-17 medium bombers (elements of KG 2, KG 3, and KG 53), flying in groups of three and manned by hand-picked crews with night-flying experience, crossed the Russo-German frontier at high altitude and headed for Soviet fighter bases between Belostok and Minsk and other key targets along the line of advance of Army Group Center. By 0315 hours, the bombers were coming in at low level, disgorging hundreds of SD-2 fragmentation bombs from their open bomb bays. The 2-kilogram bombs burst among the rows of Soviet aircraft, which were uncamouflaged and arranged wingtip to wingtip on their airfields, with personnel tents located nearby. A flurry of rapid explosions soon engulfed the rows of aircraft; airframes were shredded and fuel tanks punctured, the latter evoking multiple fireballs that tossed columns of dense black smoke up into the dawn sky. In the attendant chaos, dazed ground crews struggled frantically to put out the fires but were frustrated by delayed-action explosions. With no instructions from superior headquarters, each base coped as best it could.[70]

As the sun rose, these initial attacks were followed by the main body of the Kesselring's *Luftwaffe* strike force, consisting of hundreds of medium bombers, divebombers, fighters, and destroyer aircraft. Here, too, the weather was ideal—warm and sunny with hardly a cloud in the sky. While the paramount objectives were—as they were for the *Luftwaffe* all along the front—the destruction of the enemy air forces and the establishment of air superiority, a wide array of targets were struck in the opening assault. In addition to thirty-one airfields, these targets embraced: trains and railway cars (the Germans using incendiary bullets to destroy cars filled with fuel), gasoline and grain warehouses, fuel dumps, barracks, and bunkers. Suspected locations of senior Red Army staff were also targeted from the air, including the headquarters of Soviet 4 Army, obliterated by Ju-88 bombers at the very start of the German attack.[71] *Stuka* divebombers launched precision attacks on tanks, trucks, bridges, bunkers, fieldworks, artillery, antiaircraft sites, and other targets, while the bombers of 2 and 8 Air Corps showered cities and towns across the central front—among them, Kalvaria, Alytus, Belostok, Grodno, Vilnius, Lida, Volkovysk, Slonin, Brest-Litovsk, Kobrin, Novy Dvor, and Pinsk—with high explosive and incendiary bombs.[72]

Although *Luftwaffe* historians "tend to highlight the daring annihilation of stationary aircraft, it is worth noting what they did to towns."[73] Recalled a Russian historian who survived a raid on Minsk two days later:

> *I saw it myself, a [large group] of 96 aircraft flying over Minsk. They bombed the town all day long. The entire center was destroyed. Only a couple of large buildings were left*

standing. Everything else in the center was in ruins. When this bombing began that morning I was in the Pedagogical Institute. We were at work. During the bombardment we crept into the cellar. And then, when we came out, what did we see there! Burning houses, ashes, ruins. And corpses were everywhere in the streets. People wanted to get out of the town during the bombing. But they could not flee quickly enough since the streets were jam packed. And those that were outside were mown down by low-flying German aircraft.[74]

At 0730, Soviet 3 Army reported that, since 0300 hours, German aircraft had attacked in waves of 305 aircraft every twenty to thirty minutes—"they are bombing Grodno and Sopotskin, and in particular army headquarters." While the report no doubt grossly exaggerates the extent of German air activity in the 3 Army's area of operations (after all, Kesselring's air fleet possessed less than 1,000 operational planes to cover its entire zone of attack), it offers subjective Soviet proof of the enormous and unremitting ferocity of German 2 Air Fleet operations on this day and the panic and confusion they evoked among those on the receiving end.[75]

Additional Soviet reports on German air activity along the central front underscore the observations of 3 Army and offer further insight into the relentless nature of the German air campaign. According to an official Soviet combat report issued at 0600, German bombers had struck Grodno twice by 0416 hours, while small groups of Do-17s had bombed Lida twice by 0536 hours. German aircraft also targeted a passenger train at the Lida-Gav'ya station with bombs and strafing attacks—"10 people were wounded and the train is burning." The report also noted that Belostok and Bielsk Podlaski had been bombed, resulting in the destruction of an air observation and warning station at the latter location. The Germans savagely bombed Kobrin—one attack taking place at 0710 hours with up to thirty aircraft, followed by a series of further strikes between 0856 and 1220 hours with up to ten bombers at a time. Another report, early that afternoon, stated that "the bombing of Grodno, Lida, Kobrin and Belostok is continuing." And yet another report: "Throughout [June 22] Grodno and Lida were subjected to methodical bombing every 5–10 minutes, mainly the airfields. The Grodno bridge and electrical station have been destroyed."[76]

Depending on the distance of their bases from the front, the fighters, bombers, dive-bombers, and destroyer aircraft of Kesselring's 2 and 8 Air Corps (and those of all the air corps in the East) would fly from four to eight sorties each on June 22—an extraordinary operational tempo that the German aircrew would maintain in the days, weeks, and months ahead. These "astonishing figures [were] attributable to the simplicity of the machines, the often short distances that had to be covered, the excellence of the ground crew organization (including a specially developed apparatus that allowed nine aircraft to be refueled simultaneously), and the unparalleled determination of the crews."[77] Thus even by conservative estimates, 2 Air Fleet must have logged a minimum of 4,000 sorties on the first day of the Russian campaign.

Crossing the frontier along the 500-kilometer front of GFM von Bock's Army Group Center, Kesselring's 2 and 8 Air Corps struck any and all VVS bases that could threaten the advance of the ground forces. The 2 Air Fleet, of course, possessed many more combat aircraft than its neighbor to the north (1 Air Fleet) and the results were correspondingly greater. At the Varena airfield, southwest of Vilnius, a Bf-109F squadron of III./JG 53 (the "*Pik As*" or "Ace of Spades" fighter wing) destroyed seven Soviet bombers on the ground,[78] but this was barely a beginning. In the sector of Loerzer's 2 Air Corps, Bf-110s of I./SKG 210, led by *Major* Storp, flew the first of one hundred sorties they would carry out on June 22 with devastating effect against enemy airfields. Lifting off from their bases near Warsaw, the He-111s of KG 53 ("*Legion Condor*") flew over the Bug at 0415 hours and struck an airfield close to the border, damaging the runway and leaving at least fifteen Soviet fighters in flames.[79]

On the left wing of Army Group Center, Richthofen's 8 Air Corps launched its fighters, bombers, and divebombers from a cluster of bases within and outside the Suwalki triangle, the air corps commander focusing his attention on the Soviet 9 and 11 Composite Aviation Divisions (CAD). At the Grodno Airdrome, just as a clutch of I-16 fighters attempted to get airborne, a formation of Messerschmitts swooped down and showered them with fragmentation bombs, destroying all of the Soviet planes "in perfect take-off formation at the end of the runway"; all told, the well-timed attack demolished sixty-five of the seventy-five I-16s (all belonging to the 11 CAD) at the Grodno Airdrome. In another successful foray, Bf-109Es of II./JG 27 dropped SD-2 fragmentation bombs on airfields at Dorubanok (near Vilnius), wiping out some eighty planes on the ground.[80]

The Soviet 9 Composite Aviation Division, stationed in the Belostok area not far from the attacking armor of Hoth's 3 Panzer Group, suffered even worse. The 9 CAD was an elite unit, led by Hero of the Soviet Union General-Mayor Sergey Chernykh, a veteran of the Spanish Civil War who had shot down several Loyalist planes, including the first Bf-109 ever to be lost in combat. According to the results of an inspection carried out on the eve of the German attack, Chernykh's command was one of the finest in the entire Soviet air force—its four fighter regiments outfitted with 233 modern MiG-3 fighters (and only 156 obsolete fighters), while its bomber regiment included twenty-two experimental twin-engine Ar-2 divebombers (based on a modification of the SB "high-speed bomber"). Unfortunately, Chernykh's command had the misfortune of being thrashed by both *Fliegerkorps* of 2 Air Fleet, and sustained heavier losses than any other VVS unit on this very bloody Sunday. Simply put, all of 9 CAD's airfields were targeted by the unremitting German aerial *Blitzkrieg*. In his diary, *Leutnant* Arnold Döring, an He-111 pilot in KG 53 of Loerzer's 2 Air Corps, described the initial raid on a 9 CAD airfield at Dolubovo (south of Belostok):

The ground below is covered with haze, but the targets nevertheless are clearly visible. I am surprised that we are not met with any counteraction. This will come as a surprise to those below!

The "eggs" are released. Piles of fire and smoke, fountains of earth and dust, mixed with wreckage parts of all kinds, are shooting vertically upward. Unfortunately, our bomb rows lay to the right side of the ammunition bunkers. But a whole row of bombs goes down across the entire field and plows the runway. The take-off strip receives two hits. As the formation makes a turn I can see fifteen of the parked fighters go up in flames, plus most of the living quarters. Toni cries: "Antiaircraft fire," but we could only see one single shot more than half a mile behind us. We are already out of their shooting range. Then there is a fearsome cry over the radio: "Fighters from behind!" Our machine guns rattle. The formation tightens up. Of course, we offer a large target to the Russians, but our defensive fire is most concentrated. Bullet tracers from twenty-seven planes sprinkle against the Russians, who immediately decide to disappear diving.[81]

Throughout the day, extraordinary results were often achieved by single German bomber pilots, as was the case in the sector of 2 Air Corps, which relentlessly pressed home its attacks against both 9 and 10 Composite Aviation Divisions on the right wing of Army Group Center. In one of these attacks, a single Ju-88A piloted by *Leutnant* Ernst-Wilhelm Ihrig, commander of 3./KG 3 (the "*Blitz*" bomber wing), conducted six low-level sweeps against Pinsk Airdrome and claimed the destruction of sixty Soviet planes on the ground; VVS losses at the airdrome included forty-three SB bombers and five Pe-2 twin-engine bombers.[82]

At Brest-Litovsk Airdrome, Bf-109s in a fighter-bomber role destroyed twenty aircraft of a fighter aviation regiment belonging to the 10 Composite Aviation Division on their first mission. During a second raid against the same target, nine Bf-109s made strafing attacks for nearly forty minutes, rendering an additional twenty-one I-16 Rata fighters and five I-153 fighter/ground attack biplanes *hors de combat*. One squadron (1./SKG 210) of Bf-110s annihilated another fifty of 10 CAD's aircraft at Kobrin, location of the headquarters of both 10 CAD and 4 Army. By the end of the day, the 10 Composite Aviation Division had lost 180 of its 231 aircraft, with two of its air regiments having been totally wiped out. As for its part, *Schnellkampfgeschwader 210* (SKG 210) had logged a total of thirteen attacks on fourteen airfields (with several aircrew flying six separate missions), destroying according to its own reports no fewer than 344 Soviet planes on the ground and eight more in the air on this fateful Sunday.[83]

Despite the devastating success of Kesselring's 2 Air Fleet against Soviet air bases, the results of actual aerial combat on this day were not always so inexorably one-sided. On more than a few occasions, Soviet fighter planes gave as good as they got, while German fighter and fighter-bomber pilots encountered "unexpected difficulties" in dealing with their more agile Russian opponents:

For though the Russian I-153 and I-15 biplanes, their small and stubby Curtisses and I-16 Ratas, with their fat radial engines, were all much slower than the Messerschmitts, they were also much more maneuverable. In the words of Leutnant *Schiess, of JG 53's staff flight: "They would let us get almost into an aiming position, then bring their machines around a full 180 degrees, till both aircraft were firing at each other from head-on." JG 53's* Kommodore, *Major von Maltzahn, became so mad with frustration because again and again his opponent could turn out of his line of fire at the last moment and he himself kept grossly over-shooting.*[84]

At 9:15 in the morning, a formation of Bf-110s confronted a group of Soviet fighters near Zambrova, at the Russo-German border in Poland. Only this time the Russians were not only flying I-16s but modern MiG-3s belonging to a fighter aviation regiment of the "crack" 9 Composite Aviation Division.

Three Soviet fighters and two Bf 110s went down in flames. Having run out of ammunition (which was quite common among the Soviet fighter pilots due to their instruction to fire extremely long bursts), Mladshiy Leytenant *[Second Lieutenant] Dmitriy Kokorev cut the rudders of a third Bf 110 into pieces with the propeller of his MiG-3. The German plane went down and crashed into the ground while Kokorev managed to bring his damaged plane home to a successful landing at Vysoke-Mazovetsk Airdrome. This Soviet airman was awarded the Order of the Red Banner for the taran [air-to-air ramming]. He carried out another hundred sorties and achieved a total victory score of five before being shot down and killed in October 1941.*[85]

Another "taran" victim on this first day of the war was *Major* Wolfgang Schellmann, a Knight's Cross holder and commander of JG 27 (8 Air Corps). Schellmann had cut his teeth during the Spanish Civil War, where he had fought on the side of Franco's Loyalists and shot down twelve Republican aircraft, many of Soviet manufacture. Before the invasion of Soviet Russia, he had registered another thirteen aerial victories. On this day, however, he was suddenly engaged near Grodno in a series of aerial dogfights. After shooting down an I-16 fighter, he was rammed by a tenacious I-153 biplane piloted by *Leytenant* Petr Kuzmin. After repeated attempts, Kuzmin had managed to plow into the fuselage of his adversary's Bf-109E, dying instantly as a result. Schellmann, however, was able to bail out successfully. While nothing definitive is known of his fate, on June 28 *Pravda* carried a story about the capture of a German fighter pilot—and holder of the Knight's Cross—by the name of Franz Jord. "According to the news story, the German had served in the Mediterranean area prior to the invasion of the USSR. No German airman named Franz Jord was reported lost on the Eastern Front at this time, but *Feldwebel* Franz Jordan had served under Wolfgang Schellmann's command in *Stab*/JG 27 until he was killed over Greece in April 1941."[86]

While the brilliantly executed attacks on Soviet airfields went forward without sur-cease, other components of Kesselring's 2 Air Fleet fought above the spearheads of Army Group Center's two panzer groups. We have already seen how the effective application of German airpower—in this case, bombers and *Stuka* divebombers—played a significant role in crushing Soviet counterattacks with armor against the forwardmost elements of Guderian's 2 Panzer Group, even bombing the command post Soviet 14 Mechanized Corps and cutting its communication links (see, Chapter 4, Section 4.3). The *Luftwaffe* also came to the aid of Hoth's 3 Panzer Group when it was attacked by Soviet armor (Section 4.6),[87] while *Stukas* smashed a group of Soviet tanks in the Grodno region on the front of Strauss's Ninth Army and destroyed the headquarters of Soviet 3 Army at Grodno (Section 4.5).

Not to be overlooked for their part in the ground attack mission were the efforts of the Bf-109s armed with their powerful 20mm cannon. *Leutnant* Heinz Knoke, a Bf-109 fighter pilot in II./JG 52 (8 Air Corps), had flown four sorties by noon, drop-ping SD-2 fragmentation bombs from the rack slung under the belly of his "*Emil*" and strafing enemy positions from as little as 6 feet off the ground. Knoke and his comrades were enthusiastic about their chance to finally destroy the hated Bolshevik enemy and were duly impressed by the sinister designs they attributed to the massed Soviet col-umns they encountered:

> *The Chief sees smiling faces all round when the pilots report. At last the spell is broken. We have dreamed for a long time of doing something like this to the Bolshevists. Our feeling is not exactly one of hatred, so much as utter contempt. It is a genuine satisfaction for us to be able to trample the Bolshevists in the mud where they belong . . .*
>
> *New operation orders have arrived. Russian transport columns have been observed by our reconnaissance aircraft retreating eastward along the Grodno-Zytomia-Skidel-Szczuczyn highway, with our tanks in hot pursuit. We are to support them by bombing and strafing the Russians as they retreat. Take-off at 1007 hours [this was sortie number four for* Leutnant *Knoke], accompanied by* Stukas. *They are to dive-bomb the Russian artillery emplacements in the same area.*
>
> *We soon reach Grodno. The roads are clogged with Russian armies everywhere. The reason gradually dawns on us why the sudden surprise attack was ordered by our High Command. We begin to appreciate the full extent of the Russian preparations to attack us. We have just forestalled the Russian time-table for an all-out attack against Germany for the mastery of Europe.*[88]

Leutnant Knoke lifted off on his sixth, and final, sortie of the day at 2000 hours: "There has been no sign of the Russian air force the entire day, and we are able to do our work without encountering opposition."[89] Due to the catastrophic losses suffered by the VVS on the ground and in the air in the opening hours of the German aerial assault, several *Luftwaffe* units—like Knoke's—would manage to fly the entire day without sighting any Soviet aircraft in the air.

As noted, the *Stuka* wings of 2 Air Corps (StG 77) and 8 Air Corps (StG 1 and 2) struck a wide range of targets, with the Ju-87Bs flying seven or eight sorties per machine during the day.[90] When one considers that, between them, the two air corps boasted more than 300 operational divebombers, which collectively must have flown more than 2,000 sorties, it is remarkable that only two of the craft were lost on June 22—and one a victim of "friendly fire."[91] Hans-Ulrich Rudel, flying with *Stukageschwader 2*, the *"Immelmann"* wing (8 Air Corps), recounted his first divebomber missions on June 22 in his iconic memoir, *Stuka Pilot*. Like *Leutnant* Knoke, Rudel was awed by the massive buildup of Red Army forces at the frontier and drew the same sinister conclusions:

> *By the evening of the first day I have been out over the enemy lines four times in the area between Grodno and Volkovysk. The Russians have brought up huge masses of tanks together with their supply columns. We mostly observe the types KV-1, KV-2 and T-34. We bomb tanks, flak artillery and ammunition dumps supplying the tanks and infantry. Ditto the following day, taking off at 3:00 a.m. and coming in from our last landing often at 10:00 p.m. A good night's rest goes by the board. Every spare minute we stretch out underneath an aeroplane and instantly fall asleep. Then if a call comes from anywhere we hop to it without even knowing where it is from. We move as though in our dreams.*
>
> *On my very first sortie I notice the countless fortifications along the frontier. The fieldworks run deep into Russia for many hundreds of miles. They are partly positions still under construction. We fly over half-completed airfields; here a concrete runway is just being built; there a few aircraft are already standing on an [airdrome] . . . Flying in this way over one airfield after another, over one strongpoint after another, one reflects: "It is a good thing we struck." . . . It looks as if the Soviets meant to build all these preparations up as a base for invasion against us. Whom else in the West could Russia have wanted to attack? If the Russians had completed their preparations there would not have been much hope of halting them anywhere.*
>
> *We are fighting in front of the spearhead of our armies; that is our task . . . Our targets are always the same: tanks, motor vehicles, bridges, fieldworks and A.A. sites.*[92]

Hans-Ulrich Rudel would end the Second World War with more than 2,500 operational missions—the vast majority of those missions in the Ju-87 divebomber—and credit for destroying 519 Red Army tanks (one-third of a month's production, according to Foreign Armies East calculations on November 1, 1943); in September 1941, he helped to sink the Soviet battleship *Marat* of the Soviet Baltic Fleet by striking her with a 2,200-pound bomb.[93]

No account of Luftwaffe operations on June 22 would be complete without addressing the exploits of *Major* Werner Mölders, the commander of *Jagdgeschwader 51* (JG 51) of Loerzer's 2 Air Corps. The twenty-eight-year-old Mölders was one of Germany's top flying aces.[94] Early that morning, Mölders and his four Bf-109F *Gruppen* began operations from their cluster of bases east and southeast of Warsaw. Flying with his staff's flight (*Schwarm*) of four aircraft, alongside the pilots of II./JG 51, Mölders achieved his first kill of the day (and sixty-ninth of the war) at 0500 hours, the victim an I-153 biplane. His second and third aerial victories came at 1235 and 1236 hours, when he sent two SB bombers tumbling out of the sky. Two minutes later (1238) he recorded his fourth and final kill of the day (and seventy-second of his career)—another SB bomber. For his seventy-second aerial victory, Hitler sent him a congratulatory telegram and awarded him the Swords to the Knight's Cross with Oak Leaves.[95]

The next day (June 23), the Bf-109Fs of Mölders's fighter wing used their 20mm automatic cannon to knock out at least twenty-five Russian tanks near Pruzhany, helping to clear the way for Guderian's 2 Panzer Group; by the end of the day, Loerzer's 2 Air Corps had run up its score of VVS aircraft destroyed (in the air and on the ground) to the improbable figure of 716, against a loss of just twelve aircraft.[96] On June 30, Mölders (now promoted to *Oberstleutnant*) became the first fighter pilot of any belligerent nation to record eighty kills during the Second World War, tying him with the total of Manfred von Richthofen in World War I. Two weeks later, on the evening of July 15, 1941, Mölders shot down a Pe-2 bomber and was credited with his one hundredth aerial victory, making him the first pilot in history to reach the century mark. But for Werner Mölders, "the century carried a sting in its tail." To avoid the potential propaganda fallout from a top German ace falling into enemy hands, he was immediately banned from all operational flying. Promoted to full colonel (*Oberst*) on July 20, he became the *Luftwaffe's* first *General der Jagdflieger* on August 7. Attempting to return to Berlin after an inspection tour of front-line units in the Ukraine (November 1941), Mölders was killed when the He-111 in which he was a passenger crashed in bad weather near Breslau and broke apart.[97]

On 28 November, after laying in state at the RLM [Reichsluftfahrtministerium], where both Hitler and Göring came to pay their respects, Mölders' coffin was borne on a gun carriage, flanked by an escort of fellow Experten *[the German term for fighter aces] including Adolf Galland and Karl-Gottfried Nordmann, through the streets of Berlin. Tens of thousands of mourners lined the route as the cortège slowly made its way to the Invaliden Cemetery. Here, to the sound of a salute fired by a battery of 88mm flak guns drawn up in the nearby Tiergarten, Mölders was buried close to World War I hero* Rittmeister *Manfred* Freiherr *von Richthofen.[98]*

6.4: *LUFTWAFFE* OPERATIONS IN SUPPORT OF ARMY GROUP SOUTH

The German 4 Air Fleet (headquarters in Rzeszów) was commanded by fifty-six-year-old *Generaloberst* Alexander Löhr; his chief of staff was *Generalmajor* Korten. An Austrian (with a Russian mother), Löhr was given command of 4 Air Fleet in April 1939. During the Polish campaign, his air forces carried out a brutal bombardment of the Polish capital of Warsaw on September 25, 1939, with hundreds of bombers, divebombers, and ground attack aircraft, supported by thirty Ju-52 transport planes in a bombing role. Ironically, it was the latter, which, dropping a total of 72 tons of incendiary bombs, caused "widespread fires, havoc and human destruction." Two days later (September 27), Warsaw surrendered. During the Balkan campaign, on April 6, 1941, Löhr's air fleet smashed the Yugoslavian capital of Belgrade (it had been declared an "open city") with incendiary and explosive bombs in another terror attack (*Terrorangriff*). The rapid victory over Yugoslavia—the country capitulated on April 17—was attributed to the work of Löhr's air fleet, and on May 9, 1941, he was promoted to *Generaloberst*. Before *Barbarossa*, his 4 Air Fleet also took part in the invasion of Crete. After the war, Löhr was tried as a war criminal by Yugoslavia and executed on February 26, 1947.[99]

For the Russian campaign, Löhr's *Luftflotte 4* numbered 887 aircraft of all types, of which 694 were combat ready, the latter including 307 bombers and 272 fighter aircraft. Cooperating with—yet not subordinate to—Löhr's air fleet was a (no longer ascertainable) number of Romanian aircraft, perhaps about 600 (of which some 350 were frontline machines), organized into an air combat group consisting of several bomber and fighter wings.[100] However, as noted above (Section 5.1), because operational planning for *Barbarossa* did not place the main effort on the southern wing, Löhr's air fleet was allotted no *Stuka* divebombers and only minimal forces for the CAS mission; moreover, some of the air fleet's assets were committed to defending the Romanian oil fields from potential Soviet air attack. On the positive side, Löhr did have *Generalleutnant* Otto Dessloch's 2 Flak Corps in his order of battle, and it would play a major role supporting the advance of Kleist's 1 Panzer Group.[101]

The air units of 4 Air Fleet were organized mainly into two air corps—4 Air Corps, under *Generalleutnant* Kurt Pflugbeil; and 5 Air Corps, commanded by Air General Robert *Ritter* von Greim. In addition, there was the German *Luftwaffe* Mission Romania, led by *Generalleutnant* Hans Speidel, as well as replacement units posted in Vienna and Cracow (Kraków). The air fleet's order of battle was as follows:

4 Air Fleet

Squadron 4, Long-Range Recce Group 122 (4.(F)/122) **(Ju-88, Bf-110)**

Weather Observation Squadron 76 **(He-111H, Ju-88A, Bf-110)**

Air Transport Groups 50 and 104 **(Ju-52)**

German Luftwaffe Mission Romania

*Staff 52 Fighter Wing (JG 52), with III Group (***Bf-109E***, ***Bf-109F***)*

4 Air Corps

*Squadron 3, Long-Range Recce Group 121 (3.(F)/121) (***Ju-88A***, ***Bf-110***)*

*Staff 27 Bomber Wing (KG 27), with I, II, and III Groups (***He-111H***)*

*II Group, 4 Bomber Wing (KG 4) (***He-111H***)*

*Staff 77 Fighter Wing (JG 77), with II and III Groups (***Bf-109E***, ***Bf-109F***)*

*I Group, 2 Training Wing (LG 2) (***Bf-109E***)*

5 Air Corps

*Squadron 4, Long-Range Recce Group 121 (4.(F)/121) (***Ju-88A***)*

*Staff 55 Bomber Wing (KG 55), with I, II, and III Groups (***He-111H***, ***Bf-110***)*

*Staff 54 Bomber Wing (KG 54), with I and II Groups (***Ju-88A***)*

*Staff 51 Bomber Wing (KG 51), with I, II, and III Groups (***Ju-88A***)*

*Staff 3 Fighter Wing (JG 3), with I, II, and III Groups (***Bf-109F***)*

Air District 8 *(Cracow)*

*Replacement Fighter Training Group 3 (JG 3) (***Bf-109E***)*

*Replacement Fighter Training Group 27 (JG 27) (***Bf-109E***)*

Air District 17 *(Vienna)*

*Replacement Fighter Training Group 77 (JG 77) (***Bf-109E***)[102]*

The mission of Löhr's 4 Air Fleet in support of Field Marshal von Rundstedt's Army Group South was fourfold:

    1. Attack the Soviet air forces. Establish air superiority and thereby prevent any countermeasures by the Soviet air force against the formations of Army Group South.
    2. Provide direct and indirect support to Army Group South, with [support] concentrated on [the army group's] left wing—where Sixth Army and 1 Panzer Group are to advance toward Kiev to the Dnepr—to prevent the withdrawal of strong Soviet forces across the river.

> 3. [Conduct] attacks in the Black Sea to destroy the Soviet Black Sea Fleet and its bases.
>
> 4. Disrupt Soviet merchant shipping and transport vessels in the Black Sea and the Sea of Azov.[103]

Within this general framework, the air fleet's 4 Air Corps, from it bases in Romania, was to protect the vital oil fields (in coordination with the Royal Romanian Air Force [FARR]), while also supporting German Eleventh Army and the Romanian 3 and 4 Armies. Pflugbeil's air units were also to strike Soviet naval bases around the Black Sea. To Greim's 5 Air Corps, operating from its bases in the Zamość-Lublin region (on the left wing of Army Group South), fell the air fleet's principal task of destroying Soviet air forces and gaining air superiority along the main axis of the German advance; after this had been accomplished (most likely in three or four days), 5 Air Corps was to switch the *Schwerpunkt* of its efforts to supporting the drive of Sixth Army and 1 Panzer Group toward Kiev.[104]

Across the lengthy front of Rundstedt's army group the aerial onslaught of the bomber and fighter groups of 4 Air Fleet "unfolded in all its fury," striking some twenty-nine Soviet airfields as far south as the Black Sea coast, while the bombers ranged as far as Odessa and Sevastopol in search of their targets.[105]

> In L'vov—the city where the non-Russian population had whispered "the Germans are coming to get you" to the Russians—the "uninterrupted bombing created panic" among the civilians; German-trained "diversionists," in addition to blowing up fuel and ammunition dumps, added to the havoc as much as possible, not least by signaling the bombers and guiding them to special targets. The city commandant of L'vov was obliged to call out his military patrols and augment them with the few tanks at his disposal, in order to restore order.[106]

Keeping up with the frantic pace of German aerial operations in the central and northern combat zones, the bombers of Löhr's air fleet would fly as many as three and, in some cases, four missions throughout the day, while the fighter planes logged six to seven.[107] For the attacking fighter pilots and bomber crews flying in the southern combat zone, it was "*das alte Lied*"—the same old story of an enemy totally unprepared for the catastrophe that befell it. As *Hauptmann* Hans von Hahn, piloting his Bf-109 at the head of I./JG 3 (5 Air Corps), noted in his diary: "We hardly believed our eyes. Row after row of reconnaissance planes, bombers, and fighters stood lined up as if on parade."[108] In addition to the systematic destruction of Soviet airfields and their aircraft by both of 4 Air Fleet's air corps, the fighters and bombers of Greim's 5 Air Corps were able to intervene effectively on behalf of the ground forces, bombing and strafing Soviet troop columns and rail movements both at and behind the front, while short- and long-range recce units kept army and *Luftwaffe* commanders well informed of the whereabouts of the enemy and his intentions.[109]

Typical of the operations of 4 Air Fleet's fighter wings were those of *Major* Günther Lützow's *Jagdgeschwader 3* (5 Air Corps), made up of three Bf-109F fighter *Gruppen* and flying from bases between Zamość and Hostynne (west of Vladimir-Volynski). At 0430 hours, Lützow registered his first kill of the Russian campaign, and nineteenth overall; it was the only Russian aircraft destroyed by the four planes of Lützow's staff flight (four aircraft) on June 22. (Lützow would register his 100th and 101st aerial victories on October 24, 1941.)[110] The *Stab*/JG 3 lost one pilot and his aircraft (Bf-108) on a courier flight to Cracow, while a second aircraft (Bf-109F) was destroyed when it crash-landed after running out of fuel. The fighter wing's I Group (I./JG 3), with one squadron outfitted with bomb racks for the fighter-bomber (*Jagdbomber*) role, flew its first sorties at 0340 hours, making low-level runs with twenty-three machines against Soviet airfields at L'vov, Rava Ruska, Kamienka, Jaworow, and other locations. The fighter group was in action throughout the day, striking airfields and columns of Russian troops and vehicles east of Jaworow. By day's end, I./JG 3 had shot down eight VVS aircraft and destroyed at least thirty-six on the ground, against the loss of one pilot and his aircraft.[111]

Commanded by *Hauptmann* Lothar Keller, the Bf-109Fs of II./JG 3 lifted off from their base at Hostynne shortly before 0400 hours. Its orders: "*Frei Jadg*" (free chases) in squadron strength and low-level attacks with guns and bombs against Soviet airfields in the L'vov region.

At 0430, during one of these missions, Oblt. *Walther Dahl, who was flying with the Gruppenstab, scored the Gruppe's first victory in the east. The Staffeln of II./JG 3 flew numerous missions during the course of the day, the majority of them to the south, with emphasis on the area around L'vov. In addition to free chases and low-level attacks, in the afternoon bomber escort missions were also flown, with some pilots logging as many as five sorties. The first missions in the early morning produced little contact with Russian aircraft, however the Russian air force recovered from the initial shock remarkably quickly, and the second group of missions, which began at about 0630, resulted in several fierce air battles, in which 4 Staffel claimed three victories and the Gruppenstab four. Four more victories were claimed in an early-evening engagement. With four claims, Gruppenkommandeur Hptm. Keller was the day's most successful pilot (17–20). II./JG 3 claimed a total of 16 enemy aircraft shot down on 22 June 1941. The Gruppe's losses were comparatively light, with just one Messerschmitt written off as a result of (probable) enemy action. [Feldwebel] Hermann Freitag of 5 Staffel failed to return from a mission into the L'vov-Brody area for reasons unknown and was first reported missing. In fact Fw. Freitag was taken in by local farmers, who hid him until the arrival of German forces. As a result, he was able to rejoin the Gruppe unharmed on 2 July. For II./JG 3 this was the first example of the local population's willingness to assist. At that stage the local population still hoped that the German armies would liberate them from Soviet oppression, a hope that was to be cruelly disappointed.*[112]

The fighter wing's third fighter group (III./JG 3), commanded by *Hauptmann* Walter Oesau, went into action shortly after 0400 hours, taking off from its base at Moderowka and striking airfields along the frontier—including Dobromil and Sandor—with guns and bombs. The group flew several additional missions during the day, including an escort mission for seventeen Ju-88s of KG 51 (on a bombing run over L'vov) and more low-level attacks on VVS airfields at Sambor and Stryj, destroying a total of twelve Russian machines on the ground. Because few Soviet aircraft were encountered in the air by this fighter group, it only claimed one enemy plane shot down. As it was, June 22 turned out to be a black day (*Schwarzer Tag*) for III./JG 3. While loading one of the Messerschmitts with 50-kilogram bombs, one of the bombs exploded, killing four of the ground crew and badly damaging the aircraft. On a low-level mission near the Dnester River, the squadron chief (*Staffelkapitän*) of 8./JG 3 was hit by flak and forced to make an emergency belly landing in enemy territory, where he was captured and killed by enraged Russian soldiers. A Bf-109F belonging to 9./JG 3 was also hit by flak, resulting in the loss of the plane and the pilot. In addition, five Bf-109Fs had to be written off due to crash landings and other accidents at Moderowka.[113]

In the sector of 4 Air Corps, *Oberleutnant* Georg Schirmböck took part in the first fighter-bomber sorties of JG 77 against airfields of the Black Sea Fleet; he later told German aviation historian Jochen Prien: "Russia really was not prepared at all. Railway stations, villages, everywhere where there was light, the entire country was lit up. At railway stations we could see fully normal activity." *Leutnant* Joachim Deicke, also with JG 77, described what happened when the German *Jagdbomber* came screaming down on their targets: "The Russians came out of their barracks and waved their hands at us. Having seen this, upon return to our base, we asked ourselves if this raid wasn't a terrible mistake."[114]

While the Bf-109s of Löhr's air fleet were smashing Soviet airfields and pummeling troop and vehicle concentrations, the He-111 and Ju-88 bombers of 4 and 5 Air Corps were doing the same, and then some.[115] One of the primary targets of *Generalleutnant* Pflugbeil's bombers (4 Air Corps) was the Black Sea port city of Sevastopol, in 1941 one of the most redoubtable fortresses in the world—strongly defended by concrete bunkers, minefields, and dozens of heavy naval guns—and, most significantly, home to the Soviet Union's Black Sea Fleet. Historian Catherine Merridale, in her wonderful study of the Soviet fighting man in World War II (*Ivan's War*), describes the start of the German aerial bombardment of the port city.

In Sevastopol . . . it was, as naval officer Evseev remarked in his diary, "a wonderful Crimean evening." That Saturday, "all the streets and boulevards in the city were lit.

The white houses were bathed in light, the clubs and theaters beckoned the sailors on shore leave to come inside. There were crowds of sailors and local people, dressed in white, packing the city's streets and parks. As always, the famous Primorskii boulevard was full of people out for a stroll. Music was playing. There were jokes and happy laughter everywhere on the evening before the holiday." A week earlier, the Soviet foreign minister, Vyacheslav Molotov, had insisted that rumors of Germany's intention to break its pact with Moscow and launch an attack on the Soviet Union were completely without foundation. The temptation to believe him must have been overwhelming.

One source of all the light across the city's twin harbors that night was the Upper Inkerman lighthouse. With its help, the German planes could navigate their way unerringly toward the port. They came from the east, flying low out of the steppe, their route a great arc across Soviet space. They knew their targets in advance: the fleet, the warehouses, the antiaircraft guns. Soon the Black Sea reflected new lights from the shore: incandescent trails and flares, searchlights, the evil glow of a landscape on fire. "Are those planes ours?" someone asked Evseev as the sailors scrambled into boats to get back to their ships. "It must be another exercise." But his neighbor had been taking careful stock. "Our antiaircraft batteries are firing live rounds," he said. "And those bombs don't look at all like dummies." "So we're at war then?" said a third. "But with whom?"[116]

On its first mission of the day, KG 51 (5 Air Corps), from bases south of Rzeszów,[117] dispatched eighty Ju-88 medium bombers against a series of airfields, including Kovel', in northwestern Ukraine, and Tarnopol, 200 kilometers to the south. Fyodor Arkhipenko, operations duty officer of the 17 Fighter Aviation Regiment at Kovel' airfield, recalled what took place there:

Beginning at 0325 in the morning, about fifty German planes bombed our field, coming back four times. Only myself and the duty pilot, my squadron leader, Ibragimov, and the guards, the security forces, were there. Because it was Sunday, the rest had been allowed to go home on leave.

The airfield was small, two by three kilometers. You can imagine the kinds of horrors that took place at that airfield. Then, by afternoon, the pilots and ground crews started arriving. Many of them, their hair had turned white. And some of them had even begun to stutter from fear after experiencing that kind of bombing.[118]

The initial raids resulted in the destruction of about a hundred VVS aircraft on the ground by the bomber *Staffeln* of KG 51. The "*Edelweiss*" wing would fly three more large-scale missions (*Grossangriffe*) on June 22, yet by the end of the day it had sustained alarming losses: "When on the evening of the first day, *Oberstleutnant* Schulz-Heyn, at the wing's command post in Castle Polanka in Krosno, took stock he had to write off 15 crews with 60 experienced airmen." Fourteen bombers belonging to III./KG 51 were a total loss, in part the result of enemy action but also due to crash landings and other accidents. Indeed, it had also been a "black day" for the airmen of KG 51. In other action, KG 55 (5 Air Corps) had at least eight of its He-111s shot down by Soviet fighters and five damaged while conducting attacks on airfields of the VVS, leaving a trail of white parachutes and blazing aircraft in its wake.[119]

Despite the infrequent VVS success story, it is certainly accurate to posit that the initial Soviet reaction to the German aerial onslaught was sporadic and uncoordinated, a state of affairs exacerbated by the confusion caused by the breakdown of communications due to the unremitting air raids. Only the VVS commander of the Odessa Military District had put his command on war readiness and dispersed his units over several airfields. As a result, only six of his command's aircraft were destroyed on the ground. "But this was the only exception."[120]

By the end of June 22, the fighter and bomber groups of 4 Air Fleet had destroyed, at a minimum, 350–400 Soviet aircraft—the vast majority while standing idle on their airfields. According to official records, 4 Air Corps—by far the smaller of Löhr's two air corps—destroyed 142 planes on the ground and just sixteen in the air on *Barbarossatag*.[121] Which, of course, was also an indication of how successful the Germans were in pulling off a surprise attack. By thoroughly disabling the VVS, the initial strikes of 4 Air Fleet enabled it to gain air superiority over the front and, as planned, to devote most of its resources to supporting the panzer spearheads of Army Group South after the third day of the campaign.[122] The air fleet would easily adapt to its new primary mission of direct and indirect support of the ground forces. As recorded in a situation report of the *Luftwaffe* High Command (OKL), by June 30, 4 Air Fleet had destroyed 201 tanks, twenty-seven bunkers, and two heavily armed fortified installations; by July 3, Greim's 5 Air Corps alone had destroyed more than than 1,000 aircraft on the ground.[123] The Army High Command also took notice of 4 Air Fleet's dramatic success. On June 30, Army Chief of Staff Halder remarked in his diary that the "*Luftwaffe* is being reinforced in the sector of Army Group South and on the Romanian front. In Army Group South, very effective action by our *Luftwaffe* against enemy air force and enemy columns retreating before our troops (as many as three columns abreast are reported). A total of 200 aircraft shot down during this day. Enemy reported to be already reduced to sending very old four-engine models into the battle."[124]

6.5: *ABENDLAGE:* PRÉCIS OF *LUFTWAFFE* OPERATIONS IN SUPPORT OF *OSTHEER*
As the morning of June 22, 1941, slipped slowly by, something odd began to happen: Soviet bombers, in large numbers, apparently coming out of nowhere, began to strike at the advancing German troops or to bomb East Prussian cities and bases in German-occupied Poland.[125] The strange phenomenon is dramatically recounted by Cajus Bekker in his book, *The Luftwaffe War Diaries.*

No one knew where [the Soviet bombers] came from: whether it was from far away, from the airfields already blitzed, or from others so far undetected. In any case, they were there: ten, twenty, thirty of them, in compact formation. And they attacked.

It happened just after the Gruppen *of Major* Graf Schönborn's *Stukageschwader 77 had re-landed after their first operation against fortified lines on the River Bug. There were five explosions then five black mushrooms of smoke on the opposite boundary. Only then were the bombers sighted: six twin-engine machines turning away in a wide curve.*

At this moment two or three little dots were seen approaching the bombers at full speed: German fighters. They treated the Stuka *crews on the ground to a breath-taking spectacle. 6./StG 77's squadron commander,* Hauptmann *Herbert Pabst, reported:*

"As the first one fired, thin threads of smoke seemed to join it to the bomber. Turning ponderously to the side, the big bird flashed silver, then plunged vertically downwards with its engines screaming. As it crashed, a huge sheet of flame shot upwards. The second bomber became a glare of red, exploded as it dived, and only the bits came floating down like great autumnal leaves. The third turned over backwards on fire. A similar fate befell the rest, the last falling in a village and burning for an hour. Six columns of smoke rose from the horizon. All six had been shot down!"

This was but one example. For the same thing happened along the whole front. The Russian bombers came in, held to their course, and made no attempt to evade either flak or fighters. Their losses were frightful. When ten had already been shot down, another fifteen would appear on the scene. "They went on coming the whole afternoon," Pabst continued. "From our airfield alone we saw twenty-one crash, and not one get away."[126]

As we've seen, Field Marshal Kesselring was so bewildered by the behavior of the Soviet bomber crews, their willingness to face certain death, that he labeled it "infanticide." In his memoir, he also stated that the destruction of the Russian bomber force in the first few days of the war was so complete, so final, that it was rendered a non-factor in the months that followed.[127] Using Kesselring as his source, German military historian Horst Boog reinforced the point: "The Soviet bomber fleet had indeed been practically eliminated and hardly made its presence felt during the following months, even though it still undertook sporadic, ineffective, and costly attacks against the German rear area. At this time the Soviet air force was unable to create significant difficulties for the German army in the east."[128]

While Boog went on to admit that Soviet air units "increasingly began to offer resistance once the element of surprise had worn off," and that the VVS was "gradually able to recover thanks to its own efforts" as well as the "breathing space" provided by the poor weather in the fall of 1941,[129] the truth is that both the bomber and fighter units of the Soviet air force were far from totally neutralized as a result of the devastating

Luftwaffe victories in the first days of the war.[130] It is, of course, beyond question that the VVS suffered an enormous—and historically unprecedented—catastrophe at the start of Operation *Barbarossa*. After losing an astounding 1,811 aircraft on June 22 (322 in the air or destroyed by AA fire; 1,489 on the ground),[131] the Soviet air force had written off an additional 800 aircraft by the end of June 23, with the result that the *Luftwaffe*—or so it seemed—had gained complete air supremacy, or at least air superiority, along the entire Eastern Front.[132] On June 24, General Halder wrote in his diary that the Soviet air force was now "completely out of the picture [*völlig im Hintertreffen*] after the very high losses."[133] By June 30, 1941, the Germans were reporting the destruction of a total of 4,614 Soviet aircraft.[134]

Yet the *Luftwaffe's* achievement, extraordinary to be sure, was not nearly so absolute as it appeared to be (and as many historians have interpreted it to be). Simply put, despite its astronomical losses, the Soviet air force, from the very outset of the war, continued to make its presence felt, often significantly so. There were many reasons for this, perhaps foremost among them the fact that the *Luftwaffe*, operating along a front that grew dramatically in length the farther east the Germans went, was too small in number to maintain the requisite pressure on the VVS (the air superiority mission) while also meeting the burgeoning demands of the army for air support.[135] Another factor was the remarkable regenerative powers of the Red Army, which was able to infuse the battlefield with an unending stream of new formations, both on the ground and in the air. As a result, as early as July 4, 1941, Kesselring's air fleet was reporting that, despite the VVS's heavy losses, the number of Russian aircraft had hardly declined, while the army began to complain that, in certain sectors, the Soviets had even regained air superiority, and that the "direction of Soviet air units was increasingly marked by a 'clear-headed and aggressive leadership.'"[136]

That the Soviet air force remained active during the summer of 1941 is also supported by statistics of sorties flown across the entire Eastern Front. According to the Soviet official history of the air war, more than 47,000 sorties were logged through July 9, 1941—that is, more than 2,500 per day, including thousands flown by Soviet bombers[137]—the VVS concentrating its attacks on the German armored spearheads along all three axes. Weapons employed included high-explosive and fragmentation bombs, machine-gun fire, and rockets. The primary targets were "tanks, artillery, and mortars in firing position, tank and motorized columns, vehicle concentrations, river crossings, reserves, and troops on the battlefield."[138] Starting in July, Red Army air units also began to actively strike German airfields; on July 8, attacks were carried out all along the front against forty airfields, with the air forces of Soviet Western Front alone destroying or damaging fifty-four German planes.[139]

The point here is not that the Soviet air force saw a dramatic reversal of fortune as early as the start of July 1941—it did not, and would not until the fall/winter of 1941/42—rather, it is that the VVS was never "completely out of the picture" (to use Halder's phrase) and continued to generate a surprisingly high number of sorties per day despite the horrendous losses at the onset of the campaign. Simply put, this author has read too many accounts like the following (written on July 1 by a German doctor with Model's 3 Panzer Division at Bobruisk on the Berezina River) to believe otherwise: "Yesterday, at the edge of the forest, we again experienced many air attacks. They seemed to attack every 15 minutes. One could hardly catch a minute of sleep because of the racket. In our sector alone I saw 32 enemy planes shot down."[140]

None of the above analysis is meant to imply that the Soviet air force performed *effectively* at the start of the Russian campaign, because for the most part it did not. "On the whole," acknowledged former VVS officer M. N. Kozhevnikov, "the actions of Soviet aviation against enemy troops did not have a noticeable influence on the success of the ground troops' defensive actions in the initial period of the war. VVS efforts were often dispersed, planes were not massed adequately in the main sectors, the weapons selection and the methods and altitude of bomb strikes were not always appropriate, and the tactics of bomber and ground attack aviation did not fit the situation."[141] The assessment of a former German tank commander was equally blunt: "Our superiority in the air was quite obvious ... It soon became clear that the Russian air force had only obsolete machines at their disposal, but above all that the pilots did not function nearly as well as our fighter and dive-bomber pilots, or the pilots of our Western opponents. This was naturally a great relief to us, and when Russian aircraft appeared, we hardly bothered to take cover."[142] On the other hand, the VVS had remained largely intact despite its losses and was learning *how* to fight with remarkable dispatch.

Finally, it is noted with palpable irony that *Luftwaffe losses* at the onset of the Russian campaign were, one can reasonably argue, even more significant than those of their adversary. The seventy-eight aircraft lost on June 22—sixty-one to enemy action and seventeen to "other causes"—were equal to more than 3 percent of the *Luftwaffe's* operational strength (2,255 planes) in the Eastern Theater; numerically, they signified the greatest single day's loss since the start of World War II on September 1, 1939. Losses among aircrew were also serious, among them 113 dead or missing and dozens more wounded. By June 30, the *Luftwaffe* had already written off some 330 aircraft; and, by July 12, total losses had soared to 550 aircraft (nearly 25 percent of its operational strength at the start of the Russian campaign). In the long run, this enormous rate of attrition among German air units was unsustainable and a major reason for the ultimate failure of Hitler's attempt to enslave the Soviet Union.[143]

CHAPTER 7

Berlin, Moscow, and the First Twenty-One Hours of War on the Eastern Front

Deutsches Volk! *At this very moment a concentration of forces is underway which, in its extent and scope, is the largest the world has ever seen . . . The formations of the German* Ostfront *extend from East Prussia to the Carpathian Mountains . . . The task of this front is . . . the safeguarding of Europe and with that the salvation of all. I have, therefore, today decided to place the destiny and future of the German Reich and our* Volk *in the hands of our soldiers. May the Lord God aid us in this very struggle!*
—ADOLF HITLER'S PROCLAMATION TO THE GERMAN PEOPLE,
JUNE 22, 1941[1]

Within a few hours the first extra editions of the papers were on the streets . . . The people bought the extras almost as fast as they appeared. For the first time since the war began, there was momentary enthusiasm among the German populace . . . I listened to their conversations around the newsstands and on the subways. I talked with a number of them. For the first time they were excited about the war. "Now," they said, "we are fighting our real enemy."
—AMERICAN JOURNALIST HARRY W. FLANNERY IN BERLIN, JUNE 22, 1941[2]

In the course of the day, regular German troops fought our frontier troops and achieved minor successes in a number of sectors. In the afternoon, with advance field forces of the Red Army arriving at the frontier, the attacks of the German groups have been repelled along most of the frontier with heavy losses to the enemy.
—FIRST OFFICIAL COMMUNIQUÉ OF THE SOVIET GOVERNMENT, 10:00 P.M.,
JUNE 22, 1941[3]

On the early morning of 22 June we got a call from Milmann: The Germans have
declared war on us and bombed Soviet cities . . . We sat in front of the radio and waited
for Stalin to speak. But instead it was Molotov who spoke. He was nervous. I marveled
at his words about the breach of trust and the surprise attack . . . But what else could
one expect from the fascists? We sat by the radio for quite some time. Hitler spoke. Then
we heard a speech by Churchill. Meanwhile from Moscow we heard songs, both cheerful
and bold songs that were completely out of touch with the mood of the people. Apparently
no one had either an article or a speech prepared. Instead they played songs.
—SOVIET WRITER AND JOURNALIST ILYA EHRENBURG [4]

DURING THE AFTERNOON OF JUNE 21, THE SOVIET AMBASSADOR IN BERLIN, VLADIMIR Dekanozov, hoping to deliver his "little protest" against the ongoing violations of Soviet airspace by German aircraft, had repeatedly telephoned the German Foreign Office asking for an audience with the foreign minister. After being "fobbed off" with the word that Ribbentrop was "out of town," the Soviet envoy was finally informed at 2:00 the next morning (June 22) that the Nazi foreign minister would receive him at 4:00 A.M. at the Foreign Office in the Wilhelmstrasse. Dr. Paul Schmidt, a Foreign Office interpreter who had been Hitler's main interpreter at major prewar events, and who was present in Ribbentrop's office that morning, recalled that he had never seen his chief so agitated as he was in the few minutes before Dekanozov's arrival. Pacing back and forth in the room "like a caged animal," Ribbentrop kept repeating to himself, "the *Führer* is absolutely right [*der Führer hat Recht!*] to attack Russia now." To Schmidt it seemed as if the German foreign minister was trying to reassure himself: "The Russians would certainly themselves attack us, if we did not do so now."[5]

Punctually, at 4:00 A.M., Dekanozov was shown in and, "obviously not guessing anything was amiss, held out his hand to Ribbentrop." The three men sat down, and the Soviet ambassador attempted to relay the grievances of his government, but he hadn't gotten far when Ribbentrop, with a "stony expression," cut him off and said, "That's not the question now."[6] The smug foreign minister handed Dekanozov a copy of a declaration of the German government and informed him that, at that very instant, German troops were taking "military countermeasures" at the Russo-German frontier. The declaration accused the Soviet government of repeatedly violating the Nazi-Soviet pact of August 1939, which the Germans, it said, had adhered to faithfully. The Soviet regime was also guilty of "sabotage, terrorism and espionage" against the Reich, and had challenged Germany's best efforts to build "a stable order in Europe." More alarmingly, the Soviet Union had "menaced" Germany by concentrating "all available Russian forces on a long front from the Baltic to the Black Sea," while "reports received the last few days," it went on, "eliminate the last remaining doubts as to the aggressive character of this Russian concentration."[7]

The German declaration hurled further accusations at the Soviet government until finally asserting that Russia was "about to attack Germany from the rear," and that "the *Führer* has therefore ordered the *Wehrmacht* to oppose this threat with all the means at their disposal." It is not clear whether the stunned Soviet ambassador pored over the entire declaration at that moment. In any case, recalled Schmidt, Dekanozov "recovered his composure quickly and expressed his deep regret" at this tragic turn in German-Soviet relations, the blame for which he placed entirely on the non-cooperative posture of the Germans. "He rose, bowed perfunctorily, and left the room"—this time without offering his interlocutor a handshake.[8]

In the meantime, an equally tragic scene was unfolding in Moscow. The German ambassador there, Count Friedrich Werner von der Schulenburg, had devoted years of his life to improving German-Soviet relations; his efforts now in shambles, he had instructions from Ribbentrop to deliver to Molotov the same declaration Dekanozov was receiving in Berlin. Schulenburg arrived at the Kremlin "just as dawn was breaking" on the crisp early morning of June 22; he proceeded, with all the dignity he could muster, to read out the German declaration to the Soviet foreign minister. Molotov listened in silence. When Schulenburg finished, he replied: "It is war. Do you believe that we deserved that?" Schulenburg returned to Berlin, where he was forced to retire. He would be executed by the Gestapo on November 10, 1944, for his role in the failed July 1944 plot to assassinate Hitler.[9]

In both Berlin and Moscow the eruption of war left the remaining Soviet and German diplomats "understandably nervous, and other citizens terrified." At some point during the day, the Gestapo stormed the Soviet trade mission in Berlin and began to haul away documents, while the Russian staff sought frantically to destroy what materials they could. The courtyard at the Soviet embassy was suddenly transformed into a "gypsy encampment," as a few ("but still far too many") of the 1,000 Soviet citizens still in Germany and the occupied territories sought refuge. Eventually, the interests of the Russians in Germany were placed under the protection of Sweden, those of the 120 Germans in Russia under Bulgaria; furthermore, it was agreed that Soviet workers in the Reich and their families would be evacuated via Prague-Vienna-Belgrade as far as the Yugoslav city of Niš, in order to enable the Germans to get their people out of the Soviet Union. In subsequent days, the Soviet citizens reached Niš under SS guard. While the fate of the Russian non-diplomats is unknown, the Soviet diplomatic team managed to make its way through neutral Turkey to Moscow.[10]

7.1: BERLIN: THE REACTION TO THE FIRST SUCCESSES

After having broken the "grim news" to the Soviet ambassador, Ribbentrop summoned in "rapid succession" the representatives of Germany's allies—Italy, Japan, Hungary, Finland, and Romania—and informed them of the start of Germany's surprise attack on the Soviet Union. At 6:00 A.M., with his assembled staff at his side, the German foreign minister addressed the domestic and international press.[11] Thirty minutes earlier (5:30 A.M.), in solemn tones befitting the historic occasion, Dr. Goebbels read Hitler's "Proclamation to the German People" from his office in the Reich Ministry for Propaganda. "It was," observed historian Roger Moorhouse, "a strange document." It was also—except for a slightly different ending tailored to its audience—the same proclamation that had been read out to some three million German soldiers by their officers along the Eastern Front just hours before (see, Chapter 2, Section 2.2), with its meandering attack on Great Britain, point-by-point refutation of Soviet claims and demands, and cynical justification of the attack on Russia as a preemptive measure. The turgid and long-winded document would be repeated throughout the day on all German radio stations.[12]

Public reaction to the sudden outbreak of war with the Soviet Union was mixed. In Berlin, the official response of the public was "stoical," signaling "complete trust in our *Wehrmacht*" and that "coming events" would be faced "with calmness and martial determination."[13] Many Berliners, however—and Germans throughout the Reich—in particular those who had not seen it coming, responded with a profound sense of shock. Marie Vassiltchikov, a young White Russian émigré fortunate enough to have parlayed her language skills into a minor position at the German Foreign Office, *had* seen it coming, and yet she was still "thunderstruck" by the news of the German invasion.[14] Marianne Miethe, a twenty-year-old employee in an accountancy firm in Hirschfelde, looked toward Germany's uncertain future with dread, and a dire prediction from her father-in-law:

> How happy we were about the non-aggression pact between the German Reich and the Soviet Union, and we had no inkling that this was merely a clever move on the part of both the dictators, Hitler and Stalin, in particular to carve up Poland and win time before the outbreak of war. We thought that the non-aggression pact between the German Reich and the Soviet Union could pave the way for a peaceful solution to the whole conflict.
>
> The special announcement about the entry into war with the Soviet Union hit us like a bolt from the blue and we thought with dread back to Napoleon's Russian campaign. The critics, among them my father-in-law, said: "Now we have lost the war." We hoped that these fears would not come to pass and had no idea of the suffering that lay ahead for humanity.[15]

Yet the larger point—as illustrated by historian Ian Kershaw in his brilliant biography of Hitler—is that the war with Russia "was not inflicted by a tyrannical dictator on an unwilling country. It was acceded to, even welcomed . . . by all sections of the German elite, non-Nazi as well as Nazi. Large sections of the ordinary German population, too, including the millions who would fight in lowly ranks in the army, would . . . go along with the meaning Nazi propaganda imparted to the conflict, that of a 'crusade against Bolshevism.'"[16]

The outbreak of war in the East brought a profound sense of liberation to many Germans, as the weeks fraught with speculation and rumor were finally at an end and "Germany could at last engage with what many of them regarded as their country's most dangerous opponent. Even the less ideologically committed would have absorbed the vehement anti-Soviet rhetoric of the early 1930s and adjusted only with difficulty to the tactical alliance with Moscow that had opened the war."[17] The thoughts of Frau "A. N." on this day were far from atypical:

> *Well, I had just turned the radio on and heard this: the latest reports from the* Ostfront, *and this brings me straight to the thing that no doubt concerns every German the most today. When I switched on the radio this morning and then, totally unsuspecting, heard the* Führer's *proclamation, I was totally speechless at first. And yet, I don't know, I don't think anybody really took the friendship between the USSR and the German Reich very seriously. We all had our doubts about whether this would go well and we didn't trust the Russians.*
>
> *What it must have cost the* Führer *to have to associate with Stalin at all and to go into a friendly relationship with him! Today I came to realize with complete clarity the full extent of his diplomacy. This whole matter has been of great concern to him. You can just sense that. And when you just think about it, you feel really quite humble.*
>
> *What is our little bit of suffering, our cares, and the tiny sacrifices that have to be made in this wartime economy? But that's the way we are, really we don't reflect enough, and then we just get so wrapped up in personal matters, and life just goes by. At any rate, the struggle will surely be tough, and yet many will breathe a sigh of relief after the long weeks of suspense. For, at the end of the day, a proper soldier longs for battle and victory so that he may again go about his normal tasks.*[18]

The reader will recall that Hitler, after a long and tempestuous night pacing back and forth inside the Reich Chancellery with Propaganda Minister Goebbels and trying out new fanfares for the eastern campaign (see, Section 2.1), had finally retired to his chambers at 2:30 on the morning of June 22—yet not before assuring his adjutants that "before three months have passed, we shall witness a collapse in Russia the like of which world history has never seen!"[19] When Hitler awoke later that morning, the war in the East was already several hours old and he no doubt devoured the first reports from the front with uttermost eagerness. While no records appear to exist indicating just what those first reports to Hitler were, we can surmise with some assuredness that they would have embraced (at least) three primary themes: (a) that the German attack had taken the enemy by complete surprise, and resistance was negligible to nonexistent; (b) that all of the bridges across the main river barriers had been captured intact by the *Ostheer*'s assault detachments; and, (c) that the Russian air force had sustained frightful losses on the ground and in the air. Hitler's diplomatic liaison, Walther Hewel, recalled that a "tranquil, self-possessed mood" seemed to overcome the Chancellery on this momentous morning. Indeed, "it was almost like any other Sunday, except that Hitler and Ribbentrop fell fast asleep after lunch"[20]—no doubt reassured that all was progressing according to plan.

While the mood of Hitler's General Staff may not have been a tranquil one, it was certainly bolstered by initial reports of the army groups pouring in via telephone and teletype to OKH headquarters in Zossen, south of Berlin.[21] The reaction of the General Staff is explicitly underscored by an event that morning: Deputy Chief of Staff for Operations (*Oberquartiermeister I*), *Generalleutnant* Friedrich Paulus, the man most responsible for developing and refining operational war plans for Russia, briefed Field Marshal von Brauchitsch, C-in-C of the army, on the first reports from the East. The reports were good. Brauchitsch asked Paulus how long he thought the war against the Soviet Union would last. Paulus, a superb General Staff officer and typically sober judge of events, predicted it would all be over in just six to eight weeks. "Ja, Paulus, you are certainly correct," replied the field marshal. "We will need about eight weeks for Russia."[22]

Early in the afternoon (1330 hours), *Generaloberst* Halder recorded in his diary that the *Luftwaffe* had already destroyed 800 enemy aircraft and that, so far, only ten German planes had been lost. Army Group Center, meanwhile, was reporting "wild flight on the Brest-Litovsk–Minsk road," and that the "Russian command organization [was] in complete confusion."[23] Later that afternoon, after noting that Italy had honored her obligations and declared war on the Soviet Union,[24] the army chief of staff made his assessment of the first day of Operation *Barbarossa*—an assessment that accurately reflected the situation on the ground (including the serious plight of the Soviet military leadership) while also capturing many of the themes adumbrated throughout the combat portion of this narrative.

The overall picture [Gesamtbild] *of the first day of the offensive is as follows:*

The enemy was surprised by the German attack. His forces were not in tactical disposition for defense. The troops in the border zone were widely scattered in their quarters. The frontier itself was for the most part weakly guarded.

As a result of this tactical surprise, enemy resistance directly on the border was weak and disorganized, and we succeeded everywhere in seizing the bridges across the border rivers and in piercing the defense positions (field fortifications) near the frontier.

After the first shock [Schreckwirkung], the enemy has turned to fight [hat der Feind sich zum Kampf gestellt]. There have been instances of tactical withdrawals and no doubt also disorderly retreats, but there are no indications of an attempted operational disengagement. Such a possibility can moreover be discounted. Some enemy headquarters have been put out of action; e.g., Belostok and some sectors are deprived of high-echelon control. But quite apart from that, the impact of the shock is such that the Russian High Command could not be expected in the first few days to form a clear enough picture of the situation to make so far-reaching a decision. On top of everything, the command organization is too ponderous to effect swift operational regrouping in reaction to our attack, and so the Russians will have to accept battle in the disposition in which they were deployed.

Our divisions on the entire offensive front have forced back the enemy on an average of 10 to 12 km. This has opened the path for our armor. [Note: Halder then addresses the achievements of the individual army groups.] . . . The army groups are pursuing their original objectives. Nor is there any reason for a change. OKH has no occasion to issue any orders . . .

Luftwaffe reports 850 enemy airplanes shot down! This number includes entire bomber squadrons, committed without fighter escort, which were taken on and destroyed in the air by our fighters.[25]

In the meantime, Germany's friends and allies were offering their congratulations to Hitler and his Third Reich for the bold attack against Soviet Russia, and vying with one another to provide support, however modest. Franco's Spain was one of the first—telephoning that a volunteer legion was being recruited to join the crusade against the hated Bolshevik enemy. Slovakia offered for "immediate commitment" an armored group in the strength of about a reinforced regiment, to be ready by the evening of June 23; the offer was accepted and the group assigned to the Seventeenth Army (Army Group South). In addition, two Slovak divisions were to be "brought up to war strength immediately," and made available by June 25; they, too, were to go to Seventeenth Army.[26] Not to be outdone, an "ecstatic" Admiral Horthy, regent of Hungary, "exulted at the 'magnificent' news," informing the German ambassador that he had dreamt of this day for twenty-two years— that "mankind would thank Hitler for this deed for centuries to come." In response, Hungary broke off diplomatic relations with the Soviet Union but as yet would go no further.

At 6:00 p.m. a disappointed General Jodl telephoned his liaison officer in Budapest to remind the Hungarians of the historic importance of the hour; but Horthy had gone off to play polo, his Chief of Army Staff was "unavailable," and the defense minister had gone fishing. Just as Hitler had expected, the Hungarians, canny as ever, wanted to see the first results of "Barbarossa" before committing themselves.[27]

As was his custom, Hitler sat up late with his staff, monitoring the reports pouring in from the East. The *Luftwaffe* had struck Kiev, Kaunas, Sevastopol, Murmansk, Odessa, and other cities in European Russia, while dozens of Soviet forward air bases had been smashed and well over a thousand Red Army aircraft destroyed on the ground and in the air. Good news also arrived from North Africa, where Erwin Rommel's *Afrika Korps* was on the move. Because Hitler didn't keep a diary, and no accounts from his personal staff or military leaders appear to exist,[28] historians can only surmise how the *Führer* reacted to these reports. Adolf Hitler was not a man who was ever lost for words, yet his words on this fateful and dreadful day went unrecorded. One might venture to posit that whatever doubts he had had about attacking the Soviet Union would have yielded to a sublime confidence in a rapid and successful outcome to his *Barbarossa* gamble. Such a perspective is supported by Hewel, who wrote in his diary the next day: "11:30 a.m . . . . he [Hitler] is in a brilliant mood on account of the huge successes in Russia (*Luftwaffe*) and [at] Sollum (tanks)."[29] Moreover, there exists an effusive journal entry from Goebbels—a compulsive scribbler!—that must have closely mirrored Hitler's mood and thinking at this moment.

23 June 1941:

Yesterday: an oppressively hot day. Our troops won't have it easy in battle. Molotov gives a speech: a crazed rant, and an appeal to patriotism, maudlin complaints, the fear can be seen between the lines: "We will prevail," he says. The poor man! . . . All Europe is experiencing a wave of anti-Bolshevism. The Führer's *decision is the greatest sensation ever imaginable. Our air assault begins in grand style . . . On Russian towns, including Kiev . . . and airfields . . . The Russians are already experiencing very heavy aerial losses. During an attack on Tilsit they lost 22 out of 73 attacking planes.*

The operations are going to plan . . . The Russian troop concentrations . . . will suffer the same catastrophe [as the French in 1870]. The Russians are only putting up modest resistance for the time being. But their air force has already suffered terrible losses: 200 shot down, 200 destroyed on the ground, and 200 damaged. Those are pretty serious losses . . .

New reports arrive nearly every minute. Generally very positive. Up to this time 1000 Russian planes destroyed. That's a nasty shock . . . All of the day's objectives are achieved. No complications so far. We rest completely assured. The Soviet regime will go up like tinderwood . . . Once again it has become very late. Sleep has become a luxury for us in recent days.[30]

At midday, June 23, 1941, Hitler boarded his special train at Anhalt station in Berlin and set out for the "dark and gloomy" forests of the Mauerwald in East Prussia. Throughout the afternoon and evening, the train's twin-locomotives shepherded the *Führer* and his staff across Pomerania, past cities and fields "liberated" from the Poles in September 1939. Sometime after midnight, Hitler and the procession of vehicles making up his entourage slipped past the cordon of sentries guarding the entrance to his new military headquarters; at 1:30 in the morning (June 24), Hitler finally entered the compound. During the long train journey, Hitler had decided to call it *"Wolfsschanze,"* or "Wolf's Lair." As he explained to one of his secretaries, Wolf had been his code name during the Years of Struggle.[31]

Tucked deep inside a region of lakes, marshes, and dense forests of pine, spruce, beech, and oak, the *Wolfsschanze* sat astride the Rastenburg-Angerburg railroad 8 kilometers east of the town of Rastenburg. Built by the Todt Organization, the compound consisted of assiduously camouflaged concrete buildings and bunkers and prefabricated barracks, sealed off from the outside world by layers of barbed wire, mines, steel fences, palisades, and earthworks. Hitler would live and work with his closest military and political advisors in the main sector of the headquarters, while a smaller adjacent sector housed a contingent of the OKW Operations Staff and a signal center. Some 20 kilometers away, and also astride the railroad (which was closed to general traffic) the OKH had its own compound in the Mauerwald just beyond Angerburg.[32]

In this austere, dreary, and unhealthy atmosphere—hot, humid, plagued by swarms of mosquitoes in the summer, cold and damp in the winter—Hitler would spend the vast majority of his time over the next three-and-a-half years, fighting in vain against the Bolshevik enemy until the advance of the Red Army forced him to abandon the place in late November 1944 and return to Berlin.[33]

7.2: MOSCOW: THE RESPONSE TO THE INITIAL DEFEATS

On the evening of June 21, Stalin, now clearly worried but not yet willing to believe that Hitler was about to strike, had finally ordered General Zhukov, chief of the Army General Staff, to draft a short, general warning to the troops. Directive No. 1, a tepid and wholly insufficient response to the cataclysm now but hours away, ordered Red Army units to secretly occupy their positions and to disperse and camouflage their planes; conversely, no "provocative" actions were to be taken that might provoke a German response. Stalin had then retired to his dacha outside Moscow, while Zhukov and Defense Commissar Timoshenko had returned to the Ministry of Defense, where they remained on alert (see, Section 2.3).

At 0307 hours, Zhukov received a call over the secure, high frequency (HF) telephone line from Admiral F. S. Oktyabrsky, commander of the Black Sea Fleet, informing him that the fleet's aircraft warning system had detected large numbers of unidentified planes approaching from the sea; as a result, the fleet had been placed on full alert and its antiaircraft batteries were made ready to fire. At 0330 hours, General Klimovskikh, chief of staff of the Western Special Military District, reported to Zhukov that German air raids had taken place against cities and towns in Belorussia. Three minutes later, he fielded another call, this one from General M. A. Purkayev, chief of staff of the Kiev Special Military District, notifying him of airstrikes in the Ukraine. And, at 0340, General F. I. Kuznetsov, commander of the Baltic Special Military District, called to report enemy air raids on Kaunas and other locations.[34] At this point, we will pick up the story in Zhukov's own words:

The Defense Commissar said I should phone Stalin. I started calling. No one answered. I kept calling. Finally, I heard the sleep-laden voice of the general on duty at the security section. I asked him to call Stalin to the phone.

"What? Now? Comrade Stalin is asleep."

"Wake him at once. The Germans are bombing our towns!" About three minutes later Stalin picked up the receiver.

I reported the situation and requested permission to start retaliatory action. Stalin was silent. I heard the sound of his breathing.

"Did you hear me?"

Silence again.

At last Stalin asked:

"Where is the Defense Commissar?"

"Talking with the Kiev District on the HF."

"You and him come to the Kremlin. Tell Poskrebyshev[35] to summon all Politburo members."[36]

At 0430 hours, Zhukov and Marshal Timoshenko arrived at the Kremlin and were called in. Stalin, "his face white," was seated at a table cradling a loaded unlit pipe in both hands; among those also present were Molotov, NKVD Chief Beria, and Marshal K. E. Voroshilov, the former defense commissar who had made dancing lessons mandatory for officers of the Red Army.[37] Clearly "bewildered," the Soviet dictator continued to clutch at the desperate notion that it all might only be "a provocation of the German officers." He was, writes historian Gabriel Gordetsky:

Little moved by Timoshenko's attempts to bring him down to earth, and ignored the Marshal's insistence that rather than being a local incident this was an all-out offensive along the entire front. Stalin simply dug in his heels, suggesting that "if it were necessary to organize a provocation, then the German generals would bomb their own cities." After some reflection he added, "Hitler surely does not know about it."[38]

As a last resort, Stalin wished for Molotov to confer with the German ambassador. Between 3:00 and 4:00 A.M., a phone call had arrived at Molotov's secretariat from Schulenburg's office, requesting an urgent meeting with the Soviet foreign minister; authorized to meet with Schulenburg, Molotov departed Stalin's office and went upstairs to his office.[39] Again Zhukov:

Meanwhile, the First Deputy Chief of [the] General Staff Vatutin passed word that following a strong artillery barrage German land forces had mounted an assault at several points of the Northwestern and Western sectors.

A while later Molotov strode into the office and said: "The German Government has declared war on us."

Stalin sank in his chair, deep in thought.
There was a long and pregnant silence.
I decided to risk breaking it and suggested crashing down on the attackers with
the full strength of our frontier districts, and [to] hold up any further enemy advance.
"Annihilate, not hold up," Timoshenko corrected me.
"Issue a directive," said Stalin.[40]

At 0715 hours, the People's Commissariat of Defense (NKO) issued Directive No. 2. It ordered Red Army troops on the western frontier "in full strength and with all the means at their disposal [to] attack the enemy and destroy him in those regions where he has violated the Soviet border"; absent "special authorization," the troops were not to cross the Russo-German demarcation line. (Somehow, Stalin still entertained the illusion that war could be stopped, while the Politburo kept open the radio link to the German Foreign Ministry and asked Japan to mediate.)[41] The directive gave more forceful instructions to the Russian air force, which was to destroy German aircraft at their airfields, strike German ground forces, and bomb German cities (Memel' and Königsberg among them) up to 150 kilometers behind the front (see, Appendix 6).[42]

Yet this was beyond wishful thinking—it was "Cloud Cuckoo Land."[43] By the time the directive was given, Red Army air units along the frontier had been largely annihilated by the *Luftwaffe*. Pacing back and forth in his office, the all-powerful *vozhd* (leader) of the Soviet state asked in astonishment: "Surely the German air force didn't manage to reach every single airfield?" "Unfortunately," replied Timoshenko, "it did." "How many planes were destroyed?" "Around 700 at a first estimate," responded the defense commissar. "That's a monstrous crime," snapped Stalin. "Those guilty of it should pay with their heads." He was even more enraged when he learned that all contact had been lost with Army-General D. G. Pavlov, the commander of the Western Special Military District. "Your Pavlov needs to be asked some difficult questions!" he barked ominously.[44]

Well into the morning Stalin clung to the possibility that "Russia was being intimidated into political submission."[45] Neither he nor the Politburo had expected war to come without negotiations or an ultimatum—another reason for Stalin to refuse to accept that the catastrophe he had sought so assiduously to avoid had finally come to pass. Surely, he had done nothing to deserve it. For twenty-two months, since the war in Europe had begun, the Kremlin had gone out of its way to "cajole Berlin . . . Only a few days earlier Stalin had shipped nine tons of strategic raw materials—copper, nickel, tin, molybdenum, and wolfram—to military plants in Germany. He had personally authorized German officers to investigate Soviet border areas, allegedly to find the graves of German soldiers lost during World War I, ignoring the repeated warnings of Zhukov and Timoshenko that these trips were logistical intelligence-gathering missions."[46] At some point that morning, as the dreadful reality of war began to take hold, he muttered that the Germans "just descended on us, without using any pretexts, not carrying out any negotiations; simply attacked basely like thieves."[47]

With effectively no accurate information about the murderous battles taking shape along the frontier, about the German panzer columns and their battle-tested crews slashing across sacred Russian soil, Stalin and his government gradually began to respond. In one of his first initiatives as a wartime leader, Stalin approved orders for the mobilization of all men born between 1905 and 1918, the children of the Soviet leadership being among the first to respond.[48] Citing Article 49 of the Soviet constitution, a state of war was declared "in individual districts and across the whole of the USSR in order to guarantee social order and state security."[49]

If people thought things were bad in Stalin's Russia, they were about to get worse. One imagines that some members of the NKGB [People's Commissariat of State Security] and NKVD [People's Commissariat of Internal Affairs] were rubbing their hands with glee. Anybody due for release from prison or from a camp on 22 June or shortly thereafter had a nasty shock coming. All releases from camps, jails and colonies of "counterrevolutionaries, bandits, recidivists, and other dangerous offenders" were to be stopped. At 0700 on 22 June all operational staff of the Moscow Directorates of the NKGB and NKVD were confined to barracks while the plans to secure the capital and surrounding area were put into practice . . .

By 1700 the NKGB and NKVD had arrested 14 people but had lined up another 240 for arrest including 71 German "spies," 6 Japanese, 2 Hungarians, 4 British, 3 Italians, 2 Turks and 5 Romanians, plus hundreds of other "criminal elements." The Department for Combating Misappropriation of Socialist Property and Speculation was directed to identify speculators and black marketeers, while 114 defense and state factories and enterprises were placed under special surveillance, often by officials at deputy director level, and 472 checkpoints were set up. The guard on prisons, remand centers and detention camps was to be reinforced, and a camp for 1,000 inmates was set up to house the expected overflow from the prisons . . . A force of 492 officers was detailed to patrol railway lines and installations. Special military and police guards were placed on 14 key railway and other strategic bridges, while the much-loved traffic police (UShOSDOR) were to keep an eye out for any attempts to sabotage the roads and maintain a tighter grip on road traffic . . . Finally, a force of 1,525 police and special constables was to patrol Moscow's streets to maintain public order and also, no doubt, to reassure the public.[50]

Not until midday did the Soviet government, "through the limping phrases and halting tone of Molotov," announce to the Russian people via a radio broadcast that a state of war existed between Germany and the Soviet Union. The claim of a "provocation" was no longer credible, and Stalin, who had obstinately refused to face the truth, had no option but to admit to a state of war. After driving to the Central Telegraph Office on Gor'kiy Street, Molotov broadcast the announcement over the radio at 12:15 P.M.[51] "Men and women, citizens of the Soviet Union," he began tentatively, while striving to overcome his stutter:

> *The Soviet government and its head, Comrade Stalin, have instructed me to make the following statement:*
>
> *At four o'clock this morning [Moscow time], without declaration of war, and without any claims being made on the Soviet Union, German troops attacked our country, attacked our frontier in many places, and bombed from the air Zhitomir, Kiev, Sebastopol, Kaunas and some other places. There are over 200 dead or wounded. Similar air and artillery attacks have also been made from Romanian and Finnish territory.[52]*

It is not clear if Molotov was purposely misleading the Russian people by appearing to seriously underestimate Russian casualties in the initial air raids; in any case, reliable information on the results of the raids was hardly forthcoming at the time. The foreign minister continued, suggesting that, in its relations with Hitler's Reich, the Soviet government would have very likely entertained almost any concession in an effort to have avoided war:

> *This unheard-of attack on our country is an unparalleled act of perfidy in the history of civilized nations. This attack has been made despite the fact that there was a non-aggression pact between the Soviet Union and Germany, a pact the terms of which were scrupulously observed by the Soviet Union. We have been attacked even though, throughout the period of the Pact, the German government had been unable to make the slightest complaint about the USSR not carrying out its obligations. Therefore the whole responsibility for this act of robbery must fall on the Nazi rulers.[53]*

Molotov went on to recall the fate that had befallen Napoleon some 129 years ago in Russia during the "Patriotic War," insisting that the Red Army—and, indeed, all of the Russian people—would now wage a "*new* Patriotic War, for the Motherland [*Rodina*], for honor, for freedom." He concluded with the simple, but "soul-searing" words—"Our cause is just. The enemy will be smashed. Victory will be ours [*pobeda budet za nami*]."[54]

All across Moscow people had ceased what they were doing and listened intently to Molotov's words over the "round black loudspeakers—half a million of them—which were strung out on the streets, in public places, and in factories throughout the city." The people responded to the foreign minister's announcement with "patriotic emotion, tears and shock."[55]

People could not believe what was happening. Krylov, an official from the Commissariat of Finance, was traveling home by tram when an elderly woman told the passengers that war had begun. A well-dressed man sitting beside him accused her of provocation, and said she should be taken off to the police station. He shut up when a policeman got on at the next stop and said he had just heard Molotov's broadcast. When the news sank in, there was a wave of anger at German treachery, of passionate patriotism, and of confidence that the Red Army—with its glorious traditions and its modern equipment—would quickly see the Germans off the field. The war would be over in a month, or at the most by the end of the year. Krylov overheard one young man explaining to his girlfriend that modern technology meant that nowadays long wars were technically impossible. One factory director went too far: he announced to his workers that the Red Army had already captured Warsaw. He was arrested, but the rumor swept Moscow. It was left to those who remembered the First World War to warn that beating the Germans might not be so simple. Most people set aside their reservations about the regime: it was their country that now had to be defended from the German assault. They flocked in their tens of thousands to volunteer their services.[56]

The enthusiasm of the Muscovites, however, was hardly apparent to the foreigners living in the city. They noticed the ostensible absence of patriotic demonstrations, and dismissed the patriotic resolutions passed by factory workers. They, too, were flummoxed by the fact that Stalin had not spoken. The staff of the British embassy concluded that the Soviet dictator had simply chosen not to speak on such a grave occasion "because he knew that ordinary Russians found his thick Georgian accent somewhat comic." Yet why then, they wondered, had Stalin failed to issue a personal call to the people of Russia through the press?[57]

Meanwhile, just a few blocks away from Molotov's studio, in the "eerily self-contained world of the Kremlin fortress," Stalin was taking action that, in the final analysis, would have a direct (and salutary) impact on the outcome of the war. He ordered Politburo member Lazar Kaganovich to evacuate hundreds of factories and some twenty million people from the frontier regions; to begin this daunting operation, the two million workers in the Soviet railway system were immediately placed on a war footing.[58] The *vozhd* tasked Anastas Mikoyan, the minister for external trade, with the mission of feeding and supplying the Red Army. While Stalin was pleased with Molotov's radio address, he had, perhaps irrationally, already focused on the unfortunate General Pavlov, who was "doomed" to lose Belorussia, "as the target of his frustration and anger."[59]

If there is one overarching theme pertaining to Moscow and June 22, 1941, it is this: The day was consumed by the frantic efforts of Stalin and the Soviet military leadership[60] to get information about the rapidly changing situation at the front—efforts that were largely thwarted by the spectacular successes of the *Luftwaffe*, German special forces, and local saboteurs. With lines of communication shattered, or at least disrupted, neither the Kremlin nor the Ministry of Defense was aware that the situation was far worse than they believed. By evening, however, despite incomplete and even inaccurate reporting from the frontier, an "immediate decision" was required "to organize further resistance against the enemy."[61]

Thus at 9:15 P.M., Stalin and Timoshenko issued Directive No. 3, which called for a general counterattack along the entire Eastern Front (see, Appendix 6). The Northwestern and Western Fronts were to mount concentric thrusts by both infantry and armor from Kaunas and Grodno to Suwalki, while Western Front was also to contain the advance of German Army Group Center along the Warsaw-Minsk axis. Southwestern Front, while "holding firmly to the border with Hungary," was to "encircle and destroy the enemy grouping advancing on the Vladimir-Volynski and Krystynopol' front with concentric attacks in the general direction of Lublin." The attacks were to be supported by bombers of the Soviet Long-Range Aviation Force.[62]

The directive was broadly in line with prewar plans for Red Army counter-offensive action in the event of war. It indicates that Stalin and the High Command fully expected the Red Army would be able to cope with the German attack and to carry out its own strategic missions, including mounting an effective counter-invasion of German territory. Indeed, according to the third directive, the Red Army was expected to achieve its initial objectives in East Prussia and southern Poland within two days.[63]

Of course, this third, and final, "blundering" directive of June 21/22 bore not the slightest relationship to the events unfolding in the battlespace along the frontier, and today stands as a monument to the appalling level of ignorance that reigned in Moscow throughout this first day of the war. Simply put, its objective "was to hurl the German Army back in one massive attack, ending it all with a single blow." Soviet *front* commanders, striving desperately to maintain the cohesion of their armies in the face of fierce German ground and air assaults, had no choice but to prepare for the immense offensive operations (envisaged to a depth of 80–120 kilometers) demanded by the directive. And the ambitious initial objectives were to be gained in just forty-eight hours! "The impediments to any kind of success," averred the late John Erickson, "were enormous. Aircraft that might have covered the units during their concentration had long ago been shot to pieces on the ground; the artillery, like much of the infantry, was stuck for lack of transport; where transport existed, like many of the tanks it stood stalled for lack of fuel; where there was fuel, there was little or no ammunition. And even where all those requirements were met, there was no time."[64]

On the evening of June 22, Pavlov and his chief of staff reported to Moscow that their 3 and 10 Armies had been pushed back, but only slightly. 4 Army, they informed their superiors, "is fighting, it is estimated, on the line Mel'nik—Brest-Litovsk—Vlodava." Largely oblivious to the situation, having lost control of his armies, Pavlov was now reporting "estimates."[65]

The night brought temporary respite to some forces of the Soviet border commands. It also witnessed the first operational digest (*svodka*) from the Soviet General Staff, completed by 10:00 P.M. "Of the urgency of the situation," observed John Erickson, "it contained not the slightest trace. Blatant with complacency and swelled with ignorance, it read":

> *Regular troops of the German Army during the course of 22 June conducted operations against frontier defense units of the USSR, attaining insignificant success in a number of sectors. During the second half of the day, with the arrival of forward elements of the field forces of the Red Army, the attacks by German troops along most of the length of our frontiers were beaten off and losses inflicted on the enemy.*[66]

In the meantime, at about 1:00 that afternoon, Stalin, having arrived at the unfortunate "insight" that his commanders were simply "not up to it"—"our front commanders . . . have evidently become somewhat confused"—had decided that several very senior officers, acting as representatives of the Soviet High Command, should be dispatched to the *fronts* to find out what was going on and to offer assistance.[67] In response to Stalin's order, the men (General Zhukov among them) set out from Moscow for their separate destinations, where they were to observe firsthand just what the Germans' "insignificant success" had amounted to:

> *Even the brash and bumptious Kulik*[68] *was aghast at what he found at the battlefront. General Zhukov, however, had few illusions: now with the Southwestern Front, having fed on the tea and sandwiches the aircrew scraped up for him during his flight to Kiev, he learned from Vatutin*[69] *(now placed in charge of the General Staff) on the evening of 22 June that the General Staff lacked "accurate information" about either Soviet or German strengths and movements, that no information was to hand about losses and that there was no contact with Kuznetsov or Pavlov in the Baltic and Western theaters. In spite of this, Stalin was sticking grimly to Directive No. 3 and ordered that Zhukov's signature be added to the document even in his absence.*
>
> *From Kiev Zhukov asked Vatutin just what Directive No. 3 prescribed and on being told that it envisaged a "counter-offensive to rout the enemy in all major directions" and then an advance into enemy territory, he burst out with the remark that the Soviet command had absolutely no idea of where and in what strength the German army was attacking. Vatutin also pointed out ruefully that he would wait until the morning to issue an operational directive, but now the matter had been "decided" and for the moment there was no choice but to go along with it. It was midnight when the directive arrived at Southwestern Front HQ, whereupon Purkayev objected in the strongest terms, but the order had to be carried out.*[70]

Over the next several days, Stalin and Timoshenko would doggedly insist that Directive No. 3 be carried out, despite the fact that it had long been consigned to irrelevance by a situation shifting much too rapidly for either of them to grasp. In many cases, subordinate commanders, despite knowing the real situation, simply passed on the orders because they feared retribution should they refuse to obey them.[71] Except in the Ukraine, where Zhukov's skill and experience—and, to be sure, his ruthlessness—would weigh in the balance, contributing to the relative (albeit temporary) success of the massive armored counterthrusts carried out by Kirponos's Southwestern Front, the outcome would be uniformly disastrous. By June 23, the dangerous gap between Northwestern and Western Fronts, ripped open by the marauding German panzers, had widened to about 125 kilometers.[72] Because no one—not Stalin, not Timoshenko, not Zhukov—had anticipated the actual nature of the German attack, that the Germans "would concentrate such a mass of armored and motorized forces and hurl them in compact groups on all strategic axes on the first day," the Soviet armies at the frontier were being routed, enveloped, and destroyed.[73]

POSTSCRIPT

Reflections on Day One of the Most Destructive War in History and the Ultimate Failure of Operation **Barbarossa**

The first few days of our operations are now behind us. We young soldiers have been pretty badly shaken by powerful experiences and emotional impressions, as we were under fire for the first time. But there's nothing you can't get used to.
—LETTER FROM AN UNKNOWN GERMAN SOLDIER TO HIS PARENTS,
JUNE 26, 1941[1]

Today, after six days of fighting, a first brief greeting and the message that I'm well. We're deep in enemy territory and have achieved very nice successes, I think . . . Early on the 22nd, the fighting started in the same place where I finished in 1939. The first breakthrough occurred suddenly and had an annihilating effect.
—LETTER, PANZER GENERAL HEINZ GUDERIAN TO HIS WIFE,
JUNE 27, 1941[2]

Concerning the overall developments, one can generally say that they haven't fully met all the expectations that we—in my view, in part at least, to an extent not entirely justified—had hoped for . . . We haven't only deceived ourselves about the enemy's military strength, we've also underestimated his leadership abilities. In any case, the forces that this life and death struggle has unleashed on the other side are in this regard quite considerable.
—LETTER, MAJOR HELLMUTH STIEFF, GERMAN GENERAL STAFF OFFICER AT
OKH HEADQUARTERS IN MAUERWALD, EAST PRUSSIA, TO HIS WIFE,
AUGUST 2, 1941[3]

The survival of the Soviet Union in 1941/42 and its resilience in the face of shattering defeats can be ascribed to the character and patriotism of its people, especially the Russians, or to the draconian measures imposed by Stalin, Beria and their Lieutenants. In fact, it must be ascribed to both. During the war, an already authoritarian system became more so. In spite of the catastrophic errors that led to the events of 1941 and 1942, the system was able, using a mixture of terror and propaganda, to mobilize the latent patriotism of the nation.
—HISTORIAN CHRIS BELLAMY[4]

~~~

OVER SEVERAL DECADES OF RESEARCH INTO OPERATION *BARBAROSSA*, I HAVE SEEN MANY hundreds of photographs depicting scenes along the Eastern Front on June 22, 1941. When I began to prepare this postscript, one of them in particular came to mind. It shows what appears to be a platoon-sized group of German infantry, somewhere at the Russo-German frontier, tucked behind the shelter of a railway embankment and awaiting the signal to attack. As the first rays of sunlight wash over the railroad and telegraph lines in front of them, the men themselves are enveloped in darkness and shadows, the morning sun glinting off their steel pots. Some of the men have their heads flush against the ground, as if they may still be sleeping; others are peering off to the left, their attention captured by what we do not know. Perhaps they are observing a formation of German fighters, or bombers, as they droned on toward their targets somewhere beyond the border. The men are loaded down with weapons and equipment—rifles, machine pistols, hand grenades, mess kits, water bottles, entrenching tools, and the like. What look like ammunition boxes are discernable, as are several of the steel gasmask containers (*Tragbüchse*) strapped to the backs of the men.[5]

I've often wondered what thoughts were racing through the minds of these young soldiers, minutes away from rushing into battle against an enemy about whom they knew so very little. Some, no doubt, prayed; others thought of their wives, girlfriends, and families; many of them must have reflected on the profound historical significance of that Sunday morning. In the minutes just prior to this picture being shot, they would have completed last-minute checks of weapons and equipment. Sometime shortly after 3:00 A.M., the anonymous assault party captured in the photograph stormed across the frontier (most likely under cover of a protective artillery barrage) and began its fateful journey into the unknown.[6]

We'll never know what happened to the soldiers in this breathtaking photograph— how many of them were still alive an hour after it was taken, or still among the living at the end of the day. What we do know is that, in the first nine days of the war (through June 30, 1941), the Germans sustained a total of 25,000 dead, an average of almost 2,800 per day, across the entire Eastern Front.[7] In other words, the frightful attrition that would plague the *Ostheer* throughout the *Barbarossa* campaign was manifest from the very first day(s) of the war. The bitter house-to-house fighting for Tauroggen; the battle against the tenaciously defended bunkers at Akmenynai; the gruesome struggle inside the fortress of Brest-Litovsk; the desperate combat for the frontier town of Oleszyce in the Ukraine— these were merely the first bloody battles of a campaign that would, by the end of 1941, result in the veritable decapitation of the German army in the East. Indeed, even Army Chief of Staff Halder, in a moment of sober reflection, would admit in late November 1941 that Germany would never again possess an army as magnificent, as well trained and equipped, as the *Ostheer* in June 1941.[8]

Although attrition—of both men and matériel—among the Reich's armies in the East was to become a serious problem as the summer of 1941 wore on, it was certainly not an issue to the German High Command, or to the great majority of the *Wehrmacht*'s front-line units, on June 22. As we have seen, however, there were other disturbing realities—themes, if you will—that were readily apparent to the Germans from the first day of the war and that would characterize the conflict through all of its 1,418 barbarous days. Most notable among them, as expressed in the official war diaries of the German army—and in soldiers' letters and personal diaries—was the shocking brutality of the fighting on the Eastern Front. From the very first hours of the campaign, the Germans—the average *Landser* and field commanders alike—became acutely cognizant of the fact that the war in the East would be fundamentally different from the campaigns in the West and the Balkans that had preceded it. Simply put, the Red Army soldier would prove to be the most tenacious—and brutal—adversary encountered by the *Wehrmacht* in any major combat theater during World War II.

From the German perspective—as emphasized by many examples in this narrative—the Russian soldier fought hard, but he also fought dirty and in crass violation of the rules of war. In more than a few cases on June 22, Russian soldiers, concealed in farmsteads, wooded areas, or fields of tall grain, let their attackers go by only to fire on them from behind; they feigned death, or surrender, then tossed hand grenades or shot at their startled adversaries. It was a way of war that General Gotthard Heinrici (C-in-C, 43 Army Corps), and many other Germans, labeled "insidious" (*hintertückisch*).[9] In other instances, captured German soldiers were tortured, killed, and horribly mutilated by enraged Red Army soldiers, while German doctors and stretcher-bearers, as illustrated through the example of Dr. Heinrich Haape (Chapter 4, Section 4.6), soon discovered that their Red Cross armbands or ambulances offered no protection from Russian guns. The Germans, of course, responded to the excesses of the Red Army with excesses of their own; thus, from the very outset, a brutal dialectical logic of atrocity and reprisal resulted in a surging spiral of violence that would dramatically escalate the incidents of extra-judicial killings by both combatants. Of course, atrocities committed by German soldiers were not simply—or even primarily—a response to the excesses of the Red Army. "Hitler's war" against the Soviet Union was a genocidal war of annihilation, and while decades of research has led me to the conclusion that a large majority of *Landser* in the East fought within the rules of war, a small—albeit significant—minority, motivated by ideological and/or racial hatred, were guilty of brutal crimes from the very outset of the campaign, such as the shooting of prisoners of war.[10]

From the beginning of Operation *Barbarossa*, attacking German forces were plagued by problems due to the poor infrastructure of roads and bridges on the Soviet side of the frontier, as well as by the plentiful forests and swamps that acted as force multipliers for Russian troops. The roads, often little more than sandy tracks, were barely navigable for armored vehicles, trucks, or horse-drawn artillery, and slowed the rate of the German advance. This can be seen as a textbook example of what the great German military philosopher Carl von Clausewitz called "friction," which subjected German planning to the rigors of the real world. In addition, the heavily wooded areas (and swampy terrain) in the sectors of both Army Group North and Center offered excellent hiding places to Russian units, or individual groups of soldiers, overwhelmed by the superior attacking German forces. Beginning on June 22, German infantry, poorly trained for forest fighting, would be called upon time and again to clear the enemy from wooded terrain; in doing so, they soon discovered that the Russian soldier was a master of forest fighting, and that the lethality of Russian troops in such areas was greatly amplified by their cunning and skill at concealment and camouflage. The outcome was heavy losses for the attacking Germans.[11]

Also inflicting serious casualties on the Germans were the seemingly ubiquitous Russian snipers who, outfitted with their excellent automatic rifles with telescopic sights, struck often and without warning. Red Army snipers were a feared and deadly presence from the very start of the campaign; in fact, references to Russian snipers run like an unbroken thread through the combat portions of this narrative. As early as June 23, units of Field Marshal von Kluge's Fourth Army would complain about the sudden appearance of enemy snipers.[12] According to a statistical evaluation undertaken by the Germans in 1944, 43 percent of German soldiers who died on the battlefield (i.e., those buried without ever making it to a field hospital for care) succumbed to shots to the head—a favorite target of snipers.[13]

Finally, in examining the first day of Operation *Barbarossa* from the perspective of the attacking Germans, there is one overarching reality that eclipses all of the others, and it is this: "The German Army that plunged into the fields, forests and endless plains and steppe lands of European Russia on 22 June 1941 was perhaps the most splendid fighting force the world had yet seen . . . [T]he [more than three] million soldiers that comprised Germany's *Ostheer* . . . signified something uniquely special. In terms of doctrine, training, initiative, experience, efficacy of their weaponry and success on the battlefield, modern Europe, at least, had never seen anything like them."[14] The successes achieved on the battlefield by the attacking German ground and air forces on day one of the eastern campaign were truly remarkable and, as far as the *Luftwaffe* was concerned, wholly unprecedented. As we have seen, the most significant German victories achieved on June 22 were in the sector of Field Marshal von Bock's Army Group Center where, by day's end, the encirclement of the bulk of Soviet Western Front was already beginning to take shape, while the tank forces on Bock's left wing had torn open the junction between Soviet Northwestern and Western Fronts. Across the entire spectrum of German force application—from the sabotage actions of special forces through the impressive advances made by the panzer divisions of Army Groups North and Center—the results were spectacular.

Yet despite its auspicious beginning, Operation *Barbarossa* would end in failure in the arctic cold at the gates of Moscow. The simple truth is that there were simply too few *Landser* for the sheer enormity of the mission their political and military leadership had ordered them to carry out. As addressed in Chapter 1 (Section 1.4), the German attack on Soviet Russia was fatally underpowered. Carelessly—and arrogantly—underestimating the unprecedented challenges of a war with the Soviet Union, German military planners, from the outset, failed to equip the *Ostheer* with the resources it needed to succeed; after the campaign began, the eastern armies received but a trickle of reserves and replacements (both of men and matériel), as Hitler and his High Command, convinced of impending victory, prepared for the next stage along the Third Reich's path to world domination.

On June 22, 2016, the seventy-fifth anniversary of Hitler's surprise attack on the Soviet Union, I had the distinct honor of being in the Russian city of Rzhev, about 220 kilometers west of Moscow and the site of utterly savage fighting in 1942/43.[15] The strategic German bridgehead at Rzhev—the northernmost corner-post of Army Group Center—had pointed ominously toward the Soviet capital, and the battles there, which dragged on from January 1942 to March 1943, were characterized by appalling losses on both sides. All told, over this fifteen-month period, Russian combat losses on the Rzhev axis amounted to approximately a half million dead and at least twice as many wounded. German losses, while much smaller in number, were no less devastating, given the *Ostheer*'s chronic manpower shortages; they amounted to several hundred thousand casualties, including perhaps 100,000 fatal losses. To this day, the fields, forests, and swamps of the Rzhev region continue to disgorge the remains of German and Russian soldiers who perished in a bloodbath that rivaled in intensity the fighting at Stalingrad (1942/43) or at Verdun during World War I (1916).[16]

After the war, the dreadful meatgrinder of Rzhev was consigned to obscurity—the victim of Soviet censorship that sought to expunge from history the Red Army's epic failure to wrest the war-torn city from its tenacious German defenders.[17] As a result, this "forgotten battle" of the Russo-German War only began to come to light in the 1990s—following the demise of the Soviet Union—due in part to the pioneering efforts of retired U.S. Army colonel David M. Glantz.[18]

Sometime before June 22, 2016, Russian president Vladimir Putin had decreed that the seventy-fifth anniversary of Germany's attack was to be commemorated in all cities and towns throughout Russia. At 3:30 that morning, I was out on the street (at this latitude dawn breaks just after 3:00 A.M. in the summer) along with my German colleague and our Belorussian guide observing the solemn ceremony in Rzhev. Hundreds of people were present, soldiers and civilians alike. They had gathered in a large plaza, which was festooned with lit candles. Slowly, a large procession made its way down to the nearby Volga, where bouquets of flowers were delicately dropped from the bridge and into the mighty and historic river. Later that morning, we drove out to the "Peace Park," where German and Russian military cemeteries sit side-by-side. We looked on as the remains of

1,200 Russian soldiers—their bones sealed in large, brightly colored coffins—were laid to rest inside a cavernous trench within the Russian cemetery. It all made for a somber yet moving experience, and it reinforced an impression that I have held for some time—that is, while America may annually honor her dead at Pearl Harbor each December 7, or the boys who stormed the beaches of Normandy on June 6, for the Russian people the Second World War, and the victory over German fascism gained at such a frightful cost in human lives, remains to this day a living, breathing, tangible experience kept alive by a people who, collectively, still possess strong nationalist sentiments and a steadfast pride in their history.

The sacred occasion I witnessed in Rzhev on this remarkable day captured the melancholy yet unwavering spirit of the Russian people as they remembered the momentous events of June 22, 1941. The first day of the war was a dark day for the Russian people, but it was, as we have seen, a calamitous day for the Russian border guards and soldiers defending the frontier. With communications disrupted up and down the chain of command, the Russian defenders were left to their own devices for hours; when operational orders were finally issued, they bore no relationship to the events transpiring at lightning speed across the frontier from the Baltic Sea to the Prut River. The NKVD border detachments and Red Army troops caught in the maelstrom of the German assault were not prepared for war. As addressed at some length in this narrative, many of the T-34 and KV tank drivers had no more than a few hours' experience; some KV tanks had yet to be bore-sighted, or supplied with ammunition; many artillery and antiaircraft regiments were not at their stations but away at gunnery practice ranges; infantry battalions had left their combat zones to construct fortifications, but many of these fortifications were not manned when the Germans attacked; many officers were away from their units, having gone on weekend leave to be with their families; pilots were not yet trained to fly the new and more sophisticated aircraft now coming out of the factories; and, in general, Red Army units were widely scattered about, instead of concentrated at critical points, while key commanders were often not at their posts when war began.

The cumulative effect of these and many other unfortunate realities, coupled with the Teutonic precision and colossal violence of the *Wehrmacht*'s initial strike, was, with but few exceptions, the complete collapse and disintegration of the Red Army's border defenses. The chaos and confusion that prevailed up and down the front is recorded in fulsome detail in the dozens of Soviet archival documents used in the preparation of this narrative; and while I was able to examine but a tiny fraction of these documents (from the Russian Ministry of Defense), certain themes emerged with remarkable clarity and consistency. For example, I was struck by the constant references to German airstrikes—against towns and cities, Red Army command posts, airfields, troop concentrations, railway stations, even strikes on individual trains and strafing attacks against civilians—leaving me with the impression that the *Luftwaffe* was veritably omnipresent above the battlefield on this first day of the war and making the destruction of over 1,800 VVS aircraft all the more understandable. The detailed reports of Soviet *front* headquarters also make repeated (and false) references to major drops of German "parachutists" behind the lines—reports that simply underscore the confusion and panic among the Soviet commands, as well as the paucity of accurate information at their disposal throughout June 22, 1941.[19]

A consistent theme of day one of Operation *Barbarossa* was that Russian frontier forces were taken by complete surprise when the attack began. Account after account in this narrative has shown that, in the opening minutes—even hours—of the German assault, Soviet resistance was negligible to nonexistent. Yet as the day progressed, resistance began to stiffen, and at many points along the front, the Red Army fought with tenacity and courage. Soviet border guards and infantry units held out to the last man, even blew themselves up in their bunkers instead of surrendering. Other *Rotarmisten* dissolved into the forests or swamps, where they waged guerrilla war against the surging German columns. Soviet bomber crews bravely carried out their orders, even though their orders often signified certain death. Just as with the *Ostheer*, we'll never know how many Red Army men perished on June 22; we do know, however, that the frontier battles alone (lasting for eighteen days until July 9, 1941) resulted in the destruction of the Red Army's first strategic echelon—the Germans inflicting at least 747,870 casualties on Russian forces and eliminating 10,180 Russian tanks and 3,995 aircraft. By any measure, these losses were "both unprecedented and astounding."[20]

That the Red Army and the Soviet state were able to survive the initial German blows and eventually emerge victorious—as noted at the start of Chapter 2, the German attack was the 1941 equivalent of a nuclear first strike—was due to many factors. While an in-depth discussion of these factors is beyond the scope of this narrative, permit me a few final observations. Let us begin with the fact that Adolf Hitler's war of annihilation (*Vernichtungskrieg*) against the Soviet Union signified an enormous radicalization of World War II. Not only did Operation *Barbarossa* result in a vast geographical expansion of the war, it enabled Hitler to begin the systematic destruction of Europe's Jews (and other "undesirable" elements) by deploying the forces of the *Einsatzgruppen* (the notorious SS murder squads), which moved into Soviet Russia on the heels of the advancing *Wehrmacht*. As a result of the Reich's racist and genocidal policies, as well as Germany's refusal to abolish the hated collective farms and return the land to the peasantry, it soon became clear to the great majority of the Russian people that their only option was to unite in implacable opposition to the German invaders.

As the enormously influential German historian Andreas Hillgruber observed thirty-five years ago, what was "decisive" (*entscheidend*) from a military point of view was the remarkable ability of the Soviet Union to replace its towering and unprecedented losses by mobilizing and committing to battle millions of trained reservists in the final six months of 1941.[21] From June through December 1941, the Soviet Union generated more than fifty new field armies[22] and a total of approximately 285 rifle divisions, eighty-eight cavalry divisions, twelve re-formed tank divisions, 174 rifle brigades, and ninety-three tank brigades.[23] As noted in Chapter 1 (Section 1.4), it was "Soviet divisions, not cold weather, [that] stopped the Germans."[24]

In this narrative I have elaborated at length on the many failures of Joseph Stalin on the eve of war with Germany, and the Soviet leader's profound responsibility for the disaster that befell Russia on June 22, 1941. There is, however, another perspective that, in this context, merits our attention. Simply stated, it was the Soviet dictator (the *vozhd*) who drove policies in the late 1920s and 1930s that, although accomplished at such a terrible cost in human suffering,[25] forged Russia into a modern industrial state that, by 1941, had transformed a backward Red Army into a virtual juggernaut, endowed with larger mechanized, cavalry, and airborne forces than any other nation in the world (see, Chapter 1, Section 1.6). And it is this historical fact, more than any other, that accounts for the Soviet Union's ability to first halt, then defeat, the German *Blitzkrieg* of 1941. Even the Great Purge of the Soviet civilian and military leadership, implemented by Stalin in 1936, had an impact that, ironically, helped Soviet Russia to stave off defeat in 1941 and, in the years that followed, to triumph over Hitler's 1,000-Year Reich. This was because, by 1941, Stalin, as a result of his singularly ruthless policies, dominated the Soviet state (its leaders and its people) so thoroughly that it functioned as a single-minded manifestation of his own will.[26] "In Stalin's USSR," averred historian Constantine Pleshakov, "state brutality compensated for everything—impassable roads, broken tanks, ignorant generals, inadequate food. As long as the dictatorship was able to manipulate its own people, it *was* efficient and could sustain almost any challenge, despite a faltering economy and jamming guns."[27] In a fashion that Hitler could only have admired, Stalin ruthlessly lashed his soldiers—his people, his nation—on to final victory, in the process sparing them no indignity or sacrifice.[28] In his remarkable new book, historian Stephen Kotkin offers a more nuanced analysis of the sources of the *vozhd*'s boundless power over the Soviet state and its people:

> *Under Stalin's regime, both the apocalyptic bloodshed and the state's capacity to summon resources and popular involvement intensified, a consequence of the violent mass era that slightly predated but was blown open by the First World War, the heady promises of Marxism-Leninism, and Stalin's personal qualities. His despotic power derived not just from his control over the formidable levers of Leninist dictatorship, which he built, but from the ideology, which he shaped. His regime proved able to define the terms of public thought and individual identity, and he proved able to personify passions and dreams, to realize and represent a socialist modernity and Soviet might. With single-sentence telegrams or brief phone calls, he could spur the clunky Soviet party-state machinery into action, invoking discipline and intimidation, to be sure, but also emotionally galvanizing young functionaries who felt close personal ties to him, and millions more who would never come close to meeting him in person. Stalin was a student of historical forces, and of people, and his rule enabled those who came from nothing to feel world historically significant.[29]*

A final point: In the preface to this book, I posited—albeit without further elaboration—that the collapse of the Soviet Union and its empire decades later actually had its origins in Hitler's attack on June 22, 1941. While the Red Army was largely responsible for the defeat of the *Wehrmacht*, which sustained almost 75 percent of its total losses on the Eastern Front,[30] what is also true is that the Soviet Union never fully recovered from the much greater losses—both human and material—it suffered in 1,418 days of war against Hitler's Germany. Demographers "calculate the [USSR's] 'global loss' of population, resulting not only from excess deaths during the war, including the direct war deaths, but also the overall impact on population, resulting from couples who never met and babies not born, to have been in the order of 48 million."[31] Moreover, the Eastern European empire acquired by the USSR as a result of the war, as well as its extensive foreign commitments (e.g., Cuba, Africa, the Middle East), the latter a reflection of Russia's rise to "superpower" status in the postwar period, burdened the Soviet Union with responsibilities that, given its meager resource base, it ultimately could not bear. (After all, throughout its history the USSR remained, in most respects, little more than a third world country, albeit after 1949 a hostile Communist nation armed with nuclear weapons.) Eventually, these commitments (following in the wake of Russia's catastrophic losses in World War II), along with the ruinous arms race with the United States, exhausted and bankrupted the Soviet Union, leading to its formal dissolution in December 1991. And the first step down the long road to collapse was taken at dawn on that bloody Sunday, June 22, 1941.

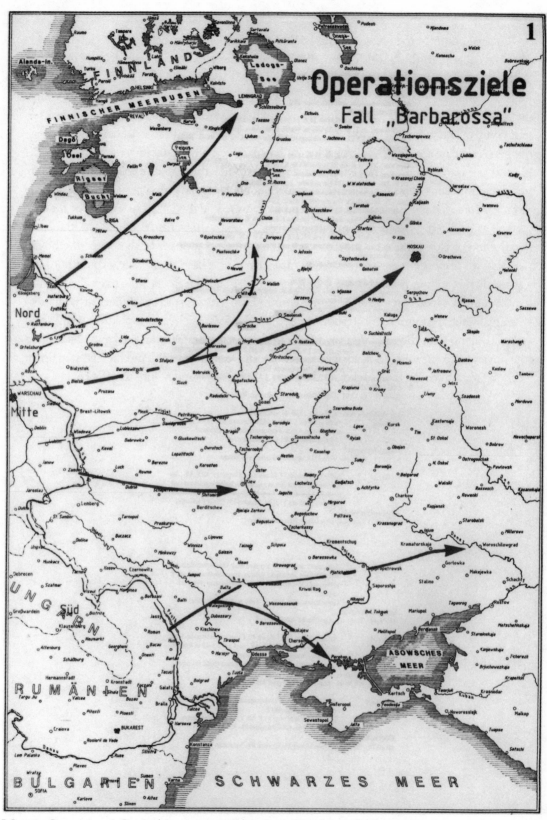

Map 1: Operational Goals (*Operationsziele*)—Case "*Barbarossa*" (1)

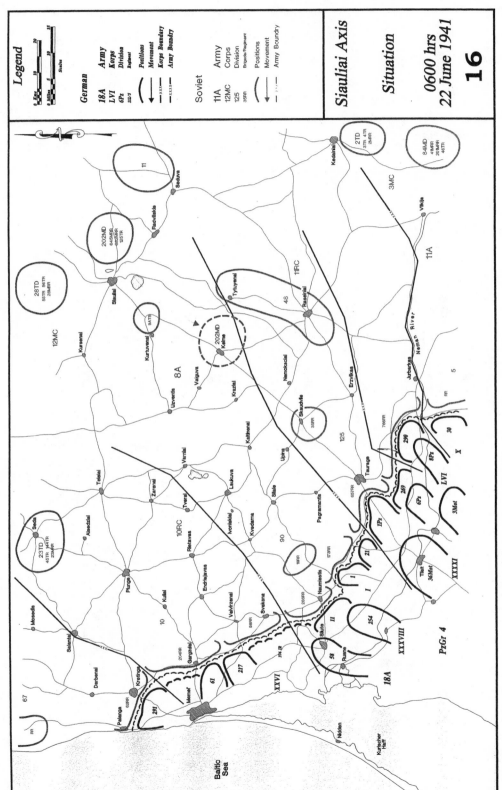

Map 2: Siauliai Axis, Situation, 0600 hrs., June 22, 1941 (2)

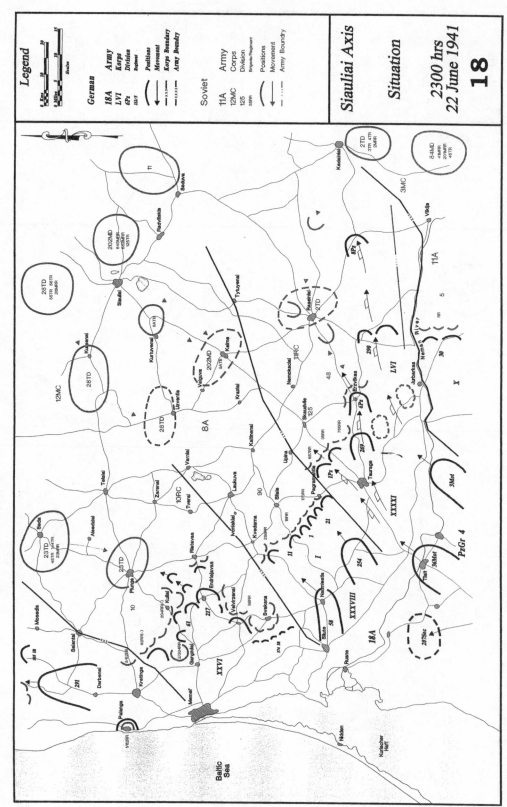

Map 3: Siauliai Axis, Situation, 2300 hrs., June 22, 1941 (2)

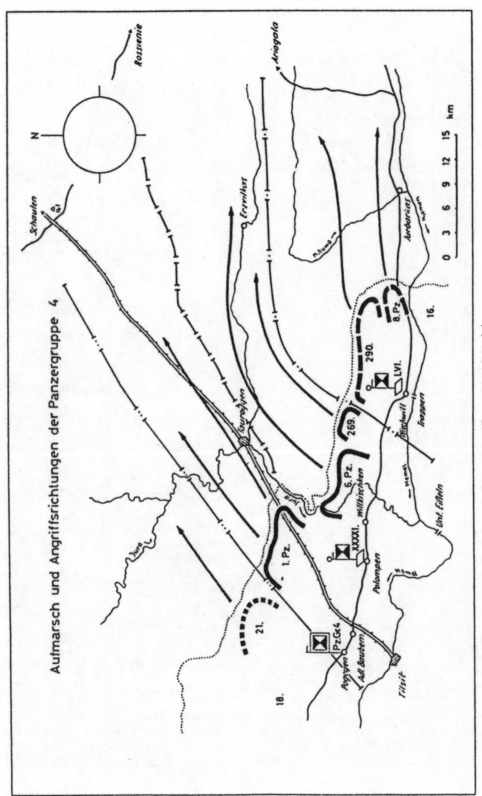

Map 4: 4 Panzer Group—Deployment and Attack Directions, June 22, 1941 (4)

Map 5: German Situation Map, Army Group North, Evening, June 22, 1941 (3)

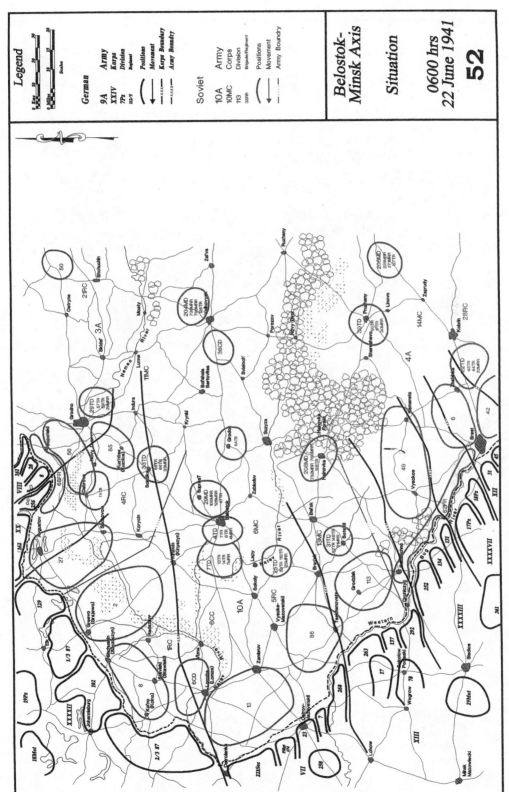

Belostok–Minsk Axis

Situation

0600 hrs
22 June 1941

52

Map 6: Belostok–Minsk Axis, Situation, 0600 hrs., June 22, 1941 (2)

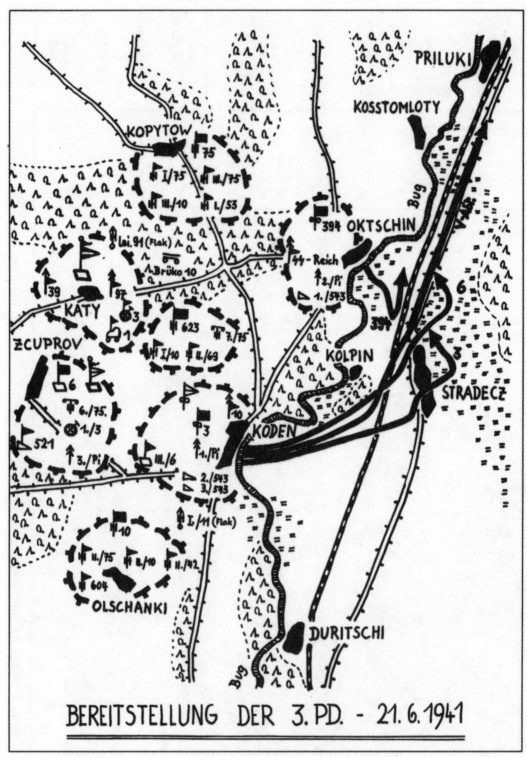

Map 7: Assembly Area of the 3 Panzer Division, June 21, 1941 (6)

Map 8: Belostok-Minsk Axis, Situation, 2300 hrs., June 22, 1941 (2)

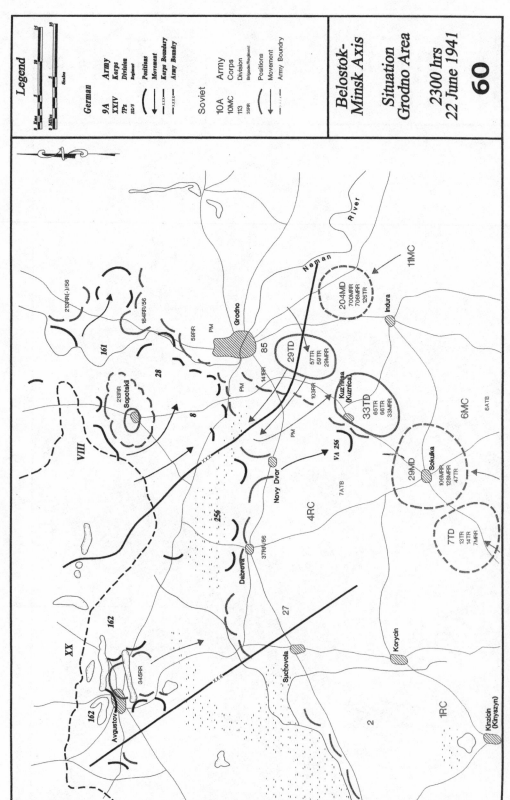

Map 9: Belostok–Minsk Axis, Situation Grodno Area, 2300 hrs., June 22, 1941 (2)

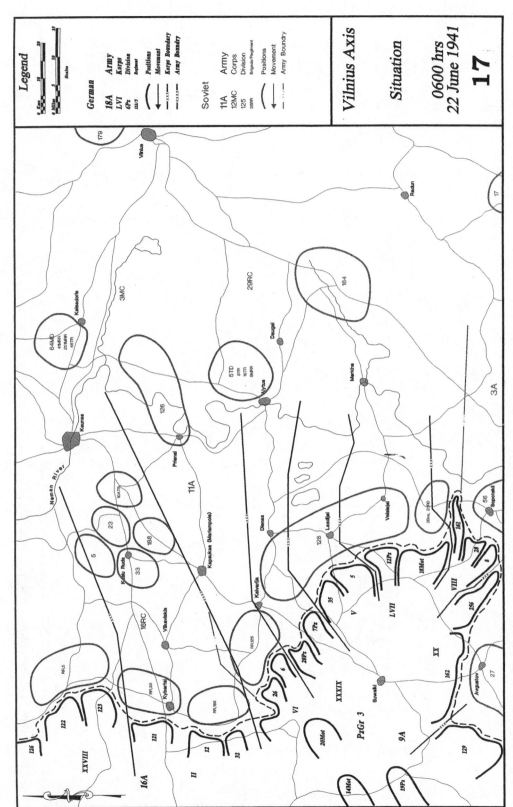

Map 10: Vilnius Axis, Situation, 0600 hrs., June 22, 1941 (2)

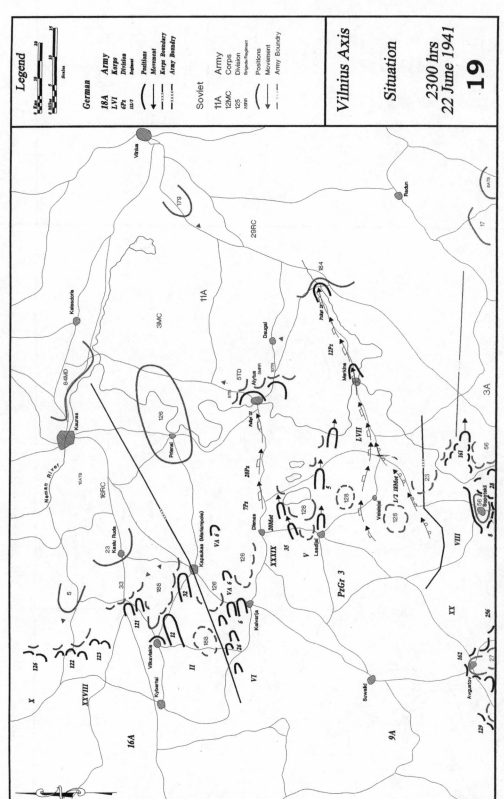

Map 11: Vilnius Axis, Situation, 2300 hrs., June 22, 1941 (2)

Map 12: German Situation Map, Army Group Center, Evening, June 22, 1941 (3)

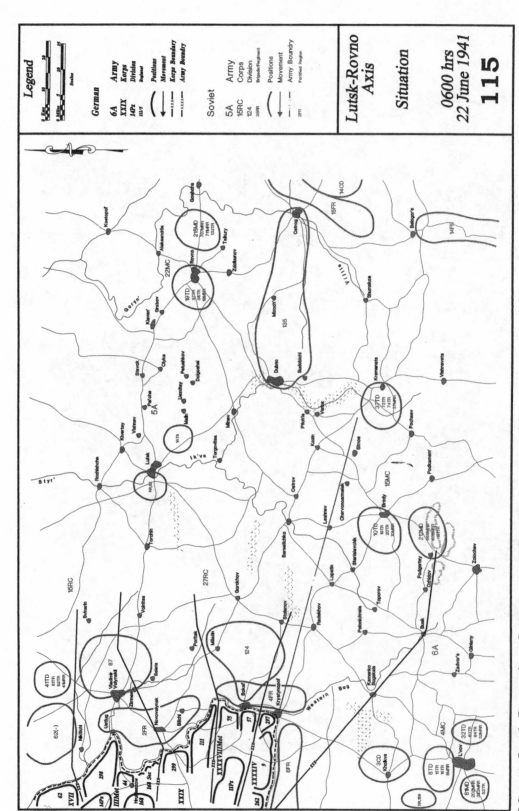

Map 13: Lutsk-Rovno Axis, Situation, 0600 hrs., June 22, 1941 (2)

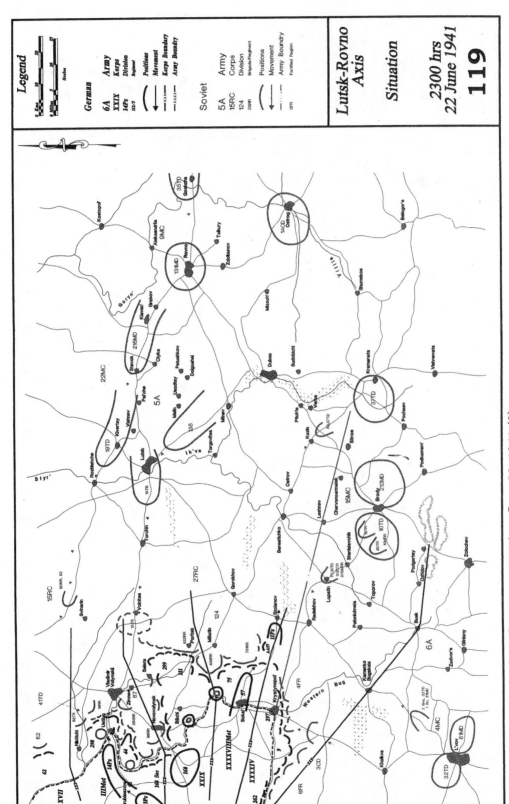

Map 14: Lutsk-Rovno Axis, Situation, 2300 hrs., June 22, 1941 (2)

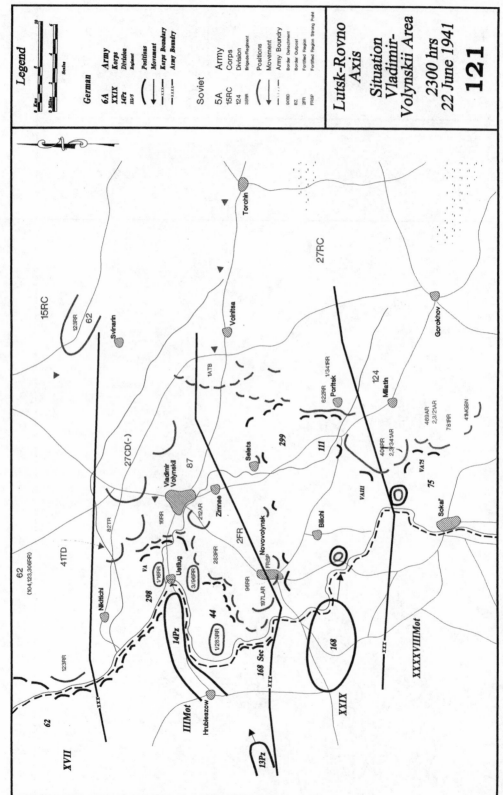

Map 15: Lutsk-Rovno Axis, Situation Vladimir-Volynski Area, 2300 hrs., June 22, 1941 (2)

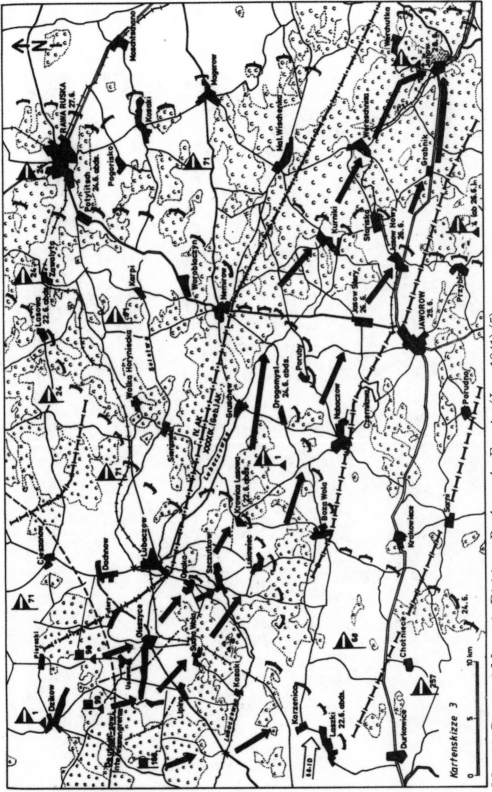

Map 16: German 1 Mountain Division—Battles at the Frontier (June 1941) (5)

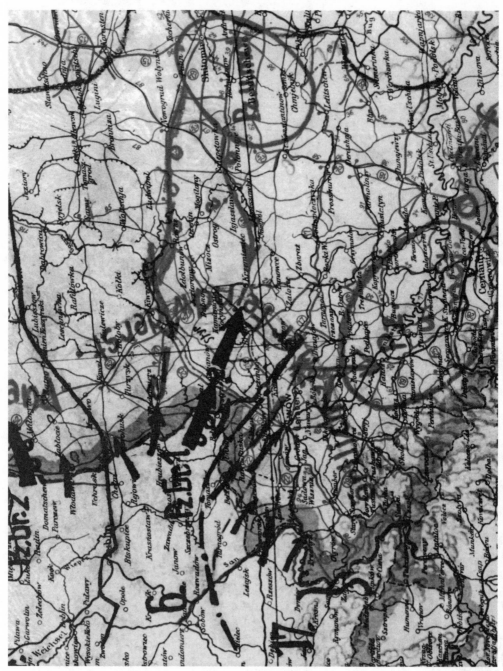

Map 17: German Situation Map, Army Group South, Evening, June 22, 1941 (3)

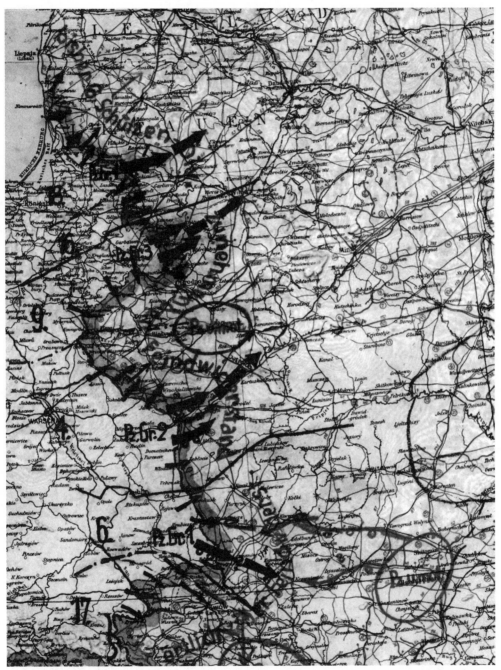

Map 18: German Situation Map, Eastern Front, Evening, June 22, 1941 (3)

APPENDIX 1
EQUIVALENT MILITARY RANKS[1]
(GERMAN/AMERICAN)

Officer Ranks:

Generalfeldmarschall	Field Marshal
Generaloberst	General
General (der Infanterie, etc.)	Lieutenant General
Generalleutnant	Major General
Generalmajor	Brigadier General
Oberst	Colonel
Oberstleutnant	Lieutenant Colonel
Major	Major
Hauptmann or Rittmeister	Captain
Oberleutnant	First Lieutenant
Leutnant	Second Lieutenant

Noncommissioned Officers (NCOs):

Stabsfeldwebel	Sergeant Major
Oberfeldwebel	Master Sergeant
Feldwebel	Technical Sergeant
Unterfeldwebel	Staff Sergeant
Unteroffizier	Noncommissioned Officer

Enlisted Men:

Stabsgefreiter	Administrative Corporal
Obergefreiter	Corporal
Gefreiter	Lance Corporal
Obersoldat	Private 1st Class
Soldat (Schütze)	Private (Rifleman)

Medical Ranks:

Oberstarzt	Colonel (med.)
Oberfeldarzt	Lieutenant-Colonel (med.)
Oberstabsarzt	Major (med.)
Stabsarzt	Captain (med.)
Oberarzt	First Lieutenant (med.)
Assistenzarzt	Second Lieutenant (med.)
Unterarzt	Noncommissioned Officer (med.)

DIRECTIVE NO. 21—CASE *BARBAROSSA*[1]
(DECEMBER 18, 1940)

Führer *and Supreme Commander*   Führer *Headquarters*
of the Armed Forces   *18 December 1940.*
                                                   9 copies

Directive No. 21
"*Case* Barbarossa"

The Wehrmacht *must be prepared, even before the conclusion of the war against* England, to crush Soviet Russia in a rapid campaign *[*Sowjetrussland in einem schnellen Feldzug niederzuwerfen*] ("Case* Barbarossa*").*

*The Army [*Heer*] will have to employ all available formations to this end, with the reservation that occupied territories must be insured against surprise attacks. The* Luftwaffe *will have to make available for this eastern campaign [*Ostfeldzug*] supporting forces of such strength that the Army will be able to bring land operations to a speedy conclusion and that Eastern Germany will be as little damaged as possible by enemy air attack. This buildup of a focal point [*Schwerpunktbildung*] in the East will be limited only by the need to protect from air attack the whole combat and arsenal area [*Rüstungsraum*] which we control, and to ensure that attacks on England, and especially upon her imports, are not allowed to lapse. The main efforts of the Navy [*Kriegsmarine*] will continue to be directed against England even during the eastern campaign.*

*In certain circumstances I shall issue orders for the deployment [*Aufmarsch*] against Soviet Russia eight weeks before the operation is timed to begin. Preparations which require more time than this will be put in hand now, in so far as this has not already been done, and will be concluded by 15 May 1941. It is of decisive importance that our intentions to attack should not be known. The preparations of the High Commands [*Oberkommandos*] will be made on the following basis:*

*I. General Intention [*Allgemeine Absicht*]:*

*The bulk of the Russian Army stationed in Western Russia will be destroyed by daring operations [*kühnen Operationen*] led by deeply penetrating armored spearheads [*Panzerkeilen*]. Russian forces still capable of giving battle will be prevented from withdrawing into the depths of Russia. The enemy will then be energetically pursued and a line will be reached from which the Russian air force can no longer attack German territory. The final objective [*Endziel*] of the operation is to erect a barrier against Asiatic Russia on the general line Volga–Archangel. The last surviving industrial area of Russia in the Urals can then, if necessary, be eliminated by the *Luftwaffe.

*In the course of these operations the Russian Baltic Fleet [*Ostseeflotte*] will quickly lose it bases and will then no longer be capable of action. The effective operation of the Russian air force is to be prevented from the beginning of the attack by powerful blows [*kraftvolle Schläge*].*

II. Probable Allies and Their Tasks

*1. On the flanks of our operations we can count on the active support of Romania and Finland in the war against Soviet Russia. The High Command of the Armed Forces [*Oberkommando der Wehrmacht*] will decide and lay down in timely fashion the manner in which the forces of these two countries will be brought under German command . . .*

4. It is possible that Swedish railways and roads may be available for the movement of the German Northern Group [Group XXI], by the beginning of the operation at the latest.

*III. Conduct of Operations [*Führung der Operationen*]:*

A. Heer (in accordance with plans submitted to me):

*In the theater of operations, which is divided by the Pripiat' Marshes into a southern and a northern sector, the main weight [*Schwerpunkt*] of attack will be delivered in the northern area. Two army groups [*Heeresgruppen*] will be employed there.*

*The more southerly of these two army groups (in the center of the whole front) will have the task of advancing with powerful armored and motorized formations from the area about and north of Warsaw, and routing the enemy forces in White Russia [*Weissrussland*]. This will make it possible for strong mobile forces to advance northwards and,* *in conjunction with the Northern Army Group operating out of East Prussia in the general direction of Leningrad, to destroy the enemy forces operating in the Baltic area. Only after the fulfillment of this first essential task, which must include the occupation of Leningrad and Kronstadt, will the attack be continued with the intention of occupying Moscow, an important center of communications and of the armaments industry. Only a surprisingly rapid collapse of Russian resistance could justify the simultaneous pursuit of both objectives . . .*

The army group operating south of the Pripiat' Marshes will also seek, in a concentric operation with strong forces on either flank, to destroy all Russian forces west of the Dnepr [River] in the Ukraine. The main attack will be carried out from the Lublin area in the general direction of Kiev, while forces in Romania will carry out a wide enclosing movement [Umfassung] across the lower Prut [River]. It will be the task of the Romanian Army to hold down Russian forces in the intervening area.

When the battles north and south of the Pripiat' Marshes are ended the pursuit [Verfolgung] of the enemy will have the following aims: In the south the early capture of the Donets Basin, important for war industry. In the north a quick advance to Moscow. The capture of this city would represent a decisive political and economic success and would also bring about the capture of the most important railway junctions.

B. Luftwaffe*:*

It will be the duty [Aufgabe] of the Luftwaffe *to paralyze and eliminate the effectiveness of the Russian air force as far as possible. It will also support the main operations of the Army, i.e., those of the Central Army Group and of the vital flank of the Southern Army Group. Russian railways will either be destroyed or, in accordance with operational requirements, captured at their most important points (river crossings!) by the bold employment [kühnen Einsatz] of parachute and airborne troops.*[2]

In order that we may concentrate all our strength against the enemy air force and for the immediate support of land operations, the Russian armaments industry [Rüstungsindustrie] will not be attacked during the main operations. Such attacks will be made only after the conclusion of mobile warfare, and they will be concentrated first on the Urals area.

C. Kriegsmarine*:*

It will be the duty of the Navy during the attack on Soviet Russia to protect our own coasts and to prevent the breakout of enemy naval units from the Baltic. As the Russian

Baltic Fleet will, with the capture of Leningrad, lose its last base and will then be in a hopeless position [hoffnungsloser Lage], major naval action will be avoided until this occurs.

After the elimination [Ausschalten] of the Russian fleet the duty of the Navy will be to protect the entire maritime traffic in the Baltic and the transport of supplies by sea to the northern flank (clearing of minefields!).

IV. All steps taken by Commanders-in-Chief on the basis of this directive must be phrased on the unambiguous assumption that they are precautionary measures [Vorsichtsmassnahmen] undertaken in case Russia should alter its present attitude toward us. The number of officers employed on preliminary preparations will be kept as small as possible and further staffs will be designated as late as possible and only to the extent required for the duties of each individual. Otherwise there is a danger that premature knowledge of our preparations, whose execution cannot yet be timed with any certainty, might entail the gravest political and military disadvantages.

V. I await submission of the plans of Commanders-in-Chief on the basis of this directive . . .

[signed] Adolf Hitler [3]

APPENDIX 3
GERMAN 6 INFANTRY DIVISION: PERSONNEL AND WEAPONS[1]
(JUNE 20, 1941)

(NOTE: THE 6 INFANTRY DIVISION [6 ID] WAS MOBILIZED IN LATE AUGUST 1939 AND transferred at once to the West Wall on the Franco-German border. The division did not participate in the Polish Campaign of September 1939, but played a role in the second phase of the French Campaign [June 1940]. Thereafter, it was transferred to the demarcation line with Vichy France and, in September 1940, to the Normandy coast, where it trained for Operation *Sealion*. In March 1941, the division was sent to East Prussia as part of the buildup for Operation *Barbarossa*. Commanded by *Generalleutnant* Helge Auleb since October 1940, 6 ID consisted of three infantry regiments [18, 37, 58 IR], along with artillery, antitank, reconnaissance, signal, engineer, supply, medical, and administrative units. On June 22, 1941, the 18,000-strong division was assigned to 6 Army Corps of *Generaloberst* Adolf Strauss's Ninth Army. Although an infantry unit, 6 ID would soon acquire a reputation as one of the finest formations in the *Ostheer*. The figures for personnel and weapons are representative of a typical full-strength German infantry division on June 22, 1941.)

COMBAT STRENGTH (*GEFECHTSSTÄRKE*)[2]
Officers: 363
Civilian Officials:[3] 13
NCOs:[4] 2,080
Enlisted Personnel:[5] 11,838
Horses: 4,468

RATION STRENGTH (*VERPFLEGUNGSSTÄRKE*)[6]
Officers: 460
Civilian Officials: 85
NCOs: 2,566
Enlisted Personnel: 15,079
HORSES: 5,555

Total Available Weapons (*Verwendungsbereite Waffen*)
(Excluding small arms)

le.MG	455
s.MG	142
le.Gr.W.	60
s.Gr.W.	56
le.IG	17
s.IG	6
Pak	74
Pz.B.	65
le.FH	36
s.FH	12
Flak 2cm	12
le.Fla.W.	12
m.Fla.W.	3

Definitions
le.MG (light machine gun)
s.MG (heavy machine gun)
le.Gr.W. (light mortar 50mm)
s.Gr.W. (medium mortar 81mm)
le.IG (light infantry gun 75mm)
s.IG (medium infantry gun 150mm)
Pak (antitank guns)
Pz.B. (light antitank rifles) (*Panzerbüchse*)
le.FH (light field howitzer 105mm)
s.FH (medium field howitzer 150mm)
Flak 2cm (antiaircraft gun 20mm)
le.Fla.W. (light antiaircraft gun)
m.Fla.W. (medium antiaircraft gun)[7]

ORDER OF BATTLE OF A GERMAN PANZER DIVISION[1]
(JUNE 1941)

Division HQ with Map Section (mot.) (2 le.MG)

Panzer Brigade Staff with,
— Signal Platoon, Light Tank Platoon (3 Pz III command tanks, 5 Pz II), Music Corps

2 Panzer Battalions[2] each with,
— 1 HQ Company (2 Pz III command tanks, 5 Pz II)
— 2 Light Tank Companies (each with 17 Pz III, 5 Pz II)
— 1 Medium Tank Company (14 Pz IV, 5 Pz II)

Rifle Brigade Staff with,
2 Rifle Regiments each with,
— HQ Company (Signal Platoon, Combat Engineer Platoon, Motorcycle Platoon, Music Corps, 3 le.MG)
— Two Rifle Battalions each with,
3 Rifle Companies (each with 18 le.MG, 2 s.MG, 3 le.Gr.W.)
1 MG Company (mot.) (8 s.MG, 6 s.Gr.W.)
1 Heavy Company (mot.) (3 37mm Pak, 2 le.IG, 4 le.MG)
— 1 Infantry Gun Company (mot.) (2 s.IG, 4. le.IG)

1 Motorcycle Battalion with,
— 3 Motorcycle Companies (weapons same as rifle battalions)
— 1 Motorcycle-MG Company (same as above)
— 1 Heavy Company (mot.) (same as above)

1 Medium Infantry Gun Company (self-propelled)
— Only for 1, 2, 5, 9, and 10 PDs (6 s.IG [SP])

1 Armored Reconnaissance Battalion with,
— Staff and Signal Platoon (mot.) (2 le.MG)
— 1 Armored Scout Company (10 KwK 20mm,[3] 25 le.MG)
— 1 Motorcycle Company (18 le.MG, 2 s.MG, 3 s.Gr.W.)
— 1 Heavy Company (mot.) (same as in rifle battalions)
— 1 Reconnaissance Column (mot.) (3 le.MG)

1 Artillery Regiment (mot.) with,
— Staff and Signal Platoon (mot.)
— 2 Light Artillery Battalions (mot.) each with,
3 Light Field Howitzer Batteries (each with 4 105mm le.FH, 2 le.MG)
— 1 Medium (*schwere*) Mixed Artillery Battalion (mot.) with,
2 Medium Field Howitzer Batteries (each with 4 150mm s.FH, 2 le.MG)
1 100mm Gun Battery (4 100mm Cannon, 2 le.MG)

1 Antitank Battalion[4] with,
— Staff and Signal Platoon (mot.)
— 3 Antitank Companies (mot.) (each with 8 37mm Pak, 3 50mm Pak, 6 le.MG)
— 1 Flak Company[5] (8 20mm flak, 2 20mm *Vierling* flak)

1 Armored Combat Engineer Battalion and Staff with,
— 2 Light Engineer Companies (mot.) (each with 9 le.MG)
— 1 Armored Combat Engineer Company (Pz Is,[6] 6 SPW[7] with 280/320mm rocket launchers)
— 1 Bridging Column "B" (mot.)
— 1 Bridging Column "K" (mot.)
— 1 Light Combat Engineer Column (mot.)

1 Armored Signal Battalion and Staff with,
— 1 Armored Telephone Company (2 le.MG)
— 1 Armored Radio Company (13 le.MG)
— 1 Light Armored Signal Column

1 Field Replacement Battalion

Supply and Rear Area Services including,
— Motor Vehicle Supply Columns
— 1 Supply Company (mot.)
— 3 Maintenance and Repair Companies (mot.)
— 2 Medical Companies
— 3 Ambulance Platoons
— 1 Bakery Company
— 1 Butchery Company
— Div. Ration Supply Office (mot.)
— Military Police (mot.) (*Feldgendarmerietrupp*)
— Field Post Service

APPENDIX 5
56 INFANTRY DIVISION'S ORDER NO. 1 FOR THE ATTACK ACROSS THE BUG RIVER[1]
(JUNE 19, 1941)

(Note: This appendix illustrates the diligent and detailed planning that was typical of German staff officers. From the length of the document, and the breadth of issues addressed, it is apparent that the individual(s) who prepared this order sought to cover every possible eventuality. Most of the document is excerpted below.)

Secret Military Document
Only for Officers

56 Infantry Division   *Div. HQ, 19 Juni 1941*
Ops. Branch No. 130/41 (Secret)

20 Copies
11th Copy

Division Order No. 1
for the Attack across the Bug [River]

1.) According to existing reports the enemy, in order to secure the border on both sides of the rail line Chelm–Luboml, has deployed elements of a rifle division and frontier guard troops in regimental strength at the Bug in a defense in depth reinforced by strong points. The forwardmost position is several hundred meters in depth and runs along the edge of the high ground . . . on the eastern bank of the Bug. Behind this line, as far as the high ground west of Luboml, which is also built up for defense, the terrain has been reinforced by numerous strong points [Widerstandsnester] of simple construction deployed in depth. Enemy artillery positions have been detected along both sides of the rail line on the level of Nowiny . . .

2.) 17 Army Corps, whose primary task is to cover the northern flank of Sixth Army against any enemy incursions out of the Pripiat' Marshes, will force a crossing of the Bug with 62 and 56 ID in the Husynne–Swierze sector, break through the enemy frontier fortifications, and secure as its objective of the day [Tagesziel] the high ground on both sides of Luboml . . .

3.) The <u>56 Inf.Div.</u> is to attack across the Bug in the sector of the rail line Chelm–Luboml–Swierze. With a strong right wing it will break through the enemy frontier fortifications on both sides of Wilczy-Przewoz and seize as its first objective Hill 192 north of Jagodzin and Hill 185 northeast of Jankowce while protecting its flank toward Rowno. From this point the division is to continue its attack toward the heights north of Luboml (205 and 215.3). The division is to secure the attack of the corps' left flank by staggering its own left wing [Linksstaffelung].

4.) <u>Combat Assignments [Kampfaufträge] of the Infantry Regiments</u>

a) The <u>reinforced 192 Inf.Rgt.</u> (192 IR, 1./Pz.Jg.Abt. 156, 1./Pi. 156), making the main effort [Schwerpunkt] of the division, is to force a crossing of the Bug at the Wilczy-Przewoz road bridge, break through the Russian frontier fortifications on the edge of the high ground astride Hill 186.5, and then advance across Nowiny as far as the high ground north of Jagodzin (Hill 192).

<u>Execution:</u>

The reinforced 192 Inf.Rgt. is to attack across the Bug at "y+3"[2] minutes west of the road bridge (breach point) with a reinforced infantry battalion and storm and seize Hill 186.5.

At the same time, a reinforced rifle company is to cross the Bug at the destroyed railroad bridge and advance along the rail embankment to the ridge line 750 meters east of the Bug. The company, by directing its fire at the southeast slope of Hill 186.5 and against the edge of the woods south of the road to Jagodzin, will support the attack of the battalion on the road bridge.

The forwardmost battalion of the regiment, after reaching the sharp bend in the road 500 meters northeast of the road bridge, is to roll up Hill 186.5 and Wilczy-Przewoz from the left, while the battalion crossing in the second attack wave is to clear the enemy from the area southeast of the bend in the road as far as the rail line.

After the elements of the regiment across the river have closed ranks, and contact with the artillery has been established, the regiment, deeply echeloned on both wings, is to expand the bridgehead by advancing to Nowiny. After reaching Nowiny, [the regiment] is to reassemble its forces and continue the attack in the direction of Hill 192 (north of Jagodzin) after elements of the artillery are across the river.

Tactical Reconnaissance [*is to be conducted*] *in the combat sector of the regiment as far as . . . Kupracze–Sawosze–Lesniaki. It is important for the division to quickly determine if Hill 192 and Hill 194 (west of Lesniaki) are occupied by the enemy.*

b) The <u>reinforced 171 Inf.Rgt.</u> *(171 IR, 3./Pz.Jg.Abt. 156 with two medium Pak, 2./ Pi. 156) is to attack across the Bug at "y hour" east of Okopy, break through the enemy border position northwest of Wilczy-Przewoz, and advance across Hill 177 as far as the heights northeast of Jankowce (Hill 185).*

Execution:

The reinforced 171 Inf.Rgt. is to attack across the Bug at "y hour" east of Okopy with two reinforced infantry battalions in the forward line and advance as far as the eastern rim of the two wooded areas north of Wilczy-Przewoz. Immediately after crossing the Bug, the infantry battalion on the right is to penetrate the northern part of Wilczy-Przewoz . . . with a rifle company and clear out the enemy there.

After the regiment has closed ranks and made contact with the artillery and the heavy infantry weapons, it is to continue the advance, with a staggered left wing, as far as Jankowce. After reaching Jankowce, the regiment will reassemble its forces and attack in the direction of Hill 185 (northeast of Jankowce) after elements of the artillery are across the river.

Tactical Reconnaissance [*is to be conducted*] *in the combat sector of the regiment up to the line Hill 194–190.6 (2.5 km southeast of Ostrowki), and, as soon as possible, toward Rowno. The division must quickly have clarity about the situation at Hill 185.*

c) The <u>reinforced 234 Inf.Rgt.</u> *(234 IR, less 1st Battalion; 2./Pz.Jg.Abt. 156; 7./AR 156) is to cross the Bug at "y hour" at Swierze and, advancing by way of the ridge line northeast of Kowal and Hill 179 (1 km northeast of Holendry-Swierzenskie), take possession of Rowno and cover the left flank of the division against enemy action from the north or northeast.*

Execution:

Covered by 7./AR 156, the regiment is to advance at "y hour" from Swierze with a reinforced infantry battalion across Holendry-Swierzenskie toward the ridge line northeast of Kowal and capture it.

A reinforced rifle company of the second infantry battalion, [after reaching] Holendry-Swierzenskie, will advance on Rowno and, supported by two batteries of I./AR 213, take possession of Hill 179 . . .

The regiment is then to advance across the line Brodki–Hill 174 toward Rowno and capture the town.

<u>*Tactical Reconnaissance:*</u> *234 IR is to conduct tactical reconnaissance as soon as possible up to the road Ostrowki–Porowa–Huszcza in order to determine if there are signs that enemy forces north of the road Luboml–Opalin will advance against the left flank of 56 ID.*

d) <u>Tactical Boundaries:</u>

As in the "Order for the Assembly for the Attack across the Bug (56 ID, Ia Nr. 100/41, secret, of 16.6.[41] . . ."

5.) <u>Conduct of Battle [Kampfführung]:</u>

a) The success of the division depends decisively on keeping the enemy guessing about the locations of the infantry crossing points and the points of penetration [Einbruchsstellen] of the regiment.

b) At 00.00 Uhr on "B"-Day, the concentration [of the troops] on the 500 meter line must be complete.

The regimental commanders are to time the final advance up to the Bug in such a manner that the pneumatic boats [Flossäcke] can be moved up to the water as follows:

1. Wave 192 IR: "<u>y Hour</u>" + <u>3 Minutes</u>
1. Wave 171 u. 234 IR: "<u>y Hour</u>"

c) At "Y-Hour" [0315 hours] the artillery and heavy infantry weapons will open fire . . .³

6.) <u>Artillerie:</u>

a) <u>Artillery Regiment 156 </u> . . . will be deployed for the attack across the Bug in the following order:

Assigned for tactical support:

I./AR 156 to 192 IR.
II./AR 156 to 171 IR.

Main Artillery Grouping [Schwerpunktgruppe]:

III./AR 156 (less 7. Battery).
IV./AR 156, 2 Batteries IV./AR 162.

b) *Artillery Regiment 156* is to support the attack of the reinforced 192 IR with the Main Artillery Grouping and I./AR 156; [and] the attack of the reinforced 171 IR with II./AR 156.

c) *Execution:*

By 192 IR: By means of a surprise barrage [Feuerüberfall] unleashed at "y hour" directly against the river bank and against and on both sides of the breach point, the opportunity will be given to the attacking battalion of 192 IR, in just three minutes, to bring the pneumatic boats to the Bug and to move into position the forwardmost heavy infantry weapons that are required for direct fire against the enemy strongpoints.

At y+3 Minutes the artillery fire will jump back 300 meters from the edge of the enemy river bank. At the same time the pneumatic boats must be put into the water. Continuation of support for 192 IR will be in accordance with the tactical fire plan [Feuerplan].

Forward observers [vorgeschobene Beobachter] of the 1st and 4th [Artillery] Battalions must cross the Bug with the first waves [of infantry]. After securing the eastern edge of Hill 186.5 it will be important that enemy counterattacks from the direction of the road to Jagodzin, or out of the woods south of Hill 177, are quickly detected by the forward observers and immediately contested [with artillery fire] . . .

7.) *Reconnaissance Battalion 156* [156 AA]:

a) 156 AA (less one bicycle troop) is to be relieved by the reinforced 234 IR in the night from B-1 to B-Day by 00.00.

b) A reinforced bicycle troop, [deployed] between 234 IR at Swierze and the right wing of the reinforced 318 IR at Hniszow is to secure the border and prevent Russian patrols *and assault units from crossing the river until the reconnaissance battalion is across the river. For this purpose the troop is being subordinated to the reinforced 234 IR.*

The [bicycle] troop is <u>not</u> to take part in the attack. It is to be deployed in the border sector and to dig in in such a manner that losses are avoided through any enemy actions.

c) The Reconnaissance Battalion 156 (less one bicycle troop) is to be assembled in the wooded area southwest of Swierze and remains at the disposal of the division.

It is the intention of the division to move the battalion forward to conduct reconnaissance up to the line Polapy–Grochowiska as soon as 234 IR has reached Rowno . . .

8.) Luftwaffe <u>and Air Defense</u>:

It is to be expected that, in the initial days, the Russian air force will intervene strongly in the ground battle.

Great care is to be taken to ensure camouflage and cover against observation from the air. There are to be no concentrations [of forces] at the bridging points and all officers and NCOs are to intervene independently and energetically against any violations. At night all sources of light are to be scrupulously blacked out [sorgfältige Verdunklung].

9.) <u>Details</u>:

The rail line Chelm–Luboml is of particular significance for supply [purposes]. Any interruption or destruction of the rail line is to be avoided in so far as the combat situation permits.

10.) <u>Signal Communications</u>:

a) The Signal Battalion 156 is to establish and maintain:

<u>Telephone Communications</u>:

From the division command post to 192, 171 and 234 Infantry Regiments and 156 Artillery Regiment.

Radio Communications:

*From the division command post to 192, 171 and 234 Infantry Regiments and Recon-
naissance Battalion 156.*

b) Radio silence [is ordered] until contact is made with the enemy! . . .

*11.) The division command post is in the woods west of Hill 177 (300 meters north
of Wolka).*

[signed] von Oven[4]

APPENDIX 6
PEOPLE'S COMMISSARIAT OF DEFENSE (NKO) DIRECTIVES 1, 2, 3 (JUNE 22, 1941)[1]

1.) NKO Directive No. 1:

"Concerning the Deployment of Forces in accordance with the plan for Covering Mobilization and Strategic Concentration."
To: The Military Councils of the Leningrad, Baltic, Western and Kiev Military Districts.
Copy to: The People's Commissar of the Navy.

1. A surprise attack by the Germans on the fronts of the Leningrad, Baltic, Western Special, Kiev Special and Odessa Military Districts is possible during the course of 22–23 June 1941.

2. The mission of our forces is to avoid provocative actions of any kind, which might produce major complications. At the same time, the Leningrad, Baltic, Western Special, Kiev Special and Odessa Military Districts' forces are to be at full combat readiness to meet a surprise blow by the Germans or their allies.

3. I order:
a) Secretly man the firing points of the fortified regions on the state borders during the night of 22 June 1941;
b) Disperse all aircraft, including military planes among field airfields and thoroughly camouflage them before dawn on 22 June 1941;
c) Bring all forces to a state of combat readiness without the additional call up of conscript personnel. Prepare all measures to black out cities and installations.

Take no other measures without special permission.

[signed] Timoshenko
Zhukov

[Note: Received by the Western Special Military District at 0045 hours June 22, 1941. Dispatched to subordinate forces at 0225–0235 hours June 22, 1941; never received by Soviet detachments on the frontier.]

2.) **NKO Directive No. 2:**

0715 hours on 22 June 1941.
To: The Military Councils of the Leningrad, Baltic, Western and Kiev Military Districts.
Copy to: The People's Commissar of the Navy.

On 22 June 1941 at 0400 hours [Moscow time] in the morning, without any cause whatsoever, German aircraft carried out flight to our airfields and cities along the western frontier and sub-jected them to bombing. Simultaneously, in a number of places German forces opened fire with artillery and crossed our border. In connection with the unprecedented attack by Germany on the Soviet Union, I ORDER:

1. Troops in full strength and with all the means at their disposal will attack the enemy and destroy him in those regions where he has violated the Soviet border. In the absence of special authorization, ground troops will not cross the frontier.

2. Reconnaissance and combat aircraft will determine the concentration areas of enemy aircraft and the deployment of his ground forces. Bomber and assault [ground-attack] aircraft will destroy the aircraft on enemy airfields by powerful strikes and will bomb concentrations of his ground forces. Mount aviation strikes on German territory to a depth of 100–150km [60–90 miles].

Bomb Königsberg and Memel'.
Do not conduct flights over Finland and Romania without special authorization.

[signed]Timoshenko
Malenkov
Zhukov

3.) **NKO Directive No. 3:**

To: The Military Councils of the Northwestern, Western, Southwestern, and Southern Fronts Concerning Force Missions on 23–26 June.
2115 hours 22 June 1941

1. Delivering main attacks from the Suwalki salient to Olita and from the Zamost'e region to the Vladimir-Volynski and Radzekhov front and secondary attacks along the Tilsit, Shauliai and Sedlits, Volkovysk axes, during the course of 22 June the enemy has achieved considerable success while suffering great losses. In the remaining sectors of the state border with Germany and on the entire state border with Romania, the enemy attacks have been beaten off with heavy losses to him.

2. I assign the forces [the following] immediate missions for 23–24 June:

    a) Encircle and destroy the enemy's Suwalki grouping by concentric, concentrated attacks by the Northwestern and Western Fronts and capture the Suwalki region by day's end on 24 June.

    b) Encircle and destroy the enemy grouping attacking in the direction of Vladimir-Volynski and Brody by powerful concentric attacks by mechanized corps, all South-western Front aircraft and other forces of the 5 and 6 Armies. Capture the Lublin region by day's end on 24 June.

3. I ORDER:

    a) The Northern Front's armies to continue to protect the state borders firmly.

    The left boundary—as exists.

    b) While firmly holding on to the coast of the Baltic Sea, the Northwestern Front's armies will deliver a powerful counterstroke from the Kaunas region against the flanks and rear of the enemy's Suwalki grouping, destroy it in cooperation with the Western Front and capture the Suwalki region by day's end on 24 June.

    The left boundary—as exists.

    c) While containing the enemy on the Warsaw axis, the Western Front's armies will deliver a powerful counterstroke with a force of no fewer than two mechanized corps and frontal aviation against the flank and rear of the enemy's Suwalki grouping, destroy it in cooperation with the Northwestern Front and capture the Suwalki region by day's end on 24 June.

    The left boundary—as exists.

    d) While holding firmly to the border with Hungary, the Southwestern Front's armies will encircle and destroy the enemy grouping advancing on the Vladimir-Volynski, Krystypol' front with concentric attacks in the general direction of Lublin with the 5 and 6 Armies, no fewer than five mechanized corps and all of the front's *aviation, and capture the Lublin region by day's end on 24 June. Cover yourself reliably along the Krakow axis.*

    e) The Southern Front's armies will prevent an enemy invasion of our territory. In the event the enemy attacks along the Chernovtsy axis or forces the Prut and Danube Rivers, destroy him by powerful flank attacks by ground forces in cooperation with aviation. Concentrate two mechanized corps in the Kishinev region and the forests northwest of Kishinev by the night of 23 June.

4. I authorize crossing of the borders along the front from the Baltic Sea to the state border with Hungary and operations without regard for the borders.

5. The Aviation of the High Command

a) Support the Northwestern Front with one flight from the 1 Long Range Aviation Corps and the Western Front with one flight from the 3 Long Range Aviation Corps while they are fulfilling their missions of destroying the enemy's Suwalki grouping.

b) Assign the 18 Long Range Aviation Corps to the Southwestern Front and support the Southwestern Front with one flight from the 2 Long Range Aviation Corps while it is fulfilling its mission of destroying the enemy's Lublin grouping; and,

c) Leave the 4 Long Range Aviation Corps at my disposal in readiness to assist the Southwestern Front and, with part of its forces, the Black Sea Fleet.

The People's Commissar of Defense   *Member of the Main Military Council*
Marshal of the Soviet Union Timoshenko   *Malenkov*

Chief of the Red Army General Staff
Army General Zhukov

[Note: Sent at 2115 hours on June 22, 1941.]

NOTES

Epigraphs

1 GFM Fedor v. Bock, *The War Diary*, Klaus Gerbet (ed.), 198 (hereafter cited as, GFM v. Bock, *War Diary*). The German text: "*Ich bin überzeugt, dass unser Angriff wie ein Hagelsturm über sie hinweggeht.*" Cited in: Lew Besymenski, *Die Schlacht um Moskau*, 32.

2 Cited in: Gabriel Gorodetsky, *Grand Delusion: Stalin and the German Invasion of Russia*, 311 (hereafter cited as, Gorodetsky, *Grand Delusion*).

3 Cited in: Karl Knoblauch, *Kampf und Untergang der 95. Infanteriedivision. Chronik einer Infanteriedivision von 1939–1945 in Frankreich und an der Ostfront*, 63. The text in English reads: "The High Command of the *Wehrmacht* announces: 'Since the early morning hours of today major combat actions have taken place at the Soviet-Russian frontier.'"

Notes on Style

1 To confirm the ranks of German general officers and the proper spelling of their names I used, *inter alia*, "*Gliederung und Stellenbesetzung des Feldheeres*," Stand: B-Tag, in: Kurt Mehner (ed.), *Die Geheimen Tagesberichte der deutschen Wehrmachtführung im Zweiten Weltkrieg 1939–1945*; and the excellent Internet site at: www.lexikon-der-wehrmacht.de.

List of Maps

1 Maps gleaned from the following sources: K.-J. Thies, *Der Zweite Weltkrieg im Kartenbild, Bd. 5: Teil 1.1: Der Ostfeldzug Heeresgruppe Mitte 21.6.1941–6.12.1941. Ein Lageatlas der Operationsabteilung des Generalstabes des Heeres* (1); David M. Glantz, *Atlas and Operational Summary. The Border Battles 22 June–1 July 1941* (2); NARA RG 242: "*Lagekarten Ost*" (Eastern Front Situation Maps) (22.6.41, abds.) (3); D. M. Glantz (ed.), *The Initial Period of War on the Eastern Front, 22 June–August 1941* (4); Charles B. Burdick, *Hubert Lanz: General der Gebirgstruppe 1896–1982* (5); Lt. Fritz Lucke, *Panzer Wedge. Volume One: The German 3rd Panzer Division and the Summer of Victory in the East* (6).

Preface

1 Ltr., Dr. Heinrich Haape to fiancée, June 21, 1941.

2 Anatolij Kazakov, "*Na toj davnijšej vojne*," in: *Zvezda, Heft* 5/2005, 61.

3 Cassidy was posted to Moscow as AP bureau chief from 1940 to 1944. His extensive collection of historical papers, covering the period 1934 to 1985, is located at the Wisconsin Historical Society.

4 Henry C. Cassidy, *Moscow Dateline 1941–1943*, 1.

5 Ibid., 2.

6 Alexander Werth, *Russia at War 1941–1945*, 125.

7 Sir Richard Stafford Cripps—British ambassador to the Soviet Union (1940–1942).

8 Cited in: Werth, *Russia at War 1941–1945*, 125.

9 According to Stephen Kotkin, "Stalin aimed not only to refute the rumors of war, again blaming them on British provocations . . . but also to elicit a German denial of any intentions to attack—or, failing that, a German presentation of its anticipated demands, which the rumors said the USSR had already received and rejected, bringing the countries to imminent military confrontation." Stephen Kotkin, *Stalin: Waiting for Hitler, 1929–1941*, 880.

10 L. M. Sandalov, *Perezhitoe* (That Which Has Been Lived Through), 78.

11 Cited in: Walter Kempowski (ed.), *Das Echolot. Barbarossa '41. Ein kollektives Tagebuch*, 13, 713 (hereafter cited as: Kempowski [ed.], *Das Echolot*).

12   See, Paul Johnson, *Modern Times: The World from the Twenties to the Nineties*, 376 (hereafter cited as, Johnson, *Modern Times*). An updated version of the book covering world events to 2000 was released in 2006.

13   Alan Clark, *Barbarossa: The Russian-German Conflict, 1941–45*, 44, 46 (hereafter cited as, Clark, *Barbarossa*).

14   Cassidy, *Moscow Dateline 1941–1943*, 40.

15   David M. Glantz, *The Soviet-German War 1941–1945: Myths and Realities: A Survey Essay*, 5 (hereafter cited as, Glantz, *The Soviet-German War: Myths and Realities*). These figures, noted David Glantz, "indicate length as the 'crow flies.' Actual length was about half again as long."

16   Dr. Craig W. H. Luther, book review of *Wehrmacht im Ostkrieg. Front und militärisches Hinterland 1941/42*, by Christian Hartmann (Munich, 2009), in: *The Journal of Military History*, January 2010 (Vol. 74, No. 1).

17   Rüdiger Overmans, *Deutsche militärische Verluste im Zweiten Weltkrieg*, 265, 277. Overmans posits total German fatal losses in the East at just under 4.0 million, a figure which, by his calculations, includes several hundred thousand who died in Soviet POW camps. Overmans's figure for POW losses, however, is quite low compared to other reliable sources, which estimate that 1.1 million German soldiers perished in Soviet captivity. Using this latter figure for POW losses, and adding to it Overmans's total of some 3.5 million German *combat* losses on the Eastern Front (including the final battles from the Oder River to Berlin), one arrives at a figure of about 4.6 million German fatal losses attributable to the war in the East. For German losses in Soviet captivity see, Franz W. Seidler (ed.), *Verbrechen an der Wehrmacht. Kriegsgreuel der Roten Armee 1941/42*, 44; also, Alfred M. de Zayas, *The Wehrmacht War Crimes Bureau, 1939–1945*, 305, f.n. 11.

18   Andreas Naumann, *Freispruch für die Deutsche Wehrmacht. "Unternehmen Barbarossa" erneut auf dem Prüfstand*, 372.

19   Approximately 5.7 million Russian soldiers were taken prisoner during the war; of these, an estimated 3.3 million died (57.8 percent) in German camps. Alfred M. de Zayas, *The Wehrmacht War Crimes Bureau, 1939–1945*, 305, f.n. 11.

20   The figure of just under 14.6 million is derived from the pioneering new study by Boris Kavalerchik and Lev Lopukhovsky: *The Price of Victory: The Red Army's Casualties in the Great Patriotic War* (Barnsley, 2017). According to the foreword by David Glantz, "the book is characterized by its sound methodology, acute accuracy, and cogent conclusions." The new figure on Soviet war losses revises steeply upward the figure of 8.7 million Soviet war dead posited in the standard work on the subject edited by G. F. Krivosheev and first published in Russian (1993) and later translated into English (1997). (See, Col.-Gen. G. F. Krivosheev (ed.), *Soviet Casualties and Combat Losses in the Twentieth Century*, 4.) That said, the issue of Soviet losses in the Great Patriotic War remains a highly politicized and contentious one, and more work clearly needs to be done on the subject.

21   Kavalerchik and Lopukhovsky, *The Price of Victory: The Red Army's Casualties in the Great Patriotic War*, 94, 150; Chris Bellamy, *Absolute War: Soviet Russia in the Second World War*, 7, 15 (hereafter cited as, Bellamy, *Absolute War*).

22   Bellamy, *Absolute War*, 13–14. Also noted by Bellamy: "Mines that had produced 100 million tons of coal and 20 million tons of iron ore were wrecked and factories that had produced 19 million tons of steel were totally or partially destroyed."

23   Craig W. H. Luther, *Barbarossa Unleashed: The German Blitzkrieg through Central Russia to the Gates of Moscow. June–December 1941* (Atglen, 2013) (hereafter cited as, Luther, *Barbarossa Unleashed*). Most of the primary materials used in the preparation of this book are in the Craig W. H. Luther Papers at the Hoover Institution Archives (Stanford University, Palo Alto, CA). The collection, which also embraces documents from an earlier book of mine (*Blood and Honor: The History of the 12th SS Panzer-Division "Hitler Youth," 1943–1945*, republished with new material by Schiffer Books in 2012), consists of fifty to sixty bankers' boxes of items provided to me by dozens of German veterans (e.g., completed questionnaires, field post letters, personal diaries, and photographs), as well as published and unpublished German unit histories, official German war diaries, rare books, and numerous other materials. At some future date, I will also donate the

German and Soviet primary materials used in the preparation of *The First Day on the Eastern Front* to my large and growing collection at the Hoover Archives.

24 All references in this book to the "Bug River" are to the "Western Bug River," not the Bug River in southern Russia (west of the Dnepr) that runs into the Black Sea.

25 The Central Archive of the Ministry of Defense = *Tsentral'nyi Arkhiv Ministerstva Oborony*, or TsAMO. The website for TsAMO is: https://pamyat-naroda.ru.

26 The website is: https://iremember.ru. The site is run by author Artem Drabkin.

27 The words are Paul Johnson's. Johnson, *Modern Times*, 374.

28 Bellamy, *Absolute War*, 19.

29 Carl von Clausewitz—the still influential nineteenth-century Prussian philosopher of war. In his most famous albeit never completed work, *On War* (*Vom Kriege*), published posthumously by his widow in 1832 following his death from cholera the year before, Clausewitz posited that war in the *abstract*—as an *ideal*—tended toward *absolute violence*. Yet in the real world, an infinite variety of factors, which he called *friction*, intervened to make war something less—often much less—than absolute in its effects. In Clausewitz's view, the wars of Napoleon actually approached his concept of absolute war. One can only speculate how he might have analyzed Operation *Barbarossa*. For an excellent introduction to Clausewitz and his military philosophy see, Peter Paret, "Clausewitz," in: *Makers of Modern Strategy: From Machiavelli to the Nuclear Age*," Peter Paret (ed.), (Princeton, 1986); also, Theodore Ropp, *War in the Modern World* (New York, 1973).

Chapter 1: Planning for Armageddon—Adolf Hitler and His General Staff Prepare to Unleash War on Soviet Russia

1 Hans-Adolf Jacobsen (ed.), *Kriegstagebuch des Oberkommandos der Wehrmacht (Wehrmachtführungsstab)*, *Bd. I: 1. August 1940–31. Dezember 1941*, 300 (hereafter cited as, *KTB OKW*, Vol. I).

2 Hans H. Hinterhuber, *Wettbewerbsstrategie*, 12, f.n. 20.

3 Ronald Lewin, *Hitler's Mistakes: New Insights into What Made Hitler Tick*, 130.

4 "*Das Jahr 1941 wird die Vollendung des grössten Sieges unserer Geschichte bringen!*" Max Domarus, *Hitler. Reden und Proklamationen 1932–1945. Bd. II: Untergang (1939–1945)*, 1649 (hereafter cited as, Domarus, *Hitler. Reden und Proklamationen*, Vol. II).

5 Ibid., 1643.

6 On September 17, 1939, pursuant to a secret clause in the Nazi-Soviet non-aggression pact, the Red Army invaded Poland from the east, eventually taking control of the country east of the agreed-upon demarcation line. Martin Gilbert, *Second World War*, 9.

7 Adam Tooze, *The Wages of Destruction: The Making and Breaking of the Nazi Economy*, 321.

8 Stephen Kotkin, *Stalin: Waiting for Hitler, 1929–1941*, 903.

9 *KTB OKW*, Vol. I: 1162 (*Chronik vom 1. September 1939 bis 31. Dezember 1941. Zusammengestellt von Andreas Hillgruber und Gerhard Hümmelchen.*)

10 Matthew Cooper, *The German Army 1933–1945*, 217.

11 William L. Shirer, *The Rise and Fall of the Third Reich*, 741–72.

12 Ibid., 742.

13 Ibid., 743.

14 Franz Halder, *The Halder War Diary, 1939–1942*, Charles Burdick and Hans-Adolf Jacobsen (eds.), 213 (hereafter cited as, Halder, *War Diary*). On July 19, 1940, Halder would be promoted to *Generaloberst* (full general).

15 *Oberkommando der Wehrmacht*, or OKW. This was Hitler's personal headquarters.

16 Shirer, *The Rise and Fall of the Third Reich*, 743–45.

17 Precise casualty figures differ somewhat, depending on the source. These are gleaned from the *Oxford Guide to World War II*, I. C. B. Dear (ed.), 326. The Germans also suffered slightly more than 13,000 missing in the French campaign.

18 Roger Moorhouse, *Berlin at War*, 65.

19 Walther Hubatsch, *Deutschland im Weltkrieg 1914–1918*, 57–58.

20 Shirer, *The Rise and Fall of the Third Reich*, 746.

21   Moorhouse, *Berlin at War*, 61.

22   *KTB OKW*, Vol. I: 1167–70 (*Chronik vom 1. September 1939 bis 31. Dezember 1941*).

23   Ian Kershaw, *Hitler 1936–1945: Nemesis*, 284.

24   Karl-Heinz Frieser, "*Die deutschen Blitzkriege: Operativer Triumph—strategische Tragödie,*" in: *Die Wehrmacht—Mythos und Realität*, Rolf-Dieter Müller and Hans-Erich Volkmann (eds.), 190 (hereafter cited as, Frieser, "*Die deutschen Blitzkriege*").

25   Luther, *Barbarossa Unleashed*, 34. Simply put, the operational level of war—as distinguished from tactics and strategy—pertains to the movement of corps, armies, and army groups on the battlefield. Operational imperatives would dominate German planning for Russia.

26   Irving, *Hitler's War*, 134.

27   "*Jetzt haben wir gezeigt, wozu wir fähig sind. Glauben Sie mir Keitel, ein Feldzug gegen Russland wäre dagegen nur ein Sandkastenspiel.*" Cited in: Frieser, "*Die deutschen Blitzkriege,*" 192. As early as June 2, 1940—that is, in the midst of the French campaign—Hitler had told General Gerd von Rundstedt, "Now that Britain will presumably be willing to make peace, I will begin the final settlement of scores with Bolshevism." Irving, *Hitler's War*, 134.

28   The words are Bernd Wegner's. See his, "*Hitlers Krieg? Zur Entscheidung, Planung und Umsetzung des 'Unternehmens Barbarossa,'*" in: *Verbrechen der Wehrmacht. Bilanz einer Debatte*, Christian Hartmann, Johannes Hürter and Ulrike Jureit (eds.), 31.

29   Ibid., 31.

30   Luther, *Barbarossa Unleashed*, 34–35.

31   Jonathan Wright, *Germany and the Origins of the Second World War*, 167–68.

32   Halder, *War Diary*, 227.

33   Ibid., 230–31. Hitler again pointed out that, in his view, Britain's position was "hopeless. The war is won by us."

34   Ibid., 231–32.

35   Irving, *Hitler's War*, 149. Apparently, Hitler also raised the topic of an autumn attack on Russia with his OKW chief, Keitel. Despite his (not undeserved) reputation as a spineless supporter of his *Führer*, Keitel stood his ground on this occasion. He argued, as had his subordinate Jodl, that the communications and supply infrastructure in occupied Poland was insufficient to serve as a base of operations against the Soviet Union, and that the war could drag on into the winter before it could be ended. Keitel's contrary opinions culminated days later in a savage rebuke from the mercurial Hitler, to which Keitel responded by offering his resignation and requesting a front-line command. While Hitler "harshly rejected" Keitel's démarche, he had no choice but to accept the professional judgment of his top military advisors. Charles von Luttichau, *The Road to Moscow. The Campaign in Russia 1941*, I: 17 (hereafter cited as, Luttichau, *The Road to Moscow*); also, Walter Görlitz (ed.), *The Memoirs of Field-Marshal Wilhelm Keitel: Chief of the German High Command, 1938–1945*, 121–23.

36   Horst Boog, et al., *Germany and the Second World War*. Vol. IV: *The Attack on the Soviet Union*, 253 (hereafter cited as, *GSWW*, Vol. IV).

37   Ibid., 253.

38   Halder, *War Diary*, 244.

39   Ibid., 245.

40   *GSWW*, Vol. IV, 254.

41   Ian Kershaw, *Fateful Choices: Ten Decisions That Changed the World, 1940–1941*, 68–69 (hereafter cited as, Kershaw, *Fateful Choices*).

42   Andreas Hillgruber, *Der Zweite Weltkrieg 1939–1945. Kriegsziele und Strategie der grossen Mächte*, 56–57.

43   Shirer, *The Rise and Fall of the Third Reich*, 803–4.

44   Gilbert, *Second World War*, 141.

45   Kershaw, *Fateful Choices*, 262.

46   Klaus-Jürgen Thies, *Der Zweite Weltkrieg im Kartenbild, Bd. 5: Teil 1.1: Der Ostfeldzug Heeresgruppe Mitte 21.6.1941–6.12.1941. Ein Lageatlas der Operationsabteilung des Generalstabes des Heeres*, vii (hereafter cited as, Thies, *Der Ostfeldzug—Ein Lageatlas*).

47   Hans-Adolf Jacobsen (ed.), *1939–1945: Der Zweite Weltkrieg in Chronik und Dokumenten*, 34; *KTB OKW*, Vol. I: 996, Document 45 (December 21, 1940).

48   For the text of the directive see, H. R. Trevor-Roper (ed.), *Hitler's War Directives 1939–1945*, 49–52. For the original German text see, Walther Hubatsch (ed.), *Hitlers Weisungen für die Kriegführung 1939–1945*, 84–88. For key excerpts from the directive see, Appendix 2.

49   Cited in: Earl F. Ziemke and Magna E. Bauer, *Moscow to Stalingrad: Decision in the East*, 15.

50   Kershaw, *Fateful Choices*, 85.

51   *GSWW*, Vol. IV: 2. *"Dieser Krieg war Hitlers eigentlicher Krieg."* Horst Boog, et al., *Das Deutsche Reich und der Zweite Weltkrieg, Bd. 4: Der Angriff auf die Sowjetunion*, xiv (hereafter cited as, *DRZW*, Vol. IV).

52   Kershaw, *Hitler 1936–1945: Nemesis*, 389.

53   Ibid., 402.

54   Guido Knopp, *Die Wehrmacht. Eine Bilanz*, 88.

55   Luther, *Barbarossa Unleashed*, 41. Hitler's words are cited in: Geoffrey P. Megargee, *War of Annihilation: Combat and Genocide on the Eastern Front, 1941*, 7 (hereafter cited as, Megargee, *War of Annihilation*).

56   Irving, *Hitler's War*, 210.

57   The "Guidelines for the Treatment of Political Commissars," the so-called "Commissar Order," was issued by OKW on June 6, 1941. The political commissars were uniformed members of the Soviet military, whose primary task was political indoctrination of the troops. The Germans "considered the commissars to be the core of the Communist military system and the 'originators of barbaric Asiatic fighting methods;'" hence, the Commissar Order enjoined front-line troops—in clear violation of international law—to immediately shoot captured commissars. Megargee, *War of Annihilation*, 38.

58   Luther, *Barbarossa Unleashed*, 41.

59   When, in 1941, the course of the war ran counter to schedule, only the first two of the "Commissariats" would be established.

60   Hillgruber, *Der Zweite Weltkrieg*, 65. "The theses presented by Andreas Hillgruber after the mid-1960s," posited German historian Bernd Wegner, "have dominated the discussion about the origins of the war between Germany and the Soviet Union and the genesis of the operational plan 'Barbarossa.' In two respects they have withstood all attemps at refutation and . . . have been essentially confirmed by more recent research. They can be summarized as follows: (1) Hitler's decision to attack the Soviet Union was the result of a mixture of ideological and strategic considerations. The idea of a large-scale colonization of the east, with the two main aims of annihilating Bolshevism and conquering 'living space' for the German nation had been, in addition to his militant anti-Semitism, the most important element in Hitler's world view since 1924/25 at the latest . . . (2) The war against the Soviet Union was of a fundamentally different nature from that of all other German campaigns in the Second World War. More than a mere military operation with a clearly defined, limited aim, it was rather a 'crusade against Bolshevism' . . . a colonial war of exploitation, and a racist war of annihilation . . . [The war in the east] was planned deliberately from the beginning with a complete disregard for internationally accepted laws of war." Although Wegner published these observations many years ago, they continue to resonate. Bernd Wegner, "The Road to Defeat: The German Campaigns in Russia 1941–1943," in: *The Journal of Strategic Studies*, Vol. 13, No. 1, March 1990, 106–8.

61   Evan Mawdsley, *Thunder in the East: The Nazi-Soviet War 1941–1945*, 12 (hereafter cited as, Mawdsley, *Thunder in the East*).

62   On July 19, 1940, in a speech to the *Reichstag*, Hitler promoted a dozen of his generals to the exalted rank of field marshal; they included the three army group commanders of the French campaign—Rundstedt, Leeb, and Bock. *Luftwaffe* commander Göring was promoted to *Reichsmarschall*, one rung higher than field marshal. Irving, *Hitler's War*, 147; Nicolaus von Below, *At Hitler's Side: The Memoirs of Hitler's Luftwaffe Adjutant 1937–1945*, 67 (hereafter cited as: Von Below, *At Hitler's Side*).

63 Hitler had carefully studied the writings of Clausewitz, Moltke, and Schlieffen. He possessed an "astounding memory" and a well-founded knowledge of both German and enemy weapons and their effects. In matters of strategy that did not pertain directly to military issues, such as politics and economics, he understood more than his generals. What Hitler did not possess, however, was an ability to coordinate the different elements of strategy; moreover, he had no sense for the physical limitations of his strategic thinking. See, Marcel Stein, *Generalfeldmarschall Walter Model. Legende und Wirklichkeit*, 225–26 (hereafter cited as, Stein, *GFM Model*).

64 Luttichau, *The Road to Moscow*, II: 1.

65 Cited in: Geoffrey P. Megargee, *Inside Hitler's High Command*, 152.

66 Ibid., 152–53.

67 *GSWW*, Vol. IV: 244–45.

68 Luttichau, *The Road to Moscow*, II: 2–3.

69 Ibid., I: 18; II: 4.

70 Mawdsley, *Thunder in the East*, 70.

71 An Army General Staff study issued just weeks before the outbreak of war put it thusly: "Central Russia is the heart of Russia, whose seizure by a very strong, armed, foreign power will paralyze all Russia and loosen the ties between all the remaining parts of the extensive Soviet empire; [its seizure] is even capable of destroying [Russia] in the long term. By far the most important objective within Central Russia is Moscow." *Generalstab des Heeres (Nur für den Dienstgebrauch!)*, "*Militärgeopolitische Angaben über das Europäische Russland, Zentral Russland (ohne Moskau)*," Berlin, May 15, 1941, cited in: Janusz Piekalkiewicz, *Die Schlacht um Moskau. Die erfrorene Offensive*, 16.

72 Keitel had been promoted to field marshal on July 19, 1940. www.lexikon-der-wehrmacht.de.

73 Luttichau, *The Road to Moscow*, I: 17. The requirement for a better rail infrastructure had become urgent by July 1940.

74 For details on the reorganization and expansion of the German tank forces prior to the start of Operation *Barbarossa* see, Burkhart Mueller-Hillebrand, *Das Heer 1933–1945, Entwicklung des organisatorischen Aufbaues, Bd. II: Die Blitzfeldzüge 1939–1941. Das Heer im Kriege bis zum Beginn des Feldzuges gegen die Sowjetunion im Juni 1941*, 76–81 (hereafter cited as, Mueller-Hillebrand, *Das Heer*, Vol. II: *Die Blitzfeldzüge*).

75 Ibid., 107.

76 Luttichau, *The Road to Moscow*, II: 10.

77 Lying between Belorussia and the western Ukraine, the Pripiat' Marshes pose the greatest single natural barrier in Russia, effectively dividing the western border region into two separate compartments. In 1941, they consisted of swampland and primeval forest about 250 kilometers in width from north to south, and some 500 kilometers in depth. The marshes began just beyond the Russo-German frontier, directly to the southeast of Brest-Litovsk; with the exception of a few man-made routes, they were virtually impassable except when frozen. The (relatively) much denser communications net (road and railroad) north of the marshes favored making the main German advance there. Luttichau, *The Road to Moscow*, II: 5–6; Albert Seaton, *The Russo-German War 1941–1945*, 55.

78 The original German in the Marcks study reads: "*Seine Eroberung zerreisst den Zusammenhang des russischen Reiches.*" Cited in: General Walther K. Nehring, *Die Geschichte der deutschen Panzerwaffe 1916–1945*, 215.

79 Luttichau, *The Road to Moscow*, II: 4–11; Williamson Murray, *Strategy for Defeat: The Luftwaffe 1933–1945*, 77.

80 Murray, *Strategy for Defeat: The Luftwaffe 1933–1945*, 77.

81 For a discussion of the so-called Lossberg study, which evinced marked parallels to the work of General Marcks see, Luther, *Barbarossa Unleashed*, 45–46.

82 Murray, *Strategy for Defeat: The Luftwaffe 1933–1945*, 77.

83 Luther, *Barbarossa Unleashed*, 45.

84 Torsten Diedrich, *Paulus: Das Trauma von Stalingrad. Eine Biographie*, 158–61.

85 Ibid., 163.

86 Ibid., 162.

87 Ibid., 162. Paulus's hopeful comments, however, failed to convince his wife. She plied her husband with books, among them Caulaincourt's account of Napoleon's disastrous campaign in Russia.

88 Ibid., 164. On December 7, 1940, a third (final) war game took place at OKH headquarters in Zossen. Ibid., 166.

89 *KTB OKW*, Vol. I: 205.

90 Ibid., 208–9.

91 *KTB OKW*, Vol. I: 209; Luttichau, *The Road to Moscow*, II: 33–34; Halder, *War Diary*, 294.

92 Luttichau, *The Road to Moscow*, II: 34.

93 Hermann Hoth, *Panzer-Operationen. Die Panzergruppe 3 und der operative Gedanke der deutschen Führung Sommer 1941*, 30–31.

94 The document was "partly the handiwork of Jodl, a master stylist whose spoken German was very clear and simple, and partly the product of Hitler's pen." Irving, *Hitler's War*, 190–91.

95 Bellamy, *Absolute War*, 126.

96 Ibid., 126.

97 Trevor-Roper (ed.), *Hitler's War Directives*, 49; Hubatsch (ed.), *Hitlers Weisungen für die Kriegführung 1939–1945*, 84.

98 Irving, *Hitler's War*, 192–93.

99 Luther, *Barbarossa Unleashed*, 57.

100 Horst Boog, "Higher Command and Leadership in the German Luftwaffe, 1935–1945," in: *Air Power and Warfare. The Proceedings of the 8th Military History Symposium, United States Air Force Academy, 18–20 October 1978*, Colonel Alfred F. Hurley and Major Robert C. Ehrhart (eds.), 150.

101 Williamson Murray and Allan R. Millett, *A War to Be Won: Fighting the Second World War, 1937–1945*, 120. Noted a highly respected German historian: "A military campaign without a clear focus [*Schwerpunkt*] beyond the first phase of the border battles could only be judged by military experts as a false construction [*Fehlkonstruktion*]." Johannes Hürter, *Hitlers Heerführer. Die deutschen Oberbefehlshaber im Krieg gegen die Sowjetunion, 1941/42*, 293 (hereafter cited as, Hürter, *Hitlers Heerführer*).

102 Irving, *Hitler's War*, 205. Addressing the campaigns in the Balkans and in North Africa, a *Wehrmacht* communiqué of June 11, 1941, had concluded: "For the German soldier nothing is impossible." Joachim C. Fest, *Hitler*, 674.

103 David M. Glantz, *Barbarossa Derailed: The Battle for Smolensk 10 July–10 September 1941*, Vol. 1: *The German Advance, the Encirclement Battle, and the First and Second Soviet Counteroffensives, 10 July–24 August 1941*, 20 (hereafter cited as, Glantz, *Barbarossa Derailed*, Vol. I).

104 Boog, "Higher Command and Leadership in the German Luftwaffe, 1933–1945," 151.

105 Christian Hartmann, *Wehrmacht im Ostkrieg. Front und militärisches Hinterland, 1941/42*, 39 (hereafter cited as, Hartmann, *Wehrmacht im Ostkrieg*).

106 For the failings of German logistical planning and execution (1941/42) see, Klaus Schüler, "The Eastern Campaign as a Transportation and Supply Problem," in: *From Peace to War: Germany, Soviet Russia and the World, 1939–1941*, Bernd Wegner (ed.), 205–22.

107 Johnson, *Modern Times*, 377.

108 Samuel W. Mitcham Jr., *The Men of Barbarossa: Commanders of the German Invasion of Russia, 1941*, 50 (hereafter cited as, Mitcham Jr., *The Men of Barbarossa*). The *Luftwaffe* order of battle for the Russian campaign was also more than inadequate—a total of about 3,000 aircraft, of which less than 2,500 were combat-ready.

109 For details see, David M. Glantz, *Barbarossa: Hitler's Invasion of Russia 1941*, 66–71 (hereafter cited as, Glantz, *Barbarossa*).

110 Walter S. Dunn, Jr., *Stalin's Keys to Victory: The Rebirth of the Red Army*, 4. According to Dunn, "The actual reason the Soviets were able to stop the Germans in late 1941 was an unbelievable mobilization of men and weapons beginning in September 1941, which created a new Red Army. The Soviets formed and sent into combat in a few months more new divisions than the United States formed in the entire war." Dunn, 4.

111   Andreas Hillgruber, *Die Zerstörung Europas. Beiträge zur Weltkriegsepoche 1914 bis 1945*, 258.

112   Bellamy, *Absolute War*, 102. The concept of preemptive war "has a respectable pedigree in international law." Bellamy, 102.

113   Luther, *Barbarossa Unleashed*, 193.

114   As Field Marshal Paulus admitted after the war, "no preparations whatever for an attack by the Soviet Union had come to our attention." Gorodetsky, *Grand Delusion*, 87.

115   Jürgen Förster, *Die Wehrmacht im NS-Staat. Eine strukturgeschichtliche Analyse*, 172.

116   Bellamy, *Absolute War*, 102. Compared to the concept of preemptive war, preventive war "enjoys less legal favor." Bellamy, 102.

117   Bogdan Musial, *Kampfplatz Deutschland. Stalins Kriegspläne gegen den Westen*, 456.

118   Luther, *Barbarossa Unleashed*, 197. Simply put, the conviction that Stalin, given the opportunity, may well have attacked in 1942, has gained increasing currency (or at very least legitimacy) among historians in recent years.

119   Murray and Millett, *A War to Be Won*, 118; Luther, *Barbarossa Unleashed*, 88.

120   The January 31, 1941, text of the deployment directive has generally been considered the final version of the document; however, the directive would go through at least two more partial rewrites by early June 1941.

121   David Stahel, *Operation Barbarossa and Germany's Defeat in the East*, 77. For the text of the deployment directive see, Franz Halder, *Kriegstagebuch: Tägliche Aufzeichnungen des Chef des Generalstabes des Heeres 1939–1942, Bd. II: Von der geplanten Landung in England bis zum Beginn des Ostfeldzuges (1.7.1940–21.6.1941)*, Hans-Adolf Jacobsen and Alfred Philippi (eds.), Appendix 2, 463–69 (hereafter cited as, Halder, *KTB*, Vol. II).

122   The missions of the army groups, armies, and panzer groups—as laid out in the deployment directive—will be covered in detail in the pertinent chapters below.

123   "*Aufmarschanweisung Barbarossa*," in: Halder, *KTB*, Vol. II: 468 (Appendix 2). *Luftwaffe* attacks on Russian industrial sites were only to begin *after* the army had reached its operational goals.

124   Ibid., Vol. II: 465 (Appendix 2). About the possible enemy use of chemical weapons, the text reads: "*Auf die Verwendung chemischer Kampfmittel auch aus der Luft durch den Gegner muss die Truppe sich einstellen.*"

125   In 1929, forty-three parties had signed the "Third Geneva Convention," which was actually two conventions providing protections for military personnel who fell into enemy hands—one addressing the issue of prisoners of war, the other care of the wounded. The United States, Germany, Italy, France, and Great Britain all signed them; Japan and the Soviet Union did not. The Soviet Union, however, had signed the 1925 Geneva protocol prohibiting the use of poison gas and bacteriological warfare. Bellamy, *Absolute War*, 20.

126   Hürter, *Hitlers Heerführer*, 231. Conferencing with the staff of Fourth Army on this day, Brauchitsch said: "The Russians will conduct the war by all possible means: Gas, spoiling of stores, and contamination of wells." Hürter, 231, f.n. 139.

127   *GSWW*, Vol. IV: 288–90.

128   Ibid., 290.

129   Hans Pottgiesser, in his study of German rail operations in the eastern campaign, concluded that the rail deployment of the eastern armies and panzer groups, their equipment and supplies, required 11,784 trains. (Hans Pottgiesser, *Die Deutsche Reichsbahn im Ostfeldzug 1939–1944*, 21–24.) According to Alfred Philippi and Ferdinand Heim, the strategic rail deployment encompassed 17,000 trains—a figure also cited by Charles von Luttichau, along with a total of 200,000 railcars. (Alfred Philippi and Ferdinand Heim, *Der Feldzug gegen Sowjetrussland 1941 bis 1945. Ein operativer Überblick*, 52 [hereafter cited as, Philippi and Heim, *Der Feldzug gegen Sowjetrussland*]; Luttichau, *The Road to Moscow*, IV: 43.) According to yet another source, some 144 trains—traveling at an average speed of 24 km/h—headed east each day as part of the buildup. Klaus-R. Woche, *Zwischen Pflicht und Gewissen. Generaloberst Rudolf Schmidt 1886–1957*, 97.

130   Luther, *Barbarossa Unleashed*, 77; Luttichau, *The Road to Moscow*, III: 28–29.

131   *GSWW*, Vol. IV: 315. The thirty-four divisions were distributed among three armies, all controlled by Army Group B.

132   Luttichau, *The Road to Moscow*, IV: 34; Jacobsen, *Der Zweite Weltkrieg in Chronik*, 35.

133   The dates for these first three phases differ slightly in other accounts; the dates used above are from Luttichau, *The Road to Moscow*, IV: 33.

134   To move a division by rail during the first three deployment phases required roughly a week from Germany and ten days from France. Typically detraining far from the eastern frontier, it then advanced farther east toward its jump-off positions in a series of phases (often involving long and arduous foot marches) in accordance with deployment timetables. Ibid., IV: 35–36.

135   For more details on the deployment effort see, Luttichau, *The Road to Moscow*, IV: 33–37; Philippi and Heim, *Der Feldzug gegen Sowjetrussland*, 52; *GSWW*, Vol. IV: 315–16.

136   On May 25, Germany shifted its railroads to a "maximum schedule." Otto Preston Chaney, Jr., *Zhukov*, 86.

137   Jacobsen, *Der Zweite Weltkrieg in Chronik*, 35; *GSWW*, Vol. IV: 316; Halder, *War Diary*, 378; Luttichau, *The Road to Moscow*, IV: 33.

138   Werner Haupt, *Die 8. Panzer-Division im Zweiten Weltkrieg*, 135. The transport of an infantry division normally required about seventy trains; that of a tank division about ninety to one hundred trains. Klaus-R. Woche, *Zwischen Pflicht und Gewissen*, 97.

139   Philippi and Heim, *Der Feldzug gegen Sowjetrussland*, 52; Foreign Military Study (FMS) P-190, Rudolf Hofmann and Alfred Toppe, "*Verbrauchs- und Verschleisssätze während der Operationen der deutschen Heeresgruppe Mitte vom 22.6.41–31.12.41*," 11.

140   *DRZW*, Vol. IV: 269; OKH Gen St d H/Op.Abt. (III), "*Kriegsgliederung Barbarossa*," Stand 18.6.41, in: Kurt Mehner (ed.), *Die Geheimen Tagesberichte der deutschen Wehrmachtführung im Zweiten Weltkrieg 1939–1945, Bd. 3: 1. März 1941–31. Oktober 1941* (hereafter cited as, "*Kriegsgliederung Barbarossa*," Stand 18.6.41, Kurt Mehner [ed.]).

141   *GSWW*, Vol. IV: 316.

142   Luttichau, *The Road to Moscow*, IV: 36–37.

143   Ibid., IV: 37.

144   For a detailed account of *Luftwaffe* preparations for the eastern campaign see, *GSWW*, Vol. IV: 353–76. Unlike the army, in 1941 the *Luftwaffe* was heavily committed to other missions—engaging Britain in the Mediterranean and the West, defense of the Reich, etc. As a result, it was only able to commit 68 percent of its total front-line strength to the Russian campaign.

145   Figures on the status of German deployments in the East on June 22, 1941, are gleaned from the following sources (all of which differ slightly): "*Gliederung und Stellenbesetzung des Feldheeres*," Stand: B-Tag, in: Kurt Mehner (ed.), *Die Geheimen Tagesberichte der deutschen Wehrmachtführung im Zweiten Weltkrieg 1939–1945*; Mueller-Hillebrand, *Das Heer*, Vol II: *Die Blitzfeldzüge*, 111; Philippi and Heim, *Der Feldzug gegen Sowjetrussland*, 52; Mawdsley, *Thunder in the East*, 33.

146   *GSWW*, Vol. IV: 485.

147   Megargee, *War of Annihilation*, 33.

148   For a detailed examination of these criminal orders, and their implementation at the start of the Russian campaign see, Luther, *Barbarossa Unleashed*, 435–58.

149   David M. Glantz (ed.), *The Initial Period of War on the Eastern Front, 22 June–August 1941. Proceedings of the Fourth Art of War Symposium*, 2 (hereafter cited as, Glantz [ed.], *Initial Period of War on the Eastern Front*).

150   The Soviet concept of "deep operations" has an interesting history. In the late 1930s it was significantly modified and even, it seems, forgotten for a time—the result, in part, of a misreading of the Red Army's experiences in Spain (1936/39), Poland (1939), and Finland (1939/40), which resulted in the temporary disbanding of its large tank corps. This decision, however, soon collided with the reality of the German *Blitzkrieg* of 1939/40. As a result, in 1940, the Red Army leadership began to hastily rebuild an armored force comprised of large tank (mechanized) corps. For more background on "deep operations" see, Luther, *Barbarossa Unleashed*, 151–52.

151   David M. Glantz, *Red Army Ground Forces in June 1941*, 48.

152 The figure of 17,000 is from Glantz; the figure of 24,000 is cited by Joachim Hoffmann. David M. Glantz, "Introduction: Prelude to Barbarossa. The Red Army in 1941," in: Glantz (ed.), *Initial Period of War on the Eastern Front*, 33; Joachim Hoffmann, "*Die Angriffsvorbereitungen des Sowjetunion 1941*," in: *Zwei Wege nach Moskau. Vom Hitler-Stalin-Pakt zum "Unternehmen Barbarossa*," Bernd Wegner (ed.), 369.

153 The secret call-up of 793,000 reservists took place at the end of May and beginning of June 1941. Dmitri Volkogonov, "The German Attack, the Soviet Response, Sunday, 22 June 1941," in: *Barbarossa: The Axis and the Allies*, John Erickson and David Dilks (eds.), 82 (hereafter cited as, Volkogonov, "The German Attack, the Soviet Response"). See also, David M. Glantz, *Stumbling Colossus: The Red Army on the Eve of World War*, 104 (hereafter cited as, Glantz, *Stumbling Colossus*).

154 Geoffrey Roberts (ed.), *Marshal of Victory*. Vol. I: *The WWII Memoirs of Soviet General Georgy Zhukov through 1941*, 233–51 (hereafter cited as, Roberts [ed.], *Marshal of Victory*. Vol. I: *WWII Memoirs of General Zhukov through 1941*).

155 Red Army rifle divisions varied greatly in strength at the start of the war, and were significantly smaller than a fully manned German infantry division. John Erickson, "Soviet War Losses," in: *Barbarossa: The Axis and the Allies*, John Erickson and David Dilks (ed.), 267.

156 John Colvin, *Zhukov: The Conqueror of Berlin*, 65.

157 Glantz, *Red Army Ground Forces in June 1941*, 20.

158 The Soviet armed forces did not include an independent air force. The Soviet air force (*Voenno-voz-dushnikh sil*, or VVS) was part of the Red Army.

159 For a much more detailed exposition of the strengths and weaknesses of the Red Army in June 1941 see, Luther, *Barbarossa Unleashed*, 139–71.

160 Mawdsley, *Thunder in the East*, 37.

161 Mawdsley, *Thunder in the East*, 40; Heinz Magenheimer, *Hitler's War: Germany's Key Strategic Decisions 1940–1945*, 76–77.

162 Revisionist historians also point to Zhukov's preemptive strike plan of May 15, 1941, as proof of Stalin's aggressive intentions. Yet if Stalin even saw the plan he did not endorse it—perhaps because he knew only too well that the Red Army was in no condition to successfully execute such an attack. Moreover, the preemptive strike plan was "conceived not as a springboard toward the seizure of the heart of Europe, but as a limited operation aimed at disrupting the German buildup and therefore of a defensive nature." Gabriel Gorodetsky, *Grand Delusion*, 322; also, Rodric Braithwaite, *Moscow 1941: A City and Its People at War*, 58 (hereafter cited as, Braithwaite, *Moscow 1941*). For an in-depth discussion of the issues of preemptive and preventive war see, Luther, *Barbarossa Unleashed*, 191–97.

163 Mawdsley, *Thunder in the East*, 40.

164 John Erickson, "Barbarossa June 1941: Who Attacked Whom?," in: *History Today*, July 2001.

165 For more details on the Stalin Line see, David M. Glantz, *The Military Strategy of the Soviet Union: A History*, 75; also, Sonja Wetzig, *Die Stalin-Linie 1941. Bollwerk aus Beton und Stahl*. The latter work includes wonderful illustrations and photographs.

166 *Frontschau Nr. 2*, "*Russischer Stellungsbau*," in: *Die Frontschau*, distributed by International Historic Films.

167 Robert Kirchubel, *Operation Barbarossa 1941 (3)*, *Army Group Center*, 27–28.

168 Klaus Latzel, *Deutsche Soldaten—nationalsozialistischer Krieg? Kriegserlebnis—Kriegserfahrung 1939–1945*, 48; Bellamy, *Absolute War*, 25; *GSWW*, Vol. IV: 514.

169 *GSWW*, Vol. IV: 514–15.

170 B. H. Liddell Hart, *The German Generals Talk*, 187–89.

Chapter 2: On the Cusp of War—Berlin, Moscow, and the Eastern Front

1 Ltr., Dr. Heinrich Haape to fiancée, June 21, 1941.

2 Bernard Häring, *Embattled Witness: Memories of a Time of War*, 4.

3 http://iremember.ru/en.

4 Glantz, *Barbarossa*, 35.

5   Four divisions committed to Operation *Barbarossa* (67,000 men) were deployed in northern Finland and assigned to the German Army of Norway (*Armeeoberkommando Norwegen*). Ziemke and Bauer, *Moscow to Stalingrad: Decision in the East*, 7; "*Die materielle Ausstattung des deutschen Ostheeres am 22. Juni 1941*," in: *DRZW*, Vol. IV: 186–87.

6   Two of these panzer divisions (2 and 5 PD) were in Germany refitting, and would not join the *Ostheer* until September 1941. *GSWW*, Vol. IV: 318.

7   *GSWW*, Vol IV: 318; *DRZW*, Vol. IV: 186–87, 270; Ziemke and Bauer, *Moscow to Stalingrad: Decision in the East*, 7; Jacobsen, *Der Zweite Weltkrieg in Chronik*, 36; "*Kriegsgliederung Barbarossa*," *Stand 18.6.41*, Kurt Mehner (ed.); *DRZW*, Vol. IV, *Beiheft*, "*Ausgangslage zum 22.6.1941*"; I. C. B. Dear (ed.), *The Oxford Guide to World War II*, 295. Order of battle figures for German and Axis troops differs slightly depending on the source.

8   For the complete Red Army order of battle on June 22, 1941, see, David M. Glantz (ed.), *Atlas and Operational Summary: The Border Battles, 22 June–1 July 1941*, 32–36 (hereafter cited as, Glantz [ed.], *Atlas and Operational Summary*).

9   A Soviet "front" was roughly equivalent to a German army group. After the 1941 campaign, the Red Army increased the number of fronts yet reduced them in size, making them about equal to German armies. Glantz, *The Soviet-German War: Myths and Realities*, 15, f.n. 1.

10   Figures on Red Army strength compiled from the following sources, all of which differ slightly in their data: Glantz, *Red Army Ground Forces in June 1941*, 3; Glantz, *Barbarossa*, 16; Bellamy, *Absolute War*, 175; Heinz Magenheimer, *Moskau 1941. Entscheidungsschlacht im Osten*, 25.

11   According to one major source, 170 divisions were stationed in the western frontier zone; of these, forty-eight divisions were deployed 10–50 kilometers, sixty-four divisions 50–150 kilometers, and fifty-six divisions 150–500 kilometers east of the Russo-German demarcation line. *GSWW*, Vol. IV: 85. The figures furnished by Glantz for the three operational belts of the first strategic echelon are fifty-seven, fifty-two, and sixty-two, respectively. Glantz, *Barbarossa*, 16.

12   Magenheimer, *Moskau 1941. Entscheidungsschlacht im Osten*, 25.

13   Glantz, *Barbarossa*, 16; Glantz, *Red Army Ground Forces in June 1941*, 3; Bellamy, *Absolute War*, 175. According to Soviet defense planning, the first strategic echelon, when fully manned, was to have consisted of 186 divisions. Concerning the second strategic echelon, seven reserve armies had been activated in accordance with a People's Commissariat of Defense (NKO) mobilization order of May 13, 1941; on June 22, however, only five of these armies were deploying along the Dvina-Dnepr lines, while two—coming from the Siberian and Arkhangel'sk Military Districts, respectively—had not yet begun to deploy when war began. In Stalin's mind, these reserve armies signified a kind of "insurance policy" against any future disaster and, even though they were not at full strength, their existence largely nullified the assumption of Hitler and his generals that they would certainly prevail if they destroyed Red Army forces west of the two main river barriers. Glantz, *Stumbling Colossus*, 102–8; Email, David M. Glantz to Dr. C. Luther, January 22, 2018.

14   Luther, *Barbarossa Unleashed*, 197; von Below, *At Hitler's Side*, 93. Recalled von Below: "Just before Hitler transferred his HQ to the southeast of the Reich, he was surprised in Berlin by a very heavy British air raid. On the night of 10 April [1941] the State Opera House, the University, the State Library and the Palace of the Crown Prince were hit. Heavy damage was caused. The Opera House was completely gutted. Hitler was outraged and as a result he had a furious argument with Göring."

15   Marie Vassiltchikov, *Berlin Diaries, 1940–1945*, 52, 54.

16   Cited in: Roger Moorhouse, *Berlin at War*, 68. As the SD report also noted, across the Reich "the Russian question is being discussed incessantly."

17   Von Below, *At Hitler's Side*, 103.

18   Irving, *Hitler's War*, 198.

19   "*Weil man so gar nichts über Russland wisse, es könne eine grosse Seifenblase sein, es könne aber auch eben-sogut anders sein.*" Cited in: Christa Schroeder, *Er war mein Chef. Aus dem Nachlass der Sekretärin von Adolf Hitler*, 113; also, Irving, *Hitler's War*, 271. Only days later, at his "Wolf's Lair" compound in East Prussia, an ebullient Hitler, reacting to the successful start of the campaign, pointed to Moscow on a large map of

Europe and said, "We'll be in Moscow in four weeks. Moscow will be razed to the ground." Schroeder, *Er war mein Chef*, 114.

20   Ralf Georg Reuth, *Goebbels. Eine Biographie*, 478–79.

21   Domarus. *Hitler. Reden und Proklamationen*, Vol. II: 1724.

22   *KTB OKW*, Vol. I: 408, 417; Irving, *Hitler's War*, 269.

23   Irving, *Hitler's War*, 268.

24   Halder, *War Diary*, 408; Irving, *Hitler's War*, 268. Hitler also dictated a proclamation to be read out to the German people; except for its ending—tailored to civilians, not soldiers—it was the same as the proclamation to the troops. For the complete text of the document see, Domarus, *Hitler. Reden und Proklamationen*, Vol. II: 1725–32.

25   Halder, *War Diary*, 409–10; Halder, *KTB*, Vol. II: 459–61.

26   Domarus, *Hitler. Reden und Proklamationen*, Vol. II: 1724; also, www.lexikon-der-wehrmacht.de.

27   John Erickson, *The Road to Stalingrad: Stalin's War with Germany:* Vol. I: 103–4 (hereafter cited as, Erickson, *The Road to Stalingrad*).

28   Shirer, *The Rise and Fall of the Third Reich*, 847–48. According to Shirer, the German attack on the Soviet Union left Schulenburg "shaken and disillusioned." He had "devoted the best years of his life to improving German-Russian relations and . . . knew that the attack on the Soviet Union was unprovoked and without justification." Schulenburg would be arrested after the July 20, 1944, plot against Hitler and executed on November 10, 1944. Shirer, 848.

29   Ibid., 849.

30   "It was not the first time that the Duce had been wakened from his sleep in the middle of the night by a message from his Axis partner, and he resented it. 'Not even I disturb my servants at night,' Mussolini fretted to Ciano, 'but the Germans make me jump out of bed at any hour without the least consideration.'" Ibid., 851.

31   Cited in: Shirer, *The Rise and Fall of the Third Reich*, 851.

32   Ralf Georg Reuth, *Hitler. Eine politische Biographie*, 520.

33   Shirer, *The Rise and Fall of the Third Reich*, 851; also, Kershaw, *Hitler 1936–1945: Nemesis*, 387.

34   Despite the "thickening rumors," Otto Dietrich, the Third Reich's press chief, had remained convinced that Hitler would never turn against Russia. Indeed, not until the night of June 21/22 did he come to realize the "frightening truth," for the "unusual bustle in the Chancellery that evening, all the coming and going and the excitement in every face, made it impossible to doubt any longer that some tremendous action against Russia was in progress." Otto Dietrich, *The Hitler I Knew*, 66.

35   Reuth, *Goebbels. Eine Biographie*, 479–80.

36   Kershaw, *Hitler 1936–1945: Nemesis*, 388.

37   Reuth, *Goebbels. Eine Biographie*, 480.

38   National Archives and Records Administration (hereafter cited as, NARA), T-315, Roll 39, *Ia KTB Ost Nr. 1, 1.Geb.Div.*, 21.6.41.

39   From an examination of several dozen German war diaries, it appears that most formations (down to division level) had received the "Dortmund" notification by early afternoon on June 21. By way of example: The code word reached HQ Army Group North at 1105 hours, Sixteenth Army (a component of Army Group North) at 1157 hours, Seventeenth Army (Army Group South) at 1107 hours, 1 Panzer Group (Army Group South) at 1145 hours, 1 Panzer Division (Army Group North) at 1241 hours, and 45 Infantry Division (Army Group Center) at 1500 hours. *Generalfeldmarschall* Wilhelm Ritter von Leeb and Georg Meyer, *Tagebuchaufzeichnungen und Lagebeurteilungen aus zwei Weltkriegen*, 274, f.n. 38 (hereafter cited as, Leeb, *Tagebuchaufzeichnungen*); NARA, T-312, Roll 543, *Ia KTB Nr. 5, AOK 16*, 21.6.41; NARA, T-312, Roll 668, *Ia KTB Nr. 1, AOK 17*, 21.6.41; NARA, T-313, Roll 3, *Ia KTB Nr. 6, Pz. AOK 1*, 21.6.41; NARA, T-315, Roll 16, *Ia KTB Nr. 6, 1.Pz.Div.*, 21.6.41; Rostislav Aliev, *The Siege of Brest 1941: The Red Army's Stand against the Germans during Operation Barbarossa*, 47 (hereafter cited as, Aliev, *The Siege of Brest 1941*).

40   Besymenski, *Die Schlacht um Moskau 1941*, 32.

41   GFM v. Bock, *War Diary*, 223; Thies, *Der Ostfeldzug—Ein Lageatlas*, "*Aufmarsch am 21.6.1941 abds., Heeresgruppe Mitte.*"

42   Mainhardt Graf von Nayhauss-Cormons, *Zwischen Gehorsam und Gewissen. Richard von Weizsäcker und das Infanterie-Regiment 9*, 130.

43   GFM v. Bock, *War Diary*, 222.

44   Volkogonov, "The German Attack, the Soviet Response," 84; Albert Kesselring, *Soldat Bis Zum Letzten Tag*, 116.

45   Kesselring, *Soldat Bis Zum Letzten Tag*, 116–17.

46   FMS D-247, Genlt. Kurt Cuno, "German Preparations for the Attack against Russia. (The German Build-up East of Warsaw)," 1; Erich Hager, *The War Diaries of a Panzer Soldier. Erich Hager with the 17th Panzer Division on the Russian Front 1941–1945*, David Garden and Kenneth Andrew (eds.), 28–29 (hereafter cited as, Hager, *The War Diaries of a Panzer Soldier*).

47   Obstlt. a.D. Joseph Dinglreiter, *Die Vierziger: Chronik des Regiments*, 39–40.

48   Philippi and Heim, *Der Feldzug gegen Sowjetrussland*, 52. As tactical terms, a "concentration area" generally denotes a position somewhat behind the front, while an "attack assembly area" is the position from which the attack is actually launched. This is an important distinction made by the late military historian R. H. S. Stolfi in his book, *German Panzers on the Offensive: Russian Front, North Africa, 1941–1942* (e.g., 149). A glance at the situation map of the German Army General Staff's Operations Branch for evening, June 21, 1941, shows that all of the *Ostheer*'s motorized infantry divisions were in concentration areas behind the front, while most of the panzer divisions (except those of Army Group South) were in attack assembly areas at the frontier. Thies, *Der Ostfeldzug—Ein Lageatlas*, "*Aufmarsch am 21.6.1941 abds., Heeresgruppe Mitte.*"

49   Bundesarchiv-Militärarchiv (BA-MA) RH 21-3/732, "*Gefechtsberichte Russland 1941/42.*"

50   Thies, *Der Ostfeldzug—Ein Lageatlas*, "*Aufmarsch am 21.6.1941 abds., Heeresgruppe Mitte.*"

51   Carl Wagener, *Heeresgruppe Süd. Der Kampf im Süden der Ostfront 1941–1945*, 49 (hereafter cited as, Wagener, *Heeresgruppe Süd*).

52   NARA, T-313, Roll 3, *Ia KTB Nr. 6, Pz. AOK 1*, 21.6.41; *DRZW*, Vol. IV, *Beiheft*, "*Ausgangslage zum 22.6.1941.*"

53   NARA, T-315, Roll 656, *Ia KTB Nr. 2, 14.Pz.Div.*, 21.6.41.

54   Erhard Raus, *Panzer Operations: The Eastern Front Memoir of General Raus, 1941–1945*, Steven H. Newton (ed.), 12 (hereafter cited as, Raus, *Panzer Operations*).

55   Lt.-Gen. A. D. von Plato and Lt.-Col. R. O. Stoves, "1st Panzer Division Operations," in: Glantz (ed.), *Initial Period of War on the Eastern Front*, 130.

56   Günther Blumentritt, "Moscow," in: *The Fatal Decisions*, William Richardson and Seymour Freidin (eds.), 46 (hereafter cited as, Blumentritt, "Moscow").

57   BA-MA MSg 1/1147: *Tagebuch* Lemelsen, 21.6.41.

58   NARA, T-312, Roll 668, *Ia KTB Nr. 1, AOK 17*, 21.6.41.

59   NARA, T-315, Roll 16, *Ia KTB Nr. 6, 1.Pz.Div.*, 21.6.41.

60   GFM v. Bock, it will be recalled, moved his headquarters from Posen to Rembertov, outside Warsaw, on June 21, 1941. GFM v. Bock, *War Diary*, 223.

61   Cited in: Ortwin Buchbender and Reinhold Sterz (eds.), *Das andere Gesicht des Krieges. Deutsche Feldpostbriefe 1939–1945*, 67 (hereafter cited as, Buchbender and Sterz [eds.], *Das andere Gesicht des Krieges*).

62   Cited in: Roland Kaltenegger, *Die Stammdivision der deutschen Gebirgstruppe. Weg und Kampf der 1. Gebirgs-Division 1935–1945*, 202–3 (hereafter cited as, Kaltenegger, *Weg und Kampf der 1. Gebirgs-Division*).

63   Craig W. H. Luther and Hugh Page Taylor, *For Germany: The Otto Skorzeny Memoirs*, 92. According to another *Waffen-SS* soldier, there was "one stubborn rumor that persisted. Namely, that there had been a treaty with Russia to permit German divisions free passage through the Ukraine, across the Caucasus and then through Turkey to Africa. There we would link up with the *Afrikakorps* and it would be all over for the British. The most fantastic part about the whole thing was that we believed it!" Helmut Günther, *Hot Motors, Cold Feet: A Memoir of Service with the Motorcycle Battalion of SS-Division "Reich" 1940-1941*," 73.

64   Gefr. Hans B. (269 ID) (38 051), Collection *Bibliothek für Zeitgeschichte* (hereafter cited as, "Collection BfZ").

65   Kirchubel, *Operation Barbarossa 1941 (3), Army Group Center*, 32.

66   Werner R. (N97.3), "*Erinnerungen*," Collection BfZ.

67   Werner Adamczyk, *Feuer! An Artilleryman's Life on the Eastern Front*, 83–84.

68   Wolfgang Schneider, *Panzer Tactics: German Small-Unit Armor Tactics in World War II*, 5.

69   Alfred Opitz, "*Die Stimmung in der Truppe am Vorabend des Überfalls auf die Sowjetunion*," in: *Der Krieg des kleinen Mannes. Eine Militärgeschichte von unten*, Wolfram Wette (ed.), 236.

70   Schneider, *Panzer Tactics*, 5; C. G. Sweeting, *Hitler's Personal Pilot: The Life and Times of Hans Baur*, 155; Kershaw, *War Without Garlands*, 10.

71   Cited in: Hans Dollinger (ed.), *Kain, wo ist dein Bruder? Was der Mensch im Zweiten Weltkrieg erleiden musste—dokumentiert in Tagebüchern und Briefen*, 78–79. The time noted by *Leutnant* Schmidt for the reading out of Hitler's proclamation (2400 hours) is the latest I've come across in any German memoir or war diary; in most cases, the proclamation was read to the troops in the afternoon, or more likely, in the evening of June 21, 1941. For example, in sectors of 45 ID, 121 ID, and Seventeenth Army, Hitler's proclamation was read out at 1400, 1600, and 2000 hours, respectively. Aliev, *The Siege of Brest 1941*, 47; *Geschichte der 121. Ostpreussischen Infanterie-Division 1940–1945*, 16 (hereafter cited as, *Geschichte der 121. Infanterie-Division*); NARA, T-312, Roll 668, *Ia KTB Nr. 1, AOK 17*, 21.6.41.

72   Cited in: Dr. Erich Bunke, *Der Osten blieb unser Schicksal 1939–1944. Panzerjäger im 2. Weltkrieg*, 208–9.

73   Hans Joachim Schröder, "*Erfahrungen deutscher Mannschaftssoldaten während der ersten Phase des Russlandkrieges*," in: *Zwei Wege nach Moskau. Vom Hitler-Stalin-Pakt zum "Unternehmen Barbarossa*," Bernd Wegner (ed.), 311.

74   One can only imagine how those discussions went! NARA, T-314, Roll 755, *Ia KTB Nr. 6, 26.AK*, 21.6.41.

75   Cited in: Hartmann, *Wehrmacht im Ostkrieg*, 248. Observed Hartmann: "Much of the evidence indicates that most of the soldiers (even those who had little to do with NS-ideology) were convinced of the necessity for such a war."

76   Hermann Frank Meyer, *Blutiges Edelweiss. Die 1. Gebirgs-Division im Zweiten Weltkrieg*, 53 (hereafter cited as, Meyer, *Die 1. Gebirgs-Division*).

77   Lt. Helmut D. (04 255 C), Collection BfZ.

78   Wilhelm Prüller, *Diary of a German Soldier*, H. C. Robbins Landon and Sebastian Leitner (eds.), 63.

79   Erich N. (18 683 C), Collection BfZ.

80   *Tagebuch*, Hptm. Dr. H.U., Collection BfZ.

81   The 98 ID was an OKH reserve division for Operation *Barbarossa*. "*Die materielle Ausstattung des deutschen Ostheeres am 22. Juni 1941*," in: *DRZW*, Vol. IV: 186–87.

82   *Gefr.* Gerhard S. (38 002), Collection BfZ.

83   The 73 ID was also an OKH reserve division for Operation *Barbarossa*. "*Die materielle Ausstattung des deutschen Ostheeres am 22. Juni 1941*," in: *DRZW*, Vol. IV: 186–87.

84   *O'Gefr.* Werner E. (21 389), Collection BfZ.

85   *True to Type: A Selection from Letters and Diaries of German Soldiers and Civilians Collected on the Soviet-German Front*, 17.

86   Cited in: Hartmann, *Wehrmacht im Ostkrieg*, 247.

87   *Gefr.* Ludwig B. (04 650), Collection BfZ.

88   G.S. (18 719 A), Collection BfZ.

89   Eberhard Krehl, *Erinnerungen eines 85 Jahre alten Mannes*, 42.

90   Cited in: Walter Bähr and Dr. Hans W. Bähr, *Kriegsbriefe Gefallener Studenten, 1939–1945*, 51–52. Hermann Stracke would be killed on the Eastern Front on September 29, 1941.

91   *Geschichte der 121. Infanterie-Division*, 16.

92   Opitz, "*Die Stimmung in der Truppe am Vorabend des Überfalls auf die Sowjetunion*," 236.

93   Wolfgang Knecht, *Geschichte des Infanterie-Regiments 77: 1936–1945*, 53. (77 IR [26 ID] was in the sector of Army Group Center.) In the area of Army Group South, the Seventeenth Army war diarist

observed that June 21 was "*heiter*," which can be translated as "clear," "bright," or "fair." NARA, T-312, Roll 668, *Ia KTB Nr. 1, AOK 17*, 21.6.41.

94 Kirchubel, *Operation Barbarossa 1941 (3), Army Group Center*, 32.

95 Siegfried Risse, "*Das IR 101 und der 2. Weltkrieg.*"

96 Knecht, *Geschichte des Infanterie-Regiments 77: 1936–1945*, 53.

97 Erickson, *The Road to Stalingrad*, 109; Bellamy, *Absolute War*, 183.

98 Bellamy, *Absolute War*, 183.

99 Adam Zamoyski, *Moscow 1812: Napoleon's Fatal March*, 78–79.

100 Erickson, *Road to Stalingrad*, 340.

101 Stephen Kotkin, *Stalin: Waiting for Hitler, 1929–1941*, 837.

102 Kershaw, *Fateful Choices*, 272–73.

103 Ibid., 284.

104 The German navy had adopted ENIGMA in 1926, the army in 1928, and the *Luftwaffe* in 1935. The Germans were well aware that their enemies were listening in on their secret radio traffic, yet they "placed absolute trust in ENIGMA," being quite convinced that their messages were undecipherable. ULTRA, the major Allied intelligence coup of the Second World War, remained a well-guarded secret until the early 1970s, with some aspects of the project concealed even into the 1980s because of their impact on operations against Soviet codes. Diane T. Putney (ed.), *ULTRA and the Army Air Forces in World War II: An Interview with Associate Justice of the U.S. Supreme Court Lewis F. Powell, Jr.*, ix–x; Johnson, *Modern Times*, 399.

105 For a splendidly detailed account of Soviet intelligence assessments of German military intentions, and how they evolved over the months prior to the start of Operation *Barbarossa*, see, Frank Ellis, *Barbarossa 1941: Reframing Hitler's Invasion of Stalin's Soviet Empire*, 164–232. According to Ellis, "Stalin was exceptionally well informed about German preparations for an attack against the Soviet Union." In fact, "by 1 June 1941, and certainly no later than that, Soviet intelligence agencies . . . had built up a detailed picture of German military intentions." Ellis, 164, 227.

106 Luther, *Barbarossa Unleashed*, 163–64. See also, Kershaw, *Fateful Choices*, 284; Musial, *Kampfplatz Deutschland*, 432–33; Constantine Pleshakov, *Stalin's Folly: The Tragic First Ten Days of WWII on the Eastern Front*, 86–87 (hereafter cited as, Pleshakov, *Stalin's Folly*); and, Rolf-Dieter Müller, "*Duell im Schnee*," in: *Der Zweite Weltkrieg. Wendepunkt der deutschen Geschichte*, Stephan Burgdorff and Klaus Wiegrefe (eds.), 114.

107 Braithwaite, *Moscow 1941*, 58.

108 Ibid., 58.

109 Pleshakov, *Stalin's Folly*, 88.

110 Braithwaite, *Moscow 1941*, 58.

111 Ibid., 58–59.

112 Ibid., 59.

113 The reference is to Stalin's famous speech in Moscow of May 5, 1941, to the new graduates of the Frunze Military Academy, the country's "most prestigious staff or war college, attended by promising captains and majors." After his forty-minute speech, in the reception that followed, he gave three short toasts. In his third and final toast he said that, while the "peace policy" had served the country well, enabling the Red Army to be rebuilt with modern weaponry, the Soviet Union would now transition from defensive to offensive operations. "The Red Army," he exclaimed, "is a modern army, but a modern army is an attacking army." Bellamy, *Absolute War*, 115; Kershaw, *Fateful Choices*, 277.

114 Braithwaite, *Moscow 1941*, 59.

115 John Erickson, *The Soviet High Command: A Military-Political History 1918–1941*, 586 (hereafter cited as, Erickson, *The Soviet High Command*).

116 Cited in: Braithwaite, *Moscow 1941*, 60. For the original source see, Winston Churchill, *The Second World War*, Vol. 4: *The Grand Alliance*, 367–68.

117 In late February 1941, soon after the start of their strategic buildup in the East, the Germans launched their most ambitious—and, surely, most successful—disinformation campaign of the war. Employing the code names "shark" (*Haifisch*) and "harpoon" (*Harpune*), its purpose was to convince the Russians that Operation *Sealion*, the planned—yet now canceled—invasion of England, was still in the

works, and that German forces massing in the East were nothing more than a ruse to convince the British that *Sealion* had been dropped. Even Stalin's conviction that any German attack would be preceded by an ultimatum, giving him time to concede, to mobilize his forces, or even to act preemptively, was a part of this German deception plan. The deception plan was also used to spread false rumors among the German troops in the East. Buchbender and Sterz (eds.), *Das andere Gesicht des Krieges*, 63–64.

118   Braithwaite, *Moscow 1941*, 61.

119   Ibid., 61.

120   Pleshakov, *Stalin's Folly*, 23–24.

121   Erickson, *The Road to Stalingrad*, 108.

122   Ibid., 108.

123   Ibid., 108.

124   Braithwaite, *Moscow 1941*, 147.

125   Gorodetsky, *Grand Delusion*, 309–10. The Soviet ambassador, Dekanozov, finally received an audience with State Secretary Ernst von Weizsäcker at 9:30 that evening, and "handed him a note, similar to the one Schulenburg had received in Moscow, specifying some 180 cases of German reconnaissance flights over Soviet territory since the latest Soviet complaint in April . . . Weizsäcker gained time by proposing that Dekanozov await the official response."

126   Ibid., 309.

127   Vatutin was the first deputy chief of the General Staff.

128   This is the time cited by Constantine Pleshakov, who had access to an impressive array of new source materials, including Stalin's office logs. According to Pleshakov, Stalin had also held a meeting earlier that evening, at which Zhukov was not present and during which, "in all likelihood Stalin ordered the pre-emptive strike—maybe in a matter of days, perhaps in a matter of a week or so" (Pleshakov, *Stalin's Folly*, 93–94). Historian Chris Bellamy supports Pleshakov on the preemptive strike: "it may be that during that meeting Stalin reluctantly ordered the still unfinished 15 May scheme for a pre-emptive strike against German forces as they assembled—he still did not know they were within nine hours of attacking—to be put into operation, as a precaution." Bellamy, *Absolute War*, 154.

129   Braithwaite, *Moscow 1941*, 67; Colvin, *Zhukov: The Conqueror of Berlin*, 65; Pleshakov, *Stalin's Folly*, 95.

130   Braithwaite, *Moscow 1941*, 67; Glantz, *Barbarossa*, 242; Pleshakov, *Stalin's Folly*, 98. For the complete text of Directive No. 1, see, Appendix 6.

131   Pleshakov, *Stalin's Folly*, 96; also, Erickson, *The Road to Stalingrad*, 115.

132   Volkogonov, "The German Attack, the Soviet Response," 85; Edwin P. Hoyt, *Stalin's War: Tragedy and Triumph 1941–1945*, 25; TsAMO RF, F. 208, Op. 2454ss, D. 26, L. 34, "*Donesenie Shtaba Zapadnogo Osobogo Voennogo Okruga Nachal'niku General'nogo Shtaba ot 21 Iyunya 1941 g. o Narushenii Gosudarstvennoi Granitsy Germanskimi Samoletami i o Snyatii Nemtsami Provolochnykh Zagrazhdenii. Sovershenno Sekretno, Vruchit' Nemedlenno*" (Report by the Staff of the Western Special Military District to the Chief of the General Staff on June 21, 1941, on the Violation of the State Border by German Aircraft and on the Removal of Wire Obstacles by the Germans. Top Secret, Deliver Immediately), in: *Sbornik Boevykh Dokumentov Velikoi Otechestvennoi Voiny* (Collection of Combat Documents of the Great Patriotic War), Vol. 35: 10–11 (hereafter cited as, SBDVOV).

133   Bellamy, *Absolute War*, 157.

134   Braithwaite, *Moscow 1941*, 68.

135   Erickson, *The Road to Stalingrad*, 109; Charles Messenger, *The Last Prussian: A Biography of Field Marshal Gerd von Rundstedt, 1875–1953*, 139 (hereafter cited as, Messenger, *A Biography of Field Marshal Rundstedt*); Heinz Guderian, *Panzer Leader*, 153. For Guderian's original account see, Heinz Guderian, *Erinnerungen eines Soldaten*, 139.

136   Pleshakov, *Stalin's Folly*, 97; Gorodetsky, *Grand Delusion*, 311; Roberts (ed.), *Marshal of Victory. Vol. I: WWII Memoirs of General Zhukov through 1941*, 280. According to Pleshakov, the German defector belonged to the 74 Infantry Division; however, no such formation existed in the German order of battle for Operation *Barbarossa*. The soldier may have belonged to 44 Infantry Division, which was posted almost

directly opposite the town of Vladimir-Volynski on June 21, 1941. *DRZW*, Vol. IV, *Beiheft*, "*Ausgangslage zum 22.6.1941.*"

137   Erickson, *The Road to Stalingrad*, 101.

138   Ibid., 97.

139   Aliev, *The Siege of Brest 1941*, 21.

140   Erickson, *The Road to Stalingrad*, 94.

141   Pleshakov, *Stalin's Folly*, 111–12. Russian journalist Rostislav Aliev, in his fine book on the battle for the fortress of Brest-Litovsk in June 1941, amplified the observations of Pleshakov: "The command staff and headquarters at every level, including the [Soviet 4 Army] level as well, didn't know how to direct the troops with the assistance of radio communications, and shunned it because of the difficulty of using radios in comparison with wire communications. The 4 Army headquarters in Kobrin handled its communications with the command of 28 Rifle Corps and the headquarters of the 6 and 42 Rifle Divisions over civilian telephone lines that had been set aside for this purpose. The 4 Army headquarters had no standing radio communications with higher or lower levels of command, or with neighboring armies. On the whole, the provision of Western Special Military District with radios was as follows: at the regimental level—41 percent of the authorized number; at the battalion level—58 percent; and at the company level—70 percent." Aliev, *The Siege of Brest 1941*, 35.

142   Glantz, *Stumbling Colossus*, 104–5.

143   For a detailed order of battle for the Baltic Special Military District (troop strength, weapons, etc.) see, Chapter 3, Section 3.1.

144   Glantz, *Stumbling Colossus*, 105.

145   Ibid., 105.

146   Erickson, *The Road to Stalingrad*, 94.

147   Ibid., 102. General Kuznetsov also ordered blackouts in the cities of Riga, Kaunas, Vilna, Daugavpils (Dvinsk) and Liepaja (Libau), while the bomber forces in his command continued with their night-training program right up to the start of the war.

148   Glantz, *Stumbling Colossus*, 105.

149   David M. Glantz, "The Border Battles on the Siauliai Axis 22–26 June 1941," in: Glantz (ed.), *Initial Period of War on the Eastern Front*, 85.

150   NARA, T-315, Roll 16, *Ia KTB Nr. 6, 1.Pz.Div.*, 21.6.41.

151   Kirchubel, *Operation Barbarossa 1941 (3), Army Group Center*, 15.

152   For a detailed order of battle for the Western Special Military District (troop strength, weapons, etc.) see, Chapter 4, Section 4.1.

153   Erickson, *The Road to Stalingrad*, 102.

154   Ibid., 101.

155   Cited in: Aliev, *The Siege of Brest 1941*, 34.

156   Ibid., 33.

157   Ibid., 42.

158   Erickson, *The Road to Stalingrad*, 101.

159   David M. Glantz, "The Border Battles on the Bialystok-Minsk Axis: 22–28 June 1941," in: Glantz (ed.), *Initial Period of War on the Eastern Front*, 189.

160   Erickson, *The Road to Stalingrad*, 104.

161   http://iremember.ru/en.

162   Erickson, *The Road to Stalingrad*, 104.

163   Pleshakov, *Stalin's Folly*, 99–100.

164   Luttichau, *The Road to Moscow*, VI: 3–4.

165   This report, no doubt, was the same one that Pavlov's chief of staff, General Klimovskikh, had sent on to Moscow on the evening of June 21 (see, Section 2.3).

166   Cited in: Pleshakov, *Stalin's Folly*, 99.

167 The intelligence report was dispatched to the deputy chief of staff of the Red Army and to the chiefs of the intelligence sections of Pavlov's 3, 4, 10, and 13 Armies. Unfortunately, the document includes what appears to be a handwritten note: "Sent at 1420 on 22 June 1941." TsAMO RF, F. 208, Op. 2454ss, D. 26, Ll. 70-73, *"Ravedivatel'naya Svodka Shtaba Zapadnogo Osobogo Voennogo Okruga o Gruppirovke Nemetskikh Voisk na 21 Iyunya 1941 g. Sovershenno Sekretno"* (Intelligence Report from the Staff of the Western Special Military District on the Disposition of German Forces on June 21, 1941. Top Secret), in: SBDVOV, Vol. 35: 13–14.

168 Cited in: Catherine Merridale, *Ivan's War: Life and Death in the Red Army, 1939–1945*, 85 (hereafter cited as, Merridale, *Ivan's War*).

169 The actual times of the German invasion on June 22, 1941, were either 0305 or 0315 hours, depending on the sector of the front.

170 Merridale, *Ivan's War*, 85.

171 Pleshakov, *Stalin's Folly*, 100–101.

172 For a detailed order of battle for the Kiev Special Military District (troop strength, weapons, etc.) see, Chapter 5, Section 5.1. No attempt is made in this chapter to examine the Odessa Military District, which covered Bessarabia and was not a factor on June 22, 1941.

173 Robert Kirchubel, *Operation Barbarossa 1941 (1), Army Group South*, 28.

174 Glantz (ed.), *Initial Period of War on the Eastern Front*, 189, 248–53; Email, David M. Glantz to Dr. C. Luther, August 22, 2017.

175 *Slaughterhouse: The Encyclopedia of the Eastern Front*, 130. In June 1945, Rokossovsky was given the "high honor" of commanding the victory parade in Moscow. Ibid., 131.

176 K. K. Rokossovsky, *Soldatskii Dolg* (A Soldier's Duty), 32–33.

177 Erickson, *The Road to Stalingrad*, 94.

178 Colvin, *Zhukov: The Conqueror of Berlin*, 66.

179 Kirchubel, *Operation Barbarossa 1941 (1), Army Group South*, 29–30.

180 NARA, T-315, Roll 1985, *298.Inf.Div. Abt.Ia Nr. 1376/41 geh., Betr.: Tagesmeldung an Gen.Kdo. 3.Pz.K.*, 20.6.41, in: *Ia Anlagen zum KTB Nr. 4: 16.6.–28.6.41.*

181 The German defector was a Corporal Alfred Liskow, a Communist furniture maker from Bavaria (Bellamy, *Absolute War*, 156). He must have been the first defector that evening that General Zhukov had telephoned Stalin about, resulting in the Soviet dictator summoning Zhukov and Timoshenko to the Kremlin. As noted (Section 2.3), Zhukov also told Stalin of a second defector (who had crossed Russian lines well north of Sokal') just after midnight.

182 Erickson, *The Road to Stalingrad*, 105.

183 Ibid., 106-7.

184 The German *Lagebericht Ost* (Situation Report East) for June 21, 1941, had detected some Red Army redeployments; the transportation of tanks along the railway between Minsk and Smolensk in the past week; and troop movements from the Far East and the Urals. In addition, major concentrations of Soviet parachute troops had been observed in the Ukraine (by a high-flying reconnaissance aircraft with Romanian markings). Yet the general situation "remained substantially unchanged, with no major modifications in Soviet strength, dispositions and apparent intentions." Ibid., 106.

185 Seaton, *The Russo-German War 1941–45*, 135; Roberts (ed.), *Marshal of Victory. Vol. I: WWII Memoirs of General Zhukov through 1941*, 280.

186 http://iremember.ru/en.

Intermezzo: Operation *Barbarossa* Begins—From the Baltic to the Black Sea

1 Franz A. P. Frisch and Wilbur D. Jones, Jr., *Condemned to Live: A Panzer Artilleryman's Five-Front War*, 69 (hereafter cited as, Frisch, *Condemned to Live*).

2 Magenheimer, *Moskau 1941. Entscheidungsschlacht im Osten*, 36–37.

3 Ziemke and Bauer, *Moscow to Stalingrad: Decision in the East*, 3; Erickson, *The Soviet High Command*, 587.

4   *KTB OKW,* Vol. I, 417.

5   Halder, *War Diary,* 410–11.

6   Bryan Fugate and Lev Dvoretsky, *Thunder on the Dnepr: Zhukov-Stalin and the Defeat of Hitler's Blitz-krieg,* 135–36; Bellamy, *Absolute War,* 184; Glantz, *Barbarossa,* 242.

7   NARA, T-311, Roll 53, *Ia KTB H.Gr.Nord,* 22.6.41.

8   According to Werner Haupt, who served with Army Group North, the barrage lasted only a few minutes. See, Werner Haupt, *Heeresgruppe Nord 1941–1945,* 25.

9   NARA, T-311, Roll 53, *Ia KTB H.Gr.Nord,* 22.6.41.

Chapter 3: Armageddon Unleashed (I)—Army Group North Goes to War

1   NARA, T-315, Roll 16, *Ia KTB Nr. 6, 1.Pz.Div.,* 22.6.41.

2   NARA, T-313, Roll 330, *Ia KTB Nr. 5, Pz. AOK 4,* 22.6.41.

3   Cited in: Werner Haupt, *Army Group North: The Wehrmacht in Russia 1941–1945,* 28 (hereafter cited as, Haupt, *Army Group North*).

4   Mitcham Jr., *The Men of Barbarossa,* 41–44; I. C. B. Dear (ed.), *The Oxford Guide to World War II,* 530; www.lexikon-der-wehrmacht.de.

5   Mawdsley, *Thunder in the East,* 82; Robert Kirchubel, *Operation Barbarossa: The German Invasion of Soviet Russia,* 126; *Voennaya Entsiklopediya,* Vol. 4: 338.

6   Brian Taylor, *Barbarossa to Berlin: A Chronology of the Campaigns on the Eastern Front 1941 to 1945,* Vol. 1: *The Long Drive East, 22 June 1941 to 18 November 1942,* 16 (hereafter cited as, Taylor, *Barbarossa to Berlin*). Aggregate personnel figures cited in this book for each of the three German army groups include: army, *Waffen SS,* assigned *Luftwaffe* units (e.g., flak battalions), and railroad troops.

7   Figures on tank strength differ slightly depending on the source. According to Eddy Bauer, 4 Panzer Group had 570 tanks on "B-Tag." See, Eddy Bauer, *Der Panzerkrieg. Die wichtigsten Panzeroperationen des zweiten Weltkrieges in Europa und Afrika, Bd. I: Vorstoss und Rückzug der deutschen Panzerverbände,* 115 (hereafter cited as, Bauer, *Der Panzerkrieg,* Vol. I). Thomas Jentz posits the figure of 602 tanks for the panzer group. Thomas L. Jentz (ed.), *Panzer Truppen: The Complete Guide to the Creation & Combat Employment of Germany's Tank Force 1933–1942,* 190–91 (hereafter cited as, Jentz [ed.], *Panzer Truppen*).

8   Before the Russian campaign the Germans introduced several effective new weapons. One of them was the "*Nebelwerfer 41,*" a six-barreled 150mm rocket launcher that hurled a high-explosive shell some 7,000 meters with devastating effect. Also available in 1941 was another version of the *Nebelwerfer* that fired 280mm (high-explosive) or 320mm (incendiary) rockets; this devastating weapon, christened "*Stuka zu Fuss*" (Stuka on foot) by the troops, had a range of about 2,000 meters. Most of the *Nebelwerfer* in service with the German army in June 1941 were the 150mm weapons; however, each panzer division had a platoon in its armored combat engineer battalion equipped with the 280/320 rockets, which were fired from crates mounted on the sides of an armored personnel carrier (APC). (See, Appendix 4.) Albert Seaton, *The German Army 1933–45,* 173; Kirchubel, *Operation Barbarossa 1941 (1), Army Group South,* 23; U.S. War Department, Technical Manual TM-E 30-451, *Handbook on German Military Forces,* 395–401 (hereafter cited as, *Handbook on German Military Forces*); Wolf Keilig, *Das Deutsche Heer 1939–1945, Bd. II, Abschnitt 103,* 6.

9   "*Kriegsgliederung Barbarossa,*" *Stand 18.6.41,* Kurt Mehner (ed.); *GSWW,* Vol. IV: 316.

10   The different types of bridge columns used by the Germans were designated by various capital letters—e.g., "B" and "K"—the letters signifying the type of bridge-building equipment used. For example, the bridge column "B" possessed sufficient equipment for building longer bridges than did the bridge column "K." However, bridges built by column "B" were of wood, while those constructed by column "K" were of steel. *Handbook on German Military Forces,* 156.

11   "*Kriegsgliederung Barbarossa,*" *Stand 18.6.41,* Kurt Mehner (ed.).

12   The short-range squadrons attached to the corps and divisions of all three of the German army groups were equipped with Henschel Hs-126 two-seat reconnaissance and observation aircraft. Long-range reconnaissance squadrons were assigned to the army groups, armies, and panzer groups; they were outfitted with

versions of the Ju-88, Do-17, and Bf-110. Franz Kurowski, *Balkenkreuz und Roter Stern. Der Luftkrieg über Russland 1941–1944*, 51–55.

13   "*Kriegsgliederung Barbarossa*," Stand 18.6.41, Kurt Mehner (ed.); "*Die materielle Ausstattung des deutschen Ostheeres am 22. Juni 1941*," in: *DRZW*, Vol. IV: 186–87.

14   *GSWW*, Vol. IV: 364; Haupt, *Army Group North*, 19; see also, Generalleutnant Hermann Plocher, *The German Air Force versus Russia, 1941*, 34.

15   *DRZW*, Vol. IV, *Beiheft*, "*Ausgangslage zum 22.6.1941*"; Clark, *Barbarossa. The Russo-German Conflict, 1941–45*, 47–48; Seaton, *The Russo-German War 1941–45*, 102; Mawdsley, *Thunder in the East*, 81.

16   "*Aufmarschanweisung Barbarossa*," in: Halder, *KTB*, Vol. II: 467 (Appendix 2). Apart from "minor amendments," the assignment of Army Group North adhered closely to the *Barbarossa* Directive No. 21 of December 18, 1940. *GSWW*, Vol. IV, 290.

17   John Keegan, *The Second World War*, 182.

18   *GSWW*, Vol. IV: 537.

19   The 3 Mechanized Corps (supporting 11 Army) was in reserve near Vilnius, while 12 Mechanized Corps (supporting 8 Army) was also stationed well back from the border near Siauliai. Taylor, *Barbarossa to Berlin*, 16.

20   Glantz, *Barbarossa*, 216 (f.n. 23), 246; Glantz, "The Border Battles on the Siauliai Axis 22–26 June 1941," in: Glantz (ed.), *Initial Period of War on the Eastern Front*, 83.

21   Glantz, *Barbarossa*, 43. On June 22, 1941, 12 Mechanized Corps fielded 30,435 men and a total of 806 tanks (the number of combat-ready tanks was somewhat lower). Most of the corps' tanks were old and obsolete, including 242 BT-7 light and 483 T-26 light tanks. Email, David M. Glantz to Dr. C. Luther, July 18, 2017.

22   Seaton, *The Russo-German War 1941–45*, 101.

23   TsAMO RF, F. 344, Op. 5554, D. 54, L. 41, "*Raspisanie Sootnosheniya Sil na Fronte 8 Armii na 21-22.6.41*" (List of the Correlation of Forces along the 8 Army's Front on June 21–22, 1941). According to this document, 8 Army was holding a front of 172 kilometers with a total strength of 103,000 men. A second (much more detailed) document states that the front of 8 Army was 158 kilometers in length, with the army's five rifle divisions composed of forty-two battalions. See, TsAMO RF, F. 221, Op. 3928ss, D. 28, L. 11, "*Sovershenno Sekretno. Tablitsa Sootnosheniya Sil na Fronte 8-i Armii k 17.00 21.6.41, Karta 100,000*" (Top Secret. The Correlation of Forces along the 8 Army's Front as of 1700 [hours] June 21, 1941, 100,000 Map), in: SBDVOV, Vol. 34: 193.

24   Glantz, "The Border Battles on the Siauliai Axis 22–26 June 1941," in: Glantz (ed.), *Initial Period of War on the Eastern Front*, 83–85.

25   Leeb, *Tagebuchaufzeichnungen*, 275–76; NARA T-311, Roll 132, *H.Gr.Nord, Ia, Geschichte Feldzug Russland*, 22.6.41.

26   Cited in Glantz, *Stumbling Colossus*, 276–79. For a detailed Soviet appreciation of German forces opposite the Baltic Special Military District as of June 17, 1941, see, TsAMO RF, F. 334, Op. 6435ss, D. 8, Ll. 9-11, "*Razvedivatel'naya Svodka Shtaba Pribaltiiskogo Osobogo Voennogo Okruga ot 18 Iyunya 1941 g. o Gruppirovke Voisk Protivnika Protiv Voisk Okruga na 17 Iyunya 1941 g.*" (Intelligence Summary by the Headquarters of the Baltic Special Military District from June 18, 1941, on the Grouping of the Enemy's Forces Opposite the District's Forces as of June 17, 1941), in: SBDVOV, Vol. 34: 18–20.

27   Glantz, *Barbarossa*, 35.

28   Personnel figures for German armies and panzer groups cited in this narrative are estimates of *organic* troop strength derived from the tables of organization of full-strength German divisions on the eve of Operation *Barbarossa*. For example, at full strength, an infantry division (three infantry regiments) consisted of about 17,000 men; a fully outfitted panzer division had an establishment of 13,300–15,600 men (depending in part on whether it had two or three tank battalions); motorized and light divisions (both with only two infantry regiments) are estimated at 14,500 men. General Headquarters (GHQ) troops, which added many thousands of additional personnel to each army and panzer group, are not included in these estimates (nor are assigned *Luftwaffe* formations). Sources used to compile the estimates include: Seaton, *The German Army 1933–45*, 263; Pier Paolo Battistelli, *Panzer Divisions: The Eastern Front 1941–43*,

13; Bauer, *Der Panzerkrieg*, Vol. I: 113; Alex Buchner, *The German Infantry Handbook 1939–1945*, 15; Nigel Thomas, *The German Army 1939–45 (3)*, *Eastern Front 1941–43*, 5–6; "*Die materielle Ausstattung des deutschen Ostheeres am 22. Juni 1941*," in: *DRZW*, Vol. IV: 186–87; *Handbook on German Military Forces*, 85–86.

29   For a terrific social history of 253 ID see, Christoph Rass, "*Menschenmaterial": Deutsche Soldaten an der Ostfront. Innenansichten einer Infanteriedivision 1939–1945*.

30   *z.V.* = *zur Verfügung*, or at the disposal of. Thus, *z.V. AOK 16* means the unit is at the disposal of (i.e., directly controlled by) Sixteenth Army HQ.

31   "*Kriegsgliederung Barbarossa*," *Stand 18.6.41*, Kurt Mehner (ed.); www.lexikon-der-wehrmacht.de.

32   *DRZW*, Vol. IV, *Beiheft*, "*Ausgangslage zum 22.6.1941*"; Glantz (ed.), *Atlas and Operational Summary*; NARA T-311, Roll 132, *H.Gr.Nord, Ia, Geschichte Feldzug Russland*, 22.6.41.

33   *GSWW*, Vol. IV: 538; Luttichau, *The Road to Moscow*, IV: 17–18.

34   "*Aufmarschanweisung Barbarossa*," in: Halder, *KTB*, Vol. II: 467 (Appendix 2).

35   See, for example, NARA, T-314, Roll 446, *Ia KTB Ost Nr. 1, 10.AK*, 22.6.41; NARA, T-315, Roll 1350, *Ia KTB Nr. 2, 126.Inf.Div.*, 22.6.41.

36   Seaton, *The Russo-German War 1941–1945*, 101; Lithuania Map, Kaunas Sheet N.E. 54/22, Series M404 (4072), Great Britain War Office, 1942–, in: Perry-Castañeda Library Map Collection, University of Texas at Austin (http://www.lib.utexas.edu/maps) (hereafter cited as the Perry-Castañeda Library Map Collection).

37   Paul Carell, *Hitler Moves East, 1941–1943*, 28.

38   NARA T-311, Roll 132, *H.Gr.Nord, Ia, Geschichte Feldzug Russland*, 22.6.41; NARA, T-312, Roll 543, *Ia KTB Nr. 5, AOK 16*, 22.6.41.

39   NARA, T-314, Roll 101, *Ia KTB Nr. 1, 2.AK*, 22.6.41.

40   Lt.-Gen. Heinz-Georg Lemm, "12th Infantry Division Operations," in: Glantz (ed.), *Initial Period of War on the Eastern Front*, 226–28. In the days before June 22, noted Lemm, "we received only poor information on the enemy and terrain in the area of attack. We had been able to recognize that the Russians had high wooden guard towers; we had been able to observe the relief of the sentries and their supply procedure, and furthermore we could see vivid entrenching activities about 800–1000 meters behind the border. From aerial photographs some firing positions of Russian field artillery were known. The division expected a troop strength of about one to two Soviet regiments in front of its sector which would presumably fight a delaying action in their field positions and developed bases. The maps we received were poorly printed and provided hardly any information on altitudes, road conditions, and forest vegetation." Glantz (ed.), *Initial Period of War on the Eastern Front*, 227.

41   NARA, T-314, Roll 101, *Ia KTB Nr. 1, 2.AK*, 22.6.41.

42   *Geschichte der 121. Infanterie-Division 1940–1945*, 16–17.

43   www.lexikon-der-wehrmacht.de.

44   *Geschichte der 121. Infanterie-Division*, 17.

45   NARA, T-312, Roll 543, *Ia KTB Nr. 5, AOK 16*, 22.6.41; Haupt, *Heeresgruppe Nord 1941–1945*, 26.

46   Gerhart Lohse, *Geschichte der rheinisch-westfälischen 126. Infanterie-Division*, 11 (hereafter cited as, Lohse, *Geschichte der 126. Infanterie-Division*). In Lohse's narrative, the Šešupė is referred to as the "*Ostfluss*" (East River), as was the German custom.

47   NARA, T-314, Roll 446, *Ia KTB Ost Nr. 1, 10.AK*, 22.6.41.

48   Lohse, *Geschichte der 126. Infanterie-Division*, 11–12.

49   Ibid., 12.

50   Bellamy, *Absolute War*, 193–95. Observed Bellamy, "preparations for armed revolt against the Soviet authorities in all the Baltic States had begun as soon as Soviet occupation forces arrived in 1940." A week before the German invasion, the Soviet authorities had begun to deport civilians from the Baltic States, including some 18,000 (5,000 of whom were children) from Lithuania.

51   NARA, T-314, Roll 446, *Ia KTB Ost Nr. 1, 10.AK*, 22.6.41; NARA, T-315, Roll 855, *Ia KTB Nr. 4, 30.Inf.Div.*, 22.6.41.

52   NARA, T-315, Roll 855, *Ia KTB Nr. 4, 30.Inf.Div.*, 22.6.41. At 0450, the division made its morning report to 10 AK, observing that the enemy opposition was apparently coming only from border guard units (*Grenzschutzeinheiten*).

53   Carell, *Hitler Moves East*, 28; Paul Carell, *Unternehmen Barbarossa: Der Marsch nach Russland*, 26–27. I have made use of Carell's original account in German to make—for the sake of accuracy—a few changes to the text quoted above.

54   NARA, T-314, Roll 446, *Ia KTB Ost Nr. 1, 10.AK*, 22.6.41.

55   Elements of the 126 ID (13./IR 424) would reach Sakiai late in the afternoon. Lohse, *Geschichte der 126. Infanterie-Division*, 12.

56   NARA T-311, Roll 132, *H.Gr.Nord, Ia, Geschichte Feldzug Russland*, 22.6.41.

57   *Geschichte der 121. Infanterie-Division*, 17.

58   Lt.-Gen. Heinz-Georg Lemm, "12th Infantry Division Operations," in: Glantz (ed.), *Initial Period of War on the Eastern Front*, 228. According to Lemm, during the battle for Kunigiskiai, "three and a half German rifle companies had wiped out two reinforced Soviet battalions except for small elements (in this connection the excellent support rendered by the batteries of 12 Artillery Regiment must not be forgotten)" Glantz (ed.), *Initial Period of War on the Eastern Front*, 230.

59   NARA, T-312, Roll 543, *Ia KTB Nr. 5, AOK 16*, 22.6.41.

60   NARA, T-311, Roll 53, *Ia KTB H.Gr.Nord*, 22.6.41.

61   TsAMO RF, F. 848, Op. 1, D. 1, L. 5, "*Razvedsvodka No. 5, Shtab 11 Armii, Kaunas, 9:00, 22.6.41*" (Intelligence Report No. 5, 11 Army Headquarters, Kaunas, 9:00 A.M., June 22, 1941).

62   TsAMO RF, F. 221, Op. 1351, D. 68, L. 28, "*Nachal'nik Shtaba PribOVO. Operativnaya Svodka No. 6, Shtab 11 Armii, Kaunas, 10:00, Polozhenie na 8:00 22.6.41*" (Chief of Staff of the Baltic Special Military District, Combat Report No. 6, Headquarters of 11 Army, Kaunas, 10:00 A.M., the Situation as of 8:00 A.M., June 22, 1941).

63   NARA, T-312, Roll 543, *Ia KTB Nr. 5, AOK 16*, 22.6.41. In the war diary of 2 Army Corps, it states that "two bunkers in Kybartai held out until late afternoon" of June 22. NARA, T-314, Roll 101, *Ia KTB Nr. 1, 2.AK*, 22.6.41.

64   Leeb, *Tagebuchaufzeichnungen*, 275; *Geschichte der 121. Infanterie-Division*, 18.

65   NARA, T-314, Roll 101, *Ia KTB Nr. 1, 2.AK*, 22.6.41.

66   Leeb, *Tagebuchaufzeichnungen*, 276. As General Wiktorin told Leeb the next day, the fighting on June 22 had been "tough" (*zäh*).

67   Carell, *Hitler Moves East*, 29. See also, Lohse, *Geschichte der 126. Infanterie-Division*, 12.

68   NARA, T-315, Roll 1350, *Ia KTB Nr. 2, 126.Inf.Div.*, 22.6.41. As the division's war diary put it: "422 IR suffered very badly on this day." (*Sehr schwer hatte an diesem Tage IR 422 zu leiden.*)

69   *Geschichte der 121. Infanterie-Division*, 18.

70   By evening, the most forward elements of 32 ID were at Mykalyne, just 5 kilometers west of Mariampole. NARA, T-314, Roll 101, *Ia KTB Nr. 1, 2.AK*, 22.6.41.

71   "Army Group North Situation Map: Evening, 22 June 1941," in: Glantz (ed.), *Initial Period of War on the Eastern Front*), 88; Lohse, *Geschichte der 126. Infanterie-Division*, 18; NARA, T-312, Roll 543, *Ia KTB Nr. 5, AOK 16*, 22.6.41.

72   NARA, T-313, Roll 330, *Ia KTB Nr. 5, Pz. AOK 4*, 22.6.41.

73   NARA, T-312, Roll 543, *Ia KTB Nr. 5, AOK 16*, 23.6.41. As noted in the war diary of 10 AK, by 1030 hours, 30 ID had already captured some 200 Russian prisoners. NARA, T-314, Roll 446, *Ia KTB Ost Nr. 1, 10.AK*, 22.6.41.

74   NARA, T-315, Roll 1351, "*Tagesmeldung*," *Ia 424.Inf.Rgt.*, 22.6.41, in: *Ia Anlagen zum KTB Nr. 2, 126. Inf.Div.*; NARA, T-314, Roll 446, *Ia KTB Ost Nr. 1, 10.AK*, 22.6.41.

75   *Gefr.* Otto S. (46 010), Collection BfZ.

76   Carell, *Hitler Moves East*, 28–29.

77   NARA, T-312, Roll 543, *Ia KTB Nr. 5, AOK 16*, 23.6.41.

78   Heinrich Bücheler, *Hoepner: Ein deutsches Soldatenschicksal des 20. Jahrhunderts*, 12 (hereafter cited as, Bücheler, *Hoepner: Ein deutsches Soldatenschicksal*). Hoepner's role in the anti-Hitler resistance was

also acknowledged by historians Samuel W. Mitcham Jr. and Gene Mueller: "Throughout the entire war Hoepner maintained connections to the conspirators and, in 1944, became a central figure in Stauffenberg's putsch attempt against Hitler." Samuel W. Mitcham Jr. and Gene Mueller, "*Generaloberst Erich Hoepner*," in: *Hitlers militärische Elite. Bd. 2: Vom Kriegsbeginn bis zum Weltkriegsende*, Gerd R. Ueberschär (ed.), 94 (hereafter cited as, *Hitlers militärische Elite*, Ueberschär [ed.]).

79   Cited in: Bücheler, *Hoepner: Ein deutsches Soldatenschicksal*, 131; see also, Mitcham Jr., *The Men of Barbarossa*, 131–32.

80   Cited in: Mitcham Jr. and Mueller, "*Generaloberst Erich Hoepner*," in: *Hitlers militärische Elite*, Ueberschär (ed.), 95. A slightly different version of Hoepner's order of the day of May 2, 1941, can be found in the records of 41 Panzer Corps, in a directive signed by the corps commander. See, "*Kampfanweisung*," *Anlage zu Festungsstab Allenstein Ia Nr. 83/41g.Kdos. (Chefs.) v. 11.5.41*, in: NARA, T-314, Roll 979, *Ia Anlagenband 1 zum KTB, 41.Pz.K.*

81   Mitcham Jr., *The Men of Barbarossa*, 235. See also, Mark M. Boatner III, *Biographical Dictionary of World War II*, 232; Ziemke and Bauer, *Moscow to Stalingrad: Decision in the East*, 128, f.n. 19; Dermot Bradley (ed.), *Deutschlands Generale und Admirale. Teil IV: Die Generale des Heeres 1921–1945, Bd. 6: Hochbaum–Klutmann*, 41.

82   To remind the reader, figures on troop strength for armies and panzer groups are estimates of organic troop strength that do not include GHQ troops.

83   "*Kriegsgliederung Barbarossa*," *Stand 18.6.41*, Kurt Mehner (ed.); Jentz (ed.), *Panzer Truppen*, 190–91; Raus, *Panzer Operations*, 11. For more specifications and background on German tank models in June 1941 see, Luther, *Barbarossa Unleashed*, 118–21.

84   "*Kriegsgliederung Barbarossa*," *Stand 18.6.41*, Kurt Mehner (ed.); Kurowski, *Balkenkreuz und Roter Stern. Der Luftkrieg über Russland 1941–1944*, 51.

85   Cited in: Bücheler, *Hoepner: Ein deutsches Soldatenschicksal*, 130–31.

86   Reinhardt's 36 Motorized Infantry Division was held in reserve behind the Neman River. Walter Chales de Beaulieu, *Generaloberst Erich Hoepner. Militärisches Porträt eines Panzer-Führers*, 134 (hereafter cited as, Chales de Beaulieu, *Hoepner*).

87   Col. Helmut Ritgen, "6th Panzer Division Operations," in: Glantz (ed.), *Initial Period of War on the Eastern Front*, 112; Lithuania Map, NN 34-3 (Siauliai), Series N501, U.S. Army Map Service, 1954, in: Perry-Castañeda Library Map Collection.

88   Cited in: Chales de Beaulieu, *Hoepner*, 133.

89   *GSWW*, Vol. IV: 538; NARA, T-313, Roll 330, *Ia KTB Nr. 5, Pz. AOK 4*, 22.6.41.

90   Chales de Beaulieu, *Hoepner*, 133. The bridge over the Dubyssa River lay 2.5 kilometers northwest of Ariogala. R. H. S. Stolfi, *German Panzers on the Offensive: Russian Front, North Africa, 1941–1942*, 149 (hereafter cited as, Stolfi, *German Panzers on the Offensive*).

91   Manstein, *Lost Victories*, 182.

92   Carell, *Hitler Moves East*, 29.

93   Chales de Beaulieu, *Hoepner*, 134; Lt.-Gen. A. D. v. Plato and Lt.-Col. R. O. Stoves, "1st Panzer Division Operations," in: Glantz (ed.), *Initial Period of War on the Eastern Front*, 127.

94   *GSWW*, Vol. IV: 537–38.

95   Bücheler, *Hoepner: Ein deutsches Soldatenschicksal*, 131.

96   Walter Chales de Beaulieu, *Der Vorstoss der Panzergruppe 4 auf Leningrad—1941*, 22 (hereafter cited as, Chales de Beaulieu, *Vorstoss der Panzergruppe 4*); Seaton, *The Russo-German War 1941–45*, 102; NARA, T-313, Roll 330, *Ia KTB Nr. 5, Pz. AOK 4*, 22.6.41.

97   Chales de Beaulieu, *Vorstoss der Panzergruppe 4*, 23; Werner Haupt, *Die 8. Panzer-Division im Zweiten Weltkrieg*, 136 (hereafter cited as, Haupt, *Die 8. Panzer-Division*); Seaton, *The Russo-German War 1941–1945*, 102.

98   Chales de Beaulieu, *Vorstoss der Panzergruppe 4*, 23.

99   NARA, T-315, Roll 16, *Ia KTB Nr. 6, 1.Pz.Div.*, 22.6.41.

100   NARA, T-313, Roll 330, *Ia KTB Nr. 5, Pz. AOK 4*, 22.6.41.

101   Erickson, *The Road to Stalingrad*, 128; Erickson, *The Soviet High Command*, 595.

102 Mitcham Jr., *The Men of Barbarossa*, 84.

103 In his postwar recollections, one former 8 PD soldier, who had served under Crisolli in France in 1940, remembered his former superior as being "unapproachable" (*unnahbar*). Werner R., "*Erinnerungen*" (N97.3), Collection BfZ.

104 All rifle regiments (*Schützen-Regimenter*) in German motorized infantry or tank divisions were fully motorized.

105 Haupt, *Die 8. Panzer-Division*, 136–37; Stolfi, *German Panzers on the Offensive*, 149.

106 NARA, T-315, Roll 1886, *Ia KTB, 290.Inf.Div.*, 22.6.41. As noted in the war diary, the lead elements of 290 ID had crossed the Mituva River by 0640.

107 NARA T-315, Roll 483, *Ia KTB, Bd. 1, 8.Pz.Div.*, 22.6.41.

108 Carell, *Hitler Moves East*, 30; Haupt, *Die 8. Panzer-Division*, 136–37; NARA, T-313, Roll 330, *Ia KTB Nr. 5, Pz. AOK 4*, 22.6.41; NARA T-315, Roll 483, *Ia KTB, Bd. 1, 8.Pz.Div.*, 22.6.41.

109 NARA T-315, Roll 483, *Ia KTB, Bd. 1, 8.Pz.Div.*, 22.6.41.

110 Haupt, *Die 8. Panzer-Division*, 137; NARA, T-313, Roll 330, *Ia KTB Nr. 5, Pz. AOK 4*, 22.6.41; NARA T-315, Roll 483, *Ia KTB, Bd. 1, 8.Pz.Div.*, 22.6.41.

111 Haupt, *Die 8. Panzer-Division*, 138; NARA T-315, Roll 483, *Ia KTB, Bd. 1, 8.Pz.Div.*, 22.6.41.

112 Stolfi, *German Panzers on the Offensive*, 154–55.

113 Haupt, *Die 8. Panzer-Division*, 138; NARA T-315, Roll 483, *Ia KTB, Bd. 1, 8.Pz.Div.*, 22.6.41.

114 NARA T-315, Roll 483, *Ia KTB, Bd. 1, 8.Pz.Div.*, 22.6.41.

115 Stolfi, *German Panzers on the Offensive*, 150.

116 Haupt, *Die 8. Panzer-Division*, 138; NARA T-315, Roll 483, *Ia KTB, Bd. 1, 8.Pz.Div.*, 22.6.41.

117 Stolfi, *German Panzers on the Offensive*, 150–51.

118 NARA T-315, Roll 483, *Ia KTB, Bd. 1, 8.Pz.Div.*, 22.6.41.

119 By evening, June 22, 290 ID had registered an impressive advance of some 30 kilometers. Chales de Beaulieu, *Vorstoss der Panzergruppe 4*, 24.

120 Manstein, *Lost Victories*, 182.

121 Stolfi, *German Panzers on the Offensive*, 151; Haupt, *Die 8. Panzer-Division*, 139–40.

122 Manstein, *Lost Victories*, 182.

123 Stolfi, *German Panzers on the Offensive*, 169.

124 Manstein, *Lost Victories*, 180–81; Erich von Manstein, *Verlorene Siege*, 178–79.

125 Jentz (ed.), *Panzer Truppen*, 190–91.

126 *DRZW*, Vol. IV, *Beiheft*, "*Ausgangslage zum 22.6.1941.*"

127 Col. Helmut Ritgen, "6th Panzer Division Operations," in: Glantz (ed.), *Initial Period of War on the Eastern Front*, 110; NARA, T-315, Roll 322, *KTB Nr. 3, 6. Schützen Brigade* [6 Rifle Brigade, 6 Panzer Division], 22.6.41.

128 Lt.-Gen. A. D. v. Plato and Lt.-Col. R. O. Stoves, "1st Panzer Division Operations," in: Glantz (ed.), *Initial Period of War on the Eastern Front*, 127.

129 Col. Helmut Ritgen, "6th Panzer Division Operations," in: Glantz (ed.), *Initial Period of War on the Eastern Front*, 110.

130 Ibid., 112.

131 NARA, T-313, Roll 330, *Ia KTB Nr. 5, Pz. AOK 4*, 22.6.41. In his personal diary, General Reinhardt noted that his panzer corps' attack began at 0305 hours supported by "very heavy artillery fire" (*ganz grosses Schiessen*). BA-MA N 245/3: *Persönliches Tagebuch Reinhardt*, 22.6.41.

132 TsAMO RF, F. 833, Op. 1, D. 13, L. 85, "*Shifrovka No. 745 iz Shtaba 8 Armii, Podana 22.6.[41]*" (Coded Message No. 745 from 8 Army Headquarters). As noted in a report by the chief of Soviet 8 Army artillery later in the day, "according to observers, 15–20% of the enemy's shells are not exploding." TsAMO, RF, F. 833, Op. 1, D. 15, L. 31, "*Opersvodka No. 2 Shtab Artillerii 8 Armii, Les Yautmel'kis (2 Kilometra Yuzhnee KURTUVENAI), 1800, 22.6.41*" (Operational Report No. 2, Artillery Headquarters of 8 Army, in the Jautmalke woods [2 kilometers south of KURTUVENAI], 1800, June 22, 1941).

133 NARA, T-313, Roll 330, *Ia KTB Nr. 5, Pz. AOK 4*, 22.6.41.

134 Raus, *Panzer Operations*, 14.

135   NARA, T-315, Roll 323, *Ia KTB, 6.Pz.Div.*, 22.6.41.

136   Seaton, *The Russo-German War 1941–45*, 102–3.

137   Seaton, *The Russo-German War 1941–45*, 102; Chales de Beaulieu, *Vorstoss der Panzergruppe 4*, 23.

138   Raus, *Panzer Operations*, 14. Battle Group von Seckendorff had been given the task of leading the attack of 6 PD and opening the road to Kongayly. The more powerful Battle Group Raus, operating on Seckendorff's left, was to attack at a later time. Raus, 12.

139   NARA, T-315, Roll 322, *KTB Nr. 3, 6. Schützen Brigade*, 22.6.41.

140   Chales de Beaulieu, *Vorstoss der Panzergruppe 4*, 23.

141   Col. Helmut Ritgen, "6th Panzer Division Operations," in: Glantz (ed.), *Initial Period of War on the Eastern Front*, 112–13.

142   Lt.-Gen. A. D. v. Plato and Lt.-Col. R. O. Stoves, "1st Panzer Division Operations," in: Glantz (ed.), *Initial Period of War on the Eastern Front*, 130, 136.

143   NARA, T-315, Roll 16, *Ia KTB Nr. 6, 1.Pz.Div.*, 22.6.41.

144   Lt.-Gen. A. D. v. Plato and Lt.-Col. R. O. Stoves, "1st Panzer Division Operations," in: Glantz (ed.), *Initial Period of War on the Eastern Front*, 132.

145   Ibid., 132–33.

146   NARA, T-315, Roll 16, *Ia KTB Nr. 6, 1.Pz.Div.*, 22.6.41.

147   The 269 ID was at the southern edge of the Soviet Sakalyne position by 0530; it would break through the position by 0900 hours and begin to move on the town of Gauré, due east of Tauroggen. At Gauré, 290 ID would encounter even tougher opposition, as it came up against exceptionally robust wooden bunker positions, cleverly adapted to the terrain, and against which the Germans had to bring up artillery in an effort to neutralize them. NARA, T-314, Roll 979, *Ia KTB, 41.Pz.K.*, 22.6.41; NARA, T-315, Roll 1858, *Ia KTB Nr. 5, 269.Inf.Div.*, 22.6.41.

148   NARA T-311, Roll 132, *H.Gr.Nord, Ia, Geschichte Feldzug Russland*, 22.6.41; NARA, T-313, Roll 330, *Ia KTB Nr. 5, Pz. AOK 4*, 22.6.41; NARA, T-315, Roll 323, *Ia KTB, 6.Pz.Div.*, 22.6.41.

149   The 489 Infantry Regiment (269 ID) had been assigned to 1 Panzer Division to support its attack across the frontier on June 22.

150   NARA, T-315, Roll 16, *Ia KTB Nr. 6, 1.Pz.Div.*, 22.6.41; NARA, T-314, Roll 979, *Ia KTB, 41.Pz.K.*, 22.6.41.

151   NARA, T-315, Roll 16, *Ia KTB Nr. 6, 1.Pz.Div.*, 22.6.41.

152   Lt.-Gen. A. D. v. Plato and Lt.-Col. R. O. Stoves, "1st Panzer Division Operations," in: Glantz (ed.), *Initial Period of War on the Eastern Front*, 132.

153   NARA, T-315, Roll 16, *Ia KTB Nr. 6, 1.Pz.Div.*, 22.6.41.

154   Glantz, *Barbarossa*, 43.

155   Taylor, *Barbarossa to Berlin*, 33; Erickson, *The Road to Stalingrad*, 128.

156   Glantz, "The Border Battles on the Siauliai Axis, 22–26 June 1941," in: Glantz (ed.), *Initial Period of War on the Eastern Front*, 87. Observed John Erickson: "Most serious was the breakdown in communications; thus, the Military Soviet of Northwestern Front, Kuznetsov, Dibrov and Klenov (Chief of Staff), drew up its counterattack plans on the evening of [June 22] in fearful ignorance of what had actually happened." Erickson, *The Road to Stalingrad*, 128.

157   TsAMO RF, F. 344, Op. 344, Op. 5554, D. 71, L. 59, "*Obstanovka na Fronte 11 Strelkovogo Korpusa k 9:00, 22.6.41*" (Situation Along the 11 Rifle Corps' Front by 0900, June 22, 1941).

158   TsAMO RF, F. 221, Op. 1351, D. 64, Ll. 2–3, "*Telegramma s Informatsiei v Shtab 8 Armii, 10:00, 22.6.41*" (A telegram with information for the headquarters of 8 Army, 1000, June 22, 1941).

159   TsAMO RF, F. 344, Op. 5554, D. 71, Ll. 60–61, "*Operativnaya Svodka No. 7, 18:00, 22.6.41, Shtab 8 Armii, Bubyai*" (Combat Report No. 7, 1800, June 22, 1941, Headquarters 8 Army, Bubiai).

160   The main components of 125 Rifle Division were 466, 657, and 749 Rifle Regiments, along with the 414 Artillery Regiment. The division was raised in Kirov, in the Ural Military District in October 1939, and assigned to the Baltic Military District in August 1940. Soon thereafter it was assigned to 8 Army in the Taurrogen region. Email, David M. Glantz to Dr. C. Luther, September 7, 2017.

161   TsAMO RF, F. 344, Op. 5554, D. 71, Ll. 63-63a, *"Boevoe Donesenie No. 1, Shtab 11 Strelkovogo Korpusa, Les Severnee Pakrazhunas, 22.6.41"* (Combat Report No. 1, Headquarters of 11 Rifle Corps, the woods north of Pakrazantis, June 22, 1941).

162   NARA, T-315, Roll 16, *Ia KTB Nr. 6, 1.Pz.Div.*, 22.6.41. As the war diary put it, "this division's artillery can be considered destroyed [*kann als aufgerieben gelten*]."

163   Robert A. Forczyk, *Tank Warfare on the Eastern Front 1941–42*, 39; Glantz, "The Border Battles on the Siauliai Axis, 22–26 June 1941," in: Glantz (ed.), *Initial Period of War on the Eastern Front*, 87. Over the next few days, the remnants of both 125 and 48 Rifle Divisions would be encircled and destroyed by the advancing German forces.

164   Erickson, *The Road to Stalingrad*, 129.

165   According to David M. Glantz, "We obtained the *Sborniki* [i.e., the collection of key Soviet military records used in this book and cited as SBDVOV] in the early 1990s, many years after [Erickson] made his judgments. [He] met with many of the Marshals of the Soviet Union, but they were restricted in what they could tell him." Email, David M. Glantz to Dr. C. Luther, October 3, 2017.

166   TsAMO RF, F. 221, Op. 2467ss, D. 39, Ll. 171-175, *"Donesenie Komanduyushchego Severo-Zapadnym Frontom ot 22 Iyunya 1941 g. Narodnomu Komissaru Oborony SSSR ob Obstanovke na 21 Chasa 22 Iyunya 1941. Sovershenno Sekretno"* (Report by the Commander of the Northwestern Front on June 22, 1941, to the USSR People's Commissar of Defense on the Situation as of 2100, June 22, 1941. Top Secret), in: SBDVOV, Vol. 34: 44.

167   NARA, T-313, Roll 330, *Ia KTB Nr. 5, Pz. AOK 4*, 22.6.41.

168   Ibid.

169   For a serious discussion of this issue, as well as several examples of major forest combat at the start of the Russian campaign see, Luther, *Barbarossa Unleashed*, 95–98, 392–96.

170   NARA, T-313, Roll 330, *Ia KTB Nr. 5, Pz. AOK 4*, 22.6.41; Wolfgang Paul, *Brennpunkte. Die Geschichte der 6. Panzerdivision (1. leichte) 1937–1945*, 106; *KTB OKW*, Vol. I: 491.

171   Col. Helmut Ritgen, "6th Panzer Division Operations," in: Glantz (ed.), *Initial Period of War on the Eastern Front*, 113. As Ritgen recalled after the war: "During the first day we captured only a few prisoners and almost no weapons. That night everybody felt that this campaign was quite different from previous campaigns."

172   NARA, T-315, Roll 322, *KTB Nr. 3, 6. Schützen Brigade*, 22.6.41. In his postwar memoir, Raus stated that his battle group "launched and sustained the division's main attack during the morning hours [of June 22]." This assertion, however, is not supported by the official records of 6 Panzer Division. See, Raus, *Panzer Operations*, 14.

173   NARA, T-315, Roll 323, *Ia KTB, 6.Pz.Div.*, 22.6.41.

174   Lt.-Gen. A. D. v. Plato and Lt.-Col. R. O. Stoves, "1st Panzer Division Operations," in: Glantz (ed.), *Initial Period of War on the Eastern Front*, 132; *KTB OKW*, Vol. I: 491.

175   NARA, T-315, Roll 16, *Ia KTB Nr. 6, 1.Pz.Div.*, 23.6.41.

176   NARA, T-313, Roll 330, *Ia KTB Nr. 5, Pz. AOK 4*, 23.6.41; Chales de Beaulieu, *Vorstoss der Panzergruppe 4*, 24.

177   NARA, T-313, Roll 330, *Ia KTB Nr. 5, Pz. AOK 4*, 22.6.41.

178   Ibid., 23.6.41.

179   The German word used by Hoepner here was *"wild,"* which can simply be translated as "wild," or "ferocious." In the context of his letter, however, "uncivilized" seemed more appropriate for the point he was trying to convey. In his personal diary, General Reinhardt (41 Panzer Corps) was rather more direct, dismissing the Russian enemy as a "base, insidious rabble" (*gemeines, heimtückisches Pack*). BA-MA N 245/3: *Persönliches Tagebuch Reinhardt*, 22.6.41.

180   Cited in: Bücheler, *Hoepner: Ein deutsches Soldatenschicksal*, 133.

181   NARA, T-312, Roll 781, *Ia KTB 4a, Bd. I, AOK 18*, 22.6.41; www.lexikon-der-wehrmacht.de.

182   *"Kriegsgliederung Barbarossa,"* Stand 18.6.41, Kurt Mehner (ed.); Haupt, *Heeresgruppe Nord 1941–1945*, 27; DRZW, Vol. IV, *Beiheft*, "Ausgangslage zum 22.6.1941." Relieved from his post as commander of the 38 Army Corps in April 1942 and transferred into the reserve pool for high-ranking officers (*Führerres-*

erve), a despondent General von Chappuis took his life on August 27, 1942. www.lexikon-der-wehrmacht .de.

183   *"Kriegsgliederung Barbarossa,"* Stand 18.6.41, Kurt Mehner (ed.).

184   Ibid.

185   The reader will recall that 1 Panzer Division, on 4 Panzer Group's left flank, had also started its attack along the Tilsit-Siauliai-Riga axis. See, Section 3.3 above.

186   *GSWW*, Vol. IV: 538; Luttichau, *The Road to Moscow*, IV: 18; *"Aufmarschanweisung Barbarossa,"* in: Halder, *KTB*, Vol. II: 467–68 (Appendix 2).

187   NARA, T-315, Roll 755, *Anlage zum KTB, 21.Inf.Div.*, 21.6.41.

188   NARA, T-315, Roll 755, *Anlage zum KTB, 21.Inf.Div.*, 21.6.41. Among the records of 21 ID are two documents that caught my attention. The first addresses the use of special units (*"Sonderkommandos"*) behind the front to seize documents (archives, files of groups hostile to Germany, etc.), diplomatic facilities, and consulates in an effort to locate materials of value to the military, counterintelligence (*Abwehr*), or the Foreign Office; the mission of these special units, which were provided by the SS Security Service (*Sicherheitsdienst*) or the Security Police (*Sicherheitspolizei*), also included the dispatch of agents into enemy territory and the capture of enemies of the Reich, such as "immigrants and saboteurs." (See, NARA, T-315, Roll 755, *"Sonderkommandos im Armeegebiet,"* *Anlage zum KTB, 21.Inf.Div.*, 21.6.41.) The second document concerns the activities of anti-Soviet groups in the Baltic States, noting that "sabotage acts will particularly be aimed at [Soviet] communications facilities and railroad lines [*Nachrichtenanlagen und Eisenbahnstränge*]." (NARA, T-315, Roll 755, *"Sabotagemassnahmen und Aktivistengruppen,"* *Anlage zum KTB, 21.Inf. Div.*, 21.6.41.)

189   NARA, T-312, Roll 781, *Ia KTB 4a, Bd. I, AOK 18*, 22.6.41.

190   Glantz, "The Border Battles on the Siauliai Axis 22–26 June 1941," in: Glantz (ed.), *Initial Period of War on the Eastern Front*, 82.

191   In its war diary, 1 Army Corps observed that enemy opposition was weak, with only scattered artillery fire (*nur vereinzelte Art.-Einwirkung*) on the left wing of 21 ID and right wing of 11 ID. NARA, T-314, Roll 39, *Ia KTB, 1.AK*, 22.6.41.

192   NARA, T-312, Roll 781, *Ia KTB 4a, Bd. I, AOK 18*, 22.6.41.

193   NARA, T-312, Roll 783, *Ia KTB 4a, AOK 18*, "Zusammenfassung, 22.6.1941."

194   Johann Christoph Allmayer-Beck and Franz Becker, *21. Infanterie-Division. Russlandfeldzug 1941*, 2 (hereafter cited as, Allmayer-Beck and Becker, *21. Infanterie-Division*).

195   Ibid., 2–3.

196   Ibid., 2. While strong enemy resistance was expected along the Jura, overall intelligence on enemy dispositions and fortifications in the sector of 21 ID (and 1 AK as a whole) remained wanting as of June 22, 1941, despite aerial reconnaissance and reports of agents. This situation was hardly unusual, as numerous German accounts—official records, personal memoirs, etc.—surprisingly reveal just how often German troops went into battle on June 22 with very little knowledge of what to expect on the other side of the frontier.

197   Ibid., 3.

198   NARA, T-315, Roll 572, *Ia KTB Nr. 4, 11.Inf.Div.*, 22.6.41.

199   NARA, T-312, Roll 781, *Ia KTB 4a, Bd. I, AOK 18*, 22.6.41; Haupt, *Heeresgruppe Nord 1941–1945*, 26.

200   Walter Hubatsch, *61. Infanterie-Division. Kampf und Opfer ostpreussischer Soldaten*, 55–56 (hereafter cited as, Hubatsch, *61. Infanterie-Division*).

201   NARA, T-315, Roll 1013, *Ia KTB Nr. 5, Bd. I, 61.Inf.Div.*, 22.6.41.

202   The bridge had been seized intact earlier in the morning (by 0405 hours). Ibid.

203   Hubatsch, *61. Infanterie-Division*, 56.

204   Ibid., 56. Unfortunately, this account by Hubatsch is quite slim; reading between the lines, however, one can assume that the executions were most likely carried out by German SS and/or police units, perhaps with the support of local anti-Soviet groups.

205   Carell, *Hitler Moves East*, 29.

206   As noted in the 291 war diary, when the attack began at 0305 hours, there was "zero visibility" (*keine Sicht*). The ground fog was so bad that the light artillery batteries were not able to support the start of the division's assault, while the medium artillery fired only on pre-designated targets. NARA, T-315, Roll 1906, *Ia KTB Nr. 1, 291.Inf.Div.*, 22.6.41.

207   "*Gefechtsbericht über das Gefecht bei Krottingen am 22.6.1941*," *504 Inf.Rgt.*, July 1941 (date partially obscured), in: NARA, T-315, Roll 1912, *Anlagen zum Ia KTB der 291 ID, Gefechtsberichte.*

208   NARA, T-315, Roll 1906, *Ia KTB Nr. 1, 291.Inf.Div.*, 22.6.41.

209   Carell, *Hitler Moves East*, 29.

210   NARA, T-312, Roll 783, *Ia KTB 4a, AOK 18*, "*Zusammenfassung, 22.6.1941*"; NARA, T-312, Roll 781, *Ia KTB 4a, Bd. I, AOK 18*, 22.6.41. The intensity of the fighting at Krottingen is reflected in the fact that 504 IR sustained twenty dead and twenty wounded on June 22. "*Gefechtsbericht über das Gefecht bei Krottingen am 22.6.1941*," *504 Inf.Rgt.*, July 1941 (date partially obscured), in: NARA, T-315, Roll 1912, *Anlagen zum Ia KTB der 291 ID, Gefechtsberichte.*

211   NARA, T-312, Roll 783, *Ia KTB 4a, AOK 18*, "*Zusammenfassung, 22.6.1941*"; NARA, T-312, Roll 781, *Ia KTB 4a, Bd. I, AOK 18*, 22.6.41; T-311, Roll 53, *Ia KTB H.Gr.Nord*, 22.6.41.

212   TsAMO RF, F. 344, Op. 5554, D. 17, L. 10, "*Zapiska dlya Komanduyushchego 8 Armii, Lichno*," 0930, *22.6.41* (A personal note for the commander of 8 Army, 0930, June 22, 1941).

213   NARA, T-312, Roll 783, *Ia KTB 4a, AOK 18*, "*Zusammenfassung, 22.6.1941*."

214   The chaos and confusion (*Wirrwarr*) among the Russian defenders caused by the sudden and over-powering German attack was reflected in intercepted radio messages. NARA, T-312, Roll 781, *Ia KTB 4a, Bd. I, AOK 18*, 22.6.41.

215   NARA, T-312, Roll 781, *Ia KTB 4a, Bd. I, AOK 18*, 22.6.41; T-311, Roll 53, *Ia KTB H.Gr.Nord*, 22.6.41. A cache of letters discovered by the Germans at the post office in Krottingen on June 22 revealed that the German attack had been expected for days.

216   Mehner (ed.), *Die Geheimen Tagesberichte*, Vol. 3: 151.

217   NARA, T-312, Roll 781, *Ia KTB 4a, Bd. I, AOK 18*, 22.6.41.

218   NARA, T-314, Roll 39, *Ia KTB, 1.AK*, 22.6.41.

219   Allmayer-Beck and Becker, *21. Infanterie-Division*, 3–4.

220   NARA, T-315, Roll 2, *Ia KTB, 1.Inf.Div.*, 22.6.41.

221   Allmayer-Beck and Becker, *21. Infanterie-Division*, 4; NARA, T-312, Roll 783, *Ia KTB 4a, AOK 18*, "*Zusammenfassung, 22.6.1941*"; NARA, T-312, Roll 781, *Ia KTB 4a, Bd. I, AOK 18*, 22.6.41.

222   At midday, 61 ID was reinforced with a 105mm gun battery (s.Art.Abt. 633) at Vezaiciai, to conduct counter-battery fire against Soviet artillery in the area. NARA, T-314, Roll 755, *Ia KTB Nr. 6, 26.AK*, 22.6.41.

223   Ibid.

224   NARA, T-315, Roll 1013, *Ia KTB Nr. 5, Bd. I, 61.Inf.Div.*, 22.6.41; Hubatsch, *61. Infanterie-Division*, 56. As recorded in the war diary of 26 AK: "13.30 . . . 61 ID reports that Gargzdai is free of the enemy; the town is burning." NARA, T-314, Roll 755, *Ia KTB Nr. 6, 26.AK*, 22.6.41.

225   NARA, T-315, Roll 1013, *Ia KTB Nr. 5, Bd. I, 61.Inf.Div.*, 22.6.41; Hubatsch, *61. Infanterie-Division*, 55–56.

226   NARA, T-315, Roll 1013, *Ia KTB Nr. 5, Bd. I, 61.Inf.Div.*, 22.6.41.

227   Haupt, *Heeresgruppe Nord 1941–1945*, 27; Leeb, *Tagebuchaufzeichnungen*, 275.

228   The 291 ID's report to Eighteenth Army headquarters was actually a little late, Lohmeyer's advance detachment having actually secured Skuodas at 1830 hours. T-315, Roll 1906, *Ia KTB Nr. 1, 291.Inf.Div.*, 22.6.41.

229   NARA, T-311, Roll 132, *H.Gr.Nord, Ia, Geschichte Feldzug Russland*, 22.6.41.

230   NARA, T-312, Roll 781, *Ia KTB 4a, Bd. I, AOK 18*, 22.6.41.

231   The 204 Rifle Regiment was part of 10 Rifle Division; the division also included the 62 and 98 Rifle Regiments, and 30 Artillery Regiment. Email, David M. Glantz to Dr. C. Luther, September 15, 2017.

232   The 90 Rifle Division was composed of the 19, 173, and 286 Rifle Regiments, and the 96 Artillery Regiment. Email, David M. Glantz to Dr. C. Luther, September 15, 2017.

233 TsAMO RF, F. 344, Op. 5554, D. 71, Ll. 60-61, "*Operativnaya Svodka No. 7, 18:00, 22.6.41, Shtab 8 Armii, Bubyai*" (Combat Report No. 7, 1800, June 22, 1941, Headquarters 8 Army, Bubiai).

234 As recorded in its war diary, 1 Army Corps incurred 106 casualties (*Ausfälle*) on June 22 (nine officers and ninety-seven NCOs and enlisted men). However, it is unclear if the figure signifies killed-in-action (KIA) only, or KIA and wounded. Most of the losses were from "well camouflaged snipers" (*Heckenschützen*) or resulted from carelessness on the part of the German soldiers themselves—many of whom had no previous combat experience and were undergoing their baptism of fire. NARA, T-314, Roll 39, *Ia KTB, 1.AK*, 22.6.41.

235 NARA, T-315, Roll 572, *Ia KTB Nr. 4, 11.Inf.Div.*, 22.6.41.

236 NARA, T-312, Roll 783, *Ia KTB 4a, AOK 18*, "*Zusammenfassung, 23.6.1941.*"

237 "Army Group North Situation Map: Evening, 22 June 1941," in: Glantz (ed.), *Initial Period of War on the Eastern Front*, 88.

238 In his diary on June 22, GFM v. Leeb wrote: "Underway, I meet the commander of Eighteenth Army, von Küchler, [who] regrets that the enemy appears to be falling back." Leeb, *Tagebuchaufzeichnungen*, 275.

239 NARA, T-311, Roll 53, *Ia KTB H.Gr.Nord*, 22.6.41.

240 Mawdsley, *Thunder in the East*, 82; Glantz, *Barbarossa*, 43; Erickson, *The Road to Stalingrad*, 146.

241 *Voennaya Entsiklopediya*, Vol. 4: 338.

Chapter 4: Armageddon Unleashed (II)—Army Group Center Goes to War

1 Cited in: Kempowski (ed.), *Das Echolot*, 23.

2 Ibid., 24–25.

3 TsAMO RF, F. 208, Op. 3038ss, D. 12, L. 1, "*Boevoe Donesenie Komanduyushchego Voiskami 4-i Armii ot 22 Iyunya 1941 g. o Napadenii Protivnika i o Deistviyakh Voisk Armii*" (Combat Report by the Commander of 4 Army on June 22, 1941, on the Enemy's Attack and the Activities of the Army's Forces), in: SBDVOV, Vol. 35: 143.

4 Mitcham Jr., *The Men of Barbarossa*, 37–38.

5 GFM v. Bock, *War Diary*, 14–15; www.lexikon-der-wehrmacht.de.

6 Mark M. Boatner III, *The Biographical Dictionary of World War II*, 49.

7 Samuel W. Mitcham Jr., *Hitler's Field Marshals and Their Battles*, 148.

8 GSWW, Vol. IV: 256–57, 315; Luttichau, *The Road to Moscow*, IV: 33–34; www.lexikon-der-wehrmacht.de. Victimized by an "old stomach problem," by late October 1940 Bock's health had deteriorated to the point that he had to temporarily relinquish command of Army Group B to GFM Wilhelm List. Bock's convalescence took several months, and he did not return to duty until the end of January 1941. GFM v. Bock, *War Diary*, 192.

9 RKKA (*Raboche-Krest'yanskaya Krasnaya Armiya*) stands for the "Workers' and Peasants' Red Army." This term was in use from 1918 to 1946, while the term "Soviet Army" was not adopted until 1946. Email, Dr. Richard Harrison to Dr. C. Luther, October 20, 2017.

10 *Voennaya Entsiklopediya*, Vol. 6: 218; Mawdsley, *Thunder in the East*, 61.

11 *Voennaya Entsiklopediya*, Vol. 6: 218; Magenheimer, *Moskau 1941. Entscheidungsschlacht im Osten*, 42. "Pavlov and his associates," observed Rodric Braithwaite, "were tried on 22 July 1941, in the middle of the first German air attack on Moscow. It is said that they asked to be sent to the front as ordinary soldiers, to atone with their blood for the defeat of their armies. If so, their plea was rejected." Braithwaite, *Moscow 1941*, 151.

12 Mawdsley, *Thunder in the East*, 61.

13 Rembertov was a village on the eastern outskirts of Warsaw; Bock had moved his headquarters there from Posen on June 21. GFM v. Bock, *War Diary*, 223; Thies, *Der Ostfeldzug—Ein Lageatlas*, "*Aufmarsch am 21.6.1941 abds., H.Gr.Mitte.*"

14 The army group's three security divisions (221, 286, 403) were under the Commander, Rear Army Area 102 (*Befehlshaber rückw. Heeresgebiet 102*).

15   *"Kriegsgliederung Barbarossa," Stand 18.6.41*, Kurt Mehner (ed.); BA-MA RH 19 II/120, *KTB H.Gr. Mitte*, 2.10.41; Jentz (ed.), *Panzer Truppen*, 190–93; Eddy Bauer, *Der Panzerkrieg. Die wichtigsten Panzeroperationen des zweiten Weltkrieges in Europa und Afrika. Bd. I: Vorstoss und Rückzug der deutschen Panzerverbände*, 116–17.

16   The *"Fla"* battalions (*Fla = Fliegerabwehr*, or antiaircraft defense) were outfitted with 20mm or 37mm AA guns; the battalions were motorized and normally organized into three companies. Ltr. Friedr.-Karl Scharffetter (*Fla-Kameradschaft*) to Dr. C. Luther, November 29, 2002.

17   Each of the "K5" pieces required two trains to move and operate and could launch a 561-pound projectile up to 37.5 miles. Kirchubel, *Operation Barbarossa (1), Army Group South*, 23.

18   *"Kriegsgliederung Barbarossa," Stand 18.6.41*, Kurt Mehner (ed.); *"Berechnung der Stärke der Heeres-Artillerie einschl. Nebeltruppen,"* 11.6.41, in: NARA, T-311, Roll 226, *Heeresgruppe Mitte / Stoart, KTB mit Anlagen*; *GSWW*, Vol. IV: 316.

19   The 750 batteries broke down as 421 light and 329 medium and heavy batteries. BA-MA RH 19 II/120, *KTB H.Gr.Mitte*, 2.10.41.

20   *"Kriegsgliederung Barbarossa," Stand 18.6.41*, Kurt Mehner (ed.).

21   A total of 244 reconnaissance and courier aircraft were assigned to Army Group Center, of which 200 were operational. One long-range reconnaissance (*Fernaufklärer*) squadron was provided to each army and panzer group. *GSWW*, Vol. IV: 364–66; also, *"Kriegsgliederung Barbarossa," Stand 18.6.41*, Kurt Mehner (ed.).

22   *GSWW*, Vol. IV: 364–66.

23   Only after introducing the 75mm antitank gun, and a more powerful 75mm tank cannon, both in 1942, were the Germans able to confront the T-34 on more equal terms. In the interim, the German *Landser* experienced many harrowing encounters with the tank that soon became their nemesis. Luther, *Barbarossa Unleashed*, 154.

24   Thies, *Der Ostfeldzug—Ein Lageatlas, "Aufmarsch am 21.6.1941 abds., H.Gr.Mitte."*

25   Ibid.

26   Minsk was roughly 250 kilometers to the east (as the crow flies) of 3 Panzer Group in the Suwalki region; from the jump-off point of 2 Panzer Group, on the right wing of Army Group Center, the city was more than 300 kilometers distant.

27   Albert Seaton, *The Battle for Moscow*, 38; *GSWW*, Vol. IV: 290; Guderian, *Panzer Leader*, 146–47.

28   Trevor-Roper (ed.), *Hitler's War Directives*, 50; *"Aufmarschanweisung Barbarossa,"* in: Halder, *KTB*, Vol. II: 466 (Appendix 2).

29   Soviet 13 Army began the war as a field headquarters only, with no forces assigned to it. Glantz, *Barbarossa*, 38, 247.

30   Ibid., 216, f.n. 7. Of the Western Front's tanks, most were obsolete models, but several hundred were new KVs and T-34s.

31   Forczyk, *Tank Warfare on the Eastern Front 1941-42*, 45.

32   Mawdsley, *Thunder in the East*, 62.

33   The town of Belostok was "strategically important to the Red Army as a rail hub, and Red Army tank and aviation units in the salient were poised to support a possible Soviet advance into southern Poland." Ibid., 62.

34   K.-J. Thies, *Der Ostfeldzug—Ein Lageatlas, "Aufmarsch am 21.6.1941 abds., Heeresgruppe Mitte."* For an in-depth look at the Western Front at the start of the Russian campaign—its strength, weaknesses, deployments, etc.—see, D. M. Glantz, "The Border Battles on the Bialystok-Minsk Axis: 22–28 June 1941," in: Glantz (ed.), *Initial Period of War on the Eastern Front*, 184–95.

35   Aliev, *The Siege of Brest*, 1941, 19–22.

36   Ibid., 22.

37   Ibid., 22–23.

38   Ibid., 23.

39   Erickson, *The Road to Stalingrad*, 109; Bellamy, *Absolute War*, 183. A combat report filed at 0600 hours by the Soviet Western Special Military District (about to become Western Front) stated that "we do not have wire communications with the armies." The report also noted German aerial bombing of cities, towns,

airfields, and the strafing of trains; in addition, there was "rifle, machine gun and artillery fire along the entire frontier." TsAMO RF, F. 208, Op. 2454ss, D. 26, Ll. 85-86, "*Boevoe Donesenie Shtaba Zapadnogo Osobogo Voennogo Okruga No. 002/op k 6 Chasam 22 Iyunya 1941g. o Boevykh Deistviyakh Protivnika Protiv Voisk Okruga. Osobo Sekretno*" (Combat Report No. 002/op by the Headquarters of the Western Special Military District as of 0600 on June 22, 1941, on the Enemy's Combat Activities Against the District's Troops. Very Secret), in: SBDVOV, Vol. 35: 15.

40 Kershaw, *War Without Garlands*, 31; Glantz, *Barbarossa*, 35.

41 BA-MA RH 21-2/927, *KTB Nr. 1, Pz.Gr. 2*, 22.6.41; Werner Haupt, *Army Group Center: The Wehrmacht in Russia 1941–1945*, 26–27; Carell, *Hitler Moves East*, 17; Luttichau, *The Road to Moscow*, VI: 8.

42 Guderian, *Erinnerungen eines Soldaten*, 139.

43 BA-MA RH 21-2/927, *KTB Nr. 1, Pz.Gr. 2*, 22.6.41; Luttichau, *The Road to Moscow*, VI: 8.

44 Carell, *Hitler Moves East*, 16–17; Carell, *Unternehmen Barbarossa*, 19.

45 BA-MA MSg 1/1147: *Tagebuch* Lemelsen, 21.6.41.

46 Blumentritt, "Moscow," 46–47.

47 The backbone of the German field artillery in WWII were the 105mm light field howitzers (le.F.H.18) (maximum range 10,700 meters) and the 150mm medium field howitzers (s.F.H.18) (maximum range 13,300 meters). The artillery regiment of a typical German infantry division was equipped with thirty-six of the 105mm guns (three battalions, each of three batteries of four guns each) and twelve of the 150mm guns (one battalion with three batteries, each of four guns). The 105mm (s. 10cm K.18) and 150mm cannons (15 cm. K.18) had maximum ranges of 19,000 and 24,700 meters, respectively. The fourth artillery battalion in some German infantry divisions was outfitted with the 105mm cannons (in place of the 150mm medium field howitzers). The 210mm heavy howitzer (21cm Mörser 18) was the German army's standard heavy howitzer; it was a very accurate and devastating weapon with a range of 16,700 meters. These heavy howitzers were normally GHQ artillery and assigned to lower echelons as required. *Handbook on German Military Forces*, 332–37; Ian Hogg, *Twentieth-Century Artillery*, 41, 53, 82; Joachim Engelmann, *German Light Field Artillery 1939–1945*, 13; Joachim Engelmann, *German Heavy Field Artillery 1934–1945*, 11–13, 46.

48 BA-MA RH 19 II/120, *KTB H.Gr.Mitte*, 2.10.41.

49 Heinrich Haape, *Moscow Tram Stop: A Doctor's Experiences with the German Spearhead in Russia*, 15 (hereafter cited as, Haape, *Moscow Tram Stop*).

50 Blumentritt, "Moscow," 47.

51 Frisch, *Condemned to Live*, 69.

52 Paul B. (46 281), Collection BfZ.

53 Helmut Pabst, *The Outermost Frontier: A German Soldier in the Russian Campaign*, 9.

54 Cited in: Ingrid Hammer and Susanne zur Nieden (eds.), *Sehr selten habe ich geweint*, 226–27.

55 Siegfried Knappe, *Soldat: Reflections of a German Soldier, 1936–1949*, 203–5.

56 Rolf Hinze, *19. Infanterie- und Panzer-Division. Divisionsgeschichte aus der Sicht eines Artilleristen*, 125–26 (hereafter cited as, Hinze, *19. Panzer-Division*).

57 Dinglreiter, *Die Vierziger: Chronik des Regiments*, 39.

58 Luttichau, *The Road to Moscow*, VI: 10.

59 Lt. Georg Kreuter, *Persönliches Tagebuch*, 22.6.41. The *Stuka* noted by Kreuter was one of only two Ju-87s lost on this first day of the war. See, Chapter 6, Section 6.3.

60 Detailed sketches of the stages of the firing plan can be found in: NARA, T-311, Roll 226, *Heeresgruppe Mitte / Stoart, KTB mit Anlagen*.

61 Dr. Rudolf Gschöpf, *Mein Weg mit der 45. Inf.-Div.*, 204.

62 Dr. Erich Bunke, *Der Osten blieb unser Schicksal, 1939–1944. Panzerjäger im 2. Weltkrieg*, 218.

63 Herbert R. (N11.15), Collection BfZ.

64 Albert Schick, *Die 10. Panzer-Division 1939–1943*, 270–71.

65 Ibid., 271.

66 Mitcham Jr., *The Men of Barbarossa*, 99.

67   Russell A. Hart, *Guderian: Panzer Pioneer or Myth Maker?*, 3 (hereafter cited as, Hart, *Guderian*). According to Hart, whose brief biography of Guderian is one of the best, the panzer general was a "good tactician and technician," who "suffered from strategic myopia." He was also "impetuous, liable to react and act instinctively, sometimes without thinking." Moreover, he "led too much from the front, which hampered the smooth functioning of his headquarters." While a "great organizer, an intellect, a theorist, and a technician," in the final analysis, "his deficiencies outweighed his strengths and he contributed directly to Germany's defeat." Hart, 115–17.

68   I. C. B. Dear (ed.), *The Oxford Guide to World War II*, 407. For Guderian's role as inspector general of panzer troops see, Hart, *Guderian*, 86–97.

69   The 267 ID was only assigned to Geyr's panzer corps for the first phase of the operation.

70   The 167 ID was only assigned to Lemelsen's panzer corps for the first phase of the operation. Stahel, *Operation Barbarossa and Germany's Defeat in the East*, 155, f.n. 9.

71   The command tanks (*Panzer Befehlswagen*) were outfitted with communications equipment and did not carry any main armament.

72   "*Kriegsgliederung Barbarossa,*" *Stand 18.6.41*, Kurt Mehner (ed.); "*Die materielle Ausstattung des deutschen Ostheeres am 22. Juni 1941,*" in: *DRZW*, Vol. IV: 186–87; Jentz, *Panzer Truppen*, 190–93.

73   The flamethrower tank battalion included: 25 Pz IIs, 42 *Flammenwerfer* tanks, and 5 Pz IIIs; it was assigned to 18 Panzer Division. Jentz, *Panzer Truppen*, 193.

74   Attached to each panzer division was at least one short-range reconnaissance squadron, most likely outfitted with the Henschel Hs-126 two-seat reconnaissance and observation aircraft. "*Kriegsgliederung Barbarossa,*" *Stand 18.6.41*, Kurt Mehner (ed.).

75   "*Kriegsgliederung Barbarossa,*" *Stand 18.6.41*, Kurt Mehner (ed.); www.lexikon-der-wehrmacht.de.

76   Karl J. Walde, *Guderian*, 119.

77   Karl J. Walde, *Guderian*, 119–20; Thies, *Der Ostfeldzug—Ein Lageatlas*, "*Aufmarsch am 21.6.1941 abds., Heeresgruppe Mitte.*"

78   The two panzer divisions of 24 Panzer Corps are not shown on this map; they would be just below Brest to the southwest.

79   Posited Colonel Albert Seaton, "the population [of Belorussia] was mainly rural and, even by the Russian standards of the time, was very poor and almost unbelievably primitive." Seaton, *The Battle for Moscow*, 41.

80   For a detailed discussion of the challenges posed by terrain and weather in Belorussia see, Luther, *Barbarossa Unleashed*, 345–50; Seaton, *The Battle for Moscow*, 41–42; Seaton, *The Russo-German War 1941–1945*, 55; Luttichau, *The Road to Moscow*, II: 5–6.

81   Forczyk, *Tank Warfare on the Eastern Front 1941–42*, 47. The 2 Air Corps was a component of Kesselring's 2 Air Fleet.

82   "*Aufmarschanweisung Barbarossa,*" in: Halder, *KTB*, Vol. II: 466 (Appendix 2).

83   A *Rollbahn*, or *Panzerstrasse*, was a road designated as a main axis of advance for panzer and motorized formations. Normally, marching infantry divisions were barred from using these "good" roads, which were vital to the forward progress of the mobile units. Johannes Steinhoff, et al. (eds.), *Voices from the Third Reich: An Oral History*, 535; FMS T-34, General Karl Allmendinger, et al., "Terrain Factors in the Russian Campaign," 52.

84   Cited in: Dinglreiter, *Die Vierziger: Chronik des Regiments*, 38.

85   Guderian, *Panzer Leader*, 153.

86   GFM v. Bock, *War Diary*, 224.

87   Kirchubel, *Operation Barbarossa 1941 (3), Army Group Center*, 32. That the German invaders were often greeted in the border regions as liberators from Soviet oppression is confirmed by numerous contemporary accounts.

88   In his memoir, Guderian stated that the barrage on the front of his panzer group lasted for an hour; however, in some sectors the barrage was of shorter duration. For example, the opening barrage along the front of 4 PD lasted for just thirty minutes. Guderian, *Panzer Leader*, 153; Joachim Neumann, *Die 4.*

Panzer-Division 1938–1943. Bericht und Betrachtung zu zwei Blitzfeldzügen und zwei Jahren Krieg in Russland, 195 (hereafter cited as, Neumann, *Die 4. Panzer-Division*).

89 Aliev, *The Siege of Brest*, 1941, xv.

90 Guderian, *Panzer Leader*, 146–47.

91 Hart, *Guderian*, 71. According to Russell A. Hart, "Guderian's squabble with von Kluge was both personal and professional. Von Kluge saw Guderian as a dangerous, impetuous innovator. Guderian saw von Kluge as intolerant, deceitful, and doctrinally opposed to maneuver warfare. He thus disliked von Kluge from the beginning and became even more distrustful, his suspicion ultimately burgeoning into hatred. Von Kluge tried repeatedly to patch up their relationship, but was rebuffed each time by Guderian. Their squabble was a fundamental clash between two different types of commanders—a calculating risk-taker vs. a prudent, yet equally distinguished, commander." Hart, 71.

92 Jentz (ed.), *Panzer Truppen*, 190; Guderian, *Panzer Leader*, 148; Colonel Horst Zobel (ret.), "3rd Panzer Division Operations," in: Glantz (ed.), *Initial Period of War on the Eastern Front*, 239 (hereafter cited as, Zobel, "3rd Panzer Division Operations").

93 Walter Görlitz, *Strategie der Defensive. Model*, 91.

94 Neumann, *Die 4. Panzer-Division*, 195.

95 Ibid., 195.

96 Hans Schäufler (ed.), *Knight's Cross Panzers: The German 35th Panzer Regiment in WWII*, 72.

97 Neumann, *Die 4. Panzer-Division*, 195–97.

98 Ibid., 197.

99 According to the war diary of 2 Panzer Group, an advance detachment of 4 Panzer Division had gained the crossroads 12 kilometers northeast of Maloryta by 2200 hours. BA-MA RH 21-2/927, *KTB Nr. 1, Pz.Gr. 2*, 22.6.41.

100 Neumann, *Die 4. Panzer-Division*, 197.

101 See, for example, the excellent, albeit rather unconventional, biography of Model by Marcel Stein. According to Stein, Model ranked alongside Manstein and Rommel as one of the three "most eminent army commanders of the *Wehrmacht* in World War II." Stein, *GFM Model*, 1.

102 *Geschichte der 3. Panzer-Division Berlin Brandenburg 1935–1945*, 108 (hereafter cited as, *Geschichte der 3. Panzer-Division*); Axel Urbanke and Dr. Hermann Türk, *Als Sanitätsoffizier im Russlandfeldzug: Mit der 3. Panzer-Division bis vor Moskaus Tore*, 35.

103 *Kampfgruppe* Kleemann included: 3 Rifle Regiment, a reinforced tank company of 6 Panzer Regiment, two antitank companies, strong combat engineer elements, construction troops, and corps bridging assets. Lt. Fritz Lucke, *Panzer Wedge. Volume One: The German 3rd Panzer Division and the Summer of Victory in the East*, 10.

104 *Kampfgruppe* Audörsch included: 394 Rifle Regiment, SS Engineer Battalion "*Das Reich*" (only for the river crossing), an antitank company, combat engineers, and construction troops. Ibid., 10.

105 BA-MA RH 27-3/14, *KTB Nr. 3, 3.Pz.Div.*, 22.6.41; Zobel, "3rd Panzer Division Operations," 241; Steven H. Newton, *Hitler's Commander: Field Marshal Walther Model—Hitler's Favorite General*, 119–20 (hereafter cited as, Newton, *Model*); *Geschichte der 3. Panzer-Division*, 108.

106 Newton, *Model*, 120.

107 The village of Stradecz was in German hands by 0715 hours. Urbanke and Türk, *Als Sanitätsoffizier im Russlandfeldzug*, 35.

108 Hans-Joachim Röll, *Oberleutnant Albert Blaich. Als Panzerkommandant in Ost und West*, 42; *Geschichte der 3. Panzer-Division*, 108.

109 *Geschichte der 3. Panzer-Division*, 109.

110 BA-MA RH 27-3/14, *KTB Nr. 3, 3.Pz.Div.*, 22.6.41; Zobel, "3rd Panzer Division Operations," 241; Stahel, *Operation Barbarossa and Germany's Defeat in the East*, 156.

111 Newton, *Model*, 122.

112 A combat report of Soviet 4 Army at 1055 hours stated: "The 14 Mechanized Corps, consisting of 22 and 30 Tank Divisions, is to concentrate in the Vidoml'–Zhabinka area and attack the enemy along the Brest axis together with the 28 Rifle Corps and the 10 Mixed Air Division and destroy him and restore the

situation." TsAMO RF, F. 208, Op. 3038ss, D. 12, Ll. 3-4, "*Boevoe Donesenie No.05, Shtarm 4, Bukhoviche, 22.6.41, 10.55, Karta 100,000*" (Combat Report No. 5, 4 Army Headquarters, Bukhoviche, June 22, 1941, 1055, 100,000 Map), in: SBDVOV, Vol. 35: 143–44.

113   Newton, *Model*, 121–22; Glantz, *Red Army Ground Forces in June 1941*, 21. The 14 Mechanized Corps should have been outfitted with 1,031 tanks.

114   Forczyk, *Tank Warfare on the Eastern Front 1941-42*, 47.

115   Glantz, "The Border Battles on the Bialystok-Minsk Axis: 22–28 June 1941," in: Glantz (ed.), *Initial Period of War on the Eastern Front*, 196.

116   Yevgenii Drig, *Mekhanizirovannye Korpusa RKKA v Boyu: Istoriya Avtobronetankovykh Voisk Krasnoi Armii v 1940–1941 Godakh* (The RKKA's Mechanized Corps in Battle: The History of the Red Army's Armored Tank Troops in 1940–1941), 377–78.

117   *Geschichte der 3. Panzer-Division*, 109–10.

118   In his memoir, L. M. Sandalov, then chief of staff of Soviet 4 Army, wrote: "At night [22 June] I had a telephone conversation with Korobkov [C-in-C, 4 Army]. He reported that only about 100 tanks remained in the 22 Tank Division, with a very small supply of shells and fuel." The division had begun the day with 187 tanks. L. M. Sandalov, *Perezhitoe* (That Which Has Been Lived Through), 117; also, Glantz, "The Border Battles on the Bialystok-Minsk Axis: 22–28 June 1941," in: Glantz (ed.), *Initial Period of War on the Eastern Front*, 191.

119   Glantz, "The Border Battles on the Bialystok-Minsk Axis: 22–28 June 1941," in: Glantz (ed.), *Initial Period of War on the Eastern Front*, 189–90, 196; Newton, *Model*, 123; Clark, *Barbarossa*, 51; Zobel, "3rd Panzer Division Operations," 242.

120   Zobel, "3rd Panzer Division Operations," 241; Stahel, *Operation Barbarossa and Germany's Defeat in the East*, 156; *Geschichte der 3. Panzer-Division*, 110.

121   BA-MA RH 27-3/14, *KTB Nr. 3, 3.Pz.Div.*, 22.6.41. As noted in the journal of 2 Panzer Group, by late evening, June 22, 1941, 3 PD's motorcycle battalion had reached the town of Bulkovo (on the Muchaviec), 15 kilometers east of Brest-Litovsk on Panzer Route 1. The division's panzer brigade was several kilometers east of Brest and approaching the *Panzerstrasse*. BA-MA RH 21-2/927, *KTB Nr. 1, Pz.Gr. 2*, 22.6.41.

122   In the opinion of historian Samuel W. Mitcham Jr., Nehring "was the best panzer commander of World War II . . . Nehring's theories included the use of dive bombers as flying artillery for the panzer units, because they could launch pinpoint attacks, as opposed to standard bombers, which could be used effectively only against area targets . . . Walther Nehring, together with [General Oswald] Lutz and Guderian, was responsible for inventing blitzkrieg warfare." For a detailed biography of Nehring see, Mitcham Jr., *The Men of Barbarossa*, 105–9.

123   Jentz (ed.), *Panzer Truppen*, 192.

124   Luttichau, *The Road to Moscow*, VI: 9.

125   FMS D-247, Genlt. Kurt Cuno, "German Preparations for the Attack against Russia. (The German Build-up East of Warsaw)," 3–4. Cuno's observations on the terrain in his division's sector were no doubt germane to 18 PD as well.

126   BA-MA RH 27-18/20, *Ia KTB, 18.Pz.Div.*, 22.6.41; Luttichau, *The Road to Moscow*, VI: 10; Guderian, *Panzer Leader*, 153; Carell, *Hitler Moves East*, 23.

127   Hager, *The War Diaries of a Panzer Soldier*, 31.

128   BA-MA RH 27-18/20, *Ia KTB, 18.Pz.Div.*, 22.6.41.

129   *Leutnant* Heinz Döll, cited in: Kempowski (ed.), *Das Echolot*, 23.

130   Carell, *Hitler Moves East*, 25.

131   Günter A. Schulze, "*General der Panzertruppe a.D. Walther K. Nehring. Der persönliche Ordonnanzoffizier berichtet von der Vormarschzeit in Russland 1941–1942.*"

132   Guderian, *Panzer Leader*, 153; Luttichau, *The Road to Moscow*, VI: 10; Wolfgang Paul, *Panzer-General Walther K. Nehring. Eine Biographie*, 118.

133   BA-MA RH 21-2/927, *KTB Nr. 1, Pz.Gr. 2*, 22.6.41; BA-MA RH 27-18/20, *Ia KTB, 18.Pz.Div.*, 22.6.41.

134   Luttichau, *The Road to Moscow*, VI:10.

135   BA-MA MSg 1/1147: *Tagebuch* Lemelsen, 25.6.41.

136   L. M. Sandalov, *Perezhitoe* (That Which Has Been Lived Through), 95.

137   Ibid., 108–9.

138   In the war diary of 18 Panzer Division Vidoml' is referred to as "Widomla" and Pilishchi as "Peliczcze." BA-MA RH 27-18/20, *Ia KTB, 18.Pz.Div.*, 22.6.41.

139   L. M. Sandalov, *Perezhitoe* (That Which Has Been Lived Through), 108.

140   Ibid., 108,

141   In its "Operational Report No. 1," Western Front headquarters noted that 14 Mechanized Corps was fighting in the "Zhabinka area" (1400 hours), while its 205 Motorized Division was in the Zaprudy-Bereza sector "preparing a defensive line along the Muchaviec River." The report also indicated that the headquarters of 4 Army at Kobrin, which had been destroyed early that morning by air attack, had been relocated to Zaprudy. TsAMO RF, F. 208, Op. 10169ss, D. 7, Ll. 1-4, "*Operativnaya Svodka Shtaba Zapadnogo Fronta No. 1 k 21 Chasam 22 Iyunya 1941 g. o Khode Boevykh Deistvii Voisk Fronta za 22 Iyunya 1941 g. Seriya 'G'*" (Operational Report No. 1 from the Western Front Headquarters at 2100 on June 22, 1941, on the Course of the Activities of the Front's Troops on June 22, 1941. Series "G"), in: SBDVOV, Vol. 35: 21–22.

142   BA-MA RH 27-18/20, *Ia KTB, 18.Pz.Div.*, 22.6.41; BA-MA RH 21-2/927, *KTB Nr. 1, Pz. Gr. 2*, 22.6.41. In the war diary of 18 PD, the figure for the division's tank losses is obscured; its losses, however, were negligible.

143   Drig, *Mekhanizirovannye Korpusa RKKA v Boyu: Istoriya Avtobronetankovykh Voisk Krasnoi Armii v 1940–1941 Godakh* (The RKKA's Mechanized Corps in Battle: The History of the Red Army's Armored Tank Troops in 1940–1941), 381.

144   While the attacks of 30 TD "halted the advance of [18 PD] for a time," by the end of the day the Soviet tank division had lost about 25 percent of its men (including three battalion and five company commanders) and 30 percent of its tanks. Ibid., 380–82.

145   Forczyk, *Tank Warfare on the Eastern Front 1941–42*, 48. According to Forczyk: "Oborin was an artilleryman with no experience in armor and he opted for the safe, textbook approach taught at the Frunze Military Academy, but he also gave Guderian a quiet night to bring the bulk of his armor across the Bug." 14 Mechanized Corps was to resume its attack at 0400, following a short artillery preparation; however, the attack did not get started until several hours later and was unsuccessful. For the 14 Mechanized Corps' plan of attack see, TsAMO RF, F. 226, Op. 2156ss, D. 67, Ll. 2-3, "*Boevoi Prikas No. 2. Shtarm 4, Zaprudy, 22.6.41, 1730*" (Combat Order No. 2 from Headquarters, 4 Army, Zaprudy, June 22, 1941, 1730), in: SBDVOV, Vol. 35: 144–45.

146   Kirchubel, *Hitler's Panzer Armies*, 63. According to Robert A. Forczyk, "the tank battles around Zhabinka, Kobrin and Pruzhany had failed to seriously delay Guderian's panzers and the defeat of the 14 Mechanized Corps sealed the fate of three Soviet armies in the Belostok salient." Forczyk, *Tank Warfare on the Eastern Front 1941–42*, 48.

147   BA-MA RH 27-18/20, *Ia KTB, 18.Pz.Div.*, 23.6.41.

148   BA-MA RH 21-2/927, *KTB Nr. 1, Pz. Gr. 2*, 22.6.41; Dinglreiter, *Die Vierziger: Chronik des Regiments*, 40; Thies, *Der Ostfeldzug—Ein Lageatlas*, "*Lage am 22.6.1941 abds., Heeresgruppe Mitte mit Feindlage.*"

149   BA-MA RH 21-2/927, *KTB Nr. 1, Pz. Gr. 2*, 22.6.41.

150   Albert Axell, *Russia's Heroes 1941–45*, 24.

151   Erickson, *The Road to Stalingrad*, 120.

152   Axell, *Russia's Heroes 1941–45*, 23–24; Kershaw, *War Without Garlands*, 29–30; Gschöpf, *Mein Weg mit der 45. Inf.-Div.*, 206–7. For a more detailed description of the fortress and its appointments see, Aliev, *The Siege of Brest 1941*, 3–5.

153   Aliev, *The Siege of Brest 1941*, ix, 24–33; Bellamy, *Absolute War*, 185.

154   Guderian, *Panzer Leader*, 147.

155   Gschöpf, *Mein Weg mit der 45. Inf.-Div.*, 202–3; Aliev, *The Siege of Brest 1941*, 7.

156   Aliev, *The Siege of Brest 1941*, 51.

157   Ibid., 13. The 600mm siege mortars belonged to 2 Battery of Heavy Artillery Battalion 833 (2./s. Art.Abt. 833). "*Kriegsgliederung Barbarossa,*" *Stand 18.6.41*, Kurt Mehner (ed.)

158   In his history of 45 ID, former division member Rudolf Gschöpf refers to the *Nebelwerfer* regiment "*mit seinem schweren Wurfgerät,*" which rather awkwardly translates as "with its heavy throwing apparatus." This means that the regiment was most likely launching 280mm and 320mm projectiles, not the 150mm rockets found in most *Nebelwerfer* batteries. Gschöpf, *Mein Weg mit der 45. Inf.-Div.*, 204–5. For a primer on the different *Nebelwerfer* weapons see, Joachim Emde (ed.), *Die Nebelwerfer: Entwicklung und Einsatz der Werfertruppe im Zweiten Weltkrieg* (Dorheim, 1979).

159   Gschöpf, *Mein Weg mit der 45. Inf.-Div.*, 204-05; Aliev, *The Siege of Brest 1941*, 7–8, 42–43. The German fire plan, which called for a "creeping concentration of artillery fire" that advanced at five-minute intervals, was likely determined by the "*Karl*" siege mortars' rate of fire. Despite the powerful artillery assembled for the opening barrage, the commander of 45 ID found it inadequate for the task at hand. According to an after-action report filed by the division: "The plan of attack for the artillery was based less on its actual physical impact [*tatsächliche Wirkung*] than on its surprise effect on the enemy. This was because the available artillery, despite repeated requests of the division, was insufficient." BA-MA RH 20-4/192, "*Gefechtsbericht über die Wegnahme von Brest Litowsk.*"

160   Cited in: Aliev, *The Siege of Brest 1941*, 64; and, Kershaw, *War Without Garlands*, 47.

161   Cited in: Aliev, *The Siege of Brest 1941*, 64–65.

162   Ibid., 66–67, 75.

163   Cited in: Paul Kohl, "*Ich wundere mich, dass ich noch lebe.*" *Sowjetische Augenzeugen berichten*, 26.

164   The first boats of 45 ID, carrying assault troops of 135 Infantry Regiment, reached the opposite bank of the Bug at 0327 hours. Aliev, *The Siege of Brest 1941*, 74, 78.

165   Aliev, *The Siege of Brest 1941*, 108; Gschöpf, *Mein Weg mit der 45. Inf.-Div.*, 206; Kershaw, *War Without Garlands*, 48; BA-MA RH 20-4/192, "*Gefechtsbericht über die Wegnahme von Brest Litowsk*"; BA-MA RH 26-45/20, *KTB 45.Inf.Div.*, 22.6.41.

166   Gschöpf, *Mein Weg mit der 45. Inf.-Div.*, 206; BA-MA RH 20-4/192, "*Gefechtsbericht über die Wegnahme von Brest Litowsk*"; BA-MA RH 26-45/20, *KTB 45.Inf.Div.*, 22.6.41.

167   TsAMO RF, F. 208, Op. 3038ss, D. 12, Ll. 3-4, "*Boevoe Donesenie No.05, Shtarm 4, Bukhoviche, 22.6.41, 10.55, Karta 100,000*" (Combat Report No. 5, 4 Army Headquarters, Bukhoviche, June 22, 1941, 1055, 100,000 Map), in: SBDVOV, Vol. 35: 143–44.

168   BA-MA RH 26-45/20, *KTB 45.Inf.Div.*, 22.6.41; Gschöpf, *Mein Weg mit der 45. Inf.-Div.*, 207.

169   Aliev, *The Siege of Brest 1941*, xvi.

170   BA-MA RH 20-4/192, "*Gefechtsbericht über die Wegnahme von Brest Litowsk*"; Luttichau, *The Road to Moscow*, VI: 11; Gschöpf, *Mein Weg mit der 45. Inf.-Div.*, 208.

171   BA-MA RH 26-45/20, *KTB 45.Inf.Div.*, 22.6.41.

172   BA-MA RH 20-4/192, "*Gefechtsbericht über die Wegnahme von Brest Litowsk*"; BA-MA RH 26-45/20, *KTB 45.Inf.Div.*, 22.6.41; Kershaw, *War Without Garlands*, 50.

173   Aliev, *The Siege of Brest 1941*, 129.

174   "*Die ersten acht Tage,*" in: *Kampf gegen die Sowjets*, OKW (ed.), 37–38.

175   Not until noon, two days later, did an assault group from 133 IR break through to the men trapped inside the church and rescue them. Gschöpf, *Mein Weg mit der 45. Inf.-Div.*, 210; BA-MA RH 20-4/192, "*Gefechtsbericht über die Wegnahme von Brest Litowsk.*"

176   Gschöpf, *Mein Weg mit der 45. Inf.-Div.*, 208.

177   George F. Nafziger, *The German Order of Battle: Infantry in World War II*, 92.

178   *DRZW*, Vol. IV, *Beiheft*, "*Ausgangslage zum 22.6.1941*"; Mitcham Jr., *The Men of Barbarossa*, 243; also, www.lexikon-der-wehrmacht.de.

179   As Kluge's aide-de-camp, *Leutnant* Boeselager was constantly with the field marshal. They ate their meals together, and Boeselager and his office mates possessed a loudspeaker that enabled them to listen in on Kluge's telephone calls, including many with Hitler. Ltr. (and papers) from Philipp *Freiherr* von Boeselager to Dr. Craig Luther, March 16, 2007.

180   Ltr. (and papers) from Philipp *Freiherr* von Boeselager to Dr. Craig Luther, March 16, 2007.

181   Ltr. (and papers) from Philipp *Freiherr* von Boeselager to Dr. Craig Luther, March 16, 2007; Philipp *Freiherr* von Boeselager, *Valkyrie: The Story of the Plot to Kill Hitler by Its Last Member*, 102–3; Mitcham Jr., *The Men of Barbarossa*, 244.

182   Opinions on Kluge varied. For example, General Halder, chief of the Army General Staff, did not rate Kluge's operational talents highly. According to Blumentritt, Kluge was "an impulsive, energetic leader of a traditional type. His talents were those of a tactician rather than a strategist." However, Kluge's former chief of staff also stated: "In a joking sort of a way he frequently compared himself with Napoleon's Marshal Ney. Like Ney, he was quite fearless, indeed oblivious to danger, and he never hesitated to fly or drive through the enemy's fire . . . He was frequently wounded and was involved in numerous car and plane crashes." Blumentritt, "Moscow," 43; Seaton, *The Battle for Moscow*, 268.

183   "Kriegsgliederung Barbarossa," *Stand 18.6.41*, Kurt Mehner (ed.); "*Die materielle Ausstattung des deutschen Ostheeres am 22. Juni 1941*," in: *DRZW*, Vol. IV: 186–87; Thies, *Der Ostfeldzug—Ein Lageatlas*, "*Aufmarsch am 21.6.1941 abds., Heeresgruppe Mitte*."

184   "*Kriegsgliederung Barbarossa*," *Stand 18.6.41*, Kurt Mehner (ed.).

185   Ibid.

186   Thies, *Der Ostfeldzug—Ein Lageatlas*, "*Aufmarsch am 21.6.1941 abds., Heeresgruppe Mitte*."

187   As discussed above, for the attack on June 22, General Schroth's 12 Army Corps, deployed on both sides of Brest-Litovsk, was assigned to Guderian's 2 Panzer Group; following the initial attack, it was to revert back to control of Fourth Army.

188   "*Aufmarschanweisung Barbarossa*," in: Halder, *KTB*, Vol. II: 467 (Appendix 2).

189   BA-MA RH 20-4/1199, *KTB AOK 4*, 22.6.41.

190   The 17 Panzer Division of Lemelsen's 47 Panzer Corps was 131 ID's neighbor on the right.

191   Max Kuhnert, *Will We See Tomorrow? A German Cavalryman at War, 1939–1942*, 71–72. Kuhnert served in the division's 432 Infantry Regiment.

192   *O'Gefr.* H.S. (04 497 A), Collection BfZ.

193   Kuhnert, *Will We See Tomorrow? A German Cavalryman at War, 1939–1942*, 75.

194   Hermann Geyer, *Das IX. Armeekorps im Ostfeldzug 1941*, 45.

195   Ibid., 34.

196   BA-MA RH 26-292/7, *KTB 292.Inf.Div.*, 22.6.41.

197   By comparison, the Bug crossings of Geyer's 263 and 292 ID were supported by nine and twenty-seven batteries, respectively. Geyer, *Das IX. Armeekorps im Ostfeldzug 1941*, 36.

198   Wilhelm Meyer-Detring, *Die 137. Infanterie-Division im Mittelabschnitt der Ostfront*, 16–17 (hereafter cited as, Meyer-Detring, *Die 137. Infanterie-Division*); Geyer, *Das IX. Armeekorps im Ostfeldzug 1941*, 35–36.

199   Cited in: Michael Jones, *The Retreat: Hitler's First Defeat*, 1.

200   Meyer-Detring, *Die 137. Infanterie-Division*, 19; BA-MA RH 26-137/4, *KTB 137.Inf.Div.*, 22.6.41.

201   Meyer-Detring, *Die 137. Infanterie-Division*, 20; BA-MA RH 26-137/4, *KTB 137.Inf.Div.*, 22.6.41.

202   Meyer-Detring, *Die 137. Infanterie-Division*, 20.

203   Thies, *Der Ostfeldzug—Ein Lageatlas*, "*Aufmarsch am 21.6.1941 abds., Heeresgruppe Mitte*."

204   Mainhardt Graf von Nayhauss-Cormons, *Zwischen Gehorsam und Gewissen. Richard von Weizsäcker und das Infanterie-Regiment 9*, 131.

205   Ibid., 131–32.

206   Werner Heinemann, *Pflicht und Schuldigkeit. Betrachtungen eines Frontoffiziers im Zweiten Weltkrieg*, 255.

207   Ibid., 256.

208   Ibid., 256–57.

209   Ibid., 257.

210   BA-MA RH 20-4/1199, *KTB AOK 4*, 22.6.41.

211   Ibid.

212   Ibid.

213   BA-MA RH 26-292/7, *KTB 292.Inf.Div.*, 22.6.41.

214 The word "*hinterhältig*" can also be translated as "underhanded," "deceitful," or "perfidious"—and, no doubt, carries those implications in Meyer-Detring's commentary.

215 Meyer-Detring, *Die 137. Infanterie-Division*, 20. In the first forty-eight hours of the campaign, 137 ID would sustain 345 casualties (seventy-three killed, 262 wounded, ten missing). BA-MA 26-137/5, "*Verlustliste der 137. Inf. Division.*"

216 Report of *Gefr.* W. Cited in: Meyer-Detring, *Die 137. Infanterie-Division*, 20–21.

217 Cited in: Kempowski (ed.), *Das Echolot*, 25.

218 Cited in: Johannes Hürter, *Ein deutscher General an der Ostfront. Die Briefe und Tagebücher des Gotthard Heinrici 1941/42*, 62–63.

219 Glantz, *Barbarossa*, 38.

220 According to a Soviet combat report issued at 1200 hours: "In view of the loss of communications with the 10 Army, deputy commander Boldin has flown to Belostok with the mission of establishing the situation along the 10 Army's front and, depending on the situation, to employ the 6 Mechanized Corps along the Grodno or Brest axes." TsAMO RF, F. 208, Op. 10169ss, D. 4, Ll. 22-24, "*Boevoe Donesenie Shtaba Zapadnogo Osobogo Voennogo Okruga No. 005/op ot 22 Iyunya 1941 g. o Khode Boevykh Deistvii Voisk Okruga. Seriya 'G'*" (Combat Report No. 005/op by the Headquarters of the Western Special Military District from June 22, 1941, on the Course of Combat Activities by the District's Troops. Series "G"), in: SBDVOV, Vol. 35: 17.

221 Glantz, "The Border Battles on the Bialystok-Minsk Axis: 22–28 June 1941," in: Glantz (ed.), *Initial Period of War on the Eastern Front*, 200.

222 Glantz, *Barbarossa*, 38–39; Glantz, *Barbarossa Derailed*, Vol. I: 31; Werth, *Russia at War 1941–1945*, 151.

223 Cited in: Bryan I. Fugate and Lev Dvoretsky, *Thunder on the Dnepr: Zhukov-Stalin and the Defeat of Hitler's Blitzkrieg*, 144–45.

224 Erwin Wagner, *Tage wie Jahre. Vom Westwall bis Moskau 1939–1949*, 27–28.

225 BA-MA RH 20-4/1199, *KTB AOK 4*, 23.6.41.

226 The notorious SS *Einsatzgruppen* operated in the wake of the advancing German armies in Russia; their mission was to rid the captured territories of all perceived enemies of the Reich. Foremost among these enemies were, of course, the Jews, but they also included Communist functionaries, the Soviet *intelligentsia*, and other so-called "undesirables." The four *Einsatzgruppen* in Russia would liquidate more than half a million Jews in the first wave of killings by the end of 1941. See, Luther, *Barbarossa Unleashed*, 446–49.

227 Mitcham Jr., *The Men of Barbarossa*, 94.

228 Stein, *GFM Model*, 67; Blumentritt, "Moscow," 44. Contributing to Strauss's decision to step down as Ninth Army commander was his poor health at the time; however, he was also angered by what he considered to be unjustified interference in his army's operations by GFM von Kluge, the new C-in-C of Army Group Center. As a result, Strauss asked to be placed on sick leave, and Kluge did not hesitate to accomodate him. Strauss was replaced by the younger, and more dynamic, Walter Model, who commanded the 3 Panzer Division at the start of the Russian campaign. Email, Dr. David Stahel to Dr. Craig Luther, January 14, 2018.

229 "*Kriegsgliederung Barbarossa*," Stand 18.6.41, Kurt Mehner (ed.).

230 Ibid.

231 Thies, *Der Ostfeldzug—Ein Lageatlas*, "*Aufmarsch am 21.6.1941 abds., Heeresgruppe Mitte.*"

232 "*Aufmarschanweisung Barbarossa*," in: Halder, *KTB*, Vol. II: 467 (Appendix 2).

233 *GSWW*, Vol. IV: 363; Richard Muller, *The German Air War in Russia*, 3.

234 James S. Corum, *Wolfram von Richthofen: Master of the German Air War*, 260–61 (hereafter cited as, Corum, *Wolfram von Richthofen*); Gerhard Hümmelchen, "*Generalfeldmarschall Wolfram Frhr. v. Richthofen*," in: *Hitlers militärische Elite*, Ueberschär (ed.), 171.

235 For more details on Soviet 3 Army deployments see, Glantz, "The Border Battles on the Bialystok-Minsk Axis: 22–28 June 1941," in: Glantz (ed.), *Initial Period of War on the Eastern Front*, 187, 191–93; Glantz, *Red Army Ground Forces in June 1941*, 21.

236 See, Section 2.2 for an explanation of the staggered start times of Operation *Barbarossa*.

237 Helmut Pabst, *The Outermost Frontier: A German Soldier in the Russian Campaign*, 5. Pabst would be killed in action in the fall of 1943.

238 Ibid., 9–10.

239 The 129 ID had three organic infantry regiments (427, 428, 430 IR). The 185 IR, in action this day with 129 ID, actually belonged to 87 ID. Nafziger, *The German Order of Battle: Infantry in World War II*, 137, 160.

240 BA-MA RH 26-129/3, *KTB 129.Inf.Div.*, 22.6.41. For more details see, Heinrich Boucsein, *Halten oder Sterben. Die hessisch-thüringische 129. Infanterie-Division im Russlandfeldzug und Ostpreussen 1941–1945*, 16–17.

241 BA-MA RH 26-129/3, *KTB 129.Inf.Div.*, 22.6.41.

242 Ibid.

243 BA-MA RH 26-256/12, *KTB 256.Inf.Div.*, 22.6.41.

244 Hans Wijers (ed.), *Chronik der Sturmgeschützabteilung 210. Tagebuchaufzeichnungen und Erinnerungen von ehem. Angehörigen*, 3. The assault gun battery also destroyed eleven Soviet tanks on June 22, 1941.

245 In 1921, there were 402 Jews in Novy Dvor, about one-third of the town's population. In October 1941, the Jews of Novy Dvor were transported to the ghetto at Ostryna, and, in the spring of 1942, to the ghetto in Sukhovolia. From there they were sent to the extermination camp at Auschwitz. Only six of the town's Jews would survive the war, three of them in the partisan movement. No Jews returned to Novy Dvor after the war. For more details see, www.shtetlinks.jewishgen.org/lida-district/now-encyc.htm, and www.jewishvirtuallibrary.org.

246 BA-MA RH 26-256/12, *KTB 256.Inf.Div.*, 22.6.41.

247 Forczyk, *Tank Warfare on the Eastern Front 1941–42*, 49; Erickson, *The Road to Stalingrad*, 129.

248 As early as 0345 hours, a combat report of Soviet 3 Army noted that the enemy had "violated the state border along the sector from Sipotski to Augustov and is bombing Grodno, particularly the army's headquarters. Wire communications with units has been disrupted and we have gone over to radio, with two radio stations destroyed." TsAMO RF, F. 208, Op. 3038ss, D. 12, L. 2, "*Boevoe Donesenie Komandu-yushchego Voiskami 3-i Armii No. 1/op k 3 Chasam 45 Minutam 22 Iyunya 1941 g. o Razvertyvanii Boevykh Deistvii Nemetsko-Fashistkimi Voiskami*" (Combat Report by the Commander of 3 Army No. 1/op at 0345 on June 22, 1941, on the Unfolding of Combat Activities by the German-Fascist Forces), in: SBDVOV, Vol. 35: 135.

249 Erickson, *The Road to Stalingrad*, 129.

250 The Soviet 3 Army commander also reported that his headquarters (in Grodno) "is ready to move to the woods near Putrishki." TsAMO RF, F. 208, Op. 10169ss, D. 4, Ll. 5-7, "*Boevoe Donesenie Shtaba Zapadnogo Osobogo Voennogo Okruga No. 004/op ot 22 Iyunya 1941 g. o Khode Boevykh Deistvii Voisk Okruga. Sov. Sekretno*" (Combat Report No. 004/op from the Headquarters of the Western Special Military District on June 22, 1941, on the Course of Combat Activities by the District's Troops. Top Secret), in: SBDVOV, Vol. 35: 16.

251 Luttichau, *The Road to Moscow*, VI: 14.

252 Ibid., 16.

253 Glantz, "The Border Battles on the Bialystok-Minsk Axis: 22–28 June 1941," in: Glantz (ed.), *Initial Period of War on the Eastern Front*, 197–200.

254 Luttichau, *The Road to Moscow*, VI: 16–17.

255 In June 1941, the 13th Company of a German infantry regiment consisted of eight infantry guns— six 75mm light guns (le.IG 18) and two 150mm medium guns (s.IG 33). The 14th Company was the antitank company. See, Luther, *Barbarossa Unleashed*, 117.

256 Colonel Dr. Alfred Durrwanger, "28th Infantry Division Operations," in: Glantz (ed.), *Initial Period of War on the Eastern Front*, 232–35. Durrwanger went on to state: "While the other regiments of my division advanced very quickly without facing great resistance, it took my regiment three days to overcome the Soviet units in front of us. They defended a line of bunkers and fortifications, partly incomplete but protected by trenches, with utmost tenacity and, let me say, with cruelty as well. The Soviets had just occu-

pied this line some days before and when attacked they had not retreated. They were very brave soldiers. Our losses were 25 soldiers killed and 125 wounded within one battalion in these three days. Evidence from prisoners confirmed that our regiment had attacked crack units (*Elite-Einheiten*) and a camp of officer candidates. In their camp they were very well equipped (soap, towels, map cases, etc.)." Durrwanger, 235.

257   Forczyk, *Tank Warfare on the Eastern Front 1941–42*, 48–49.

258   Glantz, "The Border Battles on the Bialystok-Minsk Axis: 22–28 June 1941," in: Glantz (ed.), *Initial Period of War on the Eastern Front*, 200.

259   Forczyk, *Tank Warfare on the Eastern Front 1941–42*, 48–49.

260   *KTB OKW*, Vol. I: 492.

261   Thies, *Der Ostfeldzug—Ein Lageatlas*, "Lage am 22.6.1941 abds., Heeresgruppe Mitte mit Feindlage."

262   All of Pavlov's combat reports had, hitherto, been filed under the rubric of the Western Special Military District; by now, however, his command had been re-designated as Western Front, which was issuing its first operational report.

263   For many more details see, TsAMO RF, F. 208, Op. 10169ss, D. 7, Ll. 1-4, "*Operativnaya Svodka Shtaba Zapadnogo Fronta No. 1 k 21 Chasam 22 Iyunya 1941 g. o Khode Boevykh Deistvii Voisk Fronta za 22 Iyunya 1941 g. Seriya 'G'*" (Operational Report No. 1 from the Western Front Headquarters at 2100 on June 22, 1941, on the Course of the Activities of the Front's Troops on June 22, 1941. Series "G"), in: SBDVOV, Vol. 35: 21–22.

264   Glantz, *Barbarossa*, 39–40; Seaton, *The Russo-German War 1941–1945*, 119–20.

265   David T. Zabecki (ed.), *World War II in Europe: An Encyclopedia*, Vol. I: 354; Bradley (ed.), *Deutschlands Generale und Admirale. Teil IV: Die Generale des Heeres 1921–1945, Bd. 6*: Hochbaum-Klutmann, 157–59; Blumentritt, "Moscow," 44; Mitcham Jr., *The Men of Barbarossa*, 100; www.lexikon-der-wehrmacht .de.

266   Stolfi, *German Panzers on the Offensive*, 16.

267   Jentz (ed.), *Panzer Truppen*, 190–93.

268   "*Kriegsgliederung Barbarossa*," *Stand 18.6.41*, Kurt Mehner (ed.).

269   Ibid.

270   Forczyk, *Tank Warfare on the Eastern Front 1941–42*, 44.

271   Forczyk, *Tank Warfare on the Eastern Front 1941–42*, 44; Glantz, "The Border Battles on the Vilnius Axis: 22–26 June 1941," in: Glantz (ed.), *Initial Period of War on the Eastern Front*, 158.

272   "*Aufmarschanweisung Barbarossa*," in: Halder, *KTB*, Vol. II: 466 (Appendix 2).

273   Glantz, "The Border Battles on the Vilnius Axis: 22–26 June 1941," in: Glantz (ed.), *Initial Period of War on the Eastern Front*, 155.

274   About one-third of 18 Motorized Infantry Division (57 PzK) took part in the initial attack. *DRZW*, Vol. IV, *Beiheft*, "*Ausgangslage zum 22.6.1941*."

275   NARA, T-313, Roll 225, *Ia KTB Nr. 1, 3.Pz.Gr.*, 22.6.41; BA-MA RH 21-3/732, "*Gefechtsberichte Russland 1941/42*"; Klaus-R. Woche, *Zwischen Pflicht und Gewissen. Generaloberst Rudolf Schmidt 1886–1957*, 100 (hereafter cited as, Woche, *Generaloberst Rudolf Schmidt*); Stahel, *Operation Barbarossa and Germany's Defeat in the East*, 153–55.

276   Only 19 PD's artillery supported the initial attack. Rolf Hinze, *Die 19. Panzer-Division. Bewaffnung, Einsätze, Männer. Einsatz 1941–1945 in Russland*, 11.

277   Hinze, *19. Panzer-Division*, 126.

278   Although Hoth's panzer group attacked along a "dry" front, and thus did not have to begin its attack by crossing a major river line, it still had terrain obstacles to contend with—particularly the thick belts of woodland and roads that were no more than sandy tracks, hardly suited for tanks and vehicles weighing many tons. The progress of Hoth's two panzer corps was also adversely affected by the poor march discipline evinced by some units. Luther, *Barbarossa Unleashed*, 234.

279   NARA, T-313, Roll 225, *Ia KTB Nr. 1, 3.Pz.Gr.*, 22.6.41; Hermann Hoth, *Panzer-Operationen. Die Panzergruppe 3 und der operative Gedanke der deutschen Führung Sommer 1941*, 53 (hereafter cited as, Hoth, *Panzer-Operationen*).

280   Gerhard Bopp, *Kriegstagebuch. Aufzeichnungen während des II. Weltkrieges 1940–1943*, 71.

281   Ibid., 72.

282   NARA, T-313, Roll 225, *Ia KTB Nr. 1, 3.Pz.Gr.*, 22.6.41.

283   NARA, T-313, Roll 225, *Ia KTB Nr. 1, 3.Pz.Gr.*, 22.6.41; Luttichau, *The Road to Moscow*, VI: 18.

284   TsAMO RF, F. 221, Op. 1351, D. 68, L. 28, "*Nachal'nik shtaba PribOVO. Operativnaya Svodka No. 6, Shtab 11 Armii, Kaunas, 10:00, Polozhenie na 8:00 22.6.41*" (Chief of Staff of the Baltic Special Military District, Combat Report No. 6, Headquarters of the 11 Army, Kaunas, 1000, the Situation as of 0800 June 22, 1941).

285   NARA, T-313, Roll 225, *Ia KTB Nr. 1, 3.Pz.Gr.*, 22.6.41; BA-MA RH 21-3/732, "*Gefechtsberichte Russland 1941/42*"; www.lexikon-der-wehrmacht.de.

286   Luttichau, *The Road to Moscow*, VI: 17–18.

287   Ibid., 19.

288   Ibid., 19.

289   Friedrich-Christian Stahl, "*Generaloberst Rudolf Schmidt*," in: *Hitlers militärische Elite*, Ueberschär (ed.), 219; Gerhard L. Weinberg, *A World at Arms: A Global History of World War II*, 125; www.lexikon-der-wehrmacht.de.

290   Woche, *Generaloberst Rudolf Schmidt*, 10–11, 95, 98.

291   Thies, *Der Ostfeldzug—Ein Lageatlas*, "*Aufmarsch am 21.6.1941 abds., Heeresgruppe Mitte.*"

292   Horst Ohrloff, "39 [Panzer] Corps Operations," in: Glantz (ed.), *Initial Period of War on the Eastern Front*, 170.

293   Woche, *Generaloberst Rudolf Schmidt*, 107.

294   *Oblt.* Richard D. (35 232), Collection BfZ.

295   *True to Type: A Selection from Letters and Diaries of German Soldiers and Civilians Collected on the Soviet-German Front*, 14.

296   Rolf Hinze, *Hitze, Frost und Pulverdampf. Der Schicksalsweg der 20. Panzer Division*, 25.

297   BA-MA RH 27-7/46, *Ia KTB 7.Pz.Div.*, 22.6.41.

298   NARA, T-313, Roll 225, *Ia KTB Nr. 1, 3.Pz.Gr.*, 22.6.41; Hinze, *Hitze, Frost und Pulverdampf. Der Schicksalsweg der 20. Panzer Division*, 25.

299   For a spectacular photograph of the bridge over the Neman River at Alytus see, Hasso v. Manteuffel, *Die 7. Panzer-Division. Bewaffnung, Einsätze, Männer*, 49.

300   BA-MA RH 27-7/46, *Ia KTB 7.Pz.Div.*, 22.6.41; NARA, T-313, Roll 225, *Ia KTB Nr. 1, 3.Pz.Gr.*, 22.6.41; Hoth, *Panzer-Operationen*, 54; Hasso v. Manteuffel, *Die 7. Panzer-Division. Bewaffnung, Einsätze, Männer*, 50.

301   Of 7 Panzer Division's 265 tanks, 167 of them were Pz 38(t) models, and no match for the Soviet T-34. Jentz (ed.), *Panzer Truppen*, 190.

302   Forczyk, *Tank Warfare on the Eastern Front 1941–42*, 44.

303   Ohrloff, "39 [Panzer] Corps Operations," in: Glantz (ed.), *Initial Period of War on the Eastern Front*, 173–75.

304   Forczyk, *Tank Warfare on the Eastern Front 1941–42*, 44–45.

305   BA-MA RH 27-7/46, *Ia KTB 7.Pz.Div.*, 22.6.41; Forczyk, *Tank Warfare on the Eastern Front 1941–42*, 45; Ohrloff, "39 [Panzer] Corps Operations," in: Glantz (ed.), *Initial Period of War on the Eastern Front*, 175.

306   BA-MA RH 27-7/46, *Ia KTB 7.Pz.Div.*, 22.6.41; NARA, T-313, Roll 225, *Ia KTB Nr. 1, 3.Pz.Gr.*, 22.6.41.

307   Robert Forczyk challenges the German records, at least in part, noting: "Most of the T-34s were lost due to crew errors, including two [that] sunk in the Neman River and others toppled into ditches and craters." See, Forczyk, *Tank Warfare on the Eastern Front 1941–42*, 45.

308   Apparently, a number of Soviet T-34 tanks had been adeptly integrated into Russian defensive positions along the road to Alytus. While they most likely belonged to 3 Mechanized Corps, it is unclear which division they were a part of.

309 Kirchubel, *Hitler's Panzer Armies*, 97; Stolfi, *German Panzers on the Offensive*, 17. For a photograph of destroyed German Pz 38(t)s on the approach road to Alytus see, Hasso v. Manteuffel, *Die 7. Panzer-Division. Bewaffnung, Einsätze, Männer*, 49.

310 Stolfi, *German Panzers on the Offensive*, 17.

311 NARA, T-313, Roll 225, *Ia KTB Nr. 1, 3.Pz.Gr.*, 22.6.41; Ohrloff, "39 [Panzer] Corps Operations," in: Glantz (ed.), *Initial Period of War on the Eastern Front*, 175.

312 BA-MA RH 27-7/46, *Ia KTB 7.Pz.Div.*, 28.6.41; Luther, *Barbarossa Unleashed*, 280.

313 In the words of R. H. S. Stolfi, "for most intents and purposes, 7 PD set the northern arm of the encirclement of the vast Soviet forces defending the road to Moscow." Stolfi, *German Panzers on the Offensive*, 16.

314 Erickson, *The Soviet High Command*, 595.

315 For example, fearing that some of his divisions were unreliable or even capable of treason (i.e., those manned by personnel from the Baltic States), Kuznetsov told Timoshenko on June 22 that "I cannot create a group of forces on my left flank and the boundary with Pavlov to eliminate the breakthrough. I ask that you help me." TsAMO RF, F. 221, Op. 2467ss, D. 39, Ll. 123-124, "*Donesenie Komanduyushchego Voiskami Severo-Zapadnogo Fronta ot 22 Iyunya 1941 g. Narodnomu Komissaru Oborony o Proryve Krupnykh Tankovykh i Motorizovannykh Sil Protivnika na Druskeniki i Meropriyatiyakh Komandovaniya Fronta po Organizatsii Razgrom Til'zitskoi Gruppirovki Protivnika. Sovershenno Sekretno*" (Report by the Commander of the Northwestern Front of June 22, 1941, to the People's Commissar of Defense on the Breakthrough by the Enemy's Major Tank and Motorized Forces toward Druskininkai and Measures by the Front Command to Organize the Defeat of the Enemy's Tilsit Group of Forces. Top Secret), in: SBDVOV, Vol. 34: 36.

316 At Christmas 1943, chief of the Army General Staff, *Generaloberst* Kurt Zeitzler, gifted the 6 ID's 18 Infantry Regiment 250 packages—in recognition of the regiment's "special accomplishments" and the fact that it belonged to one of the "three best divisions" of the *Ostheer*. Horst Grossmann, *Die Geschichte der rheinisch-westfälischen 6. Infanterie-Division 1939–1945*, 207 (hereafter cited as, Grossmann, *Geschichte der 6. Infanterie-Division*).

317 BA-MA RH 26-6/2, *Anlage zum Ia KTB 6.Inf.Div.*

318 Grossmann, *Geschichte der 6. Infanterie-Division*, 38.

319 D 107/56 Nr. 10: *KTB 18.Inf.Rgt.: "Der russische Sommerfeldzug mit dem I.R.18*," 20.6.41 (Staats- und Personenstandsarchiv Detmold) (hereafter cited as: D 107/56 Nr. 10: *KTB 18.Inf.Rgt.*).

320 BA-MA N 76/6: "*Kriegserinnerungen als Kommandeur der 6. Inf.Div.*," Helge Auleb (hereafter cited as: BA-MA N 76/6: "*Kriegserinnerungen*," Auleb). Special thanks to Dr. David Stahel for furnishing me with this important document.

321 Grossmann, *Geschichte der 6. Infanterie-Division*, 38.

322 As noted in the 6 ID war diary at 0330: "Everywhere resistance is negligible" (*überall nur geringe Gegenwehr*). BA-MA RH 26-6/8, *Ia KTB 6.Inf.Div.*, 22.6.41.

323 Ernst-Martin Rhein, *Das Rheinisch-Westfälische Infanterie-/Grenadier-Regiment 18 1921–1945*, 45; D 107/56 Nr. 10: *KTB 18.Inf.Rgt.*, 20.6.41; Grossmann, *Geschichte der 6. Infanterie-Division*, 37–39.

324 That the war diary of 18 Infantry Regiment survived the war was due to the efforts of Ernst-Martin Rhein, in June 1941 a company commander in the regiment and future Knight's Cross holder. He spent the final years of his long life working tirelessly through an organization he helped found (*Kuratorium Rzhew*) for reconciliation with the former Russian enemy and passed away on April 20, 2016, at the age of ninety-nine. He was a man small in physical stature, but with the heart of a lion, and this author is honored to have known him.

325 The actual text reads: "*die Masse der M.G.K.*"—most likely a reference to the Machine Gun Company, which would be the 4th Company in the battalion.

326 At 1030 hours, the war diary of 6 ID recorded that the bunkers by Akmenynai were being "tenaciously defended" (*zäh verteidigt*) and that II./IR 18 had quickly sustained serious losses. BA-MA RH 26-6/8, *Ia KTB 6.Inf.Div.*, 22.6.41.

327   As noted later in this regimental diary, for the attack on June 22, 11th Company (3rd Battalion) had been subordinated to the regiment's 2nd Battalion and took part in the costly assaults on the Soviet bunkers at Akmenynai.

328   D 107/56 Nr. 10: *KTB 18.Inf.Rgt.*, 22.6.41.

329   D 107/56 Nr. 10: *KTB 18.Inf.Rgt.*, 22.6.41; Grossmann, *Geschichte der 6. Infanterie-Division*, 40–41; BA-MA N 76/6: "*Kriegserinnerungen*," Auleb.

330   Haape, *Moscow Tram Stop*, 10; Records of the *Haape Family Archive* (courtesy of Johannes Haape).

331   Haape, *Moscow Tram Stop*, 16.

332   Ibid., 16–17.

333   Ibid., 18–19.

334   Ibid., 19–20.

335   Ibid., 20–21.

336   Ibid., 21. Haape also mentioned this tragic incident in a letter to his fiancée, noting only that six Russian "heavy bombers" were shot down, and that three men of the German artillery column "were immediately buried alive [by one of the downed Russian bombers] and completely carbonized [*verkohlten vollständig*], five others received the most severe burns." Ltr., Dr. Heinrich Haape to fiancée, June 23, 1941.

337   Most of the 6 ID's reconnaissance battalion (6 AA) had been assigned directly to 6 Army Corps, to serve as an advance detachment (*Vorausabteilung*) for the corps. All that was left of the battalion to 6 ID was a cavalry and a cycle squadron, reinforced by a mortar battery, a heavy MG battery, and an AA battery. These units were assembled under Boeselager's command. Boeselager, *Valkyrie*, 38; Grossmann, *Geschichte der 6. Infanterie-Division*, 39.

338   BA-MA RH 26-6/8, *Ia KTB 6. Inf.-Div.*, 22.6.41; Grossmann, *Geschichte der 6. Infanterie-Division*, 41–42.

339   BA-MA RH 26-6/8, *Ia KTB 6. Inf.-Div.*, 22.6.41.

340   D 107/56 Nr. 10: *KTB 18.Inf.Rgt.*, 22.6.41.

341   Haape, *Moscow Tram Stop*, 28.

342   About the doctor who'd been killed Haape wrote: "Twelve hours' warfare, a few miles into Russian territory and I had already lost one of my dearest friends. It was too much—too much for the first day of a war against a new foe." Ibid., 26–27.

343   Ltr., Dr. Heinrich Haape to fiancée, June 22, 1941.

344   Map 11 in this book ("Vilnius Axis, Situation, 2300 hrs., June 22, 1941"), shows 26 ID well short of Mariampole at the end of the day; however, the detailed color map of the German Army General Staff's Operations Branch places 26 ID just south of Mariampole. Thies, *Der Ostfeldzug—Ein Lageatlas*, "*Lage am 22.6.1941 abds., Heeresgruppe Mitte mit Feindlage*." In addition, the daily report of the General Staff's Operations Branch states that 6 Army Corps reached the line of Liudvinavas (6 ID)–Mariampole (26 ID) on June 22. *KTB OKW*, Vol. I: 491.

345   Wolfgang Knecht, *Geschichte des Infanterie-Regiments 77: 1936–1945*, 53–54.

346   Ibid., 55.

347   NARA, T-313, Roll 225, *Ia KTB Pz.Gr.3*, 22.6.41.

348   Franz Halder, *Kriegstagebuch: Tägliche Aufzeichnungen des Chef des Generalstabes des Heeres 1939–1942, Bd. III: Der Russlandfeldzug bis zum Marsch auf Stalingrad (22.6.1941–24.9.1942)*, Hans-Adolf Jacobsen and Alfred Philippi (eds.), 5.

349   Ibid., 5. In acknowledgment of Hoth having achieved complete operational freedom, Bock released 3 Panzer Group from Ninth Army control at 2400 hours on June 23, at which time it came under the direct control of Army Group Center. Guderian's 2 Panzer Group would remain under control of Fourth Army for several more days. BA-MA RH 21-3/788, *Ia KTB 3.Pz.Gr.*, 23.6.41.

350   Describing the German victory at Smolensk in early August 1941, Showalter's complete quote reads: "It was the climax of a series of virtuoso performances that combine to make a case that the relative tactical and operational superiority of the panzers over their opponents was never greater than in the first half of July 1941, on the high road to Moscow. Guderian spoke of attacks going in like training exercises." Dennis Showalter, *Hitler's Panzers: The Lightning Attacks That Revolutionized Warfare*, 170–71.

351   BA-MA RH 21-3/732, "*Gefechtsberichte Russland 1941/42.*"

352   GFM v. Bock, *War Diary*, 225.

353   Pleshakov, *Stalin's Folly*, 126.

354   Ibid., 126.

355   Ibid., 126–27.

356   V. A. Anfilov, "*Razgovor Zakonchilsya Ugrozoi Stalina*" (The Conversation Ended with Stalin's Threat), in: *Voenno-Istoricheskii Zhurnal* (Military-Historical Journal), 42–43.

357   Stahel, *Operation Barbarossa and Germany's Defeat in the East*, 156.

Chapter 5: Armageddon Unleashed (III)—Army Group South Goes to War

1   Paul R. (NO2.1), Collection BfZ.

2   *Fw.* Hans M. (28 193B), Collection BfZ. On June 22, 79 Infantry Division was an OKH reserve division with Army Group South.

3   Rokossovsky, *Soldatskii Dolg* (A Soldier's Duty), 35.

4   Mitcham Jr., *The Men of Barbarossa*, 201–2; I. C. B. Dear (ed.), *The Oxford Guide to World War II*, 755; www.lexikon-der-wehrmacht.de.

5   Mitcham Jr., *The Men of Barbarossa*, 202–3; I. C. B. Dear (ed.), *The Oxford Guide to World War II*, 755–56; www.lexikon-der-wehrmacht.de.

6   Mitcham Jr., *The Men of Barbarossa*, 202–3.

7   I. C. B. Dear (ed.), *The Oxford Guide to World War II*, 756; Rolf-Dieter Müller, *Der letzte deutsche Krieg 1939–1945*, 49.

8   I. C. B. Dear (ed.), *The Oxford Guide to World War II*, 756.

9   I. C. B. Dear (ed.), *The Oxford Guide to World War II*, 756; Messenger, *A Biography of Field Marshal Rundstedt*, 319.

10   Messenger, *A Biography of Field Marshal Rundstedt*, 309–10.

11   *Voennaya Entsiklopediya*, Vol. 4: 55–56; Mawdsley, *Thunder in the East*, 74.

12   *Voennaya Entsiklopediya*, Vol. 4: 55–56; Mawdsley, *Thunder in the East*, 74; Kirchubel, *Operation Barbarossa (1)*, *Army Group South*, 21.

13   Rokossovsky, *Soldatskii Dolg* (A Soldier's Duty), 51–52.

14   Mawdsley, *Thunder in the East*, 80; *GSWW*, Vol. IV: 875; *Voennaya Entsiklopediya*, Vol. 4: 56. As noted earlier in the text, RKKA (*Raboche-Krest'yanskaya Krasnaya Armiya*) stands for the "Workers' and Peasants' Red Army."

15   The three security divisions (213, 444, 454) were under tactical control of the Commander, Rear Army Area 103 (*Befehlshaber rückw. Heeresgebiet 103*).

16   The Germans did not inform Hungary of their decision to attack the Soviet Union until June 19, 1941, and Hungary did not declare war on the USSR until June 27. *GSWW*, Vol. IV: 1028; Ignác Romsics, "Hungary," in: *Joining Hitler's Crusade: European Nations and the Invasion of the Soviet Union, 1941*, David Stahel (ed.), 89.

17   "*Kriegsgliederung Barbarossa*," Stand 18.6.41, Kurt Mehner (ed.); "*Die materielle Ausstattung des deutschen Ostheeres am 22. Juni 1941*," in: *DRZW*, Vol. IV: 186–87; Glantz, *Barbarossa*, 217, f.n. 30; Luttichau, *The Road to Moscow*, VIII: 4; Jentz (ed.), *Panzer Truppen*, 191–92; Mitcham Jr., *The Men of Barbarossa*, 49.

18   "*Kriegsgliederung Barbarossa*," Stand 18.6.41, Kurt Mehner (ed.); Kirchubel, *Operation Barbarossa 1941 (1)*, *Army Group South*, 23; *GSWW*, Vol. IV: 316.

19   "*Kriegsgliederung Barbarossa*," Stand 18.6.41, Kurt Mehner (ed.); Luttichau, *The Road to Moscow*, IV: 9.

20   *GSWW*, Vol. IV: 363–64; Kirchubel, *Operation Barbarossa (1)*, *Army Group South*, 24; "*Kriegsgliederung Barbarossa*," Stand 18.6.41, Kurt Mehner (ed.). It is possible that 2 Flak Corps controlled as many as eight to ten flak battalions (see, Luttichau, *The Road to Moscow*, IV: 9; and, *GSWW*, Vol. IV: 370); however, the figure of six flak battalions is gleaned from the exquisitely detailed order of battle in Mehner (cited directly above).

21   *DRZW*, Vol. IV, *Beiheft*, "*Ausgangslage zum 22.6.1941.*" According to Werner Haupt, the front of Army Group South was 1,100 kilometers in length, excluding Hungary. Werner Haupt, *Die Schlachten der Heeresgruppe Süd: Aus der Sicht der Divisionen*, 16 (hereafter cited as, Haupt, *Die Schlachten der Heeresgruppe Süd*).

22 Stahel, *Operation Barbarossa and Germany's Defeat in the East*, 88–89; *GSWW*, Vol. IV: 546–47; Luttichau, *The Road to Moscow*, IV: 5–6.

23 Taylor, *Barbarossa to Berlin*, 23; Messenger, *A Biography of Field Marshal Rundstedt*, 140.

24 *GSWW*, Vol. IV; 290; Glantz, *Barbarossa*, 47; Luttichau, *The Road to Moscow*, IV: 3; *KTB OKW*, Vol. I: 425; Craig Luther, "German Armored Operations in the Ukraine 1941: The Encirclement Battle of Uman," in: *The Army Quarterly and Defence Journal*, Vol. 108, No. 4. October 1978, 454.

25 "*Aufmarschanweisung Barbarossa*," in: Halder, *KTB*, Vol. II: 465 (Appendix 2).

26 Luttichau, *The Road to Moscow*, IV: 3.

27 Glantz, *Barbarossa*, 217, f.n. 31; Mawdsley, *Thunder in the East*, 40; Magenheimer, *Moskau 1941. Entscheidungsschlacht im Osten*, 28.

28 Robert A. Forczyk, *Tank Warfare on the Eastern Front 1941–42*, 32; also, Glantz, *Red Army Ground Forces in June 1941*, 20–28.

29 *DRZW*, Vol. IV, *Beiheft*, "*Ausgangslage zum 22.6.1941*"; Kirchubel, *Operation Barbarossa 1941 (1), Army Group South*, 28.

30 Carell, *Hitler Moves East*, 37.

31 For a brief discussion of Soviet prewar planning and, particularly, why the main Red Army forces were concentrated on Kirponos's Southwestern Front see, Chapter 1 (Section 1.6).

32 *GSWW*, Vol. IV: 547; "*Kriegsgliederung Barbarossa*," *Stand 18.6.41*, Kurt Mehner (ed.); Kirchubel, *Operation Barbarossa 1941 (1), Army Group South*, 26; "*Die materielle Ausstattung des deutschen Ostheeres am 22. Juni 1941*," in: *DRZW*, Vol. IV: 187; also, www.lexikon-der-wehrmacht.de.

33 "*Kriegsgliederung Barbarossa*," *Stand 18.6.41*, Kurt Mehner (ed.); Franz Kurowski, *Balkenkreuz und Roter Stern. Der Luftkrieg über Russland 1941–1944*, 55.

34 Total Romanian forces amounted to fewer than twenty division equivalents, including several cavalry and mountain brigades; their weaponry, a patchwork of equipment from Czech, Dutch, French, German, Polish, and indigenous Romanian sources, was largely outdated, while posing a maintenance nightmare. Glantz, *Barbarossa*, 47; Ziemke and Bauer, *Moscow to Stalingrad: Decision in the East*, 7; Kirchubel, *Operation Barbarossa 1941 (1), Army Group South*, 28; Wagener, *Heeresgruppe Süd*, 47; *DRZW*, Vol. IV, *Beiheft*, "*Ausgangslage zum 22.6.1941*."

35 In late April 1941, Marshal Antonescu, in an interview with the German minister in Bucharest, Manfred *Freiherr* von Killinger, had proposed a German attack on Russia. Hitler, however, who held Antonescu in high regard, did not reveal his *Barbarossa* plan to the Romanian dictator until June 11. Luttichau, *The Road to Moscow*, IV: 25–31.

36 *GSWW*, Vol. IV: 548–49; Kirchubel, *Operation Barbarossa 1941 (1), Army Group South*, 26.

37 *DRZW*, Vol. IV, *Beiheft*, "*Ausgangslage zum 22.6.1941*."

38 "*Aufmarschanweisung Barbarossa*," in: Halder, *KTB*, Vol. II: 465 (Appendix 2).

39 Luttichau, *The Road to Moscow*, IV: 7; Glantz, *Barbarossa*, 47; Wagener, *Heeresgruppe Süd*, 47.

40 Glantz, *Barbarossa*, 53, 244; Mawdsley, *Thunder in the East*, 77; Kirchubel, *Operation Barbarossa 1941 (1), Army Group South*, 41.

41 Halder, *War Diary*, 412. Among the forces of Eleventh Army that crossed the Prut River on June 22, 1941, were elements of 305 Infantry Regiment (198 ID). For details see, Nicholas Stargardt, *The German War: A Nation Under Arms, 1939–45*, 157–58.

42 Wagener, *Heeresgruppe Süd*, 47–48.

43 *Gefr.* Franz B. (17 736), Collection BfZ.

44 Halder, *War Diary*, 414; NARA, T-311, Roll 260, *KTB H.Gr.Süd*, 22.6.41.

45 NARA, T-311, Roll 260, *KTB H.Gr.Süd*, 22.6.41.

46 *KTB OKW*, Vol. I: 425; Seaton, *The Russo-German War 1941–1945*, 136.

47 According to historian Samuel W. Mitcham Jr., Stülpnagel had run afoul of C-in-C of the army, Field Marshal von Brauchitsch, and that had resulted in his replacement. Mitcham Jr., *The Men of Barbarossa*, 188.

48 Peter Hoffmann, *The History of the German Resistance 1933–1945*, 77–78; www.lexikon-der-wehrmacht.de.

49 Hoffmann, *The History of the German Resistance 1933–1945*, 518.

50   Ibid., 529.

51   General von Briesen would be killed in action on the Eastern Front at Andrejevka on November 20, 1941. Halder, *War Diary*, 559; www.lexikon-der-wehrmacht.de.

52   *"Kriegsgliederung Barbarossa," Stand 18.6.41*, Kurt Mehner (ed.).

53   It seems one battery of Assault Gun Battalion 243 was assigned to 1 Mountain Division (49 Geb.K.) for the initial attack on June 22. See, NARA, T-315, Roll 39, *Ia KTB Ost Nr. 1, 1.Geb.Div.*, 22.6.41.

54   *"Kriegsgliederung Barbarossa," Stand 18.6.41*, Kurt Mehner (ed.).

55   *DRZW*, Vol. IV, *Beiheft*, *"Ausgangslage zum 22.6.1941"*; Haupt, *Die Schlachten der Heeresgruppe Süd*, 22.

56   Luttichau, *The Road to Moscow*, IV: 6–7; also, Luther, "German Armored Operations in the Ukraine 1941: The Encirclement Battle of Uman," 465, f.n. 5.

57   *"Aufmarschanweisung Barbarossa,"* in: Halder, *KTB*, Vol. II: 466 (Appendix 2).

58   *DRZW*, Vol. IV, *Beiheft*, *"Ausgangslage zum 22.6.1941"*; David M. Glantz, "The Border Battles on the Lutsk-Rovno Axis: 22 June–1 July 1941," in: Glantz (ed.), *Initial Period of War on the Eastern Front*, 248–52; Glantz, *Barbarossa*, 47, 248.

59   Erickson, *The Road to Stalingrad*, 121–22; Haupt, *Die Schlachten der Heeresgruppe Süd*, 16.

60   NARA, T-311, Roll 260, *KTB H.Gr.Süd*, 22.6.41.

61   NARA, T-312, Roll 668, *Ia KTB AOK 17*, 22.6.41.

62   Erickson, *The Road to Stalingrad*, 122–23.

63   Ibid., 122–23.

64   Ibid., 123.

65   As originally intended, the mission of the security divisions was behind the front lines—for example, fighting partisans or securing key terrain features, such as railroads, crossroads, bridges, and tunnels. In Russia, however, they would often find themselves in front-line combat. *"Die materielle Ausstattung des deutschen Ostheeres am 22. Juni 1941,"* in: *DRZW*, Vol. IV: 187; Nafziger, *The German Order of Battle: Infantry in World War II*, 492, 507–9.

66   Wagener, *Heeresgruppe Süd*, 48–49; *Handbook on German Military Forces*, 86.

67   Erickson, *The Road to Stalingrad*, 123.

68   Wagener, *Heeresgruppe Süd*, 49; Haupt, *Die Schlachten der Heeresgruppe Süd*, 23; Erickson, *The Road to Stalingrad*, 131; NARA, T-311, Roll 260, *KTB H.Gr.Süd*, 22.6.41; NARA, T-312, Roll 668, *Ia KTB AOK 17*, 22.6.41; *KTB OKW*, 490.

69   NARA, T-312, Roll 668, *Ia KTB AOK 17*, 22.6.41; *DRZW*, Vol. IV, *Beiheft*, *"Ausgangslage zum 22.6.1941"*; Wagener, *Heeresgruppe Süd*, 49; www.lexikon-der-wehrmacht.de.

70   Carell, *Hitler Moves East*, 27.

71   Ibid., 27.

72   NARA, T-312, Roll 668, *Ia KTB AOK 17*, 22.6.41.

73   Charles B. Burdick, *Hubert Lanz: General der Gebirgstruppe 1896–1982*, 89, 250 (hereafter cited as, Burdick, *Hubert Lanz*); Meyer, *Die 1. Gebirgs-Division*, 52; Hubert Lanz, *Gebirgsjäger. Die 1. Gebirgsdivision 1935–1945*, 134.

74   Dekan Rudolf Schwarz, *"Geprägt vom Christlichen Glauben,"* in: *Furchtlos und Treu. Zum fünfundsiebzigsten Geburtstag von General der Gebirgstruppe a.D. Hubert Lanz*, Charles B. Burdick (ed.), 44–46.

75   Burdick, *Hubert Lanz*, 99–100. Lanz was also troubled that his mountain division, which was neither trained nor equipped like a regular infantry division, was to be used as such in the first assault wave. On April 30, 1941, Lanz had met with General Kübler and appealed to him to find another use for the division. Sadly for Lanz, his démarche by Kübler failed. NARA, T-315, Roll 39, *Ia KTB Ost Nr. 1, 1.Geb.Div.*, 30.4.41. See also, Hans Steets, *Gebirgsjäger bei Uman. Die Korpsschlacht des XXXXIX. Gebirgs-Armeekorps bei Podwyssokoje 1941*, 9. Steets, who was Lanz's operations officer (Ia) at the start of the Russian campaign, noted the disadvantage of mountain divisions compared to regular infantry divisions, because the former only had two regiments instead of three, which meant they were always short of reserves in combat on regular (non-mountainous) terrain.

76   Burdick, *Hubert Lanz*, 99–102.

77   Lanz, *Gebirgsjäger. Die 1. Gebirgsdivision 1935–1945*, 134; Burdick, *Hubert Lanz*, 102; NARA, T-315, Roll 39, *Ia KTB Ost Nr. 1, 1.Geb.Div.*, 22.6.41.

78   Meyer, *Die 1. Gebirgs-Division*, 53.

79   Lanz, *Gebirgsjäger. Die 1. Gebirgsdivision 1935–1945*, 135.

80   Hubert Lanz, *Wie es zum Russlandfeldzug kam—und warum wir ihn verloren haben*, 35; NARA, T-315, Roll 39, *Ia KTB Ost Nr. 1, 1.Geb.Div.*, 22.6.41.

81   Cited in: Kaltenegger, *Weg und Kampf der 1. Gebirgs-Division*, 206–7.

82   Lanz, *Gebirgsjäger. Die 1. Gebirgsdivision 1935–1945*, 136; Burdick, *Hubert Lanz*, 102; NARA, T-315, Roll 39, *Ia KTB Ost Nr. 1, 1.Geb.Div.*, 22.6.41.

83   Burdick, *Hubert Lanz*, 102–3; Lanz, *Gebirgsjäger. Die 1. Gebirgsdivision 1935–1945*, 136.

84   NARA, T-315, Roll 39, *Ia KTB Ost Nr. 1, 1.Geb.Div.*, 22.6.41; Burdick, *Hubert Lanz*, 103; Lanz, *Gebirgsjäger. Die 1. Gebirgsdivision 1935–1945*, 136.

85   Burdick, *Hubert Lanz*, 103; Lanz, *Gebirgsjäger. Die 1. Gebirgsdivision 1935–1945*, 136. Supporting Picker's regiment in Oleszyce were combat engineers (3./Geb.Pi.Btl.54), a flak company (6./Fla.48), and a battery of 75mm assault guns (1./Stug.Abt.243). NARA, T-315, Roll 39, *Ia KTB Ost Nr. 1, 1.Geb.Div.*, 22.6.41.

86   Burdick, *Hubert Lanz*, 103.

87   Meyer, *Die 1. Gebirgs-Division*, 54; Lanz, *Gebirgsjäger. Die 1. Gebirgsdivision 1935–1945*, 136; Burdick, *Hubert Lanz*, 103–4.

88   Burdick, *Hubert Lanz*, 104; Kaltenegger, *Weg und Kampf der 1. Gebirgs-Division*, 210–11; Lanz, *Wie es zum Russlandfeldzug kam—und warum wir ihn verloren haben*, 36; NARA, T-315, Roll 39, *Ia KTB Ost Nr. 1, 1.Geb.Div.*, 22.6.41. For the elite troops of 1 Mountain Division, the difficult and costly fighting would go on in the days ahead. On June 25, 1941, the division had its initial encounter with Soviet T-34 tanks, against which, to Lanz's amazement, its 37mm AT guns were utterly useless. To defeat the T-34s, the *Gebirgsjäger* resorted to the tactic of letting the heavy Russian tanks roll over their foxholes and then attacking them from behind with grenades and explosive charges. By July 1, 1941, the division had knocked out 200 Soviet tanks, but its own losses were correspondingly high. Meyer, *Die 1. Gebirgs-Division*, 55; Kaltenegger, *Weg und Kampf der 1. Gebirgs-Division*, 215.

89   *DRZW*, Vol. IV, *Beiheft*, "*Ausgangslage zum 22.6.1941*"; NARA, T-312, Roll 668, *Ia KTB AOK 17*, 22.6.41.

90   Hans von Tettau and Kurt Versock, *Geschichte der 24. Infanterie-Division 1935–1945*, 46.

91   Ibid., 48.

92   Ibid., 48.

93   Ibid., 48.

94   Ibid., 48.

95   NARA, T-312, Roll 668, *Ia KTB AOK 17*, 22.6.41.

96   Tettau and Versock, *Geschichte der 24. Infanterie-Division 1935–1945*, 48–49; NARA, T-312, Roll 668, *Ia KTB AOK 17*, 22.6.41; Haupt, *Die Schlachten der Heeresgruppe Süd*, 22.

97   A pictorial history of 71 ID (which includes a couple of good photographs of the Russian fortifications in the border region) notes that the division suffered "losses" on June 22 during the fighting at the frontier. Hans Nölke, *Die 71. Infanterie-Division im Zweiten Weltkrieg 1939–1945*, 43.

98   The diary is typed; however, the words the diarist (or someone else on the staff) scribbled in above the sentence in question are so tiny as to be impossible to decipher. NARA, T-311, Roll 260, *KTB H.Gr.Süd*, 22.6.41.

99   TsAMO RF, F. 229, Op. 9776ss, D. 63, Ll. 5–10, "*Operativnaya Svodka Shtaba Yugo-Zapadnogo Fronta No. 1 k 19 Chasam 22 Iyunya 1941 o Boevykh Deistviyakh Voisk Fronta, Seriya 'G'*" (Operational Report No. 01, Southwestern Front Headquarters, as of 1900, June 22, 1941, on the Combat Activities of the Front's Troops, Series "G"), in: SBDVOV: Vol. 36: 12.

100   Pleshakov, *Stalin's Folly*, 168–69.

101   All told, units of 8 Mechanized Corps covered an average of 81 kilometers on June 22. TsAMO RF, F. 229, Op. 3789ss, D. 6. Ll. 116-121, "*Opisanie Komandirom 8-go Mekhanizirovannogo Korpusa Boevykh Deistvii Korpusa s 22 Iyunya po 29 Iyunya 1941 g. Sov. Sekretno*" (A Description by the Commander of the 8 Mechanized Corps of the Corps' Combat Activities from June 22 through June 29, 1941. Top Secret), in: SBDVOV, Vol. 33: 164.

102   Pleshakov, *Stalin's Folly*, 169; Forczyk, *Tank Warfare on the Eastern Front 1941–42*, 32.

103   Pleshakov, *Stalin's Folly*, 169–71.

104   Ibid., 171.

105   Ibid., 171.

106   Ibid., 172–73.

107   The 8 Mechanized Corps had been formed in July 1940. Glantz, *Red Army Ground Forces in June 1941*, 21.

108   TsAMO RF, F. 229, Op. 3789ss, D. 6. Ll. 116-121, "*Opisanie Komandirom 8-go Mekhanizirovannogo Korpusa Boevykh Deistvii Korpusa s 22 Iyunya po 29 Iyunya 1941 g. Sov. Sekretno*" (A Description by the Commander of the 8 Mechanized Corps of the Corps' Combat Activities from June 22 through June 29, 1941. Top Secret), in: SBDVOV, Vol. 33: 168–69.

109   Ibid., 169–70.

110   A. V. Egorov, *S veroj v pobedu* (*Zapiski komandira tankovogo polka*) (With the Belief in Victory [Records of the Commander of a Tank Regiment]), 15–18. It is unclear what tanks Egorov might have been referring to. The only German tanks even remotely close to Egorov's unit at this time would have belonged to 11 Panzer Division, which had crossed the frontier near Sokal'. It's possible that the "tanks" seen here by the Russians were, in fact, assault guns.

111   Because operations of Reichenau's Sixth Army and Kleist's 1 Panzer Group were so closely coordinated on June 22 (six infantry divisions of Sixth Army had been temporarily assigned to the panzer group), I considered merging their operations into a single (chapter) subsection, instead of separate subsections. After some deliberation, however, I decided for the sake of consistency to address Sixth Army and 1 Panzer Group in separate portions of this chapter. Thus, even if somewhat artificial in the case of Sixth Army, I am limiting my account of its operations to just those divisions in its official order of battle on June 22 (as I have done throughout the text for all armies and panzer groups).

112   *DRZW*, Vol. IV, *Beiheft*, "*Ausgangslage zum 22.6.1941*"; Mitcham Jr., *The Men of Barbarossa*, 182; www.lexikon-der-wehrmacht.de.

113   Mitcham Jr., *The Men of Barbarossa*, 178–79.

114   GFM von Rundstedt liked Reichenau's order so much that he sent it on to the other armies under his command. Megargee, *War of Annihilation*, 124–25; Hartmann, *Wehrmacht im Ostkrieg*, 653. For the role of Reichenau's Sixth Army in the mass killings of Jews and other "undesirables" in Russia in 1941 see, Hürter, *Hitlers Heerführer*, 575–85.

115   Halder, *War Diary*, 604; www.lexikon-der-wehrmacht.de.

116   The six infantry divisions loaned to Kleist were quickly returned to Sixth Army; an order of battle for June 27, 1941, shows the army with thirteen divisions. *GSWW*, Vol. IV: 550.

117   "*Kriegsgliederung Barbarossa*," *Stand 18.6.41*, Kurt Mehner (ed.); *DRZW*, Vol. IV, *Beiheft*, "*Schematische Kriegsgliederung Stand: B-Tag 1941 (22.6.) 'Barbarossa.'*"

118   "*Kriegsgliederung Barbarossa*," *Stand 18.6.41*, Kurt Mehner (ed.).

119   "*Kriegsgliederung Barbarossa*," *Stand 18.6.41*, Kurt Mehner (ed.); Kurowski, *Balkenkreuz und Roter Stern. Der Luftkrieg über Russland 1941–1944*, 55.

120   *DRZW*, Vol. IV, *Beiheft*, "*Ausgangslage zum 22.6.1941*"; Thies, *Der Ostfeldzug—Ein Lageatlas*, "*Aufmarsch am 21.6.1941 abds., Heeresgruppe Mitte.*"

121   "*Aufmarschanweisung Barbarossa*," in: Halder, *KTB*, Vol. II: 466 (Appendix 2); *GSWW*, Vol. IV: 548; Luttichau, *The Road to Moscow*, IV: 6.

122   Official records of 9 ID show that, on June 21, 1941, it had a combat strength (*Gefechtsstärke*) of 13,751 men (5,068 horses), and a ration strength (*Verpflegungsstärke*) of 16,015 men (5,532 horses). A typical German infantry division on the eve of the Russian campaign possessed a ration strength of about

17,000 men. NARA, T-315, Roll 514, *Ia, IIa, IIb, Anlagen zum KTB Nr. 6*, "*Gefechts- und Verpflegungsstärken der 9. Inf.-Div*," 21.6.41.

123   Wagener, *Heeresgruppe Süd*, 49–50. By 0745 hours, lead elements of 11 PD were beginning to move up toward Sokal'. NARA, T-315, Roll 1969, *Ia KTB, Bd. 2, 297.Inf.Div.*, 22.6.41.

124   www.lexikon-der-wehrmacht.de (*Lageost Karte 22.6.1941*). Late that afternoon (1607 hours), Artillery Commander 15 (*Arko 15*) and most of his GHQ artillery (including 210mm heavy howitzers and 150mm medium howitzers) was subordinated to 9 ID to support its attack, which appears to have stalled. NARA, T-315, Roll 1969, *Ia KTB, Bd. 2, 297.Inf.Div.*, 22.6.41.

125   NARA, T-315, Roll 514, *Ia, IIa, IIb, Anlagen zum KTB Nr. 6*, "*Tätigkeitsbericht der 9.Inf.Div. Abt. IIa/ IIb. 1941, Monat Juni.*"

126   Not clear from context if the fog is artificial fog, laid down by the Germans or the Russians, or simply natural fog.

127   NARA, T-315, Roll 1969, *Ia KTB, Bd. 2, 297.Inf.Div.*, 22.6.41.

128   Ibid.

129   NARA, T-315, Roll 1969, *Ia KTB, Bd. 2, 297.Inf.Div.*, 22.6.41; www.lexikon-der-wehrmacht.de (*Lageost Karte 22.6.1941*). By the close of June 22, 44 Army Corps had reached the line Parchacz-Komarow. *KTB OKW*, Vol. I: 490.

130   NARA, T-315, Roll 1028, *Ia KTB, 62.Inf.Div.*, 22.6.41; NARA, T-315, Roll 965, *Ia KTB Nr. 5, 56.Inf.Div.*, 22.6.41.

131   Anatolij Kazakov, *Na Toj Davnijšej Vojne* (In This War of Long Ago) in: *Zvezda*, 5/2005, 61.

132   The 56 ID had a ration strength of 16,837 men and 5,235 horses. "*Gefechts- und Verpflegungsstärke der 56.I.D.*," 21.6.41, in: NARA, T-315, Roll, 965, *Ia, Ic, IIa KTB und Tätigkeitsberichte mit Anlagen, 56.Inf.Div.*, 1.6.–21.6.41.

133   Carell, *Hitler Moves East*, 26; *Geschichte der 56. Infanterie-Division 1938–1945*, 28.

134   *Geschichte der 56. Infanterie-Division 1938–1945*, 31.

135   Wagener, *Heeresgruppe Süd*, 51.

136   Cited in: Wagener, *Heeresgruppe Süd*, 51–52.

137   NARA, T-315, Roll 965, *Ia KTB Nr. 5, 56.Inf.Div.*, 23.6.41; *Geschichte der 56. Infanterie-Division 1938–1945*, 30.

138   *Geschichte der 56. Infanterie-Division 1938–1945*, 30. As noted in the war diary of 56 ID: "The primary difficulties of the first day of battle were the insufficient resupply with ammunition and the lack of artillery support. The reason for this was that the bridge was occupied by the march columns of 62 ID. At 1150 hours, the division received an order from the chief of staff [of 17 Army Corps] to clear all of its march columns from the bridge to make room for the artillery of 62 ID. As a result, the artillery of 56 ID, which was already changing position, was held up. This adversely affected the 192 IR in particular, as the enemy conducted numerous counterattacks, which were only beaten off with difficulty and with serious losses due to the dwindling supply of ammunition and lack of artillery support." NARA, T-315, Roll 965, *Ia KTB Nr. 5, 56.Inf.Div.*, 22.6.41.

139   Wagener, *Heeresgruppe Süd*, 50. The lead elements of 56 ID were approaching Luboml by the end of June 22; however, it would take several more days of intense combat until the town was finally in German hands. *Geschichte der 56. Infanterie-Division 1938–1945*, 30–31.

140   "*Verlustliste 62.Inf.Div.*," in: NARA, T-315, Roll 1028, *Ia KTB, 62.Inf.Div.*, 22.6.41. Unfortunately, the war diary of 62 ID for June 22, 1941, was virtually of no use, consisting as it did of some eighty words, and making it, by a long shot, the most succinct of the dozens of German *Kriegstagebücher* I examined for this book.

141   *Geschichte der 56. Infanterie-Division 1938–1945*, 32.

142   Mitcham Jr., *The Men of Barbarossa*, 168.

143   Friedrich-Christian Stahl, "*Generalfeldmarschall Ewald von Kleist*," in: *Hitlers militärische Elite*, Ueberschär (ed.), 103.

144   Averred Mitcham Jr.: "Kleist was indeed a surprise choice [for command of the panzer group], since he had never been favorably disposed to the *Panzerwaffe* and disliked the fact that armored fighting

vehicles were replacing his beloved horses with smelly engines. Why, then, did the High Command choose Kleist? Because they thought that the appointment of a competent conservative would be an effective counterweight to the perceived rashness of Heinz Guderian and his lieutenants." Mitcham Jr., *The Men of Barbarossa*, 170.

145 Stahl, "*Generalfeldmarschall Ewald von Kleist*," in: *Hitlers militärische Elite*, Ueberschär (ed.), 101–4.

146 In 1946, Kleist was put on trial for war crimes in Yugoslavia and received a fifteen-year sentence. Two years later he was extradited to Soviet Russia and charged with alienating local Soviet populations "through mildness and kindness." I. C. B. Dear (ed.), *The Oxford Guide to World War II*, 512–13; Stahl, "*Generalfeldmarschall Ewald von Kleist*," in: *Hitlers militärische Elite*, Ueberschär (ed.), 103–5; www.lexikon-der-wehrmacht.de.

147 Both the SS "Viking" and SS "L.A.H." were elite motorized infantry divisions of the *Waffen* (Armed) SS. The SS "L.A.H." (*Leibstandarte Adolf Hitler*) motorized infantry division was—for propaganda purposes at least—the most elite unit in the German armed forces, its origins reaching back to March 1933, when Hitler established a small headquarters guard of 120 specially selected SS men for his own personal security. "*Kriegsgliederung Barbarossa*," *Stand 18.6.41*, Kurt Mehner (ed.); Jentz (ed.), *Panzer Truppen*, 191–92; *DRZW*, Vol. IV, *Beiheft*, "*Schematische Kriegsgliederung Stand: B-Tag 1941 (22.6.) 'Barbarossa.'*"

148 "*Kriegsgliederung Barbarossa*," *Stand 18.6.41*, Kurt Mehner (ed.).

149 "*Kriegsgliederung Barbarossa*," *Stand 18.6.41*, Kurt Mehner (ed.); Kurowski, *Balkenkreuz und Roter Stern. Der Luftkrieg über Russland 1941–1944*, 55.

150 As noted by Eastern Front historian Robert Kirchubel, Artemenko's 87 RD was "paired up with the 1st Antitank Brigade in the Vladimir-Volynski area"; they would, said Kirchubel, administer a rude shock to 14 Panzer Division when it crossed the frontier. Robert Kirchubel, *Hitler's Panzer Armies on the Eastern Front*, 20–21.

151 *DRZW*, Vol. IV, *Beiheft*, "*Ausgangslage zum 22.6.1941*"; Erickson, *The Soviet High Command*, 592; Glantz, "The Border Battles on the Lutsk-Rovno Axis: 22 June–1 July 1941," in: Glantz (ed.), *Initial Period of War on the Eastern Front*, 250–52.

152 "*Aufmarschanweisung Barbarossa*," in: Halder, *KTB*, Vol. II: 465–66 (Appendix 2); Kirchubel, *Hitler's Panzer Armies on the Eastern Front*, 20.

153 *Panzer-Regiment 15, Abt. 1a "Befehl für den Angriff*," 21.6.1941, cited in: G. W. Schrodek, *Ihr Glaube galt dem Vaterland. Geschichte des Panzer-Regiments 15*, 119 (hereafter cited as, Schrodek, *Geschichte des Panzer-Regiments 15*).

154 NARA, T-313, Roll 3, *Ia KTB Nr. 6, Pz.AOK 1*, 21.6.41.

155 NARA, T-315, Roll 980, *Ia KTB Nr. 5, 57.Inf.Div.*, 22.6.41; Schrodek, *Geschichte des Panzer-Regiments 15*, 123.

156 Willibald G. (N02.5), Collection BfZ.

157 NARA, T-315, Roll 980, *Ia KTB Nr. 5, 57.Inf.Div.*, 22.6.41.

158 "Kol." is the German abbreviation for "Kolchose," or collective farm. Thus, "Kol. Rawszczyzna" would be the Soviet collective farm at, or near, Rawszczyzna.

159 NARA, T-315, Roll 1074, *Ia KTB Nr. 3, 75.Inf.Div.*, 22.6.41. The war diary doesn't say just what these "special weapons" were; most likely, they were flamethrowers, explosive charges, and perhaps 210mm heavy howitzers (or other heavy artillery) in a direct fire role.

160 Christine Alexander and Mason Kunze (eds.), *Eastern Inferno: The Journals of a German Panzerjäger on the Eastern Front, 1941–43*, 26–27.

161 The bulk of the Soviet 87 Rifle Division would be encircled and destroyed by elements of both 3 PzK and 29 AK. See map, "Lutsk-Rovno Axis, Situation, 2300 hrs, 23 June 1941," in: Glantz (ed.), *Atlas and Operational Summary*.

162 NARA, T-313, Roll 3, *Ia KTB Nr. 6, Pz.AOK 1*, 22.6.41; Glantz, "The Border Battles on the Lutsk-Rovno Axis: 22 June–1 July 1941," in: Glantz (ed.), *Initial Period of War on the Eastern Front*, 255, 261.

163 Eberhard von Mackensen, *Vom Bug zum Kaukasus. Das III. Panzerkorps im Feldzug gegen Sowjetrussland 1941/42*, 11.

164 NARA, T-315, Roll 656, *Ia KTB Nr. 2, 14.Pz.Div.*, 22.6.41.

165 *Gefr.* Franz S. (06 372), Collection BfZ.
166 NARA, T-315, Roll 911, *Ia KTB Nr. 7, 44.Inf.Div.*, 22.6.41.
167 NARA, T-315, Roll 1984, *Ia KTB Nr. 4, 298.Inf.Div.*, 22.6.41.
168 Ibid.
169 In the war diary of 1 Panzer Group, it states Tartakow was taken by 48 Panzer Corps at about 1100 hours; however, the diary of 75 Infantry Division records that the town was not completely in German hands until 1330, after overcoming staunch enemy resistance. NARA, T-315, Roll 1074, *Ia KTB Nr. 3, 75.Inf.Div.*, 22.6.41.
170 NARA, T-313, Roll 3, *Ia KTB Nr. 6, Pz.AOK 1*, 22.6.41; NARA, T-311, Roll 260, *KTB H.Gr.Süd*, 22.6.41.
171 NARA, T-315, Roll 2320, *Ia KTB, 11.Pz.Div.*, 22.6.41; Schrodek, *Geschichte des Panzer-Regiments 15*, 123.
172 Schrodek, *Geschichte des Panzer-Regiments 15*, 123–24.
173 NARA, T-313, Roll 3, *Ia KTB Nr. 6, Pz.AOK 1*, 22.6.41.
174 NARA, T-315, Roll 980, *Ia KTB Nr. 5, 57.Inf.Div.*, 22.6.41.
175 NARA, T-315, Roll 1074, *Ia KTB Nr. 3, 75.Inf.Div.*, 22./23.6.41. The Soviet bunkers were eventually finished off with hollow charge explosives and concentrated charges consisting of several explosive blocks tied together (*geballte Ladung*).
176 NARA, T-315, Roll 911, *Ia KTB Nr. 7, 44.Inf.Div.*, 22.6.41.
177 In the area of 3 Panzer Corps, even Soviet air forces were active. For example, 298 ID reported several enemy aerial attacks (without any active air defense), while 14 PD, forming up to begin its thrust across the Bug, was struck several times from the air, resulting in a number of dead and wounded. "*Tagesmeldung an Gen.Kdo. 3.Pz.K.*," 22.6.41, in: NARA, T-315, Roll 1985, *Ia Anlagen zum KTB Nr. 4, 298.Inf.Div.*, 16.–28.6.41; also, NARA, T-315, Roll 656, *Ia KTB Nr. 2, 14.Pz.Div.*, 22.6.41.
178 According to one German report, Red Army commissars locked some bunker crews into their bunkers, forcing them to fight to the death. The report, however, is unconfirmed. NARA, T-315, Roll 656, *Ia KTB Nr. 2, 14.Pz.Div.*, 22.6.41.
179 NARA, T-315, Roll 1984, *Ia KTB Nr. 4, 298.Inf.Div.*, 22.6.41. For a series of combat reports pertaining to the fighting on June 22, 1941, in the sector of 298 ID see, NARA, T-315, Roll 1985, *Ia Anlagen zum KTB Nr. 4, 298.Inf.Div.*, 16.–28.6.41.
180 The "local crises" (*örtliche Krisen*) in the sector of 298 ID were noted in the war diary of 44 ID at 0445 hours on June 23, 1941. NARA, T-315, Roll 911, *Ia KTB Nr. 7, 44.Inf.Div.*, 23.6.41.
181 NARA, T-313, Roll 3, *Ia KTB Nr. 6, Pz.AOK 1*, 22.6.41.
182 "Lutsk-Rovno Axis. Situation, 2300 hrs 24 June 1941," in: Glantz (ed.), *Atlas and Operational Summary*; Mackensen, *Vom Bug zum Kaukasus. Das III. Panzerkorps im Feldzug gegen Sowjetrussland 1941/42*, 11.
183 Glantz, "The Border Battles on the Lutsk-Rovno Axis: 22 June–1 July 1941," in: Glantz (ed.), *Initial Period of War on the Eastern Front*, 255–61.
184 Schrodek, *Geschichte des Panzer-Regiments 15*, 124–28; Kirchubel, *Hitler's Panzer Armies on the Eastern Front*, 21.
185 NARA, T-311, Roll 260, *KTB H.Gr.Süd*, 22.6.41.
186 Erickson, *The Road to Stalingrad*, 121, 131, 163.
187 Ibid., 131.
188 Glantz, "The Border Battles on the Lutsk-Rovno Axis: 22 June–1 July 1941," in: Glantz (ed.), *Initial Period of War on the Eastern Front*, 259.
189 *Tagebuch*, Paul R. (N02.1), Collection BfZ.

Chapter 6: Death from the Sky: The *Luftwaffe* Wreaks Havoc and Smashes the Soviet Air Force
1 Cited in: Muller, *The German Air War in Russia*, x. After the bitter failure of aerial operations over England in 1940/41, Jeschonnek was, no doubt, anticipating with some relief the impending war against Soviet Russia, where his air forces could once again return to their primary mission of supporting Ger-

man ground forces and, thus, help to replicate the stunning victories of the *Wehrmacht* in Poland, France, and the Balkans.

2   GFM v. Bock, *War Diary*, 224; H 08-22/9, *Nachlass GFM Fedor von Bock* (entry in war diary on June 22, 1941).

3   Muller, *The German Air War in Russia*, 2.

4   Lothar von Heinemann, "*Erste Kämpfe vom 22.6. bis ca. 3.7.41*," in: Karlsruhe Document Collection. (Hereafter cited as "KDC.")

5   Pleshakov, *Stalin's Folly*, 135.

6   The VVS, or *Voenno-vozdushnikh sil* = the Soviet air force.

7   Muller, *The German Air War in Russia*, 28.

8   If an air force enjoys air superiority, it is able to conduct operations without prohibitive interference by opposing air forces. Air supremacy goes even further, and exists after all opposing air forces have been effectively neutralized. Although the *Luftwaffe* did indeed enjoy air superiority (*Luftüberlegenheit*) in the opening stages of the war, total air supremacy (*Luftherrschaft*)—that desideratum of airpower enthusiasts everywhere—was achieved only for short periods over discreet sectors of the Eastern Front in the immediate wake of the invasion. Luther, *Barbarossa Unleashed*, 157.

9   *The Rise and Fall of the German Air Force 1933 to 1945*, Reproduction of Air Ministry Pamphlet No. 248, 166.

10   "*Aufmarschanweisung Barbarossa*," in: Halder, *KTB*, Vol. II: 468 (Appendix 2).

11   *GSWW*, Vol. IV: 372.

12   *GSWW*, Vol. IV: 364; Jochen Prien, et al., *Die Jagdfliegerverbände der Deutschen Luftwaffe, Teil 6/I, Unternehmen "Barbarossa," Einsatz im Osten 22.6. bis 5.12.1941*, 28 (hereafter cited as, Prien, et al., *Die Jagdfliegerverbände der Deutschen Luftwaffe*).

13   BA-MA RL 200/17, Hoffmann von Waldau, *Tagebuch*, 22.6.41. Wrote von Waldau: "*Im Grossen ist mit durchschlagendem Erfolg zu rechnen.*"

14   *GSWW*, Vol. IV, 764; "*Der Luftkrieg im Osten gegen Russland 1941. (Aus einer Studie der 8. Abteilung 1943/1944),*" KDC; Prien, et al., *Die Jagdfliegerverbände der Deutschen Luftwaffe*, 12–13; Magenheimer, *Moskau 1941. Entscheidungsschlacht im Osten*, 36–37.

15   Prien, et al., *Die Jagdfliegerverbände der Deutschen Luftwaffe*, 12.

16   Because most Soviet fighters "were light and slow, a ram wasn't necessarily fatal for the desperate crew if they had their parachutes ready; if they didn't damage the fuel tank, they could leap from the flaming plane. Nonetheless, instant death was probable." Pleshakov, *Stalin's Folly*, 140.

17   David M. Glantz and Jonathan House, *When Titans Clashed: How the Red Army Stopped Hitler*, 38. Noted Glantz and House: "Both in Spain and in the opening battles of 1941, Red Air Force tactics tended to be very rigid. Throughout the disastrous summer of 1941, Soviet bombers stubbornly attacked at an altitude of 8000 feet, too high to ensure accurate bombing but low enough for German fighters to locate and attack them."

18   Kesselring, *Soldat Bis Zum Letzten Tag*, 120.

19   Ziemke and Bauer, *Moscow to Stalingrad: Decision in the East*, 6.

20   Muller, *The German Air War in Russia*, 31–32.

21   Ibid., 32.

22   Capt. Eric Brown, *Wings of the Luftwaffe: Flying German Aircraft of the Second World War*, 122–31; Piekalkiewicz, *Die Schlacht um Moskau. Die erfrorene Offensive*, 278.

23   David T. Zabecki (ed.), *World War II in Europe—An Encyclopedia*, 865–66; Luther, *Barbarossa Unleashed*, 131.

24   Brown, *Wings of the Luftwaffe*, 27; Maj. Friedrich Lang, *Aufzeichnungen aus der Sturzkampffliegerei*, 6–7; www.lexikon-der-wehrmacht.de.

25   Hans Joachim Schröder, *Die gestohlenen Jahre. Erzählgeschichten und Geschichtserzählung im Interview: Der Zweite Weltkrieg aus der Sicht ehemaliger Mannschaftssoldaten*, 512–14.

26   Johannes Steinhoff, et al. (eds.), *Voices from the Third Reich: An Oral History*, 137–39. The *Stuka* pilot, Siegfried Fischer, was shot down thirteen times in all.

27   Christer Bergström and Andrey Mikhailov, *Black Cross Red Star: Air War over the Eastern Front*, Vol. I: *Operation Barbarossa 1941*, 11 (hereafter cited as, Bergström and Mikhailov, *Black Cross Red Star*, Vol. I). The only significant deficiency of the Bf-109 was its relatively short range—about 600 kilometers for the Bf-109E, and 710 for the Bf-109F. *GSWW*, Vol. IV: 374–75 (Table I.iv.7).

28   Christopher Shores, *Luftwaffe Fighter Units Russia 1941–45*, 3.

29   Corum, *Wolfram von Richthofen*, 270. The SD-2 was also used against parked aircraft and airfield installations. Prien, et al., *Die Jagdfliegerverbände der deutschen Luftwaffe*, 33.

30   Prien, et al., *Die Jagdfliegerverbände der deutschen Luftwaffe*, 34–35, f.n. 101; Cajus Bekker, *The Luftwaffe War Diaries*, 219–20.

31   At the start of the Russian campaign, the *Luftwaffe* had just 102 Bf-110 *Zerstörer* aircraft in the East, of which sixty-four were operational; virtually all of these aircraft were assigned to Kesselring's 2 Air Fleet. *GSWW*, Vol. IV: 364.

32   Bergström and Mikhailov, *Black Cross Red Star*, Vol. I: 7, 11–12; Muller, *The German Air War in Russia*, 33.

33   Muller, *The German Air War in Russia*, 33–35.

34   *DRZW*, Vol. IV, *Beiheft*, "*Aufmarsch der deutschen Luftflotten 1, 2, und 4 an der Ostfront*"; Mitcham Jr., *The Men of Barbarossa*, 151; www.lexikon-der-wehrmacht.de.

35   *GSWW*, Vol. VI: 364.

36   *GSWW*, Vol. IV: 368; *DRZW*, Vol. IV: 310; Bergström and Mikhailov, *Black Cross Red Star*, Vol. I (Appendix III: *Luftwaffe* Order of Battle, 21 June 1941), 263–64. The replacement groups were essentially reserve units.

37   *GSWW*, Vol. IV: 367; Haupt, *Heeresgruppe Nord 1941–1945*, 25; Plocher, *The German Air Force Versus Russia, 1941*, 140–42; Kurowski, *Balkenkreuz und Roter Stern. Der Luftkrieg über Russland 1941–1944*, 129.

38   *GSWW*, Vol. IV: 367.

39   The precise number of *Luftwaffe* planes taking part in the first major assault wave is unclear. According to David Glantz, the attack was carried out by 500 bombers, 270 divebombers, and 480 fighters (Glantz, *Barbarossa*, 35). Martin van Creveld, however, stated that the first attack was conducted with 637 bombers (and divebombers) and 231 fighter aircraft. Creveld's figures, however, seem on the low side. (Martin van Creveld, et al., *Air Power and Maneuver Warfare*, 69.)

40   *GSWW*, Vol. IV, 764.

41   Prien, et al., *Die Jagdfliegerverbände der deutschen Luftwaffe*, 34–35; Erickson, *The Road to Stalingrad*, 113–14.

42   *GSWW*, Vol. IV: 765; Mawdsley, *Thunder in the East*, 58.

43   Luther, *Barbarossa Unleashed*, 404.

44   At 0510 hours on June 22, the Soviet Baltic Special Military District reported that enemy air forces had already bombed airfields at [Ventspils], Panevėžys, Siauliai, and Kaunas. TsAMO RF, F. 221, Op. 2467ss, D. 39, Ll. 101-103, "*Donesenie Komanduyushchego Pribaltiiskim Osobym Voennym Okrugom ot 22 Iyunya 1941 g. Narodnomu Komissaru Oborony SSSR o Nachale Nemtsami Boevykh Deistvii Protiv Voisk Okruga. Sovershenno Sekretno*" (Report by the Commander of the Baltic Special Military District on June 22, 1941, to the USSR People's Commissar of Defense on the Beginning of the Germans' Military Actions Against the District's Forces. Top Secret), in: SBDVOV, Vol. 34: 35.

45   Plocher, *The German Air Force Versus Russia, 1941*, 142.

46   NARA, T-311, Roll 53, *Ia KTB H.Gr.Nord*, 22.6.41; NARA, T-315, Roll 322, *KTB Nr. 3, 6. Schützen Brigade*, 22.6.41; *DRZW*, Vol. IV, *Beiheft*, "*Aufmarsch der deutschen Luftflotten 1, 2, und 4 an der Ostfront*." For a detailed account of the operations of Air Leader Baltic see, Plocher, *The German Air Force Versus Russia, 1941*, 144, 174–77. "On the whole," opined Plocher, "the [Air Leader] Baltic carried out successfully the assigned tasks within the limits of the forces available. Despite the very high fighting spirit of the crews and the best intentions of the command, these tasks could not be fully accomplished because the [Air Leader] Baltic had too few units and did not always have the type of planes best suited to the operations."

47   Bergström and Mikhailov, *Black Cross Red Star*, Vol. I: 30.

48   Ibid., Vol. I: 30.

49   Ibid., Vol. I: 30–31.

50   Ibid., Vol. I: 40, 42. Despite staggering losses, many Soviet fighter pilots would bravely challenge the enemy in the air throughout the day, with some pilots logging more than ten individual sorties. Yet there were, of course, many different reactions among the Soviet pilots. Some, stunned no doubt by the ferocity of the German onslaught, evinced "an increased reluctance to enter battle as the day continued." Ibid., 42.

51   Bergström and Mikhailov, *Black Cross Red Star*, Vol. I: 40; *DRZW*, Vol. IV, *Beiheft*, "*Aufmarsch der deutschen Luftflotten 1, 2, und 4 an der Ostfront*." According to one Soviet report, the VVS bombed the East Prussian city of Tilsit "throughout the day." TsAMO RF, F. 344, Op. 5554, D. 71, Ll. 60-61, "*Operativnaya Svodka No. 7, 18:00, 22.6.41, Shtab 8 Armii, Bubyai*" (Combat Report No. 7, 1800, June 22, 1941, Head-quarters 8 Army, Bubiai).

52   Bergström and Mikhailov, *Black Cross Red Star*, Vol. I: 40.

53   The Ju-88A, designed as a "fast bomber" (*Schnellbomber*), had a maximum speed of about 470 km/h. By comparison, the He-111H and Do-17Z boasted top speeds of just over 400 km/h. I. C. B. Dear (ed.), *The Oxford Guide to World War II*, 112.

54   Haupt, *Heeresgruppe Nord 1941–1945*, 26; Merridale, *Ivan's War*, 85; Taylor, *Barbarossa to Berlin*, 33; Forczyk, *Tank Warfare on the Eastern Front 1941–42*, 39; David M. Glantz, "The Border Battles, 22 June–1 July 1941," in: Glantz (ed.), *Atlas and Operational Summary*, 19.

55   TsAMO RF, F. 221, Op. 1351, D. 64, Ll. 2-3, "*Telegramma s Informatsiei v Shtab 8 Armii, 10:00, 22.6.41*" (A telegram with information for the headquarters of 8 Army); TsAMO RF, F. 344, Op. 5554, D. 71, Ll. 60-61, "*Operativnaya Svodka No. 7, 18:00, 22.6.41, Shtab 8 Armii, Bubyai*" (Combat Report No. 7, 1800, June 22, 1941, Headquarters 8 Army, Bubiai).

56   Seaton, *The Russo-German War 1941–1945*, 102–3.

57   Aerial reconnaissance would play a major role in *Luftwaffe* operations from June 22 onward. For example, photoreconnaissance, conducted by the Germans on a "grand scale," "disclosed the existence of numerous additional [Soviet] airfields, 130 of which were identified and attacked during the next few days." Creveld, et al., *Air Power and Maneuver Warfare*, 69.

58   NARA, T-311, Roll 53, *Ia KTB H.Gr.Nord*, 22.6.41; *KTB OKW*, Vol. I: 491. These tanks and other vehicles were most likely strong components of Maj.-Gen. N. M. Shestapolov's 12 Mechanized Corps.

59   Plocher, *The German Air Force Versus Russia, 1941*, 143–44. According to data of the *Luftwaffe* High Command (OKL), Förster's 1 Air Corps alone had shot down 487 Soviet planes and destroyed 1,211 more on the ground by July 13, 1941. Kurowski, *Balkenkreuz und Roter Stern. Der Luftkampf über Russland 1941–1944*, 132–33.

60   Plocher, *The German Air Force Versus Russia*, 291.

61   Mitcham Jr., *The Men of Barbarossa*, 70.

62   Recalled Kesselring, "I instructed my air force and flak generals to consider the wishes of the army as my orders, without prejudice to their subordination to me, unless serious air interests made compliance seem impracticable or detrimental. All my commanding officers and I prided ourselves on anticipating the wishes of the army and on carrying out any reasonable requests as quickly and as completely as we could." Albert Kesselring, *The Memoirs of Field-Marshal Kesselring*, 88–89.

63   Kesselring, *Soldat Bis Zum Letzten Tag*, 111–12.

64   Kesselring, *Soldat Bis Zum Letzten Tag*, 112, 116; *The Rise and Fall of the German Air Force 1933 to 1945*, Reproduction of Air Ministry Pamphlet No. 248, 165.

65   Military historian Robert A. Forczyk posits the somewhat lower figure of 273 Ju-87B divebombers in the 2 Air Fleet's inventory on June 22, 1941—158 in its 8 Air Corps, and 115 in its 2 Air Corps. Unfortunately, the author provides no source(s) to support his assertion. Forcyzk, *Tank Warfare on the Eastern Front 1941–42*, 44, 47.

66   *GSWW*, Vol. IV: 363, 366–67.

67   Sources conflict, and it is possible this bomber wing may have flown other bombers in addition to the Do-17Z.

68   *GSWW*, Vol. IV: 368–69; *DRZW*, Vol. IV: 310; Bergström and Mikhailov, *Black Cross Red Star*, Vol. I (Appendix III: *Luftwaffe* Order of Battle, 21 June 1941), 264–65.

69   Stahel, *Operation Barbarossa and Germany's Defeat in the East*, 126–27; Corum, *Wolfram von Richthofen*, 267; Murray, *Strategy for Defeat. The Luftwaffe 1933–1945*, 81. The 8 Air Corps' late deployment may also have been part of the German deception plan to conceal the buildup in the East from the Soviets as long as possible.

70   Kershaw, *War Without Garlands*, 31–33; Glantz, *Barbarossa*, 35.

71   For a graphic account of the destruction of Soviet 4 Army headquarters early on June 22 see, Pleshakov, *Stalin's Folly*, 105–6.

72   *GSWW*, Vol. IV: 764; Hoyt, *Stalin's War. Tragedy and Triumph 1941–1945*, 28–30; Hans Ulrich Rudel, *Stuka Pilot*, 17; Erickson, *The Road to Stalingrad*, 118; Haupt, *Army Group Center: The Wehrmacht in Russia 1941–1945*, 27; Corum, *Wolfram von Richthofen*, 267.

73   Michael Burleigh, *The Third Reich: A New History*, 487.

74   Cited in: Burleigh, *The Third Reich: A New History*, 488.

75   TsAMO RF, F. 208, Op. 3038SS, D. 15, L. 7, "*Boevoe Donesenie Shtaba 3-i Armii No. 2/op k 7 Chasam 30 Minutam 22 Iyunya 1941 g. Nachal'niku Shtaba Zapadnogo Osobogo Voennogo Okruga o Boevykh Deistviyakh Voisk Protivnika. Seria 'G'*" (Combat Report No. 2/op, Headquarters of 3 Army by 0730 on June 22, 1941, to the Chief of Staff of the Western Special Military District on the Combat Activities of the Enemy's Forces. Series "G"), in: SBDVOV, Vol. 35: 136.

76   TsAMO RF, F. 208, Op. 2454ss, D. 26, Ll. 85-86, "*Boevoe Donesenie Shtaba Zapadnogo Osobogo Voennogo Okruga No. 002/op k 6 Chasam 22 Iyunya 1941g. o Boevykh Deistviyakh Protivnika Protiv Voisk Okruga. Osobo Sekretno*" (Combat Report No. 002/op by the Headquarters of the Western Special Military District as of 0600 on June 22, 1941, on the Enemy's Combat Activities Against the District's Troops. Very Secret), in: SBDVOV, Vol. 35: 15; also, TsAMO RF, F. 208, Op. 10169ss, D. 4, Ll. 22-24, "*Boevoe Donesenie Shtaba Zapadnogo Osobogo Voennogo Okruga No. 005/op ot 22 Iyunya 1941 g. o Khode Boevykh Deistvii Voisk Okruga. Seriya 'G'*" (Combat Report No, 005/op by the Headquarters of the Western Special Military District from June 22, 1941, on the Course of Combat Activities by the District's Troops. Series "G"), in: SBDVOV, Vol. 35: 17; also, TsAMO RF, F. 208, Op. 3038ss, D. 15, Ll. 1-3, "*Razvedivatel'naya Svodka Shtaba Zapadnogo Fronta No. 1 k 19 Chasam 22 Iyunya 1941 g. o Deistviyakh Protivnika Protiv Voisk Fronta. Seriya 'G'*" (Intelligence Report No. 1 from the Headquarters of the Western Front by 1900 June 22, 1941, on the Enemy's Activities Against the Front's Troops. Series "G"), in: SBDVOV, Vol. 35: 19–20.

77   *GSWW*, Vol. IV: 764; Creveld, et al., *Air Power and Maneuver Warfare*, 69.

78   Bergström and Mikhailov, *Black Cross Red Star*, Vol. I: 31

79   Kurowski, *Balkenkreuz und Roter Stern. Der Luftkrieg über Russland 1941–1944*, 58–59; DRZW, Vol. IV, Beiheft, "*Aufmarsch der deutschen Luftflotten 1, 2, und 4 an der Ostfront.*"

80   Bergström and Mikhailov, *Black Cross Red Star*, Vol. I: 31–32, 40.

81   Cited in: Bergström and Mikhailov, *Black Cross Red Star*, Vol. I: 32.

82   Ibid., 32.

83   Bergström and Mikhailov, *Black Cross Red Star*, Vol. I: 32; Kurowski, *Balkenkreuz und Roter Stern. Der Luftkrieg über Russland 1941–1944*, 58–59. (Note: The "culture" of the *Luftwaffe* was such that every effort was made to accurately ascertain the destruction of enemy aircraft; a "kill" was not credited to a pilot without unequivocal evidence that it had indeed taken place.)

84   Bekker, *The Luftwaffe War Diaries*, 220–21.

85   Bergström and Mikhailov, *Black Cross Red Star*, Vol. I: 41.

86   Ibid., 37–38.

87   A subsequent report by 3 Panzer Group stated that, on June 22, 1941, cooperation with 8 Air Corps had been "particularly close and active [*besonders eng und lebendig*]," and that air supremacy (*Herrschaft im Luftraum*) had been almost completely achieved on the first day of the campaign. BA-MA RH 21-3/732, "*Gefechtsberichte Russland 1941/42.*"

88   Heinz Knoke, *I Flew for the Führer*, 46–47.

89   Ibid., 48.

90   *GSWW*, Vol. IV: 764.

91 Prien, et al., *Die Jagdfliegerverbände der deutschen Luftwaffe*, 13; see also, Luther, *Barbarossa Unleashed*, 220.

92 Rudel, *Stuka Pilot*, 16–17.

93 Muller, *The German Air War in Russia*, 122–23.

94 Mölders had scored more aerial victories (fourteen) than any other pilot in the *Legion Condor* during the Spanish Civil War. As *Gruppenkommandeur* of III./JG 53 during the western campaign of 1940 he was the first to achieve twenty kills against the western allies, for which he became the first fighter pilot to garner the prestigious Knight's Cross. By the start of the Russian campaign, he had solidified his status as a German national hero. Mölders had formally taken command of JG 51 in July 1940. John Weal, *Jagdgeschwader 51 "Mölders,"* 27.

95 Prien, et al., *Die Jagdfliegerverbände der Deutschen Luftwaffe*, 206, 220; Domarus, *Hitler. Reden und Proklamationen*, Vol. II: 1739; *DRZW*, Vol. IV, *Beiheft*, "*Aufmarsch der deutschen Luftflotten 1, 2, und 4 an der Ostfront.*"

96 BA-MA RH 20-4/1199, *KTB AOK 4*, 23.6.41.

97 Prien, et al., *Die Jagdfliegerverbände der Deutschen Luftwaffe*, 220; Weal, *Jagdgeschwader 51 "Mölders,"* 64, 73–74.

98 Weal, *Jagdgeschwader 51 "Mölders,"* 74.

99 Siegwald Ganglmair, "*Generaloberst* Alexander Löhr," in: *Hitlers militärische Elite*, Ueberschär (ed.), 123–26; Gilbert, *Second World War*, 13; *DRZW*, Vol. IV, *Beiheft*, "*Aufmarsch der deutschen Luftflotten 1, 2, und 4 an der Ostfront.*"

100 The Royal Romanian Air Force, or FARR, was outfitted with some German-made machines (He-112B single-engine fighters, similar to the Bf-109), fighters of Polish design, British-made Hawker Hurricanes, and bombers of British, French, Polish, and Italian provenance. Bergström and Mikhailov, *Black Cross Red Star*, Vol. I: 39.

101 *GSWW*, Vol. IV: 362–64. As noted in the quasi-official German history of the Second World War, a "curious aspect of the structure of 4 Air Fleet was its lack of close-combat formations, even though a dive-bomber *Gruppe* had originally been envisaged for 4 Air Corps. Instead the air fleet had at its disposal, for direct battlefield support, two Ju-88 bomber *Gruppen* equipped with dropping-devices for SD-2 anti-personnel fragmentation bombs and a fighter *Gruppe* similarly equipped." *GSWW*, Vol. IV: 365.

102 *GSWW*, Vol. IV: 369–70: *DRZW*, Vol. IV: 311; Bergström and Mikhailov, *Black Cross Red Star*, Vol. I: 265.

103 Kurowski, *Balkenkreuz und Roter Stern. Der Luftkrieg über Russland 1941–1944*, 68.

104 Ibid., 69.

105 Bergström and Mikhailov, *Black Cross Red Star*, Vol. I: 32; Erickson, *The Road to Stalingrad*, 121.

106 Erickson, *The Road to Stalingrad*, 121.

107 Kurowski, *Balkenkreuz und Roter Stern. Der Luftkrieg über Russland 1941–1944*, 70.

108 Cited in: Bergström and Mikhailov, *Black Cross Red Star*, Vol. I: 32.

109 Wagener, *Heeresgruppe Süd*, 50–51.

110 Following his 101st victory, Lützow (like Mölders before him) was immediately banned from flying further combat missions (*Feindflugverbot*). Prien, et al., *Die Jagdfliegerverbände der Deutschen Luftwaffe*, 42.

111 *DRZW*, Vol. IV, *Beiheft*, "*Aufmarsch der deutschen Luftflotten 1, 2, und 4 an der Ostfront*"; Prien, et al., *Die Jagdfliegerverbände der Deutschen Luftwaffe*, 42–51; 54.

112 Jochen Prien and Gerhard Stemmer, *Jagdgeschwader 3 "Udet" in World War II*. Vol. II: *II./JG 3 in Action with the Messerschmitt Bf 109*, 70.

113 Prien, et al., *Die Jagdfliegerverbände der Deutschen Luftwaffe*, 123.

114 Cited in: Bergström and Mikhailov, *Black Cross Red Star*, Vol. I: 34.

115 As noted in Southwestern Front's "Operational Report No. 1," issued 1900 hours, "throughout the day the enemy air force repeatedly bombed Lutsk, Luboml, Vladimir Volynski, Kovel', and Rovno." L'vov was also struck repeatedly, as were other towns and cities. TsAMO RF, F. 229, Op. 9776ss, D. 63, Ll. 5-10, "*Operativnaya Svodka Shtaba Yugo-Zapadnogo Fronta No. 1 k 19 Chasam 22 Iyunya 1941 o Boevykh Deistvi-*

yakh Voisk Fronta. Seriya 'G'" (Operational Report No. 01, Southwestern Front Headquarters, as of 1900, June 22, 1941, on the Combat Activities of the Front's Troops. Series "G"), in: SBDVOV, Vol. 36: 11–13.

116   Merridale, *Ivan's War*, 82–83. The German attack on Sevastopol was most likely conducted by 4 Air Corps' KG 27, perhaps supported by II./KG 4.

117   *DRZW*, Vol. IV, *Beiheft*, *"Aufmarsch der deutschen Luftflotten 1, 2, und 4 an der Ostfront."*

118   Cited in: Bergström and Mikhailov, *Black Cross Red Star*, Vol. I: 33.

119   Kurowski, *Balkenkreuz und Roter Stern. Der Luftkrieg über Russland 1941–1944*, 60–61; Bergström and Mikhailov, *Black Cross Red Star*, Vol. I: 36.

120   Bergström and Mikhailov, *Black Cross Red Star*, Vol. I: 34.

121   BA-MA RL 8/31, *Generalkommando des IV. Fliegerkorps Abt. Ic*, *"Lagebericht v. 22.6.41*,*"* cited in: Murray, *Strategy for Defeat*, 81, 110 (f.n. 77). According to Carl Wagener, a total of 300 VVS planes were destroyed by 4 Air Fleet on June 22, 1941, but this figure is certainly too low. Wagener, *Heeresgruppe Süd*, 50–51.

122   Kurowski, *Balkenkreuz und Roter Stern. Der Luftkrieg über Russland 1941–1944*, 70.

123   Ibid., 70.

124   Halder, *War Diary*, 438.

125   East Prussian cities struck by the Soviet air force in the opening days of the war included Königsberg, Memel', Tilsit, and Gumbinnen. Kurowski, *Balkenkreuz und Roter Stern. Der Luftkrieg über Russland 1941–1944*, 131.

126   Bekker, *The Luftwaffe War Diaries*, 221.

127   Kesselring, *Soldat Bis Zum Letzten Tag*, 120.

128   *GSWW*, Vol. IV: 766.

129   Ibid., 766.

130   Typical of the perspective that the VVS was largely a spent force (for months) after the first days of the war is this observation by historian Earl F. Ziemke: "Having committed the irreversible error of basing its main forces close to the border in anticipation of an offensive mission, the Red Army Air Force was largely demolished on the ground and in the air by nightfall on 22 June and would not recover significantly before the end of the year." Earl F. Ziemke, *The Red Army, 1918–1941: From Vanguard of World Revolution to US Ally*, 277.

131   More than 900 of the VVS losses on June 22, 1941, were attributed to the operations of Kesselring's 2 Air Fleet alone. *GSWW*, Vol. IV: 764; *"Der Luftkrieg im Osten gegen Russland 1941. (Aus einer Studie der 8. Abteilung 1943/1944)*,*"* KDC.

132   The figures on Soviet air losses were so fantastic that Air Marshal Göring initially dismissed them. Recalled Kesselring: "Reports on aircraft shot down in the air and destroyed on the ground reached approximately 2500 planes, a figure that *Reichsmarschall* Göring at first refused to believe. When, after the area had been secured, he had the figures verified, he had to tell me that the real figures were around 200–300 higher." Kesselring, *Soldat Bis Zum Letzen Tag*, 119–20.

133   Franz Halder, *Kriegstagebuch: Tägliche Aufzeichnungen des Chefs des Generalstabes des Heeres 1939–1942*, Bd. III: *Der Russlandfeldzug bis zum Marsch auf Stalingrad (22.6.1941–24.9.1942)*, Hans-Adolf Jacobsen and Alfred Philippi (eds.), 11 (hereafter cited as, Halder, *KTB*, Vol. III).

134   *GSWW*, 764.

135   Another factor contributing to the rapid recuperation of the VVS was that in the first days of war, "the numbers [of aircraft] destroyed on the ground were many times more than those shot down while airborne. One fact that should have been borne in mind, however, and that was not given enough attention by the German Command, was that in these circumstances Soviet losses in personnel were far smaller than in matériel. This explains in part the unexpectedly rapid recovery of the Soviet forces." Gen.-Lt. a.D. Walter Schwabedissen, *The Russian Air Force in the Eyes of German Commanders*, USAF Historical Studies: No. 175, 53–54.

136   *GSWW*, Vol. IV: 804–5.

137   In August and early September 1941, Soviet bombers, in retaliation for the German bombing of Moscow, conducted ten night raids on Berlin, although damage was minimal. From July 10 to September

30, 1941, Soviet Long-Range Bomber Aviation and bombers of the Red Banner Baltic and Red Banner Black Sea fleets struck enemy industrial facilities in Königsberg, Danzig, Helsinki, Warsaw, Ploesti, Bucharest, Sulina, and other cities. From July 10–30, pilots of the 4 Bomber Air Corps alone flew eight raids against petroleum industry targets in Ploesti, Constanta, and Bucharest—attacks that, according to a primary Soviet source, reduced the productive capacity of the Romanian petroleum industry (at least temporarily) by 30 percent. M. N. Kozhevnikov, *The Command and Staff of the Soviet Army Air Force in the Great Patriotic War 1941–1945*, 50.

138   Ray Wagner (ed.), *The Soviet Air Force in World War II*, 44–45. While these numbers may be exaggerated, they do offer an indication of VVS activity at the time.

139   Ibid., 45.

140   *Assistenzarzt Dr. Hermann Türk*, cited in: Kempowski (ed.), *Das Echolot*, 173.

141   M. N. Kozhevnikov, *The Command and Staff of the Soviet Army Air Force in the Great Patriotic War 1941–1945*, 39.

142   Hans von Luck, *Panzer Commander: The Memoirs of Colonel Hans von Luck*, 66. "We often had to smile," Luck continued, "when, for want of bombs, thousands of nails rained down on us from their bomb bays."

143   Prien, et al., *Die Jagdfliegerverbände der Deutschen Luftwaffe*, 12–13; *GSWW*, Vol. IV: 764.

Chapter 7: Berlin, Moscow, and the First Twenty-One Hours of War on the Eastern Front

1   Domarus, *Hitler. Reden und Proklamationen*, Vol. II: 1731–32.

2   Harry W. Flannery, *Assignment to Berlin*, 365.

3   Cited in: Werth, *Russia at War*, 157.

4   Ilya Ehrenburg, cited in: Kempowski, *Das Echolot*, 34.

5   Irving, *Hitler's War*, 272; Paul Schmidt, *Hitler's Interpreter*, 234; Domarus, *Hitler. Reden und Proklamationen*, Vol. II: 1733–34.

6   "*Darum handelt es sich jetzt nicht.*" Domarus, *Hitler. Reden und Proklamationen*, Vol. II: 1734.

7   Schmidt, *Hitler's Interpreter*, 234; Shirer, *The Rise and Fall of the Third Reich*, 847–48; Domarus, *Hitler. Reden und Proklamationen*, Vol. II: 1733–34.

8   Shirer, *The Rise and Fall of the Third Reich*, 847–48; Schmidt, *Hitler's Interpreter*, 235; Domarus, *Hitler. Reden und Proklamationen*, Vol. II: 1734.

9   Shirer, *The Rise and Fall of the Third Reich*, 847–48. According to Hitler biographer John Toland, Molotov had replied: "It is war. Your aircraft have just bombarded some 10 open villages. Do you believe that we deserved that?" John Toland, *Adolf Hitler*, 672.

10   Bellamy, *Absolute War*, 212–13.

11   Irving, *Hitler's War*, 273; Moorhouse, *Berlin at War*, 70.

12   Moorhouse, *Berlin at War*, 70. For the complete text of Hitler's proclamation see, Domarus, *Hitler. Reden und Proklamationen*, Vol. II: 1726–32.

13   *Völkischer Beobachter*, 24.6.41, 2. Cited in: Moorhouse, *Berlin at War*, 71.

14   Marie Vassiltchikov, *Berlin Diaries 1940–1945*, 55. Her complete diary entry reads: "The German army is on the offensive along the entire eastern border. Hako Czernin woke me at dawn to break the news. A new phase of the war begins. We knew it was coming. And yet we are thunderstruck!"

15   Marianne Miethe, *Memoiren 1921–1945* (unpublished document). Special thanks to *Frau* Miethe, my dear friend, for sharing her amazing memoirs with me.

16   Kershaw, *Hitler 1936–1945: Nemesis*, 389. "The more ideologically committed pro-Nazis," Kershaw continued, "would entirely swallow the interpretation of the war as a preventive one to avoid the destruction of western culture by the Bolshevik hordes. They fervently believed that Europe would never be liberated before 'Jewish-Bolshevism' was utterly and completely rooted out. The path to the Holocaust, intertwined with the showdown with Bolshevism, was prefigured in such notions."

17   Moorhouse, *Berlin at War*, 71.

18   Cited in: Buchbender and Sterz (eds.), *Das andere Gesicht des Krieges*, 70.

19   Irving, *Hitler's War*, 273.

20 Ibid., 273. In a later book, Irving offered a somewhat different translation of Hewel's words—as the "calm, mellow mood" in the Chancellery on June 22. David Irving (ed.), *Adolf Hitler: The Medical Diaries. The Private Diaries of Dr. Theo Morell*, 81.

21 For an excellent history of the German General Staff, how it was organized, and how it functioned, see, Geoffrey P. Megargee, *Inside Hitler's High Command* (Lawrence, KS: 2000).

22 According to Gerd Niepold, who worked with Paulus for most of 1941, Brauchitsch said: "*Ja, Paulus, Sie werden Recht haben, acht Wochen werden wir wohl für Russland brauchen.*" See, Georg Meyer, *Adolf Heusinger. Dienst eines deutschen Soldaten 1915 bis 1964*, 151, 850 (f.n. 23).

23 Halder, *War Diary*, 412.

24 At 3:00 that afternoon, "Rome had cabled that Italy regarded herself as at war with Russia since 5.30 that morning." Irving, *Hitler's War*, 273.

25 Halder, *War Diary*, 412–14; Halder, *KTB*, Vol. III: 5–6.

26 Irving, *Hitler's War*, 273; Halder, *War Diary*, 414. In June 1941, the Slovak army consisted of 33,676 men (1,347 officers). With the mobilization of reservists at the start of Operation *Barbarossa* (through early July 1941), the total size of the Slovak army climbed to more than 90,000 men. "Slovakia," Jan Rychlik, in: *Joining Hitler's Crusade: European Nations and the Invasion of the Soviet Union*, David Stahel (ed.), 119, 123.

27 Irving, *Hitler's War*, 273. Hungary declared war on Russia on June 27, 1941. The next day, Horthy wrote to Hitler, notifying him that the Hungarian army would fight "shoulder to shoulder with the famed and victorious German army in the crusade for the elimination of the Communist menace, and for the protection of our culture." *GSWW*, Vol. IV: 1028.

28 Hitler's *Luftwaffe* adjutant Nicolaus von Below, in the "early hours" of June 22, did hear Hitler say that the Russian campaign "will be the most difficult battle that our soldiers will have to undergo in this war." These remarks of Hitler's were most likely made before he retired to bed on the early morning of June 22; they are, however, quite revealing in light of the supremely optimistic prediction on the outcome of the campaign he also made to his adjutants early that morning (and noted in the narrative above). Taken together, Hitler's utterances exhibit an unmistakable ambivalence in his attitude toward war with Russia up to the very start of the conflict. Von Below, *At Hitler's Side*, 103.

29 Irving, *Hitler's War*, 273–74. The reference to "Sollum" is to a victory of Rommel's *Afrika Korps* in North Africa. *KTB OKW*, Vol. I: 418.

30 Ralf Georg Reuth (ed.), *Joseph Goebbels. Tagebücher 1924–1945, Bd. 4*: 1611–13.

31 Robert Payne, *The Life and Death of Adolf Hitler*, 432; Irving, *Hitler's War*, 274; Von Below, *At Hitler's Side*, 104–5; Thies, *Der Ostfeldzug—Ein Lageatlas*, vii.

32 Thies, *Der Ostfeldzug—Ein Lageatlas*, vii–ix; Luttichau, *The Road to Moscow*, VI: 27; Schroeder, *Er war mein Chef*, 111. Noted Ziemke and Bauer: "Elaborate as they were, the *Wolfsschanze* and the Mauerwald compound could only accommodate fractions of the OKW and OKH staffs; the rest stayed in and around Berlin and kept in contact with the *Wolfsschanze* by air and courier train." Ziemke and Bauer, *Moscow to Stalingrad: Decision in the East*, 4.

33 Thies, *Der Ostfeldzug—Ein Lageatlas*, vii. General Jodl, Chief, OKW Operations Staff, would later refer to the new *Führerhauptquartier* as a "mixture of cloister and concentration camp." Megargee, *Inside Hitler's High Command*, 149.

34 Roberts (ed.), *Marshal of Victory*. Vol. I: *WWII Memoirs of General Zhukov through 1941*, 281.

35 A. N. Poskrebyshev, Stalin's "all powerful" secretary. Gorodetsky, *Grand Delusion*, 312.

36 Roberts (ed.), *Marshal of Victory*. Vol. I: *WWII Memoirs of General Zhukov through 1941*, 281.

37 Roberts (ed.), *Marshal of Victory*. Vol. I: *WWII Memoirs of General Zhukov through 1941*, 282; Gorodetsky, *Grand Delusion*, 311; Braithwaite, *Moscow 1941*, 35.

38 Gorodetsky, *Grand Delusion*, 311.

39 Ibid., 312.

40 Roberts (ed.), *Marshal of Victory*. Vol. I: *WWII Memoirs of General Zhukov through 1941*, 282.

41 Halder, *KTB*, Vol. III: 4; Seaton, *The Russo-German War 1941–45*, 98. "Even at this stage," observed John Erickson, "calamitous as it was rapidly becoming, Stalin thought that he could still stop the war." Erickson, *The Road to Stalingrad*, 125.

42   Glantz, *Barbarossa*, 242; Gorodetsky, *Grand Delusion*, 313.

43   Braithwaite, *Moscow 1941*, 70.

44   Ibid., 70–71.

45   Gorodetsky, *Grand Delusion*, 313.

46   Pleshakov, *Stalin's Folly*, 7.

47   Gorodetsky, *Grand Delusion*, 313. It is a fascinating—yet for historians more than a little frustrating—fluke of history that much of what Stalin said on June 22, 1941, has been preserved, while hardly a single remark of Hitler's on this day has come down to us.

48   Braithwaite, *Moscow 1941*, 71.

49   Bellamy, *Absolute War*, 215.

50   Ibid., 215–16.

51   Erickson, *The Road to Stalingrad*, 125; Bellamy, *Absolute War*, 209.

52   Cited in Werth, *Russia at War 1941–1945*, 159.

53   Ibid., 159–60.

54   Cited in: Werth, *Russia at War*, 161; and, Bellamy, *Absolute War*, 209.

55   Braithwaite, *Moscow 1941*, 75. Molotov's announcement, alternating with martial music, was repeated in Moscow throughout the day. Nothing, however, was reported by the Soviet authorities on the situation at the front—about which, in any case, they knew little—which gave rise to rumors of all sorts. Peter Gosztony, "*Die erste Entscheidungsschlacht des Russlandfeldzuges 1941/42 (II), Moskau in der Krise 1941 (I)*," 102.

56   Braithwaite, *Moscow 1941*, 75–76.

57   Ibid., 76. According to English military historian Sir Antony Beevor, Stalin was "too traumatized" to speak to the Russian people. See his, *The Mystery of Olga Chekhova*, 165.

58   Bellamy, *Absolute War*, 209; Braithwaite, *Moscow 1941*, 260. As noted by Braithwaite, preparations for such an evacuation had begun even before the start of war with Germany: "In the spring of 1941 the General Staff told the commanders of the Military Districts in the West to make plans for the immediate evacuation of military objects and the most important industrial plants, agricultural machinery, animals and grain."

59   Bellamy, *Absolute War*, 209.

60   It should be pointed out that the USSR did not have a formal high command structure on June 22, 1941, another indication that, at the highest level, Russia was not ready for war. This oversight was remedied the next day, when the *Stavka* (Supreme High Command) was established. Initially, the *Stavka* was chaired by Timoshenko, even though real authority resided in Stalin. On July 10, the *Stavka* was reorganized and placed under Stalin's direct control. *GSWW*, Vol. IV: 836–37: Ziemke and Bauer, *Moscow to Stalingrad: Decision in the East*, 25, 30.

61   Ziemke and Bauer, *Moscow to Stalingrad: Decision in the East*, 24.

62   Glantz, *Barbarossa*, 242–43; Ziemke and Bauer, *Moscow to Stalingrad: Decision in the East*, 24.

63   Geoffrey Roberts, *Stalin's Wars: From World War to Cold War, 1939–1953*, 93. As noted by Roberts: "Confidence in victory was shared by the general Soviet population. In Moscow many people were amazed that the Germans had dared to attack, while thousands more flocked to join the armed forces and people's militias."

64   Erickson, *The Road to Stalingrad*, 132.

65   Volkogonov, "The German Attack, the Soviet Response," 89.

66   Cited in: Erickson, *The Road to Stalingrad*, 134.

67   Ibid., 126.

68   Marshal G. I. Kulik, a Soviet artillery specialist, was sent to the Western Front, along with Marshal B. M. Shaposhnikov. According to John Erickson: "Kulik was a nonentity. His prime qualification was that Stalin had known him during the days of the defense of Tsaritsyn [Stalingrad] in 1918. It was this that ultimately transformed him, in 1937, into the overlord of Soviet artillery, head of the Main Artillery Administration, Deputy Defense Commissar. There is no other evidence of his fitness for this post." Ibid., 17. Noted Simon Montefiore: "The boozy buffoon, Marshal Kulik, whose war was to be a chronicle of tragicomical blunders, outfitted himself in a pilot's fetching leathers, cap and goggles and arrived on the

Western Front like a Stalinist Biggles on the evening of 23 June. Bewildered by the rout of 10 Army, he was cut off, surrounded and almost captured." Simon Sebag Montefiore, *Stalin: The Court of the Red Tsar*, 369–70.

69   General N. F. Vatutin. According to Evan Mawdsley, Vatutin, Zhukov's deputy, would be sent to oversee the Northwestern Front. Mawdsley, *Thunder in the East*, 65.

70   Erickson, *The Road to Stalingrad*, 134. See also, Roberts (ed.), *Marshal of Victory*. Vol. I: *WWII Memoirs of General Zhukov through 1941*, 284–86.

71   Glantz, *Barbarossa*, 39.

72   Erickson, *The Road to Stalingrad*, 135.

73   The words are General Zhukov's, cited in: Kirchubel, *Operation Barbarossa 1941 (3)*, *Army Group Center*, 27.

Postscript: Reflections on Day One of the Most Destructive War in History and the Ultimate Failure of Operation *Barbarossa*

1   Cited in: Joachim Dollwet, "*Menschen im Krieg, Bejahung – und Widerstand? Eindrücke und Auszüge aus der Sammlung von Feldpostbriefen des Zweiten Weltkrieges im Landeshauptarchiv Koblenz*," in: F. J. Heyen, et al., *Jahrbuch für westdeutsche Landesgeschichte*, 298.

2   BA-MA N 802/46: "*Briefe von General Heinz Guderian an seine Frau Margarete*" (27.6.41).

3   Cited in: Horst Mühleisen (ed.). *Hellmuth Stieff Briefe*, 113.

4   Bellamy, *Absolute War*, 687.

5   As noted in Chapter 1 (Section 1.5), the Germans fully expected the Russians to use chemical or biological agents against their troops. In fact, by the start of World War II, the Soviet Union possessed some 77,000 tons of mustard gas. Agustín Sáiz, *Deutsche Soldaten. Uniforms, Equipment & Personal Items of the German Soldier 1939–45*, 95.

6   For the photograph see, Keegan, *The Second World War*, 185.

7   Rüdiger Overmans, *Deutsche militärische Verluste im Zweiten Weltkrieg*, 277. About 90 percent of these losses fell upon the army, while roughly 4 percent each were from the *Waffen-SS* and the *Luftwaffe*. The figure of 2,800 is almost equal to the size of a German infantry regiment in 1941 (3,200 men). In other words, in the first nine days of the war, the Germans incurred fatalities about equal to the total annihilation of eight full-strength infantry regiments.

8   Halder, *War Diary*, 562. On November 23, 1941, Halder jotted in his diary: "The means that are available to us for continuing the war are limited through use and the incredible strain imposed on our arms by the protected areas. Certainly the army, as it existed in June 1941, will not be available to us again." By the end of 1941, the Germans (army, *Waffen-SS*, *Luftwaffe*) had sustained 302,000 fatal losses in the East, along with two to three times as many wounded—losses from which they never fully recovered. Overmans, *Deutsche militärische Verluste im Zweiten Weltkrieg*, 277.

9   Hürter, *Ein deutscher General an der Ostfront. Die Briefe und Tagebücher des Gotthard Heinrici 1941/42*, 62.

10   As early as June 25, 1941, General Lemelsen (47 Panzer Corps), concerned about the impact of such behavior on troop discipline, intervened to stop the indiscriminate shooting of Russian POWs and civilians by his soldiers; his order, however, fell on deaf ears, compelling him to repeat it five days later (June 30). Lemelsen, however, made clear that his order did "not change anything regarding the *Führer*'s order on the ruthless action to be taken against partisans and Bolshevik commissars." BA-MA RH 27-18/24, 25.6.41, cited in: Omer Bartov, *The Eastern Front, 1941–45, German Troops and the Barbarization of Warfare*, 116–17. For a detailed comparative analysis of German and Soviet war crimes during Operation *Barbarossa* see, Luther, *Barbarossa Unleashed*, 433–72.

11   For a fascinating (albeit anonymous) study of forest fighting on the Eastern Front see, "*Der Waldkampf*," in: *Allgemeine Schweizerische Militärzeitschrift, Okt. 49 (Heft 10), Nov. 49 (Heft 11)*. The author is merely identified as a "war participant."

12   BA-MA RH 20-4/1199, *KTB AOK 4*, 23.6.41.

13   Karlheinz Schneider-Janessen, *Arzt im Krieg. Wie deutsche und russische Ärzte den zweiten Weltkrieg erlebten*, 423. *Major* Werner Heinemann, in a letter to his wife on July 11, 1941, expressed a frustration

that must have been universal among German troops in the summer of 1941: "Unfortunately snipers firing from concealed positions cause us endless problems. Two nights ago, a motor vehicle driver from my old 1st Company was murdered in the forest as he tried to repair a flat tire. He was all alone." *Feldpost*, Werner Heinemann, July 11, 1941.

14   Luther, *Barbarossa Unleashed*, 22.

15   Before the war, the civilian population of Rzhev was about 58,000; according to Russian sources, some 9,000 civilians died of hunger in the city during the German occupation, while untold others were killed in the fighting or succumbed to disease or epidemics. Of the city's 5,400 houses, only 300 were still intact when the Germans withdrew in March 1943; by that time, all but several hundred of the surviving civilians had fled or been evacuated from the city. Email, Christoph Rass to Dr. C. Luther, October 2, 2003; also, https://www.droste-haus.de.

16   According to Russian author Svetlana Gerasimova, the Red Army may well have sustained more than two million casualties during fifteen months of combat in the Rzhev bridgehead. See her book, recently translated as, *The Rzhev Slaughterhouse: The Red Army's Forgotten 15-Month Campaign against Army Group Center, 1942–1943*, 157–58.

17   The German defenders of Rzhev, unbowed and undefeated, eventually withdrew from the bridgehead on their own initiative in March 1943 in a successful effort to shorten their line and free up divisions for other tasks.

18   See, David M. Glantz, *Zhukov's Greatest Defeat: The Red Army's Epic Disaster in Operation Mars, 1942* (Lawrence, 1999); see also, his revised and expanded version of *When Titans Clashed: How the Red Army Stopped Hitler* (Lawrence, 2015; originally published in 1995).

19   For example, on the afternoon of June 22, Western Front HQ reported that "up to 400–500 parachutists landed on Nacza from 20 planes," and "300–500 parachutists at Radun from 17 planes." In another example, Southwestern Front HQ reported that, at 1520 hours, "an enemy airborne landing, involving about 18 planes, took place in the Kovel' area." However, there is absolutely no indication in surviving German military records that any such large airborne operations took place in the sectors of either Army Group Center or Army Group South on June 22, or in the days, weeks, and months that followed for that matter. TsAMO RF, F. 208, Op. 3038ss, D. 15, Ll. 1-3, "*Razvedivatel'naya Svodka Shtaba Zapadnogo Fronta No. 1 k 19 Chasam 22 Iyunya 1941 g. o Deistviyakh Protivnika Protiv Voisk Fronta. Seriya 'G'*" (Intelligence Report No. 1 from the Headquarters of the Western Front by 1900 June 22, 1941, on the Enemy's Activities Against the Front's Troops. Series "G"), in: SBDVOV, Vol. 35: 19; also, TsAMO RF, F. 229, Op. 9776ss, D. 63, Ll. 5-10, "*Operativnaya Svodka Shtaba Yugo-Zapadnogo Fronta No. 1 k 19 Chasam 22 Iyunya 1941 o Boevykh Deistviyakh Voisk Fronta, Seriya 'G'*" (Operational Report No. 1, Southwestern Front Headquarters, as of 1900, June 22, 1941, on the Combat Activities of the Front's Troops, Series "G"), in: SBDVOV: Vol. 36: 11.

20   Glantz, *Barbarossa*, 55.

21   Andreas Hillgruber, "*Die weltpolitischen Entscheidungen vom 22. Juni 1941 bis 11. Dezember 1941*," in: Andreas Hillgruber, *Der Zweite Weltkrieg 1939–1945. Kriegsziele und Strategie der grossen Mächte*, 69.

22   A Soviet army in 1941 was roughly equivalent in size to a German army corps.

23   Glantz, *Barbarossa*, 68.

24   Dunn, Jr., *Stalin's Keys to Victory: The Rebirth of the Red Army*, 4.

25   I am, of course, referring to Stalin's policies of agricultural collectivization and forced industrialization, the latter as exemplified by the Five-Year Plans. Both policies were reflections of the total mobilization of Soviet society. For an overview of the buildup of Russia's industrial base and military see, Luther, *Barbarossa Unleashed*, 140–42.

26   As I wrote in the introduction to *Barbarossa Unleashed*: "Despite [the] horrific—indeed, historically unparalleled—losses, neither Stalin's rule nor the Red Army collapsed under the repeated hammer blows of Hitler's armies. What the Germans soon began to grasp, much to their dismay, was that the Soviet system, despite its brutality and inhumanity—or perhaps *because* of it—was on a much sounder footing than realized." Luther, *Barbarossa Unleashed*, 26.

27   Pleshakov, *Stalin's Folly*, 273.

28 "Throughout the entire period [1941]," states David M. Glantz, "Stalin 'turned the screws' on Red Army troops, issuing directives that demanded absolute obedience to orders under threat of censure, arrest and even execution." Glantz, *Barbarossa*, 209.

29 Stephen Kotkin, *Stalin: Waiting for Hitler, 1929–1941*, 901.

30 Overmans, *Deutsche militärische Verluste im Zweiten Weltkrieg*, 265.

31 Bellamy, *Absolute War*, 11.

Appendix 1: Equivalent Military Ranks

1 Megargee, *Inside Hitler's High Command*, 238; *Handbook on German Military Forces*, 5–7; Buchner, *The German Infantry Handbook 1939–1945*, 6.

Appendix 2: Directive No. 21—Case *Barbarossa* (December 18, 1940)

1 This appendix has excerpts from Hitler's *Barbarossa* directive; some paragraphs have been combined to economize on space. Trevor-Roper (ed.), *Hitler's War Directives 1939–1945*, 49–52; Hubatsch (ed.), *Hitlers Weisungen für die Kriegführung 1939–1945*, 84–88.

2 Neither on June 22, 1941, nor at anytime thereafter during Operation *Barbarossa*, did the Germans ever employ "parachute and airborne troops" to capture a key geographical objective on the Eastern Front, such as a railroad bridge across a river.

3 Just nine copies of the document were issued to top German command organs. Hubatsch (ed.), *Hitlers Weisungen für die Kriegführung 1939–1945*, 88.

Appendix 3: German 6 Infantry Division: Personnel and Weapons (June 20, 1941)

1 BA-MA RH 26-6/2, *Anlage zum Ia KTB 6. Inf.-Div.*

2 Figures for "combat strength" exclude rear area services, medical personnel, and personnel belonging to the divisional baggage trains.

3 Civilian officials of the German armed forces (*Wehrmachtbeamte*) had nominal rank and wore uniforms; they were classified as combatants.

4 NCOs are "*Unteroffiziere*" and sergeants.

5 Enlisted personnel (*Mannschaften*) typically refer to those up to and including the rank of *Obergefreiter* (Corporal).

6 Figures for "ration strength" include all *Wehrmacht* personnel and horses provisioned by the 6 ID; the division's strength reports were prepared on or about the 1st, 10th, and 20th of each month, as was customary throughout the German army.

7 The final two categories ("le.Fla.W." and "m.Fla.W.") are most likely army antiaircraft weapons of the caliber 20mm and 37mm, respectively.

Appendix 4: Order of Battle of a German Panzer Division (June 1941)

1 Keilig, *Das Deutsche Heer 1939–45, Bd. II*, Abschnitt 103, 18–20. This order of battle—somewhat simplified from Keilig—portrays a "typical" German panzer division with a tank regiment of two battalions equipped with German tanks only. There were, of course, many variations to this "normal" order of battle. (*Normalgliederung*).

2 Nine panzer divisions (3, 6, 7, 8, 12, 17, 18, 19, 20 PD) had three tank battalions. Ibid., 18.

3 These were armored cars, with a 20mm main armament.

4 The actual German term, "*Panzerjäger*," literally means "tank hunter."

5 This self-propelled (SP) flak company was not in the order of battle of 3, 15, 19, and 20 Panzer Divisions; in addition, the 17 and 18 PDs were outfitted with eight 20mm flak (SP) and four 20mm flak (mot.)

6 No number given for tanks; however, this company in the Armored Combat Engineer Battalion of 4 PD (3./Pz.Pi.Btl. 79) had a dozen Pz Is and Pz IIs. Robert Michulec, *4. Panzer-Division on the Eastern Front (1) 1941–1943*, 4.

7 SPW = "*Schützenpanzerwagen*," or armored personnel carrier (APC). These vehicles (in German nomenclature Sd.Kfz. 250 or 251) offered significantly more protection than the typical troop transports

then in service and were highly valued by the *Landser* lucky enough to ride in them. However, in June 1941, most panzer and motorized divisions possessed but a small number of these SPWs. Not uncommon was the situation of 10 Panzer Division, whose entire rifle brigade had just a single company mounted in SPWs. The SPWs of the Armored Combat Engineer Battalion were used to mount the 280/320mm *Nebelwerfer* rocket launchers. Schick, *Die Geschichte der 10. Panzer-Division 1939–1943*, 263.

Appendix 5: 56 Infantry Division's Order No. 1 for the Attack across the Bug River (June 19, 1941)

1   NARA, T-315, Roll 965, *KTB und Tätigkeitsberichte mit Anlagen, 56.Inf.-Div.*, 19.6.41.
2   "y+3" would be at 0318 hours (three minutes after the start of the offensive in the sector of Army Group South).
3   In the war diary of 56 ID, it states that the artillery preparation began "according to plan" (*planmässig*) at 0318 hours. NARA, T-315, Roll 965, *Ia KTB Nr. 5, 56.Inf.Div.*, 22.6.41. See also, *Geschichte der 56. Infanterie-Division 1938–1945*, 28.
4   *Generalmajor* Karl von Oven, Commander, 56 Infantry Division.

Appendix 6: People's Commissariat of Defense (NKO) Directives 1, 2, 3 (June 22, 1941)

1   The NKO directives are gleaned from Glantz, *Barbarossa* (Appendix II), 242–43.

Select Bibliography

1   This is a copy of a document gleaned from the German Federal Military Archives (BA-MA) in Freiburg, Germany.
2   These documents were located at: https://pamyat-naroda.ru (Memory of the People.ru.). TsAMO = *Tsentral'nyi Arkhiv Ministerstva Oborony.*

Select Bibliography

Archival Materials

1. National Archives and Records Administration (NARA) (College Park, MD)

a. Still Pictures Department. RG 242-GAP-286B-4: "German troops in Russia 1941"

b. Cartographics Department. RG 373: Captured German Aerial Photography of Soviet Fortress of Brest-Litovsk.

c. Cartographics Department. RG 242: "*Lagekarten Ost*" (Eastern Front Situation Maps) (22.6.41, abds.)

d. Microfilm Department. RG 242: Captured German Records Microfilmed at Alexandria, VA.

User Guides to Records of the German Field Commands

Army Groups (T-311):
Army Group North
    Roll 53 (*Ia KTB*: 22.6.–31.8.41)
    Roll 132 (*Ia Geschichte Feldzug Russland*, 22.6.–28.7.41)
Army Group Center
    Roll 226 (*H.Gr.Mitte/Stoart KTB mit Anlagen*, 22.6.–30.6.41)
Army Group South
    Roll 260 (*KTB II. Teil, Bd. 1*: 22.6.–15.7.41)

Armies (T-312):
Sixteenth Army
    Roll 543 (*Ia KTB Nr. 5, Teil 2, Bd. I*: 21.6.–31.7.41)
Seventeenth Army
    Roll 668 (*Ia KTB Nr.1, AOK 17*: 15.5.–12.12.41)
Eighteenth Army
    Roll 781 (*Ia KTB 4a, Bd. I, AOK 18*: 21.6.–16.8.41)
    Roll 783 (*Ia KTB 4a, AOK 18*: 22.6.–31.12.41: "*Zusammenfassung*")

Panzer Armies / Panzer Groups (T-313):
1 Panzer Army (Panzer Group)
    Roll 3 (*Ia KTB Nr. 6, Pz. AOK 1*: 5.2.–31.10.41)
3 Panzer Army (Panzer Group)
    Roll 225 (*Ia KTB Nr. 1, 3. Pz. Gr*: 25.5.–31.8.41)
4 Panzer Army (Panzer Group)
    Roll 330 (*Ia KTB Nr. 5, Pz. AOK 4*: 22.6.–19.9.41)

Army Corps (T-314):
1 Army Corps
    Roll 39 (*Ia KTB Ostfeldzug Nr. 1*: 22.6.41–31.3.42)
2 Army Corps
    Roll 101 (*Ia KTB Nr. 1, Ostfeldzug, Russland 1941*: 22.6.–8.11.41)
10 Army Corps
    Roll 446 (*Ia KTB Ost Nr. 1*: 26.5.–20.7.41)
26 Army Corps
    Roll 755 (*Ia KTB Nr. 6*: Jun–Aug 41)
41 Panzer Corps
    Roll 979 (*Ia Anlagenband 1 zum KTB*: 20.4.–20.6.41)

Divisions (T-315):
1 Infantry Division
    Roll 2 (*Ia KTB* 20.6.–24.9.41)
1 Panzer Division
    Roll 16 (*Ia KTB Nr. 6*: 8.6.–19.9.41)
1 Mountain (*Gebirgs*) Division
    Roll 39 (*Ia KTB Ost Nr. 1*: 19.4.41–10.8.41)
    Roll 41 (*Anlagen Bd. 8 zum KTB Ost Nr. 1*)
6 Panzer Division
    Roll 323 (*Ia KTB*: 17.6.–15.9.41)
6 Rifle (*Schützen*) Brigade (6 Panzer Division)
    Roll 322 (*KTB Nr. 3*: 21.6.–22.11.41)
8 Panzer Division
    Roll 483 (*Ia KTB, Bd. I*: 13.6.–20.7.41)
9 Infantry Division
    Roll 514 (*Anlagen zum KTB Nr. 6*: 26.3.–31.12.41)
11 Infantry Division
    Roll 572 (*Ia KTB Nr. 4*: 22.6.–17.8.41)
11 Panzer Division
    Roll 2320 (*Ia KTB*: 1.5.–21.10.41)
14 Panzer Division
    Roll 656 (*Ia KTB Nr. 2*: 1.5.–15.12.41)
21 Infantry Division
    Roll 755 (*Anlagen zum KTB*: 1.6.–2.8.41)
30 Infantry Division
    Roll 855 (*Ia KTB Nr. 4*: 9.5.–15.12.41)
44 Infantry Division
    Roll 911 (*Ia KTB Nr. 6*: 1.4.–21.6.41)
    Roll 911 (*Ia KTB Nr. 7*: 22.6.–31.12.41)
56 Infantry Division
    Roll 965 (*KTB und Tätigkeitsberichte mit Anlagen*: 1.6.–21.6.41)
    Roll 965 (*Ia KTB Nr. 5*: 22.6.–23.7.41)
57 Infantry Division
    Roll 980 (*Ia KTB Nr. 5*: 22.6.–31.10.41)
61 Infantry Division
    Roll 1013 (*Ia KTB Nr. 5, Bd. I*: 22.6.–17.9.41)
62 Infantry Division
    Roll 1028 (*Ia KTB*: 20.5.–31.12.41)
75 Infantry Division
    Roll 1074 (*Ia KTB Nr. 3*: 10.5.–31.12.41)
126 Infantry Division
    Roll 1350 (*Ia KTB Nr. 2*: 31.3.–31.12.41)
    Roll 1351 (*Ia Anlagen zum KTB Nr. 2*: 22.6.–11.7.41)
269 Infantry Division
    Roll 1858 (*Ia KTB Nr. 5*: 22.6.–7.12.41)
290 Infantry Division
    Roll 1886 (*Ia KTB*: 19.6.–15.12.41)
291 Infantry Division
    Roll 1906 (*Ia KTB Nr. 1*: 20.6.–15.7.41)
    Roll 1912 (*Anlagen zum Ia KTB, Gefechtsberichte*, 22.6.–27.8.41)

297 Infantry Division
  Roll 1969 (*Ia KTB, Bd. 2*: 22.6.–27.6.41)
298 Infantry Division
  Roll 1984 (*Ia KTB Nr. 4*: 15.5.–29.8.41)
  Roll 1985 (*Anlagen zum Ia KTB Nr. 4*: 16.6.–28.6.41)

2. Air Force Historical Research Agency (AFHRA) (Maxwell AFB, AL)

"*Der Luftkrieg im Osten gegen Russland 1941.*" *Aus einer Studie der 8. Abteilung.* 1943/1944. (KDC: G/VI/3a).
"*Die deutschen Flugzeugverluste im ersten Monat (22.6.41–17.7.41) des Krieges gegen Russland.*" *Nach einer Zusammenstellung der 6. Abteilung des Generalstabes der deutschen Luftwaffe.* (KDC: G/VI/3a).
Heinemann, Lothar v., "*Erste Kämpfe vom 22.6. bis ca. 3.7.41.*"
———. "*Generalkommando VIII. Fliegerkorps. Operationsabschnitt: Erste Kämpfe vom 22.6. bis ca. 3.7.1941 (Doppelschlacht von Bialystok und Minsk).*" (KDC: G/VI/3a).
Plocher, Hermann. *The German Air Force versus Russia, 1941* (No. 153, 1965).
Schwabedissen, Walter. *The Russian Air Force in the Eyes of German Commanders* (No. 175, 1960).
Suchenwirth, Richard. *Command and Leadership in the German Air Force* (No. 174, 1969).

3. U.S. Army Military History Institute, Carlisle Barracks, PA

(Foreign Military Studies [FMS] prepared by former *Wehrmacht* officers in late 1940s and 1950s for the U.S. Army in Europe):
D-221: "An Artillery Regiment on the Road to Moscow (22 June to December 1941)." Genmaj. Gerhard Grassmann. 1947.
D-247: "German Preparations for the Attack against Russia (The German Build-up East of Warsaw)." Genlt. Kurt Cuno. 1947.
P-190: "*Verbrauchs- u. Verschleisssätze während der Operationen der deutschen Heeresgruppe Mitte vom 22.6.41– 31.12.41.*" General Rudolf Hofmann and Genmaj. Alfred Toppe. 1953.
T-34: "Terrain Factors in the Russian Campaign." General Karl Allmendinger, et al. 1950.

4. Bibliothek für Zeitgeschichte (BfZ) (Stuttgart, Germany)

(Field post letters [*Feldpostbriefe*] and diary entries of German soldiers who took part in the attack on Russia on June 22, 1941):

Erich N. (18 683 C)
Werner R. (N97.3)
Fw. Hans M. (28 193B)
Gefr. Franz B. (17 736)
Gefr. Franz S. (06 372)
Gefr. Gerhard S. (38 002)
Gefr. Hans B. (38 051)
Gefr. Herbert R. (N11.15)
Gefr. Ludwig B. (04 650)
Gefr. Otto S. (46 010)
G.S. (18 719 A)
Hptm. Dr. H.U. (no Signatur)
Lt. Helmut D. (04 255 C)
Oblt. Richard D. (35 232)
O'Gefr. H.S. (04 497 A)
O'Gefr. Werner E. (21 389)
Paul B. (46 281)
Paul R. (NO2.1)
Willibald G. (N02.5)

5. Bundesarchiv-Militärarchiv (BA-MA) (Freiburg, Germany)

MSg 1/1147 and 1/1148: *Tagebuch Gen. Lemelsen ("Russlandfeldzug") Band I: 6. Jun–8. Okt 41 and Band II: 10. Okt 41–24. Apr 42)*

N 76/6: *"Kriegserinnerungen als Kommandeur der 6. Inf.Div.,"* General Helge Auleb
N 245/3: *Persönliches Tagebuch*, General Georg-Hans Reinhardt
N 802/46: *"Briefe von General [Heinz] Guderian an seine Frau Margarete"*

RH 19 II/120: *KTB Hr.Gr.Mitte (Okt 41)*

RH 20-4/188: *"Die Kämpfe der 4. Armee"*
RH 20-4/192: *"Gefechtsbericht über die Wegnahme von Brest Litowsk"*
RH 20-4/337: *"Kämpfe der 4. Armee im ersten Kriegsjahr gegen den Sowjet Union"*
RH 20-4/1199: *KTB AOK 4*

RH 21-2/927: *KTB Pz.AOK 2*
RH 21-3/43, 732: *Anlagen zum KTB Pz.AOK 3 (22.6.41 & Gefechtsberichte Russland 1941)*
RH 21-3/788: *KTB Pz.Gr. 3*

RH 26-6/8: *KTB 6. ID*
RH 26-6/16: *Anlagenband 1 zum KTB Nr. 5 der 6. Inf.-Div., Ia.*
RH 26-45/20: *KTB 45. ID*
RH 26-129/3: *KTB 129. ID*
RH 26-137/4: *KTB 137. ID*
RH 26-256/12: *KTB 256. ID*
RH 26-292/7: *KTB 292. ID*

RH 27-3/14: *KTB 3. PD*
RH 27-7/46: *KTB 7. PD*
RH 27-18/20: *KTB 18. PD*

RL 200/17: *Tagebuch General von Waldau*

6. Staats- u. Personenstandsarchiv (Detmold, Germany)

D 107/56 Nr. 10: *KTB 18.Inf.Rgt.: "Der russische Sommerfeldzug mit dem I.R. 18"* (15.6.–30.9.41)

7. The Hoover Institution Archives (Stanford University, Palo Alto, CA)

H 08-22/9: *Nachlass Generalfeldmarschall Fedor von Bock (KTB 22.6.41.–5.1.42)*[1]

8. Perry-Castañeda Library Map Collection (University of Texas at Austin)

Lithuania Map, NN 34-3, Siauliai, Series N501, U.S. Army Map Service, 1954.
Lithuania Map, NN 34-6, Kaunas, Series N501, U.S. Army Map Service, 1954.
Lithuania Map, Kaunas Sheet NE 54/22, Series M404 (4072), Great Britain War Office, 1942.
Miscellaneous Maps of Baltic States and Ukraine.

9. Official Soviet Documents of the Great Patriotic War

a. TsAMO RF (Central Archive of the Ministry of Defense, Russian Federation).[2]
(Note: From this site I mostly used a handful of documents pertaining to the activities of the Soviet 8 Army [Northwestern Front].)

b. *Sbornik Boevykh Dokumentov Velikoi Otechestvennoi Voiny* (Collection of Combat Documents of the Great Patriotic War). Volumes 33–36. Voennoe Izdatel'stvo Ministerstva Oborony SSSR. Moscow, 1957–58. (Note: From this source I employed a much broader range of materials, including combat and intelligence reports of the Northwestern, Western, and Southwestern Fronts, armies attached to these fronts, and, occasionally corps-level documents.)

Primary and Secondary Sources
(Books, Personal Memoirs, Diaries—published and unpublished materials)

Adamczyk, Werner. *Feuer! An Artilleryman's Life on the Eastern Front.* Wilmington, NC: 1992.

Alexander, Christine, and Mark Kunze (eds.). *Eastern Inferno: The Journals of a German Panzerjäger on the Eastern Front, 1941–43*. Philadelphia and Newbury: 2010.

Aliev, Rostislav. *The Siege of Brest 1941: The Red Army's Stand against the Germans during Operation Barbarossa.* Mechanicsburg, PA: 2015.

Allmayer-Beck, Johann Christoph, and Franz Becker. *21. Infanterie-Division. Russlandfeldzug 1941.* Hamburg: 1960.

Axell, Albert. *Russia's Heroes 1941–45.* New York: 2001.

Bähr, Walter, and Dr. Hans W. Bähr. *Kriegsbriefe Gefallener Studenten, 1939–1945.* Tübingen and Stuttgart: 1952.

Bartov, Omer. *The Eastern Front, 1941–45, German Troops and the Barbarization of Warfare.* New York: 1985.

Battistelli, Pier Paolo. *Panzer Divisions: The Eastern Front 1941–43.* Oxford: 2008.

Bauer, Eddy. *Der Panzerkrieg. Die wichtigsten Panzeroperationen des zweiten Weltkrieges in Europa und Afrika. Bd. I: Vorstoss und Rückzug der deutschen Panzerverbände.* Bonn: 1965.

Beevor, Antony. *The Mystery of Olga Chekhova.* New York: 2004.

Bekker, Cajus. *The Luftwaffe War Diaries.* London: 1966.

Bellamy, Chris. *Absolute War: Soviet Russia in the Second World War.* New York: 2007.

Below, Nicolaus von. *At Hitler's Side: The Memoirs of Hitler's Luftwaffe Adjutant 1937–1945.* London: 2001.

Bergström, Christer, and Andrey Mikhailov. *Black Cross Red Star: Air War over the Eastern Front.* Vol. I: *Operation Barbarossa 1941.* 2000.

Besymenski, Lew. *Die Schlacht um Moskau 1941.* Cologne: 1981.

Boatner, Mark M. III. *Biographical Dictionary of World War II.* Novato, CA: 1999.

Bock, Fedor von. *Generalfeldmarschall Fedor von Bock: The War Diary 1939–1945.* Klaus Gerbet (ed.). Atglen, PA: 1996.

Boeselager, Philipp *Freiherr* von. *Valkyrie: The Story of the Plot to Kill Hitler by Its Last Member.* New York: 2009.

Boog, Horst, et al. *Das Deutsche Reich und der Zweite Weltkrieg. Bd. 4: Der Angriff auf die Sowjetunion.* Stuttgart: 1983.

———. *Germany and the Second World War*, Vol. IV: *The Attack on the Soviet Union.* Oxford: 1998.

Bopp, Gerhard. *Kriegstagebuch. Aufzeichnungen während des II. Weltkrieges, 1940–1943.* Hamburg: 2005.

Boucsein, Heinrich. *Halten oder Sterben: Die hessisch-thüringische 129. Infanterie-Division im Russlandfeldzug und Ostpreussen 1941–1945.* Potsdam, Germany: 1999.

Bradley, Dermot (ed.). *Deutschlands Generale und Admirale. Teil IV: Die Generale des Heeres 1921–1945. Bd. 6: Hochbaum-Klutmann.* Bissendorf, Germany: 2002.

Braithwaite, Rodric. *Moscow 1941: A City and Its People at War.* London: 2006.

Brown, Capt. Eric. *Wings of the Luftwaffe: Flying German Aircraft of the Second World War.* William Green and Gordon Swanborough (eds). London: 1977.

Buchbender, Ortwin, and Reinhold Sterz (eds.). *Das andere Gesicht des Krieges: Deutsche Feldpostbriefe 1939–1945.* Munich: 1982.

Bücheler, Heinrich. *Hoepner: Ein deutsches Soldatenschicksal des 20. Jahrhunderts.* Herford, Germany: 1980.

Buchner, Alex. *The German Infantry Handbook 1939–1945: Organization, Uniforms, Weapons, Equipment, Operations*. Atglen, PA: 1991.

Bunke, Dr. Erich. *Der Osten blieb unser Schicksal 1939–1944. Panzerjäger im 2. Weltkrieg*. Privately published, 1991.

Burdick, Charles B. *Hubert Lanz: General der Gebirgstruppe 1896–1982*. Osnabrück, Germany: 1988.

Burgdorff, Stephan, and Klaus Wiegrefe (eds.). *Der Zweite Weltkrieg: Wendepunkt der deutschen Geschichte*. Munich: 2005.

Burleigh, Michael. *The Third Reich: A New History*. New York: 2000.

Carell, Paul. *Hitler Moves East, 1941–1943*. Boston: 1964.

———. *Unternehmen Barbarossa: Der Marsch nach Russland*. Berlin: 1963.

Cassidy, Henry C. *Moscow Dateline: 1941–1943*. Boston: 1943.

———. *Generaloberst Erich Hoepner: Militärisches Porträt eines Panzer-Führers*. Neckargemünd, Germany: 1969.

Chales de Beaulieu, Walter. *Der Vorstoss der Panzergruppe 4 auf Leningrad—1941*. Neckargemünd, Germany: 1961.

Chaney, Otto Preston, Jr. *Zhukov*. Norman, OK: 1971.

Churchill, Winston. *The Second World War*, Vol. 4: *The Grand Alliance*. Boston: 1950.

Clark, Alan. *Barbarossa: The Russian-German Conflict 1941–45* (Reprint). Originally published, New York: 1965.

Colvin, John. *Zhukov: The Conqueror of Berlin*. London: 2004.

Cooper, Matthew. *The German Army 1933–1945: Its Political and Military Failure*. Lanham, MD: 1990.

Corum, James S. *Wolfram von Richthofen: Master of the German Air War*. Lawrence, KS: 2008.

Creveld, Martin van, et al. *Air Power and Maneuver Warfare*. Maxwell AFB, AL: 1994.

Dear, I. C. B. (ed.). *The Oxford Guide to World War II*. Oxford: 1995.

de Zayas, Alfred M. *The Wehrmacht War Crimes Bureau, 1939–1945*. Lincoln, NE: 1989.

Dieckhoff, Gerard. *3. Infanterie-Division, 3. Infanterie-Division (mot.), 3. Panzergrenadier-Division*. Göttingen, Germany: 1960.

Diedrich, Torsten. *Paulus: Das Trauma von Stalingrad. Eine Biographie*. Paderborn, Germany: 2008.

Dietrich, Otto. *The Hitler I Knew*. London: 1957.

Dinglreiter, Obstlt. a.D. Joseph. *Die Vierziger: Chronik des Regiments. Kameradschaft* Regiment 40. Augsburg, Germany: n.d.

Dollinger, Hans (ed.). *Kain, wo ist dein Bruder? Was der Mensch im Zweiten Weltkrieg erleiden musste—dokumentiert in Tagebüchern und Briefen*. Munich: 1983.

Domarus, Max. *Hitler: Reden und Proklamationen 1932–1945, Bd. II: Untergang (1939–1945)*. Würzburg, Germany: 1963.

Drig, Yevgenii. *Mekhanizirovannye Korpusa RKKA v Boyu: Istoriya Avtobronetankovykh Voisk Krasnoi Armii v 1940–1941 Godakh* (The RKKA's Mechanized Corps in Battle: The History of the Red Army's Armored Tank Troops in 1940–1941). Moscow: Tranzitkniga, 2005.

Dunn, Walter S., Jr. *Stalin's Keys to Victory: The Rebirth of the Red Army*. Westport, CT: 2006.

Egorov, A. V. *S veroj v pobedu (Zapiski komandira tankovogo polka)* (With the Belief in Victory [Records of the Commander of a Tank Regiment]). Moscow: 1974.

Ellis, Frank. *Barbarossa 1941: Reframing Hitler's Invasion of Stalin's Soviet Empire*. Lawrence, KS: 2015.

Emde, Joachim (ed.). *Die Nebelwerfer: Entwicklung und Einsatz der Werfertruppe im Zweiten Weltkrieg*. Dorheim, Germany: 1979.

Engelmann, Joachim. *German Heavy Field Artillery 1934–1945*. Atglen, PA: 1995.

———. *German Light Field Artillery 1935–1945*. Atglen, PA: 1995.

Erickson, John. *The Road to Stalingrad: Stalin's War with Germany: Volume One*. New Haven, CT: 1999.

———. *The Soviet High Command: A Military-Political History 1918–1941*. New York: 1962.

Erickson, John, and David Dilks (eds.). *Barbarossa: The Axis and the Allies*. Edinburgh: 1994.

Fest, Joachim C. *Hitler*. New York: 1974.

Flannery, Harry W. *Assignment to Berlin*. New York: 1942.

Forczyk, Robert A. *Tank Warfare on the Eastern Front 1941–42*. New York and London: 2013.

Förster, Jürgen (ed.). *Die Wehrmacht im NS-Staat: Eine strukturgeschichtliche Analyse*. Munich: 2007.
———. *Stalingrad. Ereignis—Wirkung—Symbol*. Munich: 1992.
Frisch, Franz A. P., and Wilbur D. Jones, Jr. *Condemned to Live: A Panzer Artilleryman's Five-Front War*. Shippensburg, PA: 2000.
Frontschau Nr. 2, "Russischer Stellungsbau," in: *Die Frontschau* (distributed by International Historic Films).
Fugate, Bryan I., and Lev Dvoretsky. *Thunder on the Dnepr: Zhukov-Stalin and the Defeat of Hitler's Blitzkrieg*. Novato, CA: 1997.
Gerasimova, Svetlana. *The Rzhev Slaughterhouse: The Red Army's Forgotten 15-Month Campaign against Army Group Center, 1942–1943*. Translated and edited by Stuart Britton. Solihull, England: 2013.
Geschichte der 3. Panzer-Division Berlin-Brandenburg 1935–1945. Traditionsverband der Division. Berlin: 1967.
Geschichte der 56. Infantrie-Division 1938–1945. Arbeitskreis der Division. n.d.
Geschichte der 121. Ostpreussischen Infanterie-Division 1940–1945. Traditionsverband der Division. Münster, Frankfurt, Berlin: 1970.
Geyer, Hermann. *Das IX. Armeekorps im Ostfeldzug 1941*. Neckargemünd, Germany: 1969.
Gilbert, Martin. *Second World War*. Toronto: 1989.
Glantz, David M. *Atlas and Operational Summary: The Border Battles 22 June–1 July 1941*. Privately published, 2003.
———. *Barbarossa: Hitler's Invasion of Russia 1941*. Charleston, SC: 2001.
———. *Barbarossa Derailed: The Battle for Smolensk 10 July–10 September 1941*, Vol. 1: *The German Advance, the Encirclement Battle, and the First and Second Soviet Counteroffensives, 10 July–24 August 1941*. Solihull, England: 2010.
———. *The Military Strategy of the Soviet Union: A History*. London: 1992.
———. *Red Army Ground Forces in June 1941*. Privately published, 1997.
———. *Red Army Weapons and Equipment (1941–1945)*. Privately published, 2004.
———. *The Soviet-German War 1941–1945: Myths and Realities: A Survey Essay*. Privately published, n.d.
———. *Stumbling Colossus: The Red Army on the Eve of World War*. Lawrence, KS: 1998.
Glantz, David M. (ed.). *The Initial Period of War on the Eastern Front 22 June–August 1941. Proceedings of the Fourth Art of War Symposium*. London and Portland, OR: 2001.
Glantz, David M., and Jonathan House. *When Titans Clashed: How the Red Army Stopped Hitler*. Lawrence, KS: 1995.
Görlitz, Walter. *Strategie der Defensive. Model*. Wiesbaden, Germany, and Munich: 1982.
Görlitz, Walter (ed.). *The Memoirs of Field-Marshal Wilhelm Keitel: Chief of the German High Command 1938–1945*. New York: 1966.
Gorodetsky, Gabriel. *Grand Delusion: Stalin and the German Invasion of Russia*. New Haven, CT: 1999.
Grossmann, Horst. *Die Geschichte der rheinisch-westfälischen 6. Infanterie-Division 1939–1945. Dörfler Zeitgeschichte*, n.d.; first published 1958.
Gschöpf, Dr. Rudolf. *Mein Weg mit der 45. Inf.-Div.* Nürnberg, Germany: 2002; first published 1955.
Guderian, Heinz. *Erinnerungen eines Soldaten*. Heidelberg, Germany: 1951.
———. *Panzer Leader*. New York: 1952.
Günther, Helmut. *Hot Motors, Cold Feet: A Memoir of Service with the Motorcycle Battalion of SS-Division "Reich" 1940–1941*. Winnipeg: 2004.
Haape, Heinrich (in association with Dennis Henshaw). *Moscow Tram Stop: A Doctor's Experiences with the German Spearhead in Russia*. London: 1957.
Hager, Erich. *The War Diaries of a Panzer Soldier. Erich Hager with the 17th Panzer Division on the Russian Front 1941–1945*. David Garden and Kenneth Andrew (eds.). Atglen, PA: 2010.
Halder, Franz. *The Halder War Diary 1939–1942*. Charles B. Burdick and Hans-Adolf Jacobsen (eds.). Novato, CA: 1988.
———. *Kriegstagebuch: Tägliche Aufzeichnungen des Chefs des Generalstabes des Heeres 1939–1942, Bd. II: Von der geplanten Landung in England bis zum Beginn des Ostfeldzuges (1.7.1940–21.6.1941)*. Hans-Adolf Jacobsen and Alfred Philippi (eds.). Stuttgart: 1963.

————. *Kriegstagebuch: Tägliche Aufzeichnungen des Chefs des Generalstabes des Heeres 1939–1942, Bd. III: Der Russlandfeldzug bis zum Marsch auf Stalingrad (22.6.1941–24.9.1942)*. Hans-Adolf Jacobsen and Alfred Philippi (eds.). Stuttgart: 1964.

Hammer, Ingrid, and Susanne zur Nieden (eds.). *Sehr selten habe ich geweint. Briefe und Tagebücher aus dem Zweiten Weltkrieg von Menschen aus Berlin*. Zurich: 1992.

Handbook on German Military Forces. Baton Rouge, LA: 1990. Originally published by U.S. War Department as TM-E 30-451 (March 1945).

Häring, Bernard. *Embattled Witness: Memories of a Time of War*. New York: 1976.

Hart, B. H. Liddell. *The German Generals Talk*. New York: 1948.

Hart, Russell A. *Guderian: Panzer Pioneer or Myth Maker?* Washington, DC: 2006.

Hartmann, Christian. *Halder. Generalstabschef Hitlers 1938–1942*. Paderborn, Germany, and Munich: 1991.

————. *Wehrmacht im Ostkrieg: Front und militärisches Hinterland 1941/42*. Munich: 2009.

Hartmann, Christian, Johannes Hürter, and Ulrike Jureit (eds). *Verbrechen der Wehrmacht: Bilanz einer Debatte*. Munich: 2005.

Haupt, Werner. *Die 8. Panzer-Division im Zweiten Weltkrieg*. Friedberg, Germany: 1987.

————. *Army Group Center: The Wehrmacht in Russia 1941–1945*. Atglen, PA: 1997.

————. *Army Group North: The Wehrmacht in Russia 1941–1945*. Atglen, PA: 1997.

————. *Army Group South: The Wehrmacht in Russia 1941–1945*. Atglen, PA: 1998.

————. *Heeresgruppe Nord 1941–1945*. Bad Nauheim, Germany: 1966.

————. *Die Schlachten der Heeresgruppe Süd: Aus der Sicht der Divisionen*. Friedberg, Germany: 1985.

Heinemann, Werner. *Feldpostbriefe* (collection of unpublished field post letters; courtesy of his daughter, Birgit Heinemann).

————. *Pflicht und Schuldigkeit. Betrachtungen eines Frontoffiziers im Zweiten Weltkrieg*. Berlin: 2010.

Heyen, F. J., H. W. Herrmann, and K. H. Debus (eds.). *Jahrbuch für westdeutsche Landesgeschichte*, 13. Jahrgang. Koblenz, Germany: 1987.

Hillgruber, Andreas. *Der Zweite Weltkrieg 1939–1945. Kriegesziele und Strategie der grossen Mächte*. Stuttgart: 1982.

————. *Die Zerstörung Europas. Beiträge zur Weltkriegsepoche 1914 bis 1945*. Frankfurt and Berlin: 1989.

Hinterhuber, Hans H. *Wettbewerbsstrategie*. Berlin: 1990.

Hinze, Rolf. *19. Infanterie- u. Panzer-Division: Divisionsgeschichte aus der Sicht eines Artilleristen*. Düsseldorf: 1997.

————. *Die 19. Panzer-Division. Bewaffnung, Einsätze, Männer. Einsatz 1941–1945 in Russland*. Dörfler Zeitgeschichte, n.d.

————. *Hitze, Frost und Pulverdampf: Der Schicksalsweg der 20. Panzer-Division*. 6. Auflage, 1996.

Hoffmann, Peter. *The History of the German Resistance 1933–1945*. Cambridge: 1977.

Hogg, Ian. *Twentieth-Century Artillery*. New York: 2000.

Hoth, Hermann. *Panzer-Operationen: Die Panzergruppe 3 und der operative Gedanke der deutschen Führung Sommer 1941*. Heidelberg, Germany: 1956.

Hoyt, Edwin P. *Stalin's War: Tragedy and Triumph 1941–1945*. New York: 2003.

Hubatsch, Walther. *61. Infanterie-Division. Kampf und Opfer ostpreussischer Soldaten*. Bad Nauheim, Germany: 1961.

————. *Deutschland im Weltkrieg 1914–1918*. Frankfurt, Berlin, Vienna: 1978.

Hubatsch, Walther (ed.). *Hitlers Weisungen für die Kriegsführung 1939–1945: Dokumente des Oberkommandos der Wehrmacht*. Frankfurt: 1962.

Hurley, Colonel Alfred F., and Major Robert C. Ehrhart (eds.). *Air Power and Warfare. The Proceedings of the 8th Military History Symposium, United States Air Force Academy, 18–20 October 1978*. Washington, DC: 1979.

Hürter, Johannes. *Ein deutscher General an der Ostfront. Die Briefe und Tagebücher des Gotthard Heinrici 1941/42*. Erfurt, Germany: 2001.

————. *Hitlers Heerführer. Die deutschen Oberbefehlshaber im Krieg gegen die Sowjetunion 1941/42*. Munich: 2006.

Irving, David. *Hitler's War.* New York: 1977.

Irving, David (ed.). *Adolf Hitler: The Medical Diaries. The Private Diaries of Dr. Theo Morell.* London: 1983.

Jacobsen, Hans-Adolf (ed.). *1939–1945: Der Zweite Weltkrieg in Chronik und Dokumenten.* Darmstadt, Germany: 1959.

———. *Kriegstagebuch des OKW (WFSt.), Bd. I: 1. August 1940–31. Dezember 1941.* Frankfurt: 1965.

Jentz, Thomas L. (ed.). *Panzer Truppen: The Complete Guide to the Creation & Combat Employment of Germany's Tank Force, 1933–1942.* Atglen, PA: 1996.

Johnson, Paul. *Modern Times: The World from the Twenties to the Nineties.* New York: 1991.

Jones, Michael. *The Retreat: Hitler's First Defeat.* New York: 2009.

Kaltenegger, Roland. *Die Stammdivision der deutschen Gebirgstruppe. Weg und Kampf der 1. Gebirgs-Division 1935–1945.* Graz, Austria, and Stuttgart: 1981.

Kavalerchik, Boris, and Lev Lopukhovsky. *The Price of Victory: The Red Army's Casualties in the Great Patriotic War.* Barnsley, England: 2017.

Keegan, John. *The Second World War.* New York: 1989.

Keilig, Wolf. *Das Deutsche Heer 1939–1945. Gliederung, Einsatz, Stellenbesetzung. Bd. I & II.* Bad Nauheim, Germany: 1956.

Kempowski, Walter. *Das Echolot. Barbarossa '41. Ein kollektives Tagebuch.* Munich: 2002.

Kershaw, Ian. *Fateful Choices: Ten Decisions That Changed the World, 1940–1941.* New York: 2007.

———. *Hitler 1936–1945: Nemesis.* New York: 2000.

Kershaw, Robert J. *War Without Garlands: Operation Barbarossa 1941/42.* New York: 2000.

Kesselring, Albert. *The Memoirs of Field-Marshal Kesselring.* Novato, CA: 1989.

———. *Soldat Bis Zum Letzten Tag.* Bonn: 1953.

Kirchubel, Robert. *Hitler's Panzer Armies on the Eastern Front.* U.K., 2009.

———. *Operation Barbarossa 1941 (1), Army Group South.* Oxford: 2003.

———. *Operation Barbarossa 1941 (3), Army Group Center.* Oxford: 2007.

———. *Operation Barbarossa: The German Invasion of Soviet Russia.* Oxford: 2013.

Knappe, Siegfried (with Ted Brusaw). *Soldat: Reflections of a German Soldier, 1936–1949.* New York: 1992.

Knecht, Wolfgang. *Geschichte des Infanterie-Regiments 77: 1936–1945.* 1964.

Knoblauch, Karl. *Kampf und Untergang der 95. Infanteriedivision. Chronik einer Infanteriedivision von 1939–1945 in Frankreich und an der Ostfront.* Würzburg, Germany: 2008.

Knoke, Heinz. *I Flew for the Führer.* Cassell Military Paperbacks edition, 2003; first published in English by Evans Brothers, 1953.

Knopp, Guido. *Die Wehrmacht. Eine Bilanz.* Munich: 2007.

Kohl, Paul. *"Ich wundere mich, dass ich noch lebe." Sowjetische Augenzeugen berichten.* Gütersloh, Germany: 1990.

Kotkin, Stephen. *Stalin: Waiting for Hitler, 1929–1941.* New York: 2017.

Kozhevnikov, M. N. *The Command and Staff of the Soviet Army Air Force in the Great Patriotic War 1941–1945.* Moscow: 1977.

Krehl, Eberhard. *Erinnerungen eines 85 Jahre alten Mannes. Unteroffizier beim Stab Ari.-Kdr. 121 der Panzertruppen.* Privately published memoir, 1997.

Kreuter, Lt. Georg. *Persönliches Tagebuch.* Unpublished diary.

Krivosheev, Col.-Gen. G. F. (ed.). *Soviet Casualties and Combat Losses in the Twentieth Century.* London: 1997.

Kuhnert, Max. *Will We See Tomorrow? A German Cavalryman at War 1939–42.* London: 1993.

Kurowski, Franz. *Balkenkreuz und Roter Stern. Der Luftkrieg über Russland 1941–1944.* Friedberg, Germany: 1984.

Lang, Major a.D. Friedrich. *Aufzeichnungen aus der Sturzkampffliegerei.* Christian Heine (ed.). 2002.

Lanz, Hubert. *Gebirgsjäger. Die 1. Gebirgsdivision 1935–1945.* Bad Nauheim, Germany: 1954.

———. *Wie es zum Russlandfeldzug kam—und warum wir ihn verloren haben.* Munich: n.d.

Latzel, Klaus. *Deutsche Soldaten—nationalsozialistischer Krieg? Kriegserlebnis—Kriegserfahrung 1939–1945.* Paderborn, Germany: 1998.

Leeb, Wilhelm Ritter von, and Georg Meyer. *Generalfeldmarschall Wilhelm Ritter von Leeb: Tagebuchaufzeichnungen und Lagebeurteilungen aus zwei Weltkriegen*. Stuttgart: 1976.

Lewin, Ronald. *Hitler's Mistakes: New Insights into What Made Hitler Tick*. New York: 1984.

Lohse, Gerhart. *Geschichte der rheinisch-westfälischen 126. Infanterie-Division 1940–1945*. Bad Nauheim, Germany: 1957.

Luck, Hans von. *Panzer Commander: The Memoirs of Colonel Hans von Luck*. New York: 1989.

Lucke, Lt. Fritz. *Panzer Wedge. Volume One: The German 3rd Panzer Division and the Summer of Victory in the East*. Mechanicsburg, PA: 2012.

Luther, Craig W. H. *Barbarossa Unleashed: The German Blitzkrieg through Central Russia to the Gates of Moscow. June–December 1941*. Atglen, PA: 2013.

Luther, Craig W. H., and Hugh Page Taylor (eds.). *For Germany: The Otto Skorzeny Memoirs*. San Jose, CA: 2005.

Luttichau, Charles von. *The Road to Moscow: The Campaign in Russia 1941*. Washington, DC: Office of the Chief of Military History, 1985. Unpublished Center for Military History Project 26-P.

Mackensen, Eberhard von. *Vom Bug zum Kaukasus. Das III. Panzerkorps im Feldzug gegen Sowjetrussland 1941/42*. Neckargemünd, Germany: 1967.

Magenheimer, Heinz. *Moskau 1941. Entscheidungsschlacht im Osten*. Selent, Germany: 2009.

———. *Hitler's War: Germany's Key Strategic Decisions 1940–1945*. London: 2002.

Manstein, Erich von. *Lost Victories*. Novato, CA: 1984.

———. *Verlorene Siege*. Bonn: 1998.

Manteuffel, Hasso von. *Die 7. Panzer-Division 1935–1945. Die "Gespenster-Division."* Friedberg, Germany: 1978.

———. *Die 7. Panzer-Division. Bewaffnung, Einsätze, Männer. Dörfler Zeitgeschichte*, n.d.

Mawdsley, Evan. *Thunder in the East: The Nazi-Soviet War 1941–1945*. London: 2005.

Megargee, Geoffrey P. *Inside Hitler's High Command*. Lawrence, KS: 2000.

———. *War of Annihilation: Combat and Genocide on the Eastern Front, 1941*. Lanham, MD: 2006.

Mehner, Kurt (ed.). *Die Geheimen Tagesberichte der deutschen Wehrmachtführung im Zweiten Weltkrieg 1939–1945. Bd. III: 1. März 1941–31. Oktober 1941*. Osnabrück, Germany: 1992.

Merridale, Catherine. *Ivan's War: Life and Death in the Red Army, 1939–1945*. New York: 2006.

Messenger, Charles. *The Last Prussian: A Biography of Field Marshal Gerd von Rundstedt, 1875–1953*. London: 1991.

Meyer, Georg. *Adolf Heusinger. Dienst eines deutschen Soldaten 1915 bis 1964*. Hamburg: 2001.

Meyer, Hermann Frank. *Blutiges Edelweiss. Die 1. Gebirgs-Division im Zweiten Weltkrieg*. Berlin: 2008.

Meyer-Detring, Wilhelm. *Die 137. Infanterie-Division im Mittelabschnitt der Ostfront. Dörfler Zeitgeschichte*, n.d.; first published, *Verlag der Kameradschaft* 137. I.D., 1962.

Michulec, Robert. *4. Panzer-Division on the Eastern Front (1) 1941–1943*. Hong Kong, 1999.

Miethe, Marianne. *Memoiren 1921–1945*. Unpublished memoir.

Mitcham, Samuel W., Jr. *Hitler's Field Marshals and Their Battles*. New York: 2001.

———. *The Men of Barbarossa: Commanders of the German Invasion of Russia, 1941*. Philadelphia: 2009.

Montefiore, Simon Sebag. *Stalin: The Court of the Red Tsar*. New York: 2004.

Moorhouse, Roger. *Berlin at War*. New York: 2010.

Mueller-Hillebrand, Burkhart. *Das Heer 1933–1945, Bd. II: Die Blitzfeldzüge 1939–1941. Das Heer im Kriege bis zum Beginn des Feldzuges gegen die Sowjetunion im Juni 1941*. Frankfurt: 1956.

———. *Das Heer 1933–1945, Bd. III: Der Zweifrontenkrieg. Das Heer vom Beginn des Feldzuges gegen die Sowjetunion bis zum Kriegsende*. Frankfurt: 1969.

Mühleisen, Horst (ed.). *Hellmuth Stieff Briefe*. Berlin: 1991.

Muller, Richard. *The German Air War in Russia*. Baltimore: 1992.

Müller, Rolf-Dieter. *Der letzte deutsche Krieg 1939–1945*. Stuttgart: 2005.

Müller, Rolf-Dieter, and Hans-Erich Volkmann (eds.). *Die Wehrmacht—Mythos und Realität*. Munich: 1999.

Murray, Williamson. *Strategy for Defeat: The Luftwaffe 1933–1945*. Maxwell AFB, AL: 1983.

Murray, Williamson, and Allan R. Millett. *A War to Be Won: Fighting the Second World War, 1937–1945.* Uncorrected Page Proof, 2000.

Musial, Bogdan. *Kampfplatz Deutschland. Stalins Kriegspläne gegen den Westen.* Berlin: 2008.

Nafziger, George F. *The German Order of Battle: Infantry in World War II.* London: 2000.

———. *The German Order of Battle: Panzers and Artillery in World War II.* London: 1999.

Naumann, Andreas. *Freispruch für die Deutsche Wehrmacht.* "*Unternehmen Barbarossa*" erneut auf dem Prüfstand. Tübingen, Germany: 2005.

Nayhauss-Cormons, Mainhardt Graf von. *Zwischen Gehorsam und Gewissen. Richard von Weizsäcker und das Infanterie-Regiment 9.* Bergisch Gladbach, Germany: 1994.

Nehring, General Walther K. *Die Geschichte der deutschen Panzerwaffe 1916–1945.* Stuttgart: 2000.

Neumann, Joachim. *Die 4. Panzer-Division 1938–1943. Bericht und Betrachtung zu zwei Blitzfeldzügen und zwei Jahren Krieg in Russland.* Privately published, Bonn, 1985.

Newton, Steven H. *Hitler's Commander: Field Marshal Walther Model—Hitler's Favorite General.* Cambridge, MA: 2006.

Nölke, Hans. *Die 71. Infanterie-Division im Zweiten Weltkrieg 1939–1945.* Hannover, Germany: 1984.

Oberkommando der Wehrmacht (ed.). *Kampf gegen die Sowjets. Berichte und Bilder vom Beginn des Ostfeldzuges bis zum Frühjahr 1942.* Berlin: 1943.

Overmans, Rüdiger. *Deutsche militärische Verluste im Zweiten Weltkrieg.* Munich: 2004.

Pabst, Helmut. *The Outermost Frontier: A German Soldier in the Russian Campaign.* London: 1958.

Paul, Wolfgang. *Brennpunkte. Die Geschichte der 6. Panzerdivision (1. leichte) 1937–1945.* Krefeld, Germany: 1977.

———. *Panzer-General Walther K. Nehring. Eine Biographie.* Stuttgart: 2002.

Payne, Robert. *The Life and Death of Adolf Hitler.* New York: 1973.

Philippi, Alfred, and Ferdinand Heim. *Der Feldzug gegen Sowjetrussland. 1941 bis 1945.* Stuttgart: 1962.

Piekalkiewicz, Janusz. *Die Schlacht um Moskau. Die erfrorene Offensive.* Augsburg, Germany: 1998.

Pleshakov, Constantine. *Stalin's Folly: The Tragic First Ten Days of WWII on the Eastern Front.* Boston: 2005.

Pottgiesser, Hans. *Die Deutsche Reichsbahn im Ostfeldzug 1939–1944.* Neckargemünd, Germany: 1960.

Prien, Jochen, et al. *Die Jagdfliegerverbände der Deutschen Luftwaffe 1934 bis 1943. Teil 6/1: Unternehmen "Barbarossa." Einsatz im Osten 22.6. bis 5.12.1941.* 2003.

Prien, Jochen, and Gerhard Stemmer. *Jagdgeschwader 3 "Udet" in World War II.* Vol. II: *II./JG 3 in Action with the Messerschmitt Bf 109.* Atglen, PA: 2003.

Prüller, Wilhelm. *Diary of a German Soldier.* H. C. Robbins Landon and Sebastian Leitner (eds.). New York: 1963.

Putney, Diane T. (ed.). *ULTRA and the Army Air Forces in World War II: An Interview with Associate Justice of the U.S. Supreme Court Lewis F. Powell, Jr.* Washington, DC: 1987.

Rass, Christoph. *"Menschenmaterial": Deutsche Soldaten an der Ostfront. Innenansichten einer Infanteriedivision 1939–1945.* Paderborn, Germany: 2003.

Raus, Erhard. *Panzer Operations: The Eastern Front Memoir of General Raus, 1941–1945.* Compiled and translated by Steven H. Newton. 2003.

Reuth, Ralf Georg. *Goebbels. Eine Biographie.* Munich: 1990.

———. *Hitler. Eine politische Biographie.* Munich: 2005.

Reuth, Ralf Georg (ed.). *Joseph Goebbels. Tagebücher 1924–1945, Bd. 4: 1940–1942.* Munich: 1992.

Rhein, Ernst-Martin. *Das Rheinisch-Westfälische Infanterie-/Grenadier-Regiment 18 1921–1945.* Privately published, 1993.

The Rise and Fall of the German Air Force 1933–1945. Public Record Office, 2001. Reproduction of Air Ministry Pamphlet No. 248, 1948.

Risse, Siegfried. *"Das IR 101 und der 2. Weltkrieg."* Unpublished report; courtesy of Klaus Schumann.

Roberts, Geoffrey. *Stalin's Wars: From World War to Cold War, 1939–1953.* New Haven, CT: 2006.

Roberts, Geoffrey (ed.). *Marshal of Victory.* Vol. 1: *The WWII Memoirs of Soviet General Georgy Zhukov through 1941.* Mechanicsburg, PA: 2015.

Rokossovsky, K. K., *Soldatskii Dolg* (A Soldier's Duty). Moscow: Voennoe Izdatel'stvo, 1997.

Röll, Hans-Joachim. *Oberleutnant Albert Blaich. Als Panzerkommandant in Ost und West.* Würzburg, Germany: 2009.

Rudel, Hans Ulrich. *Stuka Pilot.* New York: 1979.

Sáiz, Agustín. *Deutsche Soldaten. Uniforms, Equipment & Personal Items of the German Soldier 1939–45.* Philadelphia: 2008.

Sandalov, L. M. *Perezhitoe* (That Which Has Been Lived Through). Moscow: Voennoe Izdatel'stvo, 1966.

Schäufler, Hans (ed.). *Knight's Cross Panzers: The German 35th Panzer Regiment in WWII.* Mechanicsburg, PA: 2010.

Schick, Albert. *Die 10. Panzer-Division 1939–1943.* Cologne: 1993.

Schmidt, Paul. *Hitler's Interpreter.* New York: 1951.

Schneider, Wolfgang. *Panzer Tactics: German Small-Unit Armor Tactics in World War II.* Mechanicsburg, PA: 2000.

Schneider-Janessen, Karlheinz. *Arzt im Krieg: Wie deutsche und russische Ärzte den Zweiten Weltkrieg erlebten.* Frankfurt: 2001.

Schrodek, Gustav W. *Die 11. Panzer-Division "Gespenster Division" 1940–45. Dörfler Zeitgeschichte,* n.d.

———. *Ihr Glaube galt dem Vaterland. Geschichte des Panzer-Regiments 15.* Munich: 1976.

Schröder, Hans Joachim. *Die gestohlenen Jahre. Erzählgeschichten und Geschichtserzählung im Interview: Der Zweite Weltkrieg aus der Sicht ehemaliger Mannschaftssoldaten.* Tübingen: 1992.

Schroeder, Christa. *Er war mein Chef. Aus dem Nachlass der Sekretärin von Adolf Hitler.* Munich: 1985.

Schulze, Günter A. *"General der Panzertruppe a.D. Walther K. Nehring. Der persönliche Ordonnanzoffizier berichtet von der Vormarschzeit in Russland 1941–1942."* Unpublished manuscript.

Seaton, Albert. *The Battle for Moscow.* New York: 1983.

———. *The German Army 1933–45.* New York: 1982.

———. *The Russo-German War 1941–1945.* London: 1971.

Seidler, Franz W. (ed.). *Verbrechen an der Wehrmacht. Kriegsgreuel der Roten Armee 1941/42.* Selent, Germany: 1997.

Shilin, Oberst P. A. *Die Wichtigsten Operationen des Grossen Vaterländischen Krieges 1941–1945.* Berlin: 1958.

Shirer, William L. *The Rise and Fall of the Third Reich: A History of Nazi Germany.* New York: 1960.

Shores, Christopher. *Luftwaffe Fighter Units Russia 1941–45.* London: 1978.

Showalter, Dennis. *Hitler's Panzers: The Lightning Attacks That Revolutionized Warfare.* New York: 2009.

Slaughterhouse: The Encyclopedia of the Eastern Front. The Military Book Club (ed.). Garden City, NY: 2002.

Stahel, David. *Operation Barbarossa and Germany's Defeat in the East.* Cambridge: 2009.

Stahel, David (ed.). *Joining Hitler's Crusade: European Nations and the Invasion of the Soviet Union, 1941.* Cambridge: 2017.

Stargardt, Nicholas. *The German War: A Nation Under Arms, 1939–45.* London: 2015.

Steets, Hans. *Gebirgsjäger bei Uman. Die Korpsschlacht des XXXXIX. Gebirgs-Armeekorps bei Podwyssokoje 1941.* Heidelberg, Germany: 1955.

Stein, Marcel. *Generalfeldmarschall Walter Model. Legende und Wirklichkeit.* Bissendorf, Germany: 2001.

Steinhoff, Johannes, Peter Pechel, and Dennis Showalter (eds.). *Voices from the Third Reich: An Oral History.* Washington, DC: 1989.

Stolfi, R. H. S. *German Panzers on the Offensive: Russian Front, North Africa 1941–1942.* Atglen, PA: 2003.

Sweeting, C. G. *Hitler's Personal Pilot: The Life and Times of Hans Baur.* Washington, DC: 2000.

Taylor, Brian. *Barbarossa to Berlin: A Chronology of the Campaigns on the Eastern Front 1941 to 1945.* Vol. 1: *The Long Drive East, 22 June 1941 to 18 November 1942.* U.K.: 2003.

Tettau, Hans von, and Kurt Versock. *Geschichte der 24. Infanterie-Division 1935–1945.* Stolberg, Germany: 1956.

Thies, Klaus-Jürgen. *Der Zweite Weltkrieg im Kartenbild, Bd. 5: Teil 1:1: Der Ostfeldzug Heeresgruppe Mitte 21.6.1941–6.12.1941. Ein Lageatlas der Operationsabteilung des Generalstabes des Heeres.* Bissendorf, Germany: 2001.

Thomas, Nigel. *The German Army 1939–45 (3), Eastern Front 1941–43.* Oxford: 2002.

Toland, John. *Adolf Hitler.* New York: 1976.

Tooze, Adam. *The Wages of Destruction: The Making and Breaking of the Nazi Economy.* New York: 2006.

Trevor-Roper, H. R. (ed.). *Hitler's War Directives 1939–1945.* London: 1964.

True to Type: A Selection from Letters and Diaries of German Soldiers and Civilians Collected on the Soviet-German Front (no reference to editor, place or date of publication).

Ueberschär, Gerd R. (ed.). *Hitlers militärische Elite. Bd. 2: Vom Kriegsbeginn bis zum Weltkriegsende.* Darmstadt, Germany: 1998.

Urbanke, Axel, and Dr. Hermann Türk. *Als Sanitätsoffizier im Russlandfeldzug: Mit der 3. Panzer-Division bis vor Moskaus Tore.* Bad Zwischenahn, Germany: 2016.

Vassiltchikov, Marie. *Berlin Diaries, 1940–1945.* New York: 1987.

Voennaya Entsiklopediya. Vol. 4. Moscow: Voennoe Izdatel'stvo, 1999.

Voennaya Entsiklopediya, Vol. 6. Moscow: Voennoe Izdatel'stvo, 2002.

Wagener, Carl. *Heeresgruppe Süd. Der Kampf im Süden der Ostfront 1941–1945.* Bad Nauheim, Germany: n.d.

Wagner, Erwin. *Tage wie Jahre. Vom Westwall bis Moskau 1939–1949.* Munich: 1997.

Wagner, Ray (ed.). *The Soviet Air Force in World War II.* The Official History, Originally Published by the Ministry of Defense of the USSR. Translated by Leland Fetzer. Garden City, NY: 1973.

Walde, Karl J., *Guderian.* Frankfurt: 1976.

Weal, John. *Jagdgeschwader 51 "Mölders."* Oxford: 2006.

Wegner, Bernd (ed.). *From Peace to War: Germany, Soviet Russia and the World, 1939–1941.* Providence: 1997.

———. *Zwei Wege nach Moskau. Vom Hitler-Stalin-Pakt zum "Unternehmen Barbarossa."* Munich: 1991.

Weinberg, Gerhard L. *A World at Arms: A Global History of World War II* . Cambridge: 1994.

Werth, Alexander. *Russia at War: 1941–1945.* New York: 1964.

Wette, Wolfram (ed.). *Der Krieg des kleinen Mannes. Eine Militärgeschichte von unten.* Munich: 1992.

Wetzig, Sonja. *Die Stalin-Linie 1941: Bollwerk aus Beton und Stahl. Dörfler Zeitgeschichte,* n.d.

Wijers, Hans (ed.). *Chronik der Sturmgeschützabteilung 210. Tagebuchaufzeichnungen und Erinnerungen von ehem. Angehörigen.* 1997, 2003.

Will, Otto. *Tagebuch eines Ostfront-Kämpfers. Mit der 5. Panzerdivision im Einsatz 1941–1945.* Selent, Germany: 2010.

Woche, Klaus-R. *Zwischen Pflicht und Gewissen. Generaloberst Rudolf Schmidt 1886–1957.* Berlin-Potsdam: 2002.

Wright, Jonathan. *Germany and the Origins of the Second World War.* New York: 2007.

Zabecki, David T. (ed.), *World War II in Europe: An Encyclopedia,* Vol. I. New York and London: 1999.

Zamoyski, Adam. *Moscow 1812: Napoleon's Fatal March.* New York: 2004.

Ziemke, Earl F. *The Red Army, 1918–1941: From Vanguard of World Revolution to US Ally.* 2004.

Ziemke, Earl F., and Magna E. Bauer. *Moscow to Stalingrad: Decision in the East.* New York: 1988.

Articles and Essays

Anfilov, V. A. *"Razgovor Zakonchilsya Ugrozoi Stalina"* (The Conversation Ended with Stalin's Threat), in: *Voenno-Istoricheskii Zhurnal* (Military-Historical Journal), 1995.

Blumentritt, Günther. "Moscow," in: *The Fatal Decisions.* William Richardson and Seymour Freidin (eds.). London: 1956.

Boog, Horst. "Higher Command and Leadership in the German Luftwaffe, 1935–1945," in: *Air Power and Warfare. The Proceedings of the 8th Military History Symposium USAF Academy 18–20 October 1978.* Colonel Alfred F. Hurley and Robert C. Ehrhart (eds.). 1979.

"Der Waldkampf (Auf Grund von deutschen und russischen Erfahrungen im zweiten Weltkriege)." Von einem Kriegsteilnehmer, in: *Allgemeine Schweizerische Militärzeitschrift, Oktober 1949 (Heft 10), November 1949 (Heft 11).*

Erickson, John. "Barbarossa June 1941: Who Attacked Whom?," in: *History Today,* July 2001.

Frieser, Karl-Heinz. "*Die deutschen Blitzkriege: Operativer Triumph—strategische Tragödie*," in: *Die Wehrmacht—Mythos und Realität*. Rolf-Dieter Müller and Hans-Erich Volkmann (eds.). Munich: 1999.

Ganglmair, Siegwald. "*Generaloberst* Alexander Löhr," in: *Hitlers militärische Elite. Bd. 2: Vom Kriegsbeginn bis zum Weltkriegsende*. Gerd R. Ueberschär (ed.). Darmstadt, Germany: 1998.

Gosztony, Peter. "*Die erste Entscheidungsschlacht des Russlandfeldzuges 1941/42 (II), Moskau in der Krise 1941 (I)*," in: *Österreichische Militärische Zeitschrift, Heft 2*, 1967.

Hillgruber, Andreas. "*Die weltpolitischen Entscheidungen vom 22. Juni 1941 bis 11. Dezember 1941*," in: Andreas Hillgruber, *Der Zweite Weltkrieg 1939–1945. Kriegesziele und Strategie der grossen Mächte*. Stuttgart: 1982.

Hoffmann, Joachim. "*Die Angriffsvorbereitungen des Sowjetunion 1941*," in: *Zwei Wege nach Moskau. Vom Hitler-Stalin-Pakt zum "Unternehmen Barbarossa."* Bernd Wegner (ed.). Munich: 1991.

Kazakov, Anatolij. "*Na Toj Davnijšej Vojne*" (In This War of Long Ago), in: *Zvezda. Heft* 5/2005.

Kielmansegg, General Graf von, and Colonel Helmut Ritgen. "German Operations in the Baltic Region: The Siauliai Axis," in: David M. Glantz (ed.), *The Initial Period of War on the Eastern Front 22 June–August 1941*. London and Portland, OR: 2001.

Luther, Craig. "German Armored Operations in the Ukraine 1941: The Encirclement Battle of Uman," in: *The Army Quarterly and Defence Journal*. Vol. 108, No. 4. October 1978.

Mitcham, Samuel W., Jr., and Gene Mueller. "*Generaloberst Erich Hoepner*," in: *Hitlers militärische Elite. Bd. 2: Vom Kriegsbeginn bis zum Weltkriegsende*. Gerd R. Ueberschär (ed.). Darmstadt, Germany: 1998.

Müller, Rolf-Dieter. "*Duell im Schnee*," in: *Der Zweite Weltkrieg. Wendepunkt der deutschen Geschichte*. Stephan Burgdorff and Klaus Wiegrefe (eds.). Munich: 2005.

Opitz, Alfred. "*Die Stimmung in der Truppe am Vorabend des Überfalls auf die Sowjetunion*," in: *Der Krieg des kleinen Mannes. Eine Militärgeschichte von unten*. Wolfram Wette (ed.). Munich: 1992.

Paret, Peter. "Clausewitz," in: *Makers of Modern Strategy: From Machiavelli to the Nuclear Age*. Peter Paret (ed.). Princeton, NJ: 1986.

Plato, Lt.-Gen. A. D. von, and Lt.-Col. Rolf O. G. Stoves. "1st Panzer Division Operations," in: *The Initial Period of War on the Eastern Front 22 June–August 1941*. David M. Glantz (ed.). London and Portland, OR: 2001.

Romsics, Ignác. "Hungary," in: *Joining Hitler's Crusade: European Nations and the Invasion of the Soviet Union, 1941*. David Stahel (ed.). Cambridge: 2017.

Rychlik, Jan. "Slovakia," in: *Joining Hitler's Crusade: European Nations and the Invasion of the Soviet Union*. David Stahel (ed.). Cambridge: 2017.

Schröder, Hans Joachim. "*Erfahrungen deutscher Mannschaftssoldaten während der ersten Phase des Russlandkrieges*," in: *Zwei Wege nach Moskau. Vom Hitler-Stalin-Pakt zum "Unternehmen Barbarossa."* Bernd Wegner (ed.). Munich: 1991.

Schüler, Klaus. "The Eastern Campaign as a Transportation and Supply Problem," in: *From Peace to War: Germany, Soviet Russia and the World, 1939–1941*. Bernd Wegner (ed.). Providence: 1997.

Schwarz, Dekan Rudolf. "*Geprägt vom Christlichen Glauben*," in: *Furchtlos und Treu. Zum fünfundsiebzigsten Geburtstag von General der Gebirgstruppe a.D. Hubert Lanz*. Charles B. Burdick (ed.). Cologne: 1971.

Stahl, Friedrich-Christian. "*Generaloberst Rudolf Schmidt*," in: *Hitlers militärische Elite. Bd. 2: Vom Kriegsbeginn bis zum Weltkriegsende*. Gerd R. Ueberschär (ed.). Darmstadt, Germany: 1998.

Volkogonov, Dmitri. "The German Attack, the Soviet Response, Sunday, 22 June 1941," in: *Barbarossa: The Axis and the Allies*. John Erickson and David Dilks (eds.). Edinburgh: 1994.

Wegner, Bernd. "The Road to Defeat: The German Campaigns in Russia 1941–1943," in: *The Journal of Strategic Studies*, Vol. 13, No. 1, March 1990.

Zhukov, Georgi K. "The War Begins: June 22, 1941," in: *Battles Hitler Lost and the Soviet Marshals Who Won Them*. New York: 1986.

Websites

www.encyclopediaofukraine.com
http://iremember.ru/en
https://de.wikipedia.org/wiki/1._Gebirgs-Division_(Wehrmacht)
www.dictionary.cambridge.org
www.jewishvirtuallibrary.org
www.lexikon-der-wehrmacht.de
www.lib.utexas.edu/maps
https://pamyat-naroda.ru
www.shtetlinks.jewishgen.org/lida-district/now-encyc.htm

INDEX

Ostheer (eastern army), xxviii, xxx, 16–17, 29, 37, 68, 90, 208, 267–68, 319, 320, 334, 336–37, 339
Oven, Karl von, 265

Pabst, Helmut, 149, 187
Pabst, Herbert, 311
panzer groups: 4 Panzer Group, 47, 90–92, 94, 98, 105, 107–12, 116–17, 120–26, 129, 132, 136–37, 202, 288, 291–92; 1 Panzer Group, 47, 147, 237–39, 256, 261–63, 267–71, 274–76, 278, 304–6; 3 Panzer Group, 28, 46–47, 123, 142, 144, 148, 156, 186, 190, 193–97, 199, 202–4, 212–14, 294, 298; 2 Panzer Group, 46, 48, 65, 142, 144, 147–48, 151, 153–55, 157, 162, 165, 168, 175, 187, 196, 213, 294, 301, 303
Patriotic War, 327
Paulus, Friedrich, 17–18, 320
Pavlov, D. G., 69–72, 122, 137, 141, 144–45, 156, 183, 193–94, 204, 213–15, 236, 247, 325, 328–30; arrest of, 142
Pearl Harbor, xxviii, 338
Peremysl' Fortified Region, 31, 74, 238, 240, 246–48, 257
Pétain, Philippe, 3
Pfeffer, Max, 263
Pflugbeil, Kurt, 304, 306
Picker, Egbert, 251–53
Pleshakov, Constantine, xxxi, 281, 340
Plocher, Hermann, 292
Poland, xxviii, 2, 5, 13, 16, 21, 27, 32–33, 38–39, 44–45, 47, 49–50, 54, 60, 63, 118, 128, 136, 141, 143–45, 153, 179, 184, 200, 212, 237, 250,

254–55, 261, 285, 287, 300, 310; carving up of, 318; invasion of, 92, 234, 267
Pomerania, 322
Popov, V. S., 161
Potapov, M. I., 73, 265
Prien, Jochen, 308
Pronin, V. P., 62
Prüler, Wilhelm, 54
Puganov, V. P., 162
Purkayev, M. A., 64, 247, 323, 330
Putin, Vladimir, xxviii, 337

Raeder, Erich, 4, 8
Raus, Erhard, 47, 118
Rava Ruska Fortified Region, 31, 74, 238–40, 246–48, 254, 256–57, 262–63, 278
Red Army, xix–xx, xxix, xxx–xxxi, 14–17, 19–25, 33, 35, 49, 57–58, 60, 62, 65, 69–70, 74, 89–90, 92, 95–97, 105–6, 111, 114, 117, 123, 126, 136, 141, 144–45, 155, 160, 168, 170, 184, 189, 192, 196–98, 207, 235–36, 242, 246–48, 253, 262, 269, 275, 289, 292, 296, 302, 315, 321, 324–25, 327–30, 338, 341; atrocities of, 182–83, 335; casualties of, 339; cluster bomb, use against, 286; communication lines, problems with, 66–67; as complex fighting force, 30; confusion and fear of, 260; as inexperienced, 38; as juggernaut, 340; military components of, 30–32; provoking Germans, fear of, 260; rapid growth of, 34; readiness, xxvii, lack of, 33–34; regenerative powers